TURNING THE TIDE

ALSO BY ED OFFLEY

Scorpion Down: Sunk by the Soviets, Buried by the Pentagon, The Untold Story of the USS Scorpion

Pen & Sword: A Journalist's Guide to Covering the Military

Lifting the Fog of War
(With Admiral William A. Owens, USN)

TURNING THE TIDE

HOW A SMALL BAND OF
ALLIED SAILORS DEFEATED THE
U-BOATS AND WON THE
BATTLE OF THE ATLANTIC

ED OFFLEY

BASIC BOOKS

A Member of the Perseus Books Group
New York

Designed by Jeff Williams

Library of Congress Cataloging-in-Publication Data
Offley, Edward.
    Turning the tide : how a small band of Allied sailors defeated the U-boats and won the Battle of the Atlantic / Ed Offley.
        p. cm.
    Includes bibliographical references and index.
    ISBN 978-0-465-01397-5 (hardcover) — ISBN 978-0-465-02344-8 (e-book) 1. World War, 1939–1945—Campaigns—Atlantic Ocean. 2. World War, 1939–1945—Naval operations—Submarine. I. Title.

D770.O36 2011
940.54'293--dc22
                                                                        2010048097

10 9 8 7 6 5 4 3 2 1

This book is dedicated to the men
who fought the Battle of the Atlantic
from September 3, 1939, until May 7, 1945.

CONTENTS

A FIGHT IN THE DARK

The Battle of the Atlantic was the dominating factor all through the war. Never for one moment could we forget that everything happening elsewhere, on land, at sea, or in the air, depended ultimately on its outcome, and amid all other cares we viewed its changing fortunes day by day with hope or apprehension.

—WINSTON CHURCHILL[1]

The battle began ninety minutes after midnight. The British destroyer *HMS Hesperus* had been patrolling ten miles astern of a slow-moving Allied merchant convoy when a bright dot appeared on the ship's radarscope. The radar technician, hunched over his equipment, spoke into the speaking tube, loudly so as to be heard on the windswept navigation bridge. "Very small contact just come up, sir. Bearing 230 degrees. Range five miles." Duty watch-standers on the bridge stiffened at the words.

Hearing the technician's alert, *Hesperus* Commander Donald G. F. W. MacIntyre set a course change to race toward the as-yet unseen enemy. At the sound of the Action Stations alarm, all 145 officers and enlisted men rushed to their combat stations. Gunner's mates clambered through the access hatches into the turrets to man the warship's two 4.7-inch guns, while other sailors armed the smaller pedestal-mounted 20-mm Oerlikon cannons. Aft on the main deck, the depth charge teams checked and rechecked the massive metal cylinders on the deck rails and K-gun launchers, which sent depth charges flying out to either side of the ship.

The weather was turbulent in the first hours of May 12, 1943, as the twenty-two merchant ships of Slow Convoy 129 steamed on an east-north-east course that would take them several hundred miles northwest of the Azores. They had left Halifax, Nova Scotia nine days earlier carrying supplies for the British people and the ever-growing U.S. military force in the British Isles. The merchant ships, with a total capacity of 103,384 tons, carried grain, sugar, flour, lumber, steel, petroleum supplies, army trucks, ammunition, and explosives as well as scarce bauxite ore for the production of aluminum.[2]

Elsewhere on the North Atlantic that stormy night, eleven other Allied convoys were at sea. Including Convoy SC129, more than 517 freighters, bulk carriers, and oil tankers were proceeding in five eastbound convoys with cargo for the United Kingdom, and another seven were heading westbound in ballast from British ports for North America to pick up more materiel for the war effort. It was a typically busy night on the North Atlantic.[3]

The dozen Allied convoys were not alone as they made their way across the North Atlantic. During the past two weeks, Allied convoy planners had learned of a massive enemy formation northeast of Newfoundland: forty German *Unterseebooten,* or U-boats, arranged in three separate "wolf packs," each searching for transatlantic convoys. The threat was serious enough that U.S. Navy convoy planners had ordered Slow Convoy SC129 and fast Convoy HX237 to take a more southerly route to avoid the wolf packs in the north. SC129 had left New York on May 2 and five days later rendezvoused with MacIntyre and his British Escort Group B-2 at the designated Western Ocean Meeting Point southeast of Cape Race, Newfoundland. But the group then turned south, away from the U-boats. Although MacIntyre and his fellow escort ship commanders doubted that the maneuver would work in the long run, they had no choice but to relieve the local escort ships and proceed out into the Atlantic. Five days later, the convoy's steady speed of five knots had taken SC129 out into a perilous swath of ocean, which was called the "Greenland air gap" because patrol aircraft flying from bases in Canada, Iceland, and Northern Ireland could not reach them. For the next week, there would be no air cover. Escort Group B-2 would have to defend the convoy on its own.[4]

On the night of May 11–12 as MacIntyre and his men scanned the ocean for signs of the enemy, the U-boat Force was also on the prowl. There were 129 U-boats on patrol at sea, 114 in the North Atlantic. Alerted by German naval intelligence that two convoys were taking the southerly route, U-boat headquarters ordered twenty-three U-boats to find them. Orders transmitted via encrypted wireless Morse code separated the boats into two wolf packs, which formed a 550-mile-long line across the estimated path of the convoys. Strung out in a generally north-south direction at twenty-mile intervals, the U-boats shifted the line twenty miles south to find the forty-two vessels in fast Convoy HX237 or the twenty-two merchant ships in SC129.[5]

At nightfall on May 11, SC129 moved in standard convoy formation on a base course of 20 degrees north-northeast, proceeding in nine parallel columns of two to four ships each. Each column was separated from the next by 1,000 yards, and each ship maintained 500 yards' separation between the vessel in front and the one behind. From the air, the convoy resembled a wide rectangle with the longer sides facing forward and aft. Three to five miles outside the formation, the two destroyers, five corvettes, and two ASW (anti-submarine warfare) trawlers from Escort Group B-2 patrolled a perimeter twenty-one miles long. Between five and ten miles apart, the escorts cruised back and forth in their stations like sheepdogs guiding a herd.[6]

As senior officer of the convoy escort group, Commander MacIntyre had placed the *Hesperus* at the rear of Slow Convoy 129. That afternoon, the escort ships had detected U-boat radio signals astern of the convoy, and MacIntyre suspected that the U-boats were still trailing the formation and would most likely attack from that direction. The fateful radar sighting a half hour after midnight had confirmed his suspicions. It showed a U-boat dead astern of the convoy, close enough that its maximum surface speed of eighteen knots could bring it into torpedo range within the next ten minutes.

The U-boat commander in the darkness up ahead did not know it yet, but he was about to encounter a formidable enemy. MacIntyre, an escort group leader for the past twenty-seven months, had already presided over the destruction of four U-boats, including three by his ship. The *Hesperus* had originally been built for the Brazilian Navy, but the British Admiralty

Commander Donald MacIntyre was one of the leading U-boat killers in the Royal Navy.

Imperial War Museum, U.K.

acquired it and five sister ships at the start of the war. British shipwrights had reconfigured the 323-foot-long destroyer for convoy escort work. They installed depth-charge racks and K-guns, radar and other anti-submarine sensors, later removing the forward-most 4.7-inch cannon and replacing it with a forward-firing Hedgehog mortar. The ship was an efficient U-boat killer, and its crew were operating at the top of their deadly game.

A warship's weapons and sensors made a great difference in the fight against the U-boats, but so did the abilities of the crew. Catching a surfaced U-boat required the maximum performance by each man on the ship. As MacIntyre wrote after the war, it was imperative for each crewman to carry out his designated task as quickly and accurately as possible for the destroyer to capitalize on the brief opportunity a U-boat sighting would offer. "Naval successes are almost invariably the result of teamwork and training. . . . failure by the humblest member of the team can ruin the efforts of all." The crew's most important objective was to close with the U-boat as fast as possible before its lookouts spotted the approaching de-

The British destroyer *HMS Hesperus* at sea in late 1942.
National Archives and Records Administration

stroyer and made an emergency crash dive. The closer the distance meant higher odds that a depth-charge attack would succeed.[7]

In close-range combat, the *Hesperus* and the U-boat each had strengths and weaknesses. The *Hesperus* could easily outrace a surfaced U-boat, and so could the second destroyer in Escort Group B-2, but the six Flower-class corvettes and two smaller ASW trawlers assigned to the group could not. The escorts had to work together to take account of the smaller ships' limitations; thwarting multiple U-boat contacts around the twenty-to-forty-mile perimeter of a convoy required first-rate communications and teamwork. Both destroyers carried deck guns and lighter automatic cannons, but neither MacIntyre nor his gunner's mates had much faith in gunfire against a surfaced U-boat. In the heavy seas, the ship would not provide a stable platform, severely reducing the guns' accuracy.

Until the end of April 1943, the escorts' primary weapon had been the Mark VII depth charge. First developed as a dropping mine in 1910, the World War II depth charge was a cylindrical metal device weighing about 600 pounds and carrying 300 pounds of Torpex high explosive with a hydrostatic fuse that crewmen could set to detonate the weapon at a specific depth. Using four side-mounted K-gun launchers and the twin depth-charge rails on the stern, a destroyer could drop a diamond-shaped pattern of up to ten depth charges over the suspected U-boat location in each pass. However, since the Asdic (sonar) hydrophone system that tracked the underwater sounds of a U-boat had a blind spot directly under the ship, its operator would lose contact with the U-boat just as the destroyer reached the target area. Thus, the actual release point was always an educated guess.

Besides its conventional depth charges, the *Hesperus* sported two new anti-submarine weapons that had been rushed into service in recent months. The first was the Hedgehog, a forward-firing mortar system that could throw up to twenty-four contact-fused projectiles at a time 200 yards ahead of the launching warship. Each mortar had a shaped-charge warhead of thirty-five pounds of Torpex explosive. The Hedgehog provided MacIntyre and the other escort commanders an alternative to the standard depth charge diamond. When fired, the mortars would hit the water in an elliptical pattern 100 feet in diameter well ahead of the ship. With the Hedgehog, escort crews could target a U-boat while the Asdic system still pinpointed its underwater location. The Hedgehog was an improvement on conventional depth charges, which required the crews to fire blindly. Furthermore, the projectiles were designed to explode on contact, rather than at a given depth. If an initial salvo missed, the U-boat would hear nothing and the escort would have an additional chance to strike. The second new weapon was the massive Mark X depth charge. Designed for use against a U-boat hovering just above its 820-foot crush depth (the depth at which the submarine's hull would begin to collapse from water pressure), the Mark X featured more than a ton of high explosives. Too large to be dropped from the stern rails, it was launched from a torpedo tube, from which it sank toward a target directly beneath the attacking ship.[8]

With these two formidable weapons, the Hedgehog and the Mark X, at his disposal, MacIntyre had only to locate his target before planning his attack. Bracing himself on the exposed compass platform on the edge of the navigation bridge, from which he had the maximum possible visibility of the oncoming waters, MacIntyre reached for his most precious war souvenir: a U-boat commander's Zeiss night binoculars, which had been personally presented by Grossadmiral (Fleet Admiral) Karl Dönitz, commander in chief of the U-boat Force, to one of his favorite U-boat aces.*

MacIntyre had earned his cherished binoculars the hard way. While commanding the destroyer HMS *Walker* escorting eastbound Convoy HX112 two years earlier, MacIntyre had depth-charged and critically damaged the Type VIIB U-99 in a bitter convoy battle southeast of Iceland. The battered U-boat barely made it back to the surface, where forty of its forty-three crewmen jumped clear before their boat sank. Among those rescued was Korvettenkapitän (Commander) Otto Kretschmer, the leading ace of the U-boat Force with forty-five Allied ships totaling 258,905 tons under his belt—including six from HX112 sunk just the previous day.** As sailors leaned over to pluck Kretschmer from the water, a junior officer from the *Walker* yanked the Zeiss binoculars from around the German officer's neck and strode to the bridge to present them to his commanding officer. Now, MacIntyre raised the eyepieces and spotted a thin white line in the water nearly dead ahead. It was phosphorescent foam from the U-boat's wake lighting up the sea.[9]

As MacIntyre watched the distance between his destroyer and the surfaced U-boat shrink, he found himself in a contradictory mood. Normally, escort sailors who cornered a hated U-boat went on the attack with a sense of elation, even exhilaration. After weeks or even months of monotonous patrolling in punishing weather without so much as a glimpse of the enemy, the sudden appearance of a U-boat would send their adrenalin levels soaring, and they would race to the guns and depth-charge racks in practically a state of euphoria. Not so this night. MacIntyre was consumed with what he later described as "rage in my heart" toward the enemy.[10]

MacIntyre was furious because a U-boat had just outfoxed his escort group. Earlier that day, the veteran U-402 had carried out a submerged daylight attack—a risky move for a U-boat, given its relative daytime visibility near the surface—by getting ahead of Convoy SC129 and silently

---

*For a roster of German naval officer ranks and their British and American equivalents, see Appendix 4.

**Unless otherwise noted, the U-boats described in this book were the mainstay Type VIIC, known as the "workhorse" of the U-boat Force. For a roster of the different U-boat types in World War II, see Appendix 3.

loitering submerged until the merchantmen drew within torpedo range. At 1800 hours,* U-402, under Korvettenkapitän Siegfried von Forstner, had risen to periscope depth and fired a torpedo into the 3,082-ton Norwegian steam freighter *Grado,* carrying 1,000 tons of steel and 3,000 tons of lumber, and another into the 4,545-ton British freighter *Antigone,* with 7,800 tons of grain, general cargo, and 250 trucks. Both ships sank within minutes. The only bright spot was that the convoy rescue ship *Melrose Abbey* and two of the escorts picked up seventy-nine survivors, with only three crewmen from the *Antigone* killed. Although that U-boat had escaped, the enemy submersible looming larger and larger was still unaware of the *Hesperus*. MacIntyre hoped he could balance the books.[11]

Only a few minutes had passed since the *Hesperus*'s radar operator had spotted the blip on his scope. Rain suddenly lashed the watch-standers on the bridge as the destroyer rushed into a small squall. Emerging on the other side, MacIntyre and his lookouts saw the U-boat. It had reached ahead of the convoy's starboard flank and was on an interception course when its lookouts spotted the British destroyer closing fast. MacIntyre and his lookouts suddenly saw huge plumes of spray as the German vessel opened its vents and flooded its ballast tanks for an emergency dive. The warship raced over to the phosphorescent swirl that marked where the U-boat had just submerged. It was 0130 on Wednesday, May 12, 1943.

As MacIntyre and his crew prepared to attack the submerged U-boat, it became a matter of simple physics—and simple luck—whether the U-boat would survive. Accuracy, timing, and correct depth settings on the depth charges were essential. Guessing the right settings was only one of numerous variables that for the escorts spelled the difference between a kill and a U-boat crew rattled but free to fight another day.

Beneath the ocean surface, the U-boat frantically diving under the destroyer was the eleven-month-old U-223, the forty-first Type VIIC boat that the Germans constructed during the war. U-223's commander was Oberleutnant zur See (Lieutenant) Karl-Jürg Wächter, twenty-seven. He and his crew were twenty-six days out from port on their second combat

---

*Unless otherwise noted, all times are in Greenwich Mean Time (GMT).

The U-223 was a Type VIIC boat, the workhorse U-boat in the Battle of the Atlantic. Here, another Type VIIC, the U-701, returns to port at La Pallice, France, after a patrol.
Courtesy of Horst Degen

patrol. Despite serving in three different wolf packs, they had yet to see action.

When the *Hesperus* suddenly materialized out of the rain squall, Wächter immediately realized it had been tracking U-223 on radar. He shouted, "Alarm!" and the crew began a crash dive. The four other crewmen with Wächter on the exposed bridge jumped down the conning tower hatch, followed by Wächter himself, who spun the hatch wheel to secure the watertight fitting. The crewmen below were also scrambling to their diving stations. In the control room, Leutnant (Ingenieur) Walter Junge, the U-boat's chief engineer, shouted the order, "Flood!" and then opened the vents of the bow ballast tanks, which expelled their contents of air and began flooding with water. One of the two planesmen set the bow hydroplanes at the maximum down angle, and all other crewmen scrambled toward the bow compartment to add their weight to hasten the boat's descent. Meanwhile, at the first sound of the alarm, the diesel motor operators had closed the air induction vents to the two six-cylinder diesel motors and shut down the motors themselves, while simultaneously, in the next compartment, others activated the two electric motors. A well-trained crew could submerge its U-boat just thirty seconds after the emergency alarm and reach a depth of 300 feet in about a minute. But in this case, Wächter and his crew were too slow.[12]

As the *Hesperus* crossed the aim point, MacIntyre ordered a pattern of eight depth charges set to the shallowest settings, fifty feet. Instantly, his four K-guns blasted four depth charges to either side, and six more of the deadly canisters rolled off the stern rails. Within three to five seconds they began detonating. Years later, he described the scene: "As the depth-charges exploded, the tall columns of gleaming phosphorescent water soared up to stand momentarily like pillars of light before tumbling back into the sea in a torrent of foam." On MacIntyre's order, the *Hesperus* slowed and turned to reacquire the target on Asdic to begin another run on the U-boat. Within minutes, the tumult in the water settled down, and his Asdic operator called out a bearing angle to the enemy below.[13]

MacIntyre's first depth charge salvo had straddled U-223, and the shock waves had savagely pummeled the boat. The explosions had knocked out the lights and hurled crewmen to the deck plates and up against the bulkheads. There were leaks at the conning tower voice tube, the conning tower air intake valve, and the rudder and propeller shaft seals. Worse, the U-boat had begun an uncontrolled dive. Loss of depth control could send the U-boat falling below crush depth at 820 feet in a minute or two.

When the emergency lighting finally came on inside U-223, the crew returned to their stations and got the U-boat under control at 600 feet. Wächter and his men could hear the sharp whine of the British destroyer's Asdic pulses as they bounced off the U-boat's hull and the steadily louder beat of its propellers as it raced in for a second salvo. The roar of the warship overhead peaked then slowly subsided into silence. Reaching a terminal sinking velocity of ten feet per second, another eleven of the explosive-packed cylinders silently fell through the dark water toward the U-boat. It took a minute for them to get to U-223's depth and hammer the crewmen inside their damaged vessel. During the next hour, the *Hesperus* attacked U-223 three more times, dropping thirty-one more depth charges. The *Hesperus*'s last attack, at 0245 early Wednesday, May 12, seriously damaged the U-boat.[14]

After the last strikes by the *Hesperus*, the emergency lights went out and stayed out. By flashlight, Wächter and his men saw the depth indicator falling to 700 feet. They were approaching crush depth and would plummet through unless they could get U-233 under control. It seemed hopeless. Sailors in the torpedo compartment reported flooding. The engine room crew reported that one of the e-motors had an electrical fire. There were new leaks. Using ballast tanks and hydroplanes, however, Chief Engineer Junge somehow leveled the boat. Wächter realized there was no choice: another depth-charge pattern would finish them off. At 0250, he ordered an emergency blow of his ballast tanks and prepared to confront his enemy where the warship held all of the advantages, on the surface. The desperation maneuver saved the U-boat from its deadly freefall. Totally out of control, U-223 soared up out of the depths.[15]

After the final depth-charge salvo, MacIntyre held the *Hesperus* several hundred yards from the attack point as his crew frantically reloaded their K-guns and depth-charge racks. The ship was lurching and rolling in the heavy chop, and the depth-charge crews on the stern deck found themselves waist deep in frigid seawater as the destroyer rolled to one side or another, sending water sweeping across the deck. Suddenly, MacIntyre heard his Asdic operator shout out a report that the U-boat was blowing its ballast tanks. As the destroyer crew looked on, astonished, U-223 surfaced so close ahead of the *Hesperus* that the warship's forward 4.7-inch gun could not be depressed far enough to hit its target. The 20-mm Oerlikon cannons, however, could. MacIntyre ordered the *Hesperus* to close with the U-boat, which appeared to be dead in the water. Illuminated by the destroyer's searchlight, several crewmen were visible atop the conning tower on U-223's navigation bridge. As the escort warship surged ahead, several Oerlikon gunners swept the U-boat's conning tower and main deck with automatic fire, driving the U-boat crewmen back inside.

Passing less than fifty feet away, the *Hesperus* dropped several more depth charges set to the minimum depth right next to the U-boat, then circled around to repeat the maneuver.

Though battered, the U-223 was not finished yet. As Commander MacIntyre and his bridge watch-standers looked on from the bridge of the *Hesperus*, the U-boat suddenly began moving through the water. Wächter's engine-room crew had gotten its diesel engines started. MacIntyre ordered his gunners to open fire again, and his forward 4.7-inch gun scored several hits on the illuminated target. The beam of light dimly showed the tiny figures on the U-boat's bridge again scrambling below. But Wächter and his men were not about to go down without a fight. As the U-boat swung around in the water, MacIntyre's lookouts cried out a warning: Wächter had fired a torpedo from his stern tube, and it was racing toward the destroyer. But it missed.

MacIntyre's pursuit of the U-boat continued, and Wächter and his men were still not ready to quit. The German ordered a sharp turn to bring his bow torpedo tubes to bear, and fired four more torpedoes at the destroyer's knife-thin silhouette. All missed. With few options left, Wächter gave yet another desperation order. "Now we can only ram," he said to his crew. An 871-ton U-boat ramming a destroyer displacing nearly twice the weight was unthinkable, but Wächter had no other choice. Fortunately for MacIntyre and his men, that near-suicidal ploy proved impossible to carry out. U-223 was settling lower in the water, losing its ability to maneuver, and finally came to a dead stop. It was a prime target, but the *Hesperus* once more was too close to shell it with the ship's main battery.

For a long moment, MacIntyre stared down at U-223 and its unmanned bridge. "What in God's name do I do now?" he thought to himself. He considered ramming the boat and finishing it off but had second thoughts. The destroyer's second U-boat kill five months earlier had come from a ramming, but at a high cost. On December 26, 1942, during the battle for Convoy HX219 southwest of Iceland, the *Hesperus* was chasing a surfaced U-boat when the fleeing U-357 unexpectedly turned across the warship's bow. Seconds later, the *Hesperus* rammed it with what MacIntyre later described as "a deeply satisfying crunch." Sliced in half, U-357 sank, carrying thirty-six of its forty-two-man crew to their deaths. But the *Hesperus* had also been damaged. The collision had shredded eighty feet of its hull at the keel, flooding a number of bow compartments. Although it limped back to Liverpool to a hero's welcome, MacIntyre and his ship were sidelined for four months while shipwrights rebuilt its forward hull. Then there was the ongoing threat to Convoy SC129 to consider. "I recalled the state of *Hesperus* after the last occasion of ramming, her keel twisted back, fore compartments flooded and, above all, the Asdic dome wiped off and the Asdic out of action," MacIntyre recalled. "With the convoy still under attack and a long way to go, I could not afford that."

A ramming maneuver would likely sink the U-boat, but it would also surely prevent the *Hesperus* from completing its escort mission. Conferring with his first lieutenant, MacIntyre decided on a creative approach: a "gentle ram" aimed at capsizing the U-boat without endangering his ship. Moving at a near crawl, he nudged the destroyer's bow against the U-boat and bumped into U-223. "The submarine rolled over on to its beam ends, lay like that for a moment, but then as our bow slid down its length, sluggishly righted itself," he later recalled. "But it was obviously lying much lower in the water and I felt its end must be near." Concerned over his dwindling number of depth charges, MacIntyre once more ordered *Hesperus* to move out to bring its guns into play.[16]

Wächter realized that U-223 was doomed. If sunk, the odds of being rescued by the enemy they had been trying to kill were indeterminate. The chances of survival in the open ocean with nothing but a lifejacket were practically zero; the springtime waters of the North Atlantic were an icy forty to fifty degrees Fahrenheit and at that temperature could kill a man within hours. But there was nothing else to be done. Remaining aboard the stricken U-boat was not an option, since it was close to sinking. As the rest of the crew scrambled up through the hatches on deck, Wächter ordered Leutnant Junge and the control room's leading seaman to be "ready on the vents" to scuttle the boat by filling its ballast tanks with water and sending it to the ocean floor. Then Wächter went to join the rest of his crew atop the doomed U-boat. In the chaos on the rolling weather deck, two crewmen fell into the heavy waves. Matrosenobergefreiter (Seaman First Class) Heinz Hoog, nineteen, injured during the attacks, was hit by a wave and washed overboard. Thinking Hoog had jumped and that Wächter had given the order to abandon ship, Maschinenobergefreiter (Fireman Second Class) Gerhard Zieger, twenty-three, leaped into the ocean.[17]

MacIntyre had to choose. It was now 0253 hours, nearly ninety minutes since MacIntyre's radar operator had spotted U-223. As the *Hesperus* turned yet again to attack, MacIntyre peered at the U-boat, still illuminated by the destroyer's searchlight. Through his Zeiss binoculars, he could clearly see the German crew scrambling out on deck wearing life preservers in what obviously was an abandon-ship maneuver. As he watched, several crewmen appeared to jump into the sea. With Convoy SC129 now more than thirty miles distant and another twenty-two U-boats known to be closing in, MacIntyre gave the order to secure from Action Stations. The *Hesperus* was soon racing to the northeast at thirty-six knots to rejoin its comrades. "I left the sinking U-boat to its fate," MacIntyre recalled.

In fact, Wächter had not yet given the order for his men to jump. Stunned by the unexpected reprieve, he ordered everyone back inside the boat. For twelve hours they furiously pumped the bilges, repaired the motors, and reset the instruments. By mid-afternoon on May 12, they had salvaged their U-boat. Then they began the long crawl back to their homeport at St. Nazaire, France, one of five U-boat bases on the Brittany coast. Wächter stopped on the surface near midnight on May 12 to bury a crewman who had died from a head wound suffered during the encounter. U-223 arrived at the base twelve days later, with a tale almost unparalleled in the long and bloodstained history of the Battle of the Atlantic.[18]

Because of Escort Group B-2's aggressive reaction to each U-boat contact, Convoy SC129 safely reached Liverpool ten days after the showdown between the *Hesperus* and U-223. The convoy's twenty-four surviving merchant ships delivered 100,000 tons of supplies to the British Isles. MacIntyre and his crew, for their part, were doubly proud of their performance. In addition to their belief that they had destroyed Wächter's boat, the very next day they had located and sunk the Type IXC/40 U-186. U-186's fate was very different from that of U-223. Neither it nor any of its fifty-three crewmen were ever seen again.

The infantryman cowering in his foxhole cannot see the macro view of the battle surging around him for many miles. The bomber aircrew flying in tight aerial formation droning hundreds of miles to a target cannot comprehend the campaign in which their aircraft plays a small part. Both individuals and units engaged in the battles of World War II were locked into the moment and the proximate terrain, desperately trying to survive even as they struggled to kill their enemy. So too, Commander MacIntyre and Oberleutnant Wächter left the trackless scene of their fierce encounter that spring night in 1943 aware of little else but that they had survived to fight another day. What neither officer knew—nor could have been expected to know—was that the skirmish over Convoy SC129 occurred at the very turning point in the Battle of the Atlantic.[19]

THE BATTLE OF THE ATLANTIC was the longest and deadliest naval conflict in world history, and the crucial naval battle of the Second World War. For the British, starved by a protracted war with Germany and almost entirely dependent on supplies being rushed in by Allied ships, the Battle of the Atlantic was a last-ditch struggle for survival. For the Germans and their enemies across the Atlantic, the battle had more far-ranging significance. If the Allies could sustain the British war effort for long enough to assemble an invading force in the British Isles, they could carry the fight onto the European continent and, eventually, to Germany itself. But if the U-boats won, Germany would thwart the Allied invasion, strangle the British economy, and force the United Kingdom out of the war. The effects of this capitulation would be enormous. Without a second front to occupy the Germans in Western Europe, it was possible that the Soviet Union's Joseph Stalin might offer Germany a separate peace on the Eastern Front, giving Adolf Hitler most of the lands that the Wehrmacht, the unified German military forces, had already occupied. By the spring of 1943, the stakes in the Battle of the Atlantic were the same as the overall Allied grand strategy against the Nazis: victory or defeat. There was no middle ground.

The Battle of the Atlantic ran almost exactly as long as the war in Europe. Naval action began on September 3, 1939, eight hours and thirty-nine minutes after Great Britain had declared war on Germany following the invasion of Poland two days before. At 1839 hours on September 3, the German U-30 patrolling off the northern coast of Ireland torpedoed and sank the 13,581-ton British passenger liner *Athenia*, killing 112 of the 1,148 passengers and crew. These civilian casualties were the first of tens of thousands of lives lost in the fight for the North Atlantic, a battle that would only end with Germany's surrender more than five and a half years later.

Hunting the Allied merchant fleet was a formidable force of 830 U-boats. Commissioned over the nine-year span from 1936 to 1945, they destroyed by torpedo, gunfire, and mines 2,653 Allied merchant vessels and 175 warships worldwide, for a loss of 14.6 million gross registered tons of Allied shipping. Most of those attacks, nearly sixty percent, occurred in the North Atlantic.

The sinkings in the North Atlantic resulted in horrific loss of life. Allied and neutral merchant sailors and military gunners on merchant ships suffered extraordinarily heavy casualties during the war. Over 71,000 civilian crewmen and naval gunners perished, most in the Battle of the Atlantic. Casualty rates for merchant seamen were higher than for any other branch of the armed forces of their nation. Of 243,000 U.S. Merchant Marine crewmen who served in World War II, 9,500 died at sea from combat and shipwreck, a 3.9 percent fatality rate. That did not include 1,640 Naval Armed Guard gunners who perished at sea on the same merchant ships but were counted among navy fatalities. By contrast, the U.S. Marine Corps lost 19,733 of 669,108 active-duty personnel, a fatality rate of 2.94 percent, and the U.S. Navy, with 36,958 killed out of a wartime end-strength of 4.18 million, lost 0.88 percent of its sailors. The British Merchant Navy suffered even worse losses. A total of 37,318 British and Commonwealth merchant seamen died at sea. Of that, 22,490 British merchant sailors perished, a fatality rate of seventeen percent. In contrast, the British Army fatality rate was six percent. In addition to American, British, and Commonwealth losses, about 6,000 sailors from neutral-flag nations sailing the Allied trade routes died in attacks by U-boats, and another 10,777 merchant sailors from Nazi-occupied countries operating under British Admiralty support also lost their lives.[20]

The only military group that experienced an even higher fatality rate than Allied merchant seamen was their enemy: the men of the U-boat Force. The first U-boat lost in combat was the Type IX U-39. During an unsuccessful attempt to torpedo the aircraft carrier *HMS Ark Royal* on September 14, 1939, three of the carrier's escorts fatally damaged U-39. Its commander ordered his crew to abandon ship and set off scuttling charges. All forty-four crewmen survived as prisoners of war. Most of their comrades would not be so lucky. Over the course of the war, the U-boat Force lost 717 of its 830 commissioned U-boats, all but a handful in combat. Of 39,000 U-boat men who went to sea in World War II, 27,490 perished in combat and from accidents, a stunning seventy percent fatality rate. Of the 11,510 German crewmen who survived, some 5,000 ended the war in Allied prisoner-of-war camps.[21]

The Battle of the Atlantic shifted locations like a forest fire driven by fickle winds, as the courses of convoys, and the strategic options on both sides, changed over time. Despite the massive growth of the U-boat Force between 1939 and 1943, the Germans never had enough U-boats to impose a total quarantine on Allied shipping lanes. The ocean was just too vast. But the damage the U-boats inflicted on Allied shipping was severe, and the opposition they faced was often paltry; pressed by other wartime concerns, the Allies themselves struggled throughout the conflict to amass sufficient numbers of escorts and patrol aircraft. Due to these factors, the battle can be divided into a series of distinct periods, each of which was determined, to some extent, by developments elsewhere in the war.

From the beginning of the war, Germany's limited number of U-boats restrained its strikes against Allied merchantmen. During the first phase of the Battle of the Atlantic, running from the outbreak of the war until the German occupation of France in May 1940, Admiral Dönitz mounted limited attacks on Allied shipping by individual U-boats around the British Isles and the approaches to Gibraltar. Still, the U-boats managed to sink 148 ships for 678,130 gross tons of lost shipping during that period. German surface raiders were also active during this phase, and the Luftwaffe attacked shipping from the air. Occasionally, Hitler intervened to direct U-boat dispositions. In April 1940, for example, he personally ordered Dönitz to divert all available U-boats to Norwegian waters to support the German invasion of Norway.

The second phase of the Battle of the Atlantic saw Germany extend the reach of its naval offensives, thanks to its newfound foothold on the shore of France. This period spanned the eleven months from June 1940 to May 1941, when five U-boat bases on the French Atlantic coast became operational. The geographical advantage gained by command of the French coast helped compensate for the still lagging U-boat construction program, and the handful of U-boats then operational in the Atlantic were able to sink 381 ships, totaling two million gross tons. This period was followed by a third phase, which ran from May 1941 until the German declaration of war against the United States on December 11, 1941.

The third phase of the Battle of the Atlantic began when the U-boat bases along the French Atlantic coast were completed. Dönitz now deployed the first wolf packs against Allied convoys crossing the North Atlantic. In September 1941, one pack alone sank sixteen merchant ships from an eastbound convoy, totaling 68,259 gross tons of lost supplies. This third phase also saw the covert intervention of the U.S. Atlantic Fleet into the Allied convoy escort program, which led to several combat incidents between German U-boats and American escorts the following month. These encounters resulted in the loss of American lives when U-boats attacked the destroyers USS *Kearney* and USS *Reuben James* while they were escorting convoys. With scant publicity and in the face of avowed American neutrality in the Atlantic, the U.S. Navy had gone to war against the U-boat Force in the North Atlantic.

The fourth phase of the Battle of the Atlantic saw a stark military defeat and humiliation for the U.S. Navy, which had been unprepared for hostilities with Germany. The Japanese attack on Pearl Harbor had taken the Allies by surprise, and now Germany dispatched the first of several dozen long-range Type IX U-boats to hit U.S. and Canadian coastal shipping. They found the coastal sea lanes empty of Allied warships and aircraft, the cities brightly lit in peacetime array, and merchant ships steaming without protection. The U-boat campaign against American coastal shipping became a slaughter. During the first six months of 1942, U-boats sank 229 merchant ships along the U.S. East Coast. During the same period, U-boats in the Gulf of Mexico, Caribbean Sea, and North and Central Atlantic sank 392 ships. The overall losses were horrific, with nearly three million tons of shipping capacity destroyed.

Beginning in the fall of 1942, the fifth phase of the battle saw the U-boats focus on the North Atlantic convoy routes, with deadly results. The U-boat Force now numbered 80 to 100 boats at sea each day, allowing Germany to expand mass attacks against the trans-Atlantic convoys. More than 200 Allied warships totaling over 1.3 million tons went down from U-boat torpedoes or deck guns during the last four months of 1942. It was only because of the harsh winter storms of December 1942 through February 1943 that the Allies' losses were not greater. The coming of spring in 1943 would bring a resumption of the conflict in all its fury.[22]

The sea itself, the North Atlantic, played a vital, often decisive, role in this maritime clash. In the northern latitudes, the Atlantic can shift from tranquility to raging storm in less than a hundred heartbeats, and it is at its deadliest in the long, dark storm season running from September to May. Driven by oceanic circulation, the relatively warmer water of the North Atlantic Current sweeps up from the lower latitudes to collide with the frigid temperatures of the frozen Arctic landmass, setting off a semi-permanent center of depressed atmospheric pressure known today as the Icelandic Low. Anchored between Iceland and southern Greenland for nearly six months of the year, this meteorological engine generates the dreaded storms that whip across the North Atlantic each winter. For weeks and months that can be an eternity for the seafarer, the Icelandic Low turns the water and air into a white shroud, its winds shrieking with fury. Constant flashes of lightning and the eerie violet glow of St. Elmo's fire add to the surreal chaos of the North Atlantic storms.

The North Atlantic's harsh reality has long been ingrained in the marrow of European sailors. The fifth-century Irish, in their *curragh* boats of tanned oxen leather stretched over a wooden frame, endured the ocean's rage as they searched for the mythical Isle of the Blessed far to the west. Seven centuries later, the Viking explorers in their pine-plank *knarr* ships endured the savagery of the North Atlantic as they sailed out to settle the Faeroe Islands, Iceland, Greenland, and L'Anse aux Meadows in northern Newfoundland. So too did the famed European explorers of North America—Christopher Columbus, John Cabot, Giovanni da Verrazzano, Jacques Cartier, and others—who braved the North Atlantic in small square-rigged ships.

The North Atlantic has long had a habit of foiling the best-laid schemes of sailors and warriors. In 1588, forced to circumnavigate the British Isles after Queen Elizabeth's fleet blocked their homeward route from the Spanish Netherlands down the English Channel, the Spanish Armada succumbed to the harsh westerly gales and dozens of warships foundered on the rocky shoals of Ireland. King Philip himself later said, "I sent the Armada against men, not God's winds and waves." Four centuries later, Joseph Conrad experienced a North Atlantic storm, and lived to tell: "The Westerly Wind asserting his sway from the south-west quarter is often like a monarch gone mad, driving forth with wild imprecations the most faithful of his courtiers to shipwreck, disaster, and death."[23]

Until the twentieth century, major naval battles rarely occurred in the deep ocean. Available technology and naval architecture produced wooden, sail-powered warships that simply could not overcome the extremes of wave, wind, and temperature. It wasn't until the close of the nineteenth century that steam propulsion—achieved with coal-burning furnaces powering steam boilers—enabled the development of both trans-Atlantic merchant ships and deep-ocean navies. A half century later, the North Atlantic had been transformed from a wilderness of wind and sea to a network of established trade routes connecting North America and Europe. Thousands of freighters, bulk carriers, oil tankers, and passenger liners hastened across the Great Circle routes (the shortest, and most direct path from one point on the ocean to another) to the ports of Hampton Roads, New York, Boston, and Halifax on one side, and London, Liverpool, Rotterdam, and Brest on the other.

By the late 1930s, Great Britain relied on trans-Atlantic trade for essential food, petroleum, and raw materials. Thus, it came as no surprise that when war broke out in 1939, the U-boats went after that vital caravan of cargo. By 1941, imports had shrunk by one-third as a consequence of shipping losses and wartime requirements to bring military cargo and personnel from North America to the British Isles, and the British government warned that the country might run out of food in four months if the U-boats succeeded in a total cutoff of maritime shipments.[24]

The lumbering convoys, storm-battered escort ships, and sleek U-boats would be the instruments of Britain's fate, determined by a brutal series of skirmishes and attacks across the wide ocean. More often than not, these conflicts occurred as a violent and strangely intimate duel between a solitary Allied warship captain and his U-boat nemesis, as Commander MacIntyre and Oberleutnant zur See Wächter discovered on that rainy night in May 1943. But, taken together, these isolated encounters would determine the victor—not just in the Battle of the Atlantic—but in the entire war. The outcome of both struggles would be decided on this unforgiving expanse, by the individual men who braved it. This is their story.

Chapter 1

A CITY AT WAR

awn came cold and dreary along the Manhattan waterfront as the great city stirred to life. Deep in the shadow of the skyscrapers and office buildings, the advance guard of hundreds of thousands of people had begun pouring out of the subway entrances on their way to another day of work, dodging clumps of snow and ice from a storm two days earlier. Huddling in their winter coats against the subzero wind that blew in from the rivers, few would have noticed the flurry of activity on dozens of merchant ships as their crews prepared to cast off mooring lines or raise anchor to get under way. The preparations had, by now, become a regular sight. It was Friday, March 5, 1943, and New York was very much a city at war. Thousands of miles away, the Allies were locked in a mortal conflict with Germany, Italy, and Japan. After years of struggle and setback, they had halted the momentum of the Axis, but the much harder task of seizing the initiative and beating back the aggressors remained off in the uncertain future.

To many Americans, the conflict was a remote spectacle, but New Yorkers knew better. After four months of covert struggle between the U.S. Atlantic Fleet and the German U-boat Force, German submarines began their campaign against American shipping in the waters off New York on January 14, 1942, when the Type IXB U-123 sank the 9,577-ton Panamanian-flagged tanker *Norness* sixty miles off Montauk, Long Island. The next day, Kapitänleutnant (Lieutenant Commander) Reinhard Hardegen torpedoed the 6,768-ton British tanker *Coimbra* just twenty-seven miles south of Long Island. The towering flames from the burning ship were visible from the Hamptons, whose residents phoned authorities to notify them of the attacks.

Since the December 7, 1941 attack on Pearl Harbor, the conflict had pervaded the life of New York. Military servicemen and merchant sailors crowded the city's sidewalks. Shipyards in Brooklyn, Staten Island, and New Jersey hummed day and night with ship construction and battle repairs. Freight trains brought supplies to merchant ships docked at the city's piers. Dockyard cranes swung over boxcars and flatbeds to lift crates of ammunition, disassembled warplanes, amphibious landing craft, and army trucks into the ships' cargo holds. Crews of 200 Allied merchant ships were preparing for sea on that first Friday morning in March.[1]

New Yorkers reading the city's many newspapers during the week of March 5 were reminded of the war that dominated every aspect of American life, both in New York and across the nation. Especially chilling would have been the reports that U.S. government leaders feared Nazi Germany might somehow develop an intercontinental bomber that could attack New York and other East Coast cities. Referring to the ongoing Allied bombing campaign against Berlin and other German cities, a German government communiqué reprinted in *The New York Times* earlier that week had warned, "We should not forget that in consequence of the progress of aviation even New York with its much vaunted skyscrapers, Boston and Washington may not be safe a few months hence." In response to the threat, Mayor Fiorello La Guardia ordered a major air raid blackout drill for New York City, and Fire Commissioner Patrick J. Walsh estimated that nearly forty percent of the city's 700,000 buildings still lacked the emergency fire-fighting equipment required under a new city ordinance. Not to miss a sales opportunity, the Triangle Appliance Corp. placed an ad in the *Times* offering immediate delivery of stirrup pumps "approved by the New York Fire Dept."

While they braced to prepare for the war's possible return to American shores, New York residents also connected with the far-off fight through news reports of New York–area servicemen in action. All too often, the most visceral connection came from empathizing with a family's grief, and there was much grief to share in the first week of March. *The New York Times* briefly noted the crash of a U.S. Army Air Forces bomber in the New Mexico desert on March 3 that had killed eight crewmen, including

Cargo handlers load a disassembled fighter onto a freighter in New York for shipment to the United Kingdom.

Office of War Information

2nd Lieutenant Thomas N. La Pai of Westfield, New Jersey. In a more positive account, the War Department proudly announced that an Army Air Forces P-40 fighter group had destroyed 129 Japanese warplanes during the Allied campaign in New Guinea, citing individual performances by several New York–area pilots including Captain John H. Posten of Atlantic Highlands, New Jersey, and 2nd Lieutenant Edward M. Miller of Glen Cove, New York.[2]

By March 1943, New York itself had become the primary shipping hub for the trans-Atlantic flow of civilian aid and military supplies bound for the British Isles. Its port facilities, shipyards, and railroad terminals made the city and surrounding region the primary jumping-off point for Allied convoys. Other American and Canadian cities on the East Coast—particularly Halifax, Sydney, and Cape Breton in Nova Scotia and Hampton

Roads in Virginia—also served as convoy ports, but New York was by far the most prominent.

Although their city teemed with sailors heading for Europe, many New Yorkers were fixated on the Pacific Theater. For most Americans, New Yorkers included, the fight against the Japanese was an emotionally charged struggle that took precedence over the war in Europe. Eight months earlier, the U.S. Pacific Fleet had smashed the Japanese carrier force at Midway, inflicting catastrophic damage on Japan's navy. By the spring of 1943, the Allies had halted Japanese expansion and were now ready to begin the long and bloody counteroffensive to roll back Tokyo's occupation of half the Pacific basin. U.S. Marines and Army soldiers were consolidating their strategic stronghold on Guadalcanal after fighting there ended on February 9.

Having frozen the Japanese advance in the Pacific, by the spring of 1943, the Allies had also stopped Nazi Germany on two key fronts. In North Africa, in November 1942, first British troops, then a joint British-American force, had swarmed onto the African continent to form a western front against the Germans. By early March, the Allies had trapped the German Army's Afrika Korps in Tunisia. The battered German troops would hold out for another two months before surrendering.

The second Allied victory against Germany was even more significant than the campaign in Africa. On February 2, 1943, the German Sixth Army had surrendered to the Soviets at Stalingrad, ending one of the bloodiest battles of the war. During four months of house-to-house fighting, the Germans had lost 750,000 troops, either killed or wounded. Another 91,000 had surrendered. The victorious Red Army was itself bled dry in the siege, losing nearly 1.5 million killed, wounded, or captured. While the German Army remained capable of offensive action on the eastern front, its opportunity to destroy the Soviet Union had passed. The Allies had, it seemed, halted the German Blitzkrieg and were now preparing to reverse it.[3]

The Germans may have been down after their losses in Africa and Russia, but they were very certainly not out of the war. On February 18, Propaganda Minister Joseph Goebbels gave a passionate speech to tens of thousands of loyal Nazis at the Berlin Sports Palace. Broadcast throughout Germany, Goebbels admitted to the "disaster" in the east but used the de-

Grossadmiral Karl Dönitz, commander-in-chief of both the
German Navy and its U-boat Force
in the spring of 1943, sought to
strangle the Allied war effort by
destroying merchant ships vital to
supplying the United Kingdom.
*Clay Blair Collection, American Heritage
Center, University of Wyoming*

feat as a rallying cry to further unite the German people under Hitler and
the Nazis. "The German people face the gravest demand of the war,"
Goebbels thundered, "namely of finding the determination to use all our
resources to protect everything we have and everything we will need in the
future. . . . Total war is the demand of the hour."[4]

Despite Germany's setbacks, it still had the initiative in one area: the
sea. Grossadmiral Karl Dönitz, the U-boat Force commander-in-chief
since 1936 and the recently appointed head of the entire German Navy,
was determined to win the *guerre de course* he had launched against the
United Kingdom and its allies on the first day of the war. Britain's economy, historically dependent on foreign imports, had been ground to a nub
during their long battle with Germany. If Britain's lifeline of Allied supplies were severed, it would have to sue for peace with Germany. With
Britain out of the war, the risk of the Allies launching an amphibious invasion of the European continent would be almost nil. From the very outset
of the war, Dönitz saw this weakness in the British battle plan, and he intended to exploit it.

The German war on Allied shipping had started bit by bit. On September 3, 1939, the day Britain declared war on Germany, the U-boat Force had only fifty-seven U-boats in commission, of which only twenty were combat ready. The German Navy also had battleships, cruisers, and a small fleet of surface raiders that took part in the war on Allied shipping, although the contribution of these surface ships would quickly decline due to high losses inflicted by the Royal Navy, the lack of German escort warships, and few secure port facilities overseas. Even before the war began, Dönitz had been pleading for 300 U-boats, the minimum number he calculated was required to sever the trans-Atlantic supply pipeline to Great Britain. Competing demands by the German Army and the Luftwaffe for steel and other critical materials had delayed the planned growth of the U-boat Force. After the war began, Hitler approved an accelerated U-boat construction program, but the time lag between a U-boat's keel-laying and its initial war patrol ran between twelve and twenty-one months. Only in February 1942 did the number of U-boats reach fifty, and it was another seven months before the force topped 100 operational U-boats. Despite the slow growth of their fleet, the U-boats achieved spectacular successes against the British and neutral merchant ships during the early months of the war, for the Allies had been woefully unprepared for fighting them. Anti-submarine warfare had been a career backwater for Royal Navy officers during the interwar years, and when hostilities commenced, the fleet had too few destroyers and other escort warships.[5]

On the other side of the ocean, U.S. involvement in the Battle of the Atlantic had advanced in fits and starts, beginning fifteen months before the German declaration of war against the United States on December 11, 1941. Despite avowed American neutrality, President Franklin Delano Roosevelt had steadily supported the British against Hitler and his U-boats. In September 1940, the United States transferred fifty World War I–era destroyers to the British and Canadian navies, in return getting American military bases in Canada, Bermuda, and the Caribbean. Then, in February 1941, Roosevelt upgraded the poorly equipped and undermanned Atlantic Squadron to a full fleet headed by Admiral Ernest J. King.

America's claim of neutrality was rapidly losing any semantic value by the spring of 1941. A month after his decision to expand America's naval presence in the Atlantic, FDR took a bolder step toward supporting Great

As Atlantic Fleet commander in late 1941, Admiral Ernest J. King supervised the U.S. Navy's covert hostilities against the U-boats.

Clay Blair Collection, American Heritage Center, University of Wyoming

Britain. In March of 1941 he convinced Congress to pass the Lend-Lease Act, making American war supplies available to the British, Soviets, and, later, the Chinese and other allies. Over the course of the war, the United States would provide the British $31.4 billion (roughly $489 billion today) worth of aircraft, tanks, trucks, fuel, and other essential wartime supplies. American intervention grew in July 1941, when U.S. Marines occupied Iceland—already under British control since May 1940—to allow the Royal Army troops there to transfer to North Africa. Then, with the stroke of a pen, Roosevelt extended the declared American Neutrality Zone in the Atlantic to 26 degrees West longitude, a north-south line just to the west of Iceland. And in top-secret negotiations, U.S. and British military leaders forged a joint war plan that called for American warships to help escort Allied merchant convoys. To carry out this covert operation, Admiral King created the Atlantic Fleet Support Force, which quickly grew to twenty-seven destroyers, fifteen R-class submarines, a patrol wing of forty-eight PBY-5A Catalina flying boats, and several support and repair vessels. After a secret rendezvous with Prime Minister Winston Churchill in Placentia Bay, Newfoundland, from August 9 to 12, 1941,

President Roosevelt ordered the U.S. Navy to begin convoy escort operations with the Atlantic Fleet Support Force.[6]

It didn't take long for the first combat incident between German U-boats and Atlantic fleet warships. On September 4, Lieutenant Commander Laurence H. Frost in the twenty-two-year-old destroyer *USS Greer* was ferrying passengers and mail to Iceland when a British Lockheed Hudson patrol bomber flying overhead signaled the *Greer* that it had spotted a U-boat crash-diving ten miles ahead. The Hudson had seen U-652, commanded by Oberleutnant zur See Georg-Werner Fraatz. As the *Greer* moved in to investigate, the Hudson attacked, dropping depth charges on the U-boat. For ninety minutes, the *Greer* patiently tracked the submerged U-boat with its sonar. Both Frost and Fraatz found themselves painted into a corner. Existing Atlantic Fleet instructions did not authorize warships sailing independently to attack U-boats. Only those warships escorting convoys could do so. U-652, on the other hand, could not skulk along submerged forever, and Fraatz was well aware that *someone* up there had already fired on him.

Fraatz was unsure whether he had been attacked by the aircraft or the destroyer, but he decided to fire at the surface ship. U-652 rose to periscope depth, where Fraatz spotted a warship's silhouette identical to the fifty World War I–era destroyers that the U.S. Navy had transferred to the British. Fraatz fired a single torpedo at the *Greer*. Frost's bellowed helm order, "All ahead full speed! Right full rudder!" jerked the 314-foot-long destroyer out of the weapon's path. The *Greer*'s crew looked on, astonished, as the torpedo raced by 100 yards from the side of the ship. The *Greer* responded with depth-charge attacks against U-652, which prompted a second torpedo attack from the U-boat. The *Greer* continued to hunt the U-boat but after six hours broke off and resumed the mail run to Iceland. U-652 continued west to join a wolf pack hunting eastbound Slow Convoy 42.

Neither the destroyer nor the U-boat had suffered serious damage in the encounter, but the two sides had crossed a critical line. For the first time in World War II, an American warship and a German U-boat had traded fire. The real action took place back ashore. In a nationwide radio fireside chat, President Roosevelt announced a "shoot-on-sight order" authorizing all American warships to attack Axis U-boats and surface ships even if not provoked.[7]

Hostilities between the Support Force and the U-boats escalated after the *Greer* incident. On October 16, 1941, a Canadian escort group was guarding fifty-two Allied merchant ships in eastbound Convoy SC48 when a wolf pack of nine U-boats struck. They had already sunk three merchantmen when the *USS Kearny* and four other American destroyers arrived to reinforce the Canadian warships. Shortly after midnight on October 17, the thirteen-month-old *Kearny* was operating on the port flank of the convoy when a single torpedo struck its starboard side. The blast ripped a large hole in the side of the ship, knocking out electrical power, seriously damaging the bridge, killing eleven crewmen, and injuring another twenty-two. Postwar investigators learned that Kapitänleutnant Joachim Preuss in U-568 had attacked with three torpedoes, two of which missed. The *Kearny's* skipper, Commander Arthur Danis, restored limited power, and the destroyer limped back to Reykjavik for repairs.

Any lingering doubt that the U.S. Navy was in a shooting war with the U-boat Force vanished two weeks after the *Kearny* was torpedoed. On October 31, Kapitänleutnant Erich Topp in the U-552, one of a six-boat wolf pack attacking eastbound Convoy HX156, fired two torpedoes at the destroyer *USS Reuben James,* and at least one of them struck the warship. The blast set off the destroyer's forward ammunition magazine and blew the ship in half. The sinking killed 115 of its 160-man crew, including its commanding officer, Lieutenant Commander Heywood L. Evans, and all of the other officers aboard. It was an incident that sent shock waves throughout the United States, and Woody Guthrie soon released a folk song commemorating those who died on the *Reuben James*.[8]

Americans did not have long to mourn the *Reuben James*. When America and Germany found themselves formally at war in mid-December 1941, Dönitz moved quickly. He dispatched five of his long-range Type IX U-boats to attack merchant shipping along the U.S. East Coast and prepared another sixteen for follow-on missions. Despite unambiguous intelligence warnings by the British revealing the westward movement of the U-boats, the U.S. Navy was caught flat-footed. Hardegen in U-123 struck first, sinking the 9,076-ton British freighter *Cyclops* 125 miles

southeast of Cape Sable, Nova Scotia. The carnage of Operation Paukenschlag (Drumbeat) had begun, and several attacks off Long Island hammered home a terrifying new reality: the grey wolves were at America's
door. Between January and August 1942, when the U.S. Navy and Army
Air Forces finally secured the North American coastline by establishing a
coastal convoy system and mounting extensive aerial patrols, the U-boats
sank 609 Allied merchant ships totaling three million tons of shipping capacity. By March 1943, however, New York and other American coastal
cities could breathe a bit easier. The Battle of the Atlantic had shifted to
the northern convoy runs, and the U-boats had long since vanished from
the harbor approaches to Boston, New York, Hampton Roads, and
Florida. Now they were farther out at sea, hunting the convoys that were
keeping Britain alive.[9]

The naval battles playing out in the North Atlantic were a key part of
the Allied war plan, which called for taking the fight to Germany on the
European continent it now dominated. That meant, first and foremost,
that the Allies had to defeat the U-boats. When Roosevelt, Churchill, and
their military advisers met in Washington, D.C., several weeks after Pearl
Harbor, FDR had pledged that the United States would support the
strategic goal of "Germany first," giving priority to the defeat of the Nazi
regime over all others, including the crushing of Japan. Turning that
pledge into military reality posed two challenges for the U.S. military:
helping defend the British against the U-boat threat to its maritime trade
lifeline, while also shipping a massive force of army soldiers, airmen, and
sailors and their gear to staging bases in the United Kingdom.

To invade Europe from a staging ground in Britain, the Allies would almost certainly have to land somewhere in France, which at the narrowest
point in the English Channel is just over twenty miles from Britain. The
initial plan to invade France, drafted in early 1942 by an obscure major
general named Dwight David Eisenhower, anticipated a force of twenty-
eight U.S. Army divisions totaling nearly 400,000 men, who would fight
alongside another ten British divisions after a cross-Channel invasion.
Called Operation Sledgehammer, this plan quickly collapsed under the
weight of its own contradictions. No such U.S. Army force existed anywhere in 1942, much less in the United Kingdom. In fact, only the 1st
and 29th Infantry Divisions with a total of 28,000 troops had reached

British Prime Minister Winston Churchill and First Sea Lord Admiral Dudley Pound took a direct interest in Great Britain's response to the U-boat threat.

Clay Blair Collection, American Heritage Center, University of Wyoming

British soil by October 1942, joining a vanguard of several thousand U.S. Army Air Forces personnel assembling there for a separate, planned Anglo-American aerial bombing campaign against Germany. Fearing that further Allied delays in going to battle against the Germans might spark the Soviet Union's Joseph Stalin to make a separate peace with Hitler, the Allies opted for Operation Torch—the invasion of North Africa. As a result, the 1st Infantry Division and most of the stockpiled military supplies in Great Britain went south against the Afrika Korps, and by early March 1943 the buildup of men and equipment for the invasion of France was just starting over from scratch.[10]

Military supplies were not the only commodity desperately needed in Britain in the early spring of 1943. To be sure, the military gear that Allied merchant ships continued to haul to the United Kingdom—disassembled aircraft, bombs, artillery pieces, trucks, landing craft, ammunition, and fuel—were in high demand at the bases and military stockpiles that covered Great Britain from Londonderry to Cornwall. But a second category of cargo was just as vital to the British war effort: food, fuel, and other supplies still being sent to the civilian population under the Lend-Lease program. The initial U-boat onslaught in the Atlantic in 1940–41 had reduced British shipping capacity to the point that food and raw material imports had dropped from 43 million tons to 29.4 million tons. Strict food rationing had become a fact of life in Britain since then. On average, a British civilian could obtain twelve ounces of bread and two ounces of tea per day. Meat and eggs were in even shorter supply, with an allotment of just four ounces of ham or bacon per person each week, and one egg every two weeks—if eggs were available. Lend-Lease shipments provided much of this food, in thousands of tons of cargo that ranged from canned meat, vegetables, and fruit to condensed milk, cheese, and eggs. By early 1943, the U.S. economy was committed to providing the embattled British one-fourth of their national food supply. If the ships carrying these rations could not make it past the U-boats in the Atlantic, many Britons would starve.[11]

The Allied convoy system had risen to meet Britain's urgent needs but was still desperately short itself in several crucial respects. On paper, it had matured into a well-organized structure by March 1943. As the number of available merchant vessels steadily grew and the U-boat threat—also steadily escalating—shifted from one operational area to another, the Allied convoy system had expanded and regularly changed its routes to avoid enemy encounters. In reality, however, the Allies continuously scrambled to overcome shortages of escort warships, land-based patrol aircraft, and modern weapons and sensors to fight the U-boats.

The escort shortages that plagued the Allied convoy system had been a perennial problem since the beginning of the war. From September 1939 until March 1942, the British Admiralty and its Canadian counterpart, the Naval Service Headquarters in Ottawa, had managed the North Atlantic convoys. A shortage of surface warships had only allowed the two navies to escort eastbound convoys partway across the Atlantic, and westbound convoys only to a point west of Ireland. After these points, the escorts would turn back to port while the merchant ships dispersed to proceed independently to their ports of destination. The German U-boat Force had quickly learned of this weakness and shifted operations out into the deep Atlantic to pick off the unprotected merchant vessels. This forced the British and Canadians—and by mid-1941 in deep secrecy, the U.S. Atlantic Fleet—to come up with enough escorts to convoy the civilian ships all the way across the ocean.[12]

In organizing North Atlantic shipping, British planners devised a simple system that divided merchantmen into two groups based on the ship's top speed. Vessels that could maintain a steady speed of ten to fifteen knots would go in fast HX convoys staging out of Halifax, Nova Scotia, a major Canadian city whose port served as a gateway for resources from across the country. Those merchantmen unable to maintain at least ten knots sustained speed would travel in slow SC convoys embarking from Sydney, Cape Breton, or Halifax. Westbound convoys were similarly separated into fast Outbound (North), or ON groups and Outbound (North) Slow, or ONS formations, which left British ports to assemble in the North Channel separating Scotland and Northern Ireland.

Even under the best conditions, east- and westbound convoys often took longer to cross the Atlantic than their planners would have liked. For one thing, the average speed of a convoy was normally several knots slower than the designated rate of advance, since each formation would steam only as fast as the slowest vessel in the group. Assuming they encountered no delays from weather or U-boat attacks, the HX convoys would usually complete the 2,300-nautical-mile passage in fourteen to fifteen days depending on the specific routing, while the slow SC convoys would complete the crossing in fifteen to sixteen days. The trip would take longer if the convoy encountered storms or if its course track required significant evasive routing to the north or south of the great-circle routes between the Canadian and British ports. One formation in February 1943, Slow Convoy ONS169, was battered by a series of fierce winter gales that brought it to a standstill for days at a time. The convoy took an unprecedented twenty-seven days to reach New York.*

*For a listing of all Allied convoys between March 1 and May 24, 1943, see Appendix 2 on page 405.

By the fall of 1942, New York had become the principal staging ground for convoys departing for Britain. The U.S. Navy had assumed control over eastbound convoys in September 1942 and shifted the port of departure for both HX and SC convoys to New York. After this changeover, the fast westbound ON formations proceeded to New York, while slower ONS convoys headed for Halifax or New York, as convoy planners dictated. By early March 1943, slow convoys were departing New York and the United Kingdom at roughly eight- or nine-day intervals, while fast convoys departed about once a week. Because of their staggered departure schedules, there were always between ten and twelve eastbound and westbound convoys at sea on any given day. During the first week of March, ten North Atlantic convoys—six westbound ON/ONS formations and four eastbound HX/SC convoys—were at sea with a total of 577 ships among them.

The inexorable growth of the Allied merchant fleet had created a new problem for port authorities and convoy planners: overcrowding in New York and other ports. Collisions between ships in port had soared; in New York in February alone, thirty-one collisions involving sixty-two ships had occurred in the crowded anchorages or shipping channels. Scrambling to clear New York's congested harbor so as to avoid repair-related delays in the merchantmen's shipping schedules, convoy officials assigned eighty merchant ships apiece to the last HX and SC convoys to depart for the United Kingdom in February. Convoys SC121 and HX228 had departed on February 23 and February 28, respectively, dropping the number of merchantmen in New York to about 200. The much-needed expansion of the merchant fleet had only one downside: there would be more targets for the German wolf packs.[13]

A little over a week after the departure of fast Convoy HX228, another 118 merchant ships prepared to leave port. Three convoys were scheduled to sail during March 5–9: Slow Convoy SC122 with fifty vessels, fast Convoy HX229 with forty merchantmen, and an ad hoc fast Convoy HX229A, organized to further relieve the overcrowding. HX229A would contain another twenty-eight vessels, including thirteen large oil tankers. While each convoy's ultimate destination was the North Channel and the United Kingdom, the formations also served to move ships between three interim ports along the way. As the convoys moved past the Canadian ports of Halifax and St. John's, a number of ships were scheduled to detach from the formations, while additional ships would steam out to meet the convoys for the mid-Atlantic passage. Five ships that left New York in SC122 would detach for Halifax or St. John's, while another sixteen merchantmen would join the slow convoy from those ports. Six ships in fast Convoy HX229A likewise would break off for the Canadian ports while another eighteen merchantmen were scheduled to join up from there.

The ships waiting to depart New York in the first week of March formed a cross-section of the Allied merchant fleet. They included dry cargo freighters, refrigerated ships with cargoes of frozen meat, bulk cargo carriers laden with chemicals or grain, oil tankers, and several tank landing ships. They also came from a dozen different nations. Of 149 ships preparing to sail in the three convoys from all ports, fifty-one flew the Union Jack. There were also thirty-three American merchantmen, thirteen Panamanian-flagged vessels, eight from Norway, and seven Dutchmen. Seven other countries were represented as well, with three Icelandic ships, two apiece from Belgium, Greece, and Sweden, and one each from Canada, Denmark, and Yugoslavia. The ships flying the flags of six German-occupied countries were operating under the protection of the British Merchant Navy. Beginning with the German invasion of Norway in April 1940, the British publicly invited merchant ships at sea whose countries had been occupied to come under the protection of the Union Jack—for the duration of the war, or until they were sunk. More than 700 ships from Norway, Denmark, Belgium, the Netherlands, France, Greece, and Yugoslavia eventually joined the Allied convoy effort.[14]

Combined, convoys SC122, HX229, and HX229A would transport nearly a million tons of food, fuel, and war supplies to the British Isles. Stowed in their holds were 170,000 tons of petroleum fuels, 150,000 tons of frozen meat, and 600,000 tons of general cargo, including food, timber, ammunition, disassembled aircraft, locomotives, and tanks. The ships ranged in age from the forty-three-year-old 7,022-ton British ship *Sevilla* to eight vessels on their first voyage, including a number of American-built Liberty ships now just entering the merchant fleet. They ranged in size from the diminutive 775-ton Icelandic coastal steamer *Selfoss* to the mammoth 15,130-ton British refrigerated ship *Akaroa*.[15]

Although this trip would be the maiden voyage for some of the ships in the three convoys, many of the merchantmen bound had already traversed their fair share of treacherous waters. The Glen Line's 9,503-ton refrigerated stores ship *Glenapp* had loaded a cargo of cocoa, palm oil, and copper at Lagos, Nigeria, in November but the Admiralty had canceled the Sierra Leone–Great Britain convoy route due to the Allied invasion of North Africa. So the twenty-three-year-old British merchantman had sailed from Africa to Cuba to join the U.S. interlocking coastal convoy system, arriving in New York on Christmas 1942 with a burned-out engine that necessitated weeks of repairs before it could complete its voyage home. The Royal Mail Lines 8,174-ton *Nariva* and Donaldson Line's 7,252-ton *Coracero*—both refrigerated stores ships—had taken even longer, more wandering routes to find themselves in New York that week. Both had loaded frozen beef cargoes at Buenos Aires for Great Britain. U.S. Navy convoy planners, having received reports of a U-boat wolf pack off the Brazilian coast, ordered the two ships to make the long voyage around Cape Horn into the Pacific, then steam north along the west coast of South America until they could pass into the Caribbean via the Panama Canal. Two vessels—the Dutch 5,158-ton *Terkoelei* and New Zealander 8,695-ton *Tekoa*—were among a number of vessels that had begun their voyages in distant Australia, loading cargoes of Australian wheat, zinc, and frozen meats. The newly constructed *Fort Cedar Lake* and *Fort Anne,* both 7,134-ton freighters, had begun their trips in Vancouver, British Columbia, with cargoes of lumber, phosphates, lead, timber, and explosives.[16]

Convoy SC122 was the first of the three early March formations to depart New York. The slow convoy was scheduled to leave for the Atlantic at first light on Friday, March 5, and as New Yorkers began to fill the city's streets, the crewmen on the fifty vessels were preparing to get their ships underway. As they readied for departure, the civilian masters of the ships in SC122 would no doubt have reminded themselves of the explicit instructions presented to them by U.S. Navy authorities the day before.

On Thursday morning, with their ships topped off with fuel and last-minute extra cargo lashed to the main decks, the captains had met with U.S. Navy and civilian port officials at a formal sailing conference at the New York port director's office at 17 Battery Place. Presiding was Navy Captain F. G. Reinicke, navy director of the Port of New York. The sailing conference followed a well-established routine. Reinicke introduced the SC122 convoy commodore, retired Royal Navy Reserve Captain Samuel N. White. A veteran British merchant sea captain, White would fly his flag on the recently repaired *Glenapp*. As commodore, it was White's responsibility to coordinate the convoy's movements as directed by the commander of the escort group, and to ensure that the ships maintained proper formation and carried out emergency maneuvers passed on by a small communications staff riding with him on the flagship. The authorities at the sailing conference also introduced Commodore F. R. McNeil, master of the 2,870-ton British freighter *Boston City*, as vice commodore. His responsibility would be to take over leadership of SC122 if anything happened to Captain White or the *Glenapp*.

After the convoy's leaders had been presented, the rest of the session consisted of a review of convoy basics. SC122 would travel in fourteen columns of two to five ships each. Every ship would maintain the standard separation of 1,000 yards between vessels in the adjacent columns and 500 yards between the leading and following ships. The masters reviewed communications security, including which radio frequencies to guard and which convoy ciphers to use. Commodore White restated how important it was for each ship to avoid making excess smoke by day, and for maintaining strict darkened-ship conditions at night so as not to betray the convoy's presence to the U-boats. In addition to these security regulations, each master was informed of the position that his vessel would occupy in the convoy. Captain William Laidler, master of the 4,898-ton British freighter *Kingsbury*, learned that his ship was assigned to position 51, lead ship in the fifth (counting from port to starboard) of the fourteen columns of Convoy SC122. Thus the *Kingsbury* would be one of the first vessels to weigh anchor and get under way on Friday morning.[17]

The first leg of SC122's eastbound passage from New York promised to be uneventful. The convoy would sail several hundred miles due east from New York, then turn northeast to follow the U.S. and Canadian coastlines for about 1,200 nautical miles up toward Newfoundland, under the protection of a local escort group. When it reached the assigned Western Ocean Meeting Point, or WESTOMP, eighty-one nautical miles southeast of St. John's, Newfoundland, the formation would then rendezvous with a more powerful mid-ocean escort group assigned to shepherd it across the

North Atlantic. The U-boats had heavily attacked coastal shipping during the spring of 1942, but abandoned the inshore area in late summer after a steady buildup of coastal convoys, reinforced local escort groups, and land-based patrol aircraft. SC122 could expect a peaceful start to its long journey.*

The key piece of information that the SC122 ship captains had received at Thursday's sailing conference was not the route up to WESTOMP, however, but what would follow it: the convoy's path from WESTOMP to the North Channel. Unlike the voyage up the North American coast, this leg of the trip promised to be a treacherous one. Particularly risky was the lack of air cover for the convoys for a long stretch of their trans-Atlantic journey. In the spring of 1943, Allied land-based patrol aircraft could not cover the Greenland air gap, the broad, 600-to-800-mile swath of open ocean southwest of Iceland. While crossing this expanse of ocean, the merchantmen and their escorts could expect no air support. Unlike warships, which could have a difficult time spotting U-boats in the choppy waters of the North Atlantic even when the enemy was hovering at periscope depth, aircraft had a bird's-eye view that enabled them to quickly spot the shadows of U-boats and relay this information down to the convoy escorts. Additionally, these patrol aircraft were being equipped with airborne radar sets that could detect a U-boat on the surface even if it were cloaked in cloud cover. Without this critical air support, the defenders would have to rely on their own, imperfect methods for locating and attacking submerged U-boats.

Like the Allies, the Germans were well aware of the Greenland air gap. Swarms of U-boats assigned to different wolf packs were using it as their primary hunting ground for the North Atlantic convoys. For anywhere from three to six days, depending on convoy speed and the weather, each formation and its mid-ocean escort group would be most vulnerable to attack.

The shifting locations of U-boats in the Greenland air gap made up only one factor that convoy planners used to determine each formation's specific mid-ocean route. The navy's Convoy and Routing staffers in

---

*Allied planners designated a slightly different latitude-longitude location for each WESTOMP a convoy would use, but all were generally a day's steaming southeast from St. John's, Newfoundland.

Washington pored over Allied naval intelligence reports on the U-boat Force, studied the current weather patterns, and coordinated with their British counterparts at the Admiralty's Operational Intelligence Centre and the Admiralty Trading Division in London over the routing of other convoys. A prime concern was to avoid entangling the various east- and westbound formations with one another as they transited the Atlantic. The Great Circle route from Newfoundland to the entrance of the North Channel measured about 1,700 nautical miles. Taking this route would normally result in a seven-day journey in good weather for a fast HX convoy and nine to eleven days for a slow SC formation. This was also the least likely course track that Allied planners would ever use, for it would send the merchantmen straight through the German wolf packs lurking in the Greenland air gap. Moreover, SC122, like many convoys leaving New York, included ships bound for Halifax and St. John's in Canada, and additional ships with cargo for Great Britain coming out of those Canadian ports would join up with the HX/SC formations. Similarly, eight ships in SC122 were scheduled to detach for Iceland midway through the crossing, so the convoy's planners needed to send it close to the south of that island nation.[18]

The planners rarely plotted a straight-line course track, which would be too easy for the enemy to track if the convoy were spotted. Instead, planners devised a series of waypoints with course changes aimed at maneuvering the main convoy body, usually spanning six to seven miles in width and one mile deep, around the massed U-boats. Because of those factors, the North Atlantic convoy routes from WESTOMP to the British Isles tended to fall within a broad corridor of the ocean roughly 650 to 700 miles wide, bordered to the north by the Greenland ice pack and to the south by the current estimated position of the U-boats. In theory, there was plenty of ocean in which to steam undetected.

When the civilian masters assigned to Convoy SC122 met on March 4 and their counterparts in HX229 and HX229A met several days later, Allied planners had plotted initial courses for the three convoys. The intention was to have SC122 and HX229 gradually diverge until they were nearly 250 miles apart after passing Cape Race and entering the Greenland air gap. Upon leaving harbor, all three formations would proceed several hundred miles in a generally easterly course before turning east-northeast for the four-day passage up toward Newfoundland. However, SC122 beginning on March 8 would steer a course of 061 degrees for five days, and HX229 beginning on March 10 would hold firm to a course of 070 degrees. Even though both convoy routes passed well to the north of the Great Circle path, the two still kept well to the south of the dangerous iceberg waters off Labrador and Greenland.

Convoy HX229A would follow a significantly different course than those of SC122 and HX229. The Navy Convoy and Routing planners plotted a course that took that formation far to the north as soon as it passed Cape Race. While adding nearly 600 miles to the convoy's route, the northward track minimized the amount of time the ships would lack land-based aircraft support, while also steering the formation well clear of the known U-boat locations. Given the known risks and the continuing shortage of escorts, it was the best the planners could do for the three convoys.[19]

DEANE WYNNE came up on deck after a four-hour watch in the freighter's engine room, where he had shoveled coal nonstop into the fire boxes below the massive boilers. For the past ten days, Wynne and the other forty-three officers and merchant sailors aboard the 4,898-ton British freighter *Kingsbury* had been confined to the ship as it lay anchored in New York Harbor. They were awaiting the sailing of the next slow convoy to the United Kingdom. The harbor and docks were jammed with merchant vessels of all types and nationalities, and the ships were heavily laden with every form of cargo imaginable. It was Friday, March 5, 1943, and the crew was preparing for sea at last. Captain William Laidler, master of the *Kingsbury*, had informed his crew the afternoon before that they would be raising anchor shortly after 7:00 a.m. EST as part of eastbound Convoy SC122.

While Wynne was conscious of the cityscape he was now departing, he was just as aware of the dangerous waters through which the *Kingsbury* would soon be passing. Their ten-day sojourn in New York Harbor had been a difficult time. The *Kingsbury* had originally left New York on February 23 in Convoy SC121 but sustained minor damage in a storm that left the ship unable to keep up with the formation. Forced to return to port, the crew confronted another worry, the ice-clogged Hudson River. Massive chunks of ice continuously drifted downstream into the crowded anchorage, and the crewmen were forced to prepare for an emergency

The 4,898-ton British steam merchant *Kingsbury* in Convoy SC122 was carrying a cargo from West Africa of bauxite and bulk lumber.
Alexander Capper & Co. Ltd., U.K.

move at all hours. "Ice floes were banging against the ships' sides as the wind broke up the ice further upstream," Wynne recalled years later. Just as hazardous as the wintry weather could be the effect it had on other ships. The combination of gale-force winds and the swift river current frequently had resulted in ships dragging their anchors and sliding downstream out of control. Two ships moored near the *Kingsbury*—the 6,813-ton Dutch freighter *Zaanland* and 5,214-ton Norwegian ship *Elin K.*—had already collided when the larger ship, swinging on its anchor chain at the turn of the tide, got stuck by the bow on the harbor bottom. While the crew attempted to free their ship, the larger *Zaanland* struck the Norwegian merchantman, ripping a hole in the *Elin K.*'s forepeak that required emergency repairs.[20]

The nineteen-year-old Wynne did not know the name of the convoy in which his ship would return to the British Isles, nor did he care. As a junior member of the *Kingsbury*'s "black gang," the detachment responsible for shoveling coal into the ship's enormous furnaces, he was unaware of the ship's assigned position at the head of Column 5 in SC122. He was a lower-ranking member of the crew, privy to none of the information about the current U-boat threat or even the long-term weather predictions on the convoy's projected route. All Wynne knew was that he was finally returning to England and his widowed mother after nearly a year of non-stop convoying since signing up in the British Merchant Navy in the spring of 1942. That one year had been more than enough.

In his time at sea, Wynne had already seen the Allied shipping program from a great many angles. After signing up in the merchant navy, Wynne had briefly served as a cabin steward on a Dutch freighter plying the English coastal routes. The assignment ended abruptly when a drunken crewman assaulted him, prompting a brief hospital stay, facial stitches, and a hasty transfer to the 2,892-ton Norwegian freighter *Veni*. Wynne had crossed the North Atlantic five times on that filthy, coal-dust-ridden freighter before leaving the ship in New York in January 1943. His most recent convoy trip, the last aboard the *Veni*, had been a voyage of terror. The forty-six ships of westbound Convoy ONS154 had endured a fierce assault by two German wolf packs that sank a total of sixteen ships during December 27–30, 1942. For nearly ninety-six hours, the U-boats had out-matched and overpowered the Canadian escort group trying to protect the convoy. Wynne and the other engine-room crewmen frantically shoveled coal as the *Veni's* hull reverberated with the concussions from exploding torpedo warheads. The experience had made all too clear the dangers that awaited Wynne on the *Kingsbury's* imminent voyage.

After leaving the *Veni*, Wynne had enjoyed a six-week sabbatical ashore while waiting for a new assignment. As a British merchant sailor, he received a $3 per day allowance, which covered his meals and lodging in a New York Seaman's Mission and allowed him to explore the sights and sounds of Manhattan. Wynne's leave abruptly ended on February 23, when a British consular aide collared him at the Seaman's Mission and whisked him down to the waterfront for a boat ride out to the *Kingsbury* and its sailing with Convoy SC121.[21]

With a sudden blast of the ship's horn and a loudspeaker announcement from the bridge, the *Kingsbury* began weighing anchor around 0718 hours EST, as the first of the fifty merchantmen in Convoy SC122 began heading down the channel. Wynne turned and went below to shovel coal into the *Kingsbury's* furnaces—ready once again, after days of inactivity, for the dull routine that would consume two four-hour watches every day of the voyage. It was backbreaking work that paid relatively little. Yet apart

Deane Wynne spent most of World War II at sea on merchant ships.
Courtesy of Ruth Wynne

from the danger of being torpedoed, Wynne saw this as a far better life than fighting with the British Army in Africa or flailing about the ocean in a Royal Navy corvette.

The convoy flagship *Glenapp* went first, backing out from a wharf on the city's Upper West Side. Slowly proceeding downriver, it gathered the ships earmarked to lead the convoy's thirteen other columns. The *Kingsbury* met the procession as it passed down through New York Harbor, taking position astern of the *Glenapp* as the formation proceeded in single file through the Verrazano Narrows and down the outbound channel to the sea.

As it entered the coastal waters of the Atlantic Ocean, the captains and crews in SC122 were confident about the first leg of their journey. Dense coverage by land-based patrol aircraft and the protection afforded to convoys under the year-old coastal convoy system made it unlikely that any U-boats would interfere with the formation on the initial 1,200-nautical-mile run from New York to the designated Western Ocean Meeting Point. The convoy's diminutive escort force, three Canadian corvettes and a minesweeper, confirmed the Allies' awareness that no U-boats were in the coastal waters. Throughout the day, patrol aircraft and even a navy blimp flew overhead. It would have been a reassuring sight for veterans of previous voyages across the North Atlantic. Once they reached the deeper ocean, air cover would become more sporadic, then disappear altogether.[22]

After leaving New York harbor, Commodore White held the *Glenapp* and the column leaders on a steady easterly course and speed of five knots, while the rest of the convoy ships fell into their assigned positions. It took more than seven hours for the convoy to maneuver into its designated formation, by which point the skyscrapers of New York had faded into the distance.

As with most convoys, the ships in SC122 were assigned a position in the convoy's main body based on each vessel's intended destination, with an eye toward minimizing the disruption to the convoy as ships detached or joined the formation en route. For SC122, two vessels destined for Halifax constituted Column 1 on the convoy's port side. When they arrived at the Halifax Ocean Meeting Point on Tuesday, March 9, these ships would simply turn out of the formation to proceed to the Nova Scotia capital while the main body continued on its way. Similarly, a trio of merchantmen proceeding to St. John's occupied Column 2, which would then be the outermost port file of ships after Column 1 departed. Another six ships destined for Reyjkavik under separate escort filled Columns 3 and 4. The same planning dictated which vessels would fill the starboard columns. As the convoy neared the northern coast of Ireland, the eleven ships scheduled for Belfast, Northern Ireland, would find it easy to detach from SC122, since the planners had placed them in Columns 12 through 14 on the far right flank of the formation. The rest of the ships heading for the North Channel filled the convoy's center columns.[23]

This logical arrangement of ships brought scant comfort to veteran merchant seamen. All too often, a ship's placement in a convoy could determine its chances of surviving the trans-Atlantic voyage. Sailors like Deane Wynne were well aware of this cold fact and would have watched with apprehension as their ship maneuvered into its designated spot in the front row of the convoy. Their greatest fear was to be an easy target for a marauding U-boat, and from experience they knew that some positions in a convoy formation were significantly more dangerous than others. During his previous trans-Atlantic crossings on the Norwegian freighter *Veni*,

Wynne had quickly soaked up the conventional wisdom of which sailing positions were relatively safe, and which ones were not. Since U-boats primarily attacked convoy formations from the sides or from the front, the exposed outer columns and the leading row of ships were deemed the most dangerous places to be. Ships bringing up the rear in each column faced an additional potential danger, Wynne later recalled. "The last ship in each column was always asked if they would stop and pick up survivors," he noted. "Very few did. It was at great risk to themselves and their own crews. The value of a few lives at sea in those days was far outvalued by the cargo the ship was carrying, and indeed the ship itself, which would hopefully be available to make a few more crossings."

By late afternoon on Friday, March 5, Commodore White had Convoy SC122 in relatively good shape as the formation continued on its initial easterly track. All fifty vessels had reached their designated positions in the convoy, which was now traveling at the assigned speed of seven knots. The only glitch came when the forty-year-old Greek freighter *Georgios P.*, carrying a bulk load of sugar, signaled Commodore White that it could not maintain speed. The commodore ordered it to return to New York.

For the first few hours the convoy saw numerous patrol aircraft and several navy dirigibles overhead, but the skies grew empty as the ships continued east for the initial waypoint at 40:28 North 066:30 West, some 334 nautical miles offshore. There, the plan called for SC122 to turn to the northeast for the rendezvous four days later with fourteen ships joining from Halifax, and the handover three days after that from the Western Local Escort Force to the British mid-ocean escort group for the trans-Atlantic passage.

The first day and night at sea had passed in good weather, but late in the afternoon of Saturday, March 6, conditions began to deteriorate. As the sun dipped toward the western horizon, the winds picked up and the cloud layer thickened. A southerly gale swept in from the starboard beam and began lashing the ships. The waves grew in size until they dwarfed the merchantmen's hulls. The crewmen braced themselves for a long night. The ships began to roll and pitch in the deepening swells, and the convoy's neat pattern of rows and columns began to fall apart. The wind increased steadily until it was blowing a full gale. Watch-standers on the open navigation bridges of the four local escorts and lookouts on the merchant vessels braced themselves as the rain and spray lashed their faces. The captains of several merchant ships were forced to heave to, their bows pointed into the face of the wind, minimizing the chances that a rogue wave could capsize the ship, as the rest of the formation slowly vanished into the east.

When the sun broke through clouds on the morning of March 7, SC122 was scattered across several hundred square miles of ocean. Commodore White, however, had prepared for this eventuality. Anticipating the gale, he had sent a signal to the ships the previous afternoon identifying a rendezvous point for noon the next day, so most of the convoy was able to rejoin. When White finished counting, he found that eleven of the original forty-nine ships were still missing. He later learned that eight of them had aborted the convoy to return to port.

Two of the straggler ships rejoined SC122 two days later, prompting a message from Commodore White that perplexed many of the non-British signalmen throughout the convoy. When the 3,881-ton British bulk carrier *Vinriver* and the 3,684-ton Dutch freighter *Kedoe* finally caught up with the main body, the seas were still running high, making it difficult for them to return to their assigned stations. From his vantage point on the *Glenapp*'s bridge at the head of Column 8, White peered through binoculars as the smaller *Kedoe* struggled for more than an hour to get back to the second spot in Column 14, immediately behind the 6,198-ton American freighter *McKeesport*. When the doughty little ship finally made it, White ordered his signalman to flash a message to the Dutch captain via Aldis lamp: "Well done. Look up Luke 15:6." A short time later, the Dutch master signaled back, "I cannot find it in my Confidential Books."

The Dutchman's perplexity caused chuckling on the *Glenapp*'s bridge, for the British crew were experienced users of an informal communications technique that had evolved during the war: citing a biblical verse that contained the gist of what the sender wanted to communicate. Since most schoolchildren in British public schools studied the Bible as literature and history, many seamen found it simpler and faster to form their messages around an appropriate quotation in the Good Book. The signal itself would consist of just the particular biblical chapter and verse. British Merchant Navy veterans said the practice was popular because it offered watchstanders the chance to inject a little humor into what could be a boring or tense routine. "Captains were well versed and would turn to yeomen to look up a particular quotation applicable to a particular incident (or acci-dent)," said J. A. Bayley, a former Royal Navy signal yeoman. "Some [were] humorous, some serious, some admonishing a junior ship's captain for an error. Proverbs always were popular." In Bible Code, as British seamen called it, White had compared the straggler to the Prodigal Son: "And when he cometh home, he calleth together his friends and neighbors, say-ing unto them, rejoice with me; for I have found my sheep which was lost."

As Bayley could attest, not all messages in Bible Code were sent in a spirit of fun, however. One escort group commander reportedly became irked with the master of a coal-burning freighter that was having difficulty maintaining speed with the formation. At sunrise one morning, the de-stroyer skipper saw the elderly merchantman lagging several miles behind the other ships, and flashed it a Morse code message to keep better station. The master on the freighter signaled back that he was having trouble keeping pressure in his steam boilers but would try harder. However, on the following morning, the freighter once more had fallen behind the main body. The escort commander once more ordered the culprit to do what it took to get back in its assigned column. The civilian master meekly agreed. Then on the third morning in a row, the escort com-mander found the wrongdoer once again several miles astern of the con-voy, a ripe target for the next U-boat that might come along. "Get back in station as fast as possible," the destroyer commander signaled the freighter. "I'm doing the best I can," the freighter blinked back. Exasperated, the naval escort commander signaled, "Hebrews 13:8." The master of the freighter turned to the passage, which read: "JESUS CHRIST, the same yesterday, and today, and forever."[24]

By the end of the second day at sea, White had the convoy—now re-duced to thirty-eight ships—more or less back on track. Apart from the eight ships that had returned to port, only one, the 5,754-ton British iron ore carrier *Clarissa Radcliffe*, remained missing, and in fact, would never be seen again. The rectangular array of merchantmen, screened by the lo-cal escorts, continued plodding its way to the convoy route waypoint east of New York, where it would make the turn to the north-northeast and commence the five-day trek up to the meeting point off Newfoundland. From there, it would begin its long trek into the U-boat-infested North Atlantic.

WHILE CONVOY SC122 steamed into the early morning of March 8, heading toward the Western Ocean Meeting Point southeast of Newfoundland, several thousand other merchant crewmen and navy sailors were just beginning their preparations for the departure of fast Convoy HX229, which was slated to leave New York that same morning. In New York, Navy Signalman 3rd Class Theodore M. Schorr woke up in a strange room with a shadowy figure leaning into his bunk, shaking him hard. "You are wanted on the bridge," the sailor said. For a long moment, Schorr could not remember where he was or even how he had gotten to this unfamiliar berthing compartment. Then he remembered. His assignment to the 6,008-ton Panamanian-flagged freighter *El Mundo* had come suddenly the night before. By the time he had arrived at the ship and gotten checked in, it was already several hours past midnight. He had fallen instantly asleep upon climbing into his rack.

"Where is the bridge?" Schorr mumbled, shaking the sleep out of his head and climbing out on the linoleum tile deck. At that point, Schorr felt something strange underfoot. The ship was moving! Quickly dressing, Schorr climbed up a ladder and opened a door to the ship's rear cargo deck. He walked briskly forward toward the superstructure amidships to climb up to the ship's navigation bridge. The weather was frigid under a partial cloud layer and the ship's passage created a strong breeze that made him clench his hands together. It was Monday, March 8, 1943, and he was heading out into the North Atlantic on his first convoy.

Theodore Schorr was embarking on his initial convoy voyage, but he had been training for a long time for this moment. The son and grandson of Pittsburgh-area steel workers, the twenty-one-year-old Schorr had opted out of a safe "essential" industrial job in the Duquesne Steel Works that would have exempted him from the military draft. He had enlisted in the U.S. Navy at the end of 1942, hoping to serve on a large warship such as an aircraft carrier or battleship. Schorr soon learned that the navy had other needs and that the choice of assignment was not his to make. After boot camp at Great Lakes, Illinois, he received orders to attend a four-month signal school downstate in Champaign-Urbana, where he and dozens of other sailors were trained as signalmen. He studied Morse code, semaphore flag signaling, alphabet and numeral signal flag recognition, while taking refresher courses in reading and grammar. At the end of Jan-

Signalman 3rd Class Ted Schorr, second from right, relaxes with fellow Naval Armed Guard sailors on the freighter *El Mundo* in Convoy HX229.
Courtesy of Ted Schorr

uary 1943, Schorr and a handful of others were promoted to signalman 3rd class and assigned to the Naval Armed Guard. He had never heard of the organization.[25]

Schorr had never heard of the Naval Armed Guard because, up until recently, it hadn't existed. In January 1943, when he was assigned to that naval branch, the U.S. Navy was well into a wartime expansion program unprecedented in military history. Twelve months earlier, in the aftermath of Pearl Harbor, about 400,000 naval personnel were on active duty or in training. In the year that followed, the number of men and women in navy uniform more than tripled to 1.3 million. By July 1943, the navy would have sworn in its two millionth sailor and would continue to expand until reaching its wartime peak of 3.6 million officers and enlisted personnel on September 2, 1945, when the Japanese surrender ended the global conflict.[26]

The navy did not just assign this tidal wave of personnel to its rapidly expanding fleet of warships and auxiliaries. It also created a number of new commands to confront the many emerging threats at sea. One of these was organized to help defend merchant shipping from German U-boats, surface raiders, and aircraft, as well as Japanese forces in the Pacific theater. At the outbreak of war in Europe on September 1, 1939, the United States Merchant Marine had roughly 1,400 large merchant ships under its control. The U.S. Maritime Commission soon organized a massive civilian shipbuilding program to expand the merchant fleet, particularly the supply chain being formed between the United States and Britain. Like their Royal Navy counterparts, U.S. Navy officials after Pearl Harbor realized that to protect larger merchant ships it would be necessary to install defensive armament on board, man them with naval gunners, and provide a cadre of communications specialists to aid the civilian ship masters when steaming in formation. The navy foresaw that the need would become even greater as the American shipbuilding industry went into high gear, constructing nearly 5,000 new merchant freighters and fuel tankers to replace those lost by the enemy. The expanding merchant fleet would ferry ever larger numbers of troops, supplies, and armament across the Atlantic and Pacific to far-flung scenes of battle. Thus was born the Naval Armed Guard, the American counterpart to the British Defensively Equipped Merchant Ships (DEMS).[27]

The primary mission of Naval Armed Guard sailors was to man an array of guns that the service hastily installed aboard merchant ships. These ranged from a four-inch/.50-cal. deck gun firing high explosive shells at targets up to nine miles away, to diminutive 20-mm Oerlikon pedestal-mounted automatic cannons that a single sailor could man and fire. The navy also assigned signalmen and radio operators to aid the civilian masters as they followed their convoy commodore's orders at sea. Schorr had been trained as one of these specialists: a military serviceman who could help maintain order among the convoy of civilian merchantmen.

Like all sailors assigned to merchant ships in the Atlantic, Schorr had reported for duty at the Armed Guard Center (Atlantic), a sprawling navy complex on the Brooklyn waterfront facing New York Harbor. He arrived at the facility on February 28 and stored his sea bag and other possessions in its massive berthing compartment that could accommodate 1,700 sailors at a time. Sleep was difficult because at all hours, loudspeakers would blare out instructions to crewmen assigned to departing ships. Depending on the size of the ship and the number of guns it carried, an Armed Guard detachment could be anywhere from a dozen to as many as forty men. Schorr spent the next few days processing paperwork. After that, the master-at-arms told him to listen carefully whenever there was a loudspeaker announcement. His name would soon come up.

On Sunday evening, March 7, seven days after his arrival, Schorr had been watching a movie when the loudspeaker summoned him and two other sailors to the master-at-arms' shack. There, the grizzled chief petty officer ordered them to pack their gear. Several minutes later, the three sailors were in a station wagon driven by a Red Cross volunteer slowly heading down the Brooklyn docks. They stopped at one warehouse and wandered through to the other end, where a large door opened out onto a pier. There, Navy Ensign Leonardo DeMarco, the ship's Armed Guard detachment commander, was waiting for them. He accepted their papers and told them to board the freighter. They were last-minute replacements for three other sailors in the twenty-man Armed Guard detachment aboard, the officer said. "He explained that I was the only signalman so that my duty was to be on the bridge from before sunrise until after sunset," Schorr recalled. "The rest, he said, I would have to myself as time allowed."[28]

As Schorr made his way up to the bridge on the *El Mundo* on the morning of March 8, the forty ships of Convoy HX229 were beginning their departure from New York the same way that SC122 had done three days earlier. Starting at 0930 EST, the convoy flagship *Abraham Lincoln*, a 5,749-ton Norwegian freighter, edged out into the Hudson River and, with a loud blast of its horn, summoned the other ten column leaders to follow it downstream toward New York Harbor and the Verrazano Narrows. In charge of the merchantman was convoy Commodore Maurice J. D. Mayall, a World War I–era destroyer commander whose civilian career in the interwar years had been spent with the Canadian Pacific Lines, a freight and passenger liner company operating worldwide. The retired Royal Navy Reserve captain had returned to wartime service in November 1942 as a convoy leader. Earlier in the year, the sixty-year-old Mayall had served as vice-commodore of Convoy ON159 in the 7,248-ton British tanker *Daghestan*. The formation of twenty-nine merchantmen made the westbound crossing without incident from the North Channel to New York during January 4–20.[29]

Like his colleague Captain White in SC122, Mayall spent the better part of HX229's first day at sea organizing the eleven columns of three and four ships, with his flagship in the lead position in Column 6, dead center in the front row. He sent signal flag after signal flag soaring up the hoists, and the ship's Aldis lamp flashed continuous messages in blinking Morse code to the other vessels. Once the convoy had formed up, four local escort warships—an American destroyer, a British destroyer, and two Canadian corvettes—took station for the first leg of the journey.[30]

Signalman Ted Schorr's first watch began in total chaos. Arriving in the *El Mundo*'s pilot house several minutes after the abrupt summons, he reported to Ensign DeMarco, the detachment commander. "Schorr," the ensign told him, "someone on the beach is calling us with a flashing light." Schorr glanced around to see where the ship's Aldis lamp was mounted, so that he could prepare to flash back a response. There was no lamp in sight. Only then did DeMarco explain why Schorr had been assigned to the *El Mundo* at the last minute: the detachment signalman and two gunners had been given a four-day leave and could not return in time to make the ship's movement. Now, no one on the ship had any idea where the signalman had stowed his equipment. Everyone in the wheelhouse who was able to lend a free hand began to break into the boxes laying about, until someone found an Aldis lamp and showed Schorr where to mount it on the bridge wing and plug it into the electrical system. Schorr prompted the signaler on shore to relay the message, then turned to *El Mundo*'s master.

The signalman announced to the ship's master that an important matter had been overlooked. "Sir," Schorr said, "your degaussing system has not been turned on." This revelation caused a major commotion on the *El Mundo*. Each merchant vessel and warship carried special degaussing gear designed to neutralize the steel hull's magnetic field so as to prevent it from setting off magnetic mines. The captain barked an order, and soon the shore-based lamp blinked again, confirming that the system was now operating.

The degaussing system was working, but several minutes later came another hubbub. A lookout reported that several ships in the convoy were sending signal flag messages. Schorr asked for a pair of binoculars and read off the letters from the convoy flagship. He then went out on the bridge wing to send a confirming reply up the signal hoists, only to find that there were no signal flags in the storage boxes. This brought another hands-and-knees search in the boxes and crates before they were found. Schorr spent an hour stowing the brightly colored flags in their assigned pigeonholes. By that time, the *El Mundo* had taken Position 73 in the convoy, the third ship in the seventh column, and the other ships in convoy HX229 were continuing to assemble as the formation steamed due east from the mouth of New York Harbor. As in all convoys, the process of getting each ship to its designated place required tremendous exertion from the masters, helmsmen, lookouts, and signalmen.[31]

About three miles away from the convoy flagship, the 5,848-ton American freighter *Mathew Luckenbach* was steaming in Position 34, the last of four ships in the third column from the convoy's port beam. On the *Mathew Luckenbach's* bridge wing, Signalman 3rd Class John Orris Jackson confirmed yet another message from the flagship and turned to hand the scrawled text to Captain Antwood N. Borden, master of the twenty-five-year-old merchant ship. A native of the small farming town of Rydal, Kansas, Jackson had already made five convoy runs since joining the navy fourteen months earlier. He had sufficient experience to be wary of his new assignment on the ramshackle merchantman.

The *Mathew Luckenbach* was an old, cranky ship. It carried a single funnel amidships behind the three-level pilot house and was distinctive for its two clusters of boom cranes to service the forward and aft cargo holds. One civilian crewman years later described how he felt on first seeing the freighter about a week after Jackson himself had come on board. "I will never forget my first impression of the ship," said Able Seaman Pasquale Civitillo. "As we stepped from the warehouse onto the pier, my heart sank. There, lying low in the water, vintage World War One, a mass of rust, booms in disarray, lashings running everywhere and toilet chutes flying in the wind, was the *Mathew Luckenbach*. I felt like turning around and running; only pride kept me going."

Despite the *Mathew Luckenbach's* age and poor appearance, the navy had invested considerable expense in outfitting the ship for duty. Installed on its decks were twelve guns, including a four-inch/.50-cal. cannon on the stern, a three-inch/.50-caliber anti-aircraft gun on the foc's'le, the forward-most deck at the bow, and eight 20-mm Oerlikon cannons at stations amidship and aft. In addition to Jackson, there were twenty-one

Signalman 3rd Class John Orris Jackson, assigned to the American freighter *Mathew Luckenbach* in Convoy HX229, holds a long glass telescope used to identify signal flags from another ship.

Courtesy of the Jackson family

gunners and petty officers under the command of Ensign James H. Hammond. The ship may have been ugly, but it was doing its part in the convoy, carrying 12,000 tons of general cargo including two holds full of wheat and a dozen army trucks lashed to the weather decks.[32]

Jackson had recently returned to duty from two months of leave with his family in Kansas and was finding that he still enjoyed his war service. He had enlisted in the navy six weeks after Pearl Harbor and attended the navy's Signal School after boot camp. Receiving orders to the Naval Armed Guard—like Ted Schorr, he had never heard of the organization—Jackson had arrived at the Brooklyn center in July 1942. Several weeks later, he and thirteen other sailors had shipped out on the 7,462-ton Belgian-flagged freighter *Ville d'Anvers*, making an unremarkable run to Belfast, Northern Ireland with a cargo of steel and general supplies. Jackson's second cruise on the *Ville d'Anvers* had been a completely different experience. After steaming independently from New York to Liverpool, the ship had joined a massive southbound convoy moving supplies from Great Britain to North Africa as part of Operation Torch. Because the convoy had to run the gauntlet of both German aircraft and U-boats as it proceeded south near the Bay of Biscay, and because of German air threats in North Africa itself, the Western Approaches Command had assigned an unusually large force of escorts to protect it. Fortunately for the merchantmen, the passage was relatively uneventful, although, on November 28, Jackson had felt the deck underfoot rumble from the shock waves of depth charges that an escort had dropped on a suspected U-boat. It was his first taste of action, but it wouldn't be his last.[33]

Elsewhere in the Atlantic on the night of March 8, far from convoy HX229, another eastbound convoy was experiencing a brand of terror that Jackson had yet to encounter. Crewmen aboard the *Mathew Luckenbach* and the other HX229 merchantmen were still getting reacquainted with shipboard routine when sporadic messages came in over the BAMS circuit, a radio channel dedicated to message traffic to convoys at sea: a major U-boat attack was under way against eastbound Convoy SC121, more than 1,500 miles ahead of HX229 on the route to Great Britain. Word of the attack spread rapidly around the convoy. Although the men in HX229 were still relatively safe as they hugged the North American coastline, the coming days would require them to traverse the same expanse of water where, at this very moment, their fellow sailors were being stalked—and savaged—by the massed German wolf packs.

Chapter 2

THE ADVERSARIES

There could be no doubt about who was in charge in the massive, windowless chamber at Derby House in Liverpool. Among all the Royal Navy and Air Force officers and young uniformed members of the Women's Royal Naval Service who bustled about the crowded operations center of the Western Approaches Command, one figure often wore no signs of rank or military service. He frequently dressed, in fact, in ragged pajamas and a bathrobe—"hirsute fore and aft," as one staff aide later described it. Admiral Sir Max Kennedy Horton cut a strange and oft-commented-upon sight, but if the commander-in-chief opted to review an imminent convoy battle without bothering to dress, there was not a solitary person on his staff who was about to remind him of the Royal Navy's uniform regulations.

From their underground, armored citadel beneath Derby House, Admiral Horton and his staff directed the vast and unimaginably intricate business of protecting the flow of military supplies to the United Kingdom. Western Approaches Command monitored the movements of convoys and coordinated with the Royal Air Force Coastal Command's No. 15 Group on the disposition of land-based patrol aircraft. One of the command's primary responsibilities was the management of the Mid-Ocean Escort Force. In March 1943, the force consisted of twelve escort groups responsible for protecting east- and westbound convoys as they crossed the open waters of the North Atlantic (additional escort groups protected convoys running between Great Britain and Gibraltar, and from the United Kingdom to Soviet ports in the far north). Each of the North Atlantic

British Admiral Sir Max Horton,
commander of Western Approaches
Command in Liverpool, directed the
Allied effort against the U-boats in
the North Atlantic.
Imperial War Museum, U.K.

escort groups—seven British, four Canadian, and one American—would
rendezvous with a convoy at its assigned Western Ocean Meeting Point for
the eastbound trek to the British Isles, or at the entrance to the North
Channel for the western journey to North America. Upon arrival at St.
John's, Newfoundland, or Londonderry, Northern Ireland, an escort group
would have at least one week for crew rest and repairs before meeting its
next assigned convoy. Each of the escort groups nominally consisted of
two larger warships such as destroyers, frigates, or sloops, with a half dozen
or more smaller Flower-class corvettes filling its ranks. However, storm
damage and battle repairs usually reduced each of the escort groups to six
or seven operational warships.[1]

The Western Approaches Command, in effect, managed the British effort in the Battle of the Atlantic. Its tasks were extremely time sensitive
and required a high level of secrecy; the staff worked via a secure
teleprinter with the co-located Operational Intelligence Centre and Admiralty Trade Division in London, which helped to coordinate the move-

ment of the convoys and their escort groups by providing time-sensitive intelligence on U-boat movements.

There was a good reason for the nonstop bustle and cloak-and-dagger procedures at the Western Approaches Command headquarters. The efforts of this staff—its success or its failure—would decide the fate of Great Britain and, along with it, the ultimate outcome of the Allied war effort against Nazi Germany. In order to safeguard the trans-Atlantic convoys that sustained the civilian population, the command was charged with scrambling additional escort warships to reinforce convoys whose escorts were too weak to drive off attacking U-boats. Horton and his partners at Coastal Command would also send aircrews—stationed at airstrips from Newfoundland to Scotland—running to their VLR Liberators, Sunderland flying boats, and PBY-5A Catalinas on emergency flights to survey the waters around a convoy and drive U-boats underwater until convoys could slip past. Horton and his staff were akin to a conductor and a great orchestra whose performance requires a breathtaking degree of teamwork and cohesion. This restrained bedlam went on twenty-four hours a day, seven days a week.[2]   •

In the early morning hours of March 12, 1943, the two pin-studded, twenty-foot-tall charts that dominated the cavernous main room of Western Approaches Command headquarters showed an ocean alive with civilian shipping. Spread out across the North Atlantic were ten convoys totaling 436 ships, five westbound for New York and five eastbound for the British Isles. The eastbound convoys were laden with 2.8 million gross registered tons of cargo. About five dozen U-boat pins also adorned the North Atlantic chart; climbing a telescopic ladder, Women's Royal Naval Service members—known informally as Wrens—would add a brightly colored marker to show the location of each German U-boat as soon as it had been spotted by the Allied forces that crisscrossed the Atlantic or its location gleaned from British intelligence.

Horton had taken over as commander-in-chief, Western Approaches Command (CINCWA) just fifteen weeks earlier, on November 17, 1942, in what was then the darkest period of the Battle of the Atlantic. That month alone had brought the greatest loss of shipping tonnage since the outbreak of the war, with 126 merchant hulls totaling 802,160 gross tons of shipping falling to the seabed. Indeed, the surging losses were partially

Western Approaches Command at Derby House in Liverpool monitored the Battle of the Atlantic using oversized wall murals depicting the convoy routes.
Imperial War Museum, U.K.

what had landed Horton at Derby House. In late 1942, Prime Minister Churchill and his senior military advisers had decided that the best way to defeat Grossadmiral Dönitz and his marauding U-boat commanders was to bring in a submariner of their own, a man who inherently grasped the fundamentals of undersea warfare and who could quickly devise tactics to neutralize and defeat the threat. If there was one general consensus in the Royal Navy in those trying months, it was that Horton was the most effective submariner in British naval history.

Horton had been a part of the Royal Navy's submarine program almost since its inception. He had joined the navy at its Britannia Royal Naval College in Dartmouth in 1898, at the age of fifteen, and upon graduating had lobbied to join the service's nascent Submarine Branch. He received orders for submarine training in 1904 and, during the decade before World War I, commanded three early-model submarines and helped write the Royal Navy's book on submarine tactics. Commanding the submarine E-9 at the outbreak of the First World War, Horton had sunk a German cruiser and destroyer in the first months of the conflict, then mounted a daring offensive in which he and another submarine commander slipped into the Baltic and ran rampant against the German Baltic Fleet for the next year. His success led Germans to pick up on the British propaganda line and call the Baltic "Horton's Sea." Horton's career continued on a steady ascent after the war, but it wasn't until shortly after World War II erupted that Churchill assigned Horton to the job he had always wanted: commanding the Royal Navy's Submarine Branch.

Horton had taken part in numerous critical operations in his thirty-five-month command of the Submarine Branch, from shepherding the evacuating British and French forces at Dunkirk to defending England against an anticipated German invasion, but he made it clear that the fight raging in the Atlantic was one of the most critical of the war. In early February 1942, Horton had written a blunt memorandum to his superiors at the Admiralty. "Control of the sea is vital to the British Empire," Horton warned. "If we lose it, we lose the war." Churchill's belated response nine months later was to transfer Horton from his post at the Submarine Branch and to put him in charge of a more far-reaching operation: not only defending the flow of civilian shipping from the U-boats but organizing and carrying out the offensive against the enemy when adequate numbers of warships and aircraft finally became available.[3]

Horton's strong personality had played a role in landing him in his job at Western Approaches Command, but it also ruffled some feathers among the more than 1,000 naval and air force personnel working at Derby House. Unlike his predecessor, Admiral Sir Percy Noble, who had presided over the North Atlantic convoy escort operation for the past two years and who was regarded within the Royal Navy as an astute commander and kind, fatherly figure to his juniors, Horton was like a bull elephant. He had a short-fuse temper and was forceful, blunt, and sometimes abrasive. Whereas Noble had taken pains to get to know each man and woman with whom he had direct daily contact, Horton usually dealt only with his three immediate subordinates, as well as Air Marshal Sir John Slessor, with whom he coordinated anti-submarine aircraft patrols in the North Atlantic. Horton's idiosyncrasies were legion: he disdained the formal housing provided him and moved into a small room just off the operations center. Most days he would leave Derby House in the afternoon for a round of golf, then return for dinner and several hours of bridge. After a nap, he would materialize in the operations center around 11:30 p.m. and begin summoning the staff for updates on the convoys, firing questions nonstop until he had a clear image of the situation. After a while, the CINCWA staff took Horton's bizarre schedule for granted. "Battles were generally fought at night now," one staffer noted.[4]

The situation in the Atlantic had improved steadily since Horton had assumed command at Derby House, but the reprieve was sure to be short-lived. The fierce winter storms that raged from December through February had hampered many wolf pack attacks and caused Allied losses to drop sharply in those months, but everyone at Western Approaches knew that Dönitz and his U-boat crews would be back in full force when the weather finally moderated. And when they returned, Horton knew that he would be hard-pressed to come up with enough firepower with which to meet them.

The wall chart at Derby House in the early hours of March 12, 1943, showed an imminent crisis on the North Atlantic convoy routes. Although the number of warships in his command had steadily grown in recent months, Horton and his staff struggled to keep the escort groups fully manned with combat-ready warships. The winter storms were the main culprit; in early March, 33 of the 116 warships assigned to the command—twenty-eight percent of the force—were sidelined with storm damage. If warships were in short supply in the months leading up to March 1943, so were land-based patrol aircraft essential to convoy defense. Earlier in the war, the Allies had learned that convoys under the protection of both surface escorts and land-based aircraft had a much higher survival rate than convoys lacking air cover. The tactical equation was quite simple: the mere presence of a patrol aircraft overhead would send U-boat crewmen leaping down their conning tower hatches in an emergency crash dive. Capable of outrunning the convoys and most of their escorts on the surface, a submerged U-boat was all but immobile as long as it crouched in the deep, and the convoy could easily pass on out of sight before the U-boat commander dared come back up to periscope depth. Without patrolling aircraft to drive them underwater, however, U-boats could prowl in the vicinity of a convoy with relative impunity.

On the morning of Friday, March 12, Horton and his staff were grimly studying a new example of what the U-boats could do against inadequate convoy defenses. Two savage attacks on eastbound convoys had ended just the day before. On Derby House's two outsized wall charts, brightly colored pins marked the locations where fourteen ships from Convoy SC121 and five ships from Convoy HX228 had gone down at the hands of forty-five U-boats in three wolf packs. The ships had taken with them to the seabed 82,049 tons of cargo, making this one of the most costly convoy battles since the Germans had initiated wolf pack attacks back in August 1940. The combined SC121-HX228 battle was the third highest in tonnage losses—a somber harbinger to Horton and his staff of what the Germans might do once the winter storms abated.

The attacks on SC121 and HX228 had been a severe blow to the Allies for an additional reason: the loss of life had been particularly horrific. Of 1,114 crewmen on the nineteen stricken vessels, 740 had perished. One of those lost was a close friend of Horton's, Commander Arthur A. Tait, skipper of the destroyer *HMS Harvester* and senior officer of Escort Group B-3, which was escorting eastbound Convoy HX228.

Commander Tait's last battle was one of the more bloody encounters in the entire Battle of the Atlantic. On the morning of March 11, the U-757 had torpedoed the Liberty ship *William M. Gorgas*, killing three crewmen and forcing seventy survivors to take to lifeboats. Five hours later, the *Harvester* arrived at the scene to rescue survivors, but discovered another U-boat, U-444, proceeding on the surface. Tait ordered his destroyer to flank speed and rammed U-444. The destroyer rode up over the U-boat's hull, which became entangled in one of the destroyer's propeller shafts. After nearly an hour, the heavy waves finally broke both crippled vessels apart. Their crews were too busy attempting emergency repairs to avoid sinking to resume fighting. After several hours, Tait managed to get one propeller shaft turning, and the *Harvester*—which had rescued a German crewman thrown overboard in the ramming—limped back to the site of the *William M. Gorgas* torpedoing to rescue survivors. Of the seventy merchant seaman and Naval Armed Guard gunners who had escaped the sinking, only fifty were alive when the heavily damaged *Harvester* found them—and most of them had only a few more hours to live. The *Harvester* tried to rejoin Convoy HX228, but after several hours, the solitary propeller shaft failed, and the destroyer wallowed helplessly in the swells. Tait had earlier radioed the Free French–manned warship *Aconit* to break off from Convoy HX228 to assist, but before the corvette could arrive, two torpedoes slammed into the *Harvester*, killing 183 of the 243 men on board, including Commander Tait.

The German counterattack against Tait's destroyer came from a second U-boat, U-432, which had happened upon the immobilized *Harvester*. Its newly appointed commander, Kapitänleutnant Hermann Eckhardt, easily dispatched the British destroyer with a pair of G7es fired from 600 yards away. The twin warhead explosions blasted the 1,340-ton warship to pieces, leaving just sixty survivors (including twenty of the fifty crewmen from the Liberty ship and the U-444 crewman) floating amidst the debris.

It was now Escort Group B-3's turn for revenge. Before Lieutenant Jean Levasseur could maneuver the *Aconit* into the floating wreckage to pick up survivors, his lookouts spotted a U-boat on the surface several miles away. It was the heavily damaged U-444. After breaking free of the *Harvester*, Oberleutnant zur See Albert Langfeld had discovered his boat was unable to dive. Before Langfeld could get an emergency message dispatched to BdU Headquarters, the *Aconit* closed and rammed U-444. This time, the U-boat split in half and plunged to the seabed. Levasseur fished out three members of the U-boat's bridge watch who survived the sinking, then headed back for the *Harvester* survivors.

What happened next was a rare double-kill for one of the small Flower-class corvettes. After destroying the *Harvester*, U-432 remained at periscope depth, but Eckhardt inexplicably dismissed his crew from battle stations to celebrate the sinking of the enemy warship. While the forty-six-man crew enjoyed lunch, the *Aconit*'s Asdic operator got a firm contact on the submerged U-boat. Levasseur plastered U-432 with two salvos of ten depth charges apiece, which drove the U-boat into an uncontrollable dive that soon reached 1,000 feet, well beyond its crush depth of 960 feet. Eckhardt managed to get the boat under control and ordered an emergency blow of the ballast tanks. The *Aconit* was waiting. When U-432 popped up on the surface, the corvette was less than a half mile away. Levasseur's gunners sprayed the conning tower with four-inch gunfire, killing Eckhardt and a number of other crewmen.

In the final act of this brutal encounter, Levasseur edged his corvette up to the U-boat with plans to board and capture it. However, a heaving swell threw the 940-ton warship into the U-boat's side. U-432 sank instantly, carrying all but twenty of its forty-six-man crew down with it. Levasseur's crew fished the survivors out of the water, then returned to rescue the sixty survivors from the *Harvester*.[5]

Horton's personal loss hammered home the severity of the attacks on HX228 and SC121, but he knew that more trouble was imminent. The next eastbound convoy, SC122, was nearing its designated Western Ocean Meeting Point to rendezvous with its long-range escort group and head out into the Greenland air gap. There, more than a thousand miles from Allied air bases in Canada, Iceland, and Northern Ireland, the slow convoy could expect only minimal air support from a handful of VLR Liberators. The two following fast convoys, HX229 and HX229A, would also be vulnerable. Horton and his staff knew that the same mass of U-boats that had savaged SC121 and HX228 would regroup and take up the hunt for these next three formations as they drew to the northeast from their Newfoundland rendezvous points. There was little that the Derby House staff could do to help.

The shortage of air support had hampered Western Approaches Command since the beginning of the war. Horton's predecessor, Admiral Noble, had lobbied the Admiralty to transfer several escort aircraft carriers then under construction to protect North Atlantic convoys. Noble had also pressed the Admiralty for enough additional destroyers to form special support groups that would operate independently of the convoys in a hunter-killer role. While escort groups remained close to their assigned convoys, these support groups would comprise fast warships able to actively hunt down U-boats wherever they were sighted as well as to lend a hand in defending endangered convoys. Building on Noble's plans, Horton, from the beginning pressed his superiors to provide additional destroyers for support groups.

Thus far, the Admiralty's answer had been a firm "No." There had simply not been enough fast warships to form the proposed hunter-killer groups. Besides being denied additional destroyers, Horton was also frustrated in his attempts to obtain more air support to convoys crossing the North Atlantic. Western Approaches Command and its partner, RAF

A modified U.S. Army Air Forces B-24D Liberator, shown here, became a powerful weapon against the U-boats. By removing excess weight and adding an extra fuel tank in the aircraft's aft bomb bay, the Royal Air Force increased its combat flight radius range to over 1,000 miles, enabling the aircraft to close the feared "Greenland air gap."

Uboatarchive.net

Coastal Command Group 15, still lacked enough land-based patrol bombers that could reach the heart of the Greenland air gap. It had taken no time at all for the U-boat Force to determine the limits of Allied ground-based air coverage and for the wolf packs to set up their patrol lines and attack formations in that unguarded part of the ocean. By early 1943, a convoy would take between thirty-six and forty-eight hours to cross the 600-to-800-mile–wide Greenland air gap—more than enough time for a U-boat to sight the formation and call up the other boats in a wolf pack for a mass assault.[6]

In fact, the Allies had a weapon that, in sufficient numbers, could have closed the Greenland air gap in short order. In late 1942, British scientists and engineers had come up with a simple and brilliant solution by reconfiguring the four-engine B-24D Liberator bomber for extended patrol range. The B-24 was at that time the heaviest and longest-range bomber in the Allied inventory. Developed in 1939 to provide the U.S. Army Air Corps a more powerful weapon than the Boeing B-17, the Liberator was 67 feet long and 18 feet high, with a wingspan of 110 feet. It sported a distinct twin tail. It could carry a 4,500-pound bomb load for 800 miles to its target and have enough fuel left over to return to base. The standard air force models bristled with defensive gun turrets in the nose, top, rear, sides, and belly of the fuselage. By adding an extra fuel tank in the Liberator's rear bomb bay and stripping it of armor plating, excess gun turrets, and other unneeded weight, British scientists came up with the VLR variant, which the British named the Liberator III. It had an extended operating range of up to 2,300 nautical miles, enabling it to reach the middle of the Greenland air gap from Iceland or Northern Ireland, linger for several hours to seek and hunt any U-boats lurking in the area, and return home.[7]

The Liberator III had the necessary range to patrol the Greenland air gap, but it was an ungainly beast of an aircraft. It was a misery to fly in, its crew forced to suck oxygen through rubber facemasks and to wear bulky flight suits and jackets to ward off the subfreezing wind howling through the fuselage. The aircraft's extended range meant agonizingly long missions: most flights to the Greenland air gap and back lasted twenty hours. Worse, they often ended in disappointment. The navigational capabilities of both ships and aircraft were primitive by twenty-first-century standards. Thus, many VLR Liberators would arrive at the calculated spot to find an empty expanse of ocean, thanks to crosswind drift or inaccurate navigational fixes. Even if they were able to locate the convoys, Liberators often had to contend with local weather conditions. It was not uncommon for the crews on escort and merchant vessels to identify a Liberator only by the heavy droning of its four Pratt & Whitney R-1830-43 supercharged engines as it searched fruitlessly for them in fog banks or cloud cover that reached down to the water. Yet when the VLR Liberators did appear overhead, any U-boats in the area crash-dived, and the merchant sailors cheered.[8]

Despite its shortcomings, the VLR Liberator was the best shot the Allies had at providing continual air support for their merchant convoys. Coastal Command's new commander in 1943, Air Marshal Sir John Slessor, argued to his RAF superiors that a modest allotment of VLR-converted Liberators—one hundred at most—would enable his aircrews to close the Greenland air gap once and for all. This appeared to be an easy and straightforward solution, considering that by early 1943 Consolidated

Aircraft and three other American aircraft manufacturers had already built nearly 3,500 Liberators and were on target to construct over 19,000 by 1945. Even though hundreds of new B-24s were coming off the assembly lines in California, Michigan, Texas, and Oklahoma each month, American and British senior military commanders could not satisfy Coastal Command's plea for more.

The growing number of the new Liberators rolling out of American factories were not enough to meet the Allies' need for the aircraft. The Liberator was a very popular flying machine in early 1943. Until the advent of the Boeing B-29 Superfortress in May 1944, it remained the Allies' heaviest bomber. It was also in great demand by a number of Allied air services whose leaders argued that their priorities were much greater than that of Slessor's No. 15 Group. In early 1943, British Air Marshal Sir Arthur Harris refused to transfer any Liberators from Bomber Command to the Coastal Command to hunt U-boats, arguing that they were needed for the upcoming planned Anglo-American bombing campaign against Germany. Churchill supported Harris. General Henry H. "Hap" Arnold of the U.S. Army Air Forces, meanwhile, was deploying Liberator bomb groups overseas as fast as their crews received their aircraft and finished training. In fact, by 1944, Liberators would be operating from airfields in Alaska, Hawaii, the Southwest Pacific, India, North Africa, and Great Britain, but in the eyes of the Allies' senior commanders in March 1943, defending the trade routes in the Atlantic was simply not as critical as prosecuting the air war against the Axis.[9]

The struggle between convoy planners and other military commanders was not the only dust-up among the Allies over the dispensation of their aircraft. An equally vicious fight over the VLR Liberators pitted General Arnold against the U.S. Navy's contentious, hard-bitten commander-in-chief, Admiral Ernest J. King, who also held the title chief of naval operations. Arnold and King clashed throughout the first fifteen months of World War II over all aspects of land-based maritime patrol aircraft, particularly the VLR Liberator. This army-navy rivalry was deeply rooted in the past. Before the war, the army's aviation generals persuaded Congress to enact laws dictating that *all* land-based aircraft—particularly bombers of all makes—were to belong to the U.S. Army Air Corps (which was renamed the U.S. Army Air Forces in 1941; there was no separate U.S. Air

Force until 1947). As a consolation, the navy retained control of carrier-based aircraft and seaplanes, but the army—under its mandate to protect the continental United States from attack—got control of all land-based anti-submarine air patrols. In early 1942, King had requested 400 long-range B-24 Liberators and 900 medium-range B-25 Mitchell bombers for navy use in the anti-submarine role. General Arnold, Secretary of War Henry L. Stimson, and even President Roosevelt all rejected his request.

The navy's lack of control over land-based, U-boat-hunting bomber squadrons plagued the Allied anti-U-boat campaign throughout 1942 and the first three months of 1943. Like their navy rivals, the Army Air Forces generals found themselves ill prepared for the task of submarine hunting in the initial months of the war and were forced to scramble to devise effective tactics. Worse, the army Liberators at that stage lacked modern radar with which to spot U-boats, and the squadrons at first did not even have depth charges in their munitions bunkers, although by late 1942 this had been rectified. Army pilots themselves were often part of the problem, as well; they disdained the drudgery of long patrols along the convoy routes, and advocated sweeping the sea-lanes with aerial hunter-killer groups hunting U-boats. This dashing, take-the-offensive approach flew in the face of a British analysis showing that aircraft patrolling in the vicinity of convoys made a successful U-boat sighting for every twenty-nine hours of flight, while aircraft searching the ocean at random only found surfaced U-boats on average every 164 hours. Maintaining their offensive strategy, the army aircraft made few kills as the U-boat Force plundered the East Coast littoral in early 1942, sinking over 585 ships in six months.[10]

Even if it were able to come up with a larger number of VLR Liberators, the U.S. Navy could not be counted upon to use these aircraft to protect trans-Atlantic convoys. Admiral King desperately wanted a large force of VLR Liberators for his service's use in the Pacific, where they were well suited for long-range reconnaissance missions. Unfortunately for Western Approaches Command and its escort groups, though King had finally obtained 112 of the bombers by March 1943, he assigned seventy to the Pacific. None were flying convoy escort missions in the North Atlantic.

Early March 1943 had seen further disappointment for the convoy commodores and merchant sailors who wanted more protection by Allied aircraft. On March 1, four days before Convoy HX229 had begun its exodus of merchant ships from New York, more than a hundred U.S., British, and Canadian military leaders convened at a top-secret Atlantic Convoy Conference at U.S. Navy headquarters on Constitution Avenue in Washington, D.C. The representatives from the three nations constituted the Allies' expert leadership on anti-submarine warfare. They had thus far proven themselves unable to come up with a solution to the VLR Liberator dispute, and yet it fell to this fractious bunch to put into effect Roosevelt and Churchill's declaration at the Casablanca Conference in January 1943 that "the defeat of the U-boat must remain the first charge on the resources of the United Nations" (as the Allies had begun calling themselves at that stage of the war). Not surprisingly, the critical meetings in Washington were somber and tense. The Allies were suffering mightily in the North Atlantic, and no speedy solution was in sight.[11]

Meeting from March 1 to 12, the Allied admirals and generals did make progress on a number of contentious issues. Some hard compromises included raising the role of the Royal Canadian Navy in the Battle of the Atlantic by shifting control of convoys in the western sector from the United States to a new Canadian Northwest Atlantic Command, headquartered in Halifax. The U.S. Navy, which under Admiral King resisted the creation of multinational military commands, succeeded in thwarting a long-held British campaign to place all Allied convoy defenses under the control of Admiral Horton at Western Approaches Command. The Atlantic Convoy Conference concluded that the U.S. Navy would unilaterally manage the central Atlantic convoy routes between Hampton Roads, Virginia, and the Mediterranean, while the British and Canadians would share control over the North Atlantic routes. As a temporary aid to British escorts in the North Atlantic, Admiral King agreed to have the USS Bogue, the first of ten new escort carriers joining the fleet, operate with its escort destroyers on the North Atlantic convoy routes until the British brought their own escort carriers into operation later that spring.[12]

While the Allies agreed on who would manage the convoy routes, the Atlantic Convoy Conference failed to resolve the issue of VLR Liberator allocations. The senior generals of both the U.S. Army Air Forces and the Royal Air Force's Bomber Command still clung tightly to every B-24 that came off the production lines. The paralysis would remain long after the Atlantic Convoy Conference ended.

Thanks to the deadlock among the Allied commanders, the week that Convoys SC122, HX229, and HX229A left New York, Coastal Command had only eighteen VLR Liberators available. Twelve were operating with the RAF 120 Squadron based at Reykjavik, Iceland, from which they could make penetrating but infrequent forays into the Greenland air gap. Another six aircraft recently arrived from conversion to the VLR model were operating with the newly formed 86 Squadron based at Aldergrove, Northern Ireland, from which they could similarly reach the air gap. Since generally one-third of the planes were down for repairs or maintenance at any given time, Horton and Slessor could count on only twelve of the extended-range Liberators to come to the aid of the embattled convoys within the Greenland air gap. It was just not enough. In the spring of 1943, the continuing lack of sufficient VLR Liberators would bring great comfort to Grossadmiral Dönitz and his U-boat crews. Those woefully insufficient numbers would also play a role in the carnage that soon followed.[13]

IN THE CRAMPED operations room, a handful of senior German U-boat officers pored over a nautical chart spread before them on a large table covered with a green baize cloth. Dressed in formal blue uniforms, with most of them bearing the Knight's Cross of the Iron Cross commemorating their valor in combat, they were a far cry from their salt-stained, bedraggled comrades at sea. But the small staff at Befehlshaber der Unterseeboote (BdU), the U-boat Force Headquarters in a guarded villa adjoining the Hotel am Steinplatz in the Charlottenburg district of Berlin, was intimately involved in the day-to-day operations of the U-boats deployed across the globe. This handful of men presided over U-boat attacks on Allied merchant ships from the Arctic Ocean to the Indian Ocean.

At midmorning on Friday, March 12, 1943, several of the BdU operations staff officers were compiling attack reports from the U-boats that had assaulted the two eastbound North Atlantic convoys SC121 and HX228 over the past five days. Of thirty-nine U-boats that had attempted to intercept the two formations, twenty-two had reported successful attacks. The

U-boats that had attacked Convoy SC121 reported sinking sixteen merchant ships totaling 92,500 tons, while the U-boats that had stalked Convoy HX228 reported eight ships sunk for about 50,000 tons—a modest
exaggeration of the actual losses of thirteen ships totaling 73,000 tons from
SC121 and six ships (including a deck-stowed landing craft) totaling
25,806 tons from HX228.[14]

A trim, unsmiling admiral in his early fifties entered the operations
room. Grossadmiral Karl Dönitz was commander-in-chief of both the
German Navy and its U-boat Force, and although he had ceded day-to-
day responsibility for tactical command of the U-boats to his senior staff
since assuming command of the entire Kriegsmarine five weeks earlier,
Dönitz made a point of visiting the BdU operations center every day that
his schedule permitted. These appearances gave Dönitz the opportunity to
obtain updates on his U-boats at sea and on any ongoing or pending wolf
pack battles. Given the predominant role that the U-boats played against
Germany's maritime enemies, the staff knew that Dönitz was soaking in
every detail that the flags and pins on the charts conveyed. One observer
later described the admiral's unguarded intensity: "His eyes were rather
close together and extremely alert. His mouth was smallish and he . . .
seemed to be constantly collecting information."[15]

Admiral Dönitz and the BdU staff had a meticulous system for organizing their U-boat forces in the North Atlantic. Dominating one wall of the
operations room was an oversize copy of the "1870G Nord-Atlantischer
Ozean" chart. Unlike most nautical maps, which only relied on latitude
and longitude marks to help pinpoint ship locations, the German naval
chart also featured a dense matrix of numbered squares covering the
oceanic areas on the map. From north of Iceland to the equator, a series of
quadrants, each identified with a two-letter code and measuring 486 nautical miles per side, marked off the trackless ocean. Inside each lettered quadrant were eighty-one smaller squares identified by a two-digit number,
measuring fifty-four miles per side. And within each of those secondary
quadrants, yet another subdivision of eighty-one numbered squares
marked a relatively tiny swath of ocean measuring six by six nautical miles.
This was the German Navy's unique way of plotting U-boat positions, enemy contacts, and convoy routes.

Developed in late 1941, the Kriegsmarine's German Naval Grid system was designed to avoid identifying a designated location by latitude and longitude, a recurring numerical pattern that security officials feared would facilitate enemy code-breaking efforts. When a U-boat reported a convoy contact, or the BdU staff issued a redeployment order to a U-boat commander, the message would use the two-letter, four-number grid reference. For instance, a U-boat in the North Atlantic operating at 57:21 North 032:00 West—a position about 400 miles east-southeast of Greenland's Cape Farewell—would cite the naval grid designation AK 2799 for its position instead of the actual latitude and longitude (see Naval Grid Chart on pages 54-55). Festooning the chart were pins depicting each U-boat on patrol, as well as other markers denoting the locations of known Allied convoys.[16]

The U-boat Force was operating in full stride by March 1943. The German Navy had launched an ambitious construction plan shortly after the outbreak of war on September 3, 1939, but it had taken more than two years for the new U-boats to reach operational status. The force had steadily grown during that period. In March 1941, Dönitz, a vice admiral at the time, was able to keep an average of only thirteen U-boats deployed at sea at any one time. A year later, the average daily deployment figure was forty-eight. By March 1943, with a total of 430 in commission, Dönitz now commanded a worldwide operational force of more than 100 combat-ready U-boats at sea on any given day. The large nautical chart that morning was covered with sixty small flags showing the U-boats operating in the North Atlantic, with another sixteen returning to port. Merchant mariners and escort sailors traversing the dangerous North Atlantic convoy routes did not have access to those classified figures, but they knew well enough that the U-boats were out in unprecedented numbers as spring began.[17]

Presiding over the huddle of staff officers at U-boat Force Headquarters was Konteradmiral (Rear Admiral) Eberhard Godt, forty-two, who, as Chef der Operationsabteilung (Operations Chief), was in charge of the BdU staff on a day-to-day basis. Godt had first served in the Imperial Navy's surface fleet in the final year of World War I, then transferred to the newly formed Reichsmarine of the Weimar Republic in 1920. He had

54

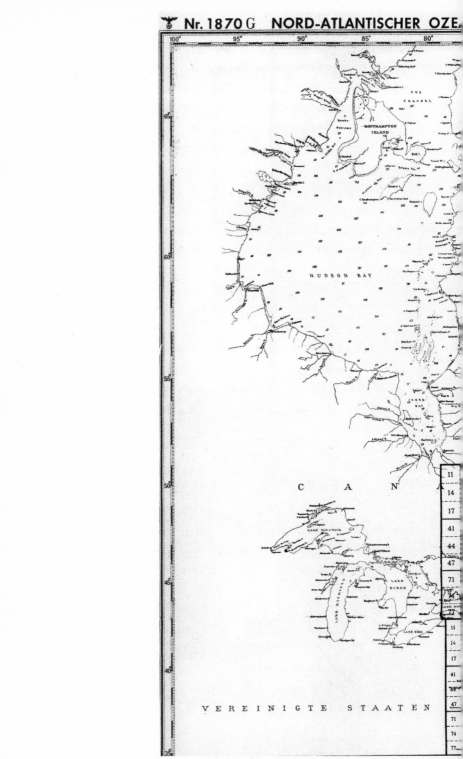

The German Naval Grid system utilized a two-letter, four-number code to indicate positions of U-boats and convoys on the nautical chart.

Her Majesty's Stationery Office, U.K.

served under Dönitz on several assignments and followed Dönitz to the newly organized U-boat Force in 1936. After commanding the Type IA U-25 and the Type IIB U-23 during the prewar naval buildup of 1936–38, Godt became the senior Admiralstabsoffizier (admiral's staff officer) to Dönitz in January 1938. The taciturn Dönitz described his deputy as "a man of unshakeable imperturbability, who was of immense assistance in arriving at a factual appreciation of any given situation."[18]

The other officers standing shoulder to shoulder with Dönitz and Godt that morning were among the most highly decorated U-boat commanders in the German Navy. They included Korvettenkapitän Günter Hessler, thirty-three, who had sunk twenty-one ships totaling 118,822 gross tons during three patrols in command of the Type IXB U-107 during seven months in 1941. Hessler had been on the BdU staff since November of that year, but he had a longer-standing connection to the admiral; he was Dönitz's son-in-law, having married the admiral's only daughter, Ursula, in 1937. Serving as convoy staff officer since October 1942 was Kapitänleutnant Adalbert Schnee, twenty-nine, another combat veteran who had already commanded three U-boats and had sunk twenty-three Allied ships for a total of 95,889 tons while commanding the Type IIC U-boat U-60 in 1939–40 and the Type VIIC U-201 in 1941–42. A relative newcomer to Dönitz's staff was Kapitänleutnant Peter-Erich Cremer. The thirty-one-year-old officer had commanded U-333 on its first four war patrols from August 1941 until October 1942, bagging six ships for a total of 26,873 tons. Cremer's crew regarded him as a good-luck charm after U-333 enjoyed several close escapes from enemy warships. Seriously wounded during an attack on his boat five months earlier, Cremer was temporarily assigned to BdU Operations pending a medical evaluation.[19]

Despite their own distinguished records, the BdU staff officers regarded the fleet admiral with respect bordering on awe. His nickname was *der Löwe*—the Lion. More than anyone else, the U-boat Force was the product of his vision and implacable drive. As a twenty-five-year-old oberleutnant zur see in World War I, Dönitz had transferred to U-boats in 1916, serving in the Mediterranean in command of the UC-25 and later in the larger UB-68. This second command ended in disaster for the skipper and his crew. While they were attacking a convoy, UB-68 experienced a major malfunction, forcing Dönitz to surface and abandon ship. He and thirty-

Admiral Dönitz tried to personally greet each U-boat crew upon their return from patrol.
Imperial War Museum, U.K.

one surviving crewmen spent the rest of the war as POWs in Britain.
Repatriated to Germany after the war, Dönitz served in the Weimar Republic Navy, steadily rising through the ranks. In July 1935, German
Navy commander-in-chief Grand Admiral Erich Räder appointed
then–Kapitän zur See (Captain) Dönitz to be the Führer der Unterseeboote (FdU, or U-boat Force Leader), responsible for bringing the U-boat
Force back to life. For nearly eight years—half in peacetime and half at
war—Dönitz had overseen the training of nearly 40,000 U-boat officers
and crewmen, and the planning for a fleet of over 430 U-boats, of which
240 were operational by the spring of 1943.[20]

Dönitz and his operations staff at BdU Headquarters kept a tight leash
on the U-boats, organizing and directing them based on the most up-to-
date information about Allied convoy movements. When German naval
intelligence anticipated a merchant convoy approaching the U-boats' location, Dönitz assigned them to temporary wolf packs to entrap the enemy
ships. Using encrypted high-frequency communications, Dönitz would
array a wolf pack in an extended patrol line several hundred miles long.

The line of U-boats would orient at a right angle to the convoy's suspected course to maximize the odds of snaring the enemy merchantmen. Each U-boat might find itself between ten and thirty miles from the next as the lookouts scanned the horizon for a forest of masts or plumes of exhaust marking the presence of the target. Once a U-boat sighted the convoy, it would radio the detection to BdU and transmit a low-frequency radio homing signal, usually a pair of letters in the alphabet. Dönitz and his staff then would order some or all of the pack to close in on the "contact keeper" U-boat. Because the first U-boat to attack a convoy usually came under fierce counterattack by the escorts that forced it to crash-dive, Dönitz imposed a stern rule that at least two boats had to be in firm contact with the enemy merchantmen before unleashing their attacks to ensure the convoy did not escape. Once enough U-boats were in visual sight of the formation, BdU would then authorize a mass assault.

By mid-1943, both sides in the convoy battles were well informed of their enemy's tactics and had adapted their own defensive countermeasures to match them. In a night attack, U-boats would attempt to swarm against the convoys from all sides in order to overwhelm the seven to ten warships constituting the convoy escort screen. The escort warships, for their part, would try to calculate the most likely approach route and, if warranted, stack the defense in that area. Dönitz had long preferred attacking on the surface at night because the U-boat's top surface speed of eighteen knots was faster than most merchant vessels, allowing the attackers to position themselves as advantageously as possible with relatively little risk of being spotted. Because the U-boat's maximum submerged speed was just between four and seven knots, slower than most convoy speeds, a daylight attack—virtually impossible for a surfaced U-boat, given the high likelihood of being spotted and forced underwater by a convoy's escorts—required the U-boat to position itself at periscope level ahead of the merchantmen in the formation's course track, and wait for the target vessels to move to within torpedo range. U-boat commanders preferred night attacks for both the cover and the maneuverability they afforded. However, substantial gains in Allied shipboard radar had stripped the U-boats of much of the cover that darkness afforded them, convincing Dönitz that the far more difficult and risky daylight maneuvers had an equal chance of success as nighttime actions.[21]

As the Battle of the Atlantic wore on, the Allies turned to radar as a means of neutralizing the U-boats' stealth characteristics and providing Allied convoy defenses with the ability to defeat the wolf packs. Radar was one of three major technological innovations installed aboard escort warships after the outbreak of World War II. The other two were the high-frequency direction-finding (HF/DF) receiver and the Talk Between Ships, or TBS. HF/DF (which its users pronounced Huff-Duff) allowed an escort warship to pinpoint a line of bearing to a U-boat when it sent an encrypted radio message. TBS was a very-high-frequency (VHF) radiotelephone system that enabled escort ship commanders to coordinate their movements and actions in a much faster and more effective manner than had been possible with older signaling devices such as blinking Morse code via the Aldis lamp or signal flags in daylight. While all three inventions significantly bolstered the convoy escort group's ability to detect U-boats and to organize a coordinated counterattack, radar was the most important, since it provided the escort group with an instant situational awareness of the convoy, its defenses, and the threat it faced.

Scientists had known about the possible uses of radar for some time before figuring out how to exploit the technology for military use. Shorthand for radio detection and ranging, radar works by sending a burst of radio wave pulses from a transmitter, and then capturing the returning echo when the radar signal strikes a solid object such as a ship or aircraft. On the radar sets developed for use during World War II, the returning pulse appeared on a cathode ray tube display in such a manner that the operator could calculate the bearing and range of the object. At the beginning of the war, however, military radar was still only a concept. American, British, and German scientists had dabbled with radar during the 1930s, but it wasn't until after the outbreak of the war that both sides realized the potential military applications of this new technology. Nevertheless, progress in developing an effective radar capability remained uneven on all sides due to the serious technical challenge of devising systems that were both accurate and either rugged enough to withstand the harsh environment of shipboard life or light enough to install in aircraft.

The breakthrough in radar came in 1940 with the British invention of the cavity magnetron, a device that generated the outgoing radar pulse at a vastly more powerful energy level and with a much narrower wavelength that significantly increased both its range and its accuracy. Whereas earlier radar sets operated on wavelengths ranging from one and one-half to seven meters, the Type 271M radar first deployed in March 1941 was stepped down to 9.7 centimeters (operators rounded up the number to ten centimeters, and called the device a "centimetric" radar). When working properly under the hands of a trained operator, the Type 271M could detect a submerged U-boat's periscope up to four miles away, a significant increase in range from the earlier systems, whose maximum range was less than two miles. By the spring of 1943, most Allied convoy escort ships had received the Type 271M system, and their crews were becoming proficient in its use.

Just as convoy escorts were benefiting from the new centimetric radar, Allied scientists had made a parallel breakthrough in radar that would prove equally valuable in the Battle of the Atlantic. In February 1943, the first ASV Mark III (for "air-to-surface vessel") centimetric radar was installed on Royal Air Force Coastal Command patrol bombers. Like ground- and ship-based sets, the earlier models were plagued with glitches and operators were not well trained in their use, but scientists and air force technicians worked hard to smooth out the wrinkles in the system. Soon, the ASV Mark III radar had become an effective tool in the fight against the U-boats. When it functioned properly, this look-down radar enabled aircrews to locate U-boats operating below the thick cloud cover that frequently blanketed the North Atlantic, and ambush them by suddenly dropping through the cloud layer to straddle the U-boat with a pattern of aerial depth charges.

German ignorance and technical shortcomings made the centimetric radar especially lethal against the U-boats. Admiral Dönitz did not fully realize the technological threat from Allied centimetric radar until May 1943, when it was all but too late to overcome the strengthened convoy defenses. Worse, German scientists were long unable to come up with a receiver that could register the centimetric radar pulses. As a result, German radar detection receivers carried on the U-boats were blind to the shorter-wavelength pulses even as the new technology stripped them of much of the cover of darkness that they relied upon to close with and attack a convoy. Even though he still did not know the specific cause, by March of 1943, Admiral Dönitz had become convinced that, because nighttime attacks were obviously losing their effectiveness, his U-boats would have to try the far more difficult and risky daylight attack at periscope depth in addition to assaulting convoys at night on the surface.[22]

At Dönitz's bidding, the wolf packs that had bloodied convoys SC121 and HX228 had carried out their attacks in the daytime as well as at night. The fierce storms that had bedeviled both convoys made the periscope-depth attacks more effective than normal, since the U-boats were cloaked by the towering swells and low clouds. The results had been astounding; the convoys' escorts, it seemed, were simply unable to fend off such a large-scale assault, regardless of the hour in which it occurred. While Grossadmiral Dönitz and the staff at BdU were tallying up the damage their U-boats had wrought upon convoys SC121 and HX228, they also had their eyes on a new target, which was even now approaching the killing fields of the North Atlantic. Neither Commodore White nor the merchant captains in SC122, or Commodore Mayall and the ship masters in HX229, realized that Dönitz and his BdU staff were aware of the movement of both convoys. The Germans had enough information on the two formations and their routes that the U-boat chief was preparing to unleash forty-six fully armed U-boats against them, in what would be the largest wolf pack attack so far in the war.[23]

Chapter 3

MOVEMENT TO CONTACT

T he Atlantic was mercifully calm after the storm that had scattered Convoy SC122 on its first day out of New York. After the gale, Commodore Samuel White on the convoy flagship *Glenapp* kept his formation in order during the rest of the seven-day voyage up through American and Canadian coastal waters. The convoy's initial four local escort warships had taken SC122 as far as the rendezvous point south of Halifax, where they handed it off to another three escorts—the destroyer *HMS Leamington* and two Canadian corvettes—on Tuesday, March 9. Two of the convoy's merchant ships broke off for Halifax, while the three new warships brought fifteen additional merchant vessels out to meet the eastbound convoy. They proceeded without a solitary Asdic or radar contact to indicate the presence of a prowling U-boat. SC122 continued toward the rendezvous with its mid-ocean escort group at the assigned Western Ocean Meeting Point at 46:45 North 051:14 West, just eighty-one nautical miles southeast of St. John's, Newfoundland.[1]

The local escorts' handoff of Convoy SC122 to the mid-ocean escorts went off without incident. The local group brought the formation to the rendezvous point at 0900 local hours (12 noon GMT) on Friday, March 12. Soon, lookouts spotted the warships of Escort Group B-5 on the port beam coming down from St. John's. Commodore White ordered the convoy to keep formation in its structure of eleven columns as two ships detached for St. John's. The whaling depot ship *Sevilla* was scheduled for that port stop, but the 3,751-ton ore carrier *PLM13* was leaving the convoy because of a malfunctioning boiler (the other two merchantmen orig-

In calm weather, ships in a North Atlantic convoy had little difficulty keeping in orderly rows and columns.

Office of War Information

inally destined for Newfoundland had aborted the convoy during the storm and returned to New York). At 0930, the single ship assigned to join the formation from St. John's, the 4,998-ton British freighter *Reaveley*, arrived and took Position 83, the third ship in Column 8.

With its merchantmen in position, Convoy SC122 prepared to begin the long trek out into the open Atlantic while its escorts completed their handoff. On the destroyer *HMS Havelock*, Commander Richard C. Boyle, senior officer of British Escort Group B-5, caught up with the *Leamington* to formally assume responsibility for SC122's protection. Lieutenant A. D. B. Campbell, in charge of the five local escorts, transferred a bulky, waterproofed packet of convoy papers to Boyle via highline. As the *Leamington* and the two Canadian corvettes reversed course for home with the two detaching merchantmen, Boyle ordered the nine other B-5 warships to take their day stations around the main body. Edging the *Havelock* up close to the *Glenapp*, Boyle and White briefly exchanged messages before preparing to guide their charges out into the deep Atlantic.[2]

While the change in escort groups marked a major milestone in the convoy's passage, few of the merchant sailors in SC122 would likely have paused in their routine to watch the handover, which occurred several miles out from the formation of civilian ships. On the British merchant-man *Kingsbury*, fireman Deane Wynne and his fellow engine room crew worked away at their four-hour shifts, ate their meals, and relaxed in their Spartan accommodations. "Being a mere fireman of course, I was not privy to what was really afoot," Wynne later wrote. Still, news had trav-eled fast through the ships of Convoy SC122 about the savaging that the two earlier convoys had endured south of Greenland and Iceland just days before, and crewmen were beginning to be anxious about the trip across the North Atlantic. "News had been passed round by the commodore that SC121 ahead of us had been attacked and badly mauled," Wynne later noted.[3]

Had they known who was guarding them, Wynne and the other mer-chant sailors would have rested a bit easier. While a relative newcomer to the North Atlantic convoy system, Commander Boyle had won a reputa-tion among his Royal Navy peers as a careful but sound escort leader who demanded top performance by all the men and ships in his group. Still, the ships and men of Escort Group B-5 had not been immune from the fierce winter storms that had ravaged the convoys and escort ships for the past five months. In his previous escort duties, Boyle and several of his fellow B-5 warship commanders had learned all too well the stakes they were up against, especially when operating with an inadequate number of escorts. While escorting a convoy in the Caribbean in early 1943 as part of a re-duced formation of Group B-5, the *Havelock* and three corvettes were shepherding nine oil tankers in Convoy TM1 from Trinidad to the Mediterranean to supply the Allied forces in North Africa. When a U-boat spotted the convoy on January 3, Dönitz ordered fourteen U-boats into the attack. The few escort ships were insufficiently armed and lacked adequate radar and radio direction-finding gear, and the result was a massacre. Dur-ing January 8–11, and in a later encounter during January 25–27, the U-boats sank seven of the nine tankers in TM1, killing ninety-seven crew-men in the process. The U-boats so outmatched the escorts that one of them openly trailed the convoy on the surface by day. That bravado led to one of the more bizarre encounters in the entire U-boat war: a frustrated officer on the *Havelock* finally ordered his signalman to flash a blinking light Morse code signal in plain English to the shadowing U-boat: "Why don't you go away?" The U-boat calmly replied, "Sorry, we have our orders."[4]

As it joined Convoy SC122, Escort Group B-5 was in better shape than during its experience with Convoy TM1, but not by much. Just four days before joining Convoy SC122, Escort Group B-5 had finished a harrowing, seventeen-day crossing of the North Atlantic with westbound Convoy ONS168. Thanks to intelligence the British had passed on to the Convoy and Routing staff at U.S. Navy headquarters in Washington, the formation had evaded several wolf packs by steering a northerly route, but became trapped in a major gale. Two stragglers, the 6,537-ton British tanker *Empire Light II* and 7,176-ton American Liberty ship *Thomas Hooker*, fell prey to the U-boats. Many of the remaining fifty-eight merchantmen and the escorts suffered serious storm damage. Working round the clock, repair crews in St. John's patched up some of the escorts during their three-day stopover. Royal Canadian Navy officials found several replacements for escorts too damaged to deploy on the next mission.

Teamwork was a critical part of any successful escort effort, but B-5 was heading out into the Atlantic with several new ships and their unfamiliar crews. Normally, B-5 consisted of the *Havelock*; two V&W-class destroyers, HMS *Volunteer* and HMS *Warwick*; and five Flower-class corvettes, HMS *Saxifrage*, HMS *Godetia*, HMS *Pimpernel*, HMS *Buttercup,* and HMS *Lavender.* The *Warwick* was sidelined for repairs, and officials had transferred the *Volunteer* to temporarily lead Escort Group B-4, whose lead ship would be delayed in a scheduled departure because of required repairs. Officials assigned the World War I–era destroyer USS *Upshur* and the River-class frigate HMS *Swale* to plug the gaps in B-5. A ninth warship, the newly built Isles-class ASW trawler HMS *Campobello*, bound for a permanent duty station in Great Britain, would also serve with B-5 on that crossing.

For the merchant ships' crews, one of the most encouraging additions to SC122 was not an escort but a rescue ship, the *Zamalek*, whose sole purpose was to rescue crewmen whose ship went down while en route to Britain. Wynne and his shipmates on the *Kingsbury* were very much aware that their convoy had the rescue ship, a former packet steamer that had operated in the Mediterranean and Black Seas prior to the war. "She had already made a name for herself by rescuing and saving the lives of many men, under the most difficult, and harrowing of times in the Russian convoys," Wynne recalled after the war. "There were a few of these small, properly equipped ships now plying the North Atlantic convoy routes. They were all very similar in size and did a magnificent job at great risk to themselves and their crews by dropping behind the convoys and searching for survivors of torpedoed ships."[5]

As SC122 DEPARTED the Western Ocean Meeting Point on March 12 for the trans-Atlantic leg of its journey, the forty merchantmen in fast Convoy HX229 were still two days from WESTOMP. While the fast convoy was lucky and missed the gale that partially scattered SC122, HX229 had struggled for several days through thick fog and heavy snow that made station keeping exceedingly difficult. However, since HX229 was not scheduled to receive any additional ships from Halifax, the local escorts did not have to execute a rendezvous as the formation passed about 100 miles south of the Nova Scotia port.

Like Deane Wynne in SC122, the men sailing in Convoy HX229 also found the passage from New York to Newfoundland relatively uneventful. The merchant seamen and escort sailors were well aware that the dangers had shifted back into the mid-Atlantic and the Greenland air gap, and so they could relax a bit as their convoy trekked up the North American coast.

For Signalman 3rd Class Ted Schorr on the freighter *El Mundo*, the only excitement thus far had been on the first day at sea when he witnessed an angry confrontation between the *El Mundo*'s master and several of the crewmen. Captain MacKenzie (Schorr never learned his first name) was a large, formidable Scotsman who had reportedly lost a leg during an attack in World War I, and it was his custom to retire to his sea cabin around noon and sleep during the afternoon while his assistants conned the ship. This would leave him alert and rested for the long, tense nighttime hours when the U-boats were most likely to attack.

MacKenzie was taking his regular afternoon nap when the second mate who was manning the bridge sent for two seamen to throw the ship's garbage over the side. It was common practice to do this during the late afternoon so that if any telltale material was still floating by the next morning, the ship would be far away. The *El Mundo* had a large pile of boxes and sacks of garbage that needed to be jettisoned. Schorr was standing on the port bridge wing when the boatswain came in with the two sailors. The two men had grim expressions and were shaking their heads. "They want to be paid overtime for this," the boatswain told the second mate. "I don't have that authority," the second mate replied. More head shaking. Finally, the second mate told Schorr to go get Captain MacKenzie. Schorr did as he was told.

MacKenzie appeared on the bridge wearing a fur jacket and a strange cap with a red tassel on top, Schorr later recalled. After the second mate explained the situation, MacKenzie glowered at the two crewmen. "Start throwing the garbage over the side," he ordered. When the two continued to refuse, the captain reached into his coat, pulled out a long-barreled revolver, cocked the hammer, and said, "I intend to shoot any man who does not throw garbage." The two immediately began hurling garbage over the rail. Even the boatswain joined in. When the deck was finally clear, MacKenzie said, "And there is no overtime pay."

Striding back into the wheelhouse, MacKenzie must have noticed the look on Schorr's face. He walked over and put a hand on the American's shoulder. "Did that scene upset you?" he asked the young navy sailor. "I have never seen anything like that in real life," Schorr said. He looked up into the Scotsman's face and asked, "Would you have really shot those men?" MacKenzie grimaced. "I have no choice," he said. "If I backed down, within the hour the crew would be dictating [orders] to me!"[6]

On the *Mathew Luckenbach*, Signalman 3rd Class John Orris Jackson had been spared the sort of mayhem that briefly threatened to erupt on the *El Mundo*. His job was relatively straightforward as he rotated his watches on the freighter's navigation bridge with two other signalmen from the Naval Armed Guard detachment. For the most part, the signals he received by flashing light Morse code from the commodore flagship *Abraham Lincoln* three miles away were routine messages regarding station keeping and anticipated course changes, and Jackson's replies were mostly acknowledgments on behalf of the *Mathew Luckenbach*'s master. Not encountering any crisis or enemy attack, he found his attention drifting back to two timeless subjects: food and the weather. "It doesn't seem to be any colder out here than it was in New York," Jackson had jotted in his diary on March 9. "All is well. There are forty-one ships in the convoy, all nice big ones, too. The weather is fine for the Atlantic. Food on the ship is fair, although the cooks aren't so hot."

By March 13, HX229 was nearing Cape Race, where lingering winter weather roughened the ocean. Two days before reaching WESTOMP, there came a minor crisis. Heavy rainfall and fog descended upon the convoy, and many of the ships fell out of formation. The confusion forced Jackson to spend an all-nighter on the *Mathew Luckenbach's* signal platform as Commodore Mayall and the local escort commander struggled to pull the ships back in line. "A lot of the [ship's] lights were on" to prevent collisions by other vessels, Jackson wrote in his diary. "We almost rammed several ships—what a mess. There were a lot of messages" to receive and send.[7]

As HX229 regained its formation and steered toward WESTOMP, a motley group of escorts was mustering to meet it. British Escort Group B-4, assigned to shepherd HX229, was in even worse shape than Commander Boyle and his B-5 escorts had been when they met SC122. B-4 was led by Commander Edward C. L. Day on the destroyer *HMS Highlander*. The escort group should have included three other destroyers— *HMS Winchelsea, HMS Vimy,* and the ex–U.S. Navy four-stack *HMS Beverley*—as well as six Flower-class corvettes: *HMS Abelia, HMS Anemone, HMS Asphodel, HMS Clover, HMS Pennywort,* and the Canadian *HMCS Sherbrooke.* But the group had been battered by a fierce storm while escorting westbound Convoy ONS169 during February 23–March 9. Five of the ten warships were unfit for sea and the rest were sorely strained from months of operating on the stormy Atlantic convoy routes.

Commander Day in B-4 found his escort group even more critically short-staffed when it came time to meet the next eastbound convoy he was assigned to protect. The escort ships themselves had been seriously damaged by the winter storms they encountered on their previous, westbound mission; by the time the escort group emerged from the last winter gale on its latest crossing, it was as beat up and scattered as the convoy itself. Day's escorts had straggled into port at St. John's during March 9–12 with four of them seriously impaired and another three still at sea. The *Highlander* and *Sherbrooke* required dry-docking in St. John's to repair their damaged Asdic domes, while the *Winchelsea* and *Clover* were also undergoing repairs for storm damage. The corvettes *Abelia, Sherbrooke,* and

Pennywort, the latter badly in need of engine repairs, were late in arriving while they continued to search for stragglers from ONS169. As for the destroyer *Vimy,* it had not even been able to finish the crossing, having been forced to abort to Iceland halfway across for storm-damage repairs. Thus, instead of a complement of ten warships, Escort Group B-4 could only muster the destroyer *Beverley* and corvette *Anemone* to stand out to meet HX229 on March 14.

Escort Group B-4's commander had enough experience and good sense to appreciate just how bad a predicament he and his ships were in. Commander Day had been on the North Atlantic convoy runs since January 1941 and was described by one fellow officer as "sound, blunt, brainy and very experienced." He also was a realist who knew that sending a major convoy into the U-boat-infested Greenland air gap with just two escorts amounted to a maritime suicide pact. After arriving at St. John's, Day lobbied Canadian Navy officials for a three-day delay in HX229's schedule to permit completion of the repairs to the *Highlander* and the other ships and to allow the other B-4 ships still escorting the remnants of ONS169 to make port for provisioning. During this time, Day suggested, HX229 could shelter in the waters of Placentia Bay, Newfoundland. Canadian Rear Admiral Leonard W. Murray in Halifax turned down the request.

With no hope for a reprieve and with the *Highlander* still undergoing repairs in St. John's, Day didn't have many choices left. He decided to remain in port with his ship and try to catch up with HX229 when repairs to the *Highlander* were complete, about thirty-six hours after his escorts were scheduled to meet up with the formation. To provide B-4 with an interim commander, the senior Canadian naval officer at St. John's transferred the British destroyer *Volunteer* from nearby Escort Group B-5 to Escort Group B-4 and appointed its commander, Lieutenant-Commander Gordon J. Luther, as acting senior escort officer in that group. On the morning of March 13, the day before HX229 was slated to arrive at WESTOMP, Day, Luther, and several staff officers from the naval command at St. John's met on the *Highlander.* The Canadians assigned the two "short-legged" destroyers HMS *Mansfield* and HMS *Witherington,* normally used for local escort duties, to fill B-4's depleted ranks. The gesture was practically useless, since these destroyers had a limited range of 600 miles, and most of the U-boats were out in the middle of the Green-

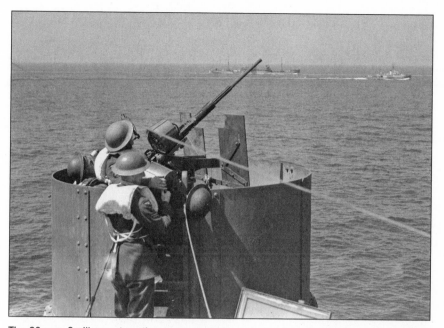

The 20-mm Oerlikon automatic cannon could be operated by a single gunner against both aircraft and surfaced U-boats and was installed on most Allied merchant ships.
Imperial War Museum, U.K.

land air gap, 700 to 1,000 miles offshore. Still, this addition gave B-4 a total of four destroyers and one corvette at the outset, with the *Highlander, Abelia, Pennywort,* and *Sherbrooke* scheduled to race to catch up with the escort group as soon as their repairs were done.[8]

For all the efforts to fill its ranks, Escort Group B-4 had other serious problems besides a shortage of ships. For one thing, HX229 lacked a dedicated rescue ship such as the *Zamalek* in Convoy SC122. If a U-boat torpedoed a merchant ship, rescuing the survivors would fall on the other civilian vessels, none of which had ever practiced the difficult task of approaching a sinking ship, heaving to, and lowering boats. To make matters worse, the escort team protecting HX229 would sail into harm's way under a commander with limited convoy escort experience and with whom none of the other warship commanders had ever served. B-4 would go into action lacking what naval experts had learned was the single most important capability in convoy defense: the cohesion of a trained team that could react effectively and quickly to the U-boat threat. This combination of shortages and insufficient cohesion would prove a recipe for disaster. Even more critical still would be the technology that B-4 was sorely lacking.[9]

By the spring of 1943, the Allies had equipped most convoy escort groups with three U-boat tracking technologies. There were Asdic underwater sounding gear and ship-based radar. The third one, high-frequency direction-finding, would make the Allied escort groups significantly more deadly against the U-boats. Ironically, throughout the war, Admiral Dönitz and his staff would focus their attention on the threat from Allied radar and largely overlook the danger from HF/DF detection. The U-boats would pay a high price for this intelligence failure.[10]

Ship-mounted HF/DF was a recent variation on a long-established system that maritime nations had devised to help ship captains navigate accurately. Beginning in the early 1930s, the major powers—Great Britain, France, Germany, and the United States—used low- and medium-range radio transmitters and shipboard listening devices as navigation aids. Shore-based transmitters at fixed sites would send out coded signals, and shipboard radio operators would take the bearings to two or more beacons that would provide them with a cross-bearing "fix" of their current location at sea. Germany had figured out a way to make even better use of this technology by specially outfitting its modern U-boat types with rotating radio direction-finding loop antennas that would pick up land-based navigation beacons when operating in coastal waters, as well as the lower-frequency homing signals each U-boat transmitted when it had firm contact with an Allied convoy.

Nearly a decade before the outbreak of the war, British and French military scientists became aware that U-boats were being equipped with high-frequency radio to transmit encrypted messages to BdU Headquarters. They began researching how to develop radio direction-finding receivers that would work in this electromagnetic spectrum so as to track U-boats at sea by their transmissions. Still, HF/DF was in its infancy when Great Britain and Germany went to war in 1939.

The principle of how wartime HF/DF worked was simple. Even if the U-boat transmission was encrypted, the signal itself would betray the U-boat's presence. A single receiver would give a line of bearing to the origination of the U-boat transmission as far as twenty miles from the convoy. Two or more intercepts caught by different ships would provide an accurate cross-bearing fix of the U-boat's position, allowing escort ships to swoop in and attack.

The early-model British receivers would not work on a warship that also had radar, due to electronic interference. Moreover, most warship commanders preferred radar to the still-untested HF/DF gear, so deployment of the Allied direction-finding sets lagged. Even when designers came up with the effective British FH-3 and FH-4 HF/DF receivers, only a small number of convoy escorts had the gear installed. By August 1942, just seventy Royal Navy ships were equipped with HF/DF gear. The U.S. Navy likewise was late to exploit ship-based HF/DF technology. The first American-built sets, based on a French design smuggled out of Paris after the German invasion in June 1940, did not come off the assembly line at the International Telephone and Telegraph Corporation's New York laboratory until October 1941.[11]

Although HF/DF was slow to catch on, by the spring of 1943 the Allies had strongly embraced it as an essential element of convoy defense. As the American, British, and Canadian navies battled the U-boat wolf packs during 1941 and 1942, their appreciation for HF/DF's ability to locate individual U-boats and gathering wolf packs had steadily grown. In June 1942, Admiral King himself became a convert and ordered that half of all newly constructed destroyers and destroyer escorts be fitted with HF/DF. Meanwhile, shipwrights on both sides of the Atlantic were busy retrofitting with HF/DF the older vessels. Both the U.S. Navy and Western Approaches Command attempted to ensure that at least two warships in every convoy escort group would have HF/DF, so as to be able to take the cross-bearings when a German commander transmitted on his radio, thus providing firm information about the transmitting U-boat's location.

Ship-mounted HF/DF allowed Allied escort groups to locate and track U-boats by exploiting a fundamental weakness in U-boat doctrine. All U-boats at sea followed an ironclad set of instructions whereby each commander was required to report his position, fuel state, and other mission details back to Berlin on a nearly daily basis via high-frequency radio. In turn, U-boat Headquarters regularly dictated intelligence findings and operational orders to the deployed boats, messages that then required confirmation of receipt. Using signals gleaned from multiple detectors, the Allied HF/DF network could triangulate each U-boat transmission as it went out, and assemble readings of multiple signals to identify areas in which wolf packs were gathering.

By 1943, Allied naval officials had realized that ship-mounted HF/DF was far more accurate and effective than the older array of shore listening stations that the United States and British had established on both sides of the Atlantic. The British had built a network of receiving stations that reached from Scotland to Land's End in Cornwall to Gibraltar, while the U.S. Navy had constructed an HF/DF network comprising more than a dozen stations from Winter Harbor, Maine, to the Caribbean. Other stations were operating in Greenland, Iceland, and Bermuda, giving the Allies blanket coverage of the North Atlantic. Unfortunately, the land-based receivers suffered from poor accuracy given the extended range at which their antennas picked up U-boat transmissions.

The Allied HF/DF system was even more effective because the U-boat Force never realized how accurate the newer ship-mounted sets had become. Locked into their reliance on high-frequency communications, Admiral Dönitz and the staff at BdU failed to detect the expanding role that Allied shipboard HF/DF was playing in convoy defense. German radio scientists assured BdU that neither the Allies nor anyone else could accurately track high-frequency transmissions. The truth—that Allied HF/DF systems could easily pick up such transmissions—was one of several nasty surprises the Germans would learn after the end of the war. In the meantime, however, Dönitz took the precaution of restricting his U-boat commanders from sending lengthy messages, and BdU devised a system of short messages that the Germans thought would further frustrate enemy radio direction-finding stations. Both the scientists and the grand admiral were mistaken.

Then–Lieutenant-Commander Donald MacIntyre, commander of Escort Group B-2 on the HMS Hesperus, had been the first Royal Navy destroyer commander to receive an HF/DF set back in March 1941. By the spring of 1943, his crew typified the central role that radio direction finding now played in Western Approaches Command. MacIntyre would frequently brag that Lieutenant Harold Walker, his lead HF/DF operator and a former civilian telegraph operator, was so attuned to the sounds in his headset he could identify individual German radio operators by their distinctive telegraph keying, and could even distinguish the difference between a U-boat signal using an aerial that was dry (a U-boat running on the surface for a while) and wet (one that had just surfaced).[12]

As Convoy HX229 turned out into the open ocean on March 14, 1943, officials at Western Approaches Command in Liverpool and U.S. Navy headquarters in Washington were hoping that the combination of shore-based and ship-mounted HF/DF would enable them to carefully monitor the U-boat situation northeast of Newfoundland. But they also knew that there was a potentially dangerous flaw in this system. To be able to use HF/DF technology effectively, two or more ships in every group had to have a set onboard.

Unfortunately for Convoy HX229, Escort Group B-4 had only one shipboard HF/DF set—on the *Volunteer*. Thus, any intercepted U-boat transmission would provide only a single line of bearing to the enemy, rather than the cross-bearing fix that could be obtained with two or more receiver sets. This lack of a second HF/DF set would make it much harder to locate U-boats approaching the convoy and make it impossible for HF/DF to provide escorts with the enemy's exact location.

HX229's lack of HF/DF would imperil it in the days to come, but the technology was able to help a different convoy outbound from New York that week. Following a day behind Convoy HX229 was the ad hoc Convoy HX229A, which would make its Atlantic crossing with the British 40th Escort Group. When shore-based HF/DF stations revealed three massive wolf packs operating ahead of the three convoys astride their initial course tracks, COMINCH ordered Commander John S. Dalison, senior officer of the 40th Escort Group, to reroute Convoy HX229A on a northerly course up toward Greenland before turning east for the British Isles. The long diversion was the first major decision by U.S. Navy convoy managers to safeguard the three eastbound formations. Because of this radical move, Convoy HX229A and its escorts circumvented the U-boats and would fortunately play no further part in the critical battles that followed. Because naval planners always tried to keep convoys from sailing close to one another so as to minimize the chance of detection, they had no choice but to keep SC122 and HX229 on a more normal northeasterly heading toward the British Isles—and proceeding directly toward the massing U-boats.[13]

Brothers Joseph and William Stilinovich were both Naval Armed Guard gunners serving on different merchant ships in Convoy HX229.
Courtesy of Gladys Stilinovich

On Sunday, March 14, the ragtag B-4 group under Luther's temporary command arrived at the designated WESTOMP at 47:38 North 049:01 West to meet HX229, but Luther found only empty ocean. B-4 had pulled out of St. John's the previous evening so as to arrive at the rendezvous at the designated hour of 1000, but when the *Volunteer*, *Beverley* and *Anemone* got there, Convoy HX229 had already come and gone. As a result of a strong following sea and winds from astern, the convoy had exceeded its designated speed of ten knots, passing the rendezvous point several hours earlier than scheduled. The three ships of B-4 chased after the convoy, finally meeting it ten hours later at 1800. Shortly after that, the stopgap destroyers *Witherington* and *Mansfield* also joined up. Luther assigned the escort ships to assemble around the main body, and HX229 continued out into the open sea.[14]

As HX229 moved out toward the Greenland air gap, two Naval Armed Guard sailors serving on different vessels in the convoy reached out to one another across nearly one and one-half miles of ocean. William Stilinovich, eighteen, and Joseph Stilinovich, twenty-one, were close brothers in a large, second-generation American family from Hibbing, Minnesota. They had grown up together, attended school and played together, and enlisted in the navy on the same day in late 1942. They attended boot camp at Great Lakes, Illinois together—sharing adjacent bunks in their barracks—and then went to Naval Armed Guard School in the same class. But when they reported in to the Armed Guard Center (Atlantic) in Brooklyn, officials had placed them on separate ships. While the navy in early 1943 did not formally prohibit siblings from serving on the same vessel, officials had begun to discourage the practice in response to the Sullivan brothers tragedy, which had occurred on November 13, 1942. The five Sullivan brothers, a sister, and their parents lived in Waterloo, Iowa. The brothers had enlisted in the navy together on condition that they be allowed to serve on the same ship. They were onboard the light cruiser *USS Juneau* near Guadalcanal when it exploded and sank after a Japanese submarine torpedo attack. All five Sullivan brothers perished.[15]

Despite their separation, the Stilinovich brothers found themselves both in Convoy HX229 when it departed New York on March 8. Joe was serving as a gunner on the 6,366-ton American freighter *Harry Luckenbach,* carrying 8,381 tons of ammunition and general cargo to Liverpool, while Bill was a 20-mm machine-gunner on the 6,125-ton American freighter *Irénée Du Pont,* loaded with 5,800 tons of general cargo and 3,200 tons of oil and carrying eleven medium bombers on its main deck. The two ships occupied the lead positions in Columns 8 and 11 on the starboard side of HX229, with two other merchantmen in between. On the afternoon of March 14, each brother persuaded a signalman from his detachment to activate his signal lantern. As the convoy headed out into the treacherous waters of the North Atlantic, Joe and Bill wished each other good luck via blinking Morse code.[16]

Chapter 4

THE U-BOAT

To the men on U-758, it would have been hard to believe that their U-boat could survive the fury of the storm. Displacing just 769 tons on the surface, the Type VIIC U-boats were all but buried by the towering seas they often encountered in the North Atlantic. The waters relentlessly crashed over their narrow hulls and exposed bridges. On its present patrol, U-758 seemed to defy nature as it battled through the mountainous waves and shrieking winds.

Down in the U-boat's cramped steel pressure hull, forty-two German sailors struggled to go about their daily tasks while their vessel rose and plunged with each passing swell. U-boats were violently tossed during storms like this, with crewmen hurled to the deck, tossed into the overhead, and sent sprawling into the metal pipes and fittings that nearly filled their space. Each time a wave crashed into the conning tower, tons of seawater would cascade down through the open bridge hatch to drench the watch-standers in the control room two levels down. They worked in a deafening bellow from the boat's two supercharged Germaniawerft diesel engines, in a foul miasma of every possible stench that dozens of men living in a steel tube could create: diesel fumes, unwashed bodies, rotting food, mold, human waste, and the sweet musk of cologne everyone wore to ward off the reek. But they carried out their wartime tasks with stoicism and resolve despite the hellish conditions in which they lived and worked.[1]

The men below deck were the fortunate ones. Four members of the crew—an officer and three lookouts—were exposed to the teeth of the storm in the small open bridge atop the U-boat's conning tower. Lashed to the superstructure by steel-reinforced safety belts, they would have endured rogue waves that buried the bridge under frigid water and threatened to rip them from their perch. As one survivor of a similar storm described it, "When we were on watch, the wind punished us with driving snow, sleet, hail, and frozen spray. It beat against our rubber diver's suits, cut our faces like a razor, and threatened to tear away our eye masks; only the steel belts around our waists secured us to boat and life."[2]

To the naked eye, U-758 would have appeared totally alone in the vast raging sea. But this was not the case. There were more than three dozen U-boats spread out over several thousand square miles of the North Atlantic on March 15, 1943. Orders from U-boat Force Headquarters in Berlin had organized them into three wolf packs to hunt the enemy convoys that German naval intelligence predicted would soon appear. Until that happened, however, the crewmen on each boat were locked in a desperate struggle, both private and communal, against the storm.

Aboard U-758, Oberfunkmaat (Radioman 2nd Class) Martin Beisheim sat hunched over his Telefunken radio receiver in the tiny radio room, his headset covering only one ear. While his assistant, Funkobergefreiter (Radioman) Karl Pauli, performed other tasks, Beisheim carefully monitored the sounds from two different worlds. With his covered ear, Beisheim listened for the faint staccato of a Morse code message from another U-boat announcing contact with the enemy, or instructions from Berlin that would send the crew to battle stations and vector them to the fight. While all wireless Morse code messages were encrypted and arrived as a series of random four-letter blocks of letters that Beisheim would have to "break" into clear text, he strained to hear the unencrypted message header—*dash-dot-dot-dot-dash*, German Morse for the Greek letter beta—that would alert all recipients that another U-boat had an enemy convoy in sight. At the same time, his uncovered left ear filtered out the boat's cacophony while awaiting one of three meaningful sounds: a cry from one of the boat's lookouts shouted down the voice tube from the conning tower to the radio room that they had visually spotted a convoy; the sudden din of the emergency alarm that would send the boat hurtling into the depths in a crash dive; or the unannounced arrival of Kapitänleutnant Helmut Manseck with an outgoing message for Beisheim to encrypt and transmit.[3]

U-758 Radio Operator Martin
Beisheim and his wife, Edith.
Courtesy of Martin Beisheim

U-758 was on patrol about 525 miles east-northeast of St. John's, New-foundland, on the early evening of Monday, March 15, thirty-four days out on its second war cruise. U-758 had left St. Nazaire, France on February 14, and over the previous three weeks, Manseck and his men had pa-trolled the western edge of the Greenland air gap with several dozen other U-boats in hopes of finding an Allied convoy heading either eastbound for the United Kingdom or westbound for North America.

U-758 was a relatively new U-boat. Constructed by the Kriegsmarine-Werft shipyard in Wilhelmshaven, Germany, it was commissioned on May 5, 1942, becoming the 448th Type VIIC model to join the U-boat Force since 1941. U-758 was 220 feet long, with a beam of twenty feet, and measuring just over thirty-one feet from the keel to the top of the conning tower; it displaced 769 tons running on the surface, and could make nearly eighteen knots. When heading toward a patrol area, the boat could cruise at ten knots for 8,500 nautical miles without refueling. Running submerged, it could travel eighty nautical miles at four knots before having to surface to recharge its batteries. In an emergency, the submerged U-boat could make seven knots, but at the risk of exhausting its electrical batteries in only a few hours' time.[4]

Like all Type VIIC U-boats, U-758's primary weapon was the anti-ship torpedo. During the first half of World War II, German U-boats relied on two main types of torpedoes, the G7a compressed-steam propulsion torpedo and the newer G7e electric introduced in early 1939. Both measured twenty-one inches in diameter and twenty-three feet in length and both carried a 618-pound high-explosive warhead. The G7a ran on a combustion engine burning alcohol that generated steam to turn a single, six-bladed propeller. Its speed could be set before launch from thirty to forty-four knots. At its slowest speed, the torpedo had a maximum range of 6.75 nautical miles and at its fastest, 3.24 miles. Its biggest liability was that the engine left a visible wake of exhaust gas that would be easily seen in daylight, but otherwise the G7a was a deadly efficient ship killer.

By the spring of 1943, most U-boats also carried the G7e electric torpedo, a new variant on the G7a. Propelled by a 100-horsepower electric motor powered by wet-cell batteries, the G7e employed a Pi 2 firing pistol that could be set for either contact or magnetic detonation. Unlike the older G7a, this torpedo had only one speed, thirty knots, and a maximum range of only 2.7 nautical miles. However, it was a much stealthier weapon that left no wake as it raced through the water toward the target. U-758 was one of three U-boats at sea on March 15 equipped with the new G7s Falke (falcon) torpedo, which featured a new passive acoustic homing device that would track the sound of a merchantman's propellers.[5]

When leaving on patrol, the Type VIIC normally carried fourteen torpedoes, one apiece in each of four bow tubes and a single stern tube, four more stored under removable deck plates in the bow compartment, another pair in the bow compartment itself, one additional torpedo stored under the deck plates in the stern torpedo room, and a pair stored in over-deck containers located fore and aft of the conning tower between the U-boat's pressure hull and the deck. The Type VIIC could also be used for mine laying, loading up to twenty-six TMA moored anti-ship mines, loaded two apiece in each torpedo tube with another ten stored in the torpedo compartment.

Martin Beisheim kept numerous photographs of the U-758 at sea during nearly three years on the boat.
Courtesy of Martin Beisheim

For surface attacks, U-758 carried a C35 88-mm deck cannon mounted on the main deck, and a 20-mm cannon for anti-aircraft defense. U-boats would later carry additional 20-mm cannons.[6]

As U-758's commander, Dönitz had assigned an experienced U-boat officer who had already had significant combat experience on another boat. Manseck, a twenty-seven-year-old native of Silesia, had served in the German surface navy for eight months in 1939–40 before joining the U-boat Force. After finishing U-boat training, he served as Erster Wachoffizier (First Watch Officer, or 1WO) under highly decorated Kapitänleutnant Karl Thurmann in U-553 for eight months during 1940–41. Manseck helped commission the boat and took part in its first two war patrols. During his tour, U-553 sank two Allied merchantmen totaling 7,945 gross tons steaming in southbound Convoy OG64 from Liverpool to Gibraltar.

With a significant amount of combat experience, Manseck was granted command of his own U-boat. He made a formal but highly respected U-boat commander, according to Martin Beisheim, who joined U-758 the day after its commissioning. "He was a role model officer, I have to say. Not only his military attitude, but also his social skills," Beisheim recalled many years later. "He fulfilled his duty as captain 100 percent, a real officer, but not one of the kind who longed to get the Knight's Cross."[7]

Manseck took the officers and men of U-758 through the U-boat Force's *Baubelehrung* (boat familiarization) program in the spring of 1942. The crew literally worked side by side with the Kriegsmarine-Werft shipwrights in the last month of construction. They scrambled through the unfinished U-boat, learning its capabilities and limits, studying the myriad components and systems as they took shape. For six months after the formal commissioning ceremony, the crew worked around the clock on training exercises in the Baltic before departing the U-boat Training School at Kiel on the boat's first war patrol on November 14, 1942. During that forty-one-day war cruise, U-758 attempted several attacks on eastbound Convoy HX217 but scored no confirmed hits. Two months after arriving at its permanent homeport at St. Nazaire, Manseck and his crew departed on February 14 for its second, current patrol.[8]

U-758 had followed the standard patrol pattern for U-boats operating in the North Atlantic during World War II. Leaving port, the boats would dash at maximum surface speed across the Bay of Biscay, off the western coast of France, so as to evade British bombers flying from southern England. Once in the open ocean, they would slow to economical cruising speed as they headed to the initial patrol area identified in sealed orders that the commander brought on board. The transit could take as long as two weeks if the U-boat was destined for the east coast of the United States or the northwest Atlantic between Greenland and Canada. Upon arrival on station, it would join a wolf pack or individually patrol the area.

A number of variable factors would determine the intensity of a patrol for a boat like U-758. If the shipping lanes were empty of Allied merchantmen, the boat might screen a specific area of ocean until the situation changed. If a wolf pack failed to find a suspected convoy because of weather conditions or a successful evasion ploy, BdU might redirect the U-boats to hunt for another suspected convoy. Sometimes Admirals

The bow compartment of a U-boat is crammed with perishable foods and spare torpedoes at the outset of a patrol.

Clay Blair Collection, American Heritage Center, University of Wyoming

Dönitz and Godt would assign individual U-boats to weather reporting duties in the North Atlantic near Greenland or Iceland. Barring mechanical breakdowns, serious battle damage, or the expenditure of its entire torpedo inventory, a Type VIIC U-boat such as U-758 could expect to remain on patrol for anywhere from four to six weeks before returning to port. Having left St. Nazaire just over a month before, U-758 could still expect to be at sea for another two weeks before being relieved.

The U-boats' long patrols seemed interminable to both newcomers and veteran crewmen alike, Beisheim later recalled. Within days, the air had gone foul and all the fresh food wore a coating of white mold. Since at least two crewmen shared each bunk, it did not take long for the sheets and pillowcases to darken with sweat, dirt, and grease stains. The crew's clothing became equally filthy. Each crewman could bring only one set of clothes onboard, given the absence of personal storage space. One wore the clothes for the first two weeks of a patrol, then turned them inside out for the last two weeks. Like the crew of sailing ships a century before, the men ate lemons to prevent scurvy. Even brushing one's teeth was a luxury. Each crewman received a daily allotment of one cup of fresh water. The choice was to drink it or use it for dental hygiene. All fifty-one crewmen from the captain to the youngest recruit had to share the one toilet available (a second toilet was filled with supplies at the start of a patrol and was unavailable to the crew until much later). The flushing mechanism required a complicated and difficult series of movements that if done incorrectly could unleash a fountain of human waste to drench the unfortunate operator. "The hygiene in a sub is a catastrophe," Beisheim later said with a shudder as he described the living conditions that he and other U-boat men were forced to endure.

For all of the monotony, physical hardship, and genuine danger at sea, Martin Beisheim loved serving in U-boats. His childhood fascination with the sea, his early training as an electrician, and his deep personal interest in radio had all but guaranteed his future service in the Kriegsmarine. As a teenager, he had joined the naval branch of the Hitler Youth—membership in Hitler Youth was mandatory for all males over the age of thirteen—and received extensive training in military radio communications as well as general military skills. When he had enlisted in the Kriegsmarine at age sixteen, however, he had not initially intended to join the U-boat Force, telling other recruits he wanted to serve on small, fast patrol boats.

If Martin Beisheim's personal experiences would eventually draw him toward the U-boat Force, the culture in which he and his generation were raised had similarly prepared them for war. Born to a middle-class family on June 23, 1921, Martin Beisheim grew up in a Germany still reeling from the impact of World War I. It was a time of widespread social and economic dislocation, which contributed to the rise of the Nazi Party in the early 1930s. After his stint in the Hitler Youth movement, Beisheim later joined the Reichsarbeitsdienst (State Labor Service), a nationwide organization that carried out massive public work projects. While he was in the labor service, Beisheim's superiors encouraged him to continue pursuing his interest in radio technology. When he finally went on active duty in the Kriegsmarine, Beisheim later recalled, he was "already almost a complete radio operator."

The German invasion of Poland on September 1, 1939 had changed the lives of all Germans, including Beisheim. Having embraced Adolf

Hitler and the Nazi Party, Germans as a whole were totally committed to the war effort. Because the Reichsarbeitsdienst was a labor auxiliary of the military, Beisheim's initial wartime service was not in the navy but on a work gang repairing damaged bridges and rebuilding roads in southern Poland in the rear of the German invasion force. The navy caught up with Beisheim after several weeks, and on October 1, 1939, he entered boot camp. After graduating two months later, he attended a series of specialized schools dealing with intelligence gathering, basic U-boat operations, and advanced radio procedures. Then one morning in late 1940, the young *Funkgefreiter* (Radioman) received orders to a new U-boat under construction at the AG Weser shipyard in Bremen.

Beishem's first U-boat assignment had placed him under the command of Kapitänleutnant Günther Müller-Stockheim aboard the Type IXC U-67, a somewhat more ungainly craft than the one on which he currently served. The Type IXC, a later model of the original Type IX boat, and Type VIIC were the two workhorse U-boats in World War II. Significantly larger than the VIIC, the Type IX models were designed for distant patrols in areas such as the Caribbean and Indian Ocean. While the U-67 was forty percent heavier than a VIIC, it could still reach eighteen knots at flank speed on the surface and nearly eight knots submerged, about the same as the smaller boat. The boat also carried twenty-two torpedoes, eight more than the VIIC.

The only disadvantage in the Type IX design was a major one: a slower rate of submergence. In a crash dive, the Type VIIC could plunge from the surface to forty-three feet down in just thirty seconds, while the larger Type IX took between thirty-five and forty seconds to reach the same depth. If a land-based patrol bomber attacked, that five-to-ten-second difference seemed an eternity to the crew. During the crisis of the Battle of the Atlantic in the spring of 1943, the Allies would sink eleven percent of the seventy Type IX boats in operation, while destroying only two percent of the more nimble Type VIIC boats. It was no secret in the U-boat Force that the best commanders preferred the VIIC.[9]

Beisheim had gotten an introduction to the harsh realities of life at sea on the U-67. Nothing could prepare a first-time U-boat sailor for the inhospitable conditions of a month-long war patrol. With its complement of twenty-two torpedoes, bunkers loaded with 209 tons of diesel fuel, and every cubic inch of space crammed with food supplies, the U-67 headed out for its shakedown cruise in the North Atlantic on August 1, 1941, moving around the British Isles to its new base in Lorient, France.

Beisheim made two war patrols on the U-67 over the course of five months during the phase of the Battle of the Atlantic that U-boat men came to call the Glückliche Zeit (the Happy Time), given the poor state of British naval defenses. Operating off the west coast of Africa during its first patrol, U-67 sank a 3,753-ton British steam merchant from Convoy SL87 on September 24, 1941. For the first time in the war, Beisheim and his crewmates listened to the dull, basso rumblings through the pressure hull marking the collapse of a sinking enemy ship's compartments. Three days later, the U-67 itself nearly met its end. While heading to rendezvous with a homebound U-boat near the Cape Verde Islands to transfer fuel and torpedoes, it suffered heavy bow damage in a collision with the British submarine HMS Clyde and had to abort the mission.

On return to port after U-67's second patrol, Beisheim found orders to attend advanced radio training. After five months of classroom work, he reported to the newly commissioned U-758 as a radioman 2nd class. The move would save his life. On July 16, 1943, four months after Beisheim's current patrol on U-758, a U.S. Navy Avenger dive-bomber from the escort carrier USS Core would sight U-67 some 850 miles west-southwest of the Azores and drop four depth charges on the boat, sinking it and killing Kapitänleutnant Müller-Stockheim and forty-seven of the crew. Three members of the bridge watch would survive and be taken prisoner. None of the three would be from the radio room.[10]

At this juncture, Beisheim of course could not foretell what would happen to his former mates on U-67, but he did know that as March 15 was ending, his U-boat had yet to sink a single enemy ship, and that this Monday was shaping up to be yet another disappointing day in an increasingly frustrating patrol. U-758's second war patrol had begun promisingly enough. Outbound from France on February 21, the U-boat had joined with eight others in Gruppe Sturmbock (Storm Support) in an attempted attack on westbound Convoy ONS167. Because of the harsh weather and an aggressive escort group protecting the convoy, however, only one U-boat in Gruppe Sturmbock, U-664, managed to sink any merchant ships at all—and it had bagged two. The convoy escorts counterattacked and drove off U-758 when Manseck attempted to close on the formation the next day. Two days afterward, BdU headquarters formed the wolf pack Gruppe Wildfang (Madcap) comprising ten U-boats, including U-758. Admiral Dönitz then paired the wolf pack with another sixteen U-boats in Gruppe Bürggraf (Fortress Chief), which he had established two days earlier northeast of Newfoundland.

Along with Gruppe Bürggraf, U-758's Gruppe Wildfang created a twenty-six-boat patrol line extending over 300 miles, oriented in a north-west-to-southeast direction, aiming to intercept an eastbound slow convoy—SC121, though no one aboard the U-boats would have known the convoy's name—that had left New York several days earlier. Dönitz ordered each U-boat to maintain an interval of twelve miles from the next one in line, increasing the chances that one or more of them would sight the convoy as it approached. A third wolf pack of eleven U-boats, Gruppe Neptun (Neptune) was holding several hundred miles north of the Wildfang-Bürggraf line as a reserve force. On March 4, Dönitz formed a fourth wolf pack, Gruppe Neuland (New Territory), out of twenty-two U-boats just entering the Atlantic from bases in France or Germany. Positioned about 300 miles farther to the east, this wolf pack would hunt for other east- and westbound convoys as opportunity permitted.

While the U-boats in the North Atlantic and BdU Headquarters were well prepared for Convoy SC121, neither of the groups had anticipated the severity of the weather in the first week of March. Unfortunately for Beisheim and his crewmates on U-758, the foul weather enabled Convoy SC121 to slip through a gap between the southernmost U-boat in the Wildfang patrol line and the northernmost boat in the Bürggraf line. The twenty-eight U-boats in Gruppen Ostmark and Westmark patrolling several hundred miles to the east-northeast would get the opportunity to attack SC121. The thirteen boats in Gruppe Neuland would also enjoy good luck, closing in and attacking eastbound Convoy HX228, which followed the Slow Convoy SC121 by a day.

After missing out on the action against Convoys SC121 and HX228, U-758 had been reassigned once more. On March 6, Dönitz had sent U-758 and a dozen other boats to the newly formed Gruppe Raubgraf (Robber Baron) and positioned them along the western edge of the Greenland air gap. Since then, Manseck and his battered lookouts had seen nothing but the towering waves and scudding clouds of the North Atlantic in winter. This wearying monotony was about to change.[11]

Aboard U-758, Martin Beisheim suddenly stiffened where he sat as the familiar cadence erupted in his headset. As the *dash-dot-dot-dot-dash* of the unencrypted beta signal message heading repeated itself, he snatched a notepad and pencil and began writing down the jumble of random letters that followed. He glanced up at a ship's clock on the curved bulkhead. It was 2018 hours Central European Time.* When finished, Beisheim told his assistant, Karl Pauli, to prepare the Funkschlüssel-M machine for decrypting what could only be another U-boat's convoy sighting report.[12]

As a senior radioman, Beisheim was responsible for operating a variety of sophisticated communications and direction-finding gear on U-758. While the captain at his periscope and the lookouts on the cramped navigational bridge served as the eyes of the boat, Beisheim and the three other radiomen aboard served as both the U-boat's voice and its ears. Each radioman stood alternating watches in the radio room. On the boat, that meant working from 0800 to 1200, followed by four hours off duty for meals and additional duties, then back to the radio gear from 1600 until 2000. At 2000 the first night watch ran six hours until 0200, with the second night watch from 0200 until 0800 the next morning. It was a demanding schedule to which the radiomen were accustomed.

Beisheim and the other radiomen were also essential in locating and attacking enemy ships. When U-758 was running submerged, Beisheim and the other radiomen operated the U-boat's passive hydrophone array to locate the position and sound bearing of an attacking enemy destroyer or the far-off murmur of dozens of churning propellers signaling a convoy on the move. These inputs gave Kapitänleutnant Manseck a clear spatial awareness of the enemy's movements against his own. Beisheim and his mates also operated a low-frequency radio transmitter critical to organizing a mass attack against a convoy. Upon sighting a convoy, Beisheim and

---

*U-boats at sea from November 2, 1942 until March 28, 1943 operated on German Summer Time, the time zone of BdU Headquarters in Berlin. This was one hour ahead of Greenwich Mean Time. From March 29 until October 4, 1943, U-boats switched to Central Europe Summer Time, two hours ahead of GMT.

The cramped radio compartment on a German U-boat.
Uboat.net

the other radiomen would tap out a Morse code letter that other U-boats would receive and use to obtain a bearing to the enemy merchant ships.

Beginning in August 1942, all U-boats were also equipped with a primitive radar-detection system intended to keep them safe from probing enemy aircraft. The system went by the formal title of Funkmessbeobachter-1, or FuMB-1 Metox, after the French manufacturer. U-boat men called it the Biscay Cross after both the antenna's shape and the increasingly dangerous conditions in the Bay of Biscay, where British bombers had begun to locate surfaced U-boats at night with the new ASV Mark III centimetric radar.

The Metox was generally dismissed as a crude, stopgap measure against Allied airborne radar, but it had already saved U-758's life. When Manseck took the boat to sea on its first patrol, a Metox unit was aboard. Beisheim and Pauli made their first intercept of an enemy aircraft radar one day as U-758 was passing between the Faeroes and Shetland Islands north of Scotland en route to the Atlantic. Beisheim was eating lunch in the petty officer's area when Pauli, monitoring the Metox, suddenly shouted for him to come forward to the radio room. Beisheim took the headset and heard the steady whine of the audio tone signaling an aircraft radar beam striking the boat. He called across the compartment where Kapitänleutnant Manseck was lying on his bunk. The skipper stood up and donned the headset. The tone was getting loud enough to hear without putting on the headgear. Manseck called up to the bridge watch for a visibility report. The answer came back: visibility only 300 meters in steady fog. In a calm voice, Manseck ordered a crash dive. The gun crews out on deck quickly secured the ready ammunition and raced down the ladder, followed by a lookout wrestling the Biscay Cross and its cable through the hatch, and lastly by the rest of the bridge watch. Scarcely had U-758 plunged below the surface when a loud explosion went off very close by. Captain and crewmen silently gaped at one another, belatedly realizing that the ad hoc device had probably just saved their lives. The radiomen now added a new word to their lexicon: "Ortung!"—"Detection!"—meant the Metox had sniffed an incoming aircraft.[13]

Aside from his navigation and detection duties, one of Beisheim's more mundane—but no less important—tasks was to serve as U-758's official diarist. Each U-boat commander kept a detailed *Kriegstagebüch* (KTB), or daily war diary, that set down the boat's position, weather conditions, fuel state, and an hour-by-hour description of the boat's activities. After each attack on an Allied merchantman or escort, the commander, his first watch officer, and the navigator would reconstruct the sequence of events in fine-grain detail, including the time of each torpedo launch, the torpedo tube used, and the identity or description of any ship it sank. The commander would also note in the KTB any mechanical breakdowns or other mishaps that occurred on the boat's patrol, and the KTB would also provide a summary of each message sent to or from the boat. As a senior radio petty officer, it was Beisheim's job to type up the top-secret daily report from the commander's notes. It was a task he hated because Manseck had terrible handwriting.[14]

From operating the hydrophone to keeping the ship's diary, the duties of Beisheim and the other U-boat radiomen were important but ancillary compared to their most critical task. They were responsible for a top-secret technology that would, in many ways, determine the outcome of the Battle of the Atlantic.

Chapter 5

THE BATTLE OF THE CODES

The Battle of the Atlantic was a conflict fought on and under the great ocean mass. But central to winning it was another battle, one fought across the electromagnetic spectrum. Its fighters included U-boat men like Oberfunkmaat Martin Beisheim on U-758 but also a wide assemblage of scientists, mathematicians, and code-breakers huddled in top-secret monitoring stations ashore.

At sea, Beisheim and other U-boat radiomen managed the encryption and transmission of operational messages between U-758 and U-boat Force headquarters. In this, the young petty officer had been entrusted with one of the most sensitive secrets in the German Navy—the Funkschlüssel-M (radio cipher), or naval Enigma machine. Resembling a bulky office typewriter with several strange electrical add-ons, the Enigma featured a keyboard and three rows of small circular windows, each marked with a letter of the alphabet. When the operator depressed a key, it closed an electrical circuit, and a small light bulb behind one of twenty-nine small glass windows (corresponding to the twenty-six-letter alphabet plus the umlauted German letters ä, ö, and ü) would illuminate. The letter that appeared in the lit window represented the encryption of the letter that the radio operator had just typed. The secret of Enigma was how the machine turned one letter—the keystroke—into a different one—the illuminated letter appearing in the circular face of one of the glow lamps—seemingly at random.

Beisheim turned on the U-758's Enigma and began the exacting procedure to decrypt the incoming message into plain-text German using his

The Marine-Funkschlüssel M, or naval Enigma machine, provided the means by which U-boats at sea could communicate with shore-based headquarters using encrypted messages.
Clay Blair Collection, American Heritage Center, University of Wyoming

notebook full of handwritten Morse code letters. He jotted down the time the transmission had begun: 1918 Central European Time (1818 hours GMT). The Enigma was the primary safeguard of war-related communications between Berlin and the U-boat fleet, and its complexity reflected this vital role. The heart of the Enigma machine in 1943 was a system of four moving electromechanical rotors that continuously changed the circuit path from keyboard to glow lamp. It was an improved model issued to the U-boats in February 1942 that replaced a three-rotor version the navy had first used in 1925. The U-boat Force provided each Enigma machine with eight different rotors, each identified with a roman numeral from I to VIII, and each of which had different letter-to-letter wiring designs; from these eight rotors, the operator would select four to install in the machine on a preplanned schedule. The sequence of Enigma rotors installed in the machine changed every other day at midnight, adding yet another layer of complexity to the system.

While it was relatively straightforward to operate, the Enigma was incredibly complicated in its internal design. The four-inch bakelite rotors were mounted on a horizontal shaft in the machine. Each rotor contained a complex arrangement of electrical wiring that formed part of the circuit connecting each letter on the Enigma keyboard with the twenty-nine glow lamps. Each rotor sported twenty-nine spring-loaded metal pins on one side and twenty-nine circular electrical contacts on the other corresponding to the German alphabet. Within each rotor, one letter position was wired to a second, different letter position, so that, for example, every time the operator pressed the letter "A" on the keyboard, the wiring in that particular rotor would direct the current to the letter "C." When pressing the letter "D," the rotor wiring might send the signal to the letter "M," and so on. A fifth circular device permanently installed in the machine was the reflector, essentially a non-moving rotor. The electrical impulse traveled from the keyboard through the four moving rotors to the reflector, which redirected it back down through a different path in each of the four rotors. Thus, when a letter emerged from the rotor system, its identity had changed nine times since the Enigma operator had pressed the typewriter key. Nor was that the end of it.[1]

Besides the rotor system, the machine's designers had added two additional layers of encryption to Enigma. One device was an "alphabet ring" mounted on each rotor and the reflector. The ring displayed the rotor position indicator letter that appeared in each of four small windows on the face of the machine. Also engraved with the twenty-nine letters of the German alphabet, the metal ring on each rotor itself could be turned until the letter designated for that day's use locked into a stud. This enabled the Enigma operator to change the rotor circuit for each letter prior to use. Another encryption layer came from a cable plug board on the front of the machine. In addition to running the typed letter through each rotor twice and the reflector once, this component added a tenth layer of encryption. The plug board had twenty-nine electrical sockets corresponding to the alphabet as well. Following another pre-planned schedule, the operator would connect pairs of letters using a series of short electrical cables with plugs on both ends.

The genius of the encryption system was that, apart from external inputs, the rotors also interacted with each other when the machine was in use. As the operator typed each succeeding letter in the message, the right-hand rotor would advance one letter position by a ratchet-and-pawl mechanism on its outer edge. The other three rotors would also advance, but only after a larger number of keystrokes had occurred. In reality, every letter of an Enigma message was encrypted by a unique code. The effect was that the same letter of the alphabet would encrypt to a different one each time the operator pressed that key.

Encrypting a message on naval Enigma was a complex process requiring careful attention to details, since a single error in a rotor setting or message key would result in gibberish at the other end. Adding to the complexity of the process was the fact that the entire procedure was reset every other day near midnight, when the U-boat Force switched to a new Enigma encryption setting. U-boats carried publications that provided the radio crews with the necessary inputs for each new forty-eight-hour period. These publications—printed in water-soluble ink for easy destruction in case of sinking or boarding by the enemy—told the radiomen which four rotors to use on any given date; the alphabet ring settings for each rotor and the reflector; the rotor sequence on the shaft; the daily four-letter "machine setting" for the rotors, and the plug board cable settings.

When Manseck had a message to dispatch to BdU Operations in Berlin, he would hand the German plain text to Beisheim. The radioman would do the rest. Encrypting the commander's handwritten notes into an Enigma message required two steps: preparing a separate message key and the message header, and encrypting the plain-text message itself using the Enigma machine. To create a message key, Beisheim would open a separate publication that contained several pages with columns of random four-letter text blocks. He would pick one at random for changing the Enigma rotor settings. From a third publication, the radioman would create a second four-letter text block indicating the radio network in use (the German Navy assigned separate networks for each geographical area such as the North Atlantic, Ireland, Africa, and the Mediterranean). On a printed message form, Beisheim would first put down the unencrypted—but scrambled in code—four-letter message key and four-letter network indicator, then the clear text of the message itself. The template required inserting the clear text in blocks of four letters without word breaks, and inserting the letter "x" to separate sentences. Next, Beisheim would sit at the Enigma machine and slowly type the header and message text. Pauli would read the encrypted letters as the glow lamps illuminated and write them down on the message form.

Despite its mind-boggling complexity and the hundreds of billions of possible letter transformations it employed, the Enigma provided a simple process by which a message's recipient could unlock the encryption. When the four rotors, rotor sequence, plug board settings, daily machine key, and message key were correctly applied, all a receiving radio operator had to do was type the garbled text into the machine and record the plain-text message as it emerged in the glow lamps. Prior to transmitting, Beisheim and his fellow radio operators would use the decryption process to check the draft message for accuracy.

Only once they had double-checked the encryption would Beisheim fire up his radio set and begin tapping the message on his telegraph key, sending it out over the airwaves in Morse code. Enigma designers calculated that the total number of possible letter conversions ran in the hundreds of billions, rendering Enigma—in the German Navy's opinion—effectively impervious to hostile penetration.[2]

In the case of the beta signal that they had begun to receive on the early evening of March 15, Beisheim and Pauli's task was much simpler than the encoding procedure they used for outgoing messages. They simply reversed the series of steps to unlock the incoming message. Rechecking the Enigma's various settings once again to ensure they conformed to the daily schedule, Beisheim slowly keyed in the blocks of random letters as Pauli transcribed the clear-text message from the Enigma glow lamps.

As the two radiomen worked to decode the incoming message, their hearts began to race. The text read, "2018 hours 1 destroyer [naval grid square] BC 3559. Northeast course; believed to be convoy. Walkerling." This meant the enemy was quite near: not only was Kapitänleutnant Heinz Walkerling in U-91 assigned to Gruppe Raubgraf, but his U-boat was only three positions away in the wolf pack patrol line! Beisheim rushed to the control room and handed the clear-text message form to Manseck. Comparing the sighting report to U-758's own navigational fix at 2000 CET, the skipper realized that the suspected enemy convoy was less than fifty miles to the south.[3]

Three hours later, another encrypted message came chattering in over Beisheim's headset. This one was from Grossadmiral Dönitz and the BdU staff in Berlin: "To Gruppe Raubgraf. Manseck, Gräf, Uphoff operate on Walkerling report." The Lion was ordering the captains of the four southernmost U-boats on the Raubgraf patrol line to go hunting. Manseck immediately ordered a fifty-eight-degree turn to starboard and the U-boat began struggling through the towering waves lashing in on its port beam. The information that propelled U-758 farther into the teeth of the storm confirmed earlier German intelligence reports that calculated the movement of at least two eastbound convoys crossing the North Atlantic on the night of March 15–16—but unbeknownst to the staff at BdU Headquarters in Berlin, the Allies were also watching U-758.[4]

As the U-boats of Gruppe Raubgraf commenced hunting for the unknown convoy, each side in the Battle of the Atlantic clung to a crucial secret: the operations staff at BdU knew the planned course track of most of the eastbound formations from their departures from New York all the way across the North Atlantic, while the operations staff at Western Approaches Command in Liverpool and their American counterparts in Washington generally knew the precise location of the massed U-boats. Neither side was aware of the other's secret knowledge, and this would have a profound impact on the course of the convoy fights to come.

Thus, there were two separate battles raging across the North Atlantic in mid-March 1943. The overt struggle took place on the convoy routes, where wolf packs maneuvered to intercept and sink Allied merchantmen, and Allied escort warships and land-based patrol bombers scrambled to strike back at the U-boats. While these sailors and servicemen fought for their lives in the North Atlantic, another, equally important struggle was going on behind impenetrable security barriers ashore. This was the clandestine attempt by the Allies and the Germans to break their enemy's encrypted naval communications so as to learn the other side's intentions, operational plans, and future movements. This information was critical to both sides' objectives. The U-boat Force desperately needed to know specific Allied convoy course tracks in order to maneuver the wolf packs to intercept them. The Allies just as anxiously needed to know the location and future movements of the wolf packs so the convoys could evade them. Like the Battle of the Atlantic itself, the struggle of the code-breakers ran nonstop throughout the course of the war.

The cryptologic conflict was a vastly different struggle from the battles unfolding out at sea. The combatants were a host of linguists, mathematicians, and cryptanalysts toiling behind closed doors at obscure facilities known only to a handful of their country's senior military and political leaders. While intelligence gained from code-breaking often resulted in evasion signals to the convoys and redeployment orders to the wolf packs, only a minimum number of people at sea on either side had access to the source of the information; the merchant sailors and escort crewmen knew nothing of the Allied campaign to break German naval communications, and the U-boat commanders had no knowledge of German successes in breaking Allied codes. These efforts remained cloaked in the highest military secrecy for the most obvious of reasons: the outcome of the Battle of the Atlantic, and probably the war itself, depended not only on the successful penetration of enemy communications but also on keeping the enemy unaware of that very success. At this juncture in the Atlantic crisis, both sides could claim significant gains.[5]

On one side of the cryptologic battle was the German Navy's Funkbeobachtungsdienst (Observation Service), or B-dienst. This branch of German naval intelligence had steadily grown since the outbreak of the war. It focused on breaking into the British and U.S. naval codes, particularly the encrypted communications servicing Allied convoy operations. By March 1943 the B-dienst, led by Kapitän zur See Heinz Bonatz, had expanded to a staff of over 6,000 linguists and cryptanalysts operating more than five dozen radio-monitoring stations from Scandinavia to the central Mediterranean. At the B-dienst facility at German Navy Headquarters in Berlin, more than 1,000 English-speaking code breakers, analysts, and radio clerks processed thousands of Allied messages each month. The top priority for B-dienst was attacking Allied messages concerning the schedules and courses of the North Atlantic convoys. Those messages that could be broken within a day or two of interception often yielded valuable tactical intelligence on a convoy's future movements. B-dienst pumped the material via a secure teleprinter line to U-boat Headquarters, where it was used to direct the U-boats out on the deep ocean.[6]

For years, ever since the seizure of several Allied codebooks, B-dienst technicians had enjoyed particular success in their effort to decipher Allied convoy communications. On July 10, 1940, the German surface raider *Atlantis* had captured the British liner *City of Baghdad* in the Indian Ocean after its crew hastily abandoned ship. A boarding team had discovered a copy of the Allied Merchant Ships' Code, a two-part code used by the British Admiralty to send coded Morse code messages via radio to convoys at sea. Four months later, the *Atlantis* crew seized another British freighter and found an updated copy of the code. Within weeks, B-dienst cryptanalysts were providing the U-boat Force with clear-text messages from the Western Approaches Command redirecting convoys at sea away from areas of suspected U-boat activity. By February 1942, German communications experts had thoroughly penetrated the primary Royal Navy codes as well. These included the Administrative Code, Auxiliary Code, Merchant Navy Code, and Naval Code No. 1. But the most valuable success came when B-dienst analysts cracked Naval Cypher No. 3, a more sophisticated code that the Admiralty had introduced in October 1941 for the use of Allied merchant convoys and their escorts. The contents of Naval Cypher No. 3 were critical to U-boat operations since they included information about convoy departures from port, their routes, and any evasion courses ordered from Washington or Liverpool.

By December 1942, the German Navy knew nearly as much about convoy operations as the Allied planners themselves. B-dienst analysts were reading eighty percent of the Naval Cypher No. 3 messages, including those transmitted to convoy escorts at sea. In an additional breakthrough, the penetration of Naval Cypher No. 3 also provided Grossadmiral Dönitz and the BdU operations staff with the daily British U-boat Situation Reports apprising escort groups of known and suspected U-boat locations. These reports allowed BdU to both remove U-boats from harm's way and place boats where they would be least expected—and most deadly. Dönitz later credited the B-dienst staff with providing him fifty percent of the operational intelligence the U-boat Force employed to hunt down Allied convoys throughout the war. For example, as a direct result of a decrypted message revealing one convoy's base course to the British Isles, thirteen U-boats in Gruppe Veilchen (Violet) had savaged eastbound Convoy SC107 in early November 1942, sinking fifteen merchant ships totaling 82,817 gross tons.[7]

Lax Allied communications security had contributed heavily to the Germans' success in the North Atlantic. After the war, Kapitän Bonatz credited Canadian Rear Admiral Leonard W. Murray's communications staff in Halifax—which supported the several hundred escort warships fer-

rying Allied convoys across the Atlantic—with giving B-dienst the means
to break the convoy codes and other encrypted communications. One of
the fastest ways to decipher an encrypted message was to identify a phrase
or block of plain text that appeared frequently in the messages, then test
that sequence of letters against the encryption. Admiral Murray's staff unintentionally provided the phrase, and B-dienst analysts were quick to
pounce. The Canadian staff each day would send out an encrypted situation report message that began the same way:

SNO [senior naval officer] HALIFAX BREAK GROUP TELEGRAM IN
[a number of] PARTS FULL STOP SITUATION . . .

Encrypted once into four-digit code groups, the Allies then "super-en-
ciphered" the text a second time by adding random numbers from a list of
5,000 number groups. This did little to strengthen the encryption of the
messages. The Germans had solved that piece of the puzzle way back in
1935, when a British naval squadron exercising in the Red Sea had used
the super-enciphering groups on a series of messages but added them to
an older naval code that the Germans had already broken, thus allowing
B-dienst to break the super-enciphering element of the message traffic.
Knowing that the clear-text Canadian daily situation report would begin
with the identical phrasing, the German cryptanalysts could easily strip
the message of the super-encipherment, then attack the encrypted message itself. By failing to vary the formatting and structure of daily communications to the convoys and by dispatching messages of identical shape
and content structure, Murray's staff gave the B-dienst analysts a handy
template for penetrating encrypted Allied communications.

As the Allies' situation in the Battle of the Atlantic grew more and more
dire, the German intelligence apparatus was only getting better and better.
In the spring of 1943, Admiral Godt and the BdU operations staff would
often receive a clear-text copy of a vital convoy message within two hours
of its interception in Berlin, with ample time to capitalize on the intelligence it provided on a given convoy's movements ten to twenty hours in
the future. When Convoy SC122 had scattered in the storm the day after
leaving New York on March 5, for instance, Commodore White sent several messages detailing which ships had straggled and which had suffered

damage requiring their return to port. Within hours, B-dienst operators had transmitted the roster of the missing SC122 merchantmen to U-boat Force headquarters. More significantly, during Convoy HX229's passage from south of Cape Sable, Nova Scotia, to its Western Ocean Meeting Point, shore-based officials had twice ordered minor changes to the convoy's route. B-dienst interceptions of eight separate signals to or from SC122 and HX229 gave Admirals Dönitz and Godt clear warning that the two eastbound convoys were heading up to Newfoundland and then out into the deep Atlantic. This series of signals had included a message confirming the departure of Commander Boyle's Escort Group B-5 from St. John's to rendezvous with Convoy SC122. Given the Germans' accumulated knowledge of North Atlantic convoy routes, this tactical warning was more than enough to trigger the U-boat redeployment that put Gruppe Raubgraf at right angles to the anticipated convoy course track.[8]

Not only were the waters into which SC122 and HX229 were steering alive with hostile U-boats, but these hunters were very much aware of the convoys steaming into their midst. What none of the German commanders knew, however, was that the Allies had intelligence of their own to help counterbalance the German threat. They had gleaned this information through an astonishing feat: breaking the impossibly complex German naval Enigma codes.

Despite the elaborate safeguards employed by the German Navy to protect naval Enigma, by March 1943, both British and American naval code breakers had penetrated the system and were harvesting the output from the U-boats' Funkschlüssel-M machines. The British had taken the lead in this effort; since 1939, before the outbreak of war, the Government Code and Cypher School at Bletchley Park, an estate fifty miles northwest of London, had begun operations aimed at deciphering German military communications. Since then, the staff at Bletchley Park had grown to more than 9,000 mathematicians, linguists, cryptanalysts, and clerks, all laboring around the clock. The staff targeted all German communications, ranging from the Luftwaffe and German Army to the SS—but one of their highest priorities was attacking the encrypted Enigma messages between Dönitz's headquarters and his U-boats at sea.

The British cryptologic campaign had gotten off to a slow start. For the first two years of the war, German naval Enigma remained extremely diffi-

cult to penetrate. The Bletchley Park staff had initially attempted decrypting the U-boat traffic by hand, using a battery of equations and guesswork
that had limited success. Subsequently, Polish and French cryptanalysts
who had purloined the blueprints of an early Enigma machine turned the
material over to the British, allowing them to construct an analog machine that would mirror the workings of the actual Enigma, but which
was nevertheless slow and inefficient.

The first big breakthrough in Britain's code-breaking effort came on
May 9, 1941, when the crew from the destroyer *HMS Bulldog* forced the
crew of the Type IXB U-110 to surface and abandon ship south of Iceland.
Without the knowledge of the U-boat's crew, a British boarding party got
inside the boat and grabbed its Enigma machine, encryption rotors, and
related documents. The seizure enabled British scientists to replicate the
Enigma machine in a device known as a "bombe," a highly advanced (for
that era) electromechanical computer that copied the Enigma machine's
rotor and plug board wiring. Massive in size—each bombe measured eight
feet in height, twelve feet wide, and three feet deep—the machine had
rows of hand-adjustable wheels corresponding to the Enigma machine rotors. By 1941 there were forty-nine bombes at Bletchley Park processing
an incoming river of encrypted German messages. Using "cribs"—extrane-
ous clues as to the contents of the encrypted text, such as a known message
header—the operators would set the bombes to the suspected Enigma rotor setting and activate the device. If the crib was on target, within several
minutes the bombe would generate a clear-text message. The Allies named
the intelligence derived from the decryption effort Ultra.[9]

After an Enigma message was successfully decrypted, it was rigorously
examined before being put to use. First the Bletchley Park staff would
transmit the clear-text message via a secure teleprinter line to the British
Admiralty's Operational Intelligence Centre at the Royal Navy's underground Citadel headquarters in London. There, a small team, led by
barrister-turned–Royal Navy Reserve Commander Rodger Winn, cross-
checked the material against other intelligence source material for further
confirmation or details. Winn and his staff then passed carefully sanitized
intelligence reports to the Admiralty Trade Division, also located in the
Citadel, and to Western Approaches Command in Liverpool. Using that
information, Admiral Horton and his operations staff would guide the

convoys and their escort groups at sea to elude the wolf packs. Beginning in late 1941, the U.S. Navy followed the British lead and organized its own code-breaking section, although for the first year it focused on Japanese naval codes.

After their initial breakthrough in May 1941, the Allied code-breakers went blind for ten long months beginning in March 1942 when the U-boat Force switched from the three-rotor to a four-rotor Enigma machine. With its bombes designed only to decrypt three-rotor Enigma, Bletchley Park could not penetrate the redesigned naval Enigma system. The resulting lack of intelligence was immediate and devastating to the Allies and directly contributed to the soaring shipping losses in much of 1942. British analysts later determined that in the fall of 1941, when Ultra decrypts of BdU message traffic enabled them to reroute convoys out of harm's way, the U-boats had succeeded in finding only one in ten convoys crossing the Atlantic. A year later, with Bletchley Park still unable to decrypt four-rotor Triton messages, the wolf packs were finding one out of three convoys. Allied merchant ship tonnage losses correspondingly soared from 750,532 tons in the last half of 1941 to 3,239,558 tons in the same period in 1942, a more than fourfold jump.[10]

Following that ten-month blackout, the British finally broke back into naval Enigma in December 1942. After a Royal Navy destroyer crippled U-559 in the eastern Mediterranean and forced its crew to abandon ship, a boarding party entered the U-boat and retrieved updated German Navy weather codes before the boat sank. These weather codes provided the clues that enabled Bletchley Park to master the four-rotor Enigma and resume deciphering German communications. By the time Britain had regained their access to Enigma communications, British and American analysts were more on par than they had been earlier in the war. The U.S. Navy had created an intelligence section known as OP-20-G, which operated its own set of bombes. The American and British code breakers, while running separate decryption efforts, had also established secure communications lines to exchange data and discuss their analysis efforts.[11]

Although Convoys SC121 and HX228 had fallen prey to Grossadmiral Dönitz's wolf packs despite the intelligence available to Allied commanders, several other convoys were able to evade those same U-boats thanks to the Ultra campaign. The U.S. Navy's Convoy and Routing staff, alerted

A U.S. Navy "bombe" used to decrypt German naval Enigma. Both the U.S. Navy and British code-breakers operated these electro-mechanical computers in a top-secret struggle against the U-boats.

Clay Blair Collection, American Heritage Center, University of Wyoming

to the location of the three wolf packs in the Greenland air gap by their radio transmissions, had diverted the ninety-two merchant ships in west-bound Convoys ONS169 and ON170 far to the north of the area. A total of eighty-eight merchant ships representing 544,817 gross tons of shipping in the two convoys made the trans-Atlantic crossing without a single loss. Evasive maneuvers, however, did not always go so smoothly. Even with renewed penetration of Enigma, there were still periods when the Bletchley Park bombes would fail to break the enciphered messages. In many instances, when the clear text finally emerged from the machine, so much time had elapsed since its interception that the information was useless.[12]

With so many factors affecting the outcome of the cryptologic battles, it was inevitable that fortune would occasionally favor one side over the other. And so it happened that, as Convoys HX229 and SC122 headed for the Greenland air gap, the Germans were holding the cryptologic advantage. The critical development that tipped the scales was a routine shift in U-boat Force communications: a preplanned change in a minor German naval weather code. This deviation from the previous Enigma coding system temporarily stripped the Allied code breakers of the ability to break four-rotor German naval Enigma. The ax fell on Tuesday, March 9, as HX229A, the last of the three eastbound convoys, pulled out of New York. The unexpected new blackout hobbled the Allied code breakers just as navy officials ashore desperately needed to know the position and movements of the Atlantic U-boats to protect the three convoys.

Because of a minor change in the German weather code, the fog of war would favor the Germans for a brief and deadly interval in mid-March, 1943. This seemingly random turn of fate would nevertheless play a major part in the Battle of the Atlantic—and in the fates of hundreds of Allied merchant sailors, naval gunners, and civilian passengers, scores of ships, and thousands of tons of Allied shipping, all of which hung in the balance as Convoys SC122 and HX229 neared the Greenland air gap.[13]

Chapter 6

THE SIGHTING

The wolf pack had scented a shepherd but had yet to find its flock. The lone destroyer that U-91 had glimpsed on the evening of March 15 almost certainly meant that a herd of vulnerable merchantmen was somewhere in the vicinity of Gruppe Raubgraf. But until the three U-boats that Grossadmiral Dönitz had dispatched could locate the merchant ships themselves, they would have to operate on U-91's report and scour the ocean for more signs of the convoy that the destroyer was presumed to be guarding.

As night gave way to the early morning hours of March 16, one U-boat in Gruppe Raubgraf was not participating in the hunt for the presumed convoy. U-653, under the command of Kapitänleutnant Gerhard Feiler, had been on patrol for forty-seven days, serving in three wolf packs with moderate success. Three weeks earlier, U-653 had damaged the 9,382-ton Dutch *Madoera*, a straggler from westbound Convoy ON166, and just four days before it had dispatched the drifting 7,176-ton American freighter *Thomas Hooker*, which had been abandoned by its crew after suffering major structural failures during the previous week. Due in part to its attacks on these two ships, by the night of March 15–16, U-653 was no longer capable of combat. It had fired all but one of its torpedoes, and both the U-boat and its crew were strained after nearly seven weeks of battling the North Atlantic storms. Admiral Godt had ordered it to return to port. Now, with U-653's fuel tanks practically empty, Feiler was heading east to rendezvous with a U-boat specially designed to refuel and rearm U-boats at sea. Concerned that the mainstay Type VIIC boats could not operate in extended patrol areas due to their maximum unrefueled range of 8,100 nautical miles, Dönitz had arranged for the construction of twenty-four Type XIV "U-tankers," of which eight were operational in March 1943. Modified from the larger Type IX hull, the U-tankers carried extra fuel, torpedoes, and food supplies that would enable the Type VIICs to extend their patrols. U-653 would take on enough fuel from the U-463, one of three U-tankers operating in support of the three wolf packs, to make the long trip back to Brest.[1]

U-653 had chosen a fateful path out of the North Atlantic hunting ground. Shortly before 0430 local time (0725 GMT) on March 16, about twelve hours after Kapitänleutnant Walkerling in U-91 had briefly sighted the lone Allied destroyer, Obersteuermann (Quartermaster Chief) Heinz Theen, the ranking member of the U-653 bridge watch, was peering through his night binoculars at the waters ahead of the eastbound U-boat. Suddenly, a light flared in the dark Atlantic night. "I saw a light directly ahead, only for about two seconds," Theen said in a postwar interview. "I think it was a sailor on the deck of a steamer lighting a cigarette. I sent a message to the captain and by the time he had come up on the bridge we could see ships all around us. There must have been about twenty, the nearest was on the port side between 500 meters and half a [nautical] mile away." Allied merchant captains mandated a strict "darkened ship" condition to minimize the chance of detection by U-boat lookouts. In this case, a sailor's violation of the rules would prove disastrous.

U-653 had stumbled into the middle of the thirty-eight ships in Convoy HX229. Feiler ordered a crash dive and took the U-boat into the cellar. As the crew quietly went to their battle stations, the U-boat vibrated with the cacophony of the merchant ships passing overhead. "We could hear quite clearly the noises of the different engines—the diesels with fast revs, the steamers with slow revs and the turbines of the escorts made a singing noise," Theen said. Feiler kept U-653 underwater for two hours, then brought it to the surface for his radioman to fire off a short encrypted "beta" contact message: they were following a convoy on course 070 degrees in naval grid square BD 1491, roughly 550 miles east of Newfoundland.

The news from U-653 had sparked a flurry of activity at U-boat Force headquarters on the morning of March 16. At 0825 Central European Time (0725 GMT), Admiral Godt immediately ordered the ten other boats still operating in Gruppe Raubgraf, including Kapitänleutnant Manseck in U-758, to head at maximum speed for U-653's homing signal and the enemy convoy.

Manseck had not waited for orders from Berlin to act on the new information from U-653. Either Martin Beisheim or Oberfunkmaat Medart Wich, the other senior radioman aboard U-758, had intercepted and decrypted Feiler's message upon its transmission, and Manseck immediately reacted to its tersely worded message: "Convoy, BD 1491, course 70 [degrees]." Upon reading it, he ordered U-758 to maximum speed on an intercept course of 102 degrees, or east-southeast. Manseck had correctly anticipated Berlin's orders.[2]

Feiler's chance sighting of HX229 had succeeded where the B-dienst cryptanalysts had not, but German analysts were still confused about the exact identity of the eastbound convoy. Thanks to their continued penetration of Naval Cypher No. 3, the Germans were aware of the course tracks of convoys HX229 and SC122 into the Greenland air gap. They had not been sure about either convoy's exact position, however, and because of the bad weather and the fruitless search for another formation, westbound Convoy ON170, BdU initially misidentified Convoy HX229 as SC122. Pushed along by the southwest gales on its east-northeast heading, SC122 had in fact passed by Gruppe Raubgraf without detection. The wolf pack, it seemed, had been too slow in moving the picket line to the southeast across SC122's suspected track. At the time U-653 spotted HX229, Convoy SC122 was already 150 miles east and slightly north of the trailing formation. However, there were another thirty U-boats in front of SC122: on March 11, Dönitz and Godt had formed Gruppe Stürmer (Forward) with nineteen U-boats, and three days later, Gruppe Dränger (Pusher), with another eleven boats, with a patrol area in the eastern edge of the Greenland air gap. On March 15, BdU had realigned the two wolf packs into a single patrol line nearly 600 miles in length, oriented on a northwest-to southeast direction with each U-boat spaced about fifteen nautical miles apart from its two neighbors in the line. Dönitz then ordered the extended line to proceed southwest to intercept the expected convoys. SC122 was not out of danger yet.[3]

Although BdU was unaware that convoy SC122 had already passed by Gruppe Raubgraf, U-653's good-luck sighting had nevertheless provided

German Rear Admiral Eberhard Godt was normally in day-to-day control of the U-boats during the spring of 1943.
Uboat.net

the wolf pack with a target, clearing the way for a large-scale assault. Admirals Dönitz and Godt knew that for the next ninety-six hours, the Allied convoy U-653 had spotted—as well as the second convoy they continued to seek—would be at maximum vulnerability as they crossed the Greenland air gap. U-653's sighting of HX229 was enough to set in motion the initial stage of battle. With any luck, the second convoy would soon be spotted, as well.[4]

Like the Germans, the Allies also had an incomplete picture of what was happening on the western edge of the Greenland air gap. COMINCH and Western Approaches Command knew that there were several dozen U-boats massing in the unprotected area, but the recent breakdown of the Enigma intercepts prevented them from pinpointing their locations. As the ten boats from Gruppe Raubgraf closed in on the signal from U-653's homing signal, neither HX229 nor its overseers in Liverpool and Washington had any idea that the U-boats were headed in for the kill.

March 15 had been a tough day for HX229 and its depleted escorts. A fierce gale had swept over the convoy, causing three ships to fall behind. Also unable to keep up was the short-legged destroyer *HMS Witherington,* temporarily assigned to Escort Group B-4. Forced by the towering waves to heave to, Lieutenant-Commander Marcus H. R. Crichton of the *Witherington* radioed Lieutenant-Commander Luther in *HMS Volunteer* that he had to break off for St. John's because of low fuel. The only good news had been the belated arrival of the corvette *Pennywort* from St. John's and the strong following seas that had increased the formation's speed to 10.5

knots. That slight boost provided the merchant captains and escort commanders the faintest hope that the Greenland air gap crossing might end several hours sooner than originally calculated.

If it had seemed possible the previous day that HX229 would make it through the Greenland air gap unscathed, the daylight hours of March 16 brought the gut-wrenching confirmation that multiple U-boats were shadowing the formation. At 0942, Feiler in U-653 had transmitted a relatively lengthy message giving the convoy's course and speed, and the *HMS Volunteer's* HF/DF operator had obtained a clear "hit" on the encrypted high-frequency signal. It was bearing 353 degrees, out on the convoy's port quarter, but since the *Volunteer* was the only escort in B-4 with an HF/DF set, it was unable to triangulate the position of the U-boat to enable a concerted attack. Nevertheless, Lieutenant-Commander Luther on the *Volunteer* ordered Lieutenant-Commander Leonard C. Hill on the destroyer *HMS Mansfield* to search out on the radio bearing for fifteen miles and hunt for the enemy until 1300. *Mansfield* had no success, in part because its radar was inoperable from storm damage, and so U-653 continued to operate with impunity.

While bad weather caused stress for the escort crews and merchantmen, good weather could, too. The overnight storm had abated by sunrise, calming the sea's forty-foot-tall waves to smooth swells of only three to four feet high. At the height of the storm, visibility had shrunk to four nautical miles, effectively shielding the convoy. Now as the day dawned, the visibility range increased to sixteen nautical miles, and the U-boat lookouts would have no difficulty spotting the Allied merchantmen.[5]

After Godt had ordered the Raubgraf boats to close on U-653, he brought a second group of U-boats into play. He selected eleven U-boats from the southern end of the Stürmer patrol line of the massive Stürmer-Dränger wolf packs, which were now about 420 miles east and northeast of HX229, and ordered them to detach and head west as fast as possible to intercept Feiler's convoy by the morning of Wednesday, March 17. He detached U-229 from Stürmer to conduct weather reports, and ordered the seven remaining Stürmer boats to race due south to close up the gap created by the diversion of the eleven boats toward HX229. Between the ten boats from Raubgraf and the eleven boats from Stürmer, there were now twenty-one U-boats hunting for the fast convoy.[6]

U-758 soon became the second boat to find HX229. At 0737 local time (1037 GMT), just three hours after intercepting Feiler's contact message, lookouts on the U-boat's heaving bridge sighted an Allied freighter steaming at a speed of ten knots. The merchant ship was steering a zigzagging course that shifted between 020 and 100 degrees in an attempt to throw off any U-boat that made a tentative sighting. For the next nine hours, Manseck and his lookouts kept the straggler in sight. A subsequent message from Feiler provided vital information that the straggler was running twenty nautical miles behind the main body of the convoy. Manseck's hastily jotted notes, later transcribed by Martin Beisheim, described the growing tension as U-758 shadowed the merchantman.

> 0737 [local, or 1137 Central European Time in Berlin] Steamer in sight bearing 170 [degrees True] 12 [nautical miles] Steamer heavily changes course between 20 and 100 degrees. Changing speed up to ten knots. Submerging for attack; steamer has sharp target angle left 10 [degrees]. Closing.
>
> 0831 [local]: Steamer has target angle right 50 [degrees], 10,000 meters, approaching.
>
> 1005 [local]: Surfaced. Chased after [the ship] on the surface. Based on the contact keeper's report the steamer is 20 nm [nautical miles] behind the convoy.
>
> 1730 [local]: Closing the steamer in twilight for an underwater attack.

Finally, just as Manseck was preparing to sharpen his teeth on the lone merchant ship, the breakthrough occurred. Manseck's lookouts spotted several dozen masts just off to port.

> 1733 [local]: Convoy in sight bearing 090 [degrees True], 12 nautical miles, course 090 [degrees], speed 7 knots. Steamer chases after the convoy.[7]

Although night had fallen in Berlin, it was still late afternoon in the North Atlantic south of Greenland when Manseck's lookouts spotted the main body of Convoy HX229. Manseck ordered a short convoy-sighting "beta" message to BdU. During the next five hours, as darkness crept over the North Atlantic, three more boats—U-664, U-615, and U-91—also sighted the merchant ships and sent contact messages.

On U-758, word that the boat was in firm contact with an enemy convoy had spread quickly among the crew. "We didn't have the name of the convoy. We just knew they were coming at approximately that course," Beisheim recalled. "We had news on that and were supposed to act on it." As the boat continued to track the merchant formation, Manseck ordered the crew to battle stations. The crewmen suppressed any feelings of excitement and quietly went about their tasks. Beisheim stepped into the sound room to don the hydrophone headset in case his commander needed an underwater bearing to the convoy. Anticipating a stiff defense by the escort warships, Beisheim and Pauli inspected the cramped sound room to make sure that all loose gear was tied down or otherwise secured to the deck and bulkhead.[8]

The Raubgraf boats that had made contact with HX229 were biding their time, waiting until the most opportune moment to attack the poorly guarded convoy. Under the *Rudeltaktik* (Pack Tactics) devised by Grossadmiral Dönitz five years earlier, the wolf pack would assemble and shadow HX229 throughout the day, waiting for night to come, then launch simultaneous assaults on the ships. U-758 and the other Raubgraf boats followed that doctrine to the letter during the daylight hours of March 16, despite the difficulties of tracking HX229 in the high seas and intermittent visibility.

Given the frequently severe weather conditions in that part of the Atlantic, keeping contact with the convoy was as much an endurance contest as a stealthy hunt. Mechanikerobergefreiter (Senior Leading Machinist's Mate) Max Zweigle, a lookout under Oberleutnant zur See Hans-Joachim Bertelsmann in the U-603, one of the last Raubgraf boats to close in on Feiler's homing signal, remembered all too well the ordeal of shadowing HX229. "We went at top speed to find it; the sea was [later in the day] 6 to 8 [on the Douglas Sea Scale, waves from fifteen to over forty-five feet in height] and the seas kept breaking over us," Zweigle recalled. "I took over the sea-watch of a sick comrade because they had talked of snow and I wanted to see snow in the North Atlantic. After an hour's watch I received a heavy sea in my back, which almost swept me away. With an iron grip I hung onto the railings of the Wintergarten [gunnery platform behind the conning tower]. After that we were ordered to strap ourselves to the railings. I survived the rest of the three hours with the thought, 'Hard as Krupp steel,' 'Tough as leather,' and so on."[9]

The increasingly heavier seas once again made it easier for the U-boats to avoid detection by the B-4 escort lookouts. "There was a very high sea, not a full gale but heavy seas," Beisheim said. "The single ship we had spotted at noon disappeared behind waves from time to time and then it reappeared. I was outside too and saw it myself. We were right next to him at the same speed and he didn't see us." Manseck himself later said that he had kept U-758 about twelve miles out on the starboard flank of HX229 throughout the day, "just keeping the smoke and the tips of the masts in sight." It was somewhat difficult, he said, because the ships were doing their utmost not to betray their positions by minimizing the thick clouds of exhaust that, left unchecked, could be visible for dozens of miles.[10]

Luther and Convoy Commodore Mayall were doing all they could to safeguard the ships, but except for trying to herd their ships away from the massing U-boats, they could not do much. Per the sailing plan, the formation had reached waypoint Position V at 49:10 North 038:01 West at 0700, and had executed a course change from 089 to 028 degrees. Reorienting the convoy in this north-northeast heading would bring the ships under Allied air coverage sooner by taking them farther up into the northern area of the Greenland air gap where the unprotected area was much narrower. Since waypoint Position V was about 200 nautical miles east of where Allied convoy officials had plotted the Raubgraf patrol area on March 13, this course change was also intended to draw the vulnerable merchant ships farther away from the most dangerous waters in the Greenland air gap. Unfortunately for HX229, the Enigma blackout prevented the convoy planners from reshaping their strategy around updated information about the U-boats' movements. Raubgraf was, by now, firmly on HX229's trail.

While taking other evasive actions to safeguard HX229 from the U-boats, Luther had unfortunately weakened the convoy even further. At 1300, Commodore Mayall ordered HX229 to make an emergency turn of 90 degrees to starboard on a new course of 118 degrees in another attempt to throw off the shadowing U-boats. Then, at 1400,

HX229 had slowly turned to resume its base course of 028 degrees. In the tension of the day, Luther forgot to radio the *Mansfield*, still searching for the U-boat aft of the formation, of the two course changes. When the destroyer returned to what Lieutenant-Commander Hill thought was the convoy's position, he found only empty ocean. The mistake would cost the convoy a precious escort warship during one of the most critical periods in its voyage; it would take the *Mansfield* until midnight on March 16 to rejoin HX229, long after the Raubgraf U-boats had already drawn first blood.

JOHN M. WATERS stood on the main deck of the Coast Guard cutter *USS (CG) Ingham*, enduring the frigid cold and incessant wind that was a harsh, nonstop phenomenon for those assigned to Iceland. Above the stocky, twenty-three-year-old Coast Guard ensign on the cutter's navigation bridge, Captain A. M. Martinson and Lieutenant J. A. Martin, the *Ingham*'s officer of the deck, waited for the harbor pilot to arrive. At 1750 hours on Tuesday, March 16, the *Ingham* was tied up along at the Reykjavik waterfront, with the World War I–era destroyer *USS Babbitt* lashed to the cutter's port side. The two warships were preparing to head south, away from their stations at Iceland and into the U-boat–infested waters of the Greenland air gap, where their presence was desperately needed.

Back at Western Approaches Command, Admiral Horton faced a grim situation. The eastbound convoys HX229 and SC122 were now well inside the Greenland air gap, and at least one appeared to have attracted the attention of a patrolling wolf pack. It was increasingly clear, moreover, that neither convoy's escorts would be sufficient to deal with the large numbers of U-boats that were currently operating in the area. Escort Group B-4's lead ship, the destroyer *HMS Highlander*, and corvettes *HMS Abelia* and *HMCS Sherbrooke*, had left St. John's the day before and were making best speed to rejoin Convoy HX229. They still had several hundred miles to go. Scrambling to find reinforcements for HX229 and SC122, Horton had also issued orders to Escort Group B-4's damaged destroyer, *HMS Vimy*, to finish its storm repairs in Iceland as soon as possible and head to sea. The destroyer would not be able to get under way until early on Thursday, March 18, however, by which point it might be too late to help SC122 and HX229.

Ensign John M. Waters Jr. battled Atlantic storms and German U-boats from the Coast Guard cutter *USS (CG) Ingham*.

Courtesy of Dr. Stephen Waters, M.D.

Aside from the four remaining members then serving with Escort Group B-4, the only other warships available to assist the imperiled convoys were the Iceland-based *Ingham, Babbitt,* and cutter *USS (CG) Bibb.* Operating from the Allied naval anchorage at Hvalfjordur, some twenty-five miles north of Reykjavik, the *Ingham* and *Babbitt* had already steamed down to the Icelandic capital on March 15 after receiving tentative warning that they might have to hurry south to reinforce the defenses of Convoys SC122 and HX229. This type of emergency summons had occurred so frequently in the past four months that it was beginning to be a routine—albeit a hellish one.[11]

The *Ingham, Babbitt, Bibb,* and a fourth ship, the destroyer *USS Schenck,* were all that remained of a once-mighty American naval task force in the northwest Atlantic. Known as Task Force 26.4, these American warships ostensibly served as the "Iceland shuttle," escorting civilian merchant ships from Iceland to join up with east- and westbound Allied trade convoys and to protect Iceland-bound merchantmen once they detached from the convoys. The Iceland shuttle was a legacy from the spring

The Coast Guard cutter *Ingham* pounds through a North Atlantic gale during the height of the Battle of the Atlantic.
Coast Guard photo courtesy of Dr. Stephen Waters, M.D.

and summer of 1941, when, at President Roosevelt's order, the U.S. Atlantic Fleet created Task Force 24, comprising several dozen Canadian-based warships, to escort convoys from North America to the eastern limit of the declared American neutrality zone just west of Iceland. In the aftermath of the Japanese attack on Pearl Harbor, growing wartime demands elsewhere had prompted Admiral King at COMINCH to reassign many of the American warships to other commands. A year later, the *Ingham*, *Bibb*, *Babbitt*, and *Schenck* were all that remained. The chronic shortage of escort warships and the escalating U-boat threat had saddled Task Force 26.4 with serving as on-call escort reinforcements for convoys passing south of Iceland.[12]

While he was sick of Iceland's harsh weather, Waters was glad to be serving on the *Ingham*. It was exactly the kind of wartime assignment he had sought. As a young North Carolina State University freshman in 1939, he had sensed that the United States would probably enter World

War II. He decided not to wait for events—or the military draft—but rather to make his own plans. That summer, he won an appointment to the U.S. Coast Guard Academy in the class of 1943. Struggling to keep up with its massive wartime expansion, Coast Guard officials accelerated the academy's training schedule. Waters and his graduating classmates joined the fleet a year early, in July 1942.

Ordered to report to the *Ingham* in Iceland that November, Waters had first witnessed the Battle of the Atlantic as a helpless bystander. He and eleven other Coast Guard officers had endured three days of sheer terror as a German wolf pack massacred eastbound Convoy SC107, in which their navy troopship, the converted Great Lakes packet steamer *USS Gemini*, was traveling. The powerlessness he had felt on the *Gemini* had haunted Waters ever since. "It is the waiting that dissolves a man's courage, and brings on cold, clammy fear clutching at his viscera," he wrote many years later. "When you have the means to hit back, it is endurable, but when defenseless, the slow dragging of time becomes an intolerable thing, clocked off by the pounding of your own heart."

Waters's first glimpse of the ship on which he would serve came on the last day of the battle for Convoy SC107. The *Ingham* and two other escorts joined the convoy on November 4 after a 600-mile trek down from Iceland. Waters watched, his heart beating hard, as the *Ingham* came sprinting down between the columns of merchant ships at flank speed, its guns manned and crew at general quarters. Nearly a half-century later, his eyes still misted up at the memory. "That was a sight," Waters said, "that I will never forget until the day I die."[13]

Like its sister ships the cutters *Campbell* and *Spencer*, the *Ingham* was well suited for convoy work. With a maximum speed of twenty knots, the 327-foot cutter could outrun a surfaced U-boat. Its elongated prow and widely curved hull enabled it to handle fierce Atlantic storms that forced the sleeker navy destroyers to slow down or heave to altogether. With a fuel capacity of 135,180 gallons, it could cruise at eleven knots—a speed higher than the fastest cargo convoys—for 8,000 nautical miles without refueling. Equipped with sonar, an SC-1 radar, and a modified British FH3 HF/DF radio-direction-finding set, the *Ingham* carried all the antisubmarine sensors critical to detecting and tracking U-boats. The warship also bristled with firepower. As a Treasury-class cutter, it carried 600- and

300-pound depth charges launched from stern racks or from six powerful K-gun launchers that threw the smaller depth charges fifty yards to either side. The *Ingham* also had a Hedgehog forward-firing anti-submarine mortar. Its upper decks bristled with two five-inch/.50-cal. deck guns, four three-inch/50-cal. anti-aircraft guns, and two 20-mm Oerlikon automatic cannons.[14]

Upon first joining the *Ingham*, Waters had been impressed not just with the ship's build and its armament but also with the crew that operated it. "The prewar crew was nearly intact, only a small portion of the enlisted men being reservists," he later recalled. "They were a tough, seasoned lot who, with their bearded faces and jungle-cloth clothing white with dried salt, would have done Captain Teach proud. Despite their piratical appearance, they were a well-trained crew of regulars on a fine, capable ship." In his four months on the *Ingham*, Waters had already seen the crew's effectiveness firsthand; he had been aboard on December 15, 1942, when the *Ingham* sank the U-626 while escorting Convoy SC112. Waters had already gone to sea with the *Ingham* to protect five separate convoys from the U-boats; now the ship and her crew were being called out to fight once again.

Growing increasingly alarmed at the three wolf packs massing in the Greenland air gap, Admiral Horton and the Western Approaches Command staff decided to scramble the Iceland-based warships *Ingham, Bibb,* and *Babbitt* to reinforce the escorts of SC122—a decision that reflected Western Approaches Command's incomplete grasp of the situation that was unfolding out in the Atlantic. Officials had originally scheduled the three ships to make a routine rendezvous with Convoy SC122 to pick up seven merchant ships that were bringing cargo to Reykjavik, but now HX229 was being trailed by multiple U-boats and direly needed additional support. Because the Allies were still unable to decipher encrypted German naval Enigma communications after the unanticipated change to the coding system, they had no way of knowing that SC122 had still gone undetected. As a result of this lack of information, Horton decided to send the *Ingham, Bibb,* and *Babbitt* down the 600-mile route to meet SC122 several days early. The *Ingham* and *Babbitt* were preparing to depart from Reykjavik; since the *Bibb* was at Hvalfjordur, it would proceed independently to meet SC122.

The summons to assist SC122 had fallen upon the *Ingham*'s exhausted crew just as they were trying to recover from an extraordinarily harsh schedule. Two weeks earlier, the *Ingham* had suffered a torn sonar dome requiring emergency repairs. The work was critically important, for without the hydrophone array, the cutter could not locate and track a submerged U-boat. For the crew, however, going into the floating drydock at Hvalfjordur had meant forty-eight hours of frigid hell with minimal heat and electricity, and no water. With the toilets out of order, the crewmen had to use an open-air privy perched out over the edge of the dry dock some eighty feet above the water. The canvas shelter did little to keep out the continuous gale-force winds.

The *Ingham*'s miserable time in the drydock was followed by two horrific experiences at sea. Twelve hours after it had edged out of the drydock to return to its anchorage site on March 3, Admiral Horton's staff ordered the *Ingham* to rush out into the Atlantic to search for survivors of an American Liberty ship torpedoed 240 miles west-southwest of Iceland. The cutter battled through twenty-foot waves in the face of a southwest gale for thirty-six hours before reaching the site. All that they found of the 7,176-ton freighter *Meriwether Lewis* was a debris field of truck tires that stretched for thirty miles across the ocean. The merchantman's sixty-seven crewmen and naval gunners had all perished. The *Ingham* crew's reward for the arduous, futile search was one day at anchor at Reykjavik—and that had come to an abrupt end when another emergency message rocketed in from Liverpool.

The aftermath of the attack on the *Meriwether Lewis* paled in comparison to what the crew of the *Ingham* encountered next. On March 7, Admiral Horton ordered the *Ingham* and *Bibb* to get under way as fast as possible to assist eastbound Convoy SC121, which had reported numerous U-boats in contact. The *Ingham* and its crew fought through gale-force headwinds and towering swells for two days before reaching the eastbound convoy at mid-afternoon on March 9. During the trek, the pounding waves damaged the cutter's sonar dome again, rendering it ineffective at any speed over six knots—and to make matters worse, the *Ingham*'s presence hadn't seemed to make a substantial difference in the battle. Despite the additional firepower that the *Ingham* brought to the convoy, SC121 suffered disastrous losses due to the fierce storm that had scattered most of the ships, making them easy targets for the U-boats. During the four-day period of March 7–10, two wolf packs totaling twenty-six U-boats sank twelve merchant ships and two landing craft for a total of 56,243 tons. Worse, 480 out of 574 crewmen from the twelve sunken ships, plus the 3,670-ton British freighter *Coulmore*—abandoned by its crew after a torpedo damaged the hull—died in the stormy waters. The crewmen on the fourteen lost ships suffered a horrific 83.6 percent fatality rate.[15]

Not only had the futile attempt to help SC121 been harrowing, but it had also taken a physical toll on the *Ingham* and its crew from which they would not be able to recuperate before heading out to assist SC122. After the *Ingham* pulled back into Hvalfjordur shortly after midnight on March 13, working parties hastily loaded provisions, ammunition, and depth charges into the cutter's holds. Then, at 1625, a navy diver from the repair ship *USS Vulcan* went under the cutter's hull to inspect its sonar dome. The news was grim. The diver found a six-inch-wide tear in the dome running from one side of the fixture to the other. Only an emergency drydocking would allow workers to repair that critical piece of equipment— but the new orders to help SC122 prevented that. Now, for a second time, the *Ingham* would have to go into battle with little or no underwater listening capability. At 1804 on March 16, the *Ingham* and *Babbitt* headed out of port on a base course of 255 degrees for what—with the necessary zigzagging to minimize the threat of German torpedo attacks—would end up being an 829-mile trek to find Convoy SC122.[16]

While the *Ingham* and *Babbitt* were heading to support the eastbound convoy, SC122 and its Escort Group B-5 warships were ending a relatively uneventful day farther to the northeast of Convoy HX229 in the Greenland air gap. For Commander Richard Boyle on the *HMS Havelock,* the major crisis of March 16 had been the loss of the 550-ton, Canadian-built ASW trawler *HMS Campobello.* Canadian Navy officials had temporarily assigned the small warship to Boyle's group during its passage to a permanent base in the United Kingdom, but the ship had suffered serious hull cracks during the furious storm that overtook the convoy on March 15. Its crew was unsuccessful in stanching the leak, so Boyle had dispatched the corvette *HMS Godetia* and its Free Belgian crew to stand by the stricken ship. Finally, in late afternoon the trawler's crewmen abandoned ship. The *Godetia* retrieved the crew and dispatched the sinking *Campobello* with a single depth charge fired by one of its K-guns, so that the ship and any of its classified sensors would not fall into the hands of the Germans. The *Godetia* then hastened back to join the convoy. B-5 was now short one escort ship, and Commander Boyle awaited the arrival of the reinforcements from Iceland more desperately than ever.

Another occasion for excitement on SC122's passage on March 16 had been a false alarm that sharpened nerves on the convoy's escorts. At 1943, the HF/DF operators reported the first of several U-boat wireless Morse code transmissions that at first appeared to be very close to the slow convoy. In actuality, the signaling U-boats were still oblivious to SC122 and had been racing after HX229 instead. When Rear Admiral Godt at BdU headquarters had detached the eleven Gruppe Stürmer U-boats to break out of the patrol line in the center of the Greenland air gap, the U-boats came within 210 miles of Boyle and his escorts while heading southwest at maximum speed. The HF/DF operators on the *Havelock, Upshur,* and *Swale* began picking up the U-boats' transmissions, as did ground-based radio direction-finding stations, causing the Admiralty to flash a message to Boyle that his convoy was likely being shadowed. It wasn't—not yet.

The responses of SC122 and their defenders to the perceived U-boat threat showed just how prepared they were for an attack. Commander Boyle passed on the message through the convoy, and crewmen in every ship checked their small "panic bags" and lifejackets to ensure both were close at hand. Commodore White on the convoy flagship *Glenapp* hoisted the signal flags W and C on the ship's mainmast, signifying that enemy submarines were in the vicinity. Boyle on the *Havelock* sent his destroyer at flank speed down the convoy lanes flying the two-flag signal. Extra lookouts assembled on every merchantman, and the escort crews held simulated Action Stations to gear up for the long, hard night ahead.[17]

ABOUT 100 NAUTICAL MILES to the west-southwest of Convoy SC122, the critical moment for Convoy HX229 finally arrived at 2200 on March 16. The local time on the convoy ships' clocks read 1900 as the thirty-seven merchant vessels and four escort warships of the formation steamed east-northeast, directly toward the Eastern Ocean Meeting Point north of Lough Foyle, Northern Ireland.

The night of March 16–17 was shaping up to be moonlit and clear— perfect weather for a U-boat attack. By nightfall, the winds had backed to the north and dropped to a light breeze. The ocean itself was still rough, with swells between twenty and twenty-five feet high. After days of rain, sleet, and snow, the skies remained cloudy but occasionally the waxing moon gleamed down on the surface and placed the ships of HX229 in sharp relief. Visibility under the bright moonlight was about twelve miles. The placid weather and occasional moonlight would normally have been a sight of stunning beauty, but the Allied sailors cursed it for casting their ships in sharp silhouettes against the horizon.[18]

In his flagship, the Norwegian freighter *Abraham Lincoln*, HX229 Commodore Mayall now hoped to rendezvous with the British local escort group in another six days. Since leaving New York eight days ago on March 8, the formation had traveled 1,735 nautical miles but still had about 1,008 more miles to go on its recently changed course—and at its current speed of 9.5 knots—before reaching the eastern rendezvous. On paper at least, HX229 had passed the halfway mark on its trans-Atlantic voyage. However, the most important measurement showed the formation just reaching the midway point. At 2400 (midnight GMT) March 16, HX229 had reached 50:38 North 034:46 West, a position 908 nautical miles south-southwest of Reykjavik. The convoy and its undermanned escorts were in the dead center of the Greenland air gap.[19]

Escort and merchant ships lookouts strained their eyes in vain, seeking a glimpse of a U-boat conning tower. Unfortunately for them, the low-lying U-boats were much harder to spot than the tall silhouettes of the ships in the convoy. Unseen to the ships, lookouts on seven U-boats firmly held the convoy in their binoculars and were counting down the minutes until the opportunity for attack would come.

Escort Group B-4 was in a bind, and Lieutenant-Commander Luther knew it. He was down to four warships, the destroyer *Mansfield* still not having returned from chasing the HF/DF contact that afternoon. With so few escorts, it would be impossible to screen the convoy's entire twenty-mile perimeter, so Luther had to gamble on which side the U-boats would most likely approach. Suspecting that most of them would converge from the port bow and flank as a result of the HF/DF intercepts earlier that day, he had placed his own ship, the *Volunteer,* on the convoy's port bow in Position M (see illustration on page 128), the destroyer *Beverley* on the starboard bow in Position B, corvette *Pennywort* on the starboard beam in Position G, and corvette *Anemone* on the port beam in Position Q. Upon rejoining the convoy, the destroyer *Mansfield* would occupy Position S, astern of the formation. Luther's reorganization of HX229's escorts accomplished little, however. The gaps between the warships were so large that the U-boats would have little difficulty slipping past the guardians to get to the convoy's main body.

The U-boat commanders saw all too well the opportunity afforded them by the widely spaced escorts. The first commander to make a move was Oberleutnant zur See Bertelsmann in U-603, one of the last Raubgraf boats to make contact with HX229. Bertelsmann opted to close from the starboard bow on a surface attack, the most maneuverable mode of nighttime assault. With the destroyer *Beverley* and corvette *Pennywort* separated by several thousand yards, U-603 easily slipped past the two escorts and Bertelsmann ordered his crew to prepare to attack.[20]

When the sighting report for HX229 had come in, U-603 was down to its last four torpedoes. Like U-653, the convoy's contact keeper, U-603 was on the last legs of its war patrol. The boat had departed Brest on February 7, joining Gruppe Ritter (Knight) in the North Atlantic for action against Convoy ON166 in the last week of February. U-603 had had moderate success in that fight, finishing off two Norwegian tankers traveling in the westbound convoy—the 5,964-ton vessel *Stigstad* on February 21 and the 6,409-ton *Glittre* on February 23—that had already been hit by other U-boats. By all measures, U-603's torpedoes had been well spent.

Bertelsmann did not consider his low reserve of torpedoes to be a handicap: he had enough for at least one attack on more than one merchant ship. He ordered his torpedo room to prepare to fire two salvoes of two torpedoes from the bow tubes and one torpedo from the stern tube at the two ships in the starboard-most column of HX229. U-603 had no path-looping Federapparat (FAT) torpedoes left, so his attack would involve two G7e electrics from the bow tubes and a G7a compressed-air torpedo from the stern.

Bertelsmann gave the order, and U-603's first watch officer, Oberleutnant Rudolf Baltz, hit the firing lever. The U-boat would have shuddered
as compressed air spat the four 3,528-pound torpedoes out of the forward
tubes, and they began running at more than thirty knots toward their two
targets. It was precisely 2200 on March 16, 1943. The decisive battle was
under way.[21]

Chapter 7

THE BATTLE OF
ST. PATRICK'S DAY

I n three years of war, the 5,214-ton Norwegian freighter *Elin K.* and its native crew of thirty-six had proven themselves survivors. When Germany invaded Norway on April 7, 1940, the ship had been moored in Durban, South Africa, one of 816 Norwegian-flagged merchant ships plying the seas at the time her home country came under enemy occupation. In response to the invasion, the British government had broadcast over the BBC an invitation for Norwegian-flagged ships at sea to join the British Merchant Fleet, offering both protection and employment for the crews. Master Robert Johannessen and his thirty-five-man crew had accepted the British offer, choosing a life of self-imposed exile on their ship rather than returning to a homeland occupied by the Nazis. During the past thirty-five months, the *Elin K.* had been outfitted with a solitary deck gun manned by six British gunners and had made eighty separate voyages carrying bulk and general cargo. Its operations had ranged from the Far East to the British Isles, from Africa to the United States, and from the Middle East to the western Pacific.

The *Elin K.* was just one of thousands of dispossessed merchant ships that had gone to work against the Axis. As the German Reich expanded its control over Europe, the vast majority of merchant ships from Denmark, Belgium, the Netherlands, France, Greece, and Yugoslavia would also join the Allied cause. In addition, Swedish merchantmen frequently traveled in Allied convoys despite their nation's formal neutrality. This influx of

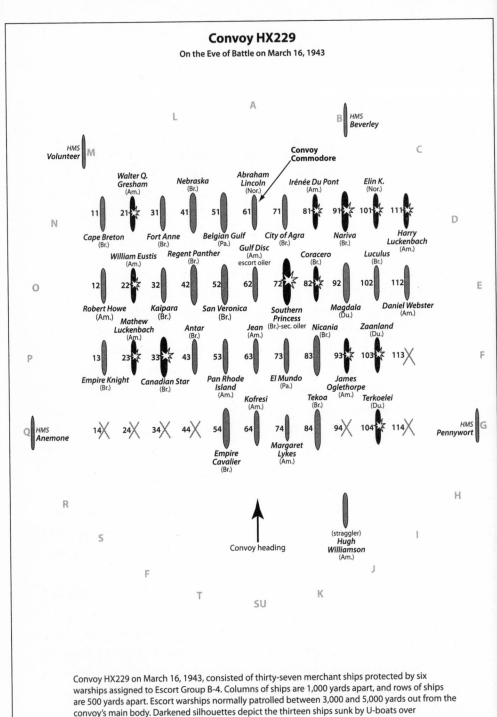

Convoy HX229

On the Eve of Battle on March 16, 1943

Convoy HX229 on March 16, 1943, consisted of thirty-seven merchant ships protected by six warships assigned to Escort Group B-4. Columns of ships are 1,000 yards apart, and rows of ships are 500 yards apart. Escort warships normally patrolled between 3,000 and 5,000 yards out from the convoy's main body. Darkened silhouettes depict the thirteen ships sunk by U-boats over the next three days.

Illustration by Robert E. Prat

vessels from ostensibly noncombatant nations had expanded the British civilian fleet from 2,969 ships flying the Union Jack to nearly 5,000 vessels. By early 1943, these volunteer ships and their crews were fully integrated into the Allied shipping effort.

THE THREE EASTBOUND CONVOYS currently crossing the Greenland air gap represented the considerable contribution of volunteer merchantmen to the Allied shipping effort. Of the 136 ships that left New York in Convoys SC122, HX229, and HX229A during March 5–9, twenty-two flew the flags of German-occupied countries, including the *Elin K.* and seven other merchantmen from Norway.

The *Elin K.*'s journey with HX229 from New York to its scheduled port of Belfast, Northern Ireland, marked the final stage of a globe-spanning trip that had begun on January 13, 1943. Loaded with 7,000 tons of wheat and manganese ore in Sydney, Australia, the ship had transited the Pacific, crossing over into the Caribbean through the Panama Canal and steaming up to New York within the American coastal convoy system. There, officials added 339 bags of mail to the cargo that the *Elin K.* would be carrying across the Atlantic to Belfast.

As occasionally happens in history, the *Elin K.*'s exemplary wartime service lends a special bitterness to the details of its fate. British shipping experts had quickly implemented the convoy system after the outbreak of war in September 1939, because they knew from their experience in World War I that ships were safer traveling in formation than sailing independently. The *Elin K.* would prove a tragic exception to the convoy-risk formula. It had sailed as an independent on seventy-five cruises, and HX229 was only the fifth convoy in which the doughty freighter had steamed.[1]

Shortly before 2200, Commodore Mayall in the *Abraham Lincoln* had ordered Convoy HX229 to make a course change from 028 to 053 degrees, and the eleven columns of ships slowly began wheeling to starboard. As the *Elin K.* was steaming in Position 101—lead ship in the tenth, or second from the starboard-most column—it was one of the first vessels to begin the turn. At that moment, the four torpedoes from Oberleutnant Bertelsmann's U-603 slashed unseen into the front of the formation from starboard. Three torpedoes narrowly missed the 6,366-ton American freighter *Harry Luckenbach* and the 7,716-ton Liberty ship *Daniel Webster*, the two leading ships in the convoy's outer column. The fourth slammed into the *Elin K.* on its starboard side, ripping open a huge gash in the No. 4 hold.

The *Elin K.*'s crew reacted calmly to the shock wave, the deafening blast, and the sudden column of water lifting high above the ship's masts. First Mate Jan Berge was on watch on the navigation bridge and took action immediately, sounding four blasts on the ship's horn, illuminating a red light on the masthead, and firing two white signal rockets to alert the flagship and escorts of a torpedo strike. By the time Captain Johannessen reached the bridge, the *Elin K.* was clearly sinking. He ordered the crew to abandon ship.

The evacuation of the *Elin K.* went smoothly, thanks to its crew's meticulous preparation and teamwork. After Captain Johannessen gave the order to abandon ship, Second Mate Hans-Henrik Smith Hansen went to his station on the main deck to prepare one of the lifeboats. It was a task he was used to performing; unlike the majority of the ship's crew, he had served on other merchant vessels since the outbreak of the war, joining the *Elin K.* in early 1942. Hansen was a survivor, having eluded death on three previous occasions when the ships on which he had been serving were sunk by the enemy. The *Elin K.* would be the fourth. Because the weather had been so bad the previous week, the *Elin K.* crew had taken extra care of the ship's survival gear. Observing many ships in the convoy losing lifeboats and rafts over the side from the pounding waves, Hansen and his mates had taken pains to tightly lash down the ship's two lifeboats. As a result, both were intact when the men needed them. The crew quickly lowered the boats, climbed aboard, and cast free. Ten minutes after the torpedo struck, all forty men were safely away in the two boats. The *Elin K.* went down fast. By the time the third ship in their column passed by, the *Elin K.*'s hull was standing vertically on end and the crew could hear its bulkheads giving way.

Not all of the ships' crews in HX229 demonstrated the good order and discipline of the *Elin K.*'s men. Commodore Mayall had directed the last ship in each column to serve as a rescue vessel should a U-boat torpedo one of the ships in line. The 5,158-ton Dutch freighter *Terkoelei* was in the last position in Column 10 and should have stopped for Captain

Johannessen and his men. Instead, Captain Albert Hocken ignored Mayall's order and, fearing that he would become a target himself, surged past the Norwegians in their lifeboats. Onboard the lead lifeboat, Second Mate Hansen recalled his experience in a prior sinking and advised Johannessen that they might not be rescued for some time given the undermanned escort group. The Norwegians began rowing in a southerly direction to come clear of the convoy and, with a little luck, to better attract an escort's attention.[2]

On the destroyer *Volunteer*, Lieutenant-Commander Luther reacted instantly to the soaring white signal rockets from *Elin K.* He ordered a Half Raspberry, a standard escort response for a U-boat night surface attack. On command, the four escorts turned outward from the convoy's main body and swept their patrol sectors. They did so without firing starshells to illuminate the surrounding water, relying instead on lookouts, radar, and Asdic.

Despite their quick response to the torpedo attack, the ships in Escort Group B-4 did not detect U-603. As soon as his torpedoes had cleared their tubes, Bertelsmann ordered a crash dive under the convoy, then let the ships pass overhead. Once they had cleared and were a safe distance away, he resurfaced and flashed a message to BdU Operations claiming one ship torpedoed and a second possibly hit. With its last torpedoes expended, U-603's radio operator began transmitting a low-frequency signal to bring up additional U-boats, and took station astern of HX229 as the contact keeper for the rest of the Gruppe Raubgraf boats.

Although B-4 failed to detect the U-boat, Luther's response had one positive result. As the corvette *Pennywort* raced back down the convoy's starboard flank, her lookouts spotted Johannessen and his men in the *Elin K.*'s two lifeboats. Canadian Lieutenant-Commander Orme G. Stuart and his crew moved in to rescue the forty crewmen and gunners.

As the *Pennywort* halted to pick up the survivors from the *Elin K.*, Convoy HX229—now with only three escorts—sailed steadily onward at its designated speed of 9.5 knots. By the time the *Pennywort* finished picking up the Norwegian crewmen and British gunners, HX229 had passed over the northeast horizon. Now, two previous missteps—the failure to provide HX229 with a sufficient number of escorts and the *Terkoelei*'s failure to rescue the Elin K. crew—led to another disaster. The *Pennywort*'s intervention had left the convoy's starboard side completely unprotected. It was an opportunity that Kapitänleutnant Helmut Manseck in U-758 was preparing to exploit.[3]

Manseck was a cautious but aggressive U-boat commander. When his lookouts had sighted a straggling freighter from Convoy HX229 earlier in the day on March 16, he had tried for nearly four hours to get into a firing position, only to be thwarted by the heavy seas and his inability to get within torpedo range while running submerged. Finally, at 1305, Manseck ordered U-758 to the surface and chased after the merchantman, aware from the contact report by U-653's Kapitänleutnant Feiler that the convoy was about twenty nautical miles ahead. For the next seven hours, the U-boat struggled through the heavy seas after Convoy HX229.

At 2030 GMT, or 1830 local, Manseck decided to take advantage of the dimming twilight conditions. He ordered U-758 to close with the steamer for a submerged attack. But three minutes later, this became unnecessary as his lookouts sighted the main body of the convoy bearing 090 degrees at a range of twelve nautical miles. Manseck's lookouts counted at least twenty merchant ships under escort by a number of destroyers and corvettes. Abandoning his plan to go after the straggler, Manseck issued helm orders to place U-758 on the starboard side of the convoy for a night surface attack under the intermittent moonlight conditions.

Manseck recalled the hunt in a postwar interview. "I had shadowed the convoy all day keeping at extreme range on the starboard side, just keeping the smoke and the tips of the masts in sight," he said. "I remember that the ships were doing well and not making much smoke. We had been about twelve miles out during the day and came in to four to five miles at dusk."[4]

As U-758 edged in to get within torpedo range of the formation, Manseck realized that he was not in his intended position ahead of and to starboard of the columns of merchant ships. "When I came in to make my attack I found that I had misjudged the speed of the convoy and that we were almost level with it," he recalled. "But I decided to attack from there rather than try to get ahead again; we came in from just ahead of 90 degrees. I could see six, eight, or ten ships and selected a solid, overlapping target of the third ships in the starboard columns."

Under the long-established tactics that Grossadmiral Dönitz had developed for the U-boat Force, U-758 had the freedom to choose the time and location of attack that Manseck thought most effective. As the U-boat steadily closed with HX229, he and First Watch Officer Leutnant zur See Bernhard Luttmann were up on the exposed bridge with four lookouts as the torpedo gang conducted last-minute checks on the five torpedoes in the bow and stern tubes. It was Luttmann's task to operate the UZO target-bearing binoculars and to press the lever that would transmit the bearing angle to each merchant ship that Manseck wanted to attack. The skipper himself was responsible for choosing the target and selecting the type of launch and specific torpedoes to be fired.

Around 2320, Manseck ordered the outer torpedo tube doors opened as the U-boat's fire-control calculator transmitted updated bearing angles from the UZO binoculars to the torpedoes. Down below in the bow compartment, Obermechanikermaat (T) (Torpedoman's Mate) Rolf Pastor turned the cranks that manually opened the torpedo tube doors. Pastor's two assistants, Mechanikerobergefreiter (T) (Torpedo Mechanic) Hans Lewald and Mechanikerobergefreiter Herbert Schulz, stood by with a group of crewmen preparing to reload the torpedo tubes on Manseck's order once U-758 got clear of the convoy and its escorts after the first salvo was fired.

Manseck selected one path-looping FAT torpedo apiece for the initial pair of targets, an 8,000-ton tanker and a 6,000-ton freighter, to be followed by a pair of G7e electric warshots aimed at two more vessels, a 7,000-ton steam merchant and a 4,000-ton freighter.

Down in U-758's radio room, Martin Beisheim tapped out the short warning message to the other Gruppe Raubgraf boats nearby that U-758 was preparing to launch a pair of FAT torpedoes, alerting them to keep clear of the convoy for at least thirty minutes in case the path-looping weapons steered through the merchant ships and emerged on the other side of the formation.

Two minutes later, Manseck leaned over the voice tube connecting the bridge and control room. "Torpedo officer—prepare tubes one to four for surface fire!" A confirmation quickly came from below, "Tubes one to four—ready for surface fire!"

Trans-Atlantic course tracks of Convoys HX229 and SC122.

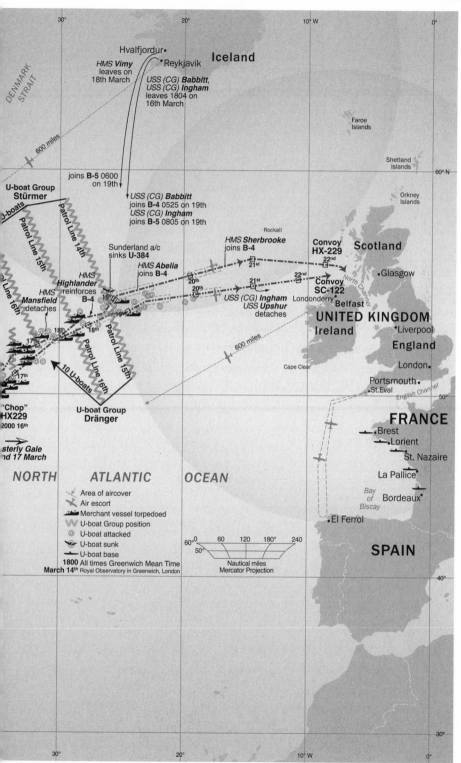

Illustration by Robert E. Pratt

On Manseck's next order, "Fire when ready!" Luttmann hit the firing lever, and the first FAT raced away toward the tanker some 5,000 yards away. A minute later, he pressed the lever a second time and the second path-looping FAT shot out of Torpedo Tube II. The two G7e torpedoes followed at 2324 and 2325. For the second time in less than ninety minutes, a U-boat had fired upon HX229.[5]

WHEN U-603's TORPEDO had struck the *Elin K.* over an hour before U-758's attack, the Panamanian-flagged freighter *El Mundo* had been steaming in Column 7, only 3,200 yards away from the Norwegian merchantman at the front of Column 10. The *El Mundo's* bridge watchstanders and lookouts had a clear view of the victim's distress rockets. Signalman 3rd Class Ted Schorr, however, did not. Exhausted from the long daylight watches on the *El Mundo's* bridge, the physical stress of functioning during the fierce storm of March 14–15, and the bitter cold that set in on the convoy after midnight, he had climbed into his rack and was sound asleep when Gruppe Raubgraf struck.

Several minutes after U-603's torpedo struck the *Elin K.*, Schorr had come awake to realize that something was wrong. The berthing compartment was empty, and only dim emergency lights provided illumination. "I looked all around and saw that there wasn't another person in the quarters," he recalled. "My next thought was that they knew that this was my first trip and this was sort of an initiation." In the haze of sleep, Schorr had mistaken the U-boat attack for a practical joke.

Donning his boots, jacket, and cap, Schorr had gone up on deck. As usual, the convoy was steaming in total darkened condition, but the moon occasionally peered out from the cloud layer and lit up the surrounding ocean. Schorr looked up at the four-inch gun where its crew was standing around the weapon. "If you guys have had your fun now, you can come down and we can all get some sleep," he called out in a mixture of irritation and humor.

"Shut up," had come the hissed reply from the gunner's mate. "A ship has been torpedoed. The Ensign has been calling for you—you're wanted on the bridge."

Schorr ran up the two flights to the wheelhouse. The entire bridge watch was wearing lifejackets. Schorr realized this was no joke at all. Ensign DeMarco walked over. "Didn't you hear the General Alarm?"

"No sir."

"Where the hell have you been?"

"Asleep in my bunk, Sir."

"Get back there and put on your heavy-duty clothing and lifejacket and get back here on the double."

Schorr dashed back down the two ladders to the main deck "in two huge leaps" and sprinted aft. At that instant, a ship three columns to starboard exploded in a huge ball of flame. He kept running. Then a second ship in the same general area went up. Schorr leaped down the ladder to the berthing compartment and seized his gear. Within a few minutes he was back on the bridge in heavy-duty clothing and lifejacket, gasping for air. Just then, Captain MacKenzie came on the ship's loudspeaker, shouting for all hands on deck to watch for white streaks in the water.[6]

FOR THREE MINUTES and fifty seconds, Manseck and the U-758's bridge team waited tensely as the torpedoes headed for the starboard ships in Convoy HX229. A series of explosions rocked the convoy as two of the torpedoes struck home.

Ten minutes after launching his attack on the convoy, Manseck ordered the U-758 to submerge after a lookout reported what he thought to be an escort aircraft overhead. The U-boat's crew could hear "loud sinking sounds" from the direction of the torpedoed merchant ships, Manseck recalled.

U-758's attack was the last of its patrol. Critically low on fuel, Manseck withdrew from the fight. U-758 hid in the cellar for four hours before surfacing again. After reporting his attack to BdU, Manseck ordered U-758 on a southeast course for the twelve-hour trek to rendezvous with the resupply tanker U-463 before beginning the six-day trip back to St. Nazaire.[7]

Manseck would later claim to have sunk three ships and damaged a fourth in the attack, but his report was unintentionally exaggerated. U-758 had only struck two ships. As in most encounters in the Battle of the Atlantic, things had not gone exactly to plan. Luttmann had used the UZO binoculars to target the first two ships in the two outermost columns. He missed three of the four. The first two torpedoes streaked past the *Harry Luckenbach, Daniel Webster,* and *Luculus,* and one of the torpedoes also narrowly missed the tanker *Magdala.* It was U-758's two

G7e electric torpedoes that hit their targets. The third torpedo fired struck the Dutch freighter *Zaanland,* the third ship in Column 10. A minute later, the fourth torpedo ran close by the *Zaanland* and crashed into the rearmost ship in Column 9, the newly built *James Oglethorpe.*[8]

The *Zaanland's* Master Gerardus Franken and his fifty-two-man crew were an experienced team that had sailed together since the prewar years. Even though this was their first time under attack they reacted without panic, just as had the crew of the *Elin K.* When Manseck's torpedo came crashing into the starboard side amidships, it wreaked fatal damage to the *Zaanland.* Franken later recalled the moment of impact: "I was standing in the starboard wing of the bridge, looking over the side towards the stem, when there was a tremendous explosion and a huge flash and a strong smell of burning," Franken said. "To my amazement I felt extremely calm; I had often wondered how I should feel if this ever happened to me. Although I had been at sea for three years prior to this, it was the first time I had been involved in a submarine attack."

The explosion blew a gaping hole in the side of the freighter, rupturing fuel tanks and causing the mainmast to collapse. Several crewmen on deck fell injured. Franken heard water loudly rushing into the engine room and saw fuel oil gushing out onto the surface of the ocean. He instantly realized the *Zaanland* was doomed. On his order, the crew put to the lifeboats, those uninjured assisting their wounded shipmates. In less than ten minutes, the stern of the *Zaanland* dropped, the bow came sharply up and the survivors heard a rumble like thunder as the ship's steam boilers crashed through the bulkheads. The men watched a final fireworks display as the anchors fell away and their chains ripped through the hawse pipes in a bright shower of sparks. The survivors then watched helplessly as, for the second time that night, the Dutch freighter *Terkoelei* steamed past a stricken ship in its column without stopping.

Just a half mile to the west-northwest of the burning *Zaanland,* a sharply different scene was unfolding on the torpedoed *James Oglethorpe.* The Liberty ship, completed just two months earlier in Savannah, Georgia, was on its maiden voyage with a newly formed and inexperienced crew of forty-three men. In addition, twenty-six Naval Armed Guard gunners were aboard to operate the one four-inch and one three-inch guns as well as eight 20-mm Oerlikon pedestal-mounted automatic cannons.

Eighteen different American shipyards mass-produced 2,751 Liberty ships during World War II. The *James Oglethorpe* and fourteen others were sunk by U-boats during the critical month of March 1943.

Clay Blair Collection, American Heritage Center, University of Wyoming

Bound for Liverpool, the *James Oglethorpe* was carrying 8,000 tons of steel, cotton, and food. Port authorities in New York had added an additional deck cargo of military aircraft, tractors, and trucks.

Captain Albert W. Long and the men aboard the *James Oglethorpe* had little time to react when they saw the explosion and flying debris from the *Zaanland;* their turn came less than a minute later. Manseck's last torpedo struck the forward section of the *James Oglethorpe's* No. 2 hold on the starboard side. The ship's steering jammed hard over to port, a fire broke out in one of the holds, and the ship began settling in the water with a starboard list. Although Long had begun a series of zigzag maneuvers when the *Elin K.* was hit, his evasive course had kept the *James Oglethorpe* relatively close to its assigned convoy position. Now, the Liberty ship fell out of formation and began to steam in large circles at the rear of the convoy.

About half of the *James Oglethorpe's* crew immediately panicked. Without waiting for an abandon-ship order, several of the mates began ordering lifeboats and rafts deployed. Several dozen crewmen hastily lowered the boats, ignoring the fact that the ship was still moving through the water. Someone cut the lines to one lifeboat prematurely and spilled the passengers into the water. Thirteen of them drowned. Thirty crewmen safely escaped in several more lifeboats. Back on board, however, Captain Long, his second officer, and thirty-one other crewmen decided to try and save the ship. They managed to extinguish the fire in the hold in fifteen minutes and struggled to restore the steering.

The loss of steering aboard the *James Oglethorpe* proved terrifying to the crewmen who had abandoned the *Zaanland*. Aboard one lifeboat, Chief Officer P. G. van Altveer was searching for signs of a rescue ship when the 441-foot-long American freighter suddenly loomed up out of the darkness. "I feared that she would overrun us; the accommodation ladder was hanging over the side and I thought we should get jammed underneath the spur [lower end] of the ladder," he recalled. "Most of my lifeboat's occupants rose from their seats to be ready for jumping overboard but I shouted, 'Sit down. Do sit down!' I feared the boat might capsize. It was a very exciting moment, she passed us on her port side at no more than five yards."

While the B-4 escorts were executing a Half-Raspberry order in response to the new U-boat attack—turning out from their patrol stations around the formation to search the immediate area for any U-boat that might be close by—the destroyer *Beverley* soon came upon the *Zaanland's* lifeboats and stopped to pick up survivors. The destroyer's crew had managed to haul nine men aboard when the corvette *Pennywort* arrived on the scene, having finished rescuing the *Elin K.'s* crew. With only the *Volunteer* and *Anemone* left to patrol the convoy perimeter, Luther ordered the destroyer to rejoin at once and for the *Pennywort* to retrieve the remaining seventy-four survivors from the *Zaanland* and *James Oglethorpe*. When all were aboard, Lieutenant-Commander Orme G. Stuart closed with the *James Oglethorpe* and hailed its master. Captain Long told Stuart that he and his diminished crew were going to try and take their damaged ship to St. John's, then 730 miles to the west. Long asked for the crewmen who had abandoned ship to rejoin him, but all refused.

Although it was a cowardly decision, the *James Oglethorpe*'s evacuees' refusal to reboard their ship saved their lives. Long and his skeleton crew turned to a course of 270 degrees for the long trek to Newfoundland and soon disappeared from sight. Neither the ship nor any of its crew were ever seen again.

The survivors from the *James Oglethorpe* were not the only ones who had been badly rattled by the assault on HX229. The torpedo attacks on three ships within a ninety-minute period had shaken the officers and crewmen throughout Escort Group B-4 and Convoy HX229. Onboard the destroyer *Volunteer,* both Luther and First Lieutenant George C. Leslie agonized over their impossible dilemma—whether to keep the understrength B-4 escorts nearby to defend the convoy's main body against another U-boat attack, or have one or two of the warships drop back to rescue survivors. Years later, Leslie vividly remembered the scene. "The Captain and I had discussed the possibility on several occasions and our conclusion was that rescue was very important at a time when the worst disaster in the Atlantic battle would be a failure of morale in the merchant ships," he said. "In the absence of a rescue ship and with the failure of the last ship in the column to stop and pick up survivors, the escort group commander had an almost impossible decision to make."

After much deliberation, Luther had opted to divert the corvette *Pennywort* to pick up the survivors. Yet now, just an hour after the attacks on the *Zaanland* and *James Oglethorpe,* another test came. U-435 under Kapitänleutnant Siegfried Strelow was the third Raubgraf boat to strike. While the *Pennywort* was still indisposed, Strelow crept in on the convoy's port side and at 0022 GMT launched two FAT torpedoes. One of them struck the 7,196-ton American freighter *William Eustis* on the starboard side of its No. 2 cargo hold, causing flooding and a major hull crack near the bridge. The newly built Liberty ship was carrying a cargo of 7,000 tons of sugar and 600 tons of food, so apart from the torpedo warhead detonation there was little fire or smoke. Still the sight would have been a terrible one for the men on board and those nearby in the formation.

Traveling directly behind the *William Eustis* on the *Mathew Luckenbach,* Signalman 3rd Class John Orris Jackson would have been an eyewitness to the sudden violence, like the other watchmen on the twenty-five-year-old freighter. Standing on the ship's navigation bridge, Jackson had seen the distant distress rockets and later learned of the loss of the *Elin K.* Then, at 2325, the *Mathew Luckenbach's* lookouts had reported the white rockets and red mast lights far off on the starboard quarter from the U-758 attack on the *Zaanland* and *James Oglethorpe*. Fifty-seven minutes after that, an explosion rocked the ship directly in front of them, throwing up a column of water more than 100 feet high. The *William Eustis* slowed and turned sideways, blocking the path of the approaching *Mathew Luckenbach*. Antwood N. Borden, the latter's master, hastily ordered a hard right turn to miss the stricken vessel, then dodged another ship in the next column. The crew watched silently as U-435's victim fell out of the formation.

"All hell broke loose," Jackson later said of the night of March 16–17. "My sea duty without action came abruptly to an end. From this minute on I got no sleep." Nor did the rest of the *Mathew Luckenbach's* forty-two crewmen and twenty-five other Naval Armed Guardsmen, who feared that their ship might be next to suffer a torpedo strike.

Because the other ships nearby had seen the attack on the *William Eustis,* its master, Cecil Desmond, apparently decided not to fire any white rockets to signal that his ship had been hit. In any event, none of the escorts were around to observe the scene. For the next half hour the Liberty ship's crew struggled to shore up the flooding vessel, but finally around 0100 Desmond ordered everyone off. Five of the six lifeboats were damaged and unusable—four because of the earlier storm and one from the torpedo impact—but all seventy-two hands safely made it into the *William Eustis's* one remaining lifeboat and four rafts. Four hours later, when Lieutenant-Commander Luther brought the *Volunteer* around the convoy in a sweep of its perimeter, the destroyer's lookouts sighted the listing *William Eustis* with its lifeboats and rafts bobbing nearby. Luther picked up the men, and the *Volunteer's* crew scuttled the wreck with gunfire and depth charges.

Overwhelmed by the impossible task of guarding all sides of the convoy with so few ships, while also having to abandon the perimeter to rescue survivors, Escort Group B-4 had managed to mount only one attack against a U-boat during this first phase of the battle for HX229. During the Half-Raspberry maneuver after the *Elin K.* was hit at 2200, the corvette *Anemone* had sighted a surfaced U-boat 3,000 yards away off the convoy's port flank. Lieutenant-Commander Patrick G. A. King immediately gave chase, but his attempt to destroy the U-boat, later identified as U-89, was plagued with misfires and bad luck. The *Anemone* managed to close within 300 yards before the U-boat suddenly crash-dived, but when King ordered a small pattern of five depth charges set to explode at fifty feet, the concussion briefly knocked out both the ship's Asdic hydrophone system and radio-telephone set. A second attack failed when a short-circuit in the *Anemone's* depth-charge alarm prematurely set off the firing bells, causing the crew to fire the K-gun launchers too soon. Again, the shock wave knocked out the corvette's Asdic gear. During one of three subsequent attacks after that, the ship tried to use its forward-firing Hedgehog, but this too malfunctioned and only four of the twenty-four projectiles left the launcher. After two hours, the *Anemone* called it quits and returned to HX229. The counterattack hadn't been a total failure. Although his boat had sustained only minor damage from the *Anemone,* Kapitänleutnant Dietrich Lohmann ordered the U-89 to quit the battle and return to port.

Following the torpedo hit on the *William Eustis* at 0022, the battle for Convoy HX229 seemed to tail off—but Commodore Mayall on the *Abraham Lincoln* knew better than to be heartened by the lull. While the main formation continued on its base course of 053 without further attacks, there was not a single escort ship from Group B-4 patrolling the perimeter until the destroyers *Beverley* and *Mansfield* rejoined. The *Beverley* had been off retrieving survivors, and the *Mansfield* finally returned after its ill-fated hunt for a U-boat contact the previous afternoon. Both destroyers caught back up with the convoy around 0230. The *Volunteer* and *Pennywort* were still retrieving survivors several miles astern, and the *Anemone* had not yet rejoined after its scrap with U-89. But as the minutes slowly passed, edgy crewmen throughout the convoy slowly relaxed. Had the U-boats lost the convoy, or had they broken off their attacks for some unknown reason? Kapitänleutnant Heinz Walkerling answered that question at 0237.

Walkerling, a twenty-seven-year native of Kiel, had commanded the U-91 since its commissioning on January 28, 1942. He and his crew had sunk two ships on their first war patrol in September 1942 and had been avidly hunting for HX229 for several days, briefly spotting one of the convoy's escorts late on March 15. Brought up by Hans-Joachim Bertels-mann's homing signal from U-603, U-91 had patiently stalked the convoy until dark along with the other Raubgraf boats and only then moved in for the kill. At a range of 2,027 yards, Walkerling launched the first of a spread of five torpedoes—two FATs and three G7es, including one from his stern tube—at the silhouetted merchant ship passing slowly from left to right.

One ship in convoy HX229 had almost certainly seen the attack com-ing. Aboard the *Harry Luckenbach,* Master Ralph McKinnon, his fifty-three crewmen, and twenty-six Naval Armed Guard gunners had strained through a nerve-wracking night as the lead ship in HX229's outermost column on the starboard side. The twenty-four-year-old steam merchant, laden with 8,381 tons of ammunition and other general cargo, had dodged at least eight torpedoes during the past three hours—including those that had gone on to strike the *Elin K., Zaanland,* and *James Oglethorpe.* Concerned that his ship's position was dangerously vulnerable, McKinnon had steamed out ahead of HX229 after the earlier attacks, zigzagging wildly to dodge the next wave of FATs and G7es, until Com-modore Mayall brusquely ordered him back in line.

McKinnon's fear for the *Harry Luckenbach* would have been under-standable to any seasoned convoy captain. Merchant sailors had nick-named the lead ship position in the outermost port and starboard columns of a convoy the "coffin corner," for the dangerous exposure of these positions to enemy attack. The nickname was no exaggeration.

At 0237 one or two of Walkerling's five torpedoes detonated against the *Harry Luckenbach's* starboard side. Unlike the *Elin K.,* which sank silently without a trace of fire or smoke, the *Harry Luckenbach*—freighted with tons upon tons of ammunition—went up in a colossal explosion that stunned sailors throughout the convoy. Despite the initial explosion and fire that followed, McKinnon managed to fire distress rockets while crew-men scrambled to launch three lifeboats. It was a frantic race against time as the *Harry Luckenbach* rapidly sank. Within four minutes the ship was gone. A large number of crewmen perished in the initial blast or because they were unable to reach lifeboats or rafts before the ship went under. What followed was even more tragic.

The destroyer *Beverley* sighted the three lifeboats from the *Harry Luckenbach* three miles behind the still-moving convoy and reported the sighting to Luther in the *Volunteer*. Luther radioed Lieutenant-Commander King on the *Anemone* to search for the survivors when he returned to the convoy, but the corvette could not locate the lifeboats. The *Pennywort*, coming back up to HX229 with 108 survivors from the earlier attacks, sighted the *Harry Luckenbach* survivors but was too full of passengers to take on any more. On the overcrowded corvette, Lieutenant-Commander Stuart tried to raise Luther by radio to have another escort pick up the drifting crewmen, but could not reach him. With multiple U-boat sightings on both sides of the convoy, the escort commander was issuing frantic orders to the other escorts to attempt to drive them off. In the confusion of the heat of battle, the three lifeboats drifted into the darkness and were never seen again.

When the *Harry Luckenbach* had exploded from U-91's torpedo attack, Naval Armed Guard gunner Bill Stilinovich could only gaze at the scene in helpless horror. The initial fireball lit up the sky and its shock wave thundered across the 3,000-yard interval between the stricken vessel and Stilinovich's ship, the *Irénée Du Pont*. The distance was too great for him to see if his brother's crew had managed to safely lower lifeboats. All Bill Stilinovich knew for sure was that the ship on which his brother, Joe, was sailing had ceased to exist. As the convoy sailed on, Stilinovich could only watch as a shroud of smoke—all that remained of the *Harry Luckenbach*—drifted into the oblivion of night.

In just four hours, over the course of some thirty nautical miles on its course track deep inside the Greenland air gap, HX229 had been badly mauled. Four Gruppe Raubgraf U-boats had torpedoed five ships totaling 32,765 tons, causing the deaths of 124 merchant sailors. And the carnage had only begun.[9]

HE HAD SEEN THE NIGHTMARE many times from afar: the sudden flash of light, the tower of foam and the rising pillar of smoke from a torpedo striking a nearby ship in his convoy. From the main deck he had watched the terror aboard a stricken ship as it fell behind the other merchantmen, its crew scrambling into lifeboats and rafts. He had witnessed the noisy fireworks display of multiple snowflake illumination rockets fired by the convoy ships and escorts in an attempt to pinpoint the attacking U-boat. When working deep in the ship's engine spaces, he had heard the blaring alarm bells summoning the crew to emergency quarters, and felt through the deck plates the muffled booms of torpedoes striking their targets. He thought that he had known what it was like to be afraid. None of that prepared Deane Wynne for the shock and horror of the actual event.

Convoy HX229 would not bear the Battle of St. Patrick's Day alone. Although the fifty-seven merchant ships in Slow Convoy SC122, steaming about 110 miles northeast of the fast convoy, had thus far evaded the scores of U-boats that Grossadmiral Dönitz had sent against the two formations in the Greenland air gap, that luck was about to change. For the more than 3,400 merchant seamen and over 800 naval escort crewmen in SC122, the reckoning came in the early morning hours of Wednesday, March 17.

At 2200 GMT, or 2000 hours local, Deane Wynne had come off a four-hour engine room watch. Exhausted and stiff from the unending labor of shoveling coal into the ship's furnaces, he paused for several minutes on the main deck to admire the large formation of darkened ships sailing in formation under the waxing moon. His ship, the British freighter *Kingsbury,* was in Position 51, making it the lead vessel in the third column from the convoy's port flank. The bulk of the convoy was in sight on the starboard beam and quarter. "There was a fair breeze blowing," Wynne described the scene many years later. "The seas were still running a bit high from the previous storms. All seemed quiet and peaceful as I watched the steady roll of our companion ships plodding their weary way home just like us." On the *Kingsbury,* Wynne turned to a shipmate standing close by at the rail and said, "I think it is a bit too rough for the U-boats to have a go at us again tonight." Wynne bade the other crewmen good night and went belowdecks, where he fell into his bunk. Within minutes, the eighteen-year-old Londoner was fast asleep.

A shattering explosion jerked Wynne awake. He lurched up and glanced at his wristwatch: it was five minutes after midnight. Suddenly everything was happening at once. The ship gave a tremendous shudder, and then the deep throbbing of its engines fell silent. Worse, the deck plates underfoot suddenly tilted as the *Kingsbury* began listing to port. Wearing only his

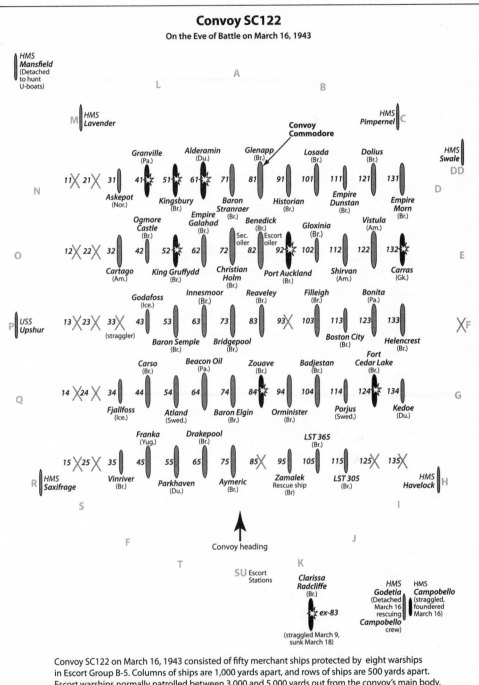

Convoy SC122

On the Eve of Battle on March 16, 1943

HMS
Mansfield
(Detached
to hunt
U-boats)

A

L   B

M | HMS
Lavender

HMS
Pimpernel | C

Convoy
Commodore

HMS
Swale
DD

Granville
(Pa.) Alderamin
(Du.) Glenapp
(Br.) Losada
(Br.) Dolius
(Br.)

N   11⨯21⨯ 31   41⚡ 51⚡ 61⚡ 71   81   91   101 111 121 131

D

Askepot
(Nor.) Kingsbury
(Br.) Baron
Stranraer
(Br.) Historian
(Br.) Empire
Dunstan
(Br.) Empire
Morn
(Br.)

Ogmore
Castle
(Br.) Empire
Galahad
(Br.) Benedick
(Br.) Gloxinia
(Br.) Vistula
(Am.)

O   12⨯22⨯ 32   42   52⚡ 62   72 Sec.
oiler 82 Escort
oiler 92⚡ 102 112 122 132⚡

E

Cartago
(Am.) King Gruffydd
(Br.) Christian
Holm
(Br.) Port Auckland
(Br.) Shirvan
(Am.) Carras
(Gk.)

Godafoss
(Ice.) Innesmoor
(Br.) Reaveley
(Br.) Filleigh
(Br.) Bonita
(Pa.)

P | USS
Upshur   13⨯23⨯ 33⨯ 43   53   63   73   83   93⨯ 103 113 123 133   ⨯F

(straggler) Baron Semple
(Br.) Bridgepool
(Br.) Boston City
(Br.) Helencrest
(Br.)

Carso
(Br.) Beacon Oil
(Pa.) Zouave
(Br.) Badjestan
(Br.) Fort
Cedar Lake
(Br.)

Q   14⨯24⨯ 34   44   54   64   74   84⚡ 94   104 114 124⚡ 134

G

Fjallfoss
(Ice.) Atland
(Swed.) Baron Elgin
(Br.) Orminister
(Br.) Porjus
(Swed.) Kedoe
(Du.)

Franka
(Yug.) Drakepool
(Br.) LST 365
(Br.)

R   15⨯25⨯ 35   45   55   65   75   85⨯ 95   105 115 125⨯ 135⨯

HMS
Saxifrage   Vinriver
(Br.) Parkhaven
(Du.) Aymeric
(Br.) Zamalek
Rescue ship
(Br) LST 305
(Br.) HMS
Havelock | H

S   I

F   Convoy heading   J

SU Escort
Stations   K

Clarissa
Radcliffe
(Br.) HMS
Godetia
(Detached
March 16
rescuing
Campobello
crew) HMS
Campobello
(straggled,
foundered
March 16)

⚡ ex-83

(straggled March 9,
sunk March 18)

Convoy SC122 on March 16, 1943 consisted of fifty merchant ships protected by eight warships
in Escort Group B-5. Columns of ships are 1,000 yards apart, and rows of ships are 500 yards apart.
Escort warships normally patrolled between 3,000 and 5,000 yards out from the convoy's main body.
Darkened silhouettes depict the nine ships sunk by U-boats over the next three days.
Columns 1 and 2 are vacant because their ships had gone to ports in Canada.

Illustration by Robert E. Pratt

underwear, Wynne leaped out of the bunk, grabbed his blue kapok life-jacket, and rushed for the starboard ladder leading up on deck.

Total chaos raged around Wynne when he emerged into the night air. The ship's master, William Laidler, had ordered all stop on the engines, but the *Kingsbury* was still making way through the rough sea. Residual high-pressure steam was blowing out of the boiler safety valves in a deaf-ening bellow. Wynne could barely hear the shouted orders and cries from dozens of crewmen emerging from below, but that didn't matter; he could see that the *Kingsbury* was sinking fast. In the bright moonlight he could see a huge, jagged hole in the main deck from the torpedo detonation. Wynne had the chilling realization that, had he run to his normal lifeboat station, he could easily have tripped over the jagged plating and fallen into the cargo hold. Wynne watched nervously as several crewmen attempted to launch a lifeboat. The painter rope securing it to the ship suddenly snapped and the boat vanished astern, bearing a solitary crewman away. He hastened along the starboard side of the ship to the other lifeboat sta-tion. Nearly paralyzed with shock and fear, Wynne watched as other crew-men wrestled with the second lifeboat.

Another *Kingsbury* fireman, escaping from his watch station deep in the belly of the ship, observed the same frantic efforts to release the lifeboats and made an impetuous decision. "I remembered that I had purchased a wedding ring in New York for my wife as she had lost her own whilst washing clothes, also I was very cold indeed not having a jacket on," Patrick Murphy said. "I made my way carefully along the sloping deck to the foc's'le and descended a few steps into the rooms. They were already awash and there was no one else there. I put a leatherette windbreaker jacket on and placed the wedding ring in my pocket. At the last moment I picked a dry blanket off a bunk in case it came in handy later on." Return-ing on deck, Murphy handed the blanket to a shipmate who, like Wynne, had fled his bunk without dressing.

As the crewmen on the *Kingsbury* struggled to put a lifeboat into the water, they could not have known that the U-boat that had ended their good fortune had done so with some luck of its own. While searching for Convoy HX229, U-338—one of the eleven Gruppe Stürmer U-boats that Dönitz had ordered west-southwest to intercept the fast convoy—had ac-cidentally stumbled upon SC122 instead.

Commanded by Kapitänleutnant Manfred Kinzel, twenty-seven, U-338 had already had an auspicious beginning to this, its first combat patrol in the North Atlantic. When shipyard workers at the Nordseewerke shipyard at Emden, Germany, were preparing the U-boat for launch on April 20, 1942, someone had cut too many of the restraining lines holding the 769-ton U-boat to the slipway. Without ceremony or a crew aboard, U-338 launched itself into the Baltic, where it promptly rammed and sank a small river craft. In appreciation for the feat, the crew nicknamed their boat *Der Wilde Esel* (the Wild Donkey) and painted a bucking donkey on the conning tower. After eight months of training in the Baltic, U-338 had been certified as ready for combat and left on its initial war patrol on February 23.

Despite the excitement of its original launch, U-338's first two weeks of patrolling had been uneventful. The U-boat had operated with the wolf packs Gruppen Neuland and Ostmark during March 7–11, but Kinzel and his 51 crewmen had not made contact with any of the convoys for which those wolf packs had hunted. U-338's crew was more than ready for action, according to Oberleutnant Herbert Zeissler, Kinzel's First Watch Officer. "It was a time of ordinary routine work with men made angry by the motion of the ship, wet clothes, a tense atmosphere between technical crew and the seamen 'who did not spot the convoy quickly enough' in order to get to the attack," Zeissler said years later. The torpedomen, in particular, yearned to fire off a volley simply so that, when they reloaded the forward tubes, there would be more room in the cramped bow compartment.[10]

The day before, on March 16, Kinzel, his crew, and ten other Stürmer boats had received orders from Dönitz to be prepared to intercept HX229 during the early daylight hours of March 17. The directive had been based on BdU's estimate of where the formation would be at that time, from U-653's contact report. Visibility was twelve nautical miles under bright moonlight as U-338 prepared to intercept HX229 early the next morning—and so it was undoubtedly with some surprise when, shortly after midnight, the lookouts unexpectedly spotted a cluster of masts dead ahead. Estimating about thirty merchantmen with an escort screen, Kinzel ordered the dispatch of a convoy sighting report, and sent his crew to battle stations. In his war diary, the kapitänleutnant wrote:

0210 [CET; 0110 GMT]: Convoy in sight bearing 200 [degrees True]. Turned off and ran ahead on an easterly course to get a view of the situation. Approximately 20–30 ships, protected by destroyers ahead and on both sides. Ships go in small line ahead, formations in fours mostly.[11]

Since Kinzel had estimated he was still 120 miles to the east of the convoy sighted by Kapitänleutnant Feiler in U-653, he immediately suspected that his lookouts had located a second formation of which BdU was still unaware. He radioed Berlin, "Convoy in sight [German naval grid] square AK 8758, course 050 [degrees], speed 7 knots." Kinzel's convoy sighting message finally cleared up the confusion at U-boat Force Headquarters, which for nearly a week had misidentified HX229 as the slow convoy that Kinzel had just spotted. Now, Konteradmiral Godt concluded, "According to boat's reports there were definitely two convoys" crossing the Greenland air gap.[12]

Having transmitted the sighting report, Kinzel swung into action. The Group B-5 corvettes *Lavender* and *Pimpernel* were maneuvering ahead of the convoy but aligned with its two sides, leaving the actual front of the formation undefended, and Kinzel deftly maneuvered U-338 through this large gap in the escort screen. There was one problem: because the UZO target-bearing binoculars were damaged, Kinzel had to fire his torpedoes from "fixed angle zero"—that is, setting their gyrocompasses to have them steer straight ahead and aiming at the ships by pointing U-338's bow directly at them. At nearly point-blank range, Oberleutnant Zeissler had done just that, hitting the firing lever two times and sending a pair of warshots heading toward the target 1,500 yards off.

"We fired the first two torpedoes at the right-hand ship we could see," Kinzel recalled. "We then had to turn to port to aim the second pair of torpedoes at the lead ship of the second column." As Kinzel's first torpedo slammed into the *Kingsbury*, U-338 launched its second pair of torpedoes at a ship fast coming up from behind in the same column. After a run of just 800 meters, nearly point-blank range, one of the second pair struck amidships and fatally damaged the 5,072-ton British freighter *King Gruffydd*.

Kinzel then ordered a turn to port to bring his stern torpedo tube on line, only to find U-338 in peril. A merchantman was close to ramming the U-boat. "During the turn to port, I come within approximately 400 meters of being rammed by the first ship from the starboard inner column," he wrote in his war diary at the time. "God, the boat turns so slowly! By just 100 meters I clear the bow of a 4,000-tonner. Still, nothing whatsoever happens, the fellow sleeps unawares."

The U-boat commander and his lookouts were transfixed by the chaos from their initial two hits, Kinzel wrote in his war diary: "Ship immediately sets two red lights in the foretop, in the starboard bridge yardarm a red flashing light. Ship immediately lists so strongly that the whole upper deck can be seen. After 5 minutes . . . one third is already under water. On surfacing [later] a freighter lies burning brightly at firing location. Suddenly it cannot be seen at a distance of 7 nm [nautical miles]. Sunk!"[13]

When U-338's stern was aligned with the next target, Zeissler launched a fifth torpedo from the stern tube. Just then, a corvette came racing in from starboard, forcing U-338 to crash-dive. Kinzel and his crew did not witness the final torpedo run, but his stern shot ran all the way through Convoy SC122 and struck the 7,134-ton British freighter *Fort Cedar Lake,* seriously damaging the ship. Kinzel and his crew thought they had sunk two ships, but in fact, had fatally struck three: the *Kingsbury, King Gruffydd,* and the 7,886-ton Dutch *Alderamin,* lead vessel in Column 6 to starboard of the *Kingsbury.* As the *Fort Cedar Lake* fell behind SC122, its master, Charles L. Collings, ordered his crew to battle a large fire that had erupted when the torpedo struck. The newly built ship kept afloat but would fall prey to another U-boat eight hours later.[14]

Back on the listing *Kingsbury,* the beautiful ocean landscape that Deane Wynne had enjoyed just a few hours ago had been transformed into a scene from hell. Two other ships close by, the *Alderamin* and *King Gruffydd,* were also afire and sinking. Flames and smoke rose up from both ships in towering plumes that stretched toward the soaring Snowflake rockets. Far off on the convoy's starboard quarter the fire on the *Fort Cedar Lake* burned brightly. The *Kingsbury's* venting steam boilers continued to scream in a deafening bellow. The sharp *crack!* and chattering staccato from the untouched ships' guns shooting wildly into the night as the gunners fired at phantom U-boats added to the bedlam.

The three ships that had been sailing behind the *Kingsbury* and *King Gruffydd* in Column 5 came up fast upon them, but then veered sharply to avoid a collision. With the rescue ship *Zamalek* assigned to SC122, the merchantmen did not need to risk stopping to help the survivors from the two ships.

A splintering crash jerked Wynne's eyes away from the chaos playing out elsewhere in the convoy. The starboard lifeboat had fallen hard into the side of the listing hull, its ropes jammed in the rigging. Wynne looked around in desperation for any sign of help. There was none. He and his shipmates had only the devil's option left: to jump into the frigid waves and get clear of the *Kingsbury* before the sinking ship sucked them down to their deaths. Scarcely believing what he was doing, Wynne put on his lifejacket, climbed up on the *Kingsbury's* scant railing, and for a moment stared at the thirty-foot waves. Then he took a deep breath, and jumped.[15]

Wynne vaguely recalled the impact of hitting the water and plunging deep under the surface, but it was hard to think coherently as he rose and fell in the thirty-foot waves. "It seemed as if I would never reach the surface again. It took an eternity to rise," he noted. "I was quite surprised when I found myself bobbing on the surface of the water, gasping for breath and being thrown about by the waves. The seawater temperature seemed to be a little warmer than the air, and probably was, albeit it was still bitterly cold." As his time in the frigid Atlantic dragged on, Wynne felt the water sapping the energy out of his body, and he could hardly feel the harsh fabric of the canvas lifejacket that was keeping him alive on the tossing ocean.

Time passed slowly as Wynne continued to tread water. All around him were signs of the chaos that had descended on Convoy SC122, and he could see the crippled ships nearby as they foundered in the water. Off to the northeast, sparkling white Snowflake rockets marked the convoy as it resolutely steamed away from the scene of battle—and the torpedoed ships' survivors.

Suddenly, Wynne was carried up by a cresting wave and slammed into a hard object. It was an overturned dinghy from the *Kingsbury,* and there were two crewmen clinging to its narrow keel. Wynne lunged and grabbed a handhold, finding himself alongside the *Kingsbury's* seventy-year-old chief engineer and a young Welsh businessman who had been taking passage on his way home to England from West Africa. At that moment, Wynne realized that the long months of backbreaking work shoveling coal on the *Veni* and *Kingsbury* had paid a dividend. "I suppose I was a pretty fit eighteen years of age at the time," he recalled. "My work had put a few muscles on my normally skinny frame." Wynne and the other two men shouted encouragement to one another above the howling wind and crashing waves, but it was hard going. "Our fingers were numb with the cold as we clung to our very slender handrail," Wynne said. "Our bodies became black and blue as we were continually bashed against the boat's side with each wave. It was very tempting to let go and pass on to heaven-sent oblivion than endure much more of this, with very little prospect of being rescued." The minutes crept slowly into hours as the men clung to the capsized jolly boat, praying for a miracle.

The faintest light of dawn was slowly breaking on the eastern horizon when Wynne saw something strange. There was a shape off in the distance that he had not noticed before. As the next wave bore up the dinghy, Wynne raised himself up for a quick look. A ship! He gave the news to the others, but their expressions did not lighten. "The question was, would she see us?" he remembered thinking. "I very much doubted she could. A small upturned dinghy in twenty-to-thirty-foot waves, in the gray light of dawn. She appeared to be quite a long way off."

Wynne and his comrades did not have to wonder for long about whether they had been spotted. Suddenly the rescue ship *Zamalek* was alongside the dingy, and Wynne could hear shouts of encouragement from above. Sailors lowered a scrambling net, and Wynne desperately lunged for it with unfeeling fingers. He felt a rope going around his waist and suddenly found himself climbing up the net with the aid of the sailors hoisting the rope. There, strong arms grabbed him and pulled him aboard. Wynne gasped out his thanks to his rescuers, then turned around to help his two shipmates. They had vanished, swept under the rescue ship's hull before they could reach the boarding net. Wynne slumped down on the deck, and wept.[16]

As DEANE WYNNE had been struggling to stay alive in the icy waters of the Atlantic, Convoy HX229 had been sailing peacefully on its base course without further interruption or crisis. After the torpedo strike and massive explosion that had sunk the *Harry Luckenbach* at 0237, it appeared once more that the U-boats had broken off contact with the fast convoy.

HX229 steamed onward for two and one-half hours without a lookout spotting torpedo wakes or a distant escort firing starshells to reveal a surfaced U-boat.

Although some of its escorts had managed to rejoin the convoy by the early hours of March 17, HX229 remained woefully unprotected. Lieutenant-Commander Luther in the destroyer *Volunteer* had rejoined the convoy at 0200 after picking up the *William Eustis's* survivors. The *Volunteer* then took station astern of the formation while the destroyers *Beverley* and *Mansfield* patrolled ahead of the outside columns. The corvette *Anemone* was also returning, but since its maximum speed was only six knots faster than the convoy's rate of advance, it would take longer for the small warship to catch up. The *Pennywort,* for its part, was nowhere to be found. It had not received the convoy course change to 053 degrees and was searching for HX229 out on the previous heading of 028 degrees, which was taking the corvette farther and farther away from the merchant ships. The absence of the *Anemone* and the *Pennywort* had left huge gaps in the convoy's defensive screen—openings through which a U-boat could easily penetrate.

For Ted Schorr on the *El Mundo's* navigation bridge, the strain of watching so many convoy merchantmen burst into flames over the course of two separate U-boat attacks had been almost unbearable. This second lull would have seemed as deceptive as the first, but as the minutes slowly dragged past, then became hours, Schorr and the other crewmen on the freighter's bridge were beginning to hope the ordeal might finally be over. They did not have long to wait before realizing their mistake.

At 0456, a spread of torpedoes raced into the formation and struck the *Irénée Du Pont* and *Nariva,* the lead ships in Columns 8 and 9, and the *Southern Princess,* 500 yards directly ahead of *El Mundo* in Column 7. The entire front of the convoy went up in flames. For the third time that night, HX229 had come under attack.

Another U-boat from Gruppe Raubgraf was behind the explosions at the front of HX229. U-600, commanded by Kapitänleutnant Bernhard Zurmühlen, had been shadowing the convoy for the past four hours. Observing the thin escort screen, the thirty-four-year-old skipper got ahead of the convoy around 0430 GMT and slipped past the *Beverley* as it patrolled ahead of the convoy's starboard side. At a range of 2,800 yards,

Zurmühlen triggered a salvo of four torpedoes—one FAT G7a and three G7e electrics—at the closest ship approaching his position then swung his boat around and loosed a fifth torpedo from the stern tube. Two of the bow tube torpedoes and the stern tube shot found targets.

The men on the *Irénée Du Pont* hadn't had time to react to the latest torpedo launch. Ensign Frank Pilling was one of nine U.S. Navy officers aboard the American freighter, all of them en route to the British Isles for new duty stations. After the chaos of the past seven hours, Pilling had joined other passengers and off-duty crewmen on deck, abandoning any thoughts of sleep. The young officer stood quietly at the starboard rail watching the setting moon, gazing at the wave tops flickering in the moonlight and imagining what an enemy torpedo wake might look like. Then, in the blink of an eye, Pilling saw something quite real. "I was not surprised when we were hit, for suddenly I saw, deep under the surface, two streaks of greasy light, parallel, moving fast, coming in at an angle," Pilling said. "There was no time to shout a warning. In one instant there were the tracks, in another a great shattering crash." Two of Kapitänleutnant Zurmühlen's FATs had struck the American freighter amidships, ripping large holes in the side at Holds No. 2 and 3.

Gunner's Mate 3rd Class Bill Stilinovich was on duty aboard the *Irénée Du Pont* when U-600 attacked. Assigned to one of the eight 20-mm Oerlikon machine guns mounted on the main deck, he had just taken a brief break to get some coffee when the world seemed to end. "The first torpedo hit us with a shattering roar," he later recalled. "I started running for the main deck hatchway and the second torpedo hit. The deck shook under my feet. The 'abandon ship' order was given and I made my way to my assigned raft. The ship was beginning to settle."

Stilinovich found Ensign Pilling and four or five other crewmen struggling to release the life raft. Its release mechanism had rusted or jammed. He watched in a daze as other crewmen gave up trying to free the raft and began jumping over the side. He made it to one of the lifeboat stations and climbed aboard, but when several crewmen went to cast loose the lines, only the bowline gave way and the boat capsized, its oars and survival supplies vanishing in the heavy seas. Stilinovich and several others managed to upright the lifeboat and climb in. Ignoring the cold water in the half-flooded boat, he looked around. The sea was alight with tiny red lights affixed to the lifejackets of *Irénée Du Pont* crewmen. A ship directly to starboard at the head of the next column was also on fire and sinking.

The 8,714-ton British stores ship *Nariva* had become U-600's second victim. The Royal Mail Lines ship, with its cargo of 5,600 tons of frozen food from Argentina, was steaming in Position 1 of Column 9 when the third FAT struck it amidships. Second Officer G. D. Williams was on duty on the port bridge wing when the warhead detonated. "A huge tower of black smoke, tons of water and debris was flung into the air just forward of the bridge," he recalled. The *Nariva*'s master, Bernard Cyril Dodds, immediately stepped out of the wheelhouse to see what had happened. "I remembered the adage that what goes up must just as assuredly come down and, without ceremony, I pushed the 'old man' back into the wheelhouse," recalled Williams, "and not a second too soon, for tons of water and debris fell on the bridge with a crunch and clatter."

With the *Nariva* settling fast, Dodds ordered the other ninety-three crewmen into the lifeboats and rafts. Williams was commanding one lifeboat when he and the others saw a horrific sight. Several men who had jumped from the rail were clinging to a life raft that had been tossed overboard. Before Williams's lifeboat could get to them, the raft was caught in an inrush of water and swept into the massive, jagged hole the torpedo had blown into the side of their ship. "I can still hear the screams of the men inside the hull," Williams said years later. Then in the next instant, however, the *Nariva* took a roll and the wave of water washed back out again, setting the raft and its passengers free. Amazingly, all ninety-four of the freighter's crew survived.

Escort Group B-4 was just scrambling to respond to the renewed U-boat assault on the *Nariva* and *Irénée Du Pont* when an even larger explosion went off. Kapitänleutnant Zurmühlen could not have chosen a better target for his fourth warshot. The 12,156-ton British tanker *Southern Princess*—a converted whaling factory ship carrying 10,053 tons of heavy fuel oil and a deck cargo of locomotives and landing craft—had been steaming in Position 2 of Column 7 when a FAT struck on the starboard side right under the bridge, rupturing the fuel tank bulkheads and igniting the oil cargo inside, which burst into a towering pillar of fire. The flames cast the entire convoy under a brilliant light that appeared almost as bright as daylight.

Schorr and the other watch-standers on the *El Mundo* stared as the fiery apparition turned broadside and went dead in the water just 500 yards ahead of their ship. With the *El Mundo* still maintaining the convoy speed of 9.5 knots, the burning *Southern Princess* grew larger by the second. Captain MacKenzie barked a helm order and his ship began turning out of column to port in order to avoid a collision. The men on *El Mundo's* bridge began feeling the high temperature from the fire as they drew close to the blazing tanker. "The heat was so intense that all hands had to run to the port side of the ship where we were protected," Schorr later said. "That ship could be seen burning all night long." Ships in the next column later reported that the fire 1,000 yards away had blistered the paintwork on their hulls and superstructures.

Despite the destruction of three ships and their valuable cargo, the loss of life from U-600's attack was remarkably small. The three ships would lose only 20 out of 288 crewman, gunners, and passengers, including 14 from the *Irénée Du Pont* and 6 from the *Southern Princess*. For the most part, this relatively low casualty count was thanks to Captain Albert Hocken in the twenty-one-year-old British freighter *Tekoa*. Assigned to the last position of Column 8, Hocken rushed his 8,695-ton vessel into the inferno of the three sinking ships as his crew prepared rope ladders and cargo nets for the survivors to grab. Over the next four hours, as HX229 and its escorts disappeared over the northeast horizon, the *Tekoa's* crew retrieved 149 survivors, 55 from the *Irénée Du Pont* and all 94 from the *Southern Princess*. The destroyer *Mansfield* and corvette *Anemone*, which had finally rejoined just before U-600's attack, also rescued survivors from the torpedoed merchantmen; the corvette retrieved all 94 of *Nariva's* crew and the destroyer picked up 16 more from *Irénée Du Pont*.

As the *Tekoa* and the *Anemone* finished their rescue work under a pale sunrise, Lieutenant-Commander Hill in the *Mansfield* decided to make one final sweep of the area, in case other survivors might still be found. After searching for an hour, the *Mansfield's* lookouts spotted a half-swamped lifeboat wallowing in the waves. Inside they found nine half-conscious *Irénée Du Pont* crewmen, including Gunner's Mate Bill Stilinovich.[17]

Chapter 8

HEAVY LOSSES

It was Wednesday, March 17, and aboard the destroyer *HMS Volunteer*, Lieutenant-Commander Gordon Luther watched the sunrise with a sense of resignation. He wrote in his journal, "Dawn broke on a somewhat decimated convoy and a scattered and rather embittered escort who felt that they had been beaten by facts outside their control and by pure weight of numbers."[1]

Convoy HX229 was barely inside the western edge of the Greenland air gap and practically helpless against the U-boat threat. Maintaining its base course of 053 degrees, at dawn the convoy reached 51 degrees North 034 degrees West, a position 761 nautical miles east-northeast of St. John's, Newfoundland, 1,000 nautical miles west of Belfast, Northern Ireland, and 876 nautical miles from Reykjavik. While its position was close enough for Very-Long-Range patrol aircraft to reach the convoy and drive the U-boats underwater, none had yet to appear.

Convoy HX229 would have to wait until later in the day for any semblance of air support to arrive. Although the ships were just coming within range of the Iceland-based VLR Liberators from RAF 120 Squadron, fierce weather at Reykjavik during the night of March 16–17 had prevented the launching of any flights. A solitary VLR Liberator from 86 Squadron had just taken off from Aldergrove, Northern Ireland, ten miles west of Belfast. It was not expected to reach the convoy until later that afternoon.

Besides lacking air cover, HX229 was also down several escorts. No additional warships had arrived to reinforce Escort Group B-4, and several of its ships had fallen behind during the attacks the previous night, after attempts to rescue the crews of the torpedoed ships and salvage one of the vessels itself.

Of the five ships torpedoed on the night of March 16, only the *James Oglethorpe* was still manned and under way, its crew trying to reach safety back in Newfoundland—but there had still seemed to be a chance that one of the torpedoed ships could be saved. The tanker *Southern Princess* had capsized after burning all night, but the abandoned freighters *Irénée Du Pont* and *Nariva* were still afloat. Although the *Nariva* had a massive hole in its side, was heavily down at the bows, and a small fire still burned on its foc's'le, Lieutenant-Commander Patrick King on the corvette *HMS Anemone* thought the *Nariva* might be capable of getting under way again. After the *Anemone*, the freighter *Tekoa*, and the destroyer *HMS Mansfield* had finished retrieving the 258 survivors from the three ships, King and his crew on the corvette remained behind as the *Mansfield* and *Tekoa* sailed off to rejoin HX229.

After a brief discussion with King aboard the *Anemone*, the *Nariva*'s Master Bernard C. Dodds, Second Officer G. D. Williams, and Second Engineer D. Brophy volunteered to reboard their Royal Mail Lines vessel to determine its seaworthiness. Taking one of the corvette's dinghies, they rowed through a debris field of frozen lamb and mutton carcasses that had floated out through the hole the torpedo had blown in the side of the ship. Climbing back aboard the *Nariva*, Dodds went up to the bridge while Brophy and Williams climbed down into the engine room. They quickly realized reviving the ship was impossible. Unattended all night, the steam boilers had consumed all of the feed water inside, allowing the furnace crowns to become red-hot. It would take hours to let the machinery cool, reload water, and bring the boilers back up to pressure—during which time the ship would remain a sitting duck for the first U-boat that happened along.

Dodds, Williams, and Brophy decided that the risks of salvaging the *Nariva* outweighed the benefits. After retrieving some personal possessions, they got back into the corvette's dinghy and were rowing back to the *Anemone* when, to their horror, the corvette suddenly went to full power and raced away.

The destroyer *HMS Volunteer* temporarily led the undermanned Escort Group B-4 to escort Convoy HX229.
National Archives and Records Administration

While Dodds and his men had been inspecting the *Nariva,* the Gruppe Raubgraf boat U-91 and Gruppe Stürmer boat U-616 had come upon the abandoned vessels from HX229. Oberleutnant Siegfried Koitschka, twenty-five, had so far had a frustrating time on U-616's first war patrol. He had become a seasoned submariner after serving under U-boat ace Kapitänleutnant Erich Topp in U-552 and been present for Topp's notorious sinking of the destroyer *USS Reuben James,* killing 115 of its 160-man crew. But since becoming U-616's second commanding officer upon its commissioning six months ago, Koitschka had yet to bring down a ship of his own. The previous night, while attempting to maneuver against HX229, he had fired four G7e torpedoes at the zigzagging destroyer *HMS Beverley,* but all had missed and the English crewmen never even knew they had come under attack. Now, Koitschka found himself just 400 yards from an enemy corvette and a damaged freighter that it was guarding. At this point-blank range, the young U-boat skipper felt he could not miss.

Koitschka ordered the crew of U-616 to set the stern tube's G7e electric torpedo to three meters depth and fired it at slow speed at the escort ship guarding the freighter. Fortunately for the *Anemone,* its lookouts were fully alert and spotted the incoming torpedo. King ordered flank speed ahead, the torpedo passed by less than 100 feet away, and the *Anemone* went sprinting back down its track searching for the U-boat. A vexed Oberleutnant Koitschka had already rushed U-616 into the cellar, however, and the *Anemone* could not detect it on Asdic. Returning to retrieve its dinghy and the three *Nariva* officers, King found that the destroyer *Mansfield* had rejoined the scene. The two escorts tried to sink the *Nariva* and the *Irénée Du Pont* by gunfire and then depth charges thrown by K-gun under each vessel, but the two freighters stubbornly refused to go under. Finally, the *Mansfield* departed once again, and the *Anemone* also set off for HX229, which by now was sixty miles away.

It would take King and his *Anemone* crew nearly eleven hours to rejoin HX229. The corvette would sight a surfaced U-boat at midday and spend nearly an hour unsuccessfully trying to locate and destroy it, leaving Escort Group B-4 undermanned for even longer. While the *Anemone* struggled to catch up with HX229, its departure from the *Nariva* also allowed U-616 to resurface for another try against the abandoned merchantman. Koitschka fired another torpedo at the ship but missed again. Thoroughly disgusted, U-616's skipper turned the boat back on course to chase after HX229. Shortly thereafter, Kapitänleutnant Walkerling in U-91 would find the two abandoned wrecks and finish them off with a torpedo apiece, adding two vessels and 14,389 tons of shipping to his record.[2]

Back at HX229, Commodore Mayall was taking steps to safeguard the convoy while it awaited the rest of its escorts and the arrival of air support. After the carnage of the night surface attacks, Commodore Mayall reorganized the formation during the morning of March 17. The loss of eight merchantmen had created gaps in six of the convoy's eleven columns, so the commodore shrank the number of columns down to nine. Mayall assigned the 5,158-ton Dutchman *Terkoelei,* which had twice the night before ignored his orders to retrieve survivors from torpedoed ships in its column, to become lead ship in Column 9 on the starboard flank, the new coffin corner. He also ordered the 7,252-ton freighter *Coracero* to move from the second position in Column 8 to serve as lead ship, replacing the *Nariva*.[3]

HX229 continued on its base course of 053 degrees for the next five hours without spotting a single U-boat. The sea had calmed, and waves of only six feet gave lookouts a visibility range of about eight miles, although the skies were cloudy. Despite the lull in U-boat activity, on the lead escort ship *Volunteer*, Lieutenant-Commander Luther faced one more challenge. Because the destroyer had limited communications capability, its radio operators could either work the HF/DF direction-finding equipment—the only set that the escort group had—to search for U-boat transmissions or use it to track the homing beacons on any VLR Liberators searching for the convoy on their long flights from land. They could not perform both tasks at once. Luther opted to use the HF/DF equipment to scan for the approach of air support. His decision would contribute to the loss of two more merchantmen.[4]

While HX229 had consolidated its remaining ships, the Germans had also regrouped. After using his last torpedoes to sink the Norwegian *Elin K.* the previous night, Oberleutnant Hans-Joachim Bertelsmann in U-603 was still shadowing the battered formation. As the morning went on, his homing signals brought up more U-boats. Many were from the two new wolf packs, Stürmer and Dränger. The Gruppe Raubgraf boats had begun breaking off contact because of low fuel or torpedoes and were heading back to France, and the first of twenty-nine U-boats assigned to the two other U-boat formations were now coming up on HX229. Two of the Stürmer boats spent the morning carefully maneuvering to get ahead of the convoy for a dangerous and risky daylight submerged attack.[5]

U-384 and U-631 were both relatively new U-boats that had had nearly identical experiences in the Battle of the Atlantic thus far. They had been commissioned two days apart in 1942 and were commanded by relatively young officers—Oberleutnant Hans-Achim von Rosenberg-Gruszcynski, twenty-five, and Oberleutnant Jürgen Krüger, twenty-four. As with all U-boats assigned to the Atlantic, on their initial deployment, they had left the training base on the Baltic a week apart in December 1942 for their first combat patrols, following a circuitous route that skirted the coast of Norway before entering the North Atlantic between the Faroes and Iceland. Once reaching the Greenland air gap, in early January 1943, the two U-boats participated in the same wolf pack and both sank their first ships. After a month at sea, U-384 arrived at its permanent base at La Pallice on February 2, and U-631 reached its new base at Brest the following day. After four weeks in port for maintenance and crew leave, they both left on patrol on March 3 and joined the seventeen other boats assigned to Gruppe Stürmer eleven days later. Now they were stalking HX229.[6]

At 1305 on March 17, torpedoes from the U-384 and U-631 struck the freighters *Coracero* and *Terkoelei* in the lead of Columns 8 and 9 at nearly the same instant. Third Officer R. McRae was on the bridge of the *Coracero* when a tremendous explosion rocked the *Terkoelei* just 1,000 yards to starboard. All he could see of the freighter was "a cloud of smoke, spray and pieces, nothing solid." Running out onto the bridge wing, McRae spotted a torpedo wake heading for the *Coracero,* and barked, "Hard-a-starboard!" to the helmsman. The 7,252-ton British freighter began swinging to the right as the torpedo converged. "It was a tense moment as our bow swung and covered the torpedo track and, for a fraction of a second, everything stopped—thoughts, blood, heartbeat—and then the track emerged on the port side," McRae recalled after the war. "We had made it." Ordering the freighter back on course, McRae reached for the lanyard to the ship's siren to sound six short blasts, the signal warning the convoy of a torpedo approaching from starboard. Before he could yank the lanyard for the third time, another torpedo slammed into his ship on the starboard side.

While McRae survived the attack, not all were so lucky. Five of the *Coracero's* crew and thirty-six from the *Terkoelei* perished. After the massive first explosion that McRae had witnessed from the bridge of the *Coracero,* the Dutch freighter sank rapidly and capsized, crushing several manned lifeboats that had not gotten clear in time. Lieutenant-Commander Luther on the *Volunteer* ordered the destroyer *Mansfield,* which had only just rejoined the convoy an hour earlier, to recover the survivors. As the *Volunteer* raced back to join the destroyer HMS *Beverley* around HX229, Lieutenant-Commander Hill and the *Mansfield's* crew went to work. They spent several hours rescuing 52 crewmen from the British ship and 55 from the Dutchman, for a total of 126 survivors including the 19 rescued from the *Irénée Du Pont* eight hours earlier. For the moment, the attacks went unavenged; the *Volunteer* and *Mansfield* had both swept the convoy flank searching for the U-boats immediately after the explosions, but von Rosenberg-Gruszcynski in U-384 and Krüger in U-631 both managed to escape undetected.[7]

The brazen daylight attack by the two U-boats put everyone's nerves on edge, and finally prompted Luther to call for help. Painfully aware that Escort Group B-4 was too weak to mount an effective defense, Luther penned an almost despairing entry in his official report: "With attacks by day and night and the escorts performing the dual role of escorting and rescue work, there was little hope of saving more than a fraction of the convoy." Several minutes later, a message from the *Volunteer* came clattering out of the teleprinter at Western Approaches Command in Liverpool.

HX229 ATTACKED, TWO SHIPS TORPEDOED. REQUEST EARLY REINFORCEMENT OF ESCORT. 51:45 NORTH, 032:36 WEST. HAVE BEVERLEY AND MANSFIELD IN COMPANY, PENNY-WORT AND ANEMONE OVERTAKING ASTERN. PERSISTENT ATTACKS WILL NOT PERMIT FUELING AND SITUATION IS BECOMING CRITICAL. D/F AND SIGHTING INDICATES MANY U-BOATS IN CONTACT.[8]

Without more warships to shore up his overstretched escort group, Luther would simply not be able to protect HX229, but there was essentially nothing more that Admiral Horton or his staff at Derby House could do. What support ships were available were already heading toward the convoy. At 1300 on March 17, Commander Day on the *Highlander* was B-4's best hope for naval reinforcement. Day was steaming at a speed of seventeen knots to catch up with his escort group but was still 287 nautical miles behind the convoy and it would not be until March 18 that the destroyer could rejoin. The slower corvettes *Abelia* and *Sherbrooke* would be even later. Luther's only hope was that a VLR Liberator might still arrive later that afternoon.

There was one other group of warships steaming in the direction of HX229, but they were destined for a different convoy. Even if Horton had been willing to send the Iceland-based escorts *Ingham* and *Babbitt* to the rescue of HX229 instead of SC122, the warships were still over 700 miles north-northeast of the fast convoy and were traveling at a reduced speed of eight knots as they battled nearly head-on into the thirty-foot waves of a Force 10 gale blowing from the southwest. When Ensign John M. Waters took over the watch on the *Ingham*'s heaving bridge at 2000, the storm had abated slightly and the cutter was able to increase speed to fifteen knots, but SC122 was still at least forty hours away. Meanwhile, the B-4 destroyer *Vimy* remained in Reykjavik as its crew hurried to complete repairs to the ship's storm damage. As with the delayed support for HX229, help from Iceland would be slow to arrive for SC122.[9]

WHEN THE SUN CAME UP on Wednesday, March 17, Convoy SC122 was in somewhat better shape than its counterpart 110 miles to the west-southwest. All but two of Escort Group B-5's eight warships were present in the convoy screen, and those two missing escorts were hurrying to catch up. The corvette *Godetia* was steaming back to rejoin after its rescue of the crew from the foundered ASW trawler *Campobello*, while the corvette *Saxifrage* and rescue ship *Zamalek*, having stopped to pick up the survivors of U-338's rampage, were farther astern. Thirty-seven of the forty-nine survivors from the *Alderamin* were crammed aboard the tiny corvette, while 131 survivors from the *Kingsbury, King Gruffydd, Alderamin,* and *Fort Cedar Lake* tried to find sitting room in the 1,527-ton rescue ship.

In the crowded lower decks of the *Zamalek*, fireman Deane Wynne wearily counted his blessings. After his rescue from the *Kingsbury* sinking, he and the other survivors had been herded down into the ship's sick bay, where a Royal Navy doctor gave him a quick checkup and a generous mug of rum. Another crewman handed Wynne a blanket, since he had come on board wearing only his underpants and a life jacket. Aching and bruised from clinging for hours to the overturned dinghy and being slammed against its wooden hull, the young merchant sailor found a spot of deck in a crowded corridor and tried to make himself comfortable. "This was to be my perch for another five days before we got into port," Wynne later said. Eventually, a crewman handed Wynne some clothes taken from another merchant sailor who had died after being brought on-board, and he was later able to go out on deck during the day for a breath of fresh air.[10]

By daylight on St. Patrick's Day some much-needed good news came for Commander Boyle, Escort Group B-5, and Convoy SC122: they were finally going to receive air support. At midnight, Coastal Command had launched an RAF 86 Squadron VLR Liberator from Aldergrove, Northern

Ireland, which would rendezvous with the slow convoy even earlier than the plane that Coastal Command had sent to find HX229.

Piloted by Australian Flying Officer Cyril Burcher and co-pilot Sergeant Jack Lloyd, a New Zealander, the VLR Liberator M/86 and its seven-man crew had been in the air for nearly eight hours when they made radio contact with Commander Boyle's radio operator. The aircraft transmitted homing beacon signals to the ship's HF/DF crew, who in turn radioed back the correct approach course to the rendezvous. Around 0600 local (0800 GMT), Burcher and Lloyd spotted a plume of smoke on the horizon up ahead. They began descending.

The VLR Liberator's timing was fortuitous, for SC122 had also failed to evade the U-boats during the night. Three from Gruppe Stürmer, including Kapitänleutnant Kinzel's U-338, were still in firm contact with the formation. Having reloaded his torpedo tubes, Kinzel was attempting to bypass the convoy out of visual sight from the escorts' masthead lookouts, so as to get ahead and set up for a daylight submerged attack. Also trailing SC122 was U-439, on its third patrol since being commissioned on December 20, 1941. This was the first operation for its new commander, twenty-five-year-old Oberleutnant Helmut von Tippelskirch. He had been up on the crowded bridge with a watch officer and four lookouts just after sunrise when one of them detected smoke on the horizon. Von Tippelskirch ordered the boat to get closer and soon identified the contact as a large freighter, apparently abandoned by its crew, on fire and down by the bows. It was the *Fort Cedar Lake,* which U-338 had torpedoed the day before. That U-boat had been forced underwater after firing a spread of five torpedoes—one of which had struck the British merchantman—and its commander had been unaware that the weapon had impacted. Now, a second U-boat was going to finish the job.

But before Tippelskirch could issue orders to torpedo the derelict freighter, a lookout cried out, "Aircraft—dead ahead!" Burcher and Lloyd had spotted U-439. Stunned at the enemy aircraft's appearance so far out in the Atlantic, von Tippelskirch shouted the order for a crash dive and leaped down the hatch with the rest of the bridge watch. U-439 quickly submerged as the VLR Liberator came roaring in, its bomb bay doors open. Burcher and Lloyd dropped four depth charges on the U-boat's swirling wake and their detonations threw up a towering column of water.

The Liberator circled the area while its pilots and five other aircrewmen stared hungrily at the churning mass of ocean for signs of debris or an oil slick; it was the first U-boat they had ever seen, much less attacked. Unfortunately for them, U-439 had made it safely into the cellar. After several more orbits, the pilots broke off the attack and headed for the convoy twenty miles away. Later that morning, the third U-boat following SC122, the eight-month-old U-665, commanded by Oberleutnant sur See Hans-Jürgen Haupt, would finish off the *Fort Cedar Lake*. It was the U-boat's first kill.[11]

The arrival of M/86 over SC122 symbolized a rare glimmer of good news for the convoys braving the Greenland air gap. Several weeks earlier, Air Vice Marshall Sir John Slessor at Coastal Command had been able to obtain more VLR Liberators, and assigned them to RAF 86 Squadron. On February 16, the unit mounted its first North Atlantic Patrol from its new base at Aldergrove, and were ready when the battle for Convoys SC122 and HX229 erupted. Along with the twelve aircraft assigned to 120 Squadron, Slessor now had twenty-three VLR Liberators, although only fourteen were in flying condition on March 17. The bad news was that this number was still too small to close the air gap completely.

When Burcher and Lloyd finally found SC122 at 0650 local time on March 17, it was the first occasion that anyone in the convoy had glimpsed a friendly aircraft since the U-boat attacks had begun over a day before. Commander Boyle immediately took advantage of the Liberator's presence, requesting that the pilots mount a Cobra search, patrolling ten miles out on each flank and ahead of the formation. On its first sweep, the aircrew sighted a second U-boat and attacked. It was U-338, still trying to get ahead of SC122. Kapitänleutnant Kinzel and his lookouts spotted the incoming bomber at 0920 local and crash-dived. The aircrew reported an oil slick after dropping its last two depth charges, but this was a ruse by the U-boat crew to bluff their attackers. Even though it was now out of depth charges, M/86 continued to patrol around the convoy for three hours in an attempt to force under any other U-boats in the vicinity. Finally, Burcher radioed Boyle that he had to break off for the seven-hour return leg to Northern Ireland.

Although they had made no kills, the bomber crew's effort had provided protection for SC122 during most of the morning. Boyle had received a message from Liverpool that a second VLR Liberator from Aldergrove was scheduled to reach the convoy in early afternoon. This gave Boyle cautious optimism that the day would pass without further incident, but he was wrong. Both U-666 and U-338 had to stay submerged until M/86 was gone, but around midday both resurfaced and resumed their hunt.[12]

News that SC122 had aerial cover had rocketed across the Atlantic, from British authorities in Liverpool to the COMINCH Combat Intelligence Center at Main Navy in Washington, D.C., but the Germans got the word nearly as fast. B-dienst code breakers failed to intercept M/86's report of the attack on U-439 transmitted at 0935, but when Burcher and his crew attacked U-338 forty-one minutes later, the German naval code breakers intercepted and decrypted the contact message from M/86 in less than two hours, immediately routing the clear text to BdU Operations in Berlin. There, Grossadmiral Dönitz and Konteradmiral Godt, along with Kapitän zur See Bonatz, the chief of the B-dienst code breakers, doubtlessly read the signal with dismay:

17/1035 [0935 GMT] 52:23N 045W. Submerging U-boat [Course] 200 [Speed] 8 knots.[13]

On just the second day of the attack against SC122, the U-boats were now operating under the Allied air umbrella. But the wolf packs would still have ample opportunities to attack, for protection for the slow convoy would be far from complete.

The sporadic appearance of coastal aircraft was simply not enough to discourage all the U-boats still swarming around the eastbound convoys, which were still only halfway through their Atlantic crossing. Shortly before noon local time, Convoy SC122 reached 52:50N 030:35W, a spot in the North Atlantic almost exactly halfway between St. John's, Newfoundland and the North Channel between Ireland and the United Kingdom. A second VLR Liberator, G/120, was en route from Aldergrove to rendezvous with the convoy, having left Northern Ireland nearly seven hours earlier—but at 1136 local, it sighted a surfaced U-boat about ten miles off the convoy's port beam and ran in for an unsuccessful depth-charge attack. However, in the 150-minute gap between the departure of M/86 and the time when G/120 arrived overhead of SC122, another U-boat had struck the slow convoy.

Capitalizing on the intermittent air coverage, U-338 had maneuvered ahead of SC122. At 1152 local (1352 GMT), Kapitänleutnant Kinzel commenced his planned assault at periscope depth. Using the attack periscope to obtain a fix on the convoy, he ordered Oberleutnant Zeissler to fire a spread of four G7e torpedoes from 2,300 yards off.

Navigators on the forty-one merchant ships had just stepped out on the navigating bridge wings with their sextants to take the noon sun shot as part of the regular ship's routine, when a large explosion rocked the lead ship in the convoy's second column. One of U-338's torpedoes had slammed into the port side of the 4,071-ton Panamanian freighter *Granville*, flooding the engine room and killing thirteen crewmen and Naval Armed Guard gunners. The twenty-year-old vessel snapped in half within two minutes and sank quickly afterward, leaving thirty-five survivors awash in several lifeboats and rafts. Fast evasive action by the master of the 5,745-ton Dutch freighter *Parkhaven* thwarted a second loss, and U-338's second and third G7e torpedoes narrowly missed the thirteen-year-old merchantman as its helmsman successfully turned away from the incoming torpedoes. Kinzel's other three torpedoes all missed their intended target.

The corvette *Godetia* and American destroyer *Upshur* raced over to locate and attack the U-boat, but once again the wily Kinzel had escaped. The crew of U-338 would have to celebrate the fourth sinking of their patrol while hiding in the cellar; the *Godetia* and *Upshur* clung to intermittent Asdic signals and held the U-boat down for four hours, allowing SC122 to slip over the horizon. The respite, however, was all too brief.[14]

SC122's torment would resume at nightfall. During the morning and afternoon, Coastal Command sent five VLR Liberators to aid SC122, and despite the poor weather that frequently blocked sight of the convoy's ships, the aircrews harassed and drove off numerous U-boats. The surface escorts were active as well, shepherding the main body as Commodore Mayall ordered an emergency course change of forty-five degrees to starboard at 1405 hours to throw off any submerged U-boats nearby. Meanwhile, the destroyers *Havelock* and *Upshur* and the frigate *Swale* pursued several U-boats in contact with SC122 as the HF/DF operators intercepted bearings from the German radio transmissions to BdU.[15]

At sunset, the weather began deteriorating around SC122, making defense more difficult. Though nothing like the North Atlantic in a full-scale winter storm, the seas were becoming rougher, the five-foot waves flecked with white tops pushed by the strengthening winds, and frequent snow squalls temporarily reduced visibility to less than a mile. Commander Boyle assigned the seven available ships of the escort group to night stations, with those warships on the convoy flanks zigzagging about two nautical miles out from the formation. Boyle himself positioned the *Havelock* about three nautical miles ahead of the convoy. The ships held station easily despite the weather, but their lookouts would have a hard time spotting the stubby superstructure of an approaching U-boat.

U-305 was one of the few Gruppe Stürmer boats that had remained in contact with Convoy SC122 during the day on March 17. Another U-boat on its first war patrol, it had left its training base at Kiel on February 27 and joined Gruppe Stürmer. Twenty-six-year-old U-boat skipper Kapitänleutnant Rudolf Bahr and his fifty crewmen were avidly anticipating their first combat action, but Bahr patiently waited for the opportunity to attack. By 2009 local time (2209 GMT), Bahr maneuvered ahead and to starboard of the merchant ships, then slowed to let the convoy come within torpedo range. Carefully watching the zigzagging escort ships *Swale* and *Pimpernel* draw near, Bahr held U-305 on a course of 310 degrees. At 2204, Leutnant zur See Johannes-Hermann Sander, Bahr's 1WO, transmitted the firing data from his UZO binoculars that would aim torpedoes toward the 7,092-ton British steamer *Empire Morn* and 5,234-ton Greek freighter *Carras* in the lead and second positions in Column 13.

Only two minutes after U-305 obtained its firing fix on the two merchantmen in SC122, the radar operator on the *Pimpernel* detected a bright blip indicating a surfaced U-boat close by. Lieutenant Hugh D. Hayes ordered the corvette to flank speed on an interception course, transmitted an Aldis lamp message to the *Havelock*, "U-boat in sight to starboard," and radioed Boyle the same alarm. But it was too late.

On U-305's bridge, Sander pressed the firing lever, and a pair of G7e torpedoes rushed out from the bow tubes toward the massed civilian ships less than a nautical mile away. A minute later, he fired a second salvo, but one of the two torpedoes jammed in the tube. Sander and the lookouts cleared the bridge in a rush, and Bahr sent U-305 hurtling down into the cellar. The *Pimpernel* and *Swale* scoured the area but could not get an Asdic signal on the submerged boat.

Sander had overestimated the convoy's speed, and U-305's three torpedoes raced into the convoy but missed their intended targets. Still, the angle of the shot was in the attackers' favor, and after three minutes and forty-seven seconds, the U-boat's crew felt a dull shock wave as one torpedo struck a merchantman's hull. Eighty seconds after that came a second rumble from another ship.

At 2014 local (2214 GMT), Bahr's first torpedo slammed into the starboard side of the 8,789-ton British refrigerated stores ship *Port Auckland* at the engine room. The explosion killed 8 of the 118 crewmen on the ship, which was carrying 7,000 tons of frozen produce and 1,000 tons of general cargo, and the merchantman began to settle rapidly. Master Arthur E. Fishwick efficiently fired off two white distress rockets and ordered the remaining 109 crewmen, gunners, and passengers to the lifeboats.

U-338's second, smaller victim had a harder fate than the *Port Auckland*'s. The 4,256-ton British freighter *Zouave* was steaming in Position 84, the fourth ship in Column 8—behind and to the port of the *Port Auckland,* in Position 93—when Bahr's second torpedo struck on its starboard side, ripping a giant breach in cargo hold 4. The weight of the ship's 7,100-ton cargo of iron ore carried it under in just five minutes. Thirteen of its forty-three-man crew perished. The survivors from the *Zouave* and the *Port Auckland* huddled in overcrowded lifeboats as the seas heaved them up wave crests that now exceeded twenty feet.

The *Zouave* sinking brought a few minutes of terror for U-305's crew, who were now passing several hundred feet under the massed merchant ships. In a postwar interview, Fähnrich zur See (Midshipman) Wolfgang Jacobsen recalled that as U-305 skulked several hundred feet beneath SC122, "One of the ships we had hit sank almost at once and we could hear the boilers blowing up under water. We had the feeling that it was coming down all around us."

Commander Boyle ordered Lieutenant Maurice A. F. Larose in the corvette *Godetia* to rescue the survivors from the two stricken ships. While this was going on, a new blast rocked the corvette. Bahr in U-305 had surfaced nearby and launched a G7e from his stern tube at the helpless *Port Auckland,* which now lay drifting and on fire. The torpedo struck the already crippled ship, opening up a second hole but failing to send it under. Larose ordered the corvette to flank speed to give chase, but Bahr crash-dived and escaped yet again. The *Godetia* returned to the wreck and pulled the last sixty-eight survivors on board.

U-305 was not the only U-boat being harried by Escort Group B-5 in the evening of March 17. At around 1944 local time (2144 GMT), as U-305 had been closing in to attack SC122, Lieutenant Leonard G. Pilcher in the corvette *Lavender* had picked up a radar contact on the convoy's port beam. The corvette had raced out to attack. Sighting the U-boat as it crash-dived, Pilcher had ordered his four-inch gun to begin firing, and the depth-charge crews had stood to their gear. They had dropped two patterns of depth charges, the second of which had caused an oil slick to rise to the surface. Down below, U-338's crew desperately worked to plug several leaks that threatened to sink their boat, and the aggressive Kapitänleutnant Kinzel was forced to temporarily withdraw from the battle.

After stanching the leaks from the depth-charge attack on U-338, Kinzel once more maneuvered his boat to close with the convoy. But when he ordered a short contact message sent to BdU Operations at midnight, the HF/DF operator on the destroyer *Havelock* got a clear bearing on his signal. Boyle sped toward the surfaced U-boat. Because of the turbulent waves, the destroyer's radar could not find U-338 in the surface clutter; Kinzel's lookouts, however, saw the incoming destroyer and he ordered yet another crash dive.

After SC122 vanished into the new storm, Kinzel resurfaced an hour later and came upon the wreck of the *Port Auckland,* which U-305 had already torpedoed twice. Kinzel launched a G7e, but the weapon passed under the hulk as it pitched and rolled in the thirty-foot waves. It didn't matter. Several minutes later, U-338's lookouts saw the ship suddenly settle by the stern, the bow rising steeply, then vanish. The U-boat crew listened to the muted thunder as its bulkheads gave way, allowing its heavy boilers and cargo to tear free in a mêlée of sound as the stricken ship plummeted to the seabed far below. Kapitänleutnant Kinzel and his men did not get the chance to add a fifth Allied merchant ship to their already impressive score.[16]

WHILE SC122 WAS TAKING A BEATING ninety nautical miles ahead of HX229, the rest of the day and that night of March 17 passed without any more sinkings for the fast convoy. Despite the grim losses of the previous twenty hours and the near certainty among the weary Escort Group B-4 crewmen that the onset of darkness would bring yet more attacks, the convoy ended up enjoying over twenty-four hours of peaceful sailing. In fact, one of the escorts had finally gotten a good lick in against Gruppe Stürmer.

The destroyer *Beverley* had taken on two U-boats at once, and severely mauled one. While the *Mansfield* and *Volunteer* had been responding to the *Terkoelei* and *Coracero* sinkings just after 1300 on March 17, Lieutenant-Commander Rodney A. Price on the *Beverley* spotted two more U-boats on the surface out in front of the convoy. Rushing out ahead of the merchantmen, the former American "four-stack" destroyer forced both U-boats to crash-dive and pounced on one of them. For the next two and a half hours, the *Beverley* pounded the Type IXC40 U-530 with a series of deliberate depth-charge attacks. Kapitänleutnant Kurt Lange and his fifty-one-man crew clung to the bulkheads and equipment as the explosives detonated close by. The blasts knocked out the U-boat's lighting, caused flooding in the torpedo compartment, and ruptured storage containers between the pressure hull and outer deck. The weight from the inrushing seawater caused the U-boat to plunge to nearly 780 feet, perilously close to crush depth. Lieutenant-Commander Price then attempted the coup de grâce with a 1,000-pound Mark X depth charge, which plummeted toward the enemy but failed to detonate. Price reluctantly turned back toward HX229 while Lange's crew, huddling in ankledeep water in the crippled U-530, began assessing the damage. Although failing to kill the enemy, Price and his crew had knocked U-530 out of its first battle and had driven off several more boats that subsequently abandoned the fight.

HX229's second piece of good luck occurred in late afternoon of March 17, when the first of two VLR Liberators finally arrived overhead. A strong storm at Reykjavik earlier that morning had forced the cancellation of the day's first two Liberator patrols—one to each convoy. However, Coastal Command's 15 Group had ordered a pair of 86 Squadron aircraft from the RAF airbase at Aldergrove to assist the two convoys. But SC122's aircraft failed to locate the slow convoy and found HX229 instead, offering brief air cover while Commander Boyle attempted to signal SC122's location to the aircrew. Then at 1908 GMT, the VLR aircraft J/120 reached HX229, bringing additional relief to the exhausted merchant sailors and escort crews.

The second Liberator that joined HX229 had an experienced crew, and Lieutenant-Commander Luther immediately put them to work. Commanded by RAF Flying Officer S. E. "Red" Esler, a veteran of thirty-one previous maritime patrols, the Liberator's seven-man crew had already attacked seven U-boats and had at least one confirmed kill. Luther on the *Volunteer* directed Esler and his men to conduct a Viper patrol, circling the merchant ships at the maximum range that kept the convoy in sight from the aircraft. During the next hour, J/120 spotted no less than five U-boats on the surface and attacked the first one, the U-221, commanded by twenty-seven-year-old Oberleutnant zur See Hans-Hartwig Trojer.

Trojer was a veteran U-boat officer who had already seen a lot of combat. A former crewmate of Radioman Martin Beisheim on U-67, where he had served as 2WO for six months in 1941, he had been commander of U-221 since its commissioning ten months earlier on May 9, 1942. Under his command, U-221 in three patrols so far had sunk seven ships plus eleven landing craft cargo for a total of 42,417 tons of Allied shipping. Trojer had also scored an unfortunate first on his previous patrol when U-221 became the first U-boat to sink another U-boat by accident. During an attempted attack on Convoy HX217 by two wolf packs comprising twenty-one U-boats, U-221 collided with and sank U-254, killing all but four of its forty-five-man crew. Upon Trojer's return to St. Nazaire, Grossadmiral Dönitz had exonerated him of any wrongdoing. "Generally speaking, it's not practical to have more than thirteen to fifteen U-boats on a single convoy," the admiral explained.[17]

The sinking of U-254 was not the only eyebrow-raising incident on U-221's wartime record: after hitting two ammunition ships—the 6,565-ton freighter *Andrea Luckenbach* and 5,412-ton *Tucurinca*—from Convoy HX228 just the week before, Trojer and his crew had nearly perished themselves. "Fired two torpedoes at two large, overlapping merchant ships," Trojer wrote in his war diary for March 10. "First torpedo hit. Ship disintegrated completely in flames and a cast cloud of smoke. . . . Shortly afterwards scored another hit on a freighter, which also exploded. From bows to bridge the ship was under water. Heavy debris crashed against my periscope, which now became difficult to turn. The whole boat re-echoed with bangs and crashes. . . . The noise inside the boat was terrific. It felt as though we were being hit by a stream of shells." Trojer and his crew were badly shaken up, but U-221 remained in the fight.[18]

Even though VLR Liberator J/120 had dropped all eight of its depth charges in the initial attacks on U-221 and a second U-boat, Esler and his crew continued to patrol the outer perimeter of HX229, swooping in to attack the enemy with their Hispano cannons and forward-firing machine guns while illuminating the U-boats' positions with marker flares. Finally, when the aircraft had become precariously low on fuel, Esler flew back to the convoy and sent a signal reporting six U-boats in sight twenty-five miles astern of the formation. He ended the message with the two-word phrase, "I go," which confirmed the aircraft had to break off patrol be-cause it had reached the limit of its fuel endurance. The *Volunteer*'s signal-man, however, erroneously deciphered the signal with the wrong distance, and handed Lieutenant-Commander Luther the message.

SIX HEARSES IN SIGHT BEARING 180 DEGREES FIVE MILES.
I GO.

Esler's garbled message caused a near-panic attack among the men on the bridge of the *Volunteer,* but subsequent HF/DF monitoring cleared up the mistake. In fact, the convoy's situation at sunset on March 17 had actually improved dramatically. The aggressive response by *HMS Beverley* in attacking U-530, along with J/120's active Viper patrol around the merchantmen, had driven off most of the U-boat swarm. HX229 would sail on its base course of 053 degrees for the rest of the night without incident.[19]

The Liberators' appearance had boosted the merchant captains' morale, but the earlier daylight attacks that had destroyed the *Terkoelei* and *Coracero* had badly shaken the resolve of several of HX229's civilian mas-ters. Aboard the 6,361-ton British freighter *City of Agra,* carrying a cargo of ammunition and general supplies, nerves were especially frayed. The *City of Agra* was the lead ship in Column 7 when U-384 and U-631 struck, and after the attacks, Captain Frank Nancollis, the ship's master, flashed Commodore Mayall a message: his ship could make a top speed of fourteen knots, five more than the convoy's current rate of advance. He requested permission to leave HX229 and proceed independently to the North Channel. On the *Abraham Lincoln*, Mayall dispatched a curt reply: "Request denied." Over in Position 23, Captain Borden on the American freighter *Mathew Luckenbach* was thinking the same thing as Captain Nancollis. Unlike Nancollis, however, Borden refrained from signaling his intentions to the convoy's commodore. He, too, had had enough of Convoy HX229 and its depleted escort group, and planned to do something about it.[20]

Chapter 9

CRISIS IN THE
NORTH ATLANTIC

D awn broke on Thursday, March 18, to find both Convoys SC122 and HX229 trapped in yet another winter gale. This time, however, the crewmen, gunners, and escort sailors welcomed the pounding waves, spraying sleet, and snow squalls, for they cloaked the vulnerable merchantmen from U-boat lookouts. In Berlin, Grossadmiral Dönitz and his sleep-deprived operations officers continued to paw through the sheaf of contact messages and torpedo-firing reports that had come in via naval Enigma over the past twenty-four hours. They knew that the convoy's air support posed as much of a challenge to their U-boats as did the storm. In the daily war diary, Konteradmiral Godt acknowledged that hunting the convoy was becoming more dangerous due to the increasing presence of VLR Liberators. "The fact that contact was lost with both sections in spite of the many boats is due to the very strong air activity by day on the 17th," Godt wrote. "Several boats were bombed and probably lagged farther and farther astern owing to constant air patrol. Radio Intelligence received eight U-boat sightings on that day."

Despite the new threat from the air, Dönitz had no intention of calling off the twin attacks on HX229 and SC122 as long as some of his boats could still close in for the kill. While twelve boats from the three wolf packs had already reported that they had broken off as a result of expended torpedoes, low fuel or battle damage, he still had twenty-nine—mostly from Gruppen Stürmer and Dränger—to carry on the fight. In fact, when three U-boats that had just entered the North Atlantic from the Bay of Biscay approached the area of the two convoys, Dönitz ordered them to stay clear. There were already more than enough U-boats stalking the merchantmen.

At Derby House in Liverpool, the Western Approaches Command staff could do little but stare at the outsized North Atlantic chart and the brightly colored flags depicting the two harried convoys and the U-boats still hunting for them. According to the staff's calculations from message traffic between the ships and headquarters, it was likely that the *HMS Highlander* would reach HX229 sometime late in the day, allowing Commander Edward C. Day to relieve the overburdened Lieutenant-Commander Luther as escort group leader. However, the cutter *Ingham*, destroyers *Babbitt* and *Vimy*, and corvettes *Sherbrooke* and *Abelia* were still at least one, and possibly two, days away from joining.

The one action the Western Approaches Command staff could take was to send as many VLR Liberators as possible from Reykjavik and Alder-grove out into the deep ocean to attempt to harass and sink the U-boats swarming around SC122 and HX229. Despite the heavy seas in the vicinity of the two formations, the weather had cleared over their airfields. Between 0146 and 0939 on March 18, five of the nine operational VLR bombers were airborne. The other four launched between 1031 and 1114 to relieve the first wave upon reaching the convoys.[1]

The mauling of Convoys HX229 and SC122 had not gone unnoticed in Washington, D.C. While the staffers at Admiral King's COMINCH headquarters were reviewing the decisions made at the Atlantic Convoy Conference that had ended the previous week, King and his hand-picked Secret Room staff were also monitoring the carnage playing out in the Atlantic. King had full access to the message traffic clattering over the teleprinters from the British Admiralty's Operational Intelligence Centre in London and Western Approaches Command in Liverpool, including distress signals from stricken merchant ships and copies of messages from the escort groups. Since the convoys had already passed the CHOP (change of operational control) line at 35 degrees West Longitude, Admiral Horton and his staff now had operational control of the two formations and their escorts, so King and his people could only watch and wait for events to unfold.

President Roosevelt and Prime Minister Churchill, shown seated during the August 1941 Atlantic Conference in Argentia Bay, Newfoundland, with then–Atlantic Fleet Commander Admiral Ernest J. King, at left, and Chief of Naval Operations Admiral Harold R. Stark standing behind. FDR and Churchill agreed that defeating the U-boat threat deserved top priority.

National Archives and Records Administration

While the British had assumed control over Convoys SC122 and HX229, there was one unexpected result in Washington from the mauling of the two formations. The bloodshed in the Atlantic had attracted the attention of the American commander-in-chief. Now, in a forceful move, President Roosevelt personally intervened in the still-unresolved stalemate between the U.S. Navy, the U.S. Army Air Forces, and the British over increasing the number of VLR Liberators assigned to convoy protection in the North Atlantic.

Roosevelt had long been personally invested in the navy, and his interest had shaped his military policies. After fifteen months of working together,

Roosevelt and King had developed a formal and correct relationship, although privately each man sometimes doubted the other's motivation and true intent. When FDR had promoted King to become COMINCH in the aftermath of Pearl Harbor, the president issued a formal executive order—drafted with King's help—giving the admiral the combined duties of both commander-in-chief of the United States Fleet and chief of naval operations. This charter gave King "supreme command of the operating forces . . . of the United States Navy" subject to the "general direction" of the navy secretary and the president. King learned to his continuing chagrin that the president regarded this general direction stipulation as boilerplate. FDR was a hands-on president. Even after he had entered the White House in 1933, Franklin Roosevelt publicly and privately identified himself as a navy man, having served as assistant secretary of the navy during 1913–20, a period that included the First World War. In formal meetings with the military service leaders, FDR would frequently say, "When I was in the Navy . . . " A despairing Army Chief of Staff General George C. Marshall would lament throughout the war that FDR always called the navy "us," and the army "them."

King's relationship with his commander-in-chief was largely positive, and was also far more effective than that which his German counterpart had with the Führer. Adolf Hitler, in 1938, had assumed personal command of all of Germany's military services, including the navy, yet remained willfully ignorant of naval strategy, tactics, and corresponding materiel requirements. At the same time, Hitler's micro-management of all things military became so all-encompassing that he decided everything, no matter how small. In order for Dönitz to keep a hospital ship stationed in Norway to service naval personnel, he had to travel to the Reich Chancellery to obtain Hitler's personal approval. And when delays were threatening the development of the T-5 Zaunkönig wake-homing torpedo, the German Navy's top admiral once more had to obtain Hitler's personal OK to win resources to fix the problem. King had more leeway than that afforded to Dönitz, making his command more flexible and adaptable in times of crisis.

For King and other naval commanders, there was a downside to FDR's boat-cloak: he occasionally regarded the navy as his personal playground. On trivial issues, this was not a problem. Roosevelt retained the right to name new warships, and assigned a new aircraft carrier with the name *Shangri-La*, after the fictitious Himalayan valley in James Hilton's 1933 novel *Lost Horizon*. FDR had long used that name for his presidential retreat in the Maryland mountains and had jested to reporters after the April 1942 Doolittle raid against Tokyo that the Army Air Forces B-25 bombers had taken off from the mythical valley (rather than the aircraft carrier *USS Hornet*). When he decided to extend the quip to the twentieth *Essex*-class aircraft carrier built in World War II, the name stuck. If King disagreed with the decision, no navy records remain to tell.

It was Roosevelt's operational advice that sometimes rankled King, but the admiral found it preferable to deflect or ignore the intrusions rather than forcing a showdown with the White House. After the debacle at Savo Island in the Pacific in August 1942 when the Japanese Navy sank four cruisers (including one Australian) and a destroyer, Roosevelt had suggested to Secretary of the Navy Frank Knox that carrier task groups use more destroyers as escorts, freeing the cruisers up for beachhead defense. King personally drafted Knox's reply to the commander-in-chief that said, in effect, the navy knew best how to organize its forces. FDR backed off, but he would not always be so accommodating.

In a bureaucratic flare-up with King in early 1942, the president had taken off the gloves. Prior to his formal appointment as both COMINCH and chief of naval operations, King and Roosevelt had discussed the specific powers the admiral would have. King even wrote a draft of the presidential Executive Order for FDR to review. The admiral had managed to slip into the text a sentence that upon careful dissection gave him the authority to reorganize the service's bureaus of ships, aeronautics, and ordnance. Neither FDR nor Navy Secretary Frank Knox noticed at the time. For decades, these antiquated offices had operated as bureaucratic fiefdoms independent of the navy's chief admiral, answering instead to powerful congressional chairmen and the White House. When FDR and Knox discovered that King was attempting to reorganize the bureaus under COMINCH authority, the president blew his stack. Roosevelt objected to the plan as eroding civilian control of the navy, and when King ignored FDR's protests, the president flatly ordered Knox to cancel every order King had made in the previous month that had anything to do with reorganizing any part of the service. FDR fumed that King's behavior had been "outrageous."[2]

Seeing that King's failure to muster VLR Liberator support for the trans-Atlantic convoys was resulting in outright slaughter, Roosevelt once again injected himself into naval affairs. After reading the latest dispatches from the HX229-SC122 battle that Thursday morning, Roosevelt confronted the navy, asking where all the U.S. Navy Liberators had been when the U-boats were ravaging the two convoys. The jibe would finally prompt the U.S. Navy and Army Air Forces to resolve their protracted standoff over controlling the anti-submarine mission. The Army Air Forces, which had long insisted on controlling all land-based patrol aircraft, shortly thereafter agreed to hand over the mission to the navy, and further agreed to hand over its current VLR Liberators in exchange for an equivalent number of future aircraft that had been designated for navy use. In addition, the joint chiefs agreed to deliver VLR bombers to the Royal Canadian Air Force (RCAF) for several squadrons based in Newfoundland and to dispatch additional Liberators to the Royal Air Force, so as to close the Greenland air gap once and for all.

Over the next month and a half, the effects of Roosevelt's intervention could be seen in the skies over the North Atlantic. By May 1943, the number of operational VLR Liberators would increase from eighteen in March to over seventy operating from bases in Canada, Iceland, and Northern Ireland. But none of this would help the two convoys still surrounded by Dönitz's U-boat wolf packs on March 18. The men in those convoys would have to make do with what little protection they had.[3]

IF THERE WAS ANY GOOD NEWS for Convoy HX229 on the morning of Thursday, March 18, it was that their escort group was finally back up to strength. Two hours after midnight, the corvettes *Pennywort* and *Anemone* rejoined with their loads of survivors, bringing Escort Group B-4 back up to five warships. But if there was any celebration among the convoy, it was short-lived; several hours later, Lieutenant-Commander Hill on the destroyer *Mansfield* signaled Luther that his fuel state had become critical and he was operating on only one engine due to a condenser failure. Despite the continuing U-boat threat, the *Mansfield* had to break off for port.

Since at sunrise the storm was still pushing into the convoy from the southwest, Hill opted to take the *Mansfield* on an 800-mile trip to Londonderry, Northern Ireland, rather than battle gale-force headwinds and

A VLR Liberator from Iceland overflies an Allied convoy in the North Atlantic. Frustration mounted for U-boat commanders in the spring of 1943 as the Allies managed to increase air cover out in the Greenland air gap.
Imperial War Museum, U.K.

heavy seas over the longer, 960-mile course back to St. John's. The *Mansfield* detached from HX229 after 0500 local (0700 GMT), bearing off the 126 survivors from the *Irénée Du Pont, Terkoelei,* and *Coracero.*

Escort Group B-4 was down to four ships again and could not count on immediate reinforcement. Luther had confidence the destroyer *Highlander* and corvette *Abelia* would rejoin in early afternoon after completing their four-day chase across the North Atlantic, but unfortunately, when the two warships radioed Luther asking for the convoy's estimated noon position, the *Volunteer* transmitted an erroneous plot about forty miles east of the correct one. As a result, the two ships would not rejoin the convoy until much later. A minor mishap on the *Highlander* further complicated things. A radioman on the destroyer was carrying two cipher books to the radio room when a rogue wave knocked him off his feet on an outside passageway. The sailor grabbed a stanchion and avoided being knocked overboard, but the two codebooks fell into the sea. This loss seriously hampered Commander Day's effort to re-establish communications with Luther when he arrived at the noon position and found only empty ocean.

For the past two days, Signalman 3rd Class John Orris Jackson had remained on the *Mathew Luckenbach*'s bridge around the clock alongside the duty bridge watch. "I had my bunk in the chart room. This was my quarters, but I had had no sleep for four days now. By this time, everyone in the ship was a wreck. Everyone was worn out from lack of sleep and we had a lot of seasickness cases," he later explained. To the crew, the only bright spot at daybreak had been that a U-boat attack in such weather was considered highly unlikely. "We definitely had thought that our troubles were over because the weather was so rough," Jackson added.[4]

As the morning wore on, it brought more frustration. The first of five VLR Liberators that Air Marshal Sir John Slessor had assigned to HX229 arrived over the convoy, but the heavy cloud cover prevented the aircrew from sighting the formation. After searching in vain for five hours, the aircrew headed back to Aldergrove. The same thing happened to the other four Liberators; poor visibility on the surface cloaked the convoy from sight. The only good news was that two of the aircraft sighted surfaced U-boats during their long flights and one of them damaged the Gruppe Dränger boat U-610 seriously enough to knock it out of the fight.

Despite the heaving ocean and poor visibility, at least one U-boat was still in contact with HX229 in the early afternoon of March 18. The resilient U-221, which had escaped serious damage the day before when jumped by a VLR Liberator, had doggedly thrashed through the twenty-foot swells after the convoy all morning and managed by 1543 to position the boat directly in front of the formation off of its port bow, where it used its periscope to watch the convoy approach. When the lead row of merchantmen closed within 2,500 yards, Oberleutnant Trojer loosed a newly deployed T4 Falke (Falcon) acoustic homing torpedo from his stern tube at a Liberty ship at the head of Column 2, then turned slightly and six minutes later fired a spread of two FATs and two G7e torpedoes at a larger merchantman at the end of Column 3.

Trojer's first torpedo sliced toward the 7,191-ton *Walter Q. Gresham*, a newly built Liberty ship traveling to the Clyde estuary with 10,000 tons of general cargo, including a large supply of powdered milk and sugar, and carrying a crew of seventy plus twenty-six Naval Armed Guardsmen. Her maiden voyage was cut short at 1346 local (1546 GMT) when Trojer's stern-tube torpedo struck and exploded on the port side at cargo hold No. 5. The blast wrecked the gunners' compartment at the stern of the ship and ripped off its solitary propeller. Survivors of the explosion managed to launch three lifeboats and two life rafts, but one of the boats capsized, pitching its passengers into the turbulent waters.

Just two-thirds of a mile away, Third Officer R. H. Keyworth was on the bridge of the 8,293-ton British freighter *Canadian Star* when he saw the *Walter Q. Gresham* suddenly lurch. "It appeared to be struck by a heavy sea throwing spray over the entire ship as high as the funnel but, when it lost way, I realized that it had been torpedoed," Keyworth later said. He rang the General Alarm bell and, as the *Canadian Star's* small gunnery detachment ran out on deck, both Keyworth and Master Robert D. Miller spotted a periscope slipping by to port. Both officers had just opened their mouths to call out the target to an Oerlikon gunner on the port wing of the bridge when two powerful explosions rocked the ship. Trojer's two G7e torpedoes had run true, striking the *Canadian Star* in the engine room and No. 5 cargo hold on the port side. The explosions killed the engines, blew the No. 5 hatch cover off, and wrecked two lifeboats. The *Canadian Star* quickly sank by the bow as the fifty-eight crewmen, eight gunners, and twenty-two passengers hurried to their lifeboat stations.

In response to the daylight submerged attack, Lieutenant-Commander Luther in the *Volunteer* immediately ordered the escorts to perform an Artichoke maneuver, in which they peeled out of formation to carry out Asdic searches astern of the convoy's main body. The *Volunteer, Anemone,* and *Pennywort* turned and raced down the main body amid the columns of ships, passing the two stricken merchantmen as they scouted the waters behind the convoy for any signs of a U-boat. The search was unsuccessful, and after a half hour, Luther sent the *Anemone* and *Pennywort* to pick up the survivors. The two corvettes managed to rescue fifty-four from the *Canadian Star* and forty-two from the *Walter Q. Gresham,* but sixty-two men, women, and children from the two ships had perished. Among these were the mother and two children of a British Army colonel on the British ship, who had drowned when their lifeboat overturned as it was being lowered, dropping them into the sea. Another female passenger died from a crushed spine after being trapped between a lifeboat and the side of the *Anemone*.

The agony for HX229 continued, but relief finally came for an exhausted and embattled Lieutenant-Commander Luther. While the rescue work was still under way, the destroyer *Highlander* finally hove into sight over the horizon, and Commander Day took over as senior officer of Escort Group B-4. His first challenge would come almost immediately.[5]

For one merchantman captain, the *Highlander's* arrival came too late. Antwood Borden, captain of the *Mathew Luckenbach,* had finally had enough of Convoy HX229. The attacks on the *Walter Q. Gresham* and *Canadian Star* were the final straw. While the weather, at least, had seemed to promise a reprieve, now a U-boat had dumped a burning, sinking merchant vessel directly in the *Mathew Luckenbach's* path for the second time in less than two days. This last attack had been particularly stressful for Borden and his crew. When Trojer's torpedo struck the *Walter Q. Gresham,* the freighter's lookouts had also spotted U-221's periscope as the Gruppe Dränger boat attempted to escape at periscope depth. The Armed Guard gunners opened fire with two 20-mm Oerlikon guns forward and the four-inch/.30 cal. gun on the aft deck but scored no hits. Borden had ordered a hard right turn after he saw the Liberty ship go dead in the water, and the *Mathew Luckenbach* had swerved out of the stricken ship's way. Seeing no emergency signals from either ship, Borden had then ordered a course to close with the convoy flagship in Position 61 some two miles ahead to starboard. Jackson signaled to the *Abraham Lincoln* asking if Commodore Mayall knew that two more ships had been hit. No response came from the *Abraham Lincoln* except a series of letter "R's" indicating the signalman's receipt of Borden's message.

With no end to the attacks in sight, and worried that the *Mathew Luckenbach* might be next, Borden decided to take a calculated risk. He would "romp" the *Mathew Luckenbach* from Convoy HX229, breaking from the formation to sail independently to its destination. It was a dangerous move, he later admitted, but one that events over the past forty hours fully justified. In a later statement to American naval authorities, Borden cited why he opted to romp: the frequent absence of the escorts from the main formation and Commodore Mayall's failure to order emergency course changes during the March 18 daylight attacks. "I considered that owing to the inadequate degree of protection that two escort ships could provide us, that we were in more danger of being torpedoed if we remained with the convoy than if we pulled out and went alone at full speed," Borden wrote. He called a meeting of his officers, crewmen, and the Naval Armed Guard detachment not on watch, and proposed abandoning HX229 to sail on independently.

Able Seaman Pasquale Civitillo vividly recalled the meeting, which took place in the ship's dining facility. Several dozen men were sitting around discussing the strikes that had sunk the *Walter Q. Gresham* and *Canadian Star* when Borden entered the room with Ensign James H. Hammond, the Armed Guard detachment commander. Borden told them that the ship was capable of fifteen knots maximum speed and that he thought remaining with the convoy and its nine-knot speed was too dangerous given the ongoing attacks. The escorts were ineffective against the subs, Borden added, and it was more than likely that the wolf packs would sink most of the remaining ships. The *Mathew Luckenbach* had run alone on other trips without mishap, and he was confident he could do it again, providing they could lose the submarine pack. He said he could do this under the cover of darkness by slipping out of the convoy and steaming ahead, leaving the U-boats to go after the convoy. "He asked for a show of hands by those in favor of it," Civitillo said. "We all raised our hands. He also had a statement written out to this effect, which he asked us all to sign. We all signed."

Signalman Jackson agreed with the vote to romp from HX229. "The captain was now ready to leave the convoy and proceed alone to England," he noted in his diary that evening. "All agreed that we should leave the convoy." Not everyone aboard the *Mathew Luckenbach*, however, agreed with the proposal; Ensign Hammond, whom Able Seaman Civitillo remembers accompanying Borden to the fated meeting, later claimed to have been opposed to Borden's idea. In his formal Voyage Report to the Third Naval District's port director, Hammond later wrote, "At 1600 [on] 18 March, I was approached by the Master of the *Luckenbach* about signing a statement that I thought we stood a better chance to get through safely if we left the convoy. I refused to sign such a statement."[6]

When Captain Borden began to carry out his romp, Commander Day, the newly arrived senior officer of Escort Group B-4, was preoccupied with plotting an emergency course change—the very maneuver that Borden would later claim might have kept him in the convoy. During the chaotic period between the U-221 attacks and sunset, Commander Day, aboard the *Highlander,* had spent several hours regrouping the escorts into a night convoy screen. Day was planning an evasive maneuver once it got thoroughly dark. He would turn the formation from its base course of 053 degrees to 080 to confuse any trailing U-boats, then after four hours steer 040, so as to bring the convoy back on its base course by dawn.

Commander Day's preparations were interrupted about 2000 hours local (2200 GMT), when a lookout reported that a merchantman in Column 2 had pulled out of the convoy. Enraged, Day ordered the *Highlander* to chase after the ship. "I saw him sneaking off, went alongside and shouted through the loud-hailer, 'Obey the last order of the Convoy Commodore,'" Day recalled in a postwar interview. Borden hailed back, "I can steam fifteen knots. I'm making my best way home." Day warned the *Mathew Luckenbach*'s captain that he was steaming into danger, but the merchantman did not turn back. It would prove to be a disastrous decision.

Borden had been overoptimistic about his ship's top speed. Apparently overburdened by the extra deck cargo that the New York authorities had loaded on the freighter at the last minute, the *Mathew Luckenbach* could only make twelve and one-half knots—just three more than HX229 itself. It took two hours for the ship to increase the distance from the convoy by five miles. At 2200 local, Borden began zigzagging on a base course of 100 degrees and finally lost sight of the formation.

As they sought to hide in the trackless Atlantic, there was much that Borden and his officers did not know. Nearly thirty U-boats were still hunting HX229 and Slow Convoy 122, which was now only eighty miles ahead of the overtaking fast convoy. Borden was unaware of this, nor did he know that, at 1832, Admiral Horton had ordered the destroyer *USS Babbitt* to steer for HX229 rather than continue its original mission of joining SC122. And while Borden and his crew knew that more than one-fourth of the convoy's forty ships had already burst into flames and had fallen out of the formation to vanish beneath the storm-tossed ocean, they did not know the precise, staggering figure of those losses. To date, eleven ships totaling 80,478 gross tons had sunk, and a twelfth—the 7,176-ton

James Oglethorpe—had broken from the convoy with torpedo damage in a desperate attempt to return through U-boat-infested waters to Newfoundland. A total of 247 merchant crewmen, naval gunners, and passengers had been killed, and another 663 survivors now huddled below decks in several overcrowded escorts and merchantmen. The men aboard the *Mathew Luckenbach* only knew the losses had been horrific. They put their trust in the darkness.[7]

The *Mathew Luckenbach* made it safely through the night of March 18, but so did the convoy they had abandoned. At dawn on Friday, March 19, the crewmen in both HX229 and SC122 came out on deck to find an Atlantic Ocean at peace. The previous day's storm had passed, the surging waves had calmed to slight swells, and the winds had died down. Only occasional rain or sleet fell down on the ships, and the lookouts enjoyed much-improved visibility.

Compared with the carnage of the previous three days, the night of March 18–19 had been relatively uneventful for the two groups. Shortly before midnight, after rescuing survivors from the *Walter Q. Gresham* and *Canadian Star,* the corvettes *Anemone* and *Pennywort* had finally rejoined HX229, bringing Escort Group B-4 up to five warships. The returning escorts immediately resumed guarding the convoy, and it wasn't long before they saw action.

With Commander Day's destroyer having rejoined Escort Group B-4, he and the other defenders were able to thwart several attacks during the night of March 18–19. At 0204 local (0404 GMT) on March 19, the *Anemone's* lookouts sighted a U-boat trailing the merchantmen, and Lieutenant-Commander King rushed in to attack, aided by the *Volunteer.* It was U-615, on its third war patrol under the command of Kapitänleutnant Ralph Kapitzky, and one of the last Gruppe Raubgraf boats to still be tracking the convoy. The two escorts executed seven different depth-charge attacks over a ninety-minute period as their Asdic operators made repeated contacts with the submerged U-boat. The *Pennywort* also found a U-boat underwater on the convoy's port side, and Commander Day on the *High-lander* located a surfaced U-boat so close aboard that lookouts could make out the commander's white cap. During the mêlée, a fifth U-boat sighted the *Highlander* and fired a spread of three torpedoes from about two nautical miles off. All missed. The escort group's strong counterattacks drove off the U-boats, damaging three of them. Commander Day was confident that HX229 had seen the worst of the fight, especially since B-4 was about to receive additional reinforcements.

Two more escort ships from Iceland, the destroyers USS *Babbitt* and B-5's storm-damaged HMS *Vimy,* were drawing near HX229 at last, and their crews were hungry for action. They would not be disappointed. The *Babbitt* was closing in on HX229 around 0525 when its radar operator called out a strong signal just one nautical mile distant. The destroyer surged to flank speed and was close to the target when the U-boat's look-outs spotted the warship and crash-dived. Lieutenant Commander Samuel F. Quarles and his crew pounded the hapless Type IXC40 U-190 for over five hours, dropping a total of fifty-three depth charges in eleven separate attacks. The blasts caused serious damage and flooding and drove the newly commissioned U-boat out of the fight—and its first war patrol—before it could ever take action against the enemy.

Convoy SC122 had a somewhat less stressful night than HX229, al-though one more of its ships fell prey to the U-boats. The first attempted attack occurred when three U-boats—including the persistent U-338, which had repaired the damage inflicted upon it by the *Lavender* on March 17—made contact with the formation. Commander Boyle and the Escort Group B-5 ships forcefully drove off all three U-boats. Then around 0300 local (0500 GMT) came welcome news: Coast Guard Captain A. M. Martinson on the *Ingham* radioed Commander Boyle that he was closing with the convoy and expected to join around 0600 local (0800 GMT), bringing a powerful reinforcement to Escort Group B-5. Boyle asked the *Ingham* to hold off at about forty miles and create a diversion by launching snowflake rockets and dropping depth charges to draw off any U-boats shadowing the convoy itself. Before Captain Martinson could give the order, the *Ingham's* lookouts saw a sudden fireworks display on the south-southwest horizon, where a cluster of snowflakes was soaring high into the night sky. Another U-boat had struck SC122.

At 0345 local (0545 GMT), the leading ship in SC122's Column 13 had gone up in a massive explosion. It was the 5,234-ton Greek freighter *Carras,* carrying a cargo of 7,000 tons of wheat. The deadly shot had come from Gruppe Stürmer boat U-666, commanded by thirty-year-old Ober-leutnant zur See Herbert Engel. Engel had fired an initial spread of five torpedoes beginning at 0017 without a hit. This time, a G7e from a second spread of four torpedoes struck its target. The twenty-five-year-old *Carras* fell out of line but did not immediately sink, giving all thirty-four crewmen time to escape in lifeboats. The Greek crewmen were picked up later by the *Zamalek* and arrived on board the rescue ship bearing bottles of liquor, which they generously shared with the other survivors already crammed below decks. At sunrise, a Belgian boat crew from the B-5 escort corvette *HMS Buttercup* would board the abandoned *Carras* to jettison its merchant codes. Afterwards, the corvette attempted to finish it off by firing at the hulk with its four-inch gun and launching a depth charge. Its efforts were unsuccessful, and the *Buttercup* gave up to rejoin the convoy.

The *Carras* would be the last merchantman sunk within the formation of either SC122 or HX229. By sunrise on March 19, the skies over the two convoys were filling with VLR Liberators and shorter-range aircraft including B-17 Fortresses, and Sunderland flying boats. Coastal Command had mounted a major air umbrella over the two convoys, which were now steaming just seventy miles apart on a roughly parallel course. The heavy air support indicated that British naval intelligence feared that Dönitz would not call off the operation just yet. As it turned out, they were right.

The U-boats had been hindered by the steady arrival of Allied bombers over the convoys, but the hunters were not quite ready to call it quits. At BdU operations near the Hotel am Steinplatz, Godt and his staff noted that at least one U-boat was shadowing each of the two convoys—U-166 clinging to SC122 and U-134, commanded by the veteran Oberleutnant zur See Hans-Günther Brosin, behind HX229. From the U-boat plot, Dönitz and Godt estimated that no fewer than ten other U-boats were in close range to the two convoys. Dönitz decided to give the wolf packs one more day. Godt entered into the BdU war diary, "Operation by day on the 20th would already bring the boats too far into the area covered by English shore-based aircraft, [so] they were ordered to break off at first light on the 20th. Any opportunity to make a day submerged attack after dawn was to be taken and the boats were then to move off to the S.W. in case there should be stragglers and damaged ships left on the convoy route."[8]

On the morning of March 19, one eastbound merchantman would not enjoy the benefit of the air support that had finally arrived for the beleaguered convoys. Sunrise on March 19 found the *Mathew Luckenbach* zigzagging on its base course of 077 degrees, which had put the ship 164 nautical miles closer to the British Isles during the previous fourteen hours. On the bridge, Captain Borden hoped that the *Mathew Luckenbach* would emerge from the U-boat-infested Greenland air gap that day, with another four days of steaming to go before reaching the North Channel and the British Isles. Around 0630 local, lookouts sighted what appeared to be several Allied escort ships in the distance and a VLR Liberator flying overhead. As a precaution, Borden sent the Armed Guardsmen to their guns. The lookouts had, in fact, spotted two of Commander Boyle's convoy screen for SC122, the *Ingham* and destroyer *Upshur*. The *Mathew Luckenbach* was far enough away from friendly forces, however, that it wasn't about to take any chances in the event a U-boat might suddenly appear.

A few miles away, another pair of eyes was carefully watching the *Mathew Luckenbach*. Kapitänleutnant Herbert Uhlig and the crew of U-527, a Type IXC40 boat on its first war patrol, had been hunting for SC122 for several days. A first-time U-boat commander, the twenty-seven-year-old Uhlig was ready for battle, having conducted extensive training in the Baltic with his fifty-two-man crew before leaving Kiel for the North Atlantic on February 9. Uhlig had already scored his first kill on a lone merchantman; on March 8, he had sighted the 5,242-ton British freighter *Fort Lamy*, which had straggled from Convoy SC121 during the fierce storm of March 5–8, and had sent her to the bottom along with her 6,333 tons of general cargo and a 291-ton landing craft that had been lashed to the freighter's main deck. Now, he was preparing to add to his record.

The *Mathew Luckenbach* would have presented an especially attractive target to Uhlig and his crew. Despite the fierce convoy attacks that had raged practically nonstop for the past three days, U-527 had yet to sight either formation. Three times in the past two days, VLR Liberators had found the boat and attacked, forcing Uhlig to crash-dive. The boat had escaped damage all three times, but the commander and his crew were feeling frustrated by the lack of action. Now, Uhlig had what appeared to be a large straggler in his periscope, but he was unable to match the freighter's speed while submerged and, seeing it steadily drawing away, he realized that any further delay would put the ship out of torpedo range. He later recounted the attack in his daily war diary. Staring through the attack periscope, Uhlig called out the firing data.

"Range one thousand, eight hundred yards, angle starboard one-oh-oh, speed ten. Bearing, mark! Three-fan spread. Tubes one, two, and four."

The torpedo petty officer reported the data was loaded into the Vorhaltrechner, and the firing-data calculator had transmitted the computed course track into the torpedo gyroscopes.

Uhlig took one last bearing then cried "Los!" ("Release!").

At 0744 local (0944 GMT), 1WO Oberleutnant zur See Karl-Hermann Behle hit the firing lever. The blasts of compressed air launched three torpedoes out of the bow tubes in three-second intervals.[9]

On the *Mathew Luckenbach,* Captain Borden had called Signalman 3rd Class John Orris Jackson up to the bridge at first light on March 19, in case Borden needed to communicate with the two distant Allied warships. Jackson later recalled that, after weeks of gale-force storms and freezing temperatures, it was a spring-like morning. The North Atlantic had calmed and the warmer temperatures prompted many of the crew to discard their heavy jackets. Jackson left the bridge for breakfast and had just returned to his post on the bridge wing when he noticed something strange. "I saw on the port quarter something that resembled a whale spraying water in the air," he said. "A minute later, I saw the wakes of two torpedoes." At the top of his voice, Jackson bellowed, "Torpedoes!" Third Mate Jerry Jones also spotted the incoming wakes and barked, "Hard right!" to the helmsman. Before the rudder had a chance to shift, the first torpedo raced by, just missing the bow.

U-527's second G7e struck on the port side at the No. 2 cargo hatch and its warhead detonated. A massive column of water and debris flew clear over the *Mathew Luckenbach*'s bridge as Jackson and the others stumbled to their knees or clung to stanchions and equipment. Down on the main deck, Able Seaman Pasquale Civitillo had heard Jackson's shouted warning. He briefly stood frozen on the spot, then realized he had left his lifebelt below in the berthing compartment. He started running across the deck but heard even more urgent cries from the lookouts. "I grabbed on to a guy wire and held on with all my might," he said. "There was a deafening roar and I was wrenched from the guy wire by tons of water and tossed head over heels across the deck until I was caught by the chain railing on the starboard side."

Borden immediately ordered two distress rockets fired and directed his crew to the lifeboats. Several seconds later, Uhlig's third torpedo struck the ship at the No. 4 hatch, and the *Mathew Luckenbach* took a sudden list to port. The crewmen made an orderly exit, Borden and others later said. "The majority of the men got into the lifeboats and life rafts but some jumped overboard," Borden added. When Jackson was asked several weeks later if he had been in a hurry to leave the stricken vessel, he replied, "No, but I passed several others who were in a hurry." Jackson made it into one of the lifeboats, where he and the others hauled in several crewmen who had jumped over the side.

Off on the distant *Ingham,* Ensign John Waters was on duty for the 0800–1200 watch as officer of the deck (OOD). So far, the morning had passed pleasantly. Waters and his men were relishing the change in weather. "After the continually terrible weather of the past four months, this day made seagoing a pleasure," he later wrote, "and in the bright sunlight, some of the bridge gang had removed their jackets and rolled up the sleeves of their dungaree shirts." At shortly after 0600 local (0800 GMT), the cutter's lookouts had reported SC122 in sight off the port bow. The *Ingham* and the convoy had been steaming on nearly reciprocal bearings so the distance between them quickly shrank. The warship had just gotten into position astern of the convoy's port corner and had slowed to twelve knots when Waters stepped out onto the port bridge wing at 0854 local time. He was scanning the horizon when, to his surprise, he saw a tall column of water soar into the air, then seconds later, two white distress rockets. Waters sounded General Quarters, informed Captain Martinson of the attack, radioed news of the incident to Commander Boyle on the *Havelock,* and ordered the cutter to flank speed on a course to the site.

The *Ingham* charged across the ocean toward the stricken *Mathew Luckenbach,* then slowed to await the destroyer *Upshur,* which would screen the area while the cutter rescued the crew. The *Ingham* quickly went to each lifeboat and raft, and in less than thirty minutes had retrieved all sixty-eight officers, crewmen, and Naval Armed Guardsmen. The only hiccup came when the cutter's crew hoisted one gunner up to the main deck. "What in hell is the Coast Guard doing picking me up out here?" the navy man asked. The *Ingham's* burly bosun's mate seized the sailor and spun him around as if to throw him overboard. "Let's wait for the navy to come get you," he snarled.

Meanwhile, the *Ingham's* Captain Martinson had been studying the *Mathew Luckenbach.* While the freighter was holed in two places, its list had all but disappeared, and it did not seem to be in imminent danger of sinking. *Ingham's* skipper met Captain Borden and his officers on the bridge and suggested the merchant crew might reboard their ship and try to get under way again. No one volunteered.

Waters was still on watch as OOD and was following the quiet but intense discussion with interest when another junior officer, Lieutenant Al Martin, piped up, "Captain, if you will give me two officers and twenty men, I'll take that ship into Iceland. The weather is good, and I think we can make it OK."

The *Ingham's* captain thought for a moment. "Well, you know we won't be able to give you an escort," Martinson said. "There aren't any lifeboats left aboard either."

Martin still wanted to try. "Yes, sir," he said. "Perhaps we can put a couple of life rafts aboard."

Waters later recalled cringing at the officer's comments. When Martin had suggested taking a prize crew aboard the crippled freighter, the lieutenant had gestured at Waters and another man as the "two officers" he wanted to go onboard the *Mathew Luckenbach.* Waters and the other officer had huddled in a corner of the bridge, questioning the lieutenant's sanity. "A freighter with two holes the size of a barn door in her, the ocean lousy with Krauts, and this weather sure as hell won't hold," Waters muttered. "What in the hell's wrong with him?"

Waters slowly edged around the bridge until he was standing directly behind Captain Martinson. He caught Lieutenant Martin's eye and vigorously shook his head from side to side while giving the "thumb's down" sign. The skipper whirled around and eyed Waters, who froze in place. Turning back to the ambitious lieutenant, Martinson said, "No. It's too much of a chance. We'll ask for a tug to come out. She looks like she'll float indefinitely."

Waters and the other junior officer exhaled in relief.[10]

THE TORPEDOING OF the *Mathew Luckenbach* on the morning of Friday, March 19, marked the final assault by Dönitz's U-boats on the ships that had sailed in Convoys SC122 and HX229. The formations were still several days from the British Isles, however, and the fighting that had marked their passage was not quite over.

SC122 and HX229 had cleared the Greenland air gap and were now close enough to the British Isles that Air Vice Marshal Slessor at Coastal Command was able to send aircraft from seven different squadrons to protect the ships. A B-17 Fortress from 206 Squadron based at Benbecula in the Outer Hebrides arrived over HX229 late on the afternoon of March 19, and Commander Day on the *Highlander* requested that it patrol around the convoy at a range of thirty miles. Within twenty minutes, B/206 came upon a thick squall line, and Pilot Officer L. G. Clark ducked into it in hopes of surprising a U-boat on the other side. His hunch was perfect.

As quickly as it had enveloped the bomber, the thick rain cloud vanished. Right below and in front of them was a surfaced U-boat. Before it could crash-dive, Clark threw the Fortress into a steep dive and straddled the U-boat with four depth charges. The dark gray hull vanished in the massive plumes of water thrown up by the explosions. Coming around on a second pass, Clark and his crew could only see a thick layer of oil spreading out on the surface. B/206 had wiped out U-384, Oberleutnant Hans-Achim von Rosenberg-Gruszcynski, and his crew of forty-six. It would be the Allies' only U-boat kill in the battles for the two convoys.

For the Allied merchantmen, the losses from HX229 and SC122 were actually greater than the commodores and merchant ship captains realized. In addition to the *James Oglethorpe,* which vanished in the Atlantic while trying to reach Newfoundland, three other ships had met their fate far from eyesight of the convoys in which they had originally sailed. The 5,754-ton British freighter *Clarissa Radcliffe*, with a crew of forty-three and twelve naval gunners, had left New York with SC122 with its cargo holds full of iron ore, but straggled from the formation on March 9 after the fierce storm that had struck the convoy four days out of port. The ship was never seen again, and it was not until a postwar examination of the U-boat archives that investigators learned that U-663, commanded by Kapitänleutnant Heinrich Schmid and operating independently in the At-

lantic on March 18, had reported to BdU that he had sunk a solitary merchant freighter steaming independently at 42 degrees North 062 degrees
West. There were no survivors. The Greek merchantman *Carras* and
American *Mathew Luckenbach,* which had been left behind as abandoned
hulks after being torpedoed by U-666 and U-527, would also be lost. Two
U-boats following in the train of the two convoys came upon the ships
late in the day on March 19 and finished them off.[11]

After the attacks on SC122 and HX229 finally ceased, it still took the
convoys three more days to make the final 450-mile passage to the designated Eastern Ocean Meeting Point rendezvous site, from which they
would head for their designated ports under local escort. The days passed
uneventfully and, with Coastal Command aircraft now thoroughly covering the two formations, the exhausted escort sailors and merchant
crewmen finally allowed themselves to relax. On eleven of the ships, however—nine escorts, the rescue ship *Zamalek* and freighter *Tekoa*—
relaxation would prove more difficult; 1,106 survivors huddled below
decks on these ships in appalling conditions. Most were grateful to have
survived the horror of a torpedo attack and did what they could to help
their hosts by cleaning the ships' spaces and assisting in daily shipboard
chores.

The rescued survivors of the U-boat assaults reached the United Kingdom ahead of the rest of their fellow merchant seamen. The destroyer
Mansfield, which had already detached from HX229 because of low fuel,
brought its 130 survivors in to the port of Gourock on the Clyde in Scotland, the principal receiving station for crewmen and passengers whose
ships had gone down en route to the British Isles. Admiral Horton at
Western Approaches Command ordered the cutter *Ingham* and destroyers
Upshur and *Babbitt* to detach from their respective convoys on March 21
and proceed directly to Londonderry to land survivors, refuel, and replenish their depth charges. The American merchant mariners and naval gunners drew new clothing and pay and settled down in temporary barracks
to await return passage to the United States. Their Allied counterparts
who had survived the loss of their ships went through a similar process at
Gourock.

HX229, which had started its trans-Atlantic crossing three days after
SC122 left on March 5, arrived at the British Isles first. It bypassed the

slower formation and met the local escort force at the rendezvous on Monday, March 22, at which point the convoy broke up into smaller sections heading for Loch Ewe, the River Clyde, Liverpool, and other ports in Wales and southern England. Once they arrived, these detachments would unload cargo and passengers, get needed repairs and fuel, and prepare to join the next westbound convoy. After handing HX229 over to local escorts, the ships of Escort Group B-4—finally at full strength with the belated arrival of the corvettes *Abelia* on March 19 and *Sherbrooke* the following day—pulled into sight of land north of Lough Foyle and the roadstead to Londonderry.

Later in the day on March 22, Commander Boyle and Escort Group B-5 led SC122 to a similar rendezvous with local escort ships, and headed in for a much-needed break. The two escort group commanders, the two convoy commodores and the commanders of the mid-ocean escort warships retired to their cabins to finish up the detailed Report of Proceedings that each officer was required to write about the convoy's passage. The commodores' reports would go to the Admiralty Trade Division in London, while the naval officers' documents would go to Derby House and a thorough vetting by Admiral Horton and his staff.

Having had to fill gaps in the two escort groups with temporary replacements, Western Approaches Command officials quickly returned those warships to their original units once the two convoys were in the hands of the local escort force. Lieutenant-Commander John Gordon Luther on *HMS Volunteer,* who as temporary senior officer of Escort Group B-4 had fought the uphill fight against the three wolf packs, obtained provisions and fuel and rejoined Escort Group B-5 for further operations. Neither Luther nor Commander Day ever met again. Lieutenant-Commander Hill's destroyer *Mansfield,* battered by the storms while crossing with Escort Group B-4, entered an English shipyard for repairs that lasted several months before it could return to Halifax and the Western Local Escort Force.

The end of the HX229-SC122 battle brought good news for the American escort crews based in Iceland. Ensign John Waters and his fellow sailors from the cutter *Ingham* and destroyers *Babbitt* and *Upshur* had originally planned to meet Convoy SC122 to escort seven ships to Reykjavik from the mid-ocean rendezvous point. Admiral Horton's decision to keep the Iceland-based escorts with the convoys meant that they would enjoy a week or two of rest in Londonderry, a welcome break from frigid Hvalfjordur. Upon reaching port, the Americans learned of even better news. As a result of the Atlantic Convoy Conference decision to remove U.S. Navy warships from close escort duties on the North Atlantic convoy routes, COMINCH headquarters sent new orders to the Iceland-based ships reassigning them to Task Force 63. This all–U.S. Navy command was responsible for escorting convoys from Hampton Roads, Virginia, to the Mediterranean across the much warmer waters of the Central Atlantic. Going forward, the only American unit operating north of latitude 40 degrees north would be the 6th Support Group, consisting of the escort carrier *USS Bogue* and six destroyers.

Like their escorts, the merchantmen in HX229 and SC122 now went their own ways. Once each convoy reached port, the individual ships scattered to assigned destinations to unload cargo and discharge passengers before starting the cycle all over again. The merchant ships and crews from HX229 and SC122 proceeded to Belfast, Loch Ewe and the Clyde in Scotland, and a number of English ports, particularly Liverpool. The freighter *El Mundo* with Signalman 3rd Class Ted Schorr aboard briefly stopped in Belfast so that Captain MacKenzie could unravel confusion over the mistaken report that his ship—and not the *Southern Princess*—had fallen victim to a U-boat on March 17. Then, the *El Mundo* proceeded down the Irish Sea to its destination of Newport, Wales.

Because of the brisk turnaround handling at British ports, a handful of ships from the same convoy would often find themselves together in the same one for the reverse crossing of the Atlantic. Two weeks after HX229 reached voyage's end, the *El Mundo* was under way with twenty-six other merchant vessels in westbound Convoy ON177 for New York. Among those making the rendezvous off Oversay were four other survivors of HX229: the Norwegian freighter *Abraham Lincoln*, again serving as convoy flagship; the two American Liberty ships *Daniel Webster* and *Hugh Williamson*; and the Dutch tanker *Magdala*. Another, most welcome addition was the rescue ship *Zamalek*, which had crossed the Atlantic with SC122.[12]

Having thus reached their destination, convoys SC122 and HX229 were disbanded. In this, an Allied convoy and a German U-boat wolf pack had one important characteristic in common. Each was an ad hoc organization designed for a specific, time-limited mission. For the fast HX and ON convoys, each group lasted only fifteen or sixteen days for a trans-Atlantic crossing in fair weather, while the slower SC and ONS formations might have a lifespan three to four days longer. These were, of course, the minimal times. When New York replaced Halifax or Sydney, Nova Scotia as the port of departure or destination, this added five to seven days to the trip; storm delays extended the time at sea even more. A U-boat wolf pack, on the other hand, lasted only as long as Grossadmiral Dönitz or Konteradmiral Godt at BdU believed it could locate and effectively attack a targeted Allied convoy. The three wolf packs that went after Convoys HX229 and SC122 were in existence for differing spans before BdU terminated the operation on March 20. Gruppe Raubgraf, which originally hunted westbound Convoys ON168, ONS169, and ON170 before targeting HX229, operated for thirteen days before BdU disbanded it. Gruppen Stürmer and Dränger, assigned specifically against HX229 and SC122, operated for nine and six days, respectively.

The survivors from the HX229-SC122 battle dispersed just as quickly as the convoys in which they had ridden. Deane Wynne reached Gourock with the rest of the *Zamalek* passengers two days after Western Approaches Command had released the rescue ship from SC122. Wynne and the other rescued merchant mariners were surprised to see that the *Zamalek* did not tie up to a pier but remained at anchor. "At last we knew we were safe," Wynne wrote years later. "We wondered why we had anchored out though! Why not get us straight ashore?" It turned out that the heavy shipping losses from the previous two weeks had severely strained the processing system. After several days, a tender came out and took the *Zamalek*'s contingent ashore. Two old Clyde paddle steamers lashed side by side at the pier served as the processing station. Wynne joined a long line of merchant sailors in one of the boats. Officials interviewed each man on the circumstances of his ship's loss. At the next station, an official issued Wynne a temporary identification card. At the next table after that, someone handed him a free rail pass. Then at the fourth table, a man gave him a small amount of subsistence money. Passing on to the second vessel, Wynne underwent a cursory medical examination, then stepped into a larger compartment where officials gave him a set of clothes, from shoes to a raincoat. "We still had not washed, let alone bathed, since we were rescued," Wynne said. "Our hair was matted with salt water, in some cases oil as well. Nevertheless, we all had new suits and raincoats."

Wynne's time ashore was well spent, but not without its frustrations. Arriving in London by train the next afternoon, he surprised his mother at her hairdressing salon for a joyous reunion. She told him that she had received an ambiguous letter from his shipping agent stating that the *Kingsbury* had sunk and that all anyone knew was that there were "some survivors." No details were available, she said, and the past two weeks had been almost unbearable. After a long overdue bath, haircut, celebratory dinner, and a good night's sleep, Wynne went to his shipping agent for back pay and another assignment the next morning. There, he learned a nasty truth about the British Merchant Navy. Wynne had calculated that his employer owed him about £13 for his three weeks aboard the *Kingsbury* and seven days in the *Zamalek* and at the Gourock processing center. Wrong. The shipping agent handed him £5, explaining that under the rules, his pay stopped the moment Kapitänleutnant Manfred Kinzel had sent a G7e torpedo crashing into the *Kingsbury's* starboard side. The shipping agent then softened the blow, telling Wynne that he could file a compensation claim with the Merchant Navy Pool Office for his lost possessions. A "thoroughly disgusted" Wynne proceeded to the office in Cable Street, Stepney, where he succeeded in getting another £20 to replace his lost clothing and personal items. The Pool Office manager further eased the strain, telling Wynne he was entitled to two week's survivor's leave at £3.10 per week, then should report back for another ship.[13]

The American survivors from HX229 and SC122 had a more limited—but no less restrained—experience than their British and other Allied compatriots. When the *Ingham* docked at Londonderry at midday on March 22, the *Mathew Luckenbach's* naval contingent and merchant marine crewmen went separate ways. Able Seaman Pasquale Civitillo and the other forty-one civilians from the ship found themselves in a large sleeping hall near the docks in Londonderry. Captain Borden arranged for a "draw" for the men—an advance on salary due them—and most of the survivors went out for an enjoyable night of pub-crawling. The only thing that marred a perfect evening back on shore was a lights-out conversation between a *Mathew Luckenbach* crewman and someone from another stricken HX229 ship. When the topic of the freighter's "romping" the convoy came up, words grew heated, then fists started flying. Only the intervention by one of the sleeping hall's night managers cooled things down.

By nightfall on March 22, Signalman 3rd Class Jackson and the other twenty-one Naval Armed Guard sailors from the *Mathew Luckenbach* found themselves in a receiving barracks at the new U.S. Navy base eight miles from their civilian shipmates in Londonderry. For the next twelve days, they relaxed, passing the time playing baseball and other sports, and taking in evening movies. Once authorities issued them new uniforms, Jackson and his mates were allowed to take liberty in Londonderry and the surrounding countryside. Then, on April 4, Jackson and ninety other Naval Armed Guard survivors were taken by truck, ferry, and train to the port of Greenock on the Clyde in Scotland. Moored out in the Clyde was the sleek, 1,031-foot-long Cunard liner *Queen Elizabeth,* painted a dull gray, having been converted before its maiden voyage from a luxury ocean liner to a troopship. In its current configuration, the *Queen Elizabeth* could carry up to 20,000 soldiers across the Atlantic at speeds exceeding twenty-six knots. That was fast enough to evade any U-boat that might have the luck to spot the liner as it raced across the open ocean. Jackson and his fellow Armed Guardsmen boarded the *Queen Elizabeth* on Wednesday, April 6, joining a motley collection of civilian and military passengers, among them Captain Borden and the other forty-one civilian crewmen from the *Mathew Luckenbach.* In midmorning the next day, the *Queen Elizabeth* headed down the Clyde for the North Channel and the five-day dash to New York. After arriving at midday on Tuesday, April 13, Jackson and the other sailors boarded trucks for the Naval Armed Guard Center in Brooklyn. The next day, he was on a train back to Kansas for nineteen days of survivor's leave and a long-overdue reunion with his family.[14]

For one survivor of Convoy HX229, rescue and repatriation brought no sense of relief, but instead, a combination of sorrow and guilt. Bill Stilinovich rode back to the United States on the *Queen Elizabeth* with a growing sense of dread. Just a week earlier, he had watched helplessly as the freighter *Harry Luckenbach* exploded and sank three minutes after being struck by two torpedoes—then had endured the sinking of his own ship, the *Irénée Du Pont*. Since arriving at Gourock on the destroyer *Mansfield*, where he was briefly hospitalized for exposure, he had heard no word about his brother, Joseph, or any other survivors from the *Harry Luckenbach*. The entire eighty-man crew had apparently vanished in the trackless North Atlantic.

Arriving in New York, Stilinovich received three weeks survivor's leave, and took the train back to Hibbing, Minnesota, to reunite with his widowed mother, Matilda Stilinovich, and other family members. It was a visit he dreaded.

Because of wartime security regulations banning discussion of ship losses, a navy officer had taken Bill Stilinovich aside and ordered him to say nothing of the *Harry Luckenbach* and its missing crew. For the entire time he spent in Hibbing, he sidestepped questions from his family and friends about Joe, even though by now he was certain his brother had perished. It was several weeks after Bill Stilinovich returned to Brooklyn and received orders to a new ship that the Navy Department telegram arrived at Matilda Stilinovich's home declaring that her other son was missing at sea.[15]

For the German sailors, the disengagement process paralleled that of their enemies in the convoys and escort groups. Once a wolf pack dissolved, BdU would send messages giving the individual U-boats new assignments. Depending on the degree of battle damage, number of torpedoes left on board, fuel state, and time at sea, the BdU operations staff would send each U-boat commander an Enigma message either assigning him to a new wolf pack, ordering his boat on an individual patrol or special operation, dispatching him to a U-tanker for refueling, or sending him back to port. Of the thirty-nine surviving U-boats from Gruppen Raubgraf, Stürmer, and Dränger, nineteen returned to their bases on the French Breton coast within a two-week period after Dönitz called off the attacks against HX229 and SC122.

The first U-boat to return to base was Kapitänleutnant Kinzel's U-338, which had been the highest-scoring U-boat in the three wolf packs. Having sunk four ships totaling 21,927 tons and damaging a fifth from SC122, Kinzel's first war cruise had been a smashing success, and he looked forward to a personal briefing with Grossadmiral Dönitz in Berlin after his arrival. Kinzel and his men, however, soon learned that the excitement was not yet over. Badly damaged in two aerial depth-charge attacks by an RAF 220 Squadron B-17 Fortress on March 19, U-338 was transiting the Bay of Biscay for St. Nazaire three days later when a British Halifax bomber swooped down to attack. Kinzel chose to fight it out on the surface, and his 20-mm gunner shot the Halifax out of the sky. U-338 rescued a wounded Australian aircrewman, the one survivor from the bomber's eight-man crew, and turned him over to security officials upon reaching port on March 24.[16]

Although Martin Beisheim's U-boat, U-758, had been one of the first to break off in the attacks against HX229 because of low fuel, Kapitänleutnant Helmut Manseck and his crew had been operating hundreds of miles to the west of U-338 and the Gruppe Stürmer boats. As a result, U-758 did not reach its temporary port at Bordeaux until March 30, thirteen days after it began its journey home. After refueling from U-463 on the return trip, Manseck had rendezvoused with Kapitänleutnant Hans-Jürgen Zetzsche in the U-591 for a prisoner transfer. Three weeks earlier, U-591 had come upon a drifting lifeboat from the sunken 9,382-ton Dutch freighter *Madoera*. He took aboard the ship's second engineer but left another four crewmen to their fates. With his patrol scheduled to last until April 7, Zetzsche handed the Dutch engineer over to Manseck for prompt delivery to the German authorities.[17]

While Manseck and his crew evaded detection by Coastal Command aircraft during the risky Bay of Biscay crossing, the last leg of the trip turned into a harrowing experience for Oberfunkmaat Beisheim. The weather turned bad with thick fog that prevented U-758's navigator from getting a position fix with his sextant. All hands were on edge because the coastal waters were heavily mined and BdU had carved out only a narrow entrance channel that they regularly swept for the explosive devices. The only navigational backup was Beisheim's radio direction-finding set, which he used to home in on several transmitter towers along the French coastline for a cross-bearing fix. Unfortunately for Beisheim, Manseck didn't believe U-758 was where his radioman's plot had placed it. Upon hearing Beisheim's calculation of their location through the speaking tube, the twenty-eight-year-old U-boat commander climbed angrily down from the bridge and confronted his radioman. "This cannot be the right position. If this was right, we would be far south of our planned position," Manseck snarled. "Take another bearing in one hour."

Beisheim's second positional reading yielded the same results as the first. "After one hour the stations synchronized and transmitted a long Victor Victor, *di di di daaa, di di di daaa,* and on the next synchronization I confirmed the position," Beisheim recalled. "The dot just moved two millimeters on the chart, both positions were correct." Before Manseck could throw a tantrum, his helmsman jumped in. "This can be right, we have a strong current here," he told Manseck. Just then, U-758 began receiving a radio homing signal from the German pilot boat that would escort them into port. The bearing was 270 degrees true, due west, and not on a heading of 090 as Manseck had anticipated. Manseck opted not to argue further. He ordered the boat on course 270, and after five and one-half hours, the *Sperrbrecher* (an auxiliary minesweeper) was suddenly alongside. "This occurrence helped my reputation with the captain a lot," Beisheim said.

Several days later, Beisheim and most of U-758's crew, clean-shaven and dressed in fresh uniforms, climbed aboard the special BdU train for three weeks of leave in Germany. Beisheim looked forward to seeing his family and fiancée, Edith Wauer, back in his hometown of Eberswalde, northeast of Berlin.[18]

THE BATTLE OF Convoy No. Nineteen, as Dönitz called the combined fight against HX229 and SC122, had been a major defeat for the Allies. It also became irresistible fodder for the propaganda mills on both sides. Even before the merchantmen made port, Dönitz gave a lengthy *Sonder-meldung* (special broadcast) direct from U-boat headquarters announcing that his U-boats had sunk thirty-two Allied merchant ships totaling 204,000 tons. These figures greatly exaggerated the results, but the true figures at Western Approaches Command and COMINCH in Washington, D.C.—twenty-one ships totaling 146,596 tons of shipping and the deaths of 373 merchant sailors, Armed Guardsmen, and passengers—were still grim enough.

Four weeks after Dönitz's celebratory Sondermeldung, the Allies put their own spin on the battle for HX229 and SC122. In a formal bulletin released by the British Admiralty and picked up by *The New York Times* on April 20, officials portrayed the HX229-SC122 battle as a major victory for land-based patrol aircraft. "U-boat Pack Loses Furious 4-Day Fight; Bombers of British Coastal Command Save Many Ships in 2 East-Bound Convoys; 4 Submarines Held Sunk," the headline read. In actuality, only the crew of B-17 Fortress B/206 had killed a U-boat, the hapless U-384. "Naturally no figures were given on the number of ships lost, nor were any exact claims made as to the U-boats destroyed," *Times* reporter Milton Bracker wrote.[19]

The Royal Navy did what it could to put a positive spin on the battles for SC122 and HX229, but behind their guarded doors at Derby House in Liverpool, the Western Approaches Command staff officers were in a bleak mood. The back-to-back battles over Convoys SC121 and HX228, and Convoys HX229 and SC122, portended a major resurgence of the U-boat threat. In those four battles alone, the U-boats had sunk thirty-eight Allied merchantmen and a Royal Navy destroyer, for a total of 227,772 gross tons. The loss of life had been unusually severe, with 1,120 merchant seamen, escort sailors, and passengers killed—some forty-three percent of all hands aboard the stricken ships. Worldwide in March 1943, the U-boats would go on to sink a total of 105 Allied merchant ships, 2 escort warships, and 3 landing craft for a total of 633,731 gross registered tons, killing 2,473 of the 6,699 crewmen, gunners, and passengers aboard, a thirty-seven-percent fatality rate overall. The worldwide shipping tonnage losses made March 1943 the third-deadliest month for the Allies since the outbreak of the war thirty-three months earlier.[20]

Two Allied intelligence estimates further heightened the pessimism that pervaded Derby House, the Admiralty in London, and Allied naval headquarters in Washington and Ottawa after the battles for Convoys SC122 and HX229. First, when on March 10 the British code breakers at Bletchley Park confirmed that the Ultra penetration of German naval Enigma had gone blind, there was a widespread fear "that the consequences would be fatal," as an official intelligence history later reported. The best guess at that time was that the Allies would be unable to break back into the German encrypted communications for several months. Equally grave was the Anglo-American estimate of German U-boat production. As Allied naval leaders conferred at the Atlantic Convoy Conference in Washington, their intelligence staffs had projected that the U-boat Force would grow to 613 boats by the end of the year, a nearly fifty-percent increase from the beginning of 1943.[21]

In his official history of the Royal Navy in World War II, Captain Stephen W. Roskill reported the shock and fear that the upsurge in U-boat attacks in March had brought to the Admiralty. He cited one particularly dire staff memorandum that concluded, "The Germans never came so near to disrupting communications between the New World and the Old as in the first twenty days of March 1943." Roskill went on to note, "No one can look back on that month [March] without feeling something approaching horror at the losses we suffered." What made the numbers truly sobering, Roskill continued, was that two-thirds of the ships lost to the U-boats had been traveling in escorted formations. "They did not know; but they must have felt," Roskill concluded, "though no one admitted it, that defeat stared them in the face."[22]

Such a defeat, the Allied naval strategists realized, was unthinkable. A U-boat victory on the North Atlantic convoy runs would leave the overarching Allied strategy—"Germany First," with a massive amphibious invasion of France planned for the near future—in ruins. By the spring of 1943, the long-planned operation to deploy American and Allied ground divisions to the United Kingdom was just beginning in earnest. During the first nine months of 1942, only two U.S. Army divisions had reached the British Isles, and one of them had been dispatched to take part in the North Africa campaign. The convoy crisis of March 1943 thus came at a critical moment in the war effort, as the United States was just starting to gear up once more for the trans-Atlantic movement of what would ultimately be a massive Allied force based in the United Kingdom: thirty-six U.S. infantry, armored, and airborne divisions and four Canadian divisions. An Allied failure to engage and destroy Germany would likely jeopardize the uneasy alliance between the West and the Soviet Union, possibly setting the stage for a separate peace between Berlin and Moscow that would mean an overall collapse of the Allied war effort. The consequences of Allied failure in the North Atlantic were unthinkable.[23]

Chapter 10

THE ALLIES FIGHT BACK

On Monday, March 22, 1943, the battered ships that had survived the U-boat attacks on Convoys SC122 and HX229 began arriving at the North Channel and dispersing to various British ports to offload passengers and supplies. As they did so, one senior Royal Navy officer decided there was a small silver lining to the black cloud of the U-boat victory. Admiral Sir Max Kennedy Horton at Western Approaches Command in Liverpool realized that the sudden crisis offered him a rare opportunity. It wasn't that the convoy system had lost its effectiveness, but simply that the convoys were not traveling with enough escort guardians. Now, Horton seized upon the HX229-SC122 battle as proof that his battered escort groups desperately needed reinforcements.

Horton had long made a racket about the need for more escort reinforcements for trans-Atlantic convoys, but he wasn't the only one. His predecessor, Admiral Sir Percy Noble, had also pressed the Admiralty for enough additional destroyers to form special support groups that would operate independently of the convoys in a hunter-killer role. Horton took this idea even further, arguing for the deployment of support groups to the Greenland air gap, where they could aid any convoy that came under attack from a wolf pack. Noble, aware of ongoing naval shipbuilding efforts, had also lobbied the Admiralty to transfer several escort aircraft carriers then under construction to convoy protection duties when they became operational.

On his first day at Derby House, November 19, 1942, Horton had pleaded with his superiors in London for additional destroyers. "The urgent need for 'support groups' to reinforce convoy escorts has been stressed by my predecessor," Horton wrote. "Unless a reasonable number of long-endurance destroyers and long-range aircraft come shortly a very serious situation will develop on the Atlantic lifeline." He seconded Noble's argument that corvettes, which constituted a majority of the escort group warships, were not fast enough to take the fight to the U-boats before they closed with a convoy. He argued that fast, long-range destroyers, frigates, and sloops should be used in the support groups, and seconded Noble's call for the new escort carriers to join the fight against the U-boats.[1]

Up until the spring of 1943, the Admiralty's answer to Noble and Horton's requests for more convoy protection had been a firm "No." There simply were not enough of the fast warships available. The losses of destroyers in the evacuation of British and French soldiers at Dunkirk and the British counterattack after the German invasion of Norway had depleted the number of combat-ready warships available to the Royal Navy. British naval commanders in the Mediterranean and other theaters had resisted the two admirals' pleas. Escort requirements for the Allied convoys to Murmansk and Royal Navy needs for the invasion of North Africa had further delayed the possibility of getting more escort ships to Western Approaches Command.

It wasn't until the battles over convoys SC122 and HX229 that the Admiralty began seriously considering the pleas emanating from Western Approaches Command. Unlike his nemesis Grossadmiral Karl Dönitz, Horton did not maintain a daily war diary at Western Approaches, so few details survive of his protracted struggle for the additional warships. However, many of Horton's subordinates and colleagues were eyewitnesses to the admiral's campaign, and at least one remembered Horton's budding optimism as he realized he had the Admiralty's collective ear. When Lieutenant-Commander Leonard C. Hill brought his destroyer, HMS *Mansfield*, to Liverpool with 126 survivors from Convoy HX229, he found orders summoning him to Derby House to present the admiral his Report of Proceedings. As Horton read over Hill's report, he remarked to the younger officer, "'I hope this will be the last picnic the Germans will have. I hope to have the escort carriers in a fortnight."[2]

While both Horton and Noble had argued for increased escort support for trans-Atlantic convoys, what convinced the Admiralty was not just the blood shed over convoys SC122 and HX229 but also a Derby House war game that proved the losses could have been avoided. On March 15, as Convoys HX229 and SC122 had headed into danger, one of Horton's duty captains at Western Approaches Command organized a detailed combat simulation exercise based on the two trans-Atlantic formations. Captain Neville Lake had been a submariner in World War I and was both a keen student of Admiral Dönitz's U-boat tactics and a fervent believer in support groups. He was aware that at least three wolf packs totaling forty-four U-boats were attempting to locate the two convoys as they neared the Greenland air gap. Sensing that a major confrontation was inevitable, Lake organized a war game that would offer realistic proof of what the additional warships could achieve.

While the Western Approaches Command staff plotted the progress of Convoys SC122 and HX229 on the oversized nautical chart of the North Atlantic that dominated one wall of the operations center, Lake added three fictional support groups to the display. His purpose was to study the probable effects that the reinforcements would have in strengthening the close escort groups, and protecting the two convoys against the swarming wolf packs. Lake filled the ranks of the hypothetical support groups with markers that represented actual British warships that were under construction or nearing operational capability. Lake dovetailed the support groups with the actual convoys and wolf packs out in the watery battlefield south-southwest of Iceland. He utilized actual weather conditions and maintained conditions of strict realism throughout the game. As Lake maneuvered the fictional support groups to the aid of HX229 and SC122 in response to the four days of attacks by the Raubgraf, Stürmer, and Dränger U-boats, he was careful to adhere to the actual limitations that the warships would experience due to fuel consumption and the depletion of depth charges.

CAPTAIN LAKE WAS UNWAVERING in his imposition of real-life limitations upon his hypothetical support groups, but even so, he found that they would have carried the day. He concluded that, with three support groups operating in the Greenland air gap, it would have been possible to keep two of them at sea and in the convoys' danger area at all times. He also reckoned that by reinforcing Escort Group B-4 with the five warships that

Royal Navy Wrens stand around the linoleum plotting surface at the Western Approaches Tactical School at Derby House. During the HX229-SC122 battle, a combat simulation exercise based on actual ongoing events proved that two support groups comprising four or five destroyers apiece would have prevented the high loss of merchant shipping.
Imperial War Museum, U.K.

constituted his initial support group, which, in the war game, rendezvoused with HX229 by March 16, the fast convoy would have avoided the staggering loss of eight ships in the initial night of battle.

Several days after the attacks on HX229 and SC122 had ended, a call came from London summoning Admiral Horton to a meeting of the cabinet-level Anti-U-boat Committee. Prime Minister Churchill had formed the interagency group in November 1942 to coordinate the anti-submarine warfare effort across the highest levels of the British government. Lake and his assistants hurriedly compiled an after-action report on the HX229-SC122 support group war game and handed it to Horton as he was leaving to board the night train to London.

Horton would later describe to Lake how, in a single meeting, the captain's after-action report had accomplished what the two admirals had not been able to do in years of trying: winning escort reinforcements for the convoys. Lake later wrote a memorandum recounting Horton's story:

[Horton] told me that the Prime Minister in a very somber mood explained the situation whereby the U-boats were threatening the very prosecution of the war. Oil stocks in the U.K. and North Africa were below danger point and there was a serious shortage of tankers. He turned to Admiral Horton and asked him what he was going to do about it. Horton replied: "Give me fifteen destroyers and we shall beat the U-boats." The Prime Minister banged the table and said: "You Admirals are always asking for more and more ships and when you get them things get no better." Admiral Horton handed him the report of the exercise and after glancing at it there was a temporary adjournment of the meeting whilst the Prime Minister and Admiral [Harold] Stark (Commander of U.S. Naval Forces in Europe) studied it. After a short while, Winston turned to Horton and said, "You can have your fifteen destroyers; we shall have to stop the Russian convoys for the present."[3]

The Russians were continuing to pressure the other Allies to support their war against the Germans along the Eastern Front, and Churchill was sure to catch hell for his decision to divert resources from the Russia-bound convoys to those heading for Britain. In the brutal calculus of war, however, his choice was a necessary one: without fuel to sustain the British war effort, the convoys for Russia would not be able to run much longer anyway. Horton told Lake that he "had never admired the Prime Minister more than at that moment" when Churchill approved the deal.

The meeting with Churchill offered Horton hope that the devastation wrought upon the March convoys would not be in vain—and that the Allies would finally get enough warships to go on the offensive in the North Atlantic. Writing to a fellow admiral several days after the meeting, Horton noted, "This job has been pretty somber up to date, because one hadn't the means to do those very simple things for which numbers are essential, and which could quash the [U-boat] menace definitely in a reasonable time; but in the last few days things are much brighter and we are to be reinforced, and I really have hopes now that we can turn from the defensive to another and better role—killing them." Nevertheless, he

The first British support group formed after the SC122-HX229 battle was commanded by Captain James A. McCoy on the destroyer *HMS Offa*.
National Archives and Records Administration

added, the HX229-SC122 battle had made that week of March 14–20 "one of the blackest on the sea."[4]

By the last week of March, Churchill had begun to make good on his promise of additional warships. Horton immediately obtained sixteen destroyers from the Scotland-based British Home Fleet, whose primary mission was to guard against a German surface navy that few expected ever to come out in force again. Temporary cancellation of the Allied convoys to Murmansk and Archangel freed up additional warships and, in a calculated risk, Horton expanded his roster of support ships even more by reducing the number of destroyers in each mid-ocean escort group by one. He hoped to have these and the other additional warships available to support all convoys as they proceeded through the Greenland air gap.

After months of frustration, Horton and his staff could finally begin assembling hunter-killer groups to safeguard the North Atlantic convoys. Forming these groups and running them through the training center at Tobermory, however, would take time. The limited support groups that Horton had already managed to deploy had shown that training was a critical part of the hunter-killers' chances of success. The American escort carrier *USS Bogue* and its escorts had begun support group operations back in early March; the carrier and two elderly World War I–era destroyers, *USS Belknap* and *USS George E. Badger,* had escorted eastbound Convoy HX228 during March 5–10, and had accompanied eastbound Convoys SC123 and HX230 during March 21–26. Because of the support group's limited state of training and the violent weather east of Newfoundland, the *Bogue* and her escorts had little to no influence on the wolf packs in that area. Storm damage during the escort of SC123 then sidelined the *Bogue* in a Boston shipyard for nearly a month.

On March 29, Horton deployed his first operational support group to the North Atlantic, just nine days after the battle for Convoys HX229 and SC122 ended. The six destroyers from this 3rd Support Group—the destroyers *HMS Offa* (with Captain James A. McCoy as senior escort officer), *HMS Impulsive, HMS Obedient, HMS Onslaught, HMS Oribi,* and *HMS Orwell*—met up with Convoy HX230 east of Newfoundland. Because air coverage from Iceland was nearly continuous, and because a fierce storm had scattered both the merchant ships and a force of forty U-boats trying to locate the convoy, there was no combat encounter between the U-boats and the escort warships.[5]

Horton and his staff sent out additional support groups at the end of March—and it wasn't long before they encountered Dönitz's U-boats. The first British hunter-killer unit to engage the U-boats was the 4th Support Group, first operational on April 3 and led by Commander Arthur G. West on the destroyer *HMS Inglefield.* The 4th Support Group had been ordered to assist Escort Group B-7 in protecting eastbound Convoy HX231, comprising sixty-six merchantmen that had left New York on March 25. When British code breakers became aware that Admiral Dönitz had organized fourteen U-boats into a wolf pack, Gruppe Löwenherz (Lion heart), to go after HX231, Horton ordered the *Inglefield* and three other destroyers from the 4th Support Group—*HMS Eclipse, HMS Fury,* and *HMS Icarus*—to race for a mid-ocean rendezvous after they finished refueling in Iceland.

The 4th Support Group would help drive off the U-boats attacking Convoy HX231 but would have less luck in their hunter-killer role. Bad weather delayed the group's join-up with HX231 until April 6, by which

The escort carrier *USS Bogue* was one of the first reinforcements sent to aid the embattled convoy escort groups in the North Atlantic.

U.S. Navy photo

time the fighting was nearly over. Seven of the fourteen boats in Gruppe Löwenherz launched nine attacks, sinking six merchantmen totaling 41,494 tons. British VLR Liberators, in turn, sank two of the attackers, U-632 and U-635. The presence of the additional warships and heavy air coverage from Iceland-based VLR Liberators did, however, thwart any further U-boat attacks, and Konteradmiral Godt called off Gruppe Löwenherz in the evening of April 7.[6]

The leader of Escort Group B-7, Commander Peter W. Gretton, later said that, with the 4th Support Group's arrival delayed, he and the other B-7 ship commanders knew the chance of heading off the U-boat attacks was slim to none. "The small number of escorts made any effective form of offensive impossible," Gretton wrote. "All we could do was to zigzag unpredictably and so try to deceive the enemy. The U-boats had grown considerably tougher and seemed to be able to stand accurate depth-charging." The escorts would need the support groups' firepower if they were to have any shot at holding off the U-boats—much less attacking and sinking them.[7]

The support groups' initial deployments were inconclusive, but their numbers steadily grew during April, promising some succor to the thinly stretched convoy escorts. By the last week in April, Western Approaches Command had five support groups available to sortie from the British Isles, Newfoundland, or Iceland. They included three units that had been deployed before April: the *Bogue* and its escorts, renamed the 6th Support Group; the 4th Support Group, which had helped HX231; and the 3rd Support Group, which had assisted Convoy HX230. Two more groups became operational on April 21 and 22. The 5th Support Group, led by Captain Edward M. C. Abel-Smith on the escort carrier *HMS Biter*, with the destroyers *HMS Obdurate*, *HMS Opportune*, and *HMS Pathfinder*, left Iceland on its maiden patrol on April 21. A day later, the 1st Support Group, led by Commander Godfrey Noel Brewer in the *Egret*-class sloop *HMS Pelican*, departed St. John's, Newfoundland to reinforce Mid-Ocean Escort Force units transiting the North Atlantic. This group had earlier served as a convoy close escort on the Liverpool–Freetown, Sierra Leone routes before being transferred to the North Atlantic. Brewer's force included the *Banff*-class sloop *HMS Sennen* and River-class frigates *HMS Jed*, *HMS Spey*, and *HMS Wear*.

With five support groups active by April 22, the Allies had gone a long way toward strengthening the protection for their trans-Atlantic convoys—and more warships were scheduled to join up in the coming weeks. The 2nd Support Group, led by the famed U-boat killer Captain Frederick "Johnny" Walker in the *Black Swan*–class sloop *HMS Starling*, was in final workups preparing for its first patrol scheduled to begin on April 30. Besides the *Starling*, the group included five additional sloops, all of them sporting distinctively avian names, the *HMS Cygnet*, *HMS Kite*, *HMS Wild Goose*, *HMS Woodpecker*, and *HMS Wren*. Horton was also preparing a third escort carrier unit for the North Atlantic convoy routes. The 4th Support Group, which was currently composed entirely of destroyers, was on schedule to receive the British escort carrier *HMS Archer* in early May. Like the *Biter* in the 5th Support Group, the *Archer* had been initially assigned to support the November 1942 Torch landings in North Africa.

Forming support groups around aircraft carriers was not a new concept, but it was one that had, up until now, been off to such a slow start as to seem not a start at all. As part of the Atlantic Convoy Conference deliberations in early March, the Royal Navy had agreed to form up to four support groups, centered on the *HMS Tracker* and other small, lightly armed escort aircraft carriers that would join the force when they became combat ready. The plan suffered serious delays, however, after an internal explosion onboard the *HMS Dasher* during flight operations in the Firth of Clyde on March 27. The carrier sank in five minutes, killing 379 of its 528-man crew. Extensive modifications to prevent further accidents delayed the additional carriers' arrivals until late summer. In the spring of 1943, the support groups would have to make do with the three carriers—the *Bogue,* the *Biter,* and soon the *Archer*—that the Royal Navy had deemed combat worthy.

For the first time since the upsurge of convoy losses in March, there was an air of cautious optimism in the giant operations center at Derby House. As a new wave of trans-Atlantic convoys began their crossings in late April, Admiral Horton had enough support group warships to attempt rolling back the U-boat threat once and for all.[8]

IF THINGS WERE LOOKING UP for the Allied commanders at Derby House, the mood change in Berlin was exactly the opposite. In the four weeks between March 20 and mid-April, the outlook of Grossadmiral Dönitz and the other commanders at BdU had passed from euphoria to uncertainty to frustration. Their wolf packs had failed to match the success of the early springtime, and the trend did not bode well for the months ahead.

The March convoy victories had given the officers at BdU headquarters a huge boost in morale following the winter slump in U-boat sinkings, and gave Dönitz and his operations staff hope that they still might repeat *Der Glückliche Zeit,* the Happy Time of the previous year. During the first half of 1942, the U-boats had encountered scant American opposition as they ravaged the U.S. East Coast, Gulf of Mexico, and Caribbean, destroying as much enemy shipping as possible as part of Operation Paukenschlag (Drumbeat). U-boats sank 567 merchant ships totaling 2.9 million gross registered tons while losing just 21 boats to the enemy. That gave Dönitz a U-boat-to-merchant-vessel exchange rate of 27 merchant ships (totaling 138,567 tons) sunk for each U-boat lost.

The Happy Time had been heady but short-lived. In the second half of 1942, the number and tonnage of Allied merchant ships destroyed by the U-boats had fallen primarily because the U.S. Navy had finally organized an effective coastal convoy system, and the Allied escort groups had steadily gained experience in how to fight back against the U-boats. As a result, Dönitz had shifted wolf pack operations back out into the North Atlantic and its Greenland air gap. During the period from July to the end of December 1942, the U-boats sank slightly more merchantmen than in the first half of the year, but U-boat losses more than tripled. The statistics for the second half of 1942 showed that the tonnage war, aimed at sinking Allied merchant ships faster than their shipbuilders could replace them, was becoming more costly to the Germans: during July through December, 588 merchant ships had been sunk worldwide for a total of 3.2 million gross registered tons, an increase of 21 ships from the previous period, but 65 U-boats had been lost to Allied warships and aircraft. The exchange rate had begun to even out, declining from 27 enemy merchantmen sunk per U-boat lost to only 9. The tonnage that the Germans could claim for each U-boat loss over that period dropped, too, from 138,567 to 49,839 gross registered tons. As long as the U-boats continued to destroy Allied merchantmen in great numbers, however, Dönitz and his subordinates had accepted the higher German losses as an unavoidable reality of the war.

If Dönitz and his staff had felt that Germany was still making headway at the end of 1942, they had cause to question that optimism as the harsh winter wore on. When compiling the statistics for February 1943, the officers at BdU headquarters found themselves scratching their heads. During that month, the Germans lost eighteen U-boats while sinking only sixty-seven Allied merchantmen, for a total of 362,081 gross registered tons. The merchantman-to-U-boat exchange rate had fallen dramatically, from nine Allied ships sunk per lost boat during July–December 1942 to 6.2 in January, and down to an appalling 3.7 in February. "Although fewer convoys were encountered in January/February 1943, due not only to the weather but to [Allied convoy tactics and land-based air patrols]," Dönitz recalled after the war, "nevertheless the danger that the surface warfare against convoys might come to an end did not appear to be immediate." Still, at one point in that bleak month he had begun to fear that the U-boat Force might be on the brink of losing the tonnage war.

In light of the fears at BdU that winter, the spike in merchant ship sinkings in March 1943 had given Dönitz and his staff renewed confidence that their *guerre de course* against the Allies might yet prevail. Dönitz seemed to have been especially moved by the wolf packs' successes in late March against HX229 and SC122; in an uncharacteristically emotional message to the attackers of those two formations, he expressed his congratulations and gratitude for their efforts: "Appreciation and recognition for the greatest success yet achieved against a convoy. After the extraordinarily successful surprise blow on the first night, tough and energetic pursuit despite strong air and surface defense brought splendid successes to the submarines in their attacks both by day and night." Dönitz's elation, however, would vanish as March passed into April, and the number of sinkings plummeted.[9]

Although the U-boat success rate left a lot to be desired, Dönitz and his operations staff had some hopes that things would improve in April. At the start of the month, they would temporarily have fewer U-boats to work with than during the March surge, but they could expect to be back up to strength by the end of the month. The number of Atlantic U-boats at sea had fallen from sixty-six on March 1 to thirty-one at month's end as most of the Gruppen Raubgraf, Stürmer, and Dränger boats returned to port for battle damage repairs and crew rest. During the first half of April, the deployed wolf packs ranged in size from ten to fourteen boats, considerably smaller than the earlier wolf packs had been. By late April, however, Dönitz intended to send dozens of other U-boats back out onto the convoy routes: the combination of veteran U-boats that would be ready to depart on patrol from the French bases, an additional twenty newly commissioned boats preparing to sail from Germany into the North Atlantic on their initial combat patrols, and a pair of U-boats transferring from the Arctic. This would boost the number of operational U-boats in the North Atlantic to fifty-five by April 20. This surge was possible in part because BdU dispatched a number of the larger and less maneuverable Type IX boats to the North Atlantic to fill in for the VIIC shortage. Dönitz also now had four oversized Type XIV "Milch Cow" U-tankers operating in the North Atlantic to replenish U-boats with fuel and torpedoes and so extend their patrols.[10]

Serving as an operations officer at BdU headquarters, Kapitänleutnant Peter-Erich Cremer shared the sense of guarded optimism that permeated Dönitz's staff as April progressed. "The British supply situation seemed seriously threatened, and voices on the island warned that with such high losses supplies would last for another two months," he later recalled. "Then that would be the end. . . . Risky as it might be, now more than ever the convoys had to sail and try to get through." If the wolf packs could match their March successes in the months ahead, the odds seemed good that Germany could force Britain out of the war. With more and more U-boats becoming combat ready, the staff at BdU seemed poised to do just that.[11]

But events did not work out the way Dönitz and his staff had hoped. During the four weeks after the HX229-SC122 battle, the U-boat campaign in the North Atlantic met with failure after failure. In contrast to the loss of twenty-one ships from the combined SC122-HX229 battle, of the twenty-three convoys that sailed during that period, eleven reached their destination without losing a single ship. Another seven convoys lost only one or two ships, most of which had straggled from the guarded main body. During that time, a total of 650 Allied merchant vessels steamed in convoy, including 86 vessels that made two crossings and another 4 that made three transits. The U-boats managed to sink only 20 ships out of that total, for an abysmal sinking rate of only 2.6 percent.[12]

Dönitz and his staff were baffled by their lack of success in April. By April 25, they had built the Atlantic U-boat Force back up to its March levels, but were not seeing the same level of performance that the boats had shown against the four March convoys. By April 26, the Atlantic U-boat Force would climb to seventy-eight operational boats, an all-time high, and would increase to eighty-seven U-boats by May 3. The growing numbers allowed Dönitz to stage multiple patrol lines up to 600 miles in length to hunt down the enemy convoys. And still his efforts were coming to naught.[13]

At first, Dönitz and his staff thought the U-boats were being thwarted by the severe weather that continued to roil the Atlantic in late March and early April. As the ships contended with fog, snow, sleet, and gale-force winds, it had been hard for either side to have a precise handle of what was happening out in the deep ocean. One particular incident highlighted the difficulty of hunting convoys in such high seas. When the U-305 had sighted eastbound Convoy HX230 on March 27, Dönitz had ordered twenty-six U-boats from Gruppen Seeteufel (Sea Devil) and Seewolf (Sea

German U-boat losses began to rise in April 1943 with sixteen boats sunk that month. Here, the Coast Guard cutter *USS (CG) Spencer* on April 17 depth-charged and sank the U-175 within sight of Convoy HX233 south of Iceland.

Clay Blair Collection, American Heritage Center, University of Wyoming

Wolf) to seek out and attack the forty-four ships. But the next day, a storm of hurricane-force velocity scattered the convoy and hid the merchantmen from the eyes of the freezing U-boat lookouts. The attack was a clear failure, with only one straggler sighted and sunk. Dönitz took the event in stride, noting in the BdU war diary that the poor visibility and high waves had made it difficult to track or attack the convoy. He followed this with a portentous note: "When the weather becomes a little calmer on the third and last day, very strong air escort appeared over the convoy, which prevented the boats from shadowing."[14]

By mid-April, BdU staffers were sensing that factors other than weather were behind the U-boats' poor performance. For a time, Dönitz and his staff thought that the rising number of inexperienced U-boat commanders on their initial patrols might be a contributing cause to the lower-than-anticipated figures. It wasn't long, however, before Dönitz realized that the change was attributable to the Allies and not to the performance of his U-boats.

A crewman from U-175 desperately waved to American sailors as he awaited rescue. Forty-one of the U-boat's fifty-four crewmen survived the loss of their Type IXC U-boat.
Clay Blair Collection, American Heritage Center, University of Wyoming

Sightings of Allied support groups provided BdU with the first evidence that the Battle of the Atlantic might be shifting. Because of the fierce storm that had thwarted the attack on HX230, the U-boats had been unaware that the 3rd Support Group had sailed to assist that convoy and eastbound SC123 during March 29–31. On March 26, however, U-664 had briefly sighted the American jeep carrier *Bogue* and its escorts in the 6th Support Group near SC123 and reported it to Dönitz, giving BdU the first clear sign that the Allied escorts were receiving reinforcements. Further confirmation came several weeks later, when U-boats shadowing the fifty-seven vessels in Convoy HX233 reported that its close escort group had been reinforced with four additional destroyers. Dönitz later noted that the "exceptionally strong escort" had prevented the wolf pack attack from scoring more than one sinking against that formation.[15]

While Admiral Horton's support groups were beginning to cause a headache for the U-boats, BdU had also noticed a second adverse trend:

the increasing presence of long-range aircraft in the Greenland air gap. Thanks to a combination of extra warplanes, aircrews' accumulating experience, and new anti-U-boat technology, the two Coastal Command squadrons operating VLR Liberators out of Aldergrove and Reykjavik were getting better at providing air cover to convoys as they crossed the 600-to-800-mile expanse of ocean. By late March, Air Marshal Sir John Slessor had managed to scrape together enough additional bombers to fill out 86 Squadron at Aldergrove to a full complement of a dozen aircraft; along with the 120 Squadron based at Reykjavik, Slessor now had two dozen of the four-engine bombers at his disposal. Although a third of them were usually grounded for repairs at any given time, Slessor could now avoid deadly gaps in air coverage. Moreover, beginning in February, the Coastal Command had begun outfitting the planes with the new ASV Mark III centimetric radar, whose 9.7-centimeter wavelength remained invisible to U-boat radar-detection devices. The new technology allowed bombers to locate surfaced U-boats without the Germans counter-detecting the aircraft. These advancements, combined with the steady improvement of Liberator air crewmen on their twenty-two-hour missions, had begun to erode the wolf packs' ability to attack the trans-Atlantic convoys.[16]

Unbeknownst to the naval commanders at BdU, the cryptologic battle had been heating up, as well. On March 20, far from the North Atlantic convoy routes, British code-breakers had managed to break back into the German naval cipher after a nerve-wracking blackout. Despite fears within the Royal Navy that the replacement of the German "short-signal" codebook for U-boat weather reports would leave Bletchley Park blind for months, the blackout had been short-lived, costing the Allies only ten days' worth of BdU-to-U-boat messages. The renewed flow of intelligence enabled COMINCH and Western Approaches Command to successfully reroute at least ten of the twenty-two convoys that sailed during late March to late April, sending them around the waiting U-boats.[17]

Dönitz finally reached his boiling point in the last week of April, when the combination of British intelligence, escort reinforcements, and air support spoiled a well-planned U-boat assault. After spotting the forty-three merchantmen in eastbound Convoy HX234, Kapitänleutnant Claus von Trotha in the U-306 had reported the sighting to BdU and began transmitting homing signals, which brought up six other boats from the eleven-day-old Gruppe Meise. But Bletchley Park had intercepted von Trotha's Enigma message to Dönitz, and the news of the impending attack triggered a fast response from Western Approaches Command. Admiral Horton's staff ordered VLR aircraft to provide air cover for HX234 and dispatched the destroyer *HMS Vimy* and three 4th Support Group destroyers—the *HMS Eclipse, HMS Inglefield,* and newly assigned *HMS Faulknor*—to reinforce the convoy's close escort warships. Commander Day, whose Escort Group B-4 had been overwhelmed by three wolf packs while shepherding Convoy HX229 five weeks earlier, now enjoyed the tactical advantage. Although six more U-boats from Gruppe Meise had arrived on the scene and the combined force of a dozen U-boats shadowed HX234 for several days, the aggressive British defense thwarted serious losses. The only U-boat victories were a pair of stragglers picked off by von Trotha in U-306 and Kapitänleutnant Ralf-Reimar Wolfram in the Type IXB U-108.[18]

As message after message streamed into BdU operations bewailing the strength of the convoy defenses, the normally taciturn Dönitz became quite shrill. At one point he praised the captain of U-306 in an attempt to shame the other U-boat skippers into trying harder: "Trotha's good shadowing must not be left without results. . . . This convoy must be plucked!" In a daily war diary entry at the time, Admirals Dönitz and Godt confirmed that the aggressive defense put on by Escort Group B-4 and its reinforcements was preventing the U-boats from attacking the convoy—or even sizing up its defenders. "The Command found it difficult to form a clear picture of the surface defense as only a few boats reported depth charge attacks," the commanders wrote. "Four boats were attacked with depth charges, one sustained considerable damage. One boat was attacked by aerial bombs. The mass attack on the convoy did not have the desired results."

As the attack on HX234 foundered, Dönitz sent a gloomy "all hands" message to the Gruppe Meise captains. "The best shadowing, without attacking results," he said, "is worthless." With hopes of a major victory against HX234 fading, the U-boats would have to bide their time until another convoy approached the hunting grounds of the Greenland air gap.[19]

RAIN, MIST, AND FOG obscured the rocky headlands of western Scotland and the distant Irish hills as the first ships of the convoy began cautiously arriving at the rendezvous. Steaming slowly in the narrow waterway of the North Channel, close to Oversay island and in sight of the looming cliffs of the Rinns of Islay behind it, the ships formed columns of threes and fours, their lookouts staring intently at the mist- and rain-shrouded water for the sudden looming of a dark shape—another vessel on a possible collision course.

On a rare, clear day, the trip north—past the Isle of Man, the Galloway coast of Scotland, Malin Head on Northern Ireland's east coast, and then the soaring Scottish headlands of the Mull of Kintyre—would have offered the merchantmen's crews some spectacular views of the northern British Isles. Not today. The distant shores remained shrouded, offering no distraction to the several thousand British and Allied merchant sailors heading back to sea. Even here in these sheltered waters, where westbound Convoy ONS5 was assembling before beginning the three-week passage to North America, a heavy swell gave hint of the southwest gales that awaited the merchantmen out in the deep Atlantic.

It was mid-morning on Thursday, April 22, 1943, a month after the disastrous U-boat attacks on Convoys SC122 and HX229. Despite the heavy shipping losses during February and March, the Allied merchant fleet was rapidly expanding thanks to the massive Allied shipbuilding campaign in the United States and British Isles. The Admiralty Trade Division and U.S. Navy Convoy and Routing staffs were struggling to manage the increasing numbers of shipments of food, fuel, military supplies, and personnel to the British Isles. To keep the massive trans-Atlantic conveyor belt running smoothly, and to keep convoys at sea spaced as far apart as possible, British officials were now dispatching a westbound ONS formation every eight days, and faster ON groups every six. So far in April, the Admiralty Trade Division had sent off three fast ON and two slow ONS convoys ranging in size from twenty-three to fifty-eight ships, for a total of 204 merchantmen. During the same three-week period, the U.S. Navy's Convoy and Routing Section in Washington, D.C., had organized five eastbound HX convoys and two SC convoys totaling 335 merchant ships from New York and Halifax to the British Isles. Those loaded-down eastbound convoys ranged in size from forty to fifty-eight ships.

ONS5 was a medium-sized convoy, with forty-four ships assigned to depart the United Kingdom for Halifax. The forty-four merchantmen now assembling off Oversay island came from five different ports scattered across the United Kingdom, from whence they had traveled a day or less to reach the rendezvous point. The vessels comprised a cross-section of the Allied merchant marine crews who participated in the North Atlantic convoy runs. Thirty of the ships flew the Union Jack, but there were also four American merchantmen, three Norwegians, two Dutchmen, a pair of Greek ships, and a Panamanian-flagged vessel in the convoy, as well as a merchantman each from Nazi-occupied Poland and Yugoslavia, now operating under protection of the Admiralty. The ships in ONS5 ranged in age from the thirty-seven-year-old Polish-flagged freighter *Modlin* to the two-year-old British freighter *Merton,* and in size from the 7,150-ton *Merton* to the barely seaworthy 1,315-ton Norwegian *Fana.* The convoy represented a combined 196,841 gross tons of shipping; most of the ships were carrying sand ballast for the westbound crossing, but seven listed a cargo of coal.[20]

Three of the ships in ONS5 were survivors of Convoy SC122's treacherous eastbound crossing the previous month. The 3,942-ton British freighter *Baron Elgin* had escaped damage in the bloody fight over SC122, discharged its cargo of sugar at Loch Ewe, and was returning in ballast to Halifax. The 5,507-ton British steam merchant *Dolius* had crossed with SC122 bearing a cargo of bauxite and general supplies to Belfast, while the 6,520-ton British merchantman *Losada* had carried general cargo for Liverpool. A fourth vessel, the 6,198-ton American freighter *McKeesport,* had started with SC122 but had been forced to return to port with storm damage. The twenty-four-year-old ship later crossed to the British Isles in Convoy SC124, arriving on April 9 with its cargo of grain and general supplies.[21]

The Convoy commodore for ONS5 was retired Royal Navy Reserve Captain J. Kenneth Brook, who with his small signal staff was embarked on the 5,242-ton Norwegian freighter *Rena.* The nineteen-year-old *Rena* was a veteran of the wartime convoy system—since joining the British Merchant Navy after the German invasion of Norway in April 1940, it had crisscrossed the globe, making ninety port calls in the British Isles, United States, South America, and Africa, and crossing the Atlantic eleven

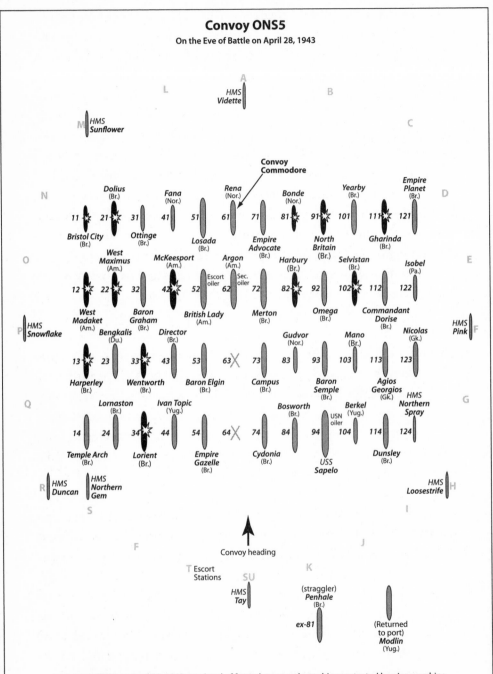

Convoy ONS5
On the Eve of Battle on April 28, 1943

Convoy ONS5 on April 28, 1943 consisted of forty-three merchant ships protected by nine warships from Escort Group B-7. Columns of ships are 1,000 yards apart. Ships in rows are 500 feet apart. Allied escort ships are 3,000–5,000 yards out from the convoy's main body. Darkened silhouettes depict the thirteen ships sunk by U-boats between April 29 and May 5.

Illustration by Robert E. Pratt

prior times, mostly on the northern convoy routes. Its service had apparently taken a strain on the ship, and engine room problems had forced a delay in the Rena's departure from Liverpool. By 2100 hours on April 21, however, the Norwegian had caught up with the ships from Liverpool and Milford Haven in Wales, the two ports furthest from the rendezvous point, as they steamed up the Irish Sea. Brook formed these two groups into three columns of ships as they proceeded north toward the rendezvous. By midday on Thursday, April 22, ONS5 had taken its near-final shape: twelve columns of merchantmen, including ten with four ships, one with three ships, and one with two. Another three merchant ships at Reykjavik were scheduled to join the convoy on Monday, April 26, four days into the convoy's trans-Atlantic voyage. Brook would be responsible for keeping these nearly four dozen merchantmen in correct formation, and for directing emergency turns to evade any U-boats along the nearly 3,000-mile route to Halifax.[22]

Also heading for the join-up that Thursday morning were the ships of British Escort Group B-7, setting out from Londonderry under the guidance of Commander Peter W. Gretton, age thirty, on the D-class destroyer HMS Duncan. Had they known who was in charge of their protection, the men in Convoy ONS5 would have been heartened. Since the outbreak of war some three and a half years ago, Gretton had made a name for himself as an adept and experienced destroyer commander. He had been at the head of B-7 when the 4th Support Group had helped it drive off the Gruppe Löwenherz U-boats ravaging Convoy HX231 in the first week of April.

The son and grandson of British Army officers, Peter Gretton had chosen a somewhat different career path, entering the Britannia Royal Naval College at Dartmouth in 1926, at the age of thirteen. He had wanted to serve in the destroyer force upon his graduation in 1930, but it took him nine years of struggle against what he called the Royal Navy's "practical-joke department"—the personnel bureaucracy—to finally win an appointment to a fleet destroyer. Gretton's opportunity finally came on September 3, 1939, soon after Great Britain declared war on Germany. Gretton found himself first lieutenant of the World War I–era Admiralty V&W-class destroyer HMS Vega, responsible for day-to-day management of the ship and its untrained, 132-man crew. Seven months later, the navy gave Gretton a "pierside jump," an unexpected reassignment, and he found himself serving as first lieutenant of *HMS Cossack,* a modern Tribal-class destroyer just twenty-two months old. Gretton reported aboard on April 5, 1940, and two days later the *Cossack* joined a British invasion force heading for Norway. It would be Gretton's introduction to naval combat. At the Second Battle of Narvik, the *Cossack* and eight other warships wiped out eight German destroyers and the Type IXB U-64 they had trapped in the narrow Norwegian fiords.

Later in 1940, Gretton had entered the Battle of the Atlantic. The Admiralty assigned the *Cossack* to a convoy escort group—but Gretton's first Atlantic crossing nearly became his last. One morning, the *Cossack* was struggling through mountainous waves when Gretton ventured onto the weather deck to monitor a group of sailors securing the lashings to one of the ship's small boats. Without warning, a wave crashed into the side of the ship, sweeping Gretton and three others over the railing into the sea. He had no time to react. Before he could cry out or even begin the futile exercise of swimming in the frigid water, another wave picked him up and dropped him back down on the *Cossack's* main deck amidships. A second crewman landed on the stern deck, but the North Atlantic swallowed the other two.[23]

Gretton survived his first exposure to the North Atlantic convoy battles and, true to his teenage ambitions, went on to serve on five Royal Navy destroyers—three of which he commanded—before the end of 1942. Shortly after his harrowing first assignment on the North Atlantic, the Royal Navy appointed him commander of the destroyer *HMS Sabre.* Commissioned in 1918, the ship was smaller than the *Cossack* but had been modified to carry out convoy escort duty with new depth charge racks, K-gun depth-charge launchers, additional deck guns, and radar. The *Sabre* soon joined an escort group based in Londonderry, shepherding convoys from the British Isles to Iceland, where it handed them over to Canadian and American local units. By late January 1942, however, the destroyer was in desperate need of repairs from a year of back-to-back convoy escort operations, so the Admiralty gave Gretton command of the V&W-class destroyer *HMS Wolverine.* In August 1942, the *Wolverine* was assigned to a naval relief force taking supplies and reinforcements to the besieged British colony of Malta in the Mediterranean. More than four dozen major warships, including four aircraft carriers, would escort the supply convoy through its hazardous journey. One night, while screening the aircraft carrier *HMS Furious,* the *Wolverine* got a radar contact of a surfaced submarine several hundred yards away. Gretton ordered the destroyer to flank speed and rammed the Italian Gemma-class submarine *Dagabur,* sending it to the bottom with its crew.[24]

Ten weeks after his quick-thinking attack on the Italian submarine, Gretton won a promotion to commander and was appointed senior officer of Escort Group B-7. It was a bittersweet moment, as he later recalled. "The *Wolverine* had had a grand ship's company with a splendid First Lieutenant and my days there had been very happy," Gretton would write. "In fact they were the last carefree days of the war, for some heavy responsibilities were ahead and the lighthearted delights of driving destroyers on my own were over forever."

Taking command of Escort Group B-7 in mid-January 1943, Gretton had found the group dispirited and worn down. His predecessor as B-7's senior escort officer had perished on December 15, 1942, when U-211 blew the destroyer *HMS Firedrake* in half with a torpedo during a fierce convoy fight. Further complicating the situation, a majority of the ships in the group were newly assigned and had not yet banded into an effective naval unit. At that time, B-7 consisted of the River-class frigate *HMS Tay,* the V&W-class destroyer *HMS Vidette,* and four Flower-class corvettes, *HMS Alisma, HMS Loosestrife, HMS Pink,* and *HMS Snowflake.* Gretton resolved to get B-7 in fighting form.

In the first four months of 1943, Gretton had honed the officers and enlisted men of Escort Group B-7 into a taut and effective fighting team. During in-port periods between convoy assignments, he dispatched his ship commanders and key enlisted crewmen to as many training schools as he could find. Of particular value was a recently established Night Escort Attack Teacher facility, where a warship's fighting team—commander, navigator, Asdic operator, HF/DF operator, radarman, and weapons controllers—would respond to simulated night surface attacks by a U-boat wolf pack. In addition to providing his men with shore-based training, Gretton also took his escort group out to sea for training sorties as often as the group's compressed schedule would allow. The Royal Navy had established a training group at the port of Larne, 12 miles north of the mouth of Belfast Lough. Using a converted yacht to represent a convoy, the escorts would practice screening procedures and coordinating with Coastal Command aircraft while several Royal Navy submarines attempted to attack. "Groups were welded together into teams, aircraft were able to carry out in practice the tactics on which they had been trained, and the results were excellent," Gretton noted.[25]

Gretton was fanatical about developing and maintaining excellent communications skills on all of his ships. Whenever Escort Group B-7 was at sea, each day at first light Gretton would send a Morse code message by Aldis lamp to the adjacent escort ship. To keep the signalmen on their toes, the text was always in Latin. The receiving ship would then retransmit the text to the next vessel as fast as possible, and so on around the convoy perimeter. "You had to produce those signals when you returned to harbor," said former Lieutenant Robert Atkinson, commander of the corvette *HMS Pink*, in a postwar interview. Gretton would pore over the copies to identify any signalman who had made a mistake. The culprit would find himself attending an additional communications training class rather than going on liberty with his mates.

Gretton was just as hard on his subordinate ship commanders as he was on the junior crewmen in his escort group. On one convoy run, Gretton flashed a message for the ships to alter course. Several weeks later, when the escorts were in port, he summoned the *Pink's* commander, Atkinson, to his sea cabin on the frigate *Tay*, Gretton's temporary lead ship at the time. Decades later, Atkinson was still able to paraphrase Gretton's first question: "On such-and-such a date and such-and-such a time, I ordered you to alter course. It took thirty-seven seconds before your mast showed a change of course. Where were you?" Atkinson, who had no recollection of the actual incident, stammered, "Well, I may have been down [below decks] for good reasons, but by and large I was on the bridge." Gretton briskly replied, "Well, you should ensure that even if you are not on the bridge, your officers alter course immediately."[26]

Gretton's meticulous command had an astonishing effect upon Escort Group B-7. In the first three months that he headed the escort group, B-7 escorted two trans-Atlantic convoys from the North Channel to WEST-OMP, and another pair from the meeting point off Newfoundland back to the British Isles, without a single loss. Under the group's protection,

184 ships totaling 1,172,099 gross registered tons of shipping safely made the trans-Atlantic crossing.

B-7's perfect record had lasted until late in March 1943, when it took over stewardship of eastbound Convoy HX231 from New York at WEST-OMP for the remainder of what would be a sixteen-day trip to the North Channel. In what Gretton later termed the "blooding" of his escort group, seven U-boats of the wolf pack Gruppe Löwenherz sank six ships totaling 41,494 tons, killing in the process 285 of the 441 merchant seamen and gunners aboard the sunken merchantmen. It hadn't been a one-sided victory; VLR Liberators had destroyed two U-boats—the U-632 and U-635—in separate aerial attacks, killing ninety-five German sailors. While the losses had been moderate compared with other convoy battles, Gretton described himself as "slightly disappointed" with B-7's overall performance. "A number of mistakes had been made which should have never occurred, and while the group had trained hard during the three months before the battle, it was evident that even more rigorous exercises were still needed," he later wrote.[27]

Gretton may have wanted to send the crews who had participated in the defense of Convoy HX231 off for even more extensive training, but that wasn't an option. Gretton and his five warship commanders had only thirteen days between Escort Group B-7's return to Londonderry and its rendezvous date with Convoy ONS5. During this time, Gretton had to oversee the intense preparations for their next mission—and, in addition to the unavoidable tasks of loading fuel, food, ammunition, and other supplies, he had to worry about integrating several new commanders and their crews into the escort group.

Two of the ships in Escort Group B-7 had new commanding officers, neither of whom were familiar with the workings of Gretton's team. After the previous convoy passage, Gretton had sacked one of his subordinate ship commanders, the captain of the corvette *Loosestrife*, for incompetence. Realizing that the officer was unsuited for convoy escort duty because he was "too old, too set in his views and who was a menace to his own ship," Gretton forced his transfer to a shore station. Replacing him was Lieutenant Herbert A. Stonehouse, a Royal Navy Reserve officer whom Gretton quickly recognized as "experienced and capable" and who would soon bring his crew up to B-7's exacting standards. Stonehouse was not the only new arrival to the group; the corvette *Sunflower* had also rejoined B-7, returning to convoy escort service with a new crew after an extensive, three-month overhaul. Gretton quickly came to admire the professionalism of the *Sunflower*'s new captain, Lieutenant-Commander James Plomer, a Royal Canadian Navy Volunteer Reserve Officer. Although Stonehouse and Plomer's newness to Escort Group B-7 could easily have become an Achilles heel for the group, Gretton quickly recognized the advantages of having both men sailing in his team.[28]

Gretton's most pressing concern had been about his new destroyer, the *HMS Duncan,* and its crew, but he soon saw that he had nothing to worry about on this front, either. After the Convoy HX231 mission had ended, Gretton had transferred to the *Duncan* from his temporary lead ship, the *Tay*. Because the *Duncan* had been decommissioned after suffering severe storm damage several months earlier, all of the ship's crewmen were newly assigned and had not yet fought as a team against a U-boat wolf pack. Gretton, for his part, had never set foot aboard the ship. The crew's lack of cohesion would have been a serious concern to any warship commander in the same situation. While Gretton and B-7 had been out on their previous convoy run, however, the Duncan's crew had undergone workup training at the Western Approaches Command training center at Tobermory on the Scottish island of Mull. When he stepped aboard the *Duncan* in the harbor at Londonderry, Gretton quickly recognized how well the instructors at Tobermory had forged its crew into a tight-knit team.

Besides being satisfied with the *Duncan*'s new crew, Gretton was also pleased with the ship itself. The Royal Navy had thoroughly modernized the ten-year-old destroyer during its overhaul. Shipyard workers had installed a forward-firing Hedgehog anti-submarine mortar launcher aboard the *Duncan,* along with a new Type 271M 10-centimeter radar with a maximum detection range of 8,000 yards. The shipwrights had also upgraded the ship's Asdic hydrophone system and installed the latest FH4 HF/DF direction-finding array. The *Duncan*'s Asdic operator was Lieutenant-Commander E. W. Morgan, Gretton's second-in-command and an expert in underwater acoustics. Since the frigate *Tay* also carried an HF/DF system, the *Duncan*'s equipment with the radar-finding gear would mean B-7 could not only track a transmitting U-boat on a line of bearing but also get an accurate cross-bearing to its location.[29]

The destroyer *HMS Duncan* was outfitted with the latest sensors and anti-submarine weapons but lacked long-range fuel endurance.
Uboat.net

Gretton's only real concern for the *Duncan* was the destroyer's "short legs." Unlike the retooled V&W-class destroyer *Vidette,* which had had one of its four boilers replaced with an extra fuel tank for extended range, naval architects had not retrofitted the D-class destroyers for trans-Atlantic convoying. As a result, his ship would have to rely on the escort group's two assigned Merchant Navy tankers, the *Argon* and *British Lady,* for underway replenishing. On the way to meet up with Convoy ONS5 after B-7's thirteen-day layover, Gretton made a point of practicing recovery of the *British Lady's* buoyant rubber fueling hose through which the fuel would flow into his tanks.

As it steamed toward the Oversay rendezvous point on the morning of April 22, Escort Group B-7 was accompanied by several specialized ships that would assist it on its mission to escort ONS5. Besides B-7's standard roster of warships—the *Duncan,* the frigate *HMS Tay* commanded by

Lieutenant-Commander Robert E. Sherwood, and the four Flower-class corvettes *Pink, Loosestrife, Sunflower,* and *Snowflake,* commanded by Lieutenant Harold Chesterman—and the two escort tankers accompanying it, Western Approaches Command at Liverpool had also assigned the anti-submarine trawlers *HMS Northern Spray* and *HMS Northern Gem* to the group as rescue ships. B-7's second destroyer, *HMS Vidette* under the command of Lieutenant Raymond Hart, had left port several days in advance to steam to Iceland, where it would escort the three merchant ships in Reykjavik designated to join ONS5 in four days.

Despite the temporary absences of its second destroyer, Escort Group B-7 was operating at a much fuller strength than had the ill-fated March Escort Group B-4, which for most of the crossing had only four warships and no rescue ship. B-5 had been more fortunate, operating with eight escorts and a rescue ship for most of its voyage. Gretton's muscular team reflected the new emphasis that Western Approaches Command was placing upon convoy protection after the devastating battles the previous month.

Commander Peter Gretton was senior officer in Escort Group B-7.

Courtesy of Vice-Admiral Michael Gretton, RN (Ret.)

The forward-firing Hedgehog fired twenty-four mortar shells ahead of the attacking warship, increasing the chances of destroying a submerged U-boat.
Imperial War Museum, U.K.

Whether they would make a difference in safeguarding Convoy ONS5 from the U-boats awaiting it in the North Atlantic, however, remained to be seen.

By mid-afternoon on April 22, Gretton's escort group had reached ONS5 at the assembly point off Oversay. Gretton edged the *Duncan* in close to the Norwegian freighter *Rena*, transferred a package of convoy documents to the flagship, and had a brief conversation with Commodore Brook via loudspeaker. While waiting for the escort force to arrive, Brook had organized ONS5 into twelve columns of three or four ships; the *Rena* itself occupied the lead position in Column 6 at the center of the formation. Gretton opted to steam the *Duncan* within the main body for the first few days, in an attempt to save the destroyer's limited fuel by traveling at the slower speed and steady course of the convoy's main body. The umbrella of air and naval cover from the British Isles extended far enough out into the Atlantic to provide protection to the formation for that time. Once ONS5 was out of range of shore-based aircraft and surface ships, however, the *Duncan* would have to take its place along the convoy's perimeter.

With all of its merchantmen and escorts in place, ONS5 was finally ready to head out into the deep Atlantic. The convoy would follow a different path than its March predecessors, however. At 1800, the formation set an initial course of 280 degrees toward a waypoint at 61:45 North 029:11 West, some 244 nautical miles west-southwest of Reykjavik and 450 miles east-northeast of Greenland's Cape Farewell. The Admiralty's Submarine Tracking Room and Admiral Horton's staff at Western Approaches Command wanted to push ONS5 literally up against the southern edge of the Greenland ice cap to elude the U-boats that Bletchley Park had identified massing in the Greenland air gap.[30]

Thanks to the Enigma intercepts, Admiral Horton knew that of 118 U-boats at sea worldwide on April 22, 64 of them were currently operating on or near the North Atlantic convoy routes. Forty U-boats had been organized into two separate wolf packs attempting to locate and destroy Allied convoys. The odds of spotting a convoy were relatively good despite the Allied re-entry into German naval Enigma: on the same day that Convoy ONS5 headed toward Greenland's Cape Farewell, from which it would turn south for Newfoundland, there were seven other convoys—totaling 264 ships and comprising 1.88 million gross registered tons of Allied shipping—steaming under mid-ocean escort protection between North America and the British Isles. The Germans hoped for another slaughter like the ones they had enjoyed the previous month.[31]

As ONS5 left Great Britain behind and approached its first waypoint off Iceland, it entered a battlefield that had been fundamentally reshaped in recent weeks. The U-boats were failing to wreak the sort of damage on the trans-Atlantic convoys that they had in March—but not because they could not find the merchant ships. In fact, one of the two wolf packs prowling the Atlantic, Gruppe Meise, was practically tripping over them. The wolf pack came upon two other convoys during the time that Convoy ONS5 was departing the British Isles: westbound Convoy ON178, a formation of fifty-six Allied merchant vessels under the protection of Escort Group B-1, and westbound Convoy ONS4, with forty-four merchantmen escorted by Commander Donald MacIntyre's Escort Group B-2. Like HX234, whose encirclement by support groups was driving Grossadmiral Dönitz to the verge of hysteria, the slow convoy had reinforced protection during its mid-ocean passage.

Whereas eastbound Convoy HX234 enjoyed the presence of shore-based VLR Liberators, Convoy ONS4 was the beneficiary of a steadier stream of air support from close by. In addition to the eight warships of Escort Group B-2, Convoy ONS4 was guarded by the jeep carrier *HMS Biter* and the other ships in the 5th Support Group, the Royal Navy's initial hunter-killer group built around an escort carrier. Though the 492-foot-long *Biter* was a pale shadow of American and British flattops, which were twice the size of an escort carrier, it could bring tactical air support to convoys even when they were out of range of all but the VLR Liberators based in Iceland and Northern Ireland. During the period from April 23 to 26, the *Biter* supported ONS4 with nine Swordfish biplane fighters and six American-built Martlets, the British version of the F4F Wildcat fighter. The destroyers *Obdurate, Opportune,* and *Pathfinder* were also on hand as part of the support group to protect the carrier and hunt any detected U-boats.[32]

The presence of an aircraft carrier alongside ONS4 guaranteed the westbound formation near-constant air coverage, a fact that dramatically changed the prospects of U-boats hoping to attack the convoy. On April 24, during the unsuccessful attempts by Gruppe Meise boats to penetrate ONS4's defenses, Oberleutnant zur See Claus-Peter Carlsen in U-732 dispatched an encrypted message to Dönitz that should have made the hairs stand up on the back of the Grand Admiral's neck: Carlsen reported being attacked and forced to dive by the appearance of a "biplane." Dönitz, however, initially concluded that the aircraft may have come from a "catapult ship," a vessel typically equipped with several older Swordfish biplanes that were launched and recovered on a makeshift flight deck. But any lingering doubt that the Allies were now protecting convoys with aircraft carriers vanished the following day, on April 25, when Kapitänleutnant Otto von Bülow in the U-404 reported that "an aircraft carrier with escort" was shadowing ONS4. Von Bülow misidentified the *Biter* as the American fleet carrier *USS Ranger,* but the point of his sighting was unmistakable: the Allies had stepped up their convoy defense considerably.

After transmitting his sighting to Berlin, von Bülow moved in for the kill. A veteran U-boat commander with thirteen Allied ships sunk during his thirteen months in command of U-404, von Bülow closed in on the boxy silhouette, hoping to rid the seas of an Allied carrier and her warplanes. At 0717 on April 25, he fired a spread of five torpedoes, including two path-looping FATs. Claiming that he had spotted two tongues of flame erupting from the target and felt "several very heavy vibrations" throughout the boat as U-404 fled from the escort warships, von Bülow later reported back to BdU that he had sunk the carrier.

News that the U-404 had sunk an Allied fleet carrier caused celebration in Berlin. Dönitz sent an Enigma message to the thirty-one-year-old Wilhelmshaven native, "Good! Good! Report whether in your opinion aircraft carrier was sunk." Von Bülow replied, "Sinking assumed." The news raced up the German chain of command to Adolf Hitler, who immediately awarded von Bülow, already a holder of the Ritterkreuz (Knight's Cross), with the next higher decoration—Der Eichenlaub zum Ritterkreuz des Eisernen Kreuz (Knight's Cross with Oak Leaves)—awarded to just twenty-nine U-boat commanders throughout the entire war.

Unfortunately for von Bülow, both the *Ranger* and the *Biter* were very much still afloat. From start to end, the sinking had been the product of the U-boat commander's fevered imagination; not only had von Bülow confused the *Biter* with a much larger American carrier, but he had mistaken the end-of-run detonation from his five torpedoes for a quadruple hit. The *Biter* sailed on, oblivious to U-404 and its attempted attack, since it made no report on the incident. Dönitz's operations officer and son-in-law, Korvettenkapitän Günter Hessler, later noted that the Grand Admiral "did not uphold the [sinking] claim and was irritated at the premature announcement" by the German Supreme Command. Several hours after von Bülow's faux attack, a *Biter* Swordfish and the destroyer *Pathfinder* collaborated in sinking another U-boat in Gruppe Meise, U-203. The *Pathfinder* rescued thirty-eight of the U-boat's forty-eight crewmen. It was the first U-boat kill from an escort carrier aircraft in the Battle of the Atlantic.[33]

The *Ranger* incident, as it quickly became known, revealed a worrisome trend within the U-boat Force. U-boat commanders were submitting inflated reports of successful ship sinkings, giving Grossadmiral Dönitz a false picture of what was actually happening at sea. Dönitz had always insisted that his U-boat commanders be conservative in their battle reports; as he later wrote, "Before the war I had always urged commanders to 'Estimate cautiously and accurately—we are an honest firm!'" Unfortunately for Dönitz and his operations staff, much of the message traffic from the wolf packs ranged from honest errors made in the heat of battle to outright fantasy. During the six-week period between the departure of Convoy ON174 from Oversay on March 20 until the arrival of Convoy ON178 in New York on May 2, U-boat commanders claimed to have sunk thirty-three Allied ships totaling 228,600 gross registered tons. In fact, they sank only twenty ships for a total of 117,862 gross registered tons, just over half the amount claimed. With Dönitz and his staff accepting as fact the destruction of 110,738 fantasy tons from the thirteen imaginary torpedoed merchantmen, both the Grand Admiral and BdU staff were dangerously deluding themselves as to the actual tactical situation developing out in the Battle of the Atlantic. The illusion, however, would not last much longer.[34]

On April 25, the same day that von Bülow claimed to have sunk the carrier escorting Convoy ONS4, Dönitz dissolved Gruppe Meise, reorganizing those U-boats that were still operational and a number of newly arrived boats into three smaller wolf packs to hunt for convoys between Newfoundland and the Denmark Strait separating Greenland and Iceland. Gruppe Amsel (Blackbird) with sixteen boats and Gruppe Specht (Woodpecker) with nineteen were strung out on an extended line running from northwest to southeast about 400 to 500 miles northeast of Newfoundland. Dönitz also organized Gruppe Star (Starling) with seventeen boats and sent it several hundred miles farther north, where it was to extend in a nearly 400-mile picket line with a north-south orientation.

As Gruppe Star took its place in the northern waters of the Atlantic, it did so beyond the gaze of Allied convoy planners. On April 26, BdU communications had ordered several changes to the daily Naval Enigma code settings, and—in a repeat of the March 10 blackout that had briefly crippled Allied intelligence—the decryption bombes at Bletchley Park suddenly went silent. When Dönitz transmitted an encrypted message ordering the formation of Gruppe Star the following day, therefore, the Allies knew nothing of this new wolf pack, its assigned operating area, or the dangers it posed to convoys plying the northernmost waters of the Atlantic.

Although the Allies were unaware of Gruppe Star, they had in fact already encountered and sunk one of its U-boats. When he organized the wolf pack on April 27, Dönitz filled it with seventeen U-boats that he knew had been operating in the North Atlantic: twelve Type VIICs, of which seven were making their first war patrols, and five newly commissioned Type IXC40s. These newer U-boats were known to have slower diving times than the VIICs and were thus dangerously vulnerable to air attack, but they would have to do; operational VIICs were still in short supply in the North Atlantic when Dönitz was reshuffling his wolf packs. In any event, even the VIIC model was not totally immune to air attacks. Unbeknownst to BdU, a Coastal Command B-17 Fortress had attacked and sunk the newly commissioned VIIC U-710 on April 24 some 300 miles east of its assigned location at the top of the north-south patrol line. When Gruppe Star arrived on station in the predawn hours of April 28, it was only sixteen boats strong.[35]

Although down one U-boat, it would not take Gruppe Star long to locate its next prey. The commodore of Convoy ONS5 and the senior officer of Escort Group B-7 did not know it, but on April 28, they were heading on a collision course toward the sixteen U-boats of Gruppe Star, which were only a few dozen miles to the east-southeast. The clash that would change the course of the Battle of the Atlantic was about to begin.[36]

Chapter 11

THE FIRST SKIRMISHES

R oiling ocean and shrieking winds, towering waves and stinging salt spray: the North Atlantic raged around the battered ships and exhausted merchant sailors, escort crews, and civilian passengers in Convoy ONS5 and Escort Group B-7. For six days and nights, the formation had clawed its way up from the North Channel on a generally northwest course track. Aware that more than fifty U-boats were operating in the Greenland air gap, the Western Approaches Command had assigned Commodore J. Kenneth Brook and senior escort officer Commander Peter W. Gretton a course that ran 600 miles north of the direct Great Circle route to Newfoundland. This move presented Convoy ONS5 with an entirely new threat. As the formation steered north to avoid the U-boats, there was a real chance that the convoy might find itself at risk in the Greenland ice pack, with its drifting icebergs.

ONS5 had had a slow and difficult voyage thus far. As storm cycles whipped across the Atlantic, the merchant ships and their escorts had labored ahead with the wind and seas hitting the formation from the port beam to dead ahead. Since ONS5 was a slow convoy, the ships assigned to it were those that could not maintain a steady speed of ten knots or more, and the convoy had been assigned a nominal speed of 7.5 knots for the crossing. The weather, however, slowed the formation further still. During this first phase of its trans-Atlantic passage, ONS5 held to an average speed of 5.8 knots over the 843 miles between Oversay and Waypoint XE, located at 61:04 North 031:10 West, roughly halfway between Iceland and the east coast of Greenland.[1]

On April 22, the convoy's first day out, the weather had deteriorated. The Polish freighter *Modlin* signaled Commodore Brook that it was experiencing engine problems and was unable to keep up with the convoy; soon thereafter, it broke off to return to port. The ballast-laden merchant vessels that remained were buffeted by the worsening storm; the ships rode higher out of the water than if fully laden with cargo, and were thus more easily scattered by the high winds and towering swells. Escort Group B-7 found itself hard-pressed to shepherd stragglers back into a semblance of the assigned formation. The westbound convoy was already showing signs of coming apart.

Over the next two days, things had only gotten worse. At dusk on April 24, a warning came from Western Approaches Command: shore-based HF/DF stations had intercepted U-boat transmissions whose bearings indicated the Germans had sighted the convoy. The message did not come as a surprise: for Gretton and his escort skippers, the issue had not been whether the U-boats would find the convoy, but when. The news from Western Approaches Command prompted Gretton to order several B-7 escorts to sweep astern of the main body in case any U-boats were stalking it from the rear. Concerned that a wolf pack might be preparing to attack and that his short-legged destroyer, the *Duncan,* would not have another chance to refuel, Gretton closed with the tanker *British Lady* to top off his tanks. There followed two frustrating hours of attempting to secure the fueling hose in the heavy swells, and the line ruptured after only a ton of fuel had been transferred. Tensions only eased two hours later, when a follow-up message from Liverpool arrived canceling the U-boat alert. The transmissions had actually been closer to Convoy SC127, on an eastward heading several hundred miles away.

Despite the continued risk of a U-boat attack, the North Atlantic weather had remained the biggest threat to ONS5. By sunset on Sunday, April 25, the storm conditions worsened even further, to the point that Commodore Brook noted that ONS5 "was experiencing considerable difficulty in steering and was to all intents and purposes hove-to" (that is, turned into the wind and practically motionless while using its engines to offset the wind and waves). The formation of columns and rows of ships had all but unraveled, as various merchantmen found it impossible to keep station in the howling winds and tumultuous seas. Gretton wrote in his daily report that on the evening of April 25, he could see "no less than eight sets of 'two red lights vertical' from ships out of control due to the weather."

Shortly before midnight on April 25, the inevitable occurred: two of the ships in Convoy ONS5 collided. The raging gale, now coming dead ahead of the convoy, had warped and twisted the actual formation as the ships struggled to make headway, and more ships were losing control. At about 2315 hours local, Third Officer A. C. Palvig was on watch on the bridge of the Danish freighter *Bornholm*, the third ship in Column 9, when a lookout on the starboard side suddenly cried out. The 1,418-ton British freighter *Mano* in the third place in Column 10, immediately to the right of the Bornholm, had illuminated its two "not under control" truck lights. Frantically trying to get out of the disabled *Mano*'s way, the ship behind it, the 2,130-ton Dutchman *Berkel*, turned hard to port, veering toward Column 9 and coming up fast on the *Bornholm*. Awakened by the frantic shouts on the bridge, the *Bornholm*'s captain came running and ordered the ship to full speed and hard to port. It was too late. ONS5 was making a speed of only two knots against the oncoming seas and gale-force winds, and the 3,177-ton *Bornholm* responded sluggishly. The *Berkel* rammed into the Danish vessel on the starboard side of its No. 4 hold, tearing open a hole in the its side ten feet above the waterline that caused flooding in the engine room. For the next fourteen hours, the Danish crew desperately manned the ship's pumps and dumped sand ballast overboard, but the influx of water exceeded their pumping capacity, and the *Bornholm* would finally detach from ONS5 for Reykjavik. The *Berkel* was luckier and sustained only minor damage, allowing it to continue with the convoy.[2]

By mid-morning on Monday, April 26, the gale had begun to ease, allowing Gretton and the other escort captains to gather up the ONS5 ships scattered all over the ocean. The detachment of the *Bornholm* left forty-two ships in convoy, but one of them, the 4,071-ton British vessel *Penhale*, had straggled so far behind ONS5 that Gretton realized it would never catch up. He ordered the anti-submarine trawler *Northern Spray* to escort the *Penhale* to Reykjavik. In the first four days of its voyage, the convoy was already down one escort ship and two merchantmen.

Although the fading storm had depleted its ranks, Convoy ONS5 and its escorts would not be shorthanded for long. Several hours after the

Northern Spray had detached for Reykjavik, the mood on the escort ships brightened: the B-7 destroyer *Vidette* had come up over the starboard horizon escorting two merchant ships and a U.S. Navy tanker from the Icelandic capital. The addition of its final destroyer brought Escort Group B-7 back up to its full strength of seven warships. The following day, the seas calmed enough for the *Duncan, Vidette,* and *Loosestrife* to refuel from the *British Lady.* The nearly continuous presence overhead of Iceland-based PBY-5A Catalinas, B-17 Fortresses, and A-29 Hudson patrol bombers further cheered the men.[3]

On the escort warships and ONS5 merchant vessels, the officers and navigators knew that the aerial support would not last long. The navigation charts showed that the convoy was approaching a pivotal milestone. The next day, April 28, Convoy ONS5 would reach Waypoint XE at 61:04 North 031:10 West, where it would alter course twenty-two degrees to port, steering from due west to west-southwest as it began the long second leg of its journey: the trip down from the northern latitudes toward Newfoundland. Ahead of them, somewhere out in the Greenland air gap, scores of German U-boats were on the prowl.[4]

OBERLEUTNANT ZUR SEE Ernst von Witzendorff and the lookouts aboard U-650 were scanning the eastern horizon around sunrise on the morning of Wednesday, April 28. For the first time in days, weather conditions were moderate. A southeast wind was blowing at around ten knots, and visibility was excellent at twelve nautical miles.

A newly commissioned Type VIIC boat, U-650 was only ten days out from Bergen, Norway, on its first North Atlantic patrol but was already fully engaged in the hunt for Allied merchant convoys. Assigned to Gruppe Star the day before, it had taken up its designated position near the very top of the wolf pack's patrol zone. All of the other Gruppe Star boats but one were stretched out in a picket line that extended nearly four hundred miles to the south. The last boat, U-710, was supposed to be the northern-most ship in the line. What neither von Witzendorff nor the operations staff back at BdU realized at that time, however, was that U-710 was at the bottom of the ocean, having been dispatched by a lone B-17 bomber four days before. Admirals Dönitz and Godt would conclude later in the day on April 28 that U-710's failure to transmit any daily position reports and a number of intercepted Allied messages of air attacks on U-boats likely meant that the U-boat had been sunk. If any Allied ships were passing to the north of the picket line, it would fall to U-650 to spot them.

At 0700 GMT (0500 local) on April 28, U-650's moment came. One of the lookouts on the bridge caught sight of a distant row of masts just edging over the northeastern horizon. For the first time in his thirty-six months as a U-boat officer, von Witzendorff stared at the enemy through his Zeiss binoculars. It was a thrilling moment for the twenty-seven-year-old skipper, who had labored for over three years in the U-boat Training Command before finally getting his own front boat just four months earlier. Von Witzendorff ordered U-650 to close with the convoy and, forty-two minutes later, made a brief encrypted sighting report to U-boat Headquarters in Berlin.[5]

Miraculously for U-650, von Witzendorff's report was not intercepted by Escort Group B-7, even though the group's two HF/DF operators were on high alert. Commander Gretton would later complain that atmospheric interference had hampered communications between the escorts and Western Approaches Command as the formation reached higher latitudes. Still, the HF/DF operators were able to catch most U-boat transmissions. At 0730 GMT, twelve minutes before von Witzendorff sent out his convoy sighting message, the two HF/DF operators in B-7 had caught an encrypted Enigma transmission bearing 159 degrees—slightly ahead of the convoy's port beam—and Gretton had ordered Lieutenant Raymond Hart in the destroyer *Vidette* to conduct a sweep down the bearing for thirty miles as a precaution. Gretton quickly concluded that the danger was not directed at his convoy, however; as he later reported, "[Convoy] SC127 was on that bearing and it soon became apparent that that convoy had been reported and not us." Shore-based HF/DF stations also confirmed that SC127 was the U-boat's target and not ONS5. Satisfied with the HF/DF reports, Gretton opted not to send out any other of his escort ships to investigate.[6]

Lost in the distant swells, von Witzendorff and his men played cat-and-mouse with Gretton's escort ships. At 0759, not long after sending off his first sighting report, von Witzendorff made a final calculation of the convoy's movement and U-650's radioman flashed a longer encrypted Enigma message to BdU:

CONVOY STEAMING AT 8–10 NAUTICAL MILES, COURSE 270 [degrees].

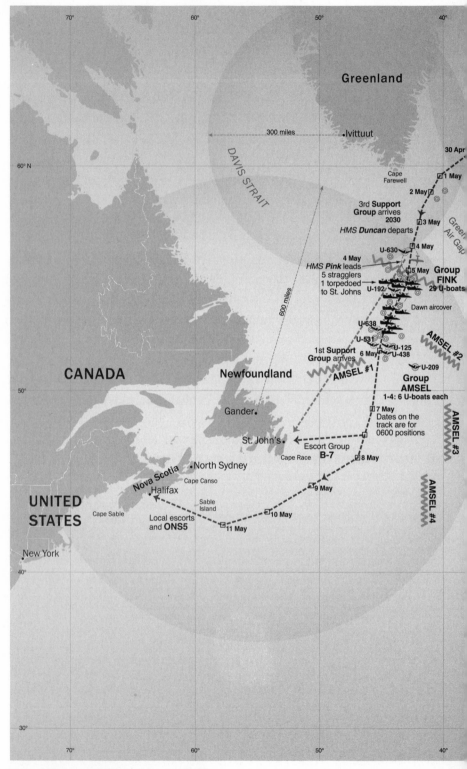

Trans-Atlantic course track of Convoy ONS5.

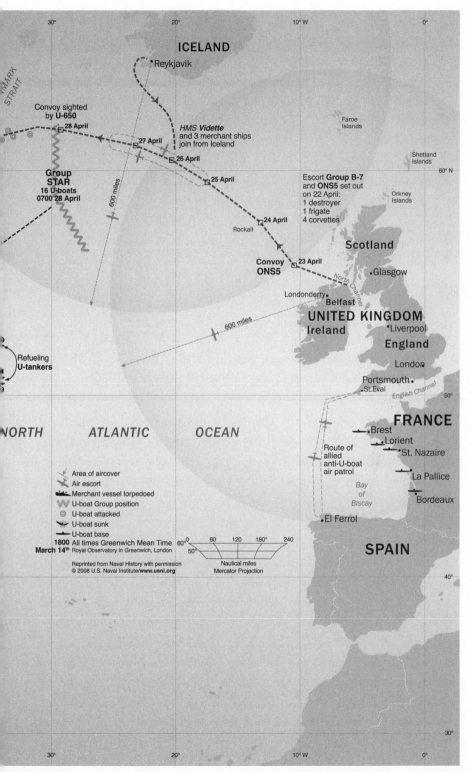

ICELAND
•Reykjavik

Convoy sighted
by **U-650**
28 April

HMS Vidette
and 3 merchant ships
join from Iceland

27 April

26 April

25 April

**Group
STAR**
16 U-boats
0700 28 April

Escort **Group B-7**
and **ONS5** set out
on 22 April:
1 destroyer
1 frigate
4 corvettes

600 miles

24 April

Rockall

Faroe
Islands

Shetland
Islands

60° N

Orkney
Islands

Scotland

Convoy
ONS5

23 April

North Channel

•Glasgow

Londonderry•

Belfast•

UNITED KINGDOM
Ireland   •Liverpool

England

600 miles

London•

Portsmouth•

•St.Eval

English Channel

50°

FRANCE

NORTH   **ATLANTIC**   **OCEAN**

Brest•

Route of
allied
anti-U-boat
air patrol

Refueling
U-tankers

•Lorient

•St. Nazaire

La Pallice

*Bay
of
Biscay*

Bordeaux

✈ Area of aircover
✈ Air escort
Merchant vessel torpedoed
W U-boat Group position
◎ U-boat attacked
U-boat sunk
U-boat base
1800 All times Greenwich Mean Time
March 14th Royal Observatory in Greenwich, London

Reprinted from Naval History with permission
© 2008 U.S. Naval Institute/www.usni.org

•El Ferrol

0 60 120 180° 240
60°
50°

Nautical miles
Mercator Projection

SPAIN

40°

30°

DENMARK STRAIT

30°   20°   10° W   0°

30°   20°   10° W   0°

Illustration by Robert E. Pratt, reprinted from Naval History with permission; © 2008 U.S. Naval Institute/www.usni.org

This transmission, like the one before it, made it past the HF/DF operators in Escort Group B-7 undetected. Forty-four minutes later, BdU
replied to U-650's first message:

GROUP STAR SHOULD ATTACK ON BASIS OF WITZENDORFF'S
REPORT. WITZENDORFF IS FREE TO ATTACK AS SOON AS AN-
OTHER BOAT HAS CONTACT.[7]

U-650 continued to shadow the plodding convoy, per his instructions.
At 1310, he updated BdU with the convoy's position, course and speed:

WESTBOUND CONVOY NOW IS [at German Naval Grid Square] AD
8728, SPEED 8 KNOTS.

Von Witzendorff's third message sent a jolt through Escort Group
B-7. The HF/DF operators on both the *Duncan* and the *Tay* caught the
signal, as did the HF/DF operator on a third warship escorting Convoy
SC127 about sixty miles south of ONS5. Using the three bearing angles
from the radio transmission, Gretton was able to triangulate its location
and deduce that at least one U-boat was close ahead of the convoy.
While they could not read the U-boat skipper's message, Gretton and
the other officers of B-7 knew exactly what it meant: a wolf pack was
very likely closing in.

With a U-boat lurking ahead of the convoy, the protectors of ONS5
sprang into action. Gretton sent the *HMS Snowflake* down the HF/DF
bearing, but Lieutenant Chesterman and his crew found nothing. At the
same time, Gretton ordered Commodore Brook to have ONS5 make an
emergency change of course thirty-five degrees to starboard, holding on
296 degrees until 1800 hours in an attempt to slip to the north of the waiting U-boat. At 1430, however, both HF/DF operators on the *Duncan* and
Tay received a new "hit" from a U-boat bearing 275 degrees true, twenty-
one degrees off to port of the new course. "I went out at full speed in the
Duncan to see if we could find anything," Gretton recalled. "We had no
success. But it was certain by then that the U-boat must have sighted or
heard us on her hydrophones, and it was clear that we were in for a heavy
attack—again that horrible sinking feeling appeared." The *Duncan*

searched out to about ten miles ahead of ONS5, then returned to its patrol station close to the main body via an evasive series of course changes intended to fool any U-boat that spotted the destroyer.

The cat-and-mouse game continued throughout the afternoon as the winds and seas picked up once again. Meanwhile, the last patrol aircraft had reached its fuel limit and broke off to return to Iceland. Aboard the *Duncan* and U-650, both Gretton and von Witzendorff felt a growing sense of frustration, though for quite different reasons. As Dönitz's response to von Witzendorff's longer message indicated, current BdU doctrine prohibited a "contact keeper" U-boat from attacking the convoy until at least one other boat made a firm sighting report. The rule aimed at maintaining contact with the target if the escorts drove the first U-boat under, but the logic of Dönitz's requirement didn't make waiting any easier. Five hours after sending his first contact message, von Witzendorff jotted into his diary, "Surfaced and sighted convoy coming directly towards. Withdrew beyond visual range. Bitterly disappointed that an attack cannot be made before another U-boat has made contact." By 1630 GMT, U-650 had managed to get ahead of the convoy, went in closer and came within one nautical mile of the destroyer *Vidette*, then screening directly ahead of the merchant ships. "The destroyer was certainly asleep," the U-boat skipper jotted in his diary. As the lead row of merchantmen neared, von Witzendorff pulled the plug and went under, his crew listening avidly to the sounds of multiple propellers as ONS5 passed by. He resurfaced and continued shadowing the formation, sending out homing signals and impatiently waiting for another U-boat to appear so that he could move in to attack.[8]

While von Witzendorff was chomping at the bit, Gretton's frustration involved more of a sense of foreboding. He had received a message from Western Approaches Command informing him that ONS5 would get no more patrol flights from Iceland due to bad weather there. From his long experience escorting North Atlantic convoys, Gretton could sense that the multiple HF/DF hits meant that U-boats were coordinating a massed night surface attack against the forty-four merchant ships that now comprised ONS5. "The weather was so bad that no flying from Iceland was possible and so we could do little to prevent the pack assembling at its leisure," he would remember. "The night promised to be a busy one."[9]

At 1800, after slightly less than five hours on the convoy's evasive northerly route, Gretton put ONS5 back on its original course of 240 degrees. The ploy seemed to have worked. At 1841, an HF/DF contact appeared just ahead of the convoy's starboard beam; then, at 1850, the HF/DF operators picked up a U-boat signal coming from astern of the convoy. The new bearing to the U-boat suggested that the boat was still searching along the convoy's original route, "indicat[ing] that the evasion had been successful," Gretton concluded. He was wrong. Von Witzendorff had indeed dropped behind the convoy, but rather than having lost its scent was now trailing ONS5 from astern.

Gretton may have believed that he had shaken the U-boat, but he wanted to be sure. He ordered Lieutenant-Commander Sherwood in the *Tay* to sweep astern for the contact, but the frigate drew a blank. Meanwhile, von Witzendorff jotted down a complaint in his diary, "Shadowing becomes difficult because of the changing visibility and the zig-zagging of the escorts." Still, U-650 managed to cling to the tail of ONS5 as dusk began to settle over the North Atlantic.[10]

Back at BdU operations in Berlin, Grossadmiral Dönitz and his staff waited apprehensively for update messages from U-650 and the other Gruppe Star boats. In one of his messages, von Witzendorff said that visibility around ONS5 had dropped to just one nautical mile in the haze, and Dönitz worried that the decreasing visibility and atmospheric interference would make it difficult to organize an effective attack. Also needling the Grossadmiral was the fact that many Gruppe Star boats were failing to acknowledge messages from BdU.

Shortly before dusk out in the Atlantic, much to Dönitz's relief, BdU obtained signals from two other U-boats confirming they had made contact with ONS5. He immediately ordered them to support von Witzendorff. Veteran U-boat commander Kapitänleutnant Erich Mäder in the U-378 and Oberleutnant zur See Hans-Albrecht Kandler in the newly commissioned U-386 were closing in on U-650's homing signals. Not far behind were two more Gruppe Star commanders: Korvettenkapitän Otto-Heinrich Junker in the new IXC40 U-532 and Kapitänleutnant Wilhelm von Mässenhausen in the veteran U-258.[11]

As Gruppe Star boats began to rally to U-650, the Allies started to pick up on the massing signals. Admiral Horton's staff at Western Approaches

Command signaled Gretton and the other escorts that shore-based HF/DF stations had detected at least thirty-two U-boats in the vicinity of ONS5. The warning mistakenly included U-boats from the Amsel-Specht wolf packs that were actually several hundred miles to the southwest, making the convoy's prospects seem even more dire than they actually were. As the light began to fade, the men of Escort Group B-7 and Convoy ONS5 began bracing for the worst.

Decades after the event, Robert Atkinson, then a lieutenant on the corvette *HMS Pink,* recalled his shock at the specificity of the intelligence that Admiral Horton's staff had been able to compile on the U-boats closing in on Convoy ONS5. "We got a signal—that was the real crisis of it all—from the commander-in-chief Western Approaches: 'Your convoy is encircled by thirty-two U-boats. You may expect attack from down-moon at approximately 0230,'" remembered Atkinson, using the convoy's local time in his description. He was doubly impressed that Admiral Horton in his operations center at Derby House more than 990 miles away had been able to assemble a situational awareness not only of the size of the threat but its location relative to the convoy. "They knew where the moon would be and when it would rise and where the U-boats might attack from—[Horton] liked a profile," Atkinson explained. "And by the feverish increased activity of the radio signaling, they knew attacks were imminent."[12]

Atkinson, who had turned twenty-seven that day, April 28, had more to worry about that night than just the approaching Germans. "A hell of a gale [was] blowing," he recalled, and the *Pink* had a rough time in such weather. "You went on the crest of a wave, you went in the trough of a wave, you thought you were never coming up again," Atkinson recalled. "On average you had a gale every four days. You pitched and rolled all the time."

If the *Pink* had such trouble in the stormy weather it encountered in its crossings, it was because the Admiralty had never planned to send the Flower-class corvettes out into the mid-Atlantic. Adapted from a modified whaling vessel design, the corvettes were built for coastal patrols and limited operations in the North Sea and Irish Sea. Each ship had only a single propeller shaft, which gave it a maximum speed of sixteen knots, slower than a Type VIIC U-boat at full speed on the surface. The corvettes were lightly armed, too; each carried a solitary four-inch deck gun. Its prime anti-submarine weapon was the depth charge rolled off the stern rails or fired from two K-gun launchers on each side. Despite their slow speed and slight armament, however, the small corvettes became effective convoy escorts when teamed up with the larger frigates and destroyers. They were versatile enough to keep station around a convoy's main body, and the Asdic and radar sets were accurate enough to offset their limited speed.

By 1943, Atkinson was a veteran of both the North Atlantic winter and the Flower-class corvette. He had joined the British merchant fleet in 1932, rising to the rank of master mariner in just four years. In 1938, as war clouds formed over Europe, Atkinson joined the Royal Navy Reserve and spent a year in officer candidate training before receiving his commission. First appointed to command the armed boarding vessel *Lorna*, a converted British yacht, Atkinson transferred to the corvette *HMS Rhododendron* as first lieutenant in 1940. On its first escort operation that November, while returning to the main body of the convoy after rescuing the crew of a torpedoed freighter, the *Rhododendron* sighted and attacked a U-boat. The Admiralty credited Atkinson's ship with a kill. The *Rhododendron's* tour ended abruptly two months later, however, when the corvette struck a mine while entering Liverpool harbor, knocking it out of service for a year. Atkinson served on three more corvettes before taking command of the *Pink* on October 20, 1942.

Atkinson and his crew loved the *Pink,* despite its limitations, cramped spaces, bad food, and eternal dampness. The conditions aboard the corvette built camaraderie between the officers and the crew. Indeed, men who served aboard the stout little warships seemed to take a masochistic pride in their experiences. Atkinson's close friend Lieutenant Harold G. Chesterman, commander of the B-7 corvette *HMS Snowflake,* said his vessel moved like "a corkscrew" in heavy seas because its wide, short hull got little traction in the water. "About the third dip [of the hull] and you get tons and tons of water come over the fo'c's'le. And if you happened to be in the waist [of the ship] . . . you probably get washed astern," he recalled. Chesterman once met one of the corvette's design engineers and later described the encounter: "He looked quite surprised when we told him how good they were. Uncomfortable and lively and wet, but safe. And it didn't matter what the weather was, we could go into the gale, down the seas, and when merchant ships were heaved to with the wind on the port bow . . . we could go anywhere."

As night was falling on April 28, Atkinson summoned all crewmen not on watch to gather in the *Pink's* small mess decks compartment. Gazing at the dozens of attentive faces before him, he held up the message from his senior escort officer. "This is the signal we've just received," Atkinson said. "I'm not sure how many of us will live to see daylight, but I intend to do so. This is what we will do." He laid out the schedule for the next hours. "We will have hands to tea at six o'clock, we'll pipe down at seven o'clock, we'll have Action Stations at one o'clock dressed in Arctic clothing. Hot chocolate will be served at two o'clock and you can expect to be there the rest of the night. God help us all." He dismissed them, and the crew quietly resumed preparing for battle.[13]

ONS5 continued on its course of 240 degrees at a speed of 7.5 knots as the North Atlantic descended into unquiet darkness. A bright moon occasionally broke through the clouds to illuminate the convoy among the rolling tops of eight- to thirteen-foot waves, propelled by a fresh southeast breeze of eighteen to twenty-four knots. On the *Pink*, the radioman handed Lieutenant Atkinson a message form. Three months of drills and actual convoy escort duty under Gretton's stern hand made a lengthy exhortation unnecessary. The commander's message contained only one word: "Anticipate."

In preparation for the inevitable attack, Gretton had ordered Escort Group B-7 into night stations. Multiple HF/DF signals had shown U-boats on the convoy's port bow, port beam, port quarter, and directly astern, suggesting that the U-boats wanted to swarm the convoy from three sides—coming either "down sea" (in the direction of the waves) or at angles to the waves to minimize spray that would betray their approach. Knowing this, Gretton oriented the close escort screen around the most likely U-boat approach routes. He sent Lieutenant Hart in the *Vidette* several miles ahead of ONS5 as a distant screen, assigned *Tay* to follow astern of the formation, and loaded the port flank with the corvettes *Sunflower*, off the port bow, and *Snowflake*, on the port beam. The *Duncan* itself would hold the port quarter. The other two corvettes, *Pink* and *Loosestrife*, held the starboard beam and quarter, respectively.

Apart from its new formation, Escort Group B-7 would employ standard night defensive tactics in protecting ONS5. Using the advantages of their HF/DF sensors to track U-boat transmissions, and their Type 271M radar sets, whose beams of energy German radar detectors could not perceive, the escorts would aggressively chase down any U-boat whose position they could plot via Asdic, radar, HF/DF, or visual sighting. They would then attack it with depth charges, Hedgehog projectiles, or gunfire to either destroy it or keep it pinned down while the convoy passed out of range. Gretton was certain from his experience that his enemy would attempt a classic night surface attack, massing on more than one side of the formation and mounting simultaneous approaches in hopes of forcing a breach in the close escort screen.[14]

Commander Gretton and the crew of the *HMS Duncan* were the first to pounce. At 2038 GMT, Gretton's HF/DF operator marked a contact showing a U-boat transmitting on the surface, close to the convoy's port bow. Gretton ordered the *Duncan* to flank speed and raced down the line of bearing, with the frigate *Tay* also heading toward the target on a parallel track.

Forty-two minutes after the initial contact, Gretton's lookouts sighted the spray from waves breaking against a U-boat's conning tower about 4,000 yards away from the *Duncan*. Several minutes later, the German lookouts spotted the approaching escort and the U-boat crash-dived. Gretton slowed the destroyer down to permit lowering the Asdic dome from its housing in order to conduct an active sonar search. The Asdic drew a blank in the turbulence of the high seas, which generated sound interference that obscured any sound generated by the U-boat's passage. Gretton fired a spread of ten depth charges at the enemy's last calculated position in hopes of keeping the U-boat under. After conducting an Operation Observant—a deliberate Asdic search across a square-shaped area two miles per side—for an hour, the *Duncan* returned to the close escort screen by 2330, leaving the *Tay* to remain behind in case the U-boat resurfaced.[15]

At 2358, just over three hours after the *Duncan's* contact, the *Sunflower* had its own U-boat encounter. When his radar operator called out a U-boat contact thirty-two degrees on the starboard bow at a range of 3,800 yards, Lieutenant-Commander James Plomer ordered the corvette out from the port bow escort station to chase it down. Before the small warship could close the distance, however, the U-boat submerged. Plomer ordered a box search of the area using Asdic and dropped two depth charges on what he later termed a "doubtful" contact. The corvette's slow speed was not its only hindrance during this response; in the excitement, a crewman had accidentally ignited a calcium flare, which brightly illuminated the corvette and the surrounding water. Plomer snarled a vicious expletive at the bridge team, but the officer of the watch explained that the flare had gone over the side as the two depth charges dropped. "That's a damn silly thing to do," Plomer said. "We'll be seen by every blasted U-boat within miles. We must go back and put it out." Before returning to the convoy, Plomer ordered the *Sunflower* to reverse course and, on the second attempt, managed to extinguish the flare by drawing it through the ship's propeller stream.[16]

Commander Gretton had long argued to his shipmates and subordinate escort commanders that the key to effective convoy defense was to react as quickly and aggressively as possible to any U-boat sighting. Shortly after returning to the port quarter station for ONS5, Gretton and the *Duncan's* crew got an opportunity to test this tactic on a massive scale. It began with a firm radar contact at 0045 on Thursday, April 29. The U-boat was bearing 100 degrees at a range of 3,500 yards, practically dead astern of the formation. Wheeling around on an intercept course, Gretton once more ordered the *Duncan* to flank speed while he radioed Lieutenant-Commander Sherwood to reposition the *Tay* from its station—codenamed Position Sugar—astern of the convoy to *Duncan's* spot on the port quarter. As Gretton headed toward the rear of the formation, the destroyer's Asdic operator picked up what he later described as a "poor" underwater contact 1,500 yards ahead. The signal faded after the ship had closed to within 1,100 yards. Hoarding his depth charges, Gretton ordered a single one dropped as a harassing measure to hold the U-boat under, then headed back to the convoy.

The *Duncan* had barely returned to the close escort screen when, at 0114, its radar operator called out a second contact 2,300 yards out and thirty-six degrees to starboard from the convoy's course track. Spotting a U-boat's wake, the *Duncan* raced toward it, but the boat quickly crash-dived. As the destroyer ran through its wake, the turbulence blanked out the Asdic's hydrophone echoes until Gretton was 500 yards from the calculated position of the U-boat. At that point, the Asdic operator reacquired the submerged U-boat, and the *Duncan's* crew dropped a full spread of ten depth charges from the stern rails and the K-guns. The ocean lit up from below with the explosions. Running out and turning to attempt to locate the target via Asdic again, Gretton was about to head in for a second spread when, at 0130, his radar operator called out a third U-boat contact, this one bearing 146 degrees at 3,000 yards. Crashing through the tall swells with a force that threw spray clear over its mainmast, the destroyer was plainly visible to lookouts on the second U-boat, which promptly vanished into the cellar. The *Duncan* dropped a single depth charge and once more turned back toward ONS5.

As the *Duncan* was nearing its position in the close screen, yet *another* bright speck flared up on its radar screen, this time 4,000 yards ahead and slightly to port. This U-boat was clearly heading toward the convoy, at a speed of twelve knots. The *Duncan* steadily closed the distance and was only 1,500 yards away before the German lookouts sighted the destroyer coming up from behind. Once again, a sleek hull plunged out of sight, but this time, Gretton's Asdic operator held a firm hydrophone contact. Gretton hastily noted that the U-boat was leaving a trail of oil on the surface, indicating it had previously suffered damage in an escort attack. At Gretton's command, the stern rails opened and the K-guns fired, and ten more depth charges went falling after the U-boat. The *Duncan* ran on for several hundred yards and turned back, its Asdic operator again making a good contact. Gretton made several unsuccessful approaches, planning to fire a spread of two dozen mortar shells ahead of the ship from the Hedgehog launcher, but gave up after the U-boat disappeared on Asdic. Gretton dropped a solitary depth charge and returned to ONS5, arriving at 0310.

Although the *Duncan* had failed to sink any of the four U-boats it had sighted so far that night, it had succeeded in driving them away from the vulnerable ships in the convoy, and Gretton later recalled with pride his crew's performance. The men were not having an easy time of it, especially not the crew manning the depth-charge launchers. "The ship was pitching and rolling badly," Gretton remembered; "the seas were washing down the quarterdeck, soaking the men there, while the heavy and cumbersome depth charges were difficult to reload." Gretton said he had made a point of broadcasting updates on the attack plan every few minutes over the loudspeaker. "There is nothing worse than working on blindly, literally in the dark as to what is happening," he said. "The crews made no mistakes, however, and were quick reloading."[17]

The *Duncan's* two-hour adventure against the four Gruppe Star U-boats ended when the destroyer resumed its regular screening pattern 5,000 yards off the convoy's port quarter at 0310. However, the action was far from over. The corvette *Snowflake's* turn came next when, at 0332, the ship's Asdic operator reported hydrophone effects dead ahead. Lieutenant Chesterman ordered his ship to make sixteen knots, the corvette's maximum speed, and moved toward the signal. Thirty seconds later, the radar operator confirmed a surfaced U-boat dead ahead, and lookouts spotted the target's silhouette moving from starboard to port at a range of 1,300 yards. Chesterman closed to about 200 yards before the U-boat detected him and crash-dived. Chesterman was preparing to order a full spread of depth charges when the *Snowflake's* helmsman, mistaking an order from the officer of the watch to the depth-charge crew for a helm order, threw the rudder hard to starboard. The turn resulted in the submerged U-boat passing down the corvette's port side 200 yards away, too far away for an effective depth-charge attack. No longer possessing the initial factor of surprise, Chesterman wrote in his log, "I maneuvered to get between the U-boat and the convoy to prevent him [from] attacking, contact having been lost."[18]

While the *Snowflake* was repositioning itself to deter a further attack, the U-boat it had just forced underwater was creeping in for a renewed frontal assault on ONS5. Korvettenkapitän Otto-Heinrich Junker was one of Admiral Dönitz's senior U-boat captains with a solid background in U-boats and torpedo development, yet this was his first wartime operation. The thirty-seven-year-old had previously commanded the Type VIIA U-33 for two prewar years during 1936–38. From there, Dönitz had assigned him as a group leader at the Torpedo Testing Branch, where he remained for four years, followed by a three-month temporary assignment at BdU Headquarters. Finally, Dönitz had given Junker command of the new Type IXC/40 U-532, which headed out on its first patrol on March 25, 1943. It had been a frustrating mission to date for both commander

Loading depth charges on an escort warship in high seas was a tough and dangerous task; here, crewmen on a British destroyer reload their stern launching rails during a hunt for a U-boat.
Imperial War Museum, U.K

and crew. Prior to assigning U-532 to Gruppe Star, BdU had included the boat in three other wolf packs—including Gruppe Löwenherz, which had gone up against Commander Gretton and Escort Group B-7 guarding Convoy HX231 just three weeks earlier. In that fight, and subsequent attempts to attack Convoys HX232 and HX234, Junker had failed to make contact with the enemy. Now, he had his chance.

At 0335, Junker came up to periscope depth, targeted a merchantman in the third spot of one of ONS5's columns, and fired a *Fäscherschuss* (fan shot) of four torpedoes from his bow tubes. A minute later, *Snowflake's* Asdic operator reacquired contact 2,000 yards away. This set off a furious, twenty-minute fight between the corvette and the U-boat.[19]

Gaining a new bearing on the U-boat he had just detected, Chesterman ordered a limited spread of three depth charges to scare it off once again. As the corvette turned to attack, however, its Asdic operator suddenly shouted, "Torpedo hydrophone effect!" Lookouts on the corvette gaped as a torpedo passed down the ship's side, missing it by a mere twenty yards. Still at periscope depth, Junker had fired torpedoes from his two stern tubes at the approaching escort, whose lookouts spotted only one of them. Chesterman ordered a blast on the ship's siren to warn ONS5 that a torpedo was inbound, and called the other escorts by radiotelephone to repeat the alert. Luckily for the *Snowflake* and ONS5, all six of U-532's torpedoes missed, and the corvette continued its attack run.

At 0343, seven minutes after Junker fired his first salvo at ONS5, the *Snowflake* closed in on the U-boat's calculated position. Junker, still at periscope depth, saw the corvette racing in and ordered the emergency alarm to crash dive. Chesterman ordered a full drop of ten depth charges, but he later reported that the attack was "not particularly accurate"; Asdic contact had been lost. Two minutes later, however, the *Snowflake* regained Asdic contact and raced toward the estimated U-boat position just 4,000 yards from the convoy, where it dropped a second ten-charge pattern. A relieved Chesterman wrote, "This attack is considered to have been accurate." Several minutes later the Asdic operator reported a "doubtful" contact, but Chesterman decided to call off the hunt. "In view of the prospect of heavy attacks by U-boats for many days to come, I could not afford to expend any more depth charges," the lieutenant wrote, "and as the U-boat was no longer in a position to menace the convoy I proceeded to rejoin."

The flurry of U-boat attempts to strike ONS5 and Escort Group B-7's furious responses during the night of April 28–29 ended inconclusively with a seventh contact with a U-boat. At 0354, the *Tay*, still patrolling Position Sugar astern of the convoy, gained a solid Asdic contact and vigorously attacked it but reported no specific damage to the target.[20]

The *Tay's* counterattack at the rear of ONS5 was the last action that Escort Group B-7 would see that night. Weary yet elated, Gretton wrote in his log, "A most successful night." The hardy escorts had beaten off no less than seven attacks by an estimated five or six U-boats without the loss of a single merchant ship. "It had been a very testing baptism of firing for the ship's company, who had behaved splendidly," Gretton said of his newly "blooded" crew.[21]

In fact, the escort group had performed better than Gretton and his commanders realized. Of the four Gruppe Star boats that had actually attempted to penetrate the convoy screen, the escorts had succeeded in mauling two. In the swirl of battle it was often impossible to assign specific credit to a particular escort, but a postwar review of British and German naval archives would reveal that the *Snowflake* had delivered a serious beating to U-532, the U-boat that had just fired at it. Junker recorded in his war diary that the depth charges had damaged his forward hydroplanes, causing them to jam and to make loud noises when moved, preventing the U-boat from changing depth without giving away its position to enemy Asdic operators. The attacks also damaged a wide range of the boat's electrical equipment, cracked a battery array that leaked acid into the bilges, and knocked out the boat's magnetic compass. Loss of the compass made it all but impossible to conduct a submerged attack, Junker reported, because the backup electrical gyrocompass generated too much noise. U-532 crouched in the cellar for fifteen hours, its exhausted crew breathing from emergency oxygen devices as they listened to B-7 depth-charging other U-boats. It wasn't until 2340 on April 29 that Junker felt safe enough to surface and set course for the boat's base at Lorient. En route, Junker radioed BdU to report he had heard "two definite detonations" from the six torpedoes he had fired at ONS5 and the *Snowflake*. Alas for him, they had been two end-of-run warhead explosions, which further padded the increasingly inaccurate tally at BdU Headquarters.[22]

After the war, Admiralty researchers would also credit Lieutenant-Commander Plomer and the corvette *Sunflower* with damaging the U-386 so severely that its commander, Oberleutnant zur See Kandler, was forced to abort his patrol as well. Despite the mishap with the flare and his Asdic operator's "doubtful" contact, Plomer's two depth-charge patterns had hammered the submerged U-boat. Kandler would manage to limp the 1,200 nautical miles to St. Nazaire, arriving twelve days later, but U-386 would cause no more trouble for ONS5.

At 0416 on April 29, with the eastern sky beginning to lighten in the dawn, Commander Gretton reassigned the escorts into their day patrol stations. Convoy ONS5 was continuing on its course of 240 degrees at a speed of seven knots. The winds had died down to a light breeze, and visibility was very good except when occasional squalls swept over the formation. So far, the convoy had avoided losing a single ship, thanks to the escort ships' aggressive response to each U-boat contact, and the skies looked even brighter ahead.

At the height of the B-7 fight against the Gruppe Star U-boats, two messages from Western Approaches Command had bolstered Gretton's confidence that ONS5 might avoid serious losses. The first had come at 0026 on April 29, informing Gretton that Admiral Horton had detached the 3rd Support Group destroyer HMS Oribi from temporary duty with the escort group for nearby Convoy SC127 to reinforce B-7 and ONS5. Lieutenant-Commander John A. C. Ingram, commander of the Oribi, had reported his departure from the eastbound convoy just over an hour later, and was currently making best speed toward ONS5. In a separate communication, Horton told Gretton that he had ordered the other destroyers in the 3rd Support Group—HMS Offa and HMS Impulsive, and two newly assigned destroyers, HMS Panther and HMS Penn—to steam as soon as possible from their homeport at St. John's to bolster B-7. Captain James A. McCoy, Offa's skipper and senior escort officer of the support group, expected it would take at least two days to make the rendezvous.[23]

Despite the anticipated arrival of reinforcements, Gretton knew that ONS5 wasn't out of the woods yet. "The night had been a busy one, the convoy unscathed and I felt that the U-boats must be discouraged by our night tactics and might try [a periscope-depth] day attack," he recalled. A submerged day attack would require the U-boat commanders to speed far ahead of the convoy, submerge in the formation's path, then hover silently as the quarry steamed into torpedo range. Under certain circumstances, such as poor visibility on the surface, U-boats could attempt periscope-depth attacks from either side of a convoy, but their slow speed submerged and limited battery life made this a difficult maneuver to carry out. Nevertheless, just in case, Gretton opted to cover the entire formation.

In light of the U-boats' possible attack vectors ahead and to each side, the nine B-7 warships had regrouped to surround ONS5 in a full circle, rather than guarding the sides calculated to be the U-boats' preferred approach route. The destroyers Duncan and Vidette were each patrolling about 5,000 yards out from the port and starboard bows of the main body, respectively, while the Sunflower, Snowflake, and Northern Gem shielded the port flank. The Loosestrife, Pink, and Northern Spray were on the starboard side. Once the *Tay* returned, it would once more occupy Position Sugar, the escort position directly behind the convoy's main body.

With the escort screen in place, Gretton finished a congratulatory message to Commodore Brook on the *Rena* and retired to his sea cabin for a much-needed nap. His rest would have to wait, however. Less than five minutes later, at 0729, the shock wave of an explosion pounded the *Duncan*'s hull and sent Gretton running from his bunk back up to the navigation bridge.[24]

The 6,198-ton American freighter *McKeesport*, one of the older merchant vessels in Convoy ONS5, had become its first casualty. Steaming in the second position in Column 4, the twenty-four-year-old merchantman had safely traveled from the United States to the British Isles in the ill-fated Convoy SC122 in March with a cargo of grain and other foodstuffs, steel tanks, and chemicals. Now, Master Oscar John Lohr and his crew of forty-three, augmented by twenty-five Naval Armed Guard gunners, were returning the ship to New York in ballast. The single torpedo that had struck the *McKeesport* blasted straight into its starboard side at the No. 1 cargo hold, which was full of sand ballast, blowing out all deck beams and cargo hatches and briefly knocking the ship's steering gear out of order. Lohr continued steaming with the convoy as his officers assessed the damage and attempted to repair the steering, but water was pouring into the *McKeesport*'s hull at an alarming rate.[25]

On the *Duncan,* Gretton grabbed the radiotelephone and ordered Operation Artichoke, the emergency response maneuver for a ship torpedoed in the convoy's main body. The frigate *Tay* sped toward the stricken freighter from its position astern of the formation, while the other escorts turned and passed down between the columns, conducting Asdic and radar searches for the U-boat. Because of conflicting reports, Gretton did not know from what side the attack had come, but six minutes after the explosion, his lookouts observed several end-of-run torpedo warhead detonations off the convoy's port quarter, indicating that the U-boat had fired from the starboard side. The escorts did not detect the U-boat that had torpedoed the McKeesport, so the *Duncan* canceled the Artichoke and ordered all of the escorts back to their day stations.

Gretton next dispatched the *Snowflake* to escort the 5,561-ton American ship *West Maximus,* which had straggled from the main body and was now five miles astern. He then brought the *Duncan* back to where the anti-submarine warfare trawler *Northern Gem* was attacking a suspected target. After an hour or so, Gretton called off the search when a new HF/DF signal intercepted at 0824 bearing 214 degrees, or twenty-six degrees to port of the convoy's path of advance, indicated a second U-boat preparing to attack. Recalling the *Snowflake* and *Tay* back to the main body, Gretton ordered the *Duncan* to flank speed and raced toward the newest target at twenty-three knots.

As Gretton was chasing the latest U-boat contact, the *Northern Gem* had pulled alongside the stricken *McKeesport*. Incredibly, Lohr and his crew had been able to keep up with ONS5 for another fifty minutes until the ship began to sink in earnest at 0815. Most of the crew had already abandoned ship into four lifeboats, but several fell into the water when the life nets became tangled. The trawler rescued all but one crewman killed in the initial explosion, although a second crewman died of exposure after being retrieved. Gretton, who had ordered Lieutenant Hart on the *Vidette* to join the *Duncan* in the sweep for the suspected U-boat, had found nothing, and by 0915, all of the escorts save the *Tay* and *Northern Gem* were back on station. When the ASW trawler finally rejoined ONS5 at 1515, Gretton became irritated when he learned that the *McKeesport* was still afloat with several confidential documents aboard, including the navigational chart and deck log. He ordered Sherwood in the *Tay* to go back and sink the hulk.[26]

The mysterious torpedo that had struck the *McKeesport* had come from Kapitänleutnant Wilhelm von Mässenhausen in U-258. The twenty-eight-year-old U-boat commander was already a relatively seasoned combat veteran, having presided over the sinking of three small Allied merchant ships while serving as 1WO aboard the U-79. Von Mässenhausen had served as commander of U-258 for one previous war patrol without sinking any ships and had been frustrated in this patrol, as well—both as part of Gruppe Meise in its unsuccessful hunts for Convoys SC126 and HX234, and as part of Gruppe Star during Escort Group B-7's aggressive maneuvering the night before. Thwarted by the dense convoy screen, von Mässenhausen had moved well out in front of ONS5 and successfully slipped under the convoy itself. He had come up between Columns 4 and 5 and fired at the *McKeesport* at point-blank range, then escaped. Later that afternoon, after resurfacing, U-258 spotted the abandoned and drifting *McKeesport*, which had resisted the *Tay*'s effort to sink it with depth charges. Von Mässenhausen fired two coup de grâce torpedoes and the old ship finally went down.[27]

For the rest of the day and night after the surprise attack on the *McKeesport*, ONS5 would be spared any further U-boat strikes. The formation, however, was about to receive a horrible test from the North Atlantic itself. In late afternoon on April 29, the weather suddenly deteriorated. A solid overcast descended and a full gale sprang up, with winds blowing over sixty miles an hour. The storm forced Coastal Command to cancel several scheduled VLR Liberator missions, and set back the scheduled rendezvous of *HMS Oribi* from Convoy SC127.

Fortunately for ONS5, the sudden storm also tore into what remained of Gruppe Star. Two HF/DF contacts at 1830 showed a pair of boats attempting to sneak up on the convoy, but when Lieutenant-Commander Plomer took the corvette *Sunflower* out on one line of bearing, his lookouts found nothing but the mountainous waves. The gale-force winds would have shrieked loudly, but as Gretton reported in his log, "There was then a silence of seven hours on H/F." Sensing that the heavy seas would mean that any new attacks would likely come from ahead instead of from the sides of the formation—the U-boat captains always avoided maneuvering against the waves to minimize creating fountains of spray that escort lookouts could readily spot—Gretton placed the *Sunflower* on the convoy's port bow, the *Duncan* dead ahead, and the *Vidette* on the starboard bow, leaving the quarters unprotected.

At 0107 on Friday, April 30, an HF/DF signal close ahead of the convoy validated Gretton's calculation. The *Duncan* chased after it and thirty minutes later dropped a full spread of ten depth charges, followed by a solitary harassing charge when the Asdic operator briefly regained contact. Meanwhile, the *Snowflake* reacted to a U-boat contact off the port beam of ONS5 and drove off the enemy with depth charges. The frigate *Tay* was still forty-nine miles astern of the formation, where Lieutenant-Commander Sherwood reported that he was attacking a suspected U-boat.

As the escorts in B-7 chased after various U-boat contacts, they finally received the first of the reinforcements that had been promised them some twenty-four hours earlier. Finishing its eleven-knot slog through the storm, the *Oribi* finally joined B-7 in the darkness. Lieutenant-Commander Ingram promptly reported to Commander Gretton that the ship was rolling so severely that three of his crewmen had suffered head injuries when a sudden lurch threw them fifteen feet against a steel bulkhead.[28]

With the *Oribi* on hand to reinforce B-7 and the *Duncan* returned from hunting after the suspected U-boat, Gretton ordered the escorts into their day stations several hours earlier than normal. He feared another wave of daylight submerged attacks from the persistent wolf pack and wanted his escorts ready before the sun came up on the convoy. But as the sky brightened slowly in the raging gale, the escorts' Asdic sets remained quiet.

The weather now became the primary concern for ONS5 and its escorts, as they were struggling to keep the formation intact. Coastal Command had managed to launch a VLR Liberator from Reykjavik that arrived overhead early that morning, despite the weather; the bomber found ONS5 at 0645 but returned to Iceland after only several passes because of the bad visibility. It may not have been the best conditions for a refueling attempt, but since the *Oribi* was a short-legged destroyer and had just made a long and grueling journey, Lieutenant-Commander Ingram requested Gretton's permission to take on fuel from the escort tanker. Falling astern of the *British Lady*, the destroyer's deck crew attempted to recover the fueling hose being dragged astern of the tanker, but it accidentally fouled the *Oribi*'s gear, making further refueling impossible for the destroyer, and forcing Gretton to transfer some of the *Duncan*'s dwindling fuel stocks to the *Oribi* when the weather temporarily improved in late morning.[29]

The afternoon and evening of April 30 passed without incident for ONS5 until 2100, when a new southwest gale came upon the convoy. Several hours later, so did several Gruppe Star U-boats. Gretton had once more stacked the escorts on the port side of the convoy, an astute move: at 0105 on Saturday, May 1, the *Snowflake*'s radar operator detected a surfaced U-boat on the port beam. Lieutenant Chesterman ordered a course change to intercept. After several minutes the German lookouts detected the *Snowflake* and with its two-knot speed advantage, the U-boat began to pull away from the slower corvette. Chesterman shouted into the engine room speaking tube that the *Snowflake* was hunting a surfaced U-boat, and his "black gang" redoubled their efforts. "Range at first opened," Chesterman dryly noted in his after-action report, "but when the engine room had been informed that we were chasing a U-boat the range subsequently closed." When reaching a distance of 3,000 yards from the U-boat, Chesterman ordered his four-inch gun to alternatively fire starshells to illuminate the target and high-explosive rounds to damage or drive it under. Crewmen manning the Oerlikon 20-mm cannons also opened up. The splashes close aboard forced the German commander to crash-dive. The *Snowflake* dropped a single harassing charge in the swirl, but lost contact. At Gretton's directive, Lieutenant Atkinson in the corvette *Pink* also joined the fray, detaching from its station on the port quarter of ONS5 to drop a small spread of harassing charges atop the U-boat's suspected location.

Nine minutes after the *Snowflake* got radar contact on its U-boat, an HF/DF intercept revealed a second U-boat very close to ONS5 just to starboard of the convoy's course track. The *Duncan* and *Vidette* turned toward the contact position, but the warships could only make eight knots headway as they struggled into the teeth of the storm. Dropping depth charges at that slow pace was "a hazardous business," since the detonations were more likely to damage the attacker than the U-boat. After the *Vidette* made its run and dropped depth charges, Gretton ordered a pair of depth charges dropped from the *Duncan*'s stern rails. The blast lifted the destroyer's stern completely out of the water, sprang leaks in the hull, and, "more serious still," Gretton quipped, smashed all the wardroom gin glasses. The U-boat disappeared and was not observed again.[30]

ONS5 was experiencing its worst storm yet. When daylight came, both the convoy and its embattled escort group were scattered over hundreds of square miles of the North Atlantic.

For Lieutenant Atkinson and the crew of the *Pink* and Lieutenant-Commander Sherwood and his men on the *Tay*, rounding up the stragglers from the raging storm would consume most of the first three days of the new month. The two escorts peeled off from the main body upon receiving Gretton's order to find the missing merchant vessels. At 0630 on May 1, Atkinson and the *Pink* quickly found the 3,862-ton freighter *Dunsley* and 3,788-ton merchantman *Omega* about ten miles astern of the main body. However, the sea conditions became so bad that the *Omega* was forced to heave to. The *Dunsley's* master, fearing that any attempt to turn into the wind would capsize his ship, decided that heaving to was not an option. He continued to run before the storm.[31]

By midday on Saturday, May 1, the gale had grown to hurricane force. Down in the boiler rooms of the forty-two merchant ships, the stokers and greasers kept steam pressure up in an attempt to drive their vessels along at the designated convoy speed of seven knots, yet the ships were all but motionless against the headwinds and advancing seas that pummeled the convoy. With scant forward motion, the merchantmen began drifting out of formation, and ONS5 slowly disintegrated. On the flagship *Rena,* Commodore Brook jotted in his logbook, "Half convoy not under command, hove to and very scattered." Gretton described the same dreary sight. "The *Duncan* was hove to first with the wind on one bow and then on the other, and we could do little except make sure of keeping reasonably close to the Commodore's ship," he wrote. "It was most frustrating to see the convoy melting away before our eyes, but we could do nothing about it."

Just as the convoy was coming apart at the seams, a 120 Squadron VLR Liberator arrived overhead with news good and bad: there were no U-boats to be seen, but icebergs lay in the convoy's path just thirty miles away. Several hours later, two U.S. Army Air Forces B-25s flew down from Greenland and circled the formation but failed to make radio contact with the escorts. Gretton successfully homed in two more VLR Liberators in late afternoon, but they too reported the ocean was empty except for the scattered ONS5 ships.

Gretton felt certain there would be no attempted attacks during such a violent tempest. Rather, he added, the U-boat commanders were probably "sitting comfortably below the waves" as they waited for the storm to abate.

For the escort crewmen, there was no relief. The night of May 1–2 was a thoroughly miserable experience for all hands on the *Pink.* As he had done regularly before, Lieutenant Atkinson bundled himself up in a heavy sweater, Royal Navy duffel coat—which he detested as "one of the worst garments ever invented"—and also donned knee-length gunboots, a knitted wool balaclava ski mask, and mitts. Thus swaddled against the lashing sleet and hail, he climbed into a chair on the elevated platform at the fore of his open navigation bridge, not far from the gyrocompass and voice pipes to the wheelhouse and navigator's station below. He tried to relax as his small warship heaved and plunged through the endless succession of towering waves.[32]

When the weather moderated in the morning of May 2, the *Pink* was in contact with five ONS5 stragglers—three British merchantmen, the *Dunsley, Omega,* and 5,107-ton *Director;* the 2,280-ton Norwegian *Gudvor;* and the 4,540-ton Greek freighter *Nicolas.* A sixth ship, the 5,565-ton American freighter *West Madaket,* joined some hours later. The small procession doggedly followed the *Pink* in the direction of the convoy fifty miles away, but the headlong seas and gales all but nullified their forward motion. At 1800 that Sunday evening, yet another hard gale blew in, and the merchant ships hove to and slowly drifted off into the gloom once more. Atkinson and his crew braced themselves for another miserable night.[33]

The long hours passed with little change. No U-boats appeared on the escort ships' radar screens, and no HF/DF intercepts occurred to confirm a transmitting U-boat close at hand.

It was on Sunday, May 2, that Gretton's chief concern shifted from the U-boat threat to the safety of his own ship. His chief engineer reported that the *Duncan's* fuel tanks were leaking oil into the forward boiler room. Gretton struggled down the ladders to inspect the damage and found a dangerous mixture of air and fuel vapor in the compartment. He reluctantly agreed to shut down the boiler, cutting the destroyer's speed in half, then wearily climbed back up onto the bridge.

As the darkened day faded into black night, the individual ships in Convoy ONS5 struggled in solitude to survive the battering waves and screaming wind. Here and there, lookouts could mark a distant pair of red truck lights on a mainmast that marked one of dozens of vessels out of control in the chaos.[34]

As they battled through the storm on May 2, the escort sailors and merchant seamen in Convoy ONS5 were totally unaware that they had finished one phase of their ordeal and were entering another. Gretton had been more right than he realized about the diminished U-boat threat; the weather on the North Atlantic had in fact been so bad that, rather than simply deterring any further attacks, it had thrown the pursuing wolf pack off ONS5's track entirely. The previous day, Grossadmiral Dönitz and Konteradmiral Godt had reluctantly decided to call off Gruppe Star's hunt for ONS5. "The continuing bad weather prevented [U-boat] contact [with ONS5] being re-established on 1st May," Godt wrote in the BdU war diary. "As there was little prospect of picking the convoy up again . . . the boats were ordered to break off the operation at dusk." Gruppe Star, like ONS5, had been thrown into disarray by the storm.

In summarizing the operations against "Convoy No. 33," Godt and Dönitz blamed atmospheric interference for obstructing their ability to receive U-boat situation reports and to direct the wolf pack. "It can therefore be said that this attack failed only because of the bad weather, not because of the enemy's defenses," the war diary entry concluded. The two German admirals would soon learn how wrong they had been on that point.[35]

ALTHOUGH BdU had dissolved Gruppe Star, the threat remained high for Convoy ONS5. Thirteen of the seventeen U-boats from that wolf pack remained on patrol in the North Atlantic. Of the other four U-boats from the group, outbound U-710 had been sunk on April 24 before joining Gruppe Star, and the other three boats—U-386, U-513, and U-528—had aborted the attack on ONS5 and were headed back to France. As they sat out the storm, the former Gruppe Star commanders and crew still on patrol waited for the BdU operations staff to identify the next approaching convoy and to assign them to a new wolf pack. In addition, there were still a host of other U-boats lurking in the Greenland air gap. Thirty-three U-boats were operating in Gruppen Amsel and Specht farther to the southwest.

By the dawn of Sunday, May 2, the storm finally showed signs of abating. The raging winds had slightly diminished, and Commodore Brook was able to increase the convoy's speed to five knots. Unfortunately, however, only twenty of the convoy's forty-one other ships were visible from the Rena's navigation bridge. Commander Gretton and the B-7 escorts faced another tough day of rounding up the others, some of which had drifted more than thirty miles downwind during the storm. Fortunately, a 120 Squadron VLR Liberator arrived overhead that morning halfway

through what would be a 1,200-mile round trip from and back to Reykjavik. After exchanging signals, the four-engine bomber began a wide
sweep of the area to locate stragglers and point them back to the formation. It greatly eased the burden of the B-7 escorts as they searched for the
rest of the merchant vessels.[36]

On the *Duncan,* Gretton was painfully aware of his ship's low fuel state.
He had not had a chance to refuel since April 26 and had been forced to
transfer some of his dwindling supplies over to the *Oribi* after her botched
refueling attempt on April 30. Now, with the weather more stable than it
had been in days, Gretton signaled the tanker *British Lady* that he was
preparing to approach from astern to refuel, and maneuvered in for the
rendezvous. The weather conditions were still against Gretton, however;
ONS5 had come close enough to the winter ice pack that the water
through which they were steaming was chockablock with pack ice that
threatened to punch a hole in a ship's hull. For several hours, Commander
Gretton and Lieutenant-Commander Morgan attempted to get close
enough to the tanker to retrieve its fuel hose, but every time they went in
for the pickup, the tanker would veer aside to miss colliding with growlers
and bergy bits. Finally emerging into a clear patch of ocean Gretton was
about to make one last effort when the weather got "impossibly bad"
within minutes, with snow and hail coming down and visibility declining.
Gretton abandoned the refueling attempt, aware that the *Duncan* would
have to abort the convoy soon if it failed to get more fuel, as would the
Vidette and *Tay.*[37]

For all of its setbacks, Escort Group B-7 received one good piece of
news on Sunday, May 2. Captain McCoy on the *Offa,* along with the *Impulsive, Panther,* and *Penn*—four destroyers from the 3rd Support Group,
the same unit as the *Oribi*—finally met up with ONS5 after departing
from St. John's some four days earlier. On April 29, the reinforcements
had been promised to B-7, but the same storm and iceberg-cluttered
ocean that had tormented the convoy had repeatedly set back the support
group's effort to make the rendezvous. Instead of joining the convoy before dark on May 1, as planned, the four destroyers did not make the rendezvous until 2000 the following day.

The arrival of the rest of the 3rd Support Group eased some of the pressure on Gretton and his escort group, although it caused a bit of profes-

sional awkwardness for Gretton. As Senior Escort Officer for B-7, he was formally responsible for the defense of Convoy ONS5 and inevitably would be required to direct McCoy and his Support Group on what actions to take against any U-boats. However, as a captain, McCoy clearly outranked Commander Gretton, and in most military organizations, junior officers do not order their seniors around. As McCoy drew the *Offa* close aboard the *Duncan* and he and Gretton exchanged greetings and transferred papers via a shot line, however, neither officer intended to let that issue grow into a problem. The two men both knew the importance of close teamwork, so when Gretton tactfully requested that McCoy and his ships take a particular action, McCoy cheerfully agreed. "It might have been embarrassing to give instructions to a vastly senior officer," Gretton recalled after the war. "But I made 'requests' and he complied with them in the most friendly way, and these unusual but necessary command arrangements worked quite admirably throughout the operation."[38]

With the *Tay* and *Pink* still absent rounding up stragglers, Gretton put the 3rd Support Group into action. He requested that McCoy's destroyers—including the *Oribi*—sweep out ahead of ONS5 at a distance of ten miles and form two groups on the port and starboard bows of the formation, in a line abreast with two miles separating each ship. They would operate throughout the night and the following morning as a distant picket line to detect any U-boats attempting to launch a daylight submerged attack.

As he wearily climbed into his sea cabin bunk late on the night of May 2, Gretton had something more positive to think about than his critical fuel state. The support group had gotten into position by 2055 and, following Gretton's directive, McCoy's warships would stay out in front of the convoy throughout the night and the following day. When B-7 shifted into its day stations around sunrise on May 3, the *Impulsive* and *Oribi* rotated to flanking positions five miles out from the convoy's port beam, while the *Penn* and *Panther* took similar stations five miles out on the starboard side. McCoy and the *Offa* moved out to the east and southeast of ONS5 to help the *Tay* and *Pink* in the search for stragglers.

On Monday, May 3, the latest storm had passed, but a cloak of fast-moving clouds whipped overhead as if to confirm the continuing instability of the North Atlantic weather. Gripping the rail on the *Duncan*'s navigation bridge, Commander Gretton now counted twenty-seven ships in loose formation, with another half-dozen fifty miles astern following the corvette *Pink*. He ordered the convoy to heave to and wait for the *Pink* and her six charges while the other escorts made another sweep for stragglers.

A moment of truth had arrived, one Gretton had been dreading for several days. The *Duncan* was down to forty percent fuel capacity and, with scant odds of being able to refuel from the escort tanker, Gretton had to make a critical decision. If he continued with Convoy ONS5 on its south-southeast course to skirt the east coast of Newfoundland, the likelihood was that the *Duncan's* fuel tanks would run dry, forcing another escort to tow the destroyer the rest of the way. The alternative was to hand over command of Escort Group B-7 to its second-ranking officer, Lieutenant-Commander Sherwood in the *Tay*, and proceed directly to St. John's. Further complicating the situation, the destroyer *Vidette* from B-7 and the five destroyers from McCoy's 3rd Escort Group were getting dangerously low on fuel, as well. At 0801, Gretton flashed a dire situation report to Admiral Horton at Derby House:

MY P/C/S 57:38 N[orth] 041:48 W[est], [Course] 202 [Speed] 3 [knots] . . . SPEED HAS DROPPED OWING TO MORE SW GALES. ABOUT 32 SHIPS IN COMPANY OUT OF 42. EG3 [3rd Escort Group] JOINED AT 2000 [GMT]/3. MY OIL FUEL PERCENTAGE REMAINING 40 [percent], VIDETTE 51 [percent]. IF WEATHER DOES NOT IMPROVE DUNCAN MUST PROCEED TO ST JOHN'S N.F. FOR FUEL AT DUSK TONIGHT . . . FOLLOWED BY VIDETTE ON WEDNESDAY. NORTHERN GEM HAS 70 SUR-VIVORS [from the *McKeesport*] ABOARD. INTEND TO SEND HER TO ST JOHN'S AT DAWN TUESDAY.[39]

Although aware that ONS5 was likely heading toward a mass of U-boats straddling the convoy's course track, Gretton also knew that he had honed Escort Group B-7 into a tough and capable fighting force. He made his decision. "After much heart-searching, I decided that the *Duncan* had to go," he later wrote. "The weather would not allow boat work [for him to transfer to another escort ship], nor transfer by a jackstay, so I had to go with her."

Lieutenant-Commander Robert Evan Sherwood, commander of *HMS Tay*, became acting senior officer Escort Group B-7 prior to the massed U-boat attacks during May 4–6, 1943.
National Museum of the Royal Navy

In Gretton's absence, Lieutenant-Commander Sherwood in the *Tay* would assume command of Escort Group B-7. Gretton called Sherwood on the radiotelephone and ordered him to return to ONS5 from hunting stragglers. At 1400, the *Tay* rendezvoused with the *Duncan* about 5,000 yards ahead of the convoy. Gretton formally ordered Sherwood to take command, and set the *Duncan* on a course of 200 degrees for St. John's. Lieutenant-Commander Robert Evan Sherwood was now in charge of a close escort group that was itself within hours of disintegrating from lack of sufficient fuel.

Had Commander Gretton enjoyed a choice of whom to select as his temporary relief commanding Escort Group B-7, it is doubtful that he would have chosen anyone other than the *Tay's* commander. A stocky thirty-six-year-old with a full beard, Sherwood had been at sea for more than half his life and was known to be an excellent seaman and an officer capable of quick and decisive action. During the long days and nights of a North Atlantic crossing, he would abandon his sea cabin, preferring to sling a hammock in the *Tay*'s cramped Asdic compartment where he would have instant oversight of any developing situation. Indeed, in the war thus far, Sherwood had seen more action than most of his contemporaries in the Royal Navy. A merchant navy sailor turned Royal Navy reservist, Sherwood had taken temporary command of a tug during the evacuation of Dunkirk in 1940, and had rescued several hundred British troops from the French beaches. He went on to command the Flower-class corvette *HMS Bluebell* in convoy escort operations from May 1940 until May 1942, during which he and his crew won renown throughout the fleet for rescuing more than 200 merchant sailors from six different ships that had fallen victim to the U-boats. Sherwood's intimate knowledge of convoy escort tactics and his lengthy experience fighting the U-boats made him an ideal commander to take the helm of Escort Group B-7. Gretton, whose personal remarks about his fellow B-7 officers were polite but understated to the point of vagueness, said of his decision to hand over the escort group to the *Tay*'s skipper, "I had been in the *Tay* with Sherwood during the last battle [of Convoy HX231] and I knew that he could compete."[40]

Not long after Gretton departed on the *Duncan,* other escorts began dropping off from Convoy ONS5. At 2140, the fuel-depleted 3rd Support Group destroyer *Impulsive* broke off for the Allied naval anchorage at Hvalfjordur, north of Reykjavik, per an order from Western Approaches Command. Although the night of May 3 passed without incident, as the convoy and escorts clawed their way into the face of the gale, daybreak on May 4 saw yet more departures. Sherwood's first task was to order the ASW trawler *Northern Gem* at 0600 to detach from the convoy for St. John's to land the sixty-seven survivors of the torpedoed freighter *McKeesport.* Two hours later, Captain McCoy ordered two more 3rd Support Group destroyers, the *Penn* and *Panther,* to break away for St. John's to refuel. Unless the weather calmed, the *Offa* and *Oribi* would have to break off no later than Wednesday morning, May 5. If that occurred, the combined Escort Group B-7 and 3rd Support Group would be down to three destroyers, one frigate, one ASW trawler and four corvettes.

At the Western Approaches Command operations center in Liverpool, there was a sudden air of crisis. Admiral Horton and his staff were well aware that ONS5 was heading into U-boat-infested waters with an escort force that was steadily shrinking to the point of being combat ineffective. Fearing that ONS5 would suffer the same fate as the scantily protected March convoys, the staff at Derby House began plans to rush a second support group to the convoy's assistance. The five warships assigned to the 1st Support Group—the sloop *HMS Pelican*; the three River-class frigates *HMS Jed, HMS Spey,* and *HMS Wear*; and the ex–U.S. Coast Guard cutter *HMS Sennen*—were ordered to depart St. John's at 1400 on May 4, and to steam at best speed to meet ONS5 and its close escort. It was all that Western Approaches could do to protect the convoy. Privately, though, they feared it might already be too late.[41]

Chapter 12

THE MÊLÉE AT
55 NORTH 042 WEST

For Grossadmiral Karl Dönitz and Konteradmiral Eberhard Godt at BdU Headquarters in Berlin, the first three days of May were a time of mounting frustration largely due to the severe weather in the North Atlantic. For two days after Kapitänleutnant von Mässenhausen in U-258 had slipped past Convoy ONS5's screen of defenders to sink the American freighter *McKeesport* on April 29, only four of the other fifteen U-boats in Gruppe Star had sighted the formation, and none could mount an effective attack in the roiling ocean. Realizing that the weather in that specific area was too harsh, the BdU leadership called off Gruppe Star's operation and dissolved the wolf pack on May 1. "The whole operation was hampered by heavy atmospherics, so that [BdU] Operational Control had no definite information on the course of the operation," Godt wrote in the command's daily war diary.

What surely must have vexed the U-boat Headquarters staff was that by May 1 they were aware of at least four more Allied convoys transiting the mid-Atlantic in addition to the just abandoned ONS5: two heavily laden eastbound convoys and two westbound formations steaming in ballast. On May 1, BdU still had the three wolf packs with forty-nine U-boats in the Greenland air gap—eighteen in Gruppe Specht and sixteen in Gruppe Amsel operating 600 miles northeast of Newfoundland, and the fifteen of the sixteen U-boats from the now-dissolved Star awaiting further orders up to the north around Cape Farewell.[1]

The harsh operating conditions at sea continued to plague Dönitz, his staff, and the U-boat commanders during the next seventy-two hours. There was only one firm convoy sighting. On May 1, B-dienst intercepted and decrypted an Allied message that helped locate the course track of an eastbound convoy several hundred miles east of Newfoundland. Then at 1900 that day, U-628, a Gruppe Specht boat, reported several plumes of smoke in naval grid BC 2215, about 300 miles east-northeast of St. John's. Dönitz scrambled all of Group Specht, and several hours later the thirteen remaining boats from the former Star formation, to go after the ships, which BdU now concluded was eastbound Convoy SC128, consisting of thirty-one merchant ships that had sailed from Halifax on April 25. But over the course of the next two days, the Allied formation, pushed along by the gale-force winds from astern its course, remained hidden in the gloom.

Despite the bad weather, Dönitz and Godt did not abandon the hunt for Convoy SC128. Instead, they re-formed the U-boats in Gruppe Specht and the former Star into a single, condensed patrol line running 190 nautical miles from 56:21 North 044:35 West to 54:57 North 044:35 West. Each of the thirty-one U-boats were stationed just 6.3 nautical miles from the next ones in line, bolstering the odds that the convoy could not pass through the line without being detected. The German admirals were confident that the eastbound convoy would inevitably fall into their carefully laid trap. What happened next was totally unexpected for the BdU staff.

Late in the day on May 3, Dönitz dispatched a message to the eighteen remaining Gruppe Specht and thirteen former Gruppe Star commanders that evinced a mixture of frustration and optimism—the same conflicted mood that pervaded his operations center at that time:

DO NOT HOLD BACK . . . SOMETHING CAN AND MUST BE ACHIEVED WITH 31 BOATS[2]

After Dönitz had rushed the U-boats in Gruppe Specht and the former Gruppe Star into the compressed picket line, on May 3 he reorganized and enlarged Gruppe Amsel (Blackbird), which had been patrolling to the southeast of Gruppe Specht, to intercept any other convoys passing through the Greenland air gap's western edge. Initially, BdU assigned five U-boats to each of the four numbered Amsel groups, but the next day added four more arriving U-boats, bringing the total in each of the small groups to six. Dönitz hoped that by breaking one large wolf pack into four smaller units and staging them several dozen miles apart from one another, he would delay Allied air patrols and shore-based direction-finding stations from discovering the actual number of U-boats in the area.

Dönitz ordered Amsel 1 and 2 to operate northeast of the Grand Banks of Newfoundland, several hundred miles to the south of Gruppe Specht, and directed Amsel 3 and 4 to patrol several hundred miles farther to the south. As with the original Amsel group, their mission was to intercept any other convoys that came along while the Specht-Star U-boats continued to hunt SC128.[3]

Unfortunately for Dönitz's newly organized U-boats, in the early hours of May 4, Convoy SC128 slipped undetected around the Specht-Star patrol line. Canadian land-based HF/DF stations had picked up on the two wolf packs' radio transmissions, and alerted the convoy. Aware of the U-boats ahead of their course track, SC128 actually turned back to the west for a time before resuming a northerly route that would circumvent the combined Specht-Star U-boats. Commander J. S. Dalison, senior officer for the 40th Escort Group protecting SC128, also came up with a ploy to further confuse the U-boats. He ordered several of his escorts to move off to the northeast from the main body, where they fired starshell rockets to mislead any U-boats close by as to the convoy's actual location and course. The maneuver went off so flawlessly that it drew grudging praise from Berlin. SC128 would reach the North Channel without losing a single ship. Grossadmiral Dönitz later acknowledged that the starshell trick had been "a skillfully executed feint" that had misled several of his U-boat captains. Meanwhile, Allied convoy planners, aware of the massive U-boat presence northeast of Newfoundland, had also routed eastbound Convoy HX236 on a more southerly course. That formation of forty-five merchantmen would make the transit in fifteen days without a single U-boat spotting it.[4]

By 1400 on May 4, Dönitz realized that Convoys SC128 and HX236 had escaped his trap. Several hours later, the BdU communications branch transmitted an encrypted order from Dönitz to the U-boats that had been hunting for SC128. The admiral was dissolving Gruppen Specht and Star and forming twenty-eight of their thirty-one U-boats into the new wolf pack Gruppe Fink (Finch). Beginning at 0800 the next morning, Fink was to maintain a new, 384-nautical-mile patrol line across the anticipated course track of the next eastbound convoy. BdU, less aware of the route the next convoy might take than it had been with Convoy SC128, was forced to spread the U-boats out in intervals about fourteen nautical miles apart, more than twice the distance employed three days earlier against the slow convoy. But before the Fink U-boats could even begin to assemble into their new formation, Convoy ONS5, still heading on course 202 degrees at seven knots, stumbled right into the midst of the massive wolf pack.[5]

AT 1757 GMT (1415 local) on May 4, Lieutenant Colonel Barry H. Moffit, commander of a Royal Canadian Air Force (RCAF) Canso A seaplane from 5 Bomber Reconnaissance Squadron, was cruising high above the North Atlantic, in the western fringe of the Greenland air gap. Moffit and his crew were nearing the end of a seven-hour patrol that had taken the aircraft more than 630 miles out into the ocean from its base at Gander, Newfoundland. At that moment, a bright blip appeared on the aircraft's ASV Mark III ten-centimeter radar screen, showing a target seven miles away from the aircraft, about twenty-five degrees off to port.

Once again, the Germans' inability to detect centimetric radar would give an Allied patrol bomber the decisive edge in combat. The U-boat had no way of detecting the aircraft's radar beam, since the U-boat Force and the rest of the German military had yet to produce a warning receiver that operated on the 10-centimeter wavelength. The Metox receivers deployed on the U-boats only worked at longer wavelengths. As the Canso A was flying in the base of solid cloud cover, it was also invisible to any German lookouts.[6]

Suspecting a surfaced U-boat, Moffit and his co-pilot moved in to investigate. They closed to within two miles of the target, then shoved the seaplane's nose down and redlined the throttles on its two Pratt & Whitney R1830-82 engines. Aircrewmen joked that the manufacturer had designed their lumbering patrol plane—the Canadian variant of the PBY-5A Catalina—so that it could operate at only one speed: "climb at ninety, cruise at ninety, and glide at ninety" knots. Now, however, Moffit's Canso A thundered down toward the water at 150 knots. As the aircraft closed in on the U-boat, the pilot and co-pilot could see through the thick haze a straggling merchant ship from Convoy ONS5 about ten miles ahead.

Leveling out at an altitude of only seventy-five feet, Moffit's crew watched as the surprised U-boat crew attempted a crash dive. They were too late. At the optimum release point several hundred feet away from the U-boat, Moffit ordered bombs away, and an electromechanical switch automatically released four wing-mounted 250-pound depth charges at intervals of forty-six feet. The first depth charge landed eighty feet in front of the boat, the second just forty feet away. The third and fourth hit within twelve feet of the boat's hull forward and aft of the conning tower. As the Canso A swooped over its target, Moffit and his crew saw a blurred confirmation that their surprise had been complete: two crewmen were clearly visible on the U-boat's bridge before the charges went off, sending up four towering columns of seawater that all but blanketed the boat. The aircrew watched the U-boat wallowing with no forward motion, then slowly sink out of sight. A large oil slick and fragments of wooden deck planking rose to the surface. Moffit circled the site for several minutes while his crew took photographs, then turned to head back to base at Gander.

Moffit's Canso A had drawn first blood against Gruppe Fink, but the U-boat did not go down as easily as it might have seemed. Unbeknownst to Moffit and his men, the boat initially survived the aerial attack. Kapitänleutnant Heinrich Brodda and his forty-five-man crew on the U-209 were experienced submariners, having made six previous patrols from Norway since U-209 was commissioned in October 1941, over the course of which they had sunk four Soviet coastal vessels. But on May 4, 1943, the lookouts' failure to spot the incoming Canso A in time would ultimately cost all forty-six crewmen their lives. With his boat devastated by the seaplane's attack and his primary radio transmitter destroyed, Brodda at 1415 on May 6 managed to use an emergency transmitter to relay a message to Berlin via the nearby U-954. He reported significant damage to U-209, including his compressed air system, radio transmitter, and exhaust valves. BdU replied three hours later, directing U-209 to break off from the wolf pack and rendezvous with the U-tanker U-119 for refueling before returning to its new homeport in Brest. U-209 never made the rendezvous with U-119, however, and was never heard from again. Both BdU and the Admiralty in London independently concluded the boat had subsequently sunk from battle damage.[7]

Moffit's devastating attack on U-209 was soon followed by another RCAF hit against Gruppe Fink. At 2045 GMT (1745 local), a second Canso A from the Canadian 5 Bomber Reconnaissance Squadron was also nearing the end of its 600-mile patrol, about sixty-three nautical miles south-southwest of U-209's location and about thirty miles ahead of Convoy ONS5. Co-pilot Flight Sergeant Mel Paul spotted a distant U-boat through his binoculars: a thin silver streak on the dull gray ocean surface, about eighteen miles off. Flight Lieutenant John W. Langmuir decided to hold off from attacking until they could position the aircraft between the U-boat and the bright afternoon sun. Reaching the right spot about eight miles from the U-boat, Langmuir and Paul turned and dove directly at their target. With the sun glaring behind the Canso A, the German lookouts did not see the diving seaplane until it was only two miles out. There was no time to crash-dive, so the U-boat gunners remained at their 20-mm anti-aircraft cannon mounted on a platform aft of the conning tower, and hastily opened fire.

Despite the fire from the U-boat's anti-aircraft cannon, Langmuir waited to trigger his four depth charges until his Canso A was just twenty feet above the U-boat. The four explosives straddled the boat and pounded it unmercifully as they detonated. The elated Canadian aircrew pulled back up to patrol altitude, where they could see the U-boat's bow rising out of the water as it seemed to be slowly sinking by the stern. Having dropped all of his depth charges, Langmuir decided to make a strafing run. Dodging a heavy burst of gunfire from the U-boat's cannon, the Canso roared in again, this time firing from the nose gun and starboard observation blister. Langmuir's nose gunner, Warrant Officer Clifford Hazlett, later claimed that he had hit two crewmen on deck and had seen them fall overboard. The aircraft circled up and around for a third pass, but by the time they prepared to make a second strafing pass, the U-boat had vanished.

The Admiralty initially credited Langmuir's aircraft with the destruction of U-438, a veteran boat on its fourth North Atlantic patrol—but this, too, was premature. At 0608 the next morning, Kapitänleutnant

Heinrich Heinsohn, U-438's commander, would report the damage to his boat to BdU:

4 BOMBS FROM CATALINA 15 METERS OFF . . . ATTACKED SEVERAL TIMES BY FLYING BOAT. NO. 40 CYLINDER COVER TORN. OTHER DAMAGES SLIGHT.

Several hours later, Heinsohn would send a follow-up message to Berlin stating that his crew could repair the damages without having to break off patrol. U-438 would remain in the fight.[8]

U-438 AND U-209 were not the only U-boats that encountered Convoy ONS5 and its escorts throughout the afternoon of May 4. At least four Gruppe Fink boats signaled to BdU between 1418 and 1817 that they had sighted one or two Allied destroyers on a generally southbound course— most likely the destroyers *Oribi* and *Offa,* which were patrolling ahead of ONS5 at the time. The convoy itself was sighted not long after. At 1817, Kapitänleutnant Heinrich Hasenschar and his lookouts in U-628 reported spotting the mast tops of a southbound convoy. The twenty-six-year-old officer, a veteran of three previous patrols, erroneously thought it was westbound fast Convoy ON180 and duly reported that in his message to Berlin.[9]

ONS5 had managed to avoid any confrontation with the U-boats after Escort Group B-7 had driven off several members of Gruppe Star on the morning of May 1. Since then, the convoy's main opponent had been the weather, but by May 4, that had become calmer. By midday, the wind had shifted to the west and was down from a strong gale to a fresh breeze of eighteen to twenty-four miles per hour. The towering waves of the night before had eased to moderate seas. The change brought much-desired relief to the exhausted and bruised merchant sailors and escort crewmen. The bad news, of course, was that it also brought back the U-boats.

Wolf pack radio activity began appearing on the ONS5's HF/DF sets. Beginning in the late morning of May 4, HF/DF operators on the *Tay* and *Oribi* had begun intercepting the signals from numerous encrypted U-boat transmissions. Somewhere nearby, U-boat commanders were sending messages back to Berlin—and the chatter could only mean that

Although designed for coastal patrols, the Flower-class corvettes were used heavily on the trans-Atlantic convoy routes. Here, a wave breaks over the bow of the *HMS Sunflower*.
Photo courtesy of Tony Cooper

ONS5 had been spotted once again. Unfortunately, voice communications between the *Tay* and *Oribi* had failed and would stay down for several critical days, making it impossible for Lieutenant-Commander Robert Sherwood on the *Tay* to get a cross-bearing HF/DF fix when a U-boat transmitted.

The renewed evidence of nearby U-boats prompted Sherwood to abandon plans to get the corvette *Pink* and its stragglers, still some fifty miles behind ONS5, to rejoin the convoy. He sent a message to Admiral Horton's staff requesting that the smaller group be designated as a separate convoy and receive separate routing directions to Newfoundland. The operations staff at Liverpool agreed. The decision would mitigate the threat to the storm-weary stragglers from ONS5, but it also meant that the larger convoy would be down one more escort as it struggled to avoid the wolf packs. Although Commander Brewer's 1st Support Group was coming as fast as possible, it was still more than a day away from reaching the convoy.[10]

As dusk closed in on May 4, the U-boats were closing in on ONS5. With HF/DF intercepts telling Sherwood there were U-boats on the convoy's port bow, port quarter, starboard beam, and starboard quarter, he decided to load the escorts at those locations. The *Sunflower, Snowflake,* and *Tay* covered the port side, while the *Vidette, Loosestrife,* and ASW trawler *Northern Spray* guarded to starboard. The support-group destroyers *Offa* and *Oribi* moved out five miles from the main body as a distant screen for the port and starboard bows of the formation. The weather remained clear with only a slight breeze of two to six miles per hour. ONS5 by now had regained its designated speed of seven knots and was on a slightly altered course of 202 degrees. Aboard the eight escort warships, crewmen stood to their battle stations. They feared that the improved nighttime visibility and gentle seas would give the U-boats the opportunity to mount simultaneous surface attacks from all points of the compass.[11]

In the cramped radio rooms of more than three dozen U-boats, an encrypted message emerged from the Funkschlüssel-M cipher machines. Grossadmiral Dönitz urged his U-boats to hurl themselves against the enemy:

YOU ARE BETTER PLACED THAN YOU EVER WERE BEFORE . . .
I AM CERTAIN THAT YOU WILL FIGHT WITH EVERYTHING
YOU'VE GOT. DON'T OVERESTIMATE YOUR OPPONENT BUT
STRIKE HIM DEAD![12]

Nine minutes after Dönitz's exhortation arrived, Oberleutnant zur See Günter Gretschel and the crew of U-707 struck at Convoy ONS5. Two hours earlier, the Gruppe Fink U-boat had run straight into the 3rd Support Group escorts, *HMS Oribi* and *HMS Offa,* patrolling five miles ahead of the main body. The twenty-eight-year-old Silesian, on his second North Atlantic patrol, was heading toward U-628's homing signals when his lookouts at 1956 sighted the two destroyers coming toward him. Gretschel quickly dived to avoid contact. At periscope depth, he watched the two destroyers proceeding on zigzag courses, seemingly oblivious to his presence. That changed in an instant, when suddenly one of them turned and came straight toward him at flank speed, blasting the U-boat with continuous Asdic signals. Gretschel ordered the boat to crash-dive from periscope depth into the cellar. His crew braced for a depth-charge attack.

On the *Oribi*, lookouts had spotted the feather wake of a periscope seven miles dead ahead of their ship. Lieutenant-Commander John Ingram instantly ordered the ship to maximum power and the *Oribi* hurtled toward the U-boat at thirty-one knots with the *Offa* coming up to help. The *Oribi* and *Offa* hunted for the U-boat for nearly three hours without regaining contact and finally resumed their forward screen at 2310.

Undeterred by the aggressive reaction of ONS5's advance guard, U-707 was continuing to stalk the convoy. The U-boat had silently crept ahead, well beneath the surface, as ONS5 and its escorts drew near. It wasn't long, however, before the warships detected U-707 and pounced on it, as well. The *Tay* picked up the U-boat on Asdic, and Lieutenant-Commander Sherwood raced the frigate in to plaster the boat with a spread of ten depth charges. Shaken but unscathed, U-707's crew listened in quiet excitement as the sound and turbulence from the attack faded, replaced by the multiple churning sounds of the propellers of several dozen merchantmen passing overhead.

At that moment, Captain John Lamsdale's freighter *North Britain* was having problems keeping up with ONS5. The 4,635-ton steam merchantman was a relatively new vessel, completed in 1940, but intermittent engine problems had plagued the ship since May 1, when it had fallen out of the convoy during the fierce storm. Lamsdale had made repairs and rejoined ONS5 earlier in the day, but once again the ship's boiler problems returned, making it unable to keep to the convoy's speed of seven knots. By 2200 on Tuesday, May 4, the freighter had fallen five miles behind the main body—not far from where U-707 was preparing to resurface.

The U-boat did not come up until the last ships in the column had passed overhead. Gretschel dictated his observations down the speaking tube to his radioman, who scribbled them into a notebook for later transcription into the boat's KTB diary:

> I am in the rear of the convoy formation. To the front are a few shadows, to starboard a corvette, astern, a large steamer. Battle stations! I attack a

modern passenger steamer of the type *City of Manchester*, with protruding bow and continuous deck, 7,500 GRT, on course 210. I launch a fan shot from Tubes I, II, and IV, bearing 90, range 1,500 meters.

The lookouts aboard the *North Britain* didn't see Gretschel's attack coming. Out of nowhere, a torpedo crashed into the freighter's starboard side, just aft of its mainmast, blasting a column of black oil and seawater high into the air. Lamsdale and thirty-four crewmen and gunners perished instantly in the attack, leaving ten crewmen and one gunner to scramble over the side. The ship was sinking rapidly under the weight of nearly 1,000 tons of ballast, and took only two minutes to disappear beneath the waves. Lieutenant F. A. J. Downer on the ASW trawler *Northern Spray* steamed over and retrieved the eleven survivors, who had made their escape in a waterlogged lifeboat and one life raft, but who were nearly unconscious from the cold. The first shot in what would become a forty-three-hour mêlée between Escort Group B-7 and the three wolf packs had occurred at 55 North 042 West, a trackless point on the North Atlantic 600 miles northeast of St. John's, Newfoundland.[13]

The attack on the *North Britain* prompted Sherwood to stack more of his defenses at the rear of the convoy. He reshuffled the close escort screen, sending Lieutenant Herbert Stonehouse in the corvette *Loosestrife* to the rear of the convoy from Position F on the starboard beam to assist the *Northern Spray*. With the corvette and ASW trawler falling astern as the convoy continued on its course at seven knots, Sherwood rotated the other escorts, dropping the *Snowflake* back from the port beam to the port quarter, Position R, while moving the *Tay* over to assume the *Loosestrife*'s original station. With the escorts repositioned in anticipation of another rear attack, there were now only four escorts guarding the rest of the convoy perimeter: the *Tay, Vidette, Sunflower,* and *Snowflake*.

Not all of the threats to ONS5 were coming from the rear, however. Up ahead of the convoy, one of the escorts had already engaged with another U-boat. At 0020, just as U-707 had begun its attack astern, Lieutenant Raymond Hart in the *Vidette* was maneuvering about 5,000 yards on the convoy's starboard bow when his radar operator gained a sharp contact bearing 205 degrees, just slightly to the right of the convoy course. Hart ordered the elderly destroyer ahead at twenty-two knots as his deck crews prepared a spread of fourteen depth charges on the stern rails and K-guns. Five minutes after the radar contact, his lookouts sighted the surfaced U-boat fleeing the destroyer at high speed.

On the Type IXC U-514, Kapitänleutnant Hans-Jürgen Auffermann, twenty-eight, had spotted the *Vidette*'s sudden course change. Auffermann was sprinting away from the warship at top speed, attempting maximum separation before pulling the plug. Eight minutes into the chase, at 0028 on Wednesday, May 5, Auffermann crash-dived. His hydrophone operator could hear the ascending screech of the *Vidette*'s propellers as the enemy warship came in for the kill. The *Vidette* had only been 700 yards behind U-514 when the U-boat's ballast tanks had vented and it had vanished in a thick plume of spray. Hart ordered the depth charges set to the shallowest setting possible and "fired by eye" at the U-boat. As the sea erupted behind the destroyer, Hart ordered the *Vidette* to move out 2,000 yards to conduct an Operation Observant via Asdic. Hart assessed that he had probably missed the target altogether. "This was not considered an accurate attack," Hart wrote in his daily report. "Although the pattern was dropped close ahead of the diving position, the U-boat had several valuable seconds in which to take drastic avoiding action under the surface."

Lieutenant Hart was felicitously mistaken about his attack on the U-boat. Several hours later, Auffermann would report to BdU that the depth charges had knocked one periscope out of order, disabled one of his two stern torpedo tubes, and caused other damage temporarily rendering his boat combat-ineffective. Auffermann moved U-514 away from the battle so that his crew could attempt repairs, and it wasn't until the early morning of Friday, May 7, that he informed BdU that the U-boat was ready for further operations. But by then, the battle would be over.

The *Vidette*'s assault on U-514 would be followed by another U-boat sighting. At 0050, just twenty minutes after it attacked U-514, a second radar contact appeared on the *Vidette*'s radar screen, this one bearing 285 degrees at a range of 3,800 yards. Hastily abandoning the Observant overwatch for the first U-boat, the destroyer rushed off on the hunt as its crew prepared to drop another fourteen-shot depth-charge pattern. Eight minutes later, at 0058, the *Vidette*'s lookouts spotted a U-boat on the surface just 1,000 yards ahead of the destroyer. Hart shouted through the ship's loudspeaker for the crew to brace themselves for a ramming, and ordered his Oerlikon gunners to open fire.

The night sky suddenly blazed with light as the *Vidette's* tracer rounds flew toward the U-boat, striking its conning tower. Surprisingly, the boat remained on the surface until the *Vidette* was just eighty yards away from ramming it, then suddenly crash-dived. This time, Hart later reported with satisfaction, his crew carried out an accurate depth-charge attack. He ordered the destroyer to sweep out again, regained Asdic contact at 0125, and dropped twelve more depth charges on what appeared to be a completely motionless U-boat hovering below the surface.

Had the commander and crew of the *Vidette* known the results of their latest round of attacks, they probably would have been as mystified as their battered foe. In their second maneuver, Hart and his crew had unwittingly attacked a third U-boat from Gruppe Fink. Their original target had been the veteran U-662, whose skipper, Kapitänleutnant Heinz-Eberhard Müller, was on his first North Atlantic patrol. Perhaps it was beginner's luck, but Müller's evasion orders during the crash dive had worked perfectly; the U-boat escaped the fury of the *Vidette's* depth-charge attack, although Müller and his crew would not be able to make contact with ONS5 again. The destroyer's aggressive response had, however, caught up with another U-boat, Oberleutnant zur See Peter Carlsen's U-732. The detonations from *Vidette's* second depth-charge attack badly shook U-732, which was already nursing several mechanical failures caused by damage suffered during an earlier convoy fight. Rattled by the latest attack, Carlsen aborted his war cruise and headed to his homeport in Brest. In just over an hour, the *Vidette* had forced three U-boats out of the fight.[14]

THE *VIDETTE'S* TRIFECTA against the U-boats ahead of ONS5 would not be the end of the fighting that night. With at least seven Gruppe Fink U-boats in firm contact with ONS5, it was only a matter of time before one or more broke through the convoy screen just as had U-707. Aboard the *Tay,* Lieutenant-Commander Sherwood found himself in a quandary similar to that which had confronted Lieutenant-Commander Gordon J. Luther seven weeks earlier, as he had tried to safeguard Convoy HX229: there were barely enough warships on hand to protect the entire convoy

perimeter. Each time an escort raced out of position to drive off a U-boat
or to pick up survivors from a torpedoed ship, it opened up that side of
the formation to a new attack.

The absence of the *Vidette* from the close escort screen offered the
U-boats a prime opportunity to penetrate ONS5's thinly stretched defenses. The U-boat that had first sighted ONS5 several hours before,
U-628, was the first to exploit the gap. Now that additional U-boats had
reported to BdU that they were in contact with ONS5, Kapitänleutnant
Hasenschar in U-628 was finally free to abandon his job as convoy contact-keeper and attempt his own strike. At 0033, thirteen minutes after
the *Vidette* had moved off to chase its radar contact with U-514, U-628
deftly slipped through the hole in the convoy screen. Over a three-minute
period beginning at 0043, Hasenschar fired five separately aimed torpedoes at five different ships from an extended range of over 4,000 yards. He
then ordered U-628 to make a high-speed run to the northeast to get
astern of the convoy escorts so that he could reload his torpedo tubes for
another attack.

Only one of Hasenschar's torpedoes hit its mark, but it would still be
enough to bring down a second ship in Convoy ONS5—its third loss of
the voyage. The 5,081-ton British freighter *Harbury* was steaming in Position 81 at the head of the third column from the convoy's starboard flank
when that single torpedo crashed into the ship's starboard side at 0050.
Captain W. E. Cook and his crew of fifty-one were caught totally unaware
by the blast, which ripped a large hole in the side at the No. 5 cargo hold.
As a result of the weight of the ship's ballast cargo of 6,820 tons of an-
thracite coal and the size of the breach in the hull, the ship began rapidly
settling by the stern. On Cook's order, his third officer fired starshell rockets and illuminated the red truck lights to signal the convoy escorts that
the ship had suffered a torpedo hit. Within twenty minutes, all but three
of the crew had abandoned ship, but four more sailors drowned after they
were forced to jump over the side. Cook and two other crewmen remained aboard until the last minute, then climbed into a life raft and cast
free of the crippled freighter. Forty-two survivors wallowed in the heavy
swells watching their ship go under.[15]

Hasenschar's attack was quickly followed by another. At 0114 on May
5, the U-264, commanded by Kapitänleutnant Hartwig Looks, had

reached a position ahead of ONS5 and, concealed by the heavy swells, slipped past the port bow and port beam escorts, the corvettes *Sunflower* and *Snowflake*. Looks, twenty-five, was on his third patrol in U-264 and had already sunk a 6,696-ton Greek freighter in the boat's initial foray in the North Atlantic; he had also experienced two dangerous Mediterranean patrols as 1WO in the U-375 in late 1941 and early 1942 before entering U-boat commander training. He used that experience to good result as he now crept up on Convoy ONS5. While he carried out his attack, Looks gave a running commentary through the speaking tube, and his radioman jotted down the commander's words:

"I have a group of five steamers ahead of me, three at approximately 1,500 meters and two behind them at about 2,500 meters. . . . I launch two fan shots at the larger two of the three nearest ships, one launch of two eels from Tubes I and III at a 6,000-tonner and another launch of two from Tubes II and IV at a 5,000-tonner. Range 1,500 meters, angle on the bow 3.8 [degrees] and 3.9 [degrees] respectively. Torpedo depth set to 3 meters. I then turn hard-a-starboard [hard to the right] and launch a fifth eel from the stern tube at a 4,500 GRT freighter. . . . The first fan launch at the 6,000-tonner detonates after runs of one minute, twenty-two seconds and one minute, twenty-six seconds, one hitting amidships and the other twenty meters from the stern. Two high smoke columns can be seen. The second fan launch hits the 5,000-tonner at the same locations on the hull after runs of one minute, forty-seven seconds and one minute, fifty-one seconds. Again there are two high detonation columns."[16]

Although Looks's fifth torpedo never hit its mark, each of his first two fan shots had gone careening into the port bow of ONS5, devastating their targets, neither of which had seen the incoming torpedo wakes.

One of U-264's first two torpedo fan shots had struck the 5,561-ton American freighter *West Maximus* on its port side near the stern, blasting a section of the hull plating away. Captain Earl E. Brooks on the *West Maximus* attempted to keep station after the first torpedo hit, but the vessel was taking on water so fast he could no longer maneuver. Brooks ordered the engines shut down and waited for assistance from one of the convoy's escorts—but, due to miscommunication or panic, a number of crewmen and gunners took to lifeboats without permission. Brooks angrily ordered them to remain alongside the freighter in case the rest of the crew had to escape. The decision may have saved his life. Several minutes passed, and then a second torpedo detonated on the *West Maximus*'s port side, near the No. 2 hold. Ten minutes later, the *West Maximus* was unmaneuverable and was sinking quickly by the bow. Captain Brooks ordered his crew to abandon ship. The fifty-six survivors—among them fifty of the crew who had remained on the ship after the first explosion—huddled in four lifeboats as ONS5 disappeared to the southwest.

Several hundred yards away, in the third position of Column 1, Captain Joseph E. Turgoose on the 4,586-ton British steam merchantman *Harperley* had seen the first torpedo strike the *West Maximus* and had ordered his crew of forty-eight to Action Stations. Several minutes later, the second pair of torpedoes from U-264 struck the *Harperley*'s port side. The first torpedo hit in the vicinity of the engine room, killing three of the ship's engineers; the second torpedo struck close to the ship's foremast. While Looks wrote in his KTB diary that there were "two high detonation columns" from the *West Maximus,* the ship's captain emerged from the fog of war with a remarkably different account. "The explosion was not very violent and appeared to be more of a dull thud," Turgoose later reported. "I did not notice a flash, neither was there a column of water thrown up, although I later learned from survivors of another vessel that they had seen a big flash."

Ravaged by the two torpedoes from U-264, the *Harperley* took on a sudden, heavy list to port. Turgoose flashed out a wireless message and a crewman fired starshell rockets to alert the convoy of the attack. While most of the ship's crewmen managed to escape from the sinking ship on three lifeboats, at least ten perished. Nearly four hours later, the *Northern Spray* rescued thirty-nine survivors from the *Harperley* and fifty-six from the *West Maximus,* bringing the total of rescued survivors aboard the diminutive warship—including eleven from the *North Britain* and forty-two from the *Harbury*—to 148 bedraggled but grateful merchant seamen, naval gunners, and passengers.[17]

WITH FOUR SHIPS in the convoy sunk since the night attacks had commenced, Escort Group B-7 and the two remaining 3rd Support Group destroyers were reacting as fast as they could to the swarm of HF/DF, radar, Asdic, and lookout sightings. Mindful of the gap in the escort screen that had been created when the *Vidette* had gone out after U-514 and U-662, Sherwood radioed Captain McCoy on the destroyer *Offa* to request that he fall back from his distant patrol and plug the hole in the convoy's close defenses. Captain McCoy and the *Offa* reached the *Vidette*'s station at 0100. In response to the initial torpedo attack on the *North Britain*, Sherwood had also ordered the first of several Half Raspberry maneuvers, in which the close escorts turned out from their patrol stations and swept their patrol sectors with radar and Asdic hydrophones, firing starshells to illuminate the area. The escorts' efforts to flush out the attacking U-boat would produce immediate results.

At 0109, Lieutenant Chesterman on the *Snowflake* was carrying out a sweep of his patrol sector on the port quarter of ONS5, firing starshells across a 120-degree arc off of the convoy's port beam, when his radar operator caught a new contact. One minute later, the corvette's Asdic operator confirmed that he had a sharp contact dead ahead at 255 degrees, at a range of 3,000 yards—and then, several seconds later, reported the sound of two torpedoes being fired. Chesterman alerted the convoy by radiotelephone and a blast of his ship's siren. Meanwhile, the *Snowflake*'s radar operator still held a firm contact on a surfaced U-boat, which had altered course to the south and was attempting to flee at high speed.

Chesterman later admitted that he did not know whether this was the same U-boat that had fired the torpedoes, or if there were two lurking in the area, but he decided to proceed with a rapid attack at the last known Asdic position. Set for shallow detonation (the lighter K-gun charges at fifty feet and heavy stern-rail charges at 140 feet), the spread of ten depth charges splashed into the water and erupted in a thundering chorus. "Ten charge pattern dropped set shallow," Chesterman wrote in his after-action report. In the heat of battle, however, the *Snowflake* had made a potentially serious error. "The explosions fractured the leads to the Asdic motor alternators and blew out the bridge fuses," Chesterman wrote. The blast had accidentally disabled the corvette's Asdic system.

As several technicians frantically worked to fix the broken Asdic set, Chesterman continued to pursue the U-boat that was still running on the surface. The *Snowflake* chased the U-boat for another twenty-four minutes, alternately firing starshells and high-explosive rounds from its four-inch main gun. With a four-knot speed advantage on the surface, however, the U-boat steadily drew off to 2,400 yards before diving. Chesterman reached the swirl and dropped five depth charges on the boat's suspected location. The U-boat skipper rewarded Chesterman's tenacity by loosing a third torpedo in his direction. The projectile missed the corvette by only 125 yards.

The *Snowflake's* crew fixed the ship's Asdic system, but the contact finally faded away, and Chesterman gave up the hunt to return to the ship's initial night station at 0235 off the convoy's port beam. The corvette skipper was not entirely pleased with the course of events: "Consider I was bluffed by the U-boat skipper into wasting [depth] charges," he wrote. After the war, Chesterman would learn that he had been chasing Kapitänleutnant Looks in U-264, just one hour after the U-boat had torpedoed the *West Maximus* and *Harperley*. Looks escaped without damage or injury.[18]

GRUPPE FINK HAD SUNK four merchantmen since the night attack had commenced, but the wolf pack was still not finished with Convoy ONS5. A little over an hour after U-628 and U-264 mounted their attacks, Kapitänleutnant Rolf Manke in the U-358 also succeeded in breaking through the convoy screen. The twenty-seven-year-old was an experienced U-boat officer, having served as 1WO of U-576 during an intense four-month period of the Battle of the Atlantic, in which he had participated in the sinking of three Allied merchant ships totaling 13,387 tons. This was Manke's second patrol since commissioning the U-358; on his initial North Atlantic foray in January 1943, he and his crew of forty-nine had sunk two ships totaling 9,677 gross tons. In the early morning hours of May 5, he intended to add to that tally.

U-358's commander would execute a textbook-perfect night surface attack. Manke had been trailing ONS5 when, at 0144, he and his lookouts on the conning tower bridge spotted several large merchant ships in the port columns of the convoy. Manke closed in to 1,600 yards, and at 0222 ordered two torpedoes fired against the first target, which he identified as an 8,000-ton *Port Hardy*–class freighter. After one minute and fifty-three seconds, the U-boat lookouts saw a violent explosion flare amidships, rocking the merchantman. Manke then sighted a second ship two columns over and in the third position. He ordered a single torpedo from his stern tube launched at that target, but the weapon jammed in the tube. One of his machinist's mates used a mine ejector device to prod the torpedo loose, and it raced off on its programmed course. After one minute and fifty-eight seconds, the U-boat crew saw a mammoth column of water and smoke erupt from the second ship's port side amidships.[19]

Manke's two concurrent attacks would nearly double his record for cargo sunk. The first ship that U-358 had struck was the 2,864-ton British freighter *Bristol City*, outbound from the British Isles for New York with a 2,500-ton cargo of general cargo and China clay. Her master, Captain A. L. Webb, had urged his lookouts to remain alert ever since the *McKeesport* sinking six days earlier, but in the heavy swells, no one saw the incoming torpedoes. Webb later described the attack in terms similar to those of the *Harperley's* Captain Turgoose. "The explosion was dull, much quieter than I would have expected," he said. "I saw a flash, and a huge column of water was thrown into the air, which cascaded down and flooded the decks." The damage was fatal. The main topmast came crashing down, cargo hatches blew open, and several lifeboats and life rafts disintegrated. The second torpedo then struck, causing even more damage and wrecking the wireless room. The ship was sinking so fast that nearly half the forty-four men on board were forced to jump over the side. Scarcely had the survivors of the torpedo impacts gone into the sea than the stricken freighter vanished beneath the waves. Fifteen of the forty-nine crewmen perished in the initial blasts or after they went into the water.

Manke's second victim had practically the same experience as his first. Even though the crew of the 5,212-ton British freighter *Wentworth* had several minutes of warning after seeing the explosions on the *Bristol City* two columns over, no one saw Manke's stern-tube shot as it raced diagonally into the convoy toward them. The ship's master, Captain Reginald G. Phillips, had darted onto the bridge after the shouted alarms from his crew in response to the attack on the *Bristol City*. Once again, master and crewmen would voice surprise at how subdued the explosion seemed. There was no fireball and the noise was not overwhelming. Yet again the strike was deadly. The torpedo ripped a twelve-foot hole in the port side of the ship, and the sea cascaded into the engine and boiler rooms. Captain Phillips gave the order to abandon ship and most of the ship's forty-seven crewmen cast off in three lifeboats that had avoided damage. Phillips remained behind with a handful of crewmen until 0350, when the hull began to split apart, at which point they made off in the port motor lifeboat. Two hours later, Lieutenant Stonehouse in the *Loosestrife* arrived and rescued the *Wentworth's* forty-two survivors. Of the five crewmen killed, four had perished instantly in the engine room when the torpedo struck, and the fifth drowned.[20]

As Manke had been wreaking havoc on the *Bristol City* and *Wentworth*, yet another U-boat had been spotted ahead of ONS5. At 0124 the *Oribi*, still patrolling well in front of the main body, had reported an HF/DF contact bearing slightly to starboard of the convoy's course track. Captain McCoy on the *Offa*, which had been holding the *Vidette's* place in the close escort screen, broke off to help hunt for the suspected U-boat, shifting his destroyer's position until he was two miles ahead of the starboardmost column. Things were quiet for just over an hour until, at 0238, the *Offa* caught a sharp radar contact bearing 152 degrees, which was fifty-seven degrees to port of the convoy course. Powering up to flank speed, McCoy raced toward the suspected U-boat. When the destroyer closed to within 900 yards of the plotted location, McCoy suddenly saw the convoy's leading row of ships looming ahead off his port bow. Instantly realizing the main body was "dangerously close," to the spot where he intended to launch depth charges, McCoy opted to drop a single harassing depth charge to keep the U-boat under, then swerved away, returning to the starboard bow escort station shortly after 0300.[21]

The next flare-up occurred at 0322 when the *Snowflake*, back in the close escort screen for less than an hour after its fruitless chase of U-264, caught a new radar signal. The contact was bearing 175 degrees at a range of 3,400 yards, about twenty-five degrees off to port of the convoy's course track. Once more, Lieutenant Chesterman peeled out of station and barreled toward the signal. Unlike the previous encounter, the corvette steadily gained on the surfaced U-boat, which was not proceeding at its fastest speed. Chesterman radioed the contact to Sherwood on the *Tay*, who in turn called Captain McCoy on the *Offa* to join the hunt. McCoy then called up Lieutenant-Commander Ingram on the *Oribi* and ordered the destroyer to assist.

The U-boat that the two warships were now after was the newly commissioned U-270, which had left Kiel on its maiden North Atlantic patrol on March 3 under the command of Kapitänleutnant Paul-Friedrich Otto. The twenty-six-year-old Otto had cut his teeth as 1WO on U-136 during two other North Atlantic patrols, in the course of which his U-boat had attacked three different convoys and several unescorted vessels, sinking seven Allied ships totaling 34,451 gross tons. Thus far on his first combat operation in command of a U-boat, Otto had yet to score a hit on any Allied convoys, even though in the eight weeks at sea U-270 had served in four separate wolf packs.

Chesterman and the *Snowflake*'s crew intended to put an end to U-270's short career. The bright blip on the corvette's radar screen was coming into range of the corvette's four-inch deck gun and, at 0358, the *Snowflake* opened up with a combination of starshells, high-explosive rounds, and 20-mm Oerlikon cannon shells. Coming up from behind, Lieutenant-Commander Ingram in the *Oribi* also lit up the sky with illumination rounds, so as to give the *Snowflake*'s gunners a clearer shot at their target.

The bright flares of starshells and the stream of incoming tracer rounds from the *Snowflake* and *Oribi* quickly caught the eye of Kapitänleutnant Otto and his lookouts, and U-270 crash-dived. Two minutes later, the corvette passed ahead of the swirl where the boat had submerged, and Chesterman, anxious about the dwindling number of depth charges in his ship, dropped a spread of only five depth charges set to 100 feet. Moving out slightly, the corvette waited for the sound turbulence to ease, and at 0414, sixteen minutes after commencing the attack, moved in on a renewed Asdic contact and let loose four heavy depth charges set for 225 feet. Ingram on the *Oribi* then took over the assault. Because his gyro compass repeaters were giving false readings, Ingram asked Chesterman to be the directing ship, passing its Asdic bearings and ranges to the destroyer. The *Oribi* then dropped two spreads of ten depth charges apiece at the U-boat lurking below them.

The depth-charge attack savaged the U-270. The initial explosions fractured the U-boat's forward pressure hull, and salt water began pouring in at a rate of several tons per hour. The blast also knocked out Otto's depth-pressure gauge and sent the boat into an uncontrolled dive. Only by

running his two E-motors at full speed astern did Otto and his men halt
the boat from sinking further. As U-270 climbed back toward the surface, it remained in a dangerous bow-down attitude. Otto ordered his
chief engineer to use the trim tanks to correct balance by shifting several
tons of water from the bow tank to its counterpart in the stern. Otto also
ordered every available crewman to the stern torpedo room to add coun-
terweight to the boat. The move worked, and the damaged U-boat safely
hovered deep under the surface. The crew of U-270 would hide in the
cellar for four hours until ONS5 and its escorts had moved on. Then,
at 0824, Otto would order U-270 to surface and begin limping back
to port.[22]

AT 0400 on Wednesday, May 5, as the *Snowflake* and the *Oribi* were
pounding U-270, Lieutenant-Commander Sherwood had ordered the escorts back to day stations. On Sherwood's frigate *Tay* and on the *Oribi*,
the HF/DF operators continued to intercept numerous U-boat messages
transmitted on the Germans' encrypted high-frequency channel. Despite
the defenders' aggressive responses, ONS5 was still being stalked.

Sherwood made no mention of the night's losses in his daily report, but
he and the other B-7 escort commanders must surely have been feeling
frustrated from the results of the night surface attacks. Five U-boats had
managed to penetrate the convoy screen and sink seven merchant ships totaling 27,939 gross tons, sending seventy-eight merchant sailors and naval
gunners down with them. And, unknown to the escorts, the actual score
was worse. Sometime during the day on May 4, the Type IXC U-125 under veteran Kapitänleutnant Ulrich Folkers had torpedoed an eighth vessel. The 4,737-ton British merchantman *Lorient*, a straggler from ONS5,
had vanished from its assigned position as last ship in Column 3 and was
never seen again. The only evidence of its loss is an encrypted message
from Folkers to BdU at 0218 on May 5 reporting that he had sunk an "independent" freighter of about 4,000 tons displacement. That loss pushed
the total to 32,676 tons and the loss of life to 118 crewmen.

Although Lieutenant-Commander Sherwood didn't know the full
scope of ONS5's losses, he was also unaware that Allied aircraft had already damaged one of the U-boats that Grossadmiral Dönitz had sent out
against ONS5. Nor did he and the other escort officers know that during

the past twelve hours, their aggressive counterattacks had forced three U-boats—U-532, U-732, and U-270—to abort their patrols. In addition, they had damaged two others (U-514 and U-413) and driven off six more (U-264, U-707, U-618, U-662, U-584, and U-260). With the exception of U-584, none of the latter eight U-boats would make subsequent contact with the convoy.[23]

At BdU Headquarters, Dönitz and Godt were obviously unhappy over the night's events. Only five out of forty U-boats would report having made successful attacks on ONS5. At 1042 on May 5, the two admirals sent a transmission to the Gruppen Amsel and Fink boats, warning them that ONS5 was approaching the coastal waters of Newfoundland. The message had a slightly hysterical tone:

IMMEDIATELY AFTER NIGHTFALL THE SOUND OF THE KETTLE DRUMS MUST BEGIN. HURRY. THERE ARE FORTY OF YOU—OTHERWISE YOU WILL LOSE THIS CONVOY. THE BATTLE CAN'T LAST LONG SINCE THE SEA SPACE LEFT IS SHORT, SO USE EVERY OPPORTUNITY TO THE FULLEST WITH ALL YOUR MIGHT.[24]

Dönitz was worried that ONS5 might get away before it could be depleted further, and rightly so. At 0800, Sherwood reported to Western Approaches Command that the convoy was still steaming on course 202 degrees in ten columns at a speed of 7.5 knots, with its position at 54:32 North 043:20 West. The coordinates placed the merchant ships 546 nautical miles northeast of St. John's, Newfoundland. The corvette *Pink,* now escorting five stragglers, was about thirty miles north-northwest of the main body, proceeding on a diverging course of 240 degrees along the separate route that Western Approaches had ordered Lieutenant Atkinson to take to St. John's.

Sherwood began the morning reorganizing the escort force. First, he ordered the designated rescue ship, *Northern Spray,* which was dangerously overcrowded with its 143 survivors on board, to detach for St. John's. The tiny, 520-ton auxiliary warship, still well astern of the convoy, acknowledged the order and changed course to make a straight-line approach to Newfoundland. Sherwood's next move was to refuel the *Tay* and the short-legged destroyers *Offa* and *Oribi* from the two escort tankers. Sherwood successfully refueled from the *British Lady,* but *Offa* only managed to take on one gallon when the fuel line snapped, forcing it to make another attempt later.

Apart from the mundane but essential provisioning, the morning of May 5 was quite busy for ONS5's escorts. At 1016, Sherwood ordered Ingram in the *Oribi* to investigate several HF/DF contacts bearing 155 degrees, about twelve miles ahead of the convoy on its port bow. The *Oribi* steamed out ahead of ONS5, and forty-seven minutes later its lookouts spotted a plume of diesel exhaust about seven miles distant. "The smoke base from her diesel [motors] was visible even before her hull had actually been spotted," Ingram wrote in his daily report.

With the U-boat's exhaust in sight, Ingram ordered his destroyer to flank speed and raced toward the contact. Within ten minutes, the *Oribi*'s lookouts sighted two more U-boats ahead—one bearing 190 degrees, six miles off, and the other bearing 145 degrees, seven miles distant—all placing themselves in position ahead of the path of the oncoming convoy for daylight submerged torpedo attacks. Lookouts on the trio of U-boats soon spotted the destroyer, and all three crash-dived. Ingram dropped a pattern of ten depth charges on the first U-boat, but aborted a second drop when it became clear from his Asdic that the boat was passing down the destroyer's port side.

The *Oribi* lost contact with its first target, but Ingram conducted a deliberate search and forty-five minutes later gained a new Asdic contact. The destroyer turned and went to the calculated location, dropping another ten depth charges. Lookouts reported an unusual aftermath to the attack, Ingram wrote. "Slightly less than two minutes after the first [depth] charge was fired, two unexplained explosions were heard, one heavy and one of less intensity, resulting in a large eruption of air." A lookout on the quarterdeck then shouted he had seen a periscope briefly appear in the disturbance.

Whatever the unusual blasts, Ingram knew he had not sunk the enemy, for at 1254, his Asdic operator reported another acoustic contact on the U-boat. The *Oribi* turned, approached the spot, and dropped a small spread of five depth charges, then left to return to ONS5. Like Lieutenant Chesterman on the *Snowflake,* Ingram was concerned about the dwindling number of depth charges in his ship. "A full pattern was not fired as it was thought essential to conserve supplies of depth charges for attacks in the vicinity of the convoy," he wrote. It was a prudent decision. Even before the *Oribi* could make its return, the U-boats struck ONS5 again.[25]

CAPTAIN GILBERT R. CHEETHAM had suffered through a stressful night on the British merchantman *Dolius*. The 5,507-ton cargo ship was outbound from the Welsh port of Milford Haven to New York in ballast, carrying a crew of fifty-seven and eight naval gunners, and until the terror of the night before had experienced only one scare since leaving port up with ONS5. On April 30, when Kapitänleutnant Wilhelm von Mässenhausen in U-258 had fired a spread of torpedoes at the convoy and sank the *McKeesport*, one of the warshots had come within twenty-five yards of the *Dolius's* stern before running out of the formation. In the early morning of May 5, however, the roof fell in. The *Dolius* occupied Position 21, lead ship in the second column of Convoy ONS5. Over a period of eighty-six minutes in the darkened early morning hours of May 5, U-boats torpedoed four ships close by, including the lead and third ships in Column 1, the vessel behind the *Dolius* in Column 2, and the third ship in Column 3. When the *Bristol City* in Position 11 failed to send any emergency signals after being struck twice, Captain Cheetham ordered his crew to fire distress rockets to alert Commodore Brook on the *Rena* to the merchant vessel's plight. The morning of May 5, however, seemed to have brought some peace back to the Atlantic. The weather was calm with a light breeze, and Cheetham looked forward to a quiet morning in his sea cabin writing letters.[26]

Unbeknownst to the crew of the *Dolius*, one of the seven U-boats still in contact with ONS5 was about to penetrate the convoy's escort screen. U-638, under the command of Kapitänleutnant Oskar Staudinger, had damaged a 6,537-ton British freighter on its first Atlantic foray eight weeks earlier on March 7. Now the U-boat was back on the North Atlantic convoy runs as part of Gruppe Amsel 1, the six-boat wolf pack Admiral Dönitz had placed to the southwest of Gruppe Fink. At 1200, Staudinger maneuvered inside ONS5 at periscope depth and, at nearly point-blank range, loosed a torpedo at the freighter leading the second column. "No one saw the track of the torpedo, which struck in the after part of the engine room on the starboard side," Captain Cheetham reported. "There was a dull explosion but no flash was seen." Racing up to the bridge wing, Cheetham saw that the blast had ripped a thirty-foot hole in the side of the ship. He ordered the engines halted. The water pouring into the massive opening immediately flooded the engine room; the ship began to list, then righted itself and began settling by the stern. Cheetham ordered his crew to abandon ship. There was a brief panic among a number of the *Dolius's* Chinese crewmen aboard, who made up nearly a third of the seventy-man complement of crewmen and naval gunners. Cheetham quickly subdued the unrest, and all but four of the crew who were killed in the torpedo detonation made an orderly departure in three surviving lifeboats. Within twenty-five minutes of the attack, the three lifeboats were standing by waiting for rescue. Sitting in one of the lifeboats, Cheetham suddenly saw a crewman appear on the stricken ship and wave urgently. Returning to the vessel, the captain found the man standing over a second, unconscious crewman who had been injured in the attack. Several crewmen reboarded the ship and helped the injured pair safely transfer to the lifeboat.[27]

Escort Group B-7 had reacted instantly to the midday attack. Commodore Brook ordered an emergency turn of the convoy to starboard, but Lieutenant-Commander Sherwood radioed him to cancel the maneuver. Instead, Sherwood ordered Operation Artichoke, the emergency response to a torpedoing of any ship in the convoy's main body. Closest to the stricken *Dolius* were Lieutenant-Commander James Plomer in the corvette *Sunflower* and Sherwood himself in the frigate *Tay.*

Sweeping down the main body between Columns 2 and 3, the *Sunflower* quickly developed an Asdic contact not far from the sinking merchantman. "The contact was most difficult to hold as there were several non-sub echoes," Plomer later reported. Asdic operators often picked up echoes from groups of fish or submerged debris drifting in the water. He ordered a full spread of ten depth charges dropped to detonate at 150 feet, and moved ahead to attempt a renewed Asdic contact when the turbulence subsided. After the initial depth-charge attack, however, Plomer's Asdic operator could detect no echo from the U-638. The *Sunflower* had become the first B-7 escort to kill a U-boat and its entire crew, but neither Lieutenant-Commander Plomer nor the *Sunflower's* crew realized it at the time. Plomer erroneously logged the result of the deadly attack as "nil," and an Admiralty assessment committee that later reviewed Escort Group B-7's attacks on the U-boats made no mention of the incident. It would not be until a postwar comparison of British and German naval records that the *Sunflower* would finally receive credit for sinking the U-boat.

For an hour after its final attack on U-638, the *Sunflower* conducted an Operation Observant with the corvette *Snowflake* in an attempt to re-acquire contact with the U-boat. Finding no trace of the submersible, Plomer retrieved the sixty-seven survivors of the nearby *Dolius,* one of whom died of his injuries aboard the corvette and was later buried at sea. Once on board the *Sunflower,* however, the survivors were grateful, volunteering to help the corvette's crew in any way they could, serving on lookout stations, performing minor maintenance tasks, and cleaning the warship from stem to stern. When it finally reached its destination at St. John's, Plomer later wrote, "The ship was sorry to see them go in spite of the overcrowding involved."[28]

COMPARED WITH THE MAIN body of Convoy ONS5 and its escorts, Lieutenant Robert Atkinson and his crew of eighty-four on the corvette *Pink* had spent the past two days uneventfully. Detached by Commander Gretton to round up stragglers from the hurricane-force storm on May 1, the *Pink* had toiled for four days to corral the struggling merchantmen, only to have them heave to or scatter when the next storm blew in several hours later. The only alarm had come the previous afternoon, when Atkinson overheard a radio report that the *Oribi* had sighted a surfaced U-boat at a position dead ahead of the straggler convoy. Atkinson ordered his group to make a course change from 235 degrees to 180 degrees for the night, and the small formation slipped past the lurking U-boat, resuming a base course of 240 degrees at 0015 on May 5.

As the sun came up on May 5, things were looking bright for the *Pink* and her charges. Atkinson cheerfully recorded in his daily log, "The weather was now good and very clear and we were making about eight knots." The only problem was that Atkinson's fuel supply had dropped to thirty percent. Since the *Pink* and its merchant ships were about eighty miles from the main body of ONS5 at sunrise, Atkinson knew he would not be able to refuel from the escort tanker, so as a precaution he had shut down one of his two steam

Lieutenant Robert Atkinson, commander of *HMS Pink*, escorted a group of stragglers from Convoy ONS5.

Courtesy of Sir Robert Atkinson

boilers to extend the corvette's range—a measure that had the effect of significantly lowering the corvette's maximum speed. The *Pink* was making a zigzag course ahead of the American 5,565-ton merchant steamer *West Madaket*, the 3,862-ton British freighter *Dunsley,* the 5,107-ton British freighter *Director,* and the 2,280-ton Norwegian steamer *Gudvor.* Sometime that morning a fifth straggler, the 5,566-ton British steamer *Yearby,* joined Atkinson's group. The ships were steaming in a line abreast several hundred yards behind the corvette when, at 0954, the passage suddenly became exciting.

Atkinson's Asdic operator shouted up through his voice tube that he had an underwater contact on the corvette's starboard bow at a range of 2,200 yards. It was, the lieutenant later said, "a most firm and excellent [U-boat] contact . . . being the sharpest and cleanest [signal] I have ever heard." As Atkinson sounded Action Stations and his crew hurried to their positions, he was mindful of a potential conflict in his choice of actions. The Atlantic Convoy Instructions under which the escorts worked required that the warships' top priority be for the safety of the merchantmen. Killing U-boats came second. The wording was unambiguous:

The safe and timely arrival of the convoy at its destination is the primary object, and nothing releases the escort commander of his responsibility in this respect. At the same time, it must be borne in mind, that, if enemy forces are reported or encountered, the escort shares with all other fighting units the duty of destroying enemy ships, provided that this duty can be undertaken without undue prejudice to the safety of the convoy.[29]

The instructions dictated that the *Pink* was only to engage with the enemy if it could do so without endangering the five merchantmen under its wing. Atkinson and his crew had yet to see action since leaving Oversay on April 22, however, and with a U-boat crisply identified by Asdic, the commander decided that the odds were in his ship's favor. He ordered full speed—a paltry eleven knots on one boiler—and headed for the U-boat's plotted location.

Closing on the site of the suspected U-boat, the *Pink* commenced a series of ever more vicious assaults. Atkinson first ordered a limited drop of three depth charges, hoping to avoid a close-in detonation like the one that had wrecked the *Snowflake's* Asdic set the night before, or had shattered the *Duncan's* wardroom gin glasses four days earlier. At 0959, just five minutes after the initial Asdic contact, the three charges fell below the smooth ocean surface and detonated in harsh *cracks* that vomited columns of water skyward. The *Pink* turned out from the swirl while her engine gang lit off the second boiler. Atkinson paused to regain an Asdic contact, then at 1007 charged in at fifteen knots for a second attack. This time he ordered a full spread—four charges from the two K-guns on each side of the corvette, and six from the stern rails—and the small warship blasted a seam in the ocean. On the *Pink's* third run, Atkinson ordered the Hedgehog crew to ready its twenty-four forward-firing mortar projectiles and gave the firing order when he estimated the corvette was 250 yards away. The mechanism misfired, however, and Atkinson ordered a new Asdic search to regain contact with the target. Eleven minutes later, at 1027, his operator reported a "firm and metallic" signal. Six minutes after that, a full spread of ten more depth charges were falling down toward the target, exploding at depths of 250 and 385 feet. The ocean astern of the corvette again crumpled and roiled, but at a lower height than the tumult caused by the earlier, shallower sets of charges.

Despite the savageness of the *Pink*'s attacks, the U-boat was still alive. Detecting acoustical signs that his target was attempting to dive even deeper, Atkinson ordered a fourth attack at 1044, with ten more depth charges set to catch the descending U-boat at 350 and 550 feet. The lieutenant called this "a most accurate and successful attack." As the warship once again moved out to reacquire the target on Asdic, the operator reported hydrophone sounds of the enemy blowing his ballast tanks. Then, 500 yards astern, three huge bubbles and a host of smaller ones broke the surface. "The water in the vicinity [was] considerably aerated in appearance and green and white like shallow water," Atkinson later wrote. "Tangible evidence of destruction was greedily and most enthusiastically searched for, but nothing further was seen."

While aware that his merchant ships had drawn considerably ahead of the site of the *Pink*'s encounter with the U-boat, Atkinson opted to make two more attacks before returning to his small convoy. A second Hedgehog attack at 1102 failed yet again when all of the projectiles detonated on impact with the water. On his final run, Atkinson ordered eight depth charges set for 350 and 550 feet, with two more set for a maximum depth of 700 feet. Once more the Atlantic boiled astern of the corvette. At 1325, Atkinson finally called off the hunt and ordered the *Pink* to rejoin the formation, which was now ten miles ahead. Then, fourteen minutes later, Atkinson recorded, "a dull and most powerful underwater explosion shook the ship, low in note and like a deep grunt." The *Pink*'s officers instantly concluded the blast had come from the U-boat. "I can only think that this was the submarine, or some part of it, exploding astern deep down, and I consider this to have been the case." Atkinson and his officers wanted badly to return to the site and look for evidence confirming the kill but decided that protecting the five merchant ships was more critical.

The object of Atkinson's combat fury was most likely the U-358, which ten hours earlier had sunk the ONS5 ships *Bristol City* and *Wentworth*. Writing in his KTB diary for May 5, Kapitänleutnant Manke reported that a "destroyer" escorting several steamers apart from the ONS5 main body had repeatedly attacked him with depth charges over a ninety-minute period. The twenty-seven-year-old U-boat officer ruefully praised the competence of the Allied escort skipper who was trying to kill him.

"The destroyer [sic] criss-crossed above the boat continuously," Manke wrote. "He must have a good hydrophone because he used Asdic only for a short time before attacking. In addition, he employed doppler effect [where the tone of the Asdic echo indicated the direction of the U-boat's underwater passage], and fifty seconds later the depth charges came."[30]

ALTHOUGH THE *PINK*'S ATTACKS would fail to sink U-358, they would knock the U-boat out of the fight. After their aggressor had departed, Manke and his men surveyed the wreckage inside their boat. Several diving cells were out of service. The conning tower hatch had sprung a bad leak. There were numerous electrical failures, four battery cells were cracked and leaking acid, and the stern hydrophones could only move ten degrees. Surfacing several hours later, Manke found that the boat could not exceed ten knots running on its diesels. He reported the situation to BdU, which ordered him to return to St. Nazaire.[31]

An hour and fourteen minutes after breaking off contact with the U-boat, Atkinson came to regret his ambitiousness. As the *Pink* strove to catch up with the convoy, her lookouts peering ahead at the distant merchant vessels steaming in line abreast, at 1452, a heavy explosion suddenly rocked one of them, sending a huge column of smoke into the sky. Another U-boat had struck with deadly effect.

While the *Pink* had been off harrying U-358, a veteran U-boat moved in on the undefended herd of merchantmen. Kapitänleutnant Joachim Deecke was on his eighth patrol in U-584; in two of his earlier cruises, Deecke had sunk two Allied merchant ships totaling 12,913 tons and the Soviet submarine M-175. In another patrol, in mid-June 1942, Deecke and his crew took part in a covert U-boat operation along the U.S. East Coast. In Operation Pastorious, Admiral Dönitz tasked the U-202 and U584 to make daring forays close to the beach to land four-man teams of German operatives who would proceed to sabotage American war facilities. U-202 landed its team by rubber raft at Amagansett Beach in eastern Long Island on June 13, 1942; four days later, Deecke and U-584 came inshore off Ponte Vedra Beach south of St. Augustine, Florida, and landed the second team of agents in the same fashion. The U-boats' part of the operation was carried out flawlessly, but the operations on land went immediately astray when two of the saboteurs betrayed the other six to the

FBI. In its current war cruise, U-584 had gone hitless in its forty-three days at sea, but its fortune changed when at 1400, Deecke spotted the *Pink* and its small convoy through his periscope.[32]

Deecke ordered a four-torpedo fanshot aimed at two of the ships. One torpedo failed in the tube, but the other three sped off toward the targets. One of them struck the *West Madaket* on its port quarter, throwing up a huge geyser of water. The freighter immediately settled by the stern. Realizing that the torpedo had broken his ship's back, Captain H. Schroeder ordered his crew of thirty-eight and twenty-two Naval Armed Guardsmen to take to the lifeboats. Atkinson, meanwhile, closed with the sinking *West Madaket*, his "worst fears" having come true, and dropped intermittent depth charges in the area to keep the U-boat under. He next retrieved the survivors from their lifeboats. Noticing that most of the crewmen had brought suitcases and other luggage, Atkinson ordered them to leave the gear behind, then told his Oerlikon gunners to take target practice on the freighted lifeboats once the survivors were safely transferred. Finally, Atkinson edged the corvette close to the listing freighter and finished it off with a pair of depth charges fired from his starboard K-guns and set to go off at fifty feet. "The result was devastating," he stated in his report of the incident. "She split as if cleaved by an ax amidships, sinking in two separate pieces and turning turtle as she sank."

STILL STEAMING ABOUT eighty nautical miles ahead of the *Pink* and her diminished convoy, ONS5 was about to get a break. At 1619 local (1919 GMT), an inbound Iceland-based 120 Squadron VLR Liberator, J/120, made radio contact with the frigate *Tay*. It was the first time in three days that the convoy had encountered a land-based aircraft. As the aircraft neared ONS5, Sherwood gave a one-word command to the pilot: "Viper." This was the code word for the Liberator to conduct a circling orbit around the convoy at the maximum range of visibility from the merchant ships. The aircraft finished the sweep fifteen minutes later without detecting any surfaced U-boats.[33]

Although the aircraft hadn't spotted any U-boats on its patrol, the wolf packs were still stalking ONS5, and one of them was about to launch a devastating attack on it. So far in the running battle between ONS5 and the four German wolf packs, all but two of the torpedoed merchant ships had been struck by Gruppe Fink U-boats. The exceptions were the erst-while Gruppe Star's U-258, which had sunk the *McKeesport* while that wolf pack was still in operation on April 29; and Gruppe Amsel 1's U-638, which had successfully attacked the *Dolius*. Nearly eight hours after the *Dolius* went down at midday on May 5, a U-boat from the fourth wolf pack, Amsel 2, would claim the highest number of merchantmen from a single strike against ONS5.

U-266 had sunk a 4,077-ton Greek freighter on its first North Atlantic patrol in December 1942, and had been trying to add to its record ever since. Kapitänleutnant Ralf von Jessen, twenty-six, had been in command of U-266 for a little under eight months since its commissioning when BdU ordered his boat to join Amsel 2 several hundred miles to the south of Gruppe Fink. The two Amsel packs were aligned generally south of Gruppe Fink, so that they could intercept any ships that eluded the larger wolf pack. The twelve U-boats had been in position for only a day when the fighting around Convoy ONS5 erupted in earnest on May 4. Upon receiving U-628's contact report that evening, BdU had ordered all forty-one U-boats from Fink, Amsel 1, and Amsel 2 to move in for the kill. Both Amsel groups headed north to intercept the convoy and were within striking range the next day. Shortly before 1630 local (1930 GMT) on May 5, von Jessen had successfully positioned his U-boat at periscope depth out in front of the convoy, which was steaming on a course of 192 degrees and was now making a speed of five and one-half knots against southwest headwinds.[34]

For most of the Atlantic crossing, the 5,136-ton British merchant steamer *Selvistan* had occupied the second position in Column 10, behind the British freighter *Yearby*. The nineteen-year-old *Selvistan* was outbound from the Scottish port of Oban to Halifax with a forty-six-man crew, including six gunners, and laden with several thousand tons of ballast. After the series of gales that began on May 1, the column leader *Yearby* had failed to rejoin the convoy along with eleven other stragglers, so Commodore Brook had ordered Captain George E. Miles to move the *Selvistan* into the lead position of Column 9.

In the late afternoon of May 5, the formation was steaming in good order under an overcast sky. A light rain was falling, but visibility was excellent and the seas had calmed into moderate swells. C. D. Head, the

Selvistan's first officer, was standing watch on the bridge when he suddenly noticed something moving between his ship and the next vessel over, the American tanker *Argon*. "At first I thought [it] was a porpoise, as it appeared to be spouting water," he later reported. "This object passed very close across the American tanker's bow, and when it was halfway between the *Selvistan* and the American ship it jumped out of the water, and then continued on its course." For a moment out of time, Head stood rooted to the deck in stunned disbelief. The approaching object was a German torpedo.

Adrenalin pounding through his body, Head ducked into the wheelhouse and rang Full Speed Ahead on the engine order telegraph while barking an order to the helmsman to turn the ship hard to port. He was too late. At 1953, the torpedo struck the freighter's port side by the No. 5 cargo hold. Five seconds later, a second torpedo slammed into the No. 4 hold forward of the first torpedo impact.

The explosions seemed muted, and Head saw no fireball, but the results were still horrific. Clinging to a stanchion, he watched the cargo hatches blow off and a huge mass of ballast stones soar high into the sky. The *Selvistan* began sinking at an alarming rate. "There was no time to lower either of the two lifeboats, but the two small bridge boats were launched," Head later testified. Captain Miles managed to get to the forward starboard life raft and cast it loose. Head made his way to one of the small bridge boats and quickly cast off as water rose to the level of the davits from which the boat was hanging. Another crewman went running toward one of the larger lifeboats, but before he could get to the station, the freighter sank out from under him. Less than two minutes after the torpedo strikes, nothing was left of the *Selvistan* but a small group of boats and life rafts, and assorted flotsam. Captain Miles and thirty-nine of his forty-five-man crew were picked up by the frigate *Tay*.[35]

The 5,306-ton British steamer *Gharinda* was about 1,000 yards to starboard of the *Selvistan*, in the lead position in Column 10, the starboardmost file in the reduced convoy, and had a clear view of the torpedoing. Captain Rodney R. Stone was on duty on the *Gharinda's* bridge when he saw the twin blasts from the torpedoes striking the *Selvistan*. Before he or any of his eight-one-man crew could react, a single torpedo struck their ship on the port side at 1955. Unlike the dull, muted thud reported by the

Selvistan's first officer, and although the *Gharinda* was carrying only ballast, the torpedo that struck the twenty-four-year-old merchantman went off in a deafening explosion and bright fireball. A huge column of water thrown into the air by the blast cascaded down on the bridge, followed by a cargo hatch, which landed on the bridge's roof. The *Gharinda* began settling rapidly at the bow. Recognizing that the torpedo hit had been fatal, Stone ordered his crew to abandon ship. They successfully lowered four of the six lifeboats, and all hands—including the ship's ten naval gunners— safely got away. By the time Stone had cast off in the last lifeboat, the *Gharinda* had settled by the bow to the point that its propeller and rudder were completely out of the water.

In the chaotic aftermath of the torpedo hit on the *Gharinda*, Stone noticed a fourth torpedo strike the Norwegian freighter *Bonde*, traveling in the last position of Column 8. Several *Bonde* crewmen later said they had seen a periscope close on their starboard beam and engaged it with machine-gun fire but were hit by the torpedo just several seconds later. It detonated on the starboard side of the tiny, 1,570-ton vessel, indicating that the U-boat had likely fired from close range in between the two columns, using the four bow tubes for the two British vessels and his stern tube for the Norwegian. The U-boat was prowling through the very midst of ONS5.[36]

The *Bonde* sank even quicker than the *Gharinda*, as Captain John Gates of the 3,242-ton British freighter *Baron Graham*, steaming several columns over, later recalled. "There was an explosion and [the *Bonde*] seemed to jump up in the water," he said. "When the smoke and spray of the explosion had cleared away, the *Bonde* was already standing on her end with her bow and foredeck vertically out of the water. I looked away for a few seconds and in that time the ship sank." Those who survived the explosion had jumped for it, since there had been no time to lower lifeboats.[37]

On the *Tay*, Sherwood was struggling to respond to a major problem on his frigate: around the time that the three ships were struck, the *Tay's* Asdic transponder malfunctioned, preventing the ship from sending acoustic pulses out to bounce off submerged U-boats' hulls. While the Asdic operator could still listen passively for sounds generated by a submerged U-boat, the warship was unable to prosecute any attacks against the U-boats swarming around ONS5. When U-266 struck the three freighters, Sherwood ordered Lieutenant Hart on the *Vidette* to carry out an Operation Artichoke, searching down the convoy columns for the attacker. Within a minute, at 1954, aircraft J/120 reappeared overhead, having found no U-boats in the course of its Viper operation. Sherwood now requested a different search: "Mamba 020," which would send the VLR Liberator down a line of bearing 020 degrees for twenty miles to search for a suspected U-boat whose transmission the HF/DF operators had just tracked on that vector. Sherwood also tasked Ingram on the *Oribi* and McCoy on the *Offa* to carry out an Operation Observant around the wrecks of the *Bonde* and *Gharinda* while he maneuvered the *Tay* to retrieve the survivors.

On the *Offa*, Captain McCoy had just finished his much-delayed refueling from the escort oiler *British Lady* when the four sharp blasts of torpedo hits had erupted off to the starboard side of the convoy. Ordered by Sherwood to assist the *Oribi* in an Operation Observant around the sites of the *Bonde* and *Gharinda* strikes, McCoy rushed across the two-mile distance from the tanker's position to the attack site. There, he met Ingram's *Oribi,* and the two warships began a careful search for ONS5's latest assailant.[38]

While awaiting rescue in one of his ship's lifeboats, Captain Stone decided to return to the *Gharinda* to see if it might still somehow be saved. At that moment, however, the frigate *Tay* raced up and began retrieving survivors from the lifeboats and rafts. "We were literally lifted bodily on board the *Tay*," Stone reported. "In fact, I was hauled up by the scruff of my neck." Despite its captain's resolve, the *Gharinda* would soon be at the bottom of the Atlantic. Over the course of forty minutes, the *Tay's* crew rescued 144 men from the three ships: 40 from the *Selvistan,* 12 from the *Bonde,* and all 92 men from the *Gharinda.* The U-boat attack had killed 14 *Bonde* crewmen and 6 from the *Selvistan.*[39]

As the *Tay* was finishing up its rescue operations, J/120 returned from its second operation. "Your Mamba, nil seen," the pilot reported to Sherwood at 2023. The lieutenant-commander requested a second Viper, and the four-engine Liberator made another sweep at maximum visible range from the convoy. Having flown 970 miles from Reykjavik to the convoy's current location, however, the Liberator could not remain overhead for very long, and at 2038, just seventy minutes after reaching ONS5, the pilot radioed Sherwood, "Don't want to go, but have to." Sherwood replied, "Thank you for your help." The deep drone of the bomber's engines faded as the aircraft turned to a northeast heading for the long trip back to Iceland.

As the VLR Liberator was departing the convoy, the destroyers *Offa* and *Oribi* were well into their Operation Observant around the wrecks of the *Bonde* and *Gharinda*. At 2039, the *Offa* was just about to turn from a westerly leg of its search toward the north when McCoy's Asdic operator called out a firm contact bearing 270 degrees at a range of 1,500 yards. "This was only two miles from the nearest wreck," McCoy reported. Suspecting this was the same U-boat that had just attacked the convoy, and fearing it might now attempt to sink the *Tay* or finish off the two crippled freighters, McCoy raced in and, three minutes after detecting the U-boat, dropped a full spread of depth charges over its calculated location.

Several minutes after the attack, the *Offa's* lookouts reported a large series of air bubbles breaking the surface at the site, but McCoy suspected a ruse. Over the next ninety minutes, he plastered the submerged U-boat with four more depth charge patterns. Next, he ordered Ingram on the *Oribi,* whose Asdic operator could not acquire the U-boat, to position the destroyer between the U-boat location and the wrecks. Finally, at 2215, McCoy called it quits. It was 1915 local time, and the skies were darkening. The escorts had to reorganize themselves for what all feared would be a violent and bloody night. "Heavy [encrypted high-frequency] activity indicated that the convoy was threatened with annihilation," McCoy later explained. "I considered it imperative to return to it before dark."

At least one of the HF/DF signals beaming across the Atlantic did not represent a further threat to ONS5, however. As the *Offa* and *Oribi* hurried back to Convoy ONS5 at twenty knots, Kapitänleutnant von Jessen and the U-266 crewmen were quietly limping away to repair the extensive damage that McCoy's five depth charge attacks had caused. Von Jessen reported to BdU that a diving tank, trim cells, an air compressor, and one E-motor had been wrecked in the pounding, and he was being forced to withdraw from the fight and return to port.

As both the U-boats and the convoy escorts regrouped on the evening of May 5, lookouts on both sides noticed that a light fog was settling in over the surface of the ocean. Within minutes, visibility shrank to just one mile. The shroud of moisture grew steadily thicker until, several hours later, lookouts could not see anything more than 100 yards away. No one realized it at first, but this simple weather phenomenon would dictate the rest of the battle over Convoy ONS5.[40]

Chapter 13

BATTLE IN THE FOG

As darkness fell on Thursday, May 5, Lieutenant-Commander Sherwood harbored a growing sense of resignation that the coming hours were going to be a bloody repetition of the previous night. There were at least nine U-boats in firm contact with the convoy, and more than two dozen others in the vicinity; the steady bursts of encrypted wireless transmissions intercepted by the HF/DF operators on Sherwood's frigate, the *Tay*, and the destroyer *Oribi*, showed the presence of U-boats on all sides of the formation. Sherwood was preparing for their inevitable assault as best he could, but with the frigate *Tay*'s Asdic set still unable to transmit active sonar pulses and the corvette *Pink* guarding a group of stragglers some eighty miles astern, Sherwood knew his escort group would be hard-pressed to stave off another mass attack. With the ship losses and stragglers from the wave of storms, the main body of ONS5 was down to twenty-three ships reorganized into ten columns, proceeding on a course of 202 degrees at a speed of seven and one-half knots.[1]

There was one factor that would have heartened Sherwood and the other ship commanders in Escort Group B-7 and the 3rd Support Group. Sherwood noted in his daily log that the weather had moderated, with a calm sea, no wind, and a steady drizzle. This normally would have given the U-boats a keen advantage in night attacks, except for one factor: the mist that had begun rolling in before dusk was getting thicker, and visibility had shrunk to half a mile. The U-boat lookouts would have extreme difficulty sighting the convoy. The radar operators in Escort Group B-7 would have no difficulty pinpointing U-boats on the surface.[2]

Despite the weather conditions that favored the escort warships, the U-boats were very much still on the hunt. At 1752 local time (2152 GMT), in response to the triple torpedo attack that had sunk the *Selvistan, Gharinda,* and *Bonde,* Convoy ONS5 Commodore Brook on the *Rena* ordered an emergency turn, and the twenty-three ships still steaming in the main body turned forty-five degrees to port on a new course of 156 for the next fifty minutes. The ploy had little effect in fooling the U-boats now surrounding ONS5. As the light had dimmed over the misty, drizzle-flecked ocean, Sherwood ordered the escorts to their night stations. Even with seven escorts on hand to protect the convoy, the large number of U-boats forced Sherwood to order several minor changes from the standard night patrol assignments. With his frigate's malfunctioning Asdic gear capable only of passive listening, Sherwood placed the *Tay* in Station A ahead of the front center of the convoy to serve, in his words, as an "Asdic listening watch only." Sherwood then shifted the corvettes *Snowflake* and *Loosestrife* back from the convoy's port and starboard beams, respectively, to its port and starboard quarters. He kept the corvette *Sunflower* off the port bow and the destroyer *Vidette* off the starboard bow in the standard format. When the *Offa* and *Oribi* returned from the hunt for U-266, Sherwood planned to have them to take station once again in a distant barrier about five miles ahead of the main body. This left the port and starboard beams and the rear of the convoy unprotected. Any U-boat attack from those directions would require the escorts to break station and rush over to intervene.[3]

While Lieutenant-Commander Sherwood and the other escort commanders braced themselves for a night of battle, in far distant Berlin, tensions were also high. Admirals Dönitz and Godt stared at the outsized 1870G Nord-Atlantischer Ozean chart: they could see that the westbound convoy that Gruppen Fink, Amsel 1, and Amsel 2 were hunting was drawing near to Newfoundland and within range of Allied land-based patrol planes there. Incoming weather messages from the U-boats stalking ONS5 revealed the second complicating factor—the steadily deteriorating visibility. Dönitz and Godt had already decided that the battle against "Convoy No. 36"—they still were unaware the convoy was ONS5 and not, as they thought, westbound ON180—would have to end the next day. "There was no prospect of the weather improving, as the convoy was approaching the Newfoundland Banks," Godt wrote in the BdU War Diary.

Having made the decision to continue the attack during the night of May 5–6, BdU sent out a series of encrypted Enigma messages urging the Fink and Amsel U-boat commanders to attack without letup. Identifying ONS5 by the name of the U-boat commander who had made the initial contact report, Dönitz ordered the U-boats to hold nothing back:

HASENSCHAR CONVOY BOATS SHOULD REPORT THEIR CONTACTS AND POSITIONS MORE FREQUENTLY. ALL ARE TO MAKE THE MOST OF THE GREAT OPPORTUNITY TONIGHT OFFERS.

Another BdU screed encouraged U-boats not to crash-dive if sighted by land-based aircraft:

TONIGHT'S OPPORTUNITY MUST IN NO EVENT BE AL-LOWED TO BE SPOILED BY AIRCRAFT BEFORE THE BEGIN-NING OF DARKNESS. BOATS WHOSE ANTIAIRCRAFT ARMAMENT IS CLEAR, REMAIN ON THE SURFACE IN THE PRESENCE OF AIRCRAFT AND SHOOT. THEN THE PLANE WILL SOON STOP ATTACKING.

In a final exhortation, Dönitz added an order that the U-boats go after the B-7 escort ships with warheads set to go off when passing through the magnetic fields generated by the surface ships' steel hulls:

IF THERE ARE NO MORE MERCHANTMEN THERE TO BE SHOT UP SINK THE ESCORT VESSELS MAKING FULL USE OF MAGNETIC EXPLODERS.[4]

The fog cloaking Convoy ONS5 now dictated the course of battle. With visibility down to less than 1,000 yards, the weather put the Germans at a potentially devastating disadvantage. The fog had all but blinded the U-boat lookouts, whose commanders depended upon them for guidance as they attempted to maneuver through the B-7 convoy screen and attack the merchantmen. Oberleutnant Gretschel on U-707, who had sunk the *North Britain* just after midnight the day before, would bitterly observe at one point on the night of May 5 that he and seven other U-boats had managed to position themselves ahead of ONS5 but had little hope of actually executing an attack. "The weather has thwarted our plans," Gretschel wrote. "The visibility has gotten very bad, with fog and drizzle, and this makes any attack impossible in the pitch-black night."[5]

While they were well aware of the frequent harsh storms in the North Atlantic, Dönitz and Godt had not anticipated the particular conditions that had descended upon the course track of ONS5. Unbeknownst to them, moreover, by the time their last message had gone out at 2333, their exhortations were unnecessary. Despite the fog, the rain, and the darkness, the climax of the battle for "Convoy No. 36" had already begun.

As Escort Group B-7 girded for battle, crewmen on many of the warships scrambled to repair a rash of mechanical malfunctions that had occurred during the U-boat night attacks of May 4–5 and the fighting during the day on May 5. On the corvette *Sunflower*, in the evening of May 5, Lieutenant-Commander James Plomer reported that his ship's magnetic compass "had become completely unreliable," forcing the *Sunflower* to plot ship positions and attack routes by radar. In addition, the buzzer system for signaling the deck crew to fire the K-guns and drop depth charges from the stern rails had become inoperable, forcing Plomer and his officers to shout the firing commands down to the stern via a voice tube. Still, the corvette's crew was ready for a fight, and soon they would get one.

At 2240, the *Sunflower*'s radar operator gained an initial surface contact off the port bow. The corvette went to its maximum speed of fourteen knots toward the suspected enemy. Seven minutes later, as the *Sunflower* approached the U-boat, it suddenly dived. The Asdic operator held a firm contact, and, at 2252, Plomer dropped a spread of ten depth charges set for 150 feet. Meanwhile, the radar operator called out a second U-boat blip straight ahead at 3,400 yards. "Course was maintained to attack the next submarine," Plomer reported. Three minutes after the second U-boat was located on radar, the *Sunflower*'s Asdic operator shouted out a warning: "Torpedo fired from Red twenty!" (that is, twenty degrees to starboard of the ship's bow). Ahead to starboard, a U-boat had launched a warshot at the corvette. Plomer ordered a slight turn toward the incoming threat, and the lookouts saw a torpedo wake pass down the corvette's port side.

Plomer radioed Sherwood that he had sighted and was chasing a second U-boat, which was still on the surface. This alert triggered a flurry of messages as the escorts rushed to respond to the *Sunflower*'s contacts. As the two U-boats were off the convoy's port bow, Sherwood called convoy Commodore Brook on the *Rena* and ordered ONS5 to make an emergency turn to starboard, in an attempt to steer clear of the threat.

At 2258, the *Sunflower*'s lookouts sighted the enemy. As the silhouette of a surfaced U-boat emerged from the mist, Plomer opened fire with high-explosive shells from the corvette's four-inch cannon but it jammed on the third shot. He instantly realized that the *Sunflower* could not catch up with the accelerating U-boat for a depth-charge attack, so he turned the corvette to pursue another U-boat that had just come up on the radar screen. Another shout from the Asdic operator: "Full salvo of torpedoes!" Four more German torpedoes were running hot. This time, Plomer ordered a hard turn to port to aim his bow at the oncoming eels. Before the *Sunflower* could complete the maneuver, lookouts watched several wakes rush down the port side of the ship.

After reacting to the flurry of U-boat radar contacts and incoming torpedoes, Plomer alerted Lieutenant-Commander Sherwood on the *Tay* to the suddenly escalating situation on the convoy's port bow. He picked up his radiotelephone handset. His voice crackled out of the speaker on the frigate *Tay*'s bridge seven miles away. "Have broken off chase, fired two H.E.'s [high explosive rounds]. Could not gain," Plomer reported. A *Tay* crewman jotted down the terse exchange in the frigate's radiotelephone log.

"Confirm there were three subs," Sherwood ordered.

"Hearse confirmed," Plomer initially replied, using the Allied code word for a U-boat. Several minutes later, he amplified the report: "Dropped pattern on one contact, chased sub on surface, escaped two torpedoes, estimate three subs in vicinity."

With no other U-boat contacts reported in the vicinity of the convoy at that moment, Sherwood decided to send the *Sunflower* assistance from another B-7 escort warship. He told Plomer he was sending the *Snowflake* up from the convoy's port quarter to assist. Scarcely had Lieutenant Chesterman ordered the *Snowflake* to maximum power, however, than the *Sunflower's* skipper reported that the U-boats had eluded further detection and that he was returning to his night station. With so many U-boats in the area, Plomer did not want to leave the convoy's flank exposed unless he was in firm contact with the enemy. It did not take long for the threat to re-emerge. The crew of the *Snowflake* was able to stand easy for all of three minutes. At 2323, the corvette's radar operator called out a U-boat contact bearing 190 degrees at 2,400 yards.

The *Snowflake* responded instantly to the report of the U-boat contact. It ran down the bearing of the radar signal, and within two minutes had narrowed the range to 2,100 yards. Chesterman ordered his forward four-inch gun to alternate firing starshells and high-explosive rounds. The dazzling illumination rounds lit up the mist, and the corvette's lookouts saw the U-boat crash-dive.

While the U-boat was no longer in position to attack the merchant ships in ONS5, it still posed a threat to the corvette hunting it. The *Snowflake* was now directly astern of the submerged U-boat, and Chesterman suddenly realized the danger of his position; if the U-boat commander came up to periscope depth, he could easily fire a torpedo from his stern tube at close range. When another radar contact revealed a second U-boat on the surface nearby, Chesterman ordered his helmsman to turn away from the submerged target and chase the new one. He later explained his decision: after the U-boat had fired on the *Sunflower* as it chased from astern, the other B-7 warship commanders were aware that they, too, were vulnerable to this aggressive tactic by the enemy. "Altered course toward second U-boat as the danger from torpedo attack was too great to warrant carrying out an attack with one or two [depth] charges on the first U-boat," Plomer explained.

Lieutenant Chesterman and the other B-7 commanders were reacting as aggressively to the U-boats as they could, but the Germans were also acting with cunning and skill. When the *Snowflake* closed to within 1,800 yards of its new target, at 2334, the second U-boat dived. The corvette swooped in to drop several depth charges. Informed by his Asdic operator that the U-boat was drawing from right to left, and anticipating that the

German would make a hard turn to port when the corvette passed over-head, Chesterman ordered his portside K-gun crews to aim thirty degrees ahead to compensate for the U-boat's anticipated turn. *Snowflake's* skipper guessed wrong and was forced to abort the depth-charge attack. "The U-boat did in fact turn hard-a-starboard and passed down the [*Snowflake's*] starboard side," Chesterman later wrote. "No charges dropped."

Because of the numerous U-boats known to be hunting ONS5, it was not possible for the B-7 warships to engage in a protracted search once a U-boat faded from the Asdic screen, since each engagement left a large gap in the convoy's protective screen. Breaking off his pursuit, Chester-man ordered the corvette to pass over the last calculated position of the first U-boat while returning to Position M on the convoy's port bow. Ar-riving at the U-boat's suspected location, he ordered a single depth charge dropped to keep the boat submerged. Continuing back toward the main body of ONS5, the *Snowflake* gained a weak Asdic signal suspected to be the second U-boat. Chesterman dropped a pair of depth charges to hold that one under as well. After an hour of chasing the two U-boats, at 0030 on Friday, May 6, the *Snowflake* was back in Position R. Conditions on the convoy's port bow were quiet, but the battle was raging in full fury elsewhere along the formation's perimeter. While Chesterman and his crew had not destroyed either U-boat, they had succeeded in preventing at least two of the enemy from attacking ONS5 through the *Snowflake's* patrol area.[6]

THE NEXT CONFRONTATION between Escort Group B-7 and Gruppe Fink occurred off the convoy's starboard bow, with disastrous results for the Germans. At 2309, Lieutenant Hart and his crew of 133 on the destroyer *Vidette* were patrolling in Position C off the starboard bow of ONS5 when Hart's radar operator called out a contact nearly dead ahead at a range of 5,100 yards. Hart sent his men to battle stations and ordered his engines to full power. The elderly warship kicked up a huge wake as it surged to twenty knots. Then, eight minutes after the first contact, the radar opera-tor called out a second slightly to port and 2,100 yards farther out. Hart ignored the new target as the *Vidette* pulled closer and closer to the first one, a U-boat steaming away from ONS5 at about eighteen knots.

Kapitänleutnant Herbert Neckel, commander of the U-531, was a veteran of the Battle of the Atlantic, and had served under several esteemed commanders before taking control of his own U-boat. The twenty-six-year-old had joined the U-boat Force in April 1940, and five months later had reported as 1WO to the famed Kapitänleutnant Fritz-Julius Lemp in the Type VIIA U-30, the U-boat that had kicked off the Battle of the Atlantic on September 3, 1939, with the sinking of the British passenger liner *Athenia*. During three patrols under Lemp's command, Neckel had participated in the sinking of eight Allied ships totaling 35,419 gross tons. In March 1941, Neckel had transferred to the Type IXB U-108. His second U-boat was commanded by Korvettenkapitän Klaus Scholtz, one of only thirty-five U-boat skippers who would sink over 100,000 tons of enemy shipping during the war. Neckel had served with this boat for three patrols during 1941 and racked up another seven ships for an additional 26,931 tons. Upon commissioning U-531 on October 28, 1942, Neckel could already claim credit for helping sink fifteen ships for 62,350 tons. Although he had yet to sink any ships in U-531, his record indicated that his tally would not lag for long.[7]

Neckel and his bridge lookouts reacted quickly when they realized the *Vidette* was approaching, making a crash dive as soon as the destroyer materialized out of the fog. Here, however, Neckel's experience and tactical brilliance would fail him, for U-531 was one of the clumsy Type IXC40 boats that Grossadmiral Dönitz had packed off to the North Atlantic convoy routes despite its inability to dive fast enough.

The *Vidette* executed a textbook attack with quick and deadly results. It closed to just 700 yards behind the U-boat when the latter disappeared in a violent swirl of water. Hart ordered a ten-charge pattern readied with the explosives set at "ramming settings"—fifty feet. The depth charges flew out to the side as the K-guns barked, and Hart's deck crew trundled the other six charges off the stern rails over a twenty-five-second period. The ocean behind the destroyer bucked and heaved as the charges blasted columns of water skyward. Hart later described what happened next. "Almost one minute after the depth charges had exploded, a large explosion was heard by bridge personnel, [depth-charge] crews and engine room ratings," he wrote. "The Engineer Officer, who was at the top of the engine room hatch at the time . . . observed a column of water with dark appearance astern at a distance varying between 300 and 600 yards astern." U-531, its distinguished commander, and his fifty-three crewmen were dead.[8]

Lieutenant Hart did not circle around for another Asdic search or to look for debris that would confirm the kill, for he still had another U-boat on radar at a range of 2,000 yards, and intended to attack that one as well. When the *Vidette* had closed to 900 yards, its lookouts suddenly saw the U-boat emerge from the haze. The boat turned thirty degrees to port and crash-dived. The *Vidette's* crew dropped a spread of five depth charges at 2333, but then lost the Asdic contact. After several attempts to reacquire the U-boat, Hart ordered the destroyer back to Position C, arriving on station at 0125 on May 6.

The long night battle for Convoy ONS5 showed no signs of abating, and for the crew of the *Vidette*, there was no letup in the action. Over the next two hours and twenty minutes, the destroyer chased several more radar contacts without result. Then, at 0406, while the *Vidette* was returning from yet another sweep back toward ONS5, Hart's Asdic operator called out a firm acoustic contact close aboard, bearing 097 degrees and only 800 yards distant.

Several hundred feet down, U-630 was maneuvering quietly on its electric motors in an attempt to escape the harsh *ping!* . . . *ping!* . . . *ping!* from the Vidette's Asdic transponder. Both the U-boat and its forty-seven-man crew were relatively new to the war. Oberleutnant zur See Werner Winkler had joined the Kriegsmarine in 1936 at the age of nineteen, serving on surface warships for three years before attending U-boat training in 1941. He served as 1WO aboard the U-569 for five months in early 1942, and finally commissioned U-630 on July 9, 1942. While this was the first North Atlantic patrol for U-630, it was not the first encounter between the U-boat and Escort Group B-7. Four weeks earlier, while operating in the wolf pack Gruppe Löwenherz, Winkler and his crew had sunk the 5,529-ton British freighter *Shillong*, which had been sailing under B-7's protection. Carrying a load of 4,000 tons of zinc concentrate and another 3,000 tons of general cargo, the four-year-old merchantman sank within two minutes. All but seven of its seventy-eight-man crew drowned in the frigid Atlantic. Now without realizing it, Lieutenant Hart on the *Vidette* was about to exact B-7's revenge.[9]

Hart set up for a Hedgehog attack on the creeping U-boat and maneuvered the *Vidette* so that the twenty-four mortar projectiles would have the
best chance of a hit. Since the U-boat was moving slowly from left to
right, Hart adjusted the trajectory of the mortar shells to compensate for
the moving target. He later said, "I put the gun on a bearing of 111 degrees, that is, allowing a three-degree throw-off to the right" to offset the
changing relative positions of the two. At 0408, Hart gave the command,
and the Hedgehog operator triggered the launcher. Two dozen Hedgehog
bombs soared up and ahead of the destroyer, creating a large oval of turbulence where they struck the water. Just three seconds after the mortars' impact with the water, the Asdic operator reported two distinct underwater
explosions, and lookouts said they had seen the underwater flashes as the
warheads exploded on contact with the U-boat's hull. The Asdic operator
reported the U-boat had blown its ballast tanks. A large swirl of air appeared off the *Vidette's* starboard side, but the U-boat never came up.
Soon after, the Asdic operator said he could find no echo from the target.
Lieutenant Hart and his crew had killed their second U-boat in less than
five hours.[10]

DURING MAY 4 AND 5, the Fink and Amsel U-boats had steadily hacked
away at Convoy ONS5. They had sunk twelve merchantmen for a total
shipping loss of 55,760 tons, killed 142 merchant sailors and naval gunners, and deprived the Allied war effort of tens of thousands of tons of vital shipping capacity. Convoy ONS5 had run a gauntlet of over 572
nautical miles from the first sighting by U-650 on April 28 until the attack by U-266 that sank the *Gharinda, Bonde,* and *Selvistan* six days later.
No doubt each U-boat commander still hunting the convoy hoped that
his skill and a bit of luck would allow him to penetrate the convoy screen
and empty his torpedo tubes at the vulnerable merchantmen. What was
now happening came as a shock and surprise to the U-boat crews, escort
sailors, and merchant seamen alike.

In a matter of hours, the battle had turned into a rout for the Germans.
The sudden fog that had unexpectedly cloaked the battlefield had blinded
only one side of the fight. The U-boats suddenly found themselves naked
to the Allied escort ships' Type 271M radar sets, which operated on a ten-
centimeter wavelength that German scientists had so far been unable to

The shock wave expands from an aerial depth charge dropped by a U.S. Navy PBY-5A
Catalina, a frequent participant in Atlantic convoy fights.
National Archives and Records Administration

detect. The eight escort ships, chasing the bright blips on their radar
screens, could instantaneously and accurately determine the location of
each surfaced U-boat without its commander or lookouts knowing it. It
was a powerful advantage, and the defenders seized it with vigor and resolve after so many long nights of frustration and loss. Indeed, the combination of advanced technology and poor visibility had made possible the
realization of Commander Peter Gretton's avowed tactic for contending
with multiple U-boat attacks from all points of the compass. As Lieutenant-Commander Sherwood on the *Tay* put it, the goal was "hitting all
submarines quickly and hard and then rejoining [the convoy] at full
speed"—and the escorts had proven themselves able to do just that.[11]

The decision by Admirals Dönitz and Godt to extend the Fink and
Amsel attacks until the morning of May 6 would prove to be a monumen-
tal error. Prior to the battle on the night of May 5–6, the Germans had already suffered considerably at the hands of the Allied warships and
aircraft: a Coastal Command 206 Squadron B-17 and the corvette *Sunflower* had sunk two U-boats (U-710 and U-638, respectively, on April 24

and May 5), while Escort Group B-7 had heavily damaged four U-boats to the point that they were forced to abort their patrols (U-386, U-528, and U-532 during April 28–29, and U-358 on the afternoon of May 5). The *Vidette* itself had just sunk two more U-boats. Now, locked in fierce battle on the fog-shrouded Atlantic, the escorts added to the German toll.

The next two U-boat fatalities came at the hands of two B-7 corvettes and a destroyer from the 3rd Support Group. At 0030, the *Loosestrife's* radar operator identified a surfaced U-boat bearing 095 degrees, 5,200 yards out on the corvette's port beam. Closing to 500 yards, the escort and U-boat lookouts sighted the other craft at the same instant. The Type IXC40 U-192 fired two torpedoes from its stern tubes at the *Loosestrife* and began an aggressive series of zigzag turns to avoid gunfire. Its commander, Oberleutnant sur See Werner Happe, then ordered a crash dive, but before the boat could reach a safe depth, the *Loosestrife* blanketed it with a spread of ten depth charges. The detonations forced the U-boat briefly back to the surface, where the corvette's lookouts observed it violently shake from an internal explosion. U-192, just twenty-two days out on its first North Atlantic patrol, was dead along with its fifty-five-man crew.[12]

Just over two hours later, at 0252, the destroyer *Oribi* was patrolling five miles out from the convoy's port bow at a clip of twenty-two knots when its Asdic operator reported an underwater contact close to starboard. Lieutenant-Commander Ingram swung the 1,540-ton destroyer hard to starboard to intercept the submerged target, but, just minutes later, a surfaced U-boat slid out of the fog, crossing from right to left just 600 feet away and apparently oblivious to the enemy warship. Ordering his crew via loudspeaker to brace for collision, Ingram watched intently as his warship's bow aimed directly at the U-boat's hull, just aft of the conning tower. The destroyer slammed into the veteran Type IXC U-125 with a loud crunching sound. "The force of the collision slewed [the U-boat] round to port and she passed down the port side, heeled over with her bows and conning tower out of the water," Ingram reported. The *Oribi* then lost visual contact as Ingram's crew hastily went to work patching up the ship's crushed bow.

On the mauled U-125, Kapitänleutnant Ulrich Folkers, a veteran of the deadly Operation Drumbeat against U.S. East Coast shipping the year before, frantically dispatched an encrypted message to BdU Headquarters:

HAVE BEEN RAMMED–AM UNABLE TO DIVE. [Location on the German Naval Grid Chart] AJ 8652. REQUEST ASSISTANCE. COURSE 090 DEGREES.

Grossadmiral Dönitz ordered six nearby U-boats to render help; then, several hours later, narrowed the list to four: U-552, U-381, U-413, and U-260. The boats would comb the area for U-125 without finding it. The *Snowflake*, as it turned out, had gotten to U-125 first.

Patrolling Position R at the convoy's port quarter, Lieutenant Chesterman peeled off at 0330 to investigate a radar contact bearing 030 degrees at 4,000 yards. En route, two more U-boats appeared on the corvette's radar screen. Because the *Snowflake* had expended all but its last depth charge, Chesterman ordered his four-inch gun to fire at the first two targets. The two U-boats dived, and at 0354, as the *Snowflake* was searching for them on Asdic, the corvette got a radar contact of a fourth U-boat on the surface. Chesterman closed for the kill, and as the range quickly decreased to 100 yards, he ordered his starboard searchlight turned on. In the bright beam, the bridge watch could see a heavily damaged U-boat moving from port to starboard.

The *Snowflake* opened up on the vulnerable U-boat with every gun that could bear. Chesterman attempted to ram the crippled U-boat, but it turned and the two vessels ended up alongside one another. Chesterman realized the enemy was gradually sinking. He later described the damage: "The conning tower was buckled, periscope standards twisted," he wrote. "A.A. [anti-aircraft] gun wrecked . . . and the lid of the after hatch appeared to have been blown away."

Chesterman edged the corvette slowly away from the U-boat so as to allow his guns to bear again, but as he did so, the corvette crew saw the U-boat crewmen, all wearing lifejackets, appear on deck as if abandoning ship. Several Germans made as if to man the U-boat's deck gun, but the *Snowflake*'s gunners sprayed them with machine-gun fire. Chesterman decided to ram the U-boat, and turned away to make a run in—but nearly crashed into the *Sunflower*. Lieutenant-Commander Sherwood on the *Tay*, upon receiving Chesterman's report of multiple U-boat radar contacts, had ordered Lieutenant-Commander Plomer on the *Sunflower* to go to the *Snowflake*'s assistance. The two corvettes nearly collided in the fog, but

Chesterman ordered his helmsman to make a sharp turn to port, and the two warships narrowly missed one another.

The end for U-125 came quickly. Chesterman ordered the *Snowflake* on an interception course for the U-boat, but before the corvette regained visual contact, Chesterman and his crew heard five scuttling charges go off. At 0415, the *Snowflake* reached the area where U-125 had been several minutes earlier. The corvette's searchlights illuminated a number of survivors swimming in a large oil slick. With the *Sunflower* still nearby to provide cover, Chesterman radioed Lieutenant-Commander Sherwood on the *Tay:* "Shall I pick up survivors?"

Sherwood's decision on whether or not to rescue the U-boat's survivors was a deliberate, cold-blooded one made in the heat of battle. With dozens of U-boats still swarming around the convoy, a rescue pickup was too dangerous. "Not approved to pick up survivors," he replied. As a consequence, Kapitänleutnant Folkers and his fifty-four crewmen perished in the still-frigid water. The Admiralty would later give the *Oribi* and *Snowflake* equal credit for the destruction of U-125.[13]

At 0443, the *Sunflower* had returned from assisting the *Snowflake* and was holding its patrol station at Position N on the convoy's port bow. Suddenly the corvette's Asdic operator called out a submerged contact at 1,200 yards. Minutes later, the target appeared on radar as the U-boat surfaced. Lieutenant-Commander Plomer put the corvette to maximum speed, and the escort churned through the fog at fourteen knots. Plomer ordered the searchlight illuminated, and his lookouts spotted the U-boat.

The lookouts on the Type IXC40 U-533 could not avoid sighting the blinding light that suddenly pierced the fog, and Kapitänleutnant Helmut Hennig, the boat's commander, ordered a crash dive. He was too late. The *Sunflower* rammed U-533 between the conning tower and stern, the corvette's bow riding up and over the U-boat's hull. As it passed over the U-boat's submerged afterdeck, Plomer ordered two depth charges dropped at shallow settings. Before they could detonate, however, the corvette's crew heard what they thought was a distinct explosion inside the U-boat. Miraculously undamaged from the collision, the *Sunflower* ran out to prepare for another attack. The corvette's lookouts caught one last sight of U-533. It appeared fatally damaged, with its stern raised eight feet out of the water at a forty-five-degree angle. Moments later, the enemy vanished below the surface. No Asdic contact appeared. The *Sunflower's* commander, believing he had torn the U-boat in half, claimed a firm kill and ordered his helmsman to steer a course back to the convoy. A subsequent analysis of intercepted U-boat communications, however, prompted the Admiralty to disallow Plomer's claim. U-533 had miraculously survived the ramming with only minor damage.[14]

The final combat encounters between the U-boats and the Allied escorts occurred during the morning of May 6, but credit for this battle would go to an entirely separate group of warships than those in Escort Group B-7 or the 3rd Support Group. Commander Godfrey Noel Brewer in the sloop *Pelican* was coming up from Newfoundland on a course of 030 degrees to reinforce Convoy ONS5 with the frigates *Wear, Jed,* and *Spey.* The group, which made up the majority of the 1st Support Group, had traveled nearly 400 nautical miles since their hasty departure from St. John's at midday on May 4. The group's fifth warship, the ex–U.S. Coast Guard cutter *Sennen,* had a top speed several knots slower than the other vessels and was on a different course to join up with the corvette *Pink* and its group of stragglers. On its way, it would make two radar contacts and attack U-650 and U-575, slightly damaging both U-boats.

While the *Sennen* was dealing with the two U-boats, Brewer's group had continued its course toward Convoy ONS5. Steaming in line abreast with four miles of separation between each ship, the formation was making sixteen knots across the still-fog-draped surface. The *Pelican's* HF/DF operator was homing in on the frigate *Tay,* when the *Wear* called at 0550 to report its radar operator had sighted Convoy ONS5 bearing 330 degrees at eight miles. Two minutes later, Brewer's own radar operator called out a contact bearing 040 degrees at 5,300 yards, a suspected U-boat on the surface. Subsequent radar fixes confirmed the U-boat was heading away from the convoy, as if proceeding to position itself directly in the formation's path for a periscope-level torpedo attack. Brewer ordered the *Pelican* to close in, and at 500 yards his lookouts spotted a U-boat conning tower. The U-boat lookouts failed to sight the *Pelican* until the sloop was a mere 100 yards away, then attempted a crash dive. Three of the sloop's guns opened fire, but the U-boat vanished in a swirl of foam. It was too late, however, for the German crew.

Brewer swung the *Pelican* in a hard turn to port and, once over the U-boat's calculated location, dropped a spread of ten depth charges set to go off at 50 and 150 feet. Unsure if the depth charges had been close enough, Brewer ordered a second spread at 150 and 300 feet depth. As the tumult in the water subsided, the *Pelican's* Asdic operator reported a series of three "small, sharp" explosions, followed nine minutes later by a pair of larger blasts, one of which rocked the 1,200-ton warship several hundred yards away. While no oil or debris rose to the surface, Brewer claimed a kill. The Admiralty assessment committee later concluded that the *Pelican* had destroyed U-438—slightly damaged by the Canadian Canso A seaplane just two days earlier—and its crew of forty-eight. "This was a good example of a support group arriving at just the right moment to achieve complete surprise," Brewer wrote in his daily log. "The U-boat, proceeding at about nine knots, probably thought herself clear of immediate danger."[15]

Brewer and his five warships had arrived at a propitious moment. Although the nightlong battle had been an unqualified Allied victory, with six U-boats sunk and another nine damaged or driven off, the escort ships had themselves taken a beating from the harsh maneuvering. The frigate *Tay's* Asdic remained partially inoperative, greatly weakening the group's capability to defend against a U-boat attack. The corvette *Snowflake* was down to its last depth charge. Despite the crew's attempts to plug the leaks, the *Oribi* was taking on water from its crushed bow from the collision with U-125. The *Sunflower* had also suffered slight hull damage in its ramming of U-533. Now that reinforcements were on hand, some of the most worn-out escorts could break off for port. At 0809, Captain McCoy on the *Offa* ordered Lieutenant-Commander Ingram on the damaged *Oribi* to detach from ONS5 to return to St. John's. Low on fuel himself, McCoy told Lieutenant-Commander Sherwood that the *Offa* would escort the *Oribi* to St. John's.

The last attack around the main body of Convoy ONS5 occurred at 0940, when the frigate *Spey* picked up a radar contact while sweeping astern of the formation. Caught on the surface, U-634 attempted a crash dive. Before the U-boat could fully submerge, however, one of the *Spey's* four-inch gun crews landed two hits on the conning tower. The *Spey* mounted several subsequent depth-charge attacks, but U-634 suffered only minor damage and lived to fight another day.[16]

At 1140 on May 6, Grossadmiral Dönitz finally decided to call off the three wolf packs. Battered but victorious, Escort Group B-7 and the remaining merchant vessels held to a course of 156 degrees for the final day of steaming toward the Western Ocean Meeting Point, where they would hand off the convoy's main body to the Western Local Escort Force and guide a half-dozen remaining stragglers into St. John's.

The battle for Convoy ONS5 had been one of the largest and most violent encounters of the Battle of the Atlantic thus far. A total of forty-six U-boats organized in four separate wolf packs—Gruppen Star, Fink, Amsel 1, and Amsel 2—had battled the nine warships of Escort Group B-7, later reinforced by the five destroyers of the 3rd Support Group and five warships from the 1st Support Group. During five days of contact, the escorts mounted seventy-seven separate attacks on suspected U-boats. In turn, the U-boats mounted at least forty-five torpedo attacks on the convoy or its escorts, thirteen of which were successful.

While ONS5 had suffered the sinking of the thirteen merchant ships totaling 61,958 gross registered tons, the battle fell far short of the defeat that the escorts of Convoys HX229 and SC122 had suffered seven weeks earlier. During that battle they had lost a total of twenty-two ships totaling 146,596 gross registered tons. On the German side, the results were far worse: in contrast to the HX229-SC122 battle, where only the U-384 and its crew of forty-seven perished, the aggressive response by Escort Group B-7 and the 1st and 3rd Support Groups resulted in the sinking of seven U-boats, killing 348 of Dönitz's elite submariners. This did not include two related losses: U-710, destroyed by a Coastal Command B-17 Fortress on April 24 before it could join Gruppe Star, and U-528, damaged by a U.S. Navy PBY-5A Catalina on April 28, and later attacked and forced to scuttle on May 11 as it was limping back to France. Those two sinkings killed another fifty-six U-boat men, with forty-five survivors from U-528.[17]

The exhausted but proud escort sailors could now look forward to a joyful reunion with Commander Peter Gretton and the crew of the destroyer *Duncan* in St. John's, and some long-overdue rest and recovery ashore. Their victory was complete.[18]

Chapter 14

DEFEAT OF THE U-BOATS

The men of Escort Group B-7 would have less than a week to enjoy the modest delights of St. John's, Newfoundland. Chained to the inexorable Allied convoy schedule, they had to accomplish all repairs and provisioning by Friday, May 14. Then it would be time to cast off and head out to meet the next eastbound convoy destined for the British Isles. In the meantime, if they could find time between the work assignments, they might hope for a chance to take liberty in the port town, which one Royal Navy petty officer had described as having "the appearance of an outpost in the Canadian North," with narrow streets, steep hills, and mostly wooden buildings that had "a makeshift, impermanent air about them." To the exhausted sailors, however, the town was a beacon of light after the long weeks they had spent battling storms and wolf packs.

The luckiest men in B-7 would have six days in St. John's. The frigate *Tay* and corvettes *Snowflake* and *Sunflower* reached port first, on Sunday, May 8, after breaking off from Convoy ONS5 the afternoon before. The destroyer *Vidette* and corvettes *Loosestrife* and *Pink* arrived at St. John's the following day, having escorted a half dozen of the merchantmen from the Western Ocean Meeting Point to St. John's. They would have only five days to prepare for the next crossing.

For Commander Peter Gretton and his escort commanders, the port stay passed in a blur of hasty repairs, paperwork, and supervision of the loading of depth charges, Hedgehog mortar shells, four-inch and 20-mm ammunition, food, and fuel oil. Shipyard officials had informed Lieutenant-Commander James Plomer that repairs to the *Sunflower*'s damaged

Asdic dome would require putting the corvette into dry dock, a procedure that would delay the ship's departure for one day after B-7 left for the rendezvous with the next eastbound convoy. Gretton, meanwhile, set about fixing the destroyer *Duncan* himself. The ship's tendency to roll hard in heavy seas had alarmed captain and crew during the major storms of May 1–3; now, studying the ship's diagrams, Gretton realized that during the *Duncan's* previous refits, shipwrights had added tons of "top hamper"— equipment, machinery and storage lockers—that made the vessel unstable. His solution was to form a massive working party to haul tons of worn-out gear and supplies onto the pier, over the objections of his petty officers who wanted to keep the spare materials aboard. The group's roughly 700 enlisted crewmen did most of the hard work but also got to enjoy a few precious hours ashore on liberty for their efforts.[1]

Before the next convoy, one necessary task for the ship commanders was to prepare their formal "Record of Proceedings" of the seventeen-day Atlantic crossing. These included a chronological account of each day's events, an analysis of the U-boats' tactics, and detailed narratives of each attempted attack on a suspected U-boat. Because the struggle between the U-boat Force and Allied naval commands was constantly evolving, the escort ship commanders and their superiors took great pains to provide as many details as possible about each U-boat attack and escort counterattack. The reports also contained mundane logs citing all HF/DF intercepts, radiotelephone conversations, and wireless messages to and from the ship. Once completed, these reports went up the chain of command, first to Rear-Admiral Leonard W. Murray at the newly formed Canadian Northwest Atlantic Command in Halifax, then to Captain G. W. G. Simpson in Londonderry, who as "Commodore D" (an informal Royal Navy title) commanded the escort groups, then to Admiral Horton at Western Approaches Command. The higher-ups would review the reports and add their endorsements and comments before intelligence officials and tactical specialists pored over the paperwork for any sign of a new U-boat weapon, sensor, communications protocol, or combat tactic. The unlucky captains of the thirteen torpedoed merchantmen—those who had survived—were also expected to summarize their experiences in formal interviews with Admiralty officials.[2]

Lieutenant-Commander Sherwood, who had seen command of Escort Group B-7 thrust into his hands with scant notice on May 3, praised the close teamwork of the ships under his authority. By working together, he said, the eight B-7 warships and the two support groups had thwarted the massed U-boat attacks the night of May 5–6 and the following morning. "All ships worked hard, capably and with intelligence, and considerable humour, and the situation was always well in hand," Sherwood concluded. Commander Gretton, in turn, lavishly praised his stand-in's performance. "Lieutenant-Commander Sherwood . . . handled a very dangerous situation with ability and coolness," Gretton wrote. "I consider he did exceptionally well, being ably backed up by the group." Captain Simpson in Londonderry, while undercounting the overall ship losses by two, agreed. "Although eleven [sic] merchant vessels were lost from this convoy, the final showing can still be considered a major victory," Simpson wrote. He also congratulated the escorts for dropping a total of 340 depth charges during the series of skirmishes with only two failed launches. "This in itself is a fine achievement . . . and is definitely the result of stiff training."

While they had many commendations for the escorts of ONS5, neither Gretton nor his superiors in the chain of command sugarcoated their remarks on things that had not gone well on the convoy's passage. Gretton himself complained that the decision by Western Approaches Command to route ONS5 as far north as Greenland's Cape Farewell had done more harm than good, exposing the formation to the series of storms that badly scattered the merchant vessels, preventing the successful refueling of the escorts on several occasions, and playing havoc with their communications with shore commands. In his assessment, Rear-Admiral Murray agreed with Gretton. Given the number of U-boats operating in the Greenland air gap, he wrote, such an evasive route was "not worth the candle."

Gretton had other critiques besides the routing of the convoy. While praising the "magnificent performance" of the Iceland-based VLR Liberators, he expressed disappointment that they were "laid on too late to get any sightings" of U-boats. And Gretton said it had been "incorrect" for Lieutenant Atkinson on the corvette *Pink* to have continued to attack U-358 on May 5, thereby enabling U-584 to torpedo and sink the *West*

Madaket. Gretton softened the blow with this caveat: "I would have hated to leave it myself."

For his part, Commodore Simpson gently chided Lieutenant-Commander Sherwood for keeping the 3rd Support Group destroyers *Offa* and *Oribi* stationed five miles ahead of the convoy during the night of May 4–5. "It is noticed," Simpson wrote "that losses to the convoy did not occur until the close screen had been reduced to five escorts." He suggested that if Sherwood had recalled the two destroyers from their distant patrol stations to the main body that night, "better protection" would have resulted. Simpson also noted, however, that on at least five occasions during the foggy night battle of May 5–6, the escort ships had clearly caught the U-boats unaware. "This seems to indicate that all U-boats are not fitted with RDF [radar] and presumably will have to rely on their hydrophones to receive warning of the approach of escorts," he added.

After reviewing these multiple second-look analyses of the escorts' performance, Admiral Horton at Western Approaches Command concluded that, despite the losses suffered by the merchantmen, their protectors had done a fine job. "The skill and determination of all escorts engaged in this operation leaves little to be desired," Horton stated flatly. Writing to his superiors at the Admiralty, Horton ventured an assessment that no one would have imagined just six weeks earlier, in the aftermath of the savage March convoy battles. "It may well be," he wrote, "that the heavy casualties inflicted on the enemy have gravely affected his morale and will prove to have been a turning point in the Battle of the Atlantic." Heralding the escorts' counterattacks as a significant blow against the U-boat Force, Horton proposed that the Admiralty commission a documentary film on the ONS5 battle for training purposes. Their Lordships declined the request.[3]

UNLIKE IN THE WAKE of the battles for HX229 and SC122, there was no backslapping at the BdU operations center in Berlin. Radio Berlin broadcast no Sondermeldung from Dönitz heralding the exploits of Gruppen Fink, Amsel 1, and Amsel 2. No congratulatory message arrived at BdU from the Supreme Headquarters of the Führer. Instead, the mood of the sleep-deprived BdU operations staff in the cramped headquarters was a mixture of shock, grief, and worry as they reviewed the results of the attack against ONS5.

In the official BdU war diary, Dönitz and Godt noted that the initial phase of the attack had gone relatively well. "During the first night, eight boats were able to sink thirteen ships straight away, probably mainly because of the suddenness of the attack," the two admirals concluded, citing the inflated total from the U-boats at sea, which was six more than the seven merchantmen that actually went down. "Between picking up the convoy and darkness there were only five hours, these circumstances are always favorable, as the anti-submarine defenses are not usually reinforced for action for about a day." On May 5, Dönitz and Godt went on to note, two more submerged attacks brought down another four merchantmen. Up until this point, the attack had been relatively successful, they concluded. So long as the escort group had had to fight the wolf packs on the latter's terms, the U-boats could operate with relative impunity.[4]

The mistake, the BdU leaders conceded, had been to extend the convoy fight into the night of May 5–6. The thick fog that had suddenly rolled in off the Newfoundland Grand Banks had effectively ended their killing spree and exposed the U-boats to surprise attacks. "If the fog had held off for six hours, many more ships would certainly have been sunk. As it was, the fog ruined everything and no further successes were scored," the two German admirals groused. "Merely during this period, fifteen boats were depth-charged, and six of these were suddenly attacked with gunfire by locating destroyers. As they had no countermeasures against location, the boats were definitely at a disadvantage and had little prospect of success." The U-boats had earlier in the war enjoyed the protection of the improvised "Biscay cross" radar warning receiver against probing Allied radar, but now, with the Allies' development of shorter-wavelength radar sets, this countermeasure had suddenly become ineffective.

The war diary's dry narrative of the convoy battle did not bother to mention that the U-boat Force had lost 348 of its skilled officers and crewmen in the battle. Nor did the BdU Kriegstagebüch mention the loss of one of the few remaining aces from the "Happy Time" of 1942, Kapitänleutnant Ulrich Folkers. A Ritterkreuz holder and veteran of the Operation Drumbeat campaign along the U.S. East Coast, Folkers had amassed a record of seventeen ships sunk totaling 82,873 tons thus far in the war, but his death passed unnoted by Dönitz and Godt.[5]

Despite Dönitz and Godt's claim that "the fog ruined everything" on the last night of attacks against ONS5, one BdU staffer recognized that the U-boats' defeat had as much to do with the increasing lethality of the Allied escort ships as it did the bad weather. Korvettenkapitän Günter Hessler was a senior operations officer at BdU during that climactic week and, as a highly decorated U-boat commander with twenty-one sunken Allied ships totaling 118,822 tons to his credit, Hessler had no trouble reading between the lines of the various U-boat reports and the BdU war diary. "In the past, [Dönitz] had believed that the normal surface escorts of a convoy could be effectively scattered if sufficient U-boats were around," Hessler observed in a postwar history of the U-boat war. Prior to Convoy ONS5, he added, BdU officials had thought that the primary threat to the U-boats came from Allied patrol aircraft operating in bad weather that cloaked their approach. "But in this last operation," Hessler observed, "the surface escorts alone had sufficed to inflict grave losses on an exceptionally strong concentration of attackers. The U-boats were blind in the fog, whereas the escorts could attack them with radar-controlled gunfire." New radar systems, and the escorts' use of that technology to mount quick, surprise strikes against the U-boats, had wreaked havoc on the wolf packs.[6]

The realization that escort warships and aircraft were now using undetectable radar was a severe blow to the staff at BdU. In the aftermath of the battle over ONS5, Grossadmiral Dönitz and Konteradmiral Godt attempted to reassure the U-boat commanders that the Kriegsmarine was doing all it could to find a warning and detection countermeasure against the Allied ten-centimeter radar. "All responsible departments are working at high pressure on the problem of again providing the submarine with gear capable of establishing whether the enemy is using radar," the two admirals pointed out in a message to the U-boat commanders, adding that—although radar detection was the most critical goal—research was also being done on developing a system that could actually make the U-boats invisible to radar. The admirals attempted to end their message on a upbeat note: "To sum up: the U-boat's struggle is now harder than ever, but all departments are working full out to assist the boats in their task and to equip them with better weapons."[7]

If BdU hoped to keep up with advances in Allied technology, it would have its work cut out for it. While they were grudgingly familiar with the new Hedgehog mortar launcher and Mark X depth charge, both of which had been in use for months, the Germans were still ignorant of two other anti-submarine weapons that would soon tip the scales even further toward the Allies. The first was the Mark XXIV "Fido" air-dropped acoustic homing torpedo. This top-secret weapon had been under development by the United States since late 1941. For security reasons officials had deliberately misidentified it as an aerial mine. The Allied patrol squadrons had obtained the Fido in late March 1943, but Western Approaches Command did not approve the first operational deployment until May 6, the day the battle of Convoy ONS5 came to an end. On May 7, an RAF 86 Squadron VLR Liberator made the initial sortie with two Fidos and four depth charges, but spotted no U-boats. It would not be long, however, before the new weapon claimed its first victim. The second new weapon was a British-designed air-to-surface rocket used by carrier-based aircraft that Admiral Horton rushed into production and deployment in just a six-week period. The U-boats on North Atlantic patrol would not have to wait very long to experience this deadly threat, either.[8]

Dönitz and Godt had more problems to contend with than their enemy's technological advancements—for it was becoming apparent that the Allies' tactics had themselves improved dramatically. The battle over Convoy ONS5 had made clear that the Allies had conceived of a new strategy for not just fending off the U-boats, but destroying them altogether. Reviewing reports from the deployed U-boats, BdU finally realized that Western Approaches Command had created support groups to reinforce convoys and their escort warships when steaming deep in the Greenland air gap. The additional warships could beef up the perimeter around an otherwise exposed convoy, but that was not the only problem. Several of these support groups also included escort carriers—meaning that convoys that would otherwise be out of range of all but the VLR Liberators now would benefit from tactical air cover for as long as an escort carrier accompanied them. The additional warships for which Horton and his predecessors had fought so hard were now being put to use in the North Atlantic with devastating results to the U-boats.

While the Allies had assembled the well-armed support groups to assist the convoy escort groups, these units had also improved their organization and responses to U-boat attacks. In their patrol reports, surviving U-boat commanders confirmed that the Allied escort groups had honed their defensive tactics into an effective and aggressive counter to mass night surface attacks and daylight submerged approaches. This revelation had an immediate impact on BdU's deployment of its U-boats. Citing the unusually high percentage of losses involving the larger and clumsier Type IX U-boats in April and in the ONS5 battle, Dönitz on May 5 reversed his earlier order using them on the North Atlantic convoy runs and dispatched them to other theaters of the "tonnage war" where Allied opposition was less organized.

Despite the Allies' new technology, tactics, and defenders, BdU's single largest failing was not that it overlooked these emerging new threats. Rather, Dönitz and his staff continued to be blind to two pre-existing Allied successes that were steadily undercutting the U-boat Force's effectiveness: ship-mounted HF/DF technology and the ongoing campaign to intercept and decrypt German naval wireless transmissions. Although the British had been using shipboard HF/DF technology to track U-boats since March 1940, Dönitz and his staff still did not understand the full extent of the role that this technology was playing in the Battle of the Atlantic. By allowing escorts to pinpoint the location of U-boats when they were transmitting radio reports back to Berlin, ship-mounted HF/DF receivers provided the escort warships with the ability to make a rapid and accurate attack.

The German inability to recognize the HF/DF threat was not a simple intelligence failure. It was not just a case where the B-Dienst cryptanalysts overlooked or did not intercept information regarding Allied warship direction-finding capabilities. In fact, several weeks before the ONS5 fight, Kapitän zur See Bonatz's staff decrypted three separate Allied radio messages that stated which ships in an escort group were equipped with high-frequency direction-finding sets. Neither the BdU staff nor German naval intelligence ever realized that HF/DF was providing vital tactical intelligence on the U-boats.[9]

High-frequency direction-finding technology was a critical addition to the Allies' strategic arsenal, but so was their program to break the Ger-

mans' codes. In fact, the ongoing operation at Bletchley Park to crack encrypted Enigma messages, and the U.S. Navy's parallel effort to do the
same, were providing the Allies with even more critical information that
allowed the convoys to evade the wolf packs and to organize effective attacks by escort and support groups. The Allied code breakers would occasionally find themselves frozen out of the Funkschlüssel-M wireless
traffic, or sometimes would not fully decrypt particular messages until
days after they had lost any tactical value. Yet, the overall "take" still provided Western Approaches Command, the escort and support groups,
and the land-based patrol squadrons with a steady and accurate picture of
where the wolf packs were operating. As the U-boats organized their assaults on trans-Atlantic convoys in the late spring of 1943, therefore, they
were often met by escorts whose commanders fully knew what their
enemy was doing.

While the Germans remained unaware of some of the most fundamental sources of Allied intelligence about the U-boats' movements, they were
also woefully ignorant of the true outcomes of the convoy battles. The
barrage of inflated sinking reports by U-boat commanders had continued
unabated throughout the spring of 1943, and effectively blinded BdU to
the deteriorating situation at sea. Convoy ONS5 had been no exception:
the Fink and Amsel skippers had reported sinking sixteen of the convoy's
ships for a total of 90,000 tons. In reality, the U-boats sank thirteen merchantmen totaling 61,598 tons. One unintended effect of these exaggerated claims was that they masked the first signs of a reversal of fortune in
the Allies' favor. Writing in retrospect, former Korvettenkapitän Hessler
ruefully concluded, "[O]ur curve of effectiveness showed a positive tendency which concealed the true facts and gave [Grossadmiral Dönitz] no
warning of the imminent collapse" of the U-boat campaign. In the aftermath of the battle for Convoy ONS5, it still seemed to the BdU staff that
the U-boats could regain the advantage in the convoy fights. It would be
one of their final errors in the Battle of the Atlantic.[10]

THE SURVIVING U-BOAT COMMANDERS in Gruppen Fink, Amsel 1, and
Amsel 2 may have been frustrated by the Allies' newfound tactics, and
senior BdU staff officers may have been muttering into their beer steins
about the stiffening of Allied convoy defenses, but one fact remained

unchanged in the aftermath of the fight over Convoy ONS5: the Battle of the Atlantic would go on. The Allied maritime conveyor belt of food, fuel, supplies, and munitions to Great Britain remained in high gear. The day that the fighting over ONS5 ended on May 6, seven other convoys were at sea making the Atlantic transit, and another five were scheduled to depart within the next seven days. Totaling 505 merchant vessels with a combined cargo capacity of 3,183,083 gross registered tons, each of these twelve convoys would be a rich target for the victory-starved U-boats.

Despite the losses suffered during the ONS5 battle, BdU's Atlantic U-boat Force was still out on the high seas in greater numbers than ever before. The week of May 3, Dönitz had 136 operational U-boats at sea, of which 104 were assigned to the North Atlantic convoy runs. Seventeen were returning to port at the end of their patrol, leaving eighty-seven armed and fueled U-boats looking for the next fight.[11]

On May 7, the day after Dönitz dissolved Gruppen Fink, Amsel 1, and Amsel 2, he formed two more large wolf packs, named after German rivers. He reassigned seventeen U-boats from Fink, Amsel 1, and Amsel 2 to Gruppe Elbe and another twelve boats from the wolf packs Amsel 3 and 4 to Gruppe Rhein. When intercepted Allied message traffic revealed that eastbound Convoys HX237 and SC129 were attempting to steam to Britain via a more southerly route, Dönitz sent these two new wolf packs to the southeast, where they formed an extended 550-mile-long patrol line to intercept the two convoys.[12]

Convoy HX237 had departed New York on May 1 with fifty-one merchant ships. They carried a cornucopia of war supplies ranging from bulk cargoes of sulfur, grain, and fuel oil to ammunition, military vehicles, and landing craft. This convoy was larger than Convoys SC122, HX229, and ONS5 and was a more valuable target since it included seventeen oil tankers in the formation. After four ships returned to port with various mechanical problems, HX237 met up with Canadian Escort Group C-2 in heavy fog at the designated Western Ocean Meeting Point southeast of Newfoundland.

While HX237 was rendezvousing with its escorts on May 7, the twenty-five merchantmen of Convoy SC129 were already moving out into the Atlantic. SC129 had met up with British Escort Group B-2 on May 6, after pulling out of Halifax on May 2 and steering for its designated WESTOMP 200 miles southeast of St. John's with a cross-section of military and economic cargo totaling 122,202 gross registered tons. As the two convoys proceeded out into the Atlantic, however, the faster HX237 steadily pulled ahead of SC129 because of the three-knot difference in their assigned speeds.[13]

Goaded by incessant messages from BdU, the Rhein wolf pack hunted in foul weather for HX237 for several days without success. Then on Sunday, May 9, Oberleutnant zur See Heinz Förster in the U-359 spotted HX237 in heavy seas 200 miles north of the Azores and transmitted a sighting report. Sensing an opportunity to trap HX237 between two wolf packs, Admiral Dönitz ordered a third wolf pack, Gruppe Drossel (Thrush), to abandon its current operational area in the eastern Atlantic near Gibraltar and to move north-northwest at high speed to reinforce the Rhein and Elbe boats. On May 10, BdU reorganized Rhein and Elbe into two new wolf packs, Elbe 1 and 2, some 650 miles away from Gruppe Drossel.[14]

As Admirals Dönitz and Godt reorganized the North Atlantic U-boats to go after the next Allied convoys entering the Greenland air gap, Admiral Horton in Liverpool was taking steps that would significantly increase the power of the convoy escorts. While the Germans prepared to launch an attack on HX237, the ships of the 5th Support Group, consisting of the British escort carrier *HMS Biter* and three destroyers, were shadowing the convoy as well. The *Biter's* aircraft overhead and the escort group's skill with HF/DF tracking—as well as stormy weather, recurring fog, and sheer bad luck—would thwart the two new wolf packs' planned attack before Gruppe Drossel could even arrive.

The first U-boat attempt against HX237 would reveal the presence of the *Biter's* air wing providing cover for the eastbound convoy. On the morning of May 10, the U-403, on its seventh patrol under Kapitänleutnant Heinz-Ehlert Clausen, spotted the escort tug *HMS Dextrous* steaming astern of Convoy HX237. Clausen decided to shadow the tug in hopes of finding the main body, but several other escorts spotted the U-boat first. They went to maximum speed to give chase, but before they could close on the target, one of the *Biter's* Swordfish biplane aircraft swooped down and dropped depth charges, forcing Clausen to crash-dive. Upon surfacing several hours later, Clausen reported to Berlin that a "wheeled" aircraft had attacked U-403. Then Kapitänleutnant Burckhard Hackländer, a veteran U-boat skipper in his ninth patrol in U-454 and operating in Gruppe Rhein, reported to BdU that his lookouts had spotted a "carrier borne plane" while they were chasing an Allied merchantman steaming independently of HX237. Dönitz and Godt seemed to miss the dire implications of the messages from Clausen and Burckhard; the BdU war diary merely concluded that Gruppe Rhein was still over ninety miles astern of HX237 and its chances of catching the fast convoy were slim to none. Dönitz then directed the Rhein boats to go after SC129 and ordered Gruppe Drossel to stay on course for HX237.[15]

Dönitz hoped that Gruppe Drossel would succeed where Rhein had failed. Next morning, on May 11, Drossel was close enough to HX237 that the convoy escorts picked up multiple HF/DF contacts. The heavy seas and foul weather cloaked the convoy from its hunters, however, and the day passed without incident. The next day, however, blood would be drawn on both sides.

It was a violent encounter between a Drossel boat and another *Biter* aircraft the next day that finally knocked the blinders off the BdU staff. During the morning of Wednesday, May 12, a Swordfish from the 5th Support Group carrier jumped U-230 on the surface. The U-boat's deck gunners shot the aircraft down, but the incident could easily have been disastrous for U-230. As it fell from the sky after its engine quit, one of the biplane's wings clipped the U-boat's conning tower before it plunged into the sea close aboard. Horrified bridge watch-stander Leutnant zur See Herbert A. Werner observed as the British pilot, who had been cast out of his cockpit, waved for help, then vanished in a fireball as the aircraft's four depth charges exploded simultaneously. Shaken but undamaged, U-230 fled the scene at maximum speed. Several hours later, Kapitänleutnant Paul Siegmann reported the clash to BdU. The downed airman's comrades in the *Biter's* biplane squadron exacted their revenge later that day, when a Squadron 811 Swordfish sighted U-89 on the surface, forced it under with depth charges, and summoned two surface escorts who finished off the U-boat. The BdU war diary for May 12 admitted that HX237 was all but untouchable due to the heavy aerial protection, "Both carrier borne and four-engined land based planes were reported with the convoy," Dönitz and Godt wrote. "They made it very difficult for the few U-boats operating to launch an attack on the convoy."[16]

Later in the day on May 12, the Allied escort groups also got their first U-boat kill with the new Fido homing torpedo. Liberator B/86 from the RAF 86 Squadron at Aldergrove was flying an extended-range mission in support of HX237 when, eight hours into the flight, its aircrew spotted a surfaced U-boat. As U-456 crash-dived, Flight Lieutenant John Wright dropped one of the homing torpedoes. Several minutes later, the aircrew observed a large swirl of brown oil—and then U-456 resurfaced as its commander, Kapitänleutnant Max-Martin Teichert, urgently radioed Berlin for help. The Fido had blown a hole in the U-boat's pressure hull. Before any other U-boat could respond, several of the convoy escorts spotted the stricken boat and rushed toward it. For reasons no one could fathom, Teichert again ordered U-456 under, and the boat promptly sank to the ocean floor, killing its entire forty-nine-member crew.

The wolf packs' final loss against HX237 came on May 13, when a British Sunderland amphibious patrol bomber spotted U-753 on the surface well astern of the convoy and engaged the boat with depth charges and machine-gun fire. Alerted to the encounter, two of HX237's escorts closed in and finished off U-753 with depth charges.[17]

While HX237's escorts had been thrashing the Rhein and Drossel U-boats, Convoy SC129 was also seeing action 200 miles farther south as it followed the same general route as the fast convoy. Escort Group B-2, under Commander Donald G. F. W. MacIntyre on the destroyer *Hesperus*, found itself fully engaged with two new wolf packs, Elbe 1 and 2, which Admiral Dönitz had formed out of the original Elbe and Rhein groups on May 10. Six of the original U-boats were forced to break off from low fuel, but twenty boats remained to battle the slow convoy.

SC129's only run of bad luck came on May 11, but it was soon reversed. The veteran U-boat skipper Korvettenkapitän Siegfried von Forstner in U-402 made a daring daylight submerged attack and managed to sink two merchantmen, the 4,545-ton British steam merchant *Antigone* and the 3,082-ton Norwegian freighter *Grado*. Fortunately for the Allies, the loss of life was small; only three of the *Antigone's* forty-six-man complement died in the attack, and all thirty-six of the crew and gunnery detachment safely

escaped in lifeboats. But U-402's triumph was short lived. Just minutes after U-402's torpedoes struck the two merchantmen, one of MacIntyre's
corvettes, the *HMS Gentian*, picked up U-402 on sonar and savaged the
boat so badly that von Forstner had to abort his patrol and limp home to
La Pallice for four months of repair work.

SC129's winning streak continued in the night of May 11–12. MacIntyre in the destroyer *Hesperus* had a knife-fight battle with Kapitänleutnant Karl-Jürg Wächter in U-223 (as described in the Introduction to this
book). After using depth charges, four-inch guns, Oerlikon 20-mm cannons, and finally his own ship as a weapon, MacIntyre was confident the
U-223 was finished—but Wächter and most of his crew survived and
would make it back to France in their battered but still functional U-boat.
After steaming off to rejoin the convoy, MacIntyre then located and destroyed the contact-keeper Type IXC U-186 several hours later, in a second, fierce encounter that ended with 53 dead U-boat sailors.

Dönitz and Godt called off the hunt for HX237 on Thursday, May 13,
and recalled the two Elbe groups from SC129 the following day. U-642
had sighted the approaching escort carrier *Biter*, which had been detached
from HX237 to lend aid to the slow convoy. When U-642 flashed a warning to Berlin, BdU ordered the wolf packs to back off.[18]

The five-day U-boat hunt against Convoys HX237 and SC129
amounted to another major defeat for the U-boat Force. Gruppen Elbe,
Rhein, and Drossel had been able to sink just five merchant vessels totaling 29,016 tons, while the convoy escort groups, the 5th Support Group,
and land-based aircraft had sunk five U-boats and heavily damaged at
least two more. Losing a U-boat for each Allied merchant vessel sunk was
a ruinous exchange rate—one that Dönitz and Godt could not tolerate for
long.[19]

While the southern mass of U-boats had been floundering around
against HX237 and SC129, an equally frustrating hunt was occurring
nearly 900 miles to the northwest near Cape Farewell, Greenland. When
Dönitz had called off the ONS5 attacks on May 6, the U-boats from
Gruppe Star that had moved southwest to form Gruppe Fink had left a
void along the northern convoy routes. To fill that gap in the hope of intercepting future westbound ON and ONS convoys, BdU created a new
northern U-boat Force, consisting of twenty-four U-boats divided into

five small wolf packs also named after German rivers—Gruppen Iller, Inn, Isar, Lech, and Naab. Eight of the boats—U-258, U-378, U-381, U-413, U-552, U-707, U-952, and U-954—came from one of the four wolf packs that had battled ONS5 during April 29–May 6. For the next five days, the small wolf packs held station south of the Greenland ice cap, on an extended patrol line with a general north-northwest to south-southeast orientation. Their lookouts found nothing but endless wave tops.[20]

Finally, on May 12, the northern U-boats found a target. Oberleutnant zur See Karl-Heinz Nagel in the U-640, outbound from Kiel on its first patrol in Gruppe Iller, reported a convoy on a northerly course in German Naval Grid Square AL 1265, approximately 220 miles south of Iceland. It was westbound Convoy ONS7, fifty merchant ships traveling with British Escort Group B-5 under Commander Richard C. Boyle. This was B-5's second convoy run since escorting Convoy SC122 through the maelstrom of attacks in mid-March.

With Gruppe Iller not yet in place, BdU authorized U-640 to conduct a solitary attack against ONS7, while moving the other four wolf packs west to form a blocking line. Nagel closed on the convoy and fired a pair of torpedoes. Poor visibility made the aiming difficult, however, and Nagel hit nothing. For the next two days, U-640 chased after the convoy. Its luck ran out on May 14, when a U.S. Navy PBY-5A Catalina from Patrol Squadron VP-84 surprised Nagel on the surface. When the twenty-six-year-old commander ordered a crash-dive, the Catalina dropped a Fido homing torpedo after him. Nagel and his forty-eight crewmen perished on the thirteenth day of their first war cruise.

The U-boats only scored one hit on ONS7, and it was a decidedly Pyrrhic victory. Three days after Nagel and his crew went down, thirty-three-year-old Korvettenkapitän Heinrich Göllnitz in U-657 sank the 5,200-ton British freighter *Aymeric*, killing fifty-three of its seventy-eight-man crew. Escort Group B-5 counterattacked fiercely, and the frigate *Swale* fatally depth-charged U-657, killing all forty-seven aboard.

The *Aymeric* and its fifty-three slain crewmen were the only casualties in ONS7. Thanks to shrewd work by Boyle's HF/DF operators and the timely arrival of the destroyers *Offa*, *Panther*, and *Penn* from Captain James A. McCoy's 3rd Support Group, Convoy ONS7 made it to Halifax without any more losses.[21]

The U-boat fatalities were rising at an alarming rate, but BdU was not ready to give up just yet. On May 15, confident that more westbound convoys would soon pass close to Cape Farewell, Admiral Godt realigned four of the five small wolf packs into two formations of eleven and twelve U-boats. He ordered Gruppen Donau 1 and Donau 2 (named for the River Danube) to form an extended picket line blocking the anticipated convoy routes southeast of Greenland. A flurry of concern soon followed when, on Monday, May 17, B-dienst decrypted an Allied "Admiralty U-boat Situation Report" transmitted to escort groups at sea. Still oblivious to the ongoing Allied penetration of naval Enigma, Godt wrote that the enemy "surprisingly knew exactly the disposition of the Groups 'Danube 1 and 2.'" This disclosure led BdU staffers to surmise that eastbound Convoy HX238 and westbound Convoy ON183 had probably given them the slip as well.

There was one bright spot in the gloom, Godt noted. The intercepted report provided the position, course, and speed of a slow eastbound convoy of thirty-seven merchant ships that had sailed from New York on Tuesday, May 11. Given their grasp of Allied convoy procedures, the BdU staffers were confident that, by moving the extended Donau patrol line to the south, they could ensnare that eastbound convoy in the center of the twenty-three U-boats within the next twenty-four hours. A faint sense of hope still lingered in U-boat Force Headquarters.[22]

PATCHED UP, REARMED, and refueled, Escort Group B-7 cast off from the piers at St. John's on Friday, May 14. Its next convoy mission was to escort Convoy SC130 from the nearby WESTOMP to the British Isles. B-7 would begin its latest journey without all of its usual ships, but with the addition of two important new members to the escort team.

Several changes to Escort Group B-7's makeup reflected both the punishment that the unit had sustained on its voyage with Convoy ONS5 and the challenges that still awaited other formations out in the Atlantic. The ASW trawler *Northern Gem* would remain behind in St. John's pending a new assignment, and the corvette *Sunflower* was still undergoing repairs to its Asdic dome; Lieutenant-Commander Plomer was scheduled to depart with the ship the next day and catch up with the convoy. Meanwhile, a temporary attachment, the *HMCS Kitchener*, cast off from the pier at

St. John's with the destroyers *Duncan* and *Vidette;* corvettes *Loosestrife,* *Pink,* and *Snowflake*; and ASW trawler *Northern Spray* as scheduled. A Canadian Flower-class corvette, the *Kitchener* was en route to a permanent assignment with another escort group in the British Isles and would serve with B-7 during the crossing.

To Commander Gretton's relief, the Canadian Northwest Atlantic Command had also assigned the rescue ship *Zamalek* to support SC130. Gretton and his subordinates were well aware of the converted British steamer's heroic feats on its eighteen previous Atlantic crossings. In particular, the *Zamalek* had picked up 131 survivors from four torpedoed ships in Convoy SC122 eight weeks earlier. The rescue ship's presence in SC130 also meant that there was a third ship in the convoy with an HF/DF receiver. Also heading out with B-7 were two American merchantmen that were joining the convoy, the 6,197-ton American freighter *Winona* with a cargo of phosphates and the 7,176-ton American Liberty ship *Joseph Warren* carrying steel and general cargo.[23]

Spring was finally coming to the North Atlantic, but the confluence of warm ocean currents and still-frigid air cloaked the first two days of B-7's passage in a thick fog. Gretton and his escorts also had to dodge the ever-present icebergs that were still breaking off from the Greenland ice cap eight weeks after the vernal equinox. The escort ships arrived at the designated rendezvous southeast of St. John's at 0655 the following morning, May 15, and executed what Gretton called an "unpleasant" rendezvous with the local escorts and main body in the midst of an impenetrable fog bank. "Luckily we succeeded in meeting the convoy on time, for despite the fog, they were in exactly the right place," Gretton later recalled. "The first confirmation of our radar's accuracy [was] the sound of their sirens booming across the water."

After exchanging official documents with convoy Commodore J. Forsythe, a retired Royal Navy Reserve captain, in the convoy flagship, the 4,814-ton British freighter *Sheaf Holme*, Gretton passed a private note urging him to keep the merchantmen in line so that SC130 would make landfall as scheduled on May 25. The reason, Gretton confided, was that he had an appointment to marry his fiancée, Royal Navy Wren Judy DuVivier, on May 29 at St. Mary's Catholic Church on Cadogan Square in London. Back across on the messenger line came a note from the commodore pledging his best efforts: he himself had a golf match scheduled for the same day! The formalities complete, Escort Group B-7 took day stations and Convoy SC130 headed out for the Greenland air gap on course 081 degrees at a designated speed of 7.5 knots.[24]

The only scare to arise in SC130's first few days at sea came the night after B-7 took over the convoy escort. Sometime after midnight on Sunday, May 16, the *Vidette* was steaming as an advance guard several miles ahead of the formation when Lieutenant Hart called Gretton on the radiotelephone. The fog was still an opaque blanket over the ocean, but his radar operator had just detected a large iceberg dead ahead of the convoy's track. Gretton ordered Hart to place his ship between the iceberg and the approaching convoy. Hart ordered every exterior light on the destroyer turned on, illuminated the iceberg with the ship's searchlight, and had the ship's siren blast a series of the letter "U" (*Dot-dot-dash! Dot-dot-dash!*), the signal for "standing into danger." A long hour later, Gretton and every other ship captain breathed a sigh of relief as the last ships in the column safely steered past the menace glowing dimly from the *Vidette's* searchlight.[25]

By mid-morning on May 16, the fog lifted and the escort crewmen and merchant sailors were delighted to see the bright sun poised in a cloudless sky. After what seemed to have been an eternal winter of hurricane-force storms, howling winds, sleet, and spray, the North Atlantic now showed its rarer, benevolent face. The good weather also made it possible for Lieutenant-Commander Plomer in the *Sunflower* to rejoin B-7 after a dash through the fog from St. John's. The only thing that marred the perfect day was that two merchantmen reported mechanical problems, and both detached to return to St. John's. With the convoy otherwise in good order, the temperatures fair, and the sun warming the faces of the sailors, Gretton now put every crewman on the *Duncan* not on watch to work completing one last, delayed task. When Gretton and his officers had huddled back in St. John's to see how they could reduce the destroyer's excessive weight topside, one idea had been to remove tons of paint that had accumulated over the years to keep the warship looking smart. With hammers and chisels, the *Duncan's* crewmen now set to work stripping the destroyer of its old coats of paint.

The fine weather and peaceful sailing continued through May 18. Still smarting from what he described as an "ignominious retreat" from Convoy ONS5 when the *Duncan* had run critically short of fuel, Gretton once more decided to extend his destroyer's range by steaming within the convoy body itself during the day, while the other escorts conducted the endless zigzag maneuvers screening the formation. He felt confident, after B-7's performance against the U-boats two weeks previously, that SC130's security was not endangered by his fuel-saving ploy. The continuing good weather meant that SC130 also enjoyed strong air coverage from Canadian-based B-17 Fortresses on May 17, and the following day, Gretton seized the opportunity to order his warships to top off from the 5,722-ton British escort oiler *Bente Maersk*. Gretton felt further comforted by the fact that Admiral Horton's staff at Derby House had a firm intelligence assessment on the U-boat threat. As a result of the intelligence reports, Horton ordered one of the support groups that had reinforced B-7 during the ONS5 battle to steam from St. John's to back up the convoy defenses for the voyage ahead. For the second time in two weeks, Commander Godfrey Brewer and four of the five warships of the 1st Support Group were riding hard to reinforce Gretton's escort group.[26]

By dusk on May 18, Convoy SC130 received signs of the enemy's presence. Lieutenant-Commander Morgan at the *Duncan's* HF/DF station reported to Gretton that a U-boat was transmitting an encrypted Enigma message close off the convoy's port bow. Within the next three hours, three more U-boat signals went off at short range. Gretton and his officers knew that it was just a matter of time before the enemy attacked. Rather than feeling fear or dread, the commander later said, he and his crew patiently waited for the first contact. "I rather looked forward to a battle now, and there was no longer that sinking feeling of anticipation," Gretton said, "for we were well on top of the enemy, we had a good escort and we were full of confidence." Adding to their sense of certainty were the calm seas, clear skies, and a bright moon just one day from full. B-7's lookouts would have an excellent chance of spotting the U-boats as they maneuvered around the convoy. Back at BdU Operations in Berlin, Konteradmiral Godt on May 18 noted the same weather from several of the Donau boats' reports, and entered a foreboding note in the daily war diary: "The operational conditions for the boats are especially unfavorable owing to specially calm weather." Godt's prognosis was grimly correct; twelve days after losing a major battle in the fog, the U-boats were finding it a major challenge to fight in fair weather. The increasing capabilities of Allied radar, HF/DF, Asdic, and patrol aircraft were steadily making it difficult, if not impossible, for the U-boats to attack the convoys under *any* conditions.

By 2316 on May 18, the escorts' HF/DF reports showed that there were at least two U-boats directly ahead of SC130 and one on each quarter of the formation. They did not attack, however. Then, just over two hours later, HF/DF operators on the *Duncan, Tay,* and *Zamalek* got a cross-bearing fix on a U-boat four miles ahead of the main body off the port bow.

With a firm plot of the U-boat's location, Gretton ordered the *Duncan* to flank speed and went tearing out ahead of the convoy on an intercept course. When the range was down to two miles, the U-boat's lookouts spotted the destroyer and it crash-dived. Failing to get a firm Asdic contact, Gretton dropped a short spread of five depth charges over the U-boat's calculated location to keep the boat down, while Commodore Forsythe put the convoy into an evasive turn to starboard. After several hours, Gretton rejoined the convoy, and it returned to its base course to the east-northeast. Anticipating that several U-boats had probably already gotten well ahead of SC130 to position themselves for daylight periscope-depth attacks, Gretton ordered the convoy to make two more turns to starboard shortly before sunrise, then once more had SC130 resume its base course of 081 degrees.[27]

Gretton's ploy worked far better than he had hoped. At 0640 on May 19, VLR Liberator T/120 from the Coastal Command's 120 Squadron at Reykjavik arrived in the area and sighted a U-boat in what Gretton later said "would have been the ideal firing position" had the convoy not executed those three predawn turns. U-731 under Oberleutnant zur See Werner Techand was three weeks out from Kiel on its first North Atlantic patrol when its lookouts spotted the incoming bomber. As the U-boat crash-dived, the VLR Liberator straddled it with three 250-pound depth charges. On the next pass, the bomber dropped two of the new Fidos into the swirl from the U-boat. Only by making radical evasive maneuvers after submerging did U-731 manage to escape the attack.

Less than an hour after it had attacked U-731 on the convoy's original course track, T/120 spotted two more U-boats on the surface astern of

SC130. Having dropped all of its ordnance, pilot Flight Sergeant W. Stoves ordered a mock attack that prompted the two boats to crash-dive. Stoves dropped a smoke float at the spot and notified Gretton by radio about the two U-boats.

At 0824, T/120 next sighted a fourth U-boat, and Flight Sergeant Stoves went in for another mock bombing run. To his surprise, the U-boat did not crash-dive; instead, its gunners opened up on the aircraft. Passing over the surfaced boat, Stoves and his co-pilot yanked their yokes over hard and the Liberator turned sharply to port. The rear gunner raked the U-boat with machine-gun fire, finally prompting its commander to dive. Stoves dropped another smoke marker and reported the attack to Gretton, who ordered Lieutenant Hart in the *Vidette* to hasten to the site. The destroyer found the marker but failed to raise any contact on its Asdic set, so turned to rejoin SC130.

Liberator T/120's patrol was not over yet. Soon after its run on the fourth U-boat, the aircrew sighted a fifth that was in the act of submerging about fourteen miles ahead of the convoy, obviously in anticipation of a daylight attack from periscope depth. Once again, the aircrew dropped a smoke marker and called in their report. Gretton ordered Lieutenant Atkinson on the *Pink* to investigate. The corvette ran out, found the marker, and let loose a small spread of depth charges to keep the U-boat's head under. Meanwhile, SC130 executed an emergency turn to starboard at 0942 to move away from the U-boat. Although the crewmen in T/120 were close to their fuel limit, they spotted a sixth U-boat about ten miles ahead of the convoy's course at 0948 and forced that U-boat to crash-dive with another mock bombing run. Flight Sergeant Stoves and his crew returned to Reykjavik proud to have sighted and attacked or forced under six U-boats threatening SC130 during the three hours of patrolling around the convoy.[28]

While T/120 was attacking its U-boat targets some ten miles out from the convoy, the close escorts were having a very busy day themselves. Lieutenant Chesterman's corvette *Snowflake* was reacting to an 0850 radar contact when his lookouts suddenly sighted a periscope just fifty yards off the ship's starboard beam, well inside the convoy formation. The *Snowflake* blanketed the U-boat with a spread of depth charges, but Commander Gretton raced over in the *Duncan* to relieve the corvette, ordering

Chesterman back into his patrol station. Gretton later acknowledged that his takeover of the attack came as a "disappointment" for the eager corvette crew but said the tradeoff was essential given the dire conditions at that time. "A destroyer has more speed to rejoin and only one ship could possibly be spared," he explained.

The *Duncan* continued to track the submerged U-boat as the columns of SC130 merchantmen passed by at 7.5 knots. Gretton ordered a full spread of depth charges dropped, which badly shook up the civilian ships and briefly knocked out the destroyer's own steering gear. On the next pass, Gretton ordered his Hedgehog team to prepare a full salvo of twenty-four of the mortar shells. The initial attempt missed, but on the third attack, Gretton scored at least one hit. "We saw oil rising, and soon left the spot at full speed back to the convoy," he later recalled. The *Duncan* came through two of the columns of SC130 at flank speed, flying a pennant that signaled "KILL." Merchant seamen from a number of the ships waved and cheered.

Hardly had the *Duncan* returned to its patrol station when a young telephone operator on the destroyer's navigation bridge shouted and pointed to a U-boat conning tower on the horizon dead ahead. The *Duncan* sped out again while Commodore Forsythe signaled the convoy to make another evasive turn. Gretton lingered in the suspected location of the U-boat long enough for SC130 to disappear over the horizon.[29]

While the *Duncan* was busy chasing down one U-boat after another, the HF/DF and radar operators on the escort ships were reciting a litany of contacts. When another 120 Squadron Liberator, P/120, called in to report his arrival from Iceland, Gretton warned the pilot not to drop all of his depth charges and Fido torpedoes at the first one. "We quickly gave him three bearings to look at and within ten minutes he had no less than three submarines in sight," Gretton recalled. After a brief but intense discussion over which U-boat was the priority target, the pilot quipped, "As Mae West said, one at a time, gentlemen, please." The Liberator then proceeded to drive all three U-boats under, dropping a spread of four depth charges on the first U-boat, then watching the other two crash-dive before it could attack.

By mid-afternoon on May 19, the U-boats temporarily ceased their attempts to penetrate SC130's convoy screen. Gretton and his subordinate commanders were elated that they had kept the wolf packs from launching a single successful attack. In fact, the only explosions the lookouts had seen were a pair of blasts quite far from the formation, likely end-of-run detonations from a U-boat commander who had fired from well out of range of the merchant ships.

The good news didn't end for B-7. About that time in mid-afternoon, Gretton also took a radiotelephone call from Commander Brewer informing him that two of the 1st Support Group frigates, *Jed* and *Wear*, had just caught several U-boats by surprise on the surface well astern of the convoy. "It must have been most depressing for the submarine captains," Gretton wrote, "to surface for repairs well astern of the convoy after a frustrating morning's work to find yet another team of ships bearing down upon them from a quite unexpected direction."[30]

One of the U-boats that the 1st Support Group had come upon happened to include among its crew a person of deep personal interest to the U-boat Force commander-in-chief. U-954 was one of eleven U-boats that Grossadmiral Dönitz and Konteradmiral Godt had assigned to Gruppe Donau 2 on the boat's initial North Atlantic patrol. Commissioned on December 23, 1942, the boat and its crew underwent three months of workup training in the Baltic under the command of Kapitänleutnant Odo Loewe, twenty-eight, who had transferred from the German surface fleet into the U-boat branch in March 1941. Loewe's previous U-boat had been so savagely depth-charged by an escort warship that it was struck from the naval register instead of being repaired and replaced with another boat, the still-under-construction U-954. Among Loewe's watch officers was Oberleutnant zur See Peter Dönitz, twenty-one, the grossadmiral's younger son.[31]

At 1230, the 1st Support Group had been closing in on SC130 from astern in line abreast with four miles of separation between each warship. Lookouts on the frigate *Wear* sighted a surfaced U-boat twelve miles ahead. The formation had gotten within 3,000 yards of the boat when it suddenly crash-dived. The *Jed* and *Wear* had just begun a box search using Asdic when lookouts sighted a second U-boat. The two frigates tore after this new contact, but it too crash-dived. Then, at 1327, lookouts on the *Jed* spotted a third U-boat eight miles away. The two escorts chased this newest contact at flank speed, the *Jed* ahead of the *Wear*, when lookouts sighted several incoming torpedoes. The ships turned into the torpedo tracks, and all missed. The *Jed* then sighted a *fourth* U-boat five miles distant and broke off to attack, but Lieutenant George D. Edwards on the *Wear* remained behind to search for the boat that had fired on the two frigates. The former U.S. Coast Guard Cutter *Sennen*, commanded by Lieutenant-Commander Frederick H. Thornton, came up to assist. After several hours of tracking the boat on Asdic and dropping depth charges, the two ships saw a very large oil patch emerge on the surface with scattered debris floating in it. U-954 and its crew of forty-seven—Peter Dönitz among them—were dead.[32]

By sunset on May 19, the escorts' aggressive attacks and the blanket coverage of the convoy by the Iceland-based aircraft had destroyed or driven off most of the Donau 1 and Donau 2 U-boats. Only a handful of sightings occurred that evening and during the night. The easing of tensions allowed Gretton to arrange for his warships to refuel from the escort oiler. Western Approaches Command, observing the arrival of the support group, directed Gretton to detach the Canadian corvette *Kitchener* to join westbound Convoy ON184, then passing close by SC130. In the late afternoon and evening of May 19, several more VLR Liberators arrived and flew various patrol patterns around SC130, driving under several U-boats.

The Donau skippers were dismayed by the saturated air cover around SC130. Oberleutnant zur See Otto Ferro in U-645 signaled BdU Operations:

UP TO NOW HAVE BEEN DRIVEN UNDER WATER CONTINU-
ALLY BY AIRCRAFT OUT OF LOW CLOUDS AND BY DESTROY-
ERS. . . . LOCATED BY AIRCRAFT.

Similar reports flowed in to BdU operations from Oberleutnant Günter Gretschel in U-707, Kapitänleutnant Heinz Koch in U-304, and others. The gist was the same: SC130 was impenetrable because of the VLR Liberators overhead.[33]

Faced with a clearly superior enemy defense, the BdU staffers in Berlin threw up their hands in frustration. As Dönitz and Godt conceded in the daily war diary, "Several boats reported strong continual air cover over the convoy and the approach of land-based aircraft from low-lying clouds. For this reason continuous contact with the convoy was apparently not possible. In addition, the boats reported good cooperation between air and escort units."

The news from the U-boat commanders was discouraging, but Dönitz was not done yet. At 1946 GMT (1746 local time), he flashed an encrypted wireless message to all of the Gruppe Donau boats:

MOVE OFF AND PROCEED AHEAD AROUND THE CONVOY AT BEST SPEED OUTSIDE CLOSE AIR (ESCORTS), I.E. PRESUMABLY AT A DISTANCE OF ABOUT THIRTY OR FORTY MILES, IN ORDER TO DIVE AHEAD OF THE CONVOY FOR DAY ATTACK.[34]

Thanks to the BdU order, the ships of Convoy SC130, Escort Group B-7, and the 1st Support Group would experience a rare period of quiet out in the Greenland air gap during the night of May 19–20. Not only did no further attempted U-boat attacks take place, but the radar screens remained empty of contacts throughout the hours of darkness. "We all thought we were in for a bad night because conditions for the submarines were ideal and a hard-pressed attack must have succeeded," Gretton later wrote. "But they had been so shaken by their harrying both from the air and from the surface that only one U-boat ever reached the close screen." Receiving a solitary HF/DF contact from that U-boat, one of the escorts quickly forced it under.

On Thursday, May 20, the weather began to deteriorate, but the defenders continued their watch, and the VLR Liberators soon began appearing overhead again. Aircraft N/120 arrived shortly after dawn and began patrolling. In regular succession over the next four hours it sighted five U-boats, attacked one, and forced the other four to crash-dive, where they then lost contact with the convoy. The surface escorts also made several HF/DF and radar contacts, and forced the Donau boats to submerge.

In the early afternoon of May 20, a second VLR Liberator, P/120, took over from N/120 and continued harassing the Gruppe Donau boats, making one notable strike against the wolf pack. After P/120 had expended its depth charges, the bomber caught U-258 on the surface and drove it under after two passes in which the Liberator used its machine guns to sweep the conning tower and gun platforms. Coming around on another pass as the U-boat submerged, P/120 dropped a Fido. The homing torpedo destroyed the U-boat, killing its crew of forty-nine, including Kapitänleutnant Wilhelm von Mässenhausen. Twenty-one days earlier, von Mässenhausen and U-258 had been a part of Gruppe Star and had drawn first blood against Escort Group B-7, sinking the American freighter *McKeesport* in Convoy ONS5 on April 29. Now the Allies had taken their revenge.[35]

On Thursday, May 20, the Donau boats found themselves just as helpless against the escort ships and VLR Liberators as they had been the day before. The weather continued to decline over the day, and the number of attempted attacks fell off and then ceased altogether. The BdU orders to continue pressing home against the slow convoy would remain in place until early on May 21, but for all practical purposes, the battle was over. In Berlin, personal sadness added to the air of frustration; after failing to receive several required situation report messages from U-954, the BdU staff declared its loss with all hands—including Dönitz's son—as "certain."

On Saturday, May 22, with the U-boats gone and a fresh gale blowing, Gretton dispatched Commander Brewer's support group to assist another convoy. Three uneventful days later, Gretton turned the convoy into the North Channel, where the merchantmen split up to head to their respective ports of destination. Lieutenant Stonehouse in the corvette *Loosestrife* detached with a handful of merchant ships bound for the northern Scottish port of Loch Ewe, while Lieutenant Hart in the destroyer *Vidette* took the lead and escorted the rest of the main body down to the Mull of Kintyre, where the ships anchored while awaiting directions to proceed to port. Commander Gretton led the remaining ships of Escort Group B-7 to the small port of Moville on Northern Ireland's Lough Foyle for rest, refit, and—for its senior escort officer—a dash by ferry and train to his appointment at the altar at St. Mary's in London.[36]

In Grossadmiral Dönitz's U-boat Headquarters, the mood was funereal. The admiral's youngest son was dead, and the trap that had been laid for Convoy SC130 was in pieces. Shortly before ordering the U-boats of the two Donau wolf packs to break off the hunt, Dönitz transmitted a blistering message to all commanders at sea to make one final effort against the enemy. BdU ordered the two wolf packs to hunt for Convoy HX239,

Following his successful defense of Convoy SC130, Commander Peter W. Gretton married Judith DuVivier in London on May 29, 1943.
Courtesy of Vice-Admiral Michael Gretton, RN (Ret.)

which had left New York on May 13 with forty-four merchant ships and was now believed to be the next eastbound convoy heading into the Greenland air gap:

NOW IF THERE IS ANYONE WHO THINKS THAT COMBATING CONVOYS IS THEREFORE NO LONGER POSSIBLE, HE IS A WEAKLING AND NO TRUE U-BOAT CAPTAIN. THE BATTLE IN THE ATLANTIC IS GETTING HARDER BUT IT IS THE DETERMINING ELEMENT IN THE WAGING OF THE WAR. . . . DO YOUR BEST WITH THIS CONVOY. WE MUST SMASH IT TO BITS.[37]

As with Convoy SC130, the U-boats located HX239 but failed to sink a single one of its ships. Twenty-one U-boats in Gruppe Mosel (named after the German river), including most of the surviving Donau boats, spent several days attempting to penetrate the convoy screen under yet another smothering blanket of land-based patrol aircraft. Two boats—U-569 and U-752—would be added to the German fatalities for the blood-drenched month of May 1943. HX239 would escape unscathed.

Like the hunt for Convoys HX237 and SC129, the attempts on Convoys ONS7, SC130, and HX239 had been an unequivocal disaster for the U-boat Force. The two Donau wolf packs had lost four boats in their failed attacks on Convoys ONS7 and SC130—U-657, U-954, U-258, and U-381—with the loss of 190 officers and crewmen. The only Allied loss was the British freighter *Aymeric* in ONS7.

As May drew to a close, Dönitz and Godt were forced to admit that there had been a profound shift in fortunes out on the North Atlantic convoy runs. During April 29 to May 23, U-boats in the North Atlantic had hunted after thirteen convoys, made contact with only six of them, and managed to sink only nineteen Allied merchant ships totaling 96,170 gross tons. Discounting the thirteen ships sunk from ONS5, this meant the Atlantic U-boats during this period were able to attack only five other convoys, and from them, sink only *six* Allied merchant vessels out of the 562 crossing the North Atlantic. In that same time span, Allied escorts and aircraft destroyed thirty-five U-boats worldwide, killing 1,555 of Dönitz's elite volunteers, including fifteen that went down in the North Atlantic for a loss of some 750 crewmen. The numbers were staggering.[38]

On Monday, May 24, 1943, Dönitz finally threw in the towel. Recognizing that the U-boat Force faced a "crisis" in the North Atlantic, he signaled to his U-boat commanders that he was ordering "decisive measures" to protect the remaining U-boats until German scientists and weapons developers could devise countermeasures to Allied radar and land-based aircraft. His first step was to get the U-boats out of the Greenland air gap. Rather than a target-rich hunting ground for the wolf packs, it had now become a killing field for the embattled U-boats.

Dönitz ordered the four dozen U-boats still operating in the Greenland air gap to disengage from attacking the convoys and to withdraw southeast toward the Central Atlantic convoy routes between Hampton Roads, Virginia, and the Strait of Gibraltar, areas of the Atlantic where BdU believed enemy aircraft patrols were less common. The situation, Dönitz explained in the message, "now forces a temporary shifting of operations to areas less endangered by aircraft. The following areas come into consideration: the Caribbean Sea, the area off Trinidad, the area off the Brazilian and West African coasts." Dönitz also directed a number of the retreating

U-boats to broadcast multiple, fictitious wireless signals as they left, so as to mislead the Allies of this redeployment.

Having called off the campaign to strangle Great Britain out of the war, Dönitz tried to assuage his commanders' pain with a pledge that the Battle of the Atlantic would resume in the future. The move away from the North Atlantic convoy routes was only temporary, Dönitz assured his captains, and would end as soon as the U-boats could be outfitted with new weapons and equipment that would allow them to achieve a higher and more sustainable rate of merchant ship sinkings. "It is, however, clearly understood," he continued, "that the main operational area of U-boats is, as it always was, in the North Atlantic and that operations must be resumed there with every determination as soon as the U-boats are given the necessary weapons for this [effort]." The U-boats' primary purpose, Dönitz knew, was to prevent critical supplies from reaching the British Isles, and the grossadmiral and his headquarters staff still desperately hoped for some technological miracle that would enable the U-boats to make a comeback and sever the Allies' lifeline once and for all.[39]

Years later, long after the Allies had completed their British-based invasion of Europe and defeated Germany, Dönitz would remember the spring of 1943 in a different light. In his postwar memoirs, written after serving a ten-year prison sentence for war crimes as decreed by the International Military Tribunal at Nuremberg, Dönitz finally accepted what had happened out in the storm-tossed ocean between mid-March and late May 1943: "We had lost the Battle of the Atlantic."[40]

EPILOGUE

On Monday, May 31, 1943, seven days after withdrawing from the Battle of the Atlantic, a dejected Grossadmiral Karl Dönitz took off from Berlin in a light military aircraft on the 350-mile flight to the Berghof, Adolf Hitler's mountain retreat in the Bavarian Alps. The Führer had summoned his naval commander-in-chief to discuss the overall situation at sea. It was a topic in which Hitler—although personally in direct command of the entire German military, the Wehrmacht, since 1938—rarely showed interest. With North American supplies flowing freely to Britain, however, the Führer had apparently taken notice of the crisis that the U-boat Force was facing.

In addition to Hitler and Dönitz, several others were present in the Berghof's spacious conference room when the meeting commenced. Field Marshal Wilhelm Keitel was chief of the High Command of the German Armed Forces and therefore, officially, the Reich's minister of war. In reality, the sixty-year-old general was merely responsible for carrying out Hitler's orders, policies, and personal whims, a task he executed so efficiently that his subordinates nicknamed him *Lakaitel*—"little lackey"— punning on the sound of his surname. Two other functionaries were there as well to take notes and countersign the minutes: Generalleutnant (Lieutenant General) Walter Warlimont, forty-eight, a senior aide to Keitel, and Navy Kapitän zur See Karl-Jesco von Puttkamer, forty-three, Hitler's naval adjutant.

Admiral Dönitz did not mince words with his Führer. He blamed the "present crisis in U-boat warfare" on a combination of increased Allied air power over the North Atlantic and an as-yet unidentified "new location device"—in actuality a combination of the Allies' centimetric radar and HF/DF direction-finding—that enabled enemy ships and aircraft to locate U-boats without German counterdetection. Dönitz specifically cited the recent furious battle over Convoy ONS5 as evidence of the calamitous improvements in Allied air power and surveillance technology. He also enumerated the soaring number of U-boat losses during the month of May, and emphasized the need to conserve the U-boat Force until German scientists could come up with countermeasures to the Allies' new technology.

The discussion between Dönitz and Hitler continued for some time, as the admiral reviewed other aspects of the U-boat situation and briefed Hitler on a number of planned new weapons and sensors. He described the development of two new acoustic homing torpedoes, the G7e (T4) Falke (Falcon) and G7s (T5) Zaunkönig (Wren), both designed to attack Allied escort warships. He updated the Führer on the ongoing plan to install quadruple-barrel anti-aircraft cannon on all U-boats to increase their firepower against the aerial threat. He described a new radar-deception device called Aphrodite that would be carried under a lighter-than-air balloon flown astern of a surfaced boat. It would reflect back a ship or aircraft radar beam to create a false image. Then, as Hitler exercised control over every military decision, however minuscule, Dönitz formally requested approval to deploy the radar-reflection devices. The conference minutes noted, "The Führer gives permission."

Dönitz attempted to reassure Hitler that the U-boat Force was only temporarily abandoning the North Atlantic convoy routes, not abdicating the war against Great Britain and the United States, but this brought a harsh interruption by the Führer. "There can be no talk of a let-up in U-boat warfare," Hitler barked. "The Atlantic is my first line of defense in the West, and even if I have to fight a defensive battle there, that is preferable to waiting to defend myself on the coast of Europe. The enemy forces tied up by our U-boat warfare are tremendous, even though the actual losses inflicted by us are no longer great." The outburst made the message painfully clear: even if Dönitz's U-boats were unable to sink the merchant ships feeding Britain, they still had a use as cannon fodder for the ships that would otherwise be committed to the Allied war effort elsewhere.[1]

A combination of tougher escort groups and stronger coverage by land-based aircraft helped to turn the tide against the U-boats in the Atlantic. Here, the U-118 desperately tries to avoid machine-gun fire and depth charges from *USS Bogue* aircraft that attacked it on June 12, 1943. Moments later, the U-boat sank, killing all but sixteen of its fifty-nine crewmen.

Clay Blair Collection, American Heritage Center, University of Wyoming

Grossadmiral Dönitz returned to BdU Headquarters with a radically different goal for the U-boats. The tonnage war was over, lost. For now, the U-boat crews would carry on a grim war of attrition in other, less protected parts of the ocean until the anticipated new weapons and sensors enabled them to return to the North Atlantic. Instead of seeking victory, BdU would now settle for delaying as best they could the buildup of troops, aircraft, and supplies in the British Isles as the Allies prepared for the invasion of the Continent. His best hope was that the U-boats would continue to tie down an estimated 1,300 Allied aircraft and 3,300 warships assigned to convoy defenses that otherwise would be redeployed to the fight against Germany itself.[2]

Despite the cloud that had settled over BdU, Dönitz pledged anew to his U-boat commanders that German science and industry could yet save the day. Germany would produce new torpedoes, anti-aircraft guns, hoped-for radar warning receivers that would work—and perhaps a revolutionary new U-boat design that would transform the war at sea.

The transforming vision that Dönitz, Godt, and the BdU staff long cherished throughout the Battle of the Atlantic was a true submarine, not the diesel-and-electric submersibles that characterized the U-boat fleet. As far back as 1934, Germany's famed U-boat designer Helmut Walter had proposed a 1,485-ton U-boat that would operate on hydrogen peroxide fuel in a closed propulsion system that allowed practically indefinite operations submerged. Bypassing the inefficient use of electric motors powered by rechargeable batteries, Walter foresaw an advanced boat that could travel 3,000 miles at seventeen knots on the surface. While the mainstay Type VIIC had a greater cruising range of 8,500 nautical miles at a fuel-efficient speed of ten knots, the Walter design's higher cruising speed offered significant tactical advantages, even though its maximum operating range was less than half that of the VIIC. It was underwater where the Walter boat would potentially neutralize the Allied anti-submarine warfare campaign: the new hull design and hydrogen peroxide propulsion system would power it for 500 miles nonstop at an incredible top speed of twenty-four knots—equal to or faster than the swiftest Allied escort ships. If such a design were to come to fruition in the German Baltic naval shipyards, Dönitz would be able—literally—to run circles around the Allied convoys.

Fortunately for the Allies, the Walter vision never materialized. The primary reason was that Germany did not have the capability to manufacture sufficient quantities of the exotic fuel for both the planned U-boats and the critically important research into ballistic missile technology that would produce the V-2 rocket in 1944. Walter's design team encountered a second, all-but-insurmountable problem involving refueling the U-boats at sea. Whereas the electric storage batteries in the conventional boats were rechargeable, consumption of the hydrogen peroxide fuel would require somehow reloading a Walter boat's fuel tanks with the highly flammable liquid from another U-boat or a surface supply ship. Moreover, by the summer of 1943, Dönitz and his staff realized that it would be impossible to build sufficient numbers of the new design to have a significant impact on the war.

What followed was a compromise: German shipwrights would take the Walter's streamlined hull and add massive storage batteries to create an advanced U-boat called the Type XXI. A smaller, 234-ton Type XXIII electro-boat built, on a similar design, would operate in coastal waters. Even such a compromise improvement, Dönitz hoped, would allow the U-boats to stalk the Allied convoys more stealthily—and safely—than before. In the summer of 1943, Hitler approved an ambitious construction plan for 700 of the Type XXI and 250 of the smaller Type XXIII boats, with the first ones becoming operational by the summer of 1944.[3]

For now, the U-boat Force remained trapped in a strategically vulnerable position, with no solution in sight. Thus, Admiral Dönitz's rhetoric remained just that: words. His only military asset on the last day of May 1943 was the unyielding loyalty of his battered U-boat crews to their commander-in-chief. As the summer of 1943 commenced, and Dönitz's U-boats continued to be clearly outmatched by the Allied convoy escort groups and VLR bombers, the faithful crewmen faced a hopeless task that could only lead one way: to their deaths.

HAVING MADE THE PAINFUL DECISION to abandon the North Atlantic convoy runs, Admirals Dönitz and Godt saw only one target-rich opportunity for the U-boats: the Central Atlantic convoy routes running east and west along the 36th Parallel between Hampton Roads, Virginia, and Gibraltar. "For the boats already at sea there was only one possibility," BdU operations officer Günter Hessler later explained, "to send them to the southwest of the Azores, where they could operate against the U.S.-Gibraltar convoys." The only alternative, he added, would have been total abandonment of the war at sea.[4]

The Central Atlantic pipeline was organized by the U.S. Navy in late 1942 to ship war supplies to the Anglo-American force that had landed in North Africa as Operation Torch beginning on November 11, 1942. It now provided critical support for the Allies as they prepared to mount the planned invasion of Sicily from bases in North Africa in July 1943. Thus far, the eastbound UGF (United States–Gibraltar—Fast) and UGS (United States–Gibraltar—Slow) Convoys had already made twenty passages by the time Dönitz suspended operations in the Greenland air gap. During that same six-month period since the convoy route opened, westbound GUF (Gibraltar–United States—Fast) and GUS (Gibraltar–United States—Slow) formations had made nineteen passages. The convoys ranged in size from as few as fifteen to as many as seventy ships.[5]

Dönitz and Godt were well aware that the Central Atlantic convoys generally enjoyed stronger protection than the North Atlantic convoys and their storm-wracked escort groups. The U.S. Atlantic Fleet, and not the storm-stressed Western Approaches Command, controlled these convoys and provided stiff protection with anywhere from twelve to several dozen U.S. Navy warships for each passage. Moreover, Atlantic Fleet Commander Admiral Royal E. Ingersoll assigned several battleships and cruisers to augment the firepower of the several dozen destroyers and Coast Guard cutters protecting these shipments. The only glimmer of hope for the Germans was that the distance factors would prevent land-based air coverage for much of the crossing. While the routes passed close to the Portuguese-held Azores, Lisbon's neutrality thus far had precluded the Allies from developing air bases on the island chain.[6]

The German admirals organized a two-pronged operation to shift away from the North Atlantic to the warmer southern waters. On May 24, they ordered nineteen U-boats—seventeen from the disbanded Gruppen Donau 2 and Mosel, and two newly deployed U-boats—to proceed to the south toward an area about 600 miles west-southwest of the Azores, where they would re-form as Gruppe Trutz (Defiance) on June 1, awaiting the arrival of eastbound Convoy UGS9. This was a formation of seventy-seven merchant ships totaling 565,301 gross registered tons of shipping bound for Gibraltar and various ports in North Africa.[7]

In an attempt to disguise this withdrawal from the North Atlantic, Dönitz ordered thirteen other U-boats from former Gruppen Donau 2 and Mosel to remain there to carry out a deception operation against the Allies. He sent the U-boats to pre-assigned positions in a 500-by-600-mile swath of the Greenland air gap. Dispersed between 70 and 200 miles apart from one another, the U-boats were to transmit multiple messages as if each one were four or five different boats. Another thirty-one U-boats that had been at sea on May 24 were returning to their bases in France.[8]

Both the deception operation and the Gruppe Trutz mission to the Central Atlantic would prove abject failures. The Allies quickly learned of both plans from decrypted naval Enigma messages and from HF/DF intercepts as the Trutz boats proceeded to their patrol area. Allied ships or aircraft sank three of the deception boats, U-202, U-304, and U-467. And when

Gruppe Trutz attempted to attack Convoy UGS9, the U-boats came under heavy attack from aircraft operating off the *USS Bogue*. An Avenger dive bomber from the escort carrier sank the Type VIID U-217 with all hands. The wolf pack would not sink a single Allied merchant ship.[9]

In the same week that Admiral Dönitz met with Hitler to explain his decision to abandon the convoy fights, Admiral Sir Max Horton at Western Approaches sent a message to all Allied units operating under his command. "The Battle of the Atlantic has taken a definite turn in our favor during the past two months," Horton wrote, "and the returns show an ever-increasing toll of U-boats and decreasing losses of merchant ships in convoy." Horton firmly believed, however, that Grossadmiral Dönitz and the U-boat Force were still in the fight and would return to the North Atlantic as soon as they came up with new weapons to use against the convoys. For that reason, Horton said, Western Approaches Command would remain vigilant. "The tide of battle has been checked, if not turned, and the enemy is showing signs of strain. . . . Now is the time to strike and strike hard."[10]

During the summer of 1943, the escort and support groups had little opportunity to act upon their commander-in-chief's urging to hunt down the U-boats. There were hardly any U-boats around to destroy. Over the seventeen weeks after U-657 sank the British merchantman *Aymeric* in Convoy ONS7 on May 17, the Allies were able to sail sixty-two eastbound and westbound convoys along the North Atlantic routes without sustaining a single loss to a U-boat. In thirty eastbound HX and SC convoys, 1,872 merchant ships delivered a staggering 12,015,945 tons of supplies to the United Kingdom.

The surge in shipping in the summer of 1943 was partly due to the decision by American and British convoy planners to seize the advantage provided by the U-boats' withdrawal. Officials quickly expanded the size of each formation. During the critical months of March and April 1943, the North Atlantic convoys had averaged forty-three ships per formation. By the first week in June, the number soared to an average of sixty-two merchantmen per convoy. The gross tonnage of supplies per convoy also skyrocketed. Whereas the forty merchantmen of Convoy HX229 had left New York on March 8 with a total of 284,613 gross tons of shipping, the summertime convoys averaged 400,532 gross registered tons.[11]

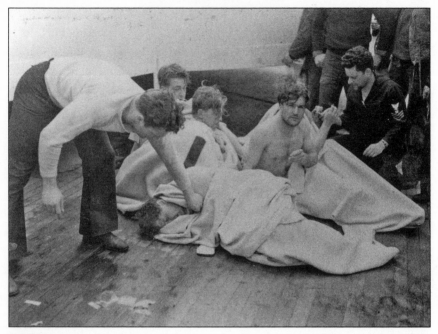

The lucky ones: survivors of the U-175 huddle on the deck of the Coast Guard cutter *USS Spencer.*
Clay Blair Collection, American Heritage Center, University of Wyoming

The escalating volume of trans-Atlantic shipping did not just add to the stockpiles of gear under Operation Bolero, the massive buildup of Allied troops and airmen in the British Isles. It also eased the dire predicament of the British people. With the U-boats gone, they began enjoying once more a balanced diet and adequate supplies of heating oil and gasoline. After all those long months of worry and fear over merchant shipping losses, Prime Minister Churchill finally decided to celebrate publicly. He stood in the House of Commons on September 21, 1943, and declared, "For the four months which ended on 18th September, no merchant vessel was sunk by enemy action in the North Atlantic. . . . During the first fortnight in this September, no Allied ships were sunk by U-boat action in any part of the world. . . . The House will also realize that we have taken full advantage of the lull in the U-boat attack to bring the largest possible convoys, and that we have replenished the reserves in these Islands of all essential commodities, especially fuel oil." The members of the House of Commons responded "with loud and prolonged cheering." The U-boats' stranglehold over everyday British life was, it seemed, over for the moment.[12]

Along with expanded convoy traffic came long-awaited reinforcements for the defenders of the merchant formations crossing the Atlantic. After months, and in some cases years, of delay, the American shipyards and aircraft factories finally began to deliver warships and aircraft that had been so desperately needed earlier in the year. The escort carrier *USS Bogue* and its British counterpart, *HMS Biter*, had been protecting North Atlantic convoys since March. Now just three months later, the *Bogue*'s sister ships *USS Card* and *USS Santee* began operating with the *Bogue* along the Central Atlantic convoy routes while the second British escort carrier, *HMS Archer*, also led a support group there. Their carrier-based aircraft quickly disabused the U-boat commanders in the Central Atlantic of Dönitz's belief that the new hunting grounds were less dangerous than those up north. The new American *Evarts-* and *Buckley*-class destroyer escorts also began appearing as convoy escorts in late spring. Their much-delayed production brought to the fleet a cadre of destroyers that would ultimately expand to a force of 260 warships. A third gain in Allied anti-submarine warfare also came in June of 1943: additional deliveries of VLR-configured B-24 Liberators. After months of contentious arguments over command, control, and tactics, the U.S. Army Air Forces agreed to transfer a group of Liberators from Bermuda to Newfoundland. During the same period, the Royal Canadian Air Force began receiving its initial allotment of the extended-range patrol aircraft. While the two units would not become fully operational for some time, and while there were currently no U-boats menacing the merchantmen crossing the North Atlantic, the moves signaled to the Germans that the Allies had closed the Greenland air gap for good.

Two other events occurred during late May 1943 that would have dire consequences for the U-boat Force. On May 1, U.S. Navy commander-in-chief Admiral Ernest King formally had created a special strategic group in his Washington headquarters to coordinate all aspects of anti-submarine warfare. Personally commanded by Admiral King, the U.S. Tenth Fleet was responsible for research, training, intelligence gathering, and operational control of the U.S. Navy's war against the U-boats, as well as the actual deployment of ASW forces. The new command would ensure that the fight against the U-boats was even more concerted and Allied teamwork even more efficient and deadly than it had been in the past. By the end of the month, the new command was up and running in full gear.

The new, more focused anti-submarine command under Admiral King had grave consequences for the Germans, but so did the Allies' growing advantage in the cryptologic war that had guided the battles at sea. In late May 1943, the Allies finally confirmed that the German B-dienst had long before penetrated British Naval Cypher No. 3, the code widely used to communicate with convoys at sea. BdU cryptanalysts had exploited their breakthrough to reposition wolf packs to intercept the merchant formations. Now, the U.S. and Royal navies quickly switched to a newer code, Naval Cypher No. 5, and the B-dienst operators went blind and deaf for good.[13]

As the U-boat Force continued to struggle with the ever-growing anti-submarine threat, far more dangerous developments confronted Germany, Italy, and Japan. On June 10, 1943, the Anglo-American Combined Chiefs of Staff unleashed an around-the-clock bomber offensive against Germany. This was another decision that British and American generals had agreed upon during January's Casablanca Conference, at which they had wrangled over the disposition of aircraft and warships for convoy defense. For the Allies, it was payback for Germany's earlier aerial atrocities, particularly the Blitz of 1940–41 when the Luftwaffe bombed London and twenty-five other cities, killing 43,000 civilians. On July 24, more than 3,000 British bombers began a seven-day bombing campaign against the port city of Hamburg. During one nighttime raid, they used incendiary bombs that sparked a massive firestorm, torching eight square miles of the city and killing over 50,000 people, many of them skilled shipwrights in the city's four U-boat shipyards.

At the same time, the two-year German invasion of the Soviet Union finally ran out of steam. On July 4, Hitler had ordered a massive armored thrust against the Red Army, an assault that became known as the Battle of Kursk. In an attempt to trap the Russians, the Germans advanced with thirty-five divisions organized into two pincers. The Russians countered with an equally large force, setting off the largest tank battle of the war. Some 6,000 tanks and 4,000 aircraft took part in the fight. When the smoke cleared in mid-August, the German Army had fallen back on Hitler's orders because of a new Allied threat in the Mediterranean, the

The Type IXC/40 U-185 sinks in the mid-Atlantic after being bombed and strafed by carrier aircraft from the *USS Card.*

Uboatarchive.net

imminent invasion of Sicily. In what turned out to be its last offensive on the eastern front, Germany lost over 70,000 troops captured or killed and nearly 3,000 tanks and 1,400 aircraft destroyed.

The Allied liberation of Sicily was Hitler's third nightmare in the summer of 1943. The invasion had also been decided upon at the Casablanca summit six months earlier. On the night of July 10, the first of 160,000 Allied troops launched a parachute assault and amphibious landing on the island, backed by a powerful naval force and air cover overhead. Steadily seizing terrain, the Allies forced the German and Italian defenders eastward toward the Strait of Messina. The only good news for Hitler was that his generals successfully evacuated over 100,000 German troops to the Italian mainland. Otherwise, the news was grim. High-ranking Italian fascists deposed and arrested dictator Benito Mussolini after the fall of Sicily and on September 8 secretly negotiated Italy's surrender to the Allies.[14]

As Germany lost its footing in Italy and Russia, the Allied slaughter of the U-boats continued apace. None of Dönitz's proposed stopgap solutions worked. When BdU "up-armed" the U-boats with the four-barreled 20-mm cannons and ordered them to fight it out against Allied aircraft, the fighters and patrol bombers quickly adjusted their tactics and neutralized the threat. Instead of a single TBF Avenger racing in to drop its depth charges after sighting a surfaced U-boat, the dive bomber would circle out of anti-aircraft range while two or more FM2 Wildcat fighters would simultaneously strafe the enemy from opposite directions, thus overwhelming the gunners and clearing the way for the Avenger to attack.[15]

When the U-boats attempted a comeback in the North Atlantic with the Zaunkönig torpedo, which became operational in September 1943, they achieved initial surprise against Convoy ON202. During a series of attacks between September 20 and 23, four of the twenty-one U-boats in Gruppe Leuthen (named for a small town in Germany) attacked the convoy's escorts with the acoustic torpedo. They sank the Canadian destroyer *HMCS St. Croix*, frigate *HMS Itchen,* and corvette *Polyanthus* and seriously damaged the frigate *HMS Lagan*. The loss of life for the escort sailors was horrific. The *Lagan* lost 30 of its 140-man crew in the torpedo strike. Sixty-six crewmen on the *St. Croix* perished in the initial torpedo explosion, and all but one of the *Polyanthus's* eighty-five crewmen died when the Zaunkönig struck. Nor was that all. The eighty-two survivors from the *St. Croix* and the *Polyanthus* were rescued by the *Itchen,* which was itself struck by another Zaunkönig three days later. Only 3 of the 222 crewmen and survivors aboard the frigate survived the attacks. In addition, the U-boats sank six merchant ships totaling 36,422 tons, although killing relatively fewer crewmen from the larger vessels—42 of 347 merchant seamen and naval gunners combined.[16]

While the spike in sinkings and the loss of four warships came as a harsh surprise to Western Approaches Command, Grossadmiral Dönitz and BdU would see no comeback for the U-boat Force from the Zaunkönig. The Allies quickly equipped the convoy escorts with a towed noisemaker called the "foxer," which deceived the torpedo's acoustic homing warhead by foiling its ability to home in on the warships' wakes.

Other U-boat innovations like the Zaunkönig also had little effect on the war at sea. Dönitz would next have most of the operational U-boats retrofitted with air-breathing snorkels, in the hopes that the devices would enable them to elude the ever-growing air threat by remaining submerged for longer periods. The snorkel, a retractable tube that allowed the boat to use its diesel motors while running at periscope depth, was adequate as a defensive measure but would severely limit the U-boats' combat capabilities by reducing its speed from seventeen knots on the surface to only five knots submerged. On another front, in 1944, German scientists finally built a radar detector that could capture the ten-centimeter radar signal, but the Allies were already shifting to an even shorter three-centimeter radar set that would elude German detection as its predecessor had done.

The danger in combat operations against clearly superior Allied convoy defenses was not the only source of fear and stress for most U-boat sailors. As 1944 began and the Allied aerial assault on the German homeland continued, the sailors' once-pleasant return trips to Germany while on leave now simply meant exposure to a new battlefield. The massive Allied bombing campaigns were slowly but steadily grinding Germany into rubble. U-boat men could see with their own eyes that the Allies were winning the war, and that their loved ones at home were in as much danger as the seamen were on the hostile ocean.

Leutnant zur See Herbert A. Werner felt the pain of the home front especially keenly. During a two-year period beginning in September 1942, Werner, then twenty-three, was able to make eight visits back to his hometown of Frankfurt after war patrols on the three U-boats in which he served. Each successive trip revealed the worsening landscape of war. On his first trip, Werner traveled to the southern German town of Ueberlingen to attend his sister's wedding. "It was so peaceful I hesitated before stepping off the train," he later recalled. "It was as if I would be contaminating the tranquility of the place with my warlike presence." Six months later, U-230, Werner's U-boat, returned from the massive March convoy battles against eastbound Convoys SC121, HX228, HX229, and SC122. He found a letter from his girlfriend in Berlin, who wrote that her best friend had perished in an air raid. Returning to his homeport of Brest in late May after the next patrol, Werner took the train to his hometown of Frankfurt and then went on to Berlin. The destruction was extensive, and Werner discovered that, to his horror, his girlfriend had died in another air raid. Four months after that, Werner visited Frankfurt and his family once again, only to find that the destruction from the air had reached "grotesque proportions." And it would only get worse.

After Werner's U-boat made a dangerous redeployment from France into the Mediterranean in January 1944, the young U-boat officer traveled from Marseilles up to Germany to attend U-boat commander's training. This time, the train was delayed just outside Frankfurt because of a heavy air raid in progress. Werner reached his family home to find that a bomb had ripped away the entire rear wall of the building, but that his parents and sister were uninjured. Two months later, following his completion of the commander's course, Werner was on a two-week skiing trip in the Alps prior to taking command of the U-415 based in Brest, when he heard a radio report of another massive Allied bombing attack against Frankfurt. He raced home and found that, this time, his family home had been completely destroyed. His family had lost most of their belongings and were huddled in a tiny hotel room.

Assuming command of another U-boat, U-953, in August 1944, Werner found orders to take the boat from Brest to its new homeport in Bergen, Norway. The D-Day invasion of Normandy on June 6 had forced the U-boats to abandon the French Atlantic bases they had used since overrunning the country in 1940. U-953 was the last boat to escape. Werner and his crew spent forty-two days creeping around the British Isles, running submerged as the crew and diesel engines breathed air through the U-boat's snorkel. There was no reward for the accomplishment. Traveling back to Germany on leave after reaching Norway, Werner had a chance encounter with a family friend on a train. She told him that everyone in his family was dead. With nowhere else to go, Werner returned to Ueberlingen, where several relatives lived. He tried to put the devastation of the war out of his mind with another skiing trip, but something new had come to the southern Alps: the continuous mutter and rumbling of American artillery as it fired against German defenses less than forty miles away.[17]

With U-953's arrival in Norway, all of the surviving Atlantic U-boats had regrouped, but Grossadmiral Dönitz's once-powerful U-boat Force would pose only a minimal threat to the Allies for the remainder of the war. The Germans' wonder weapons, the Type XXI and XXIII electroboats, never reached the U-boat Force in any significant numbers. The Allied bombing of Germany had so disrupted Hitler's transportation infrastructure that it seriously delayed delivery of the components for the new U-boats. Only two Type XXIs ever deployed on patrol, and neither sank an Allied ship. Eight of the smaller Type XXIII boats got to sea, and between them sank just four Allied merchant ships totaling 7,392 tons.[18]

The U-boat men's undertaking in the twenty-four months after May 1943 amounted to an orchestrated exercise in mass suicide. Attempts to sink Allied merchant shipping became more and more futile with every passing day. U-boats continued to sink enemy merchant ships in other areas such as the South Atlantic, Indian Ocean, and Caribbean, but new Allied merchant ship construction vastly surpassed those losses. The dispersed U-boat Force managed to destroy 192 merchant ships totaling 682,977 gross tons from May 24 to December 31, 1943. That constituted an average of .86 ships sunk per day—a paltry rate when contrasted with the 4.2 ships that the force had been sinking daily in November 1942, its best month. While the U-boats destroyed 6.14 million gross registered tons of Allied shipping in 1943, American shipbuilders alone delivered over 18 million tons of new merchant ships to the war effort during that period. The gap in tonnage gained versus tonnage lost would continue in 1944 and 1945. And while the U-boat men were failing to sink as many Allied merchantmen as were necessary to sustain the tonnage war, they were also perishing in droves.[19]

During the six-month period after the apex of the Battle of the Atlantic, from May 24 to December 31, 1943, the Allies inflicted a catastrophic blow against the German Ubootwaffe. They destroyed 151 U-boats, bringing the annual losses for 1943 to 238 boats and 10,051 U-boat crewmen killed. Of the 1,842 Germans who survived the sinkings, most were taken prisoner. The year 1944 would be even worse for U-boat losses, with 250 destroyed, though fewer crewmen, 7,976, perished. The only positive trend was that because most U-boats were forced to operate in coastal waters around Norway or the United Kingdom by this time, relatively more crewmen survived the sinking of their boats. In 1943, some 1,842 U-boat men survived, while the following year, that number grew to 2,349. The trend did not continue. During the last five months of the war, from January to May 1945, the Allies sank another 123 U-boats, killing 4,011 men with only 396 surviving the attacks.

The U-boat Force suffered casualties far greater than any branch of arms on either side of World War II. Of 1,149 U-boats that entered service during the war, 711 were lost in combat or accidents or destroyed in the bombing of shipyards, a sixty-one percent destruction rate. Personnel losses were even higher: of 39,000 U-boat men who went to sea in World War II, 27,490 perished in combat and from accidents, a stunning seventy percent fatality rate. Of the 11,510 crewmen who survived, some 5,000 ended the war in Allied POW camps. Just 6,510 of the elite sailors who had volunteered to serve on the U-boats would end the war alive and with their freedom. The others would be rewarded for their bravery with imprisonment or death.[20]

The U-boats that fought in the March attacks on Convoys SC122 and HX229, and the boats that were later deployed to hunt for Convoys ONS5 and SC130 in May, suffered even higher casualties than the force overall. Of the 111 U-boats that took part in the attacks on those four convoys, 98 were lost in various combat incidents by the end of the war. That was an astonishing loss rate of eighty-eight percent. Sixty-six of those lost U-boats, nearly sixty percent, went down with all hands. Of that group, 4,051 of the 5,574 U-boat officers and enlisted men serving on the 111 boats perished, a fatality rate of nearly seventy-three percent. Another 1,523 survived, including 193 taken prisoner of war after their boats sank.

The stepped-up anti-submarine effort by the Allies had one especially grim consequence for the U-boat men. After the late spring of 1943, the level of combat experience of a U-boat crew meant little for its odds of survival. In terms of the battles over Convoys SC122, HX229, ONS5, and SC130 alone, thirty-seven of the participating U-boats that were on their initial North Atlantic patrols did not survive the war. Another twenty-seven of the participating U-boats had three or more prior patrols and yet were *also* lost before the war's end. Among those killed in the battle of ONS5 were Kapitänleutnant Ulrich Folkers and the crew of the U-125, veterans of the 1942 Operation Drumbeat attacks on American coastal shipping. Other subsequent losses included two U-boats—U-107 and U-202—that each had eight prior patrols, and another five boats that had previously made seven war cruises. Their fates were the same: sunk with all hands.

For the men of the U-boats, valor and initiative in combat proved to be as poor a guarantee of survival as was overall combat experience. Kapitän-leutnant Manfred Kinzel in U-338 won high praise from Admiral Dönitz after sinking four ships and damaging a fifth in his bold series of attacks against Convoy SC122. He and his crew perished two patrols later, on September 23, 1943, in an attack by an RAF 120 Squadron VLR Libera-tor. Oberleutnant zur See Hans Hartwig Trojer and his crew on U-221 had enjoyed a similarly distinguished patrol in February and March 1943, sinking six ships totaling 34,658 tons, including three from Convoy HX228 and two from HX229 a week later. Trojer and his crew got to live just four days longer than Kapitänleutnant Kinzel and the crew of U-338. A British Halifax bomber sank U-221 with all fifty crewmen on Septem-ber 27, 1943.

Only fourteen U-boats from the four critical convoy battles of March and May escaped destruction in battle. They were a small minority of the 111 U-boats assigned to the nine wolf packs that had witnessed the turn-ing of the tide of war. Of the fourteen, five were decommissioned from obsolescence or from battle damage sustained in bombing of their ship-yards. The crewmen of another two boats were interned in the neutral countries of Ireland and Spain. The crews of three other boats opted to scuttle their damaged boats to prevent them from falling into the hands of the Allies. Only four boats—U-190, U-218, U-530, and U-532—lasted long enough to be surrendered to the Allies or neutral countries after Germany capitulated on May 8, 1945.[21]

Radioman Martin Beisheim and others aboard the U-758 were in the small group of survivors from the U-boats that had gone up against Con-voys SC122, HX229, ONS5, and SC130. After returning to Bordeaux from the battle of Convoy HX229 on March 30, 1943, Beisheim and his fellow sailors had received an extended, two-month reprieve from sea duty while shipwrights installed one of the first four-barrel 20-mm anti-aircraft guns on U-758. The crew deployed on its next patrol on May 26, 1943, heading to Trinidad. The U-758 was proceeding north of the Azores on June 8 when a TBF Avenger dive-bomber from the carrier *Bogue* sighted the surfaced U-boat. Kapitänleutnant Manseck, following orders to remain on the surface and fight, fended off a swarm of Avengers and F4F Wildcat fighters during an intense, two-hour fight. While Manseck's gunners forced several aircraft to abort their attacks, a pair of Avengers straddled his boat with depth charges. The damage nearly sank U-758. Eleven crewmen, including Manseck, were wounded, four critically. Manseck managed to rendezvous with the old Type XB U-118, then serving as a U-tanker, and transferred the four most seriously injured crewmen to it. He then aborted his patrol, and U-758 limped back to port. The *Bogue's* aircraft found U-118 four days later and sank it, killing all aboard, including the four critically injured crewmen from U-758.

U-758 made four more combat patrols in the war, with little to show for them. In September 1943, it took part in the attack on Convoy ON202 in which several U-boats fired Zaunkönig torpedoes for the first time. Manseck, Beisheim, and the other U-758 crewmen long claimed to have sunk a freighter and the Polish-crewed destroyer *ORP Borkan* with a pair of Zaunkönigs, but the official British after-action report concluded that both shots had missed. After a fifth patrol in December 1943 brought no success, U-758 and other boats scrambled to sea in June 1944 to serve as a defense against enemy warships heading to France as part of the Normandy invasion. Facing an overwhelming Allied air and sea presence, they spent nine days cowering on the English Channel seabed.

U-758's last patrol was a final exercise in futility. Equipped with a new snorkel and with a new commander aboard, Oberleutnant zur See Hans-Arend Feindt, the boat attempted to hunt Allied ships near the Bristol Channel separating southern England and Ireland. They found nothing. After fifty-eight days at sea, U-758 returned to Norway. Two weeks after that, Oberleutnant Feindt brought his aging and battered U-boat into the Baltic, where it rested at pierside for five months before being decommissioned.

Beisheim and most of the crew of U-758 ended the war ashore, serving in a land-based tank destroyer unit as the British Army swept across northern Germany in late March and early April 1945. After Germany surrendered on May 8, the sailors were confined in a detention camp until finally being released in August 1945. Returning home to Edith Wauer Beisheim, whom he had married on leave in July 1943, Martin Beisheim quietly celebrated one accomplishment that the vast majority of U-boat sailors had failed to achieve. He, Kapitänleutnant Manseck, and his fellow crewmen had survived.[22]

ALTHOUGH GERMANY, for all practical purposes, lost the Battle of the Atlantic in May 1943, the decision by Hitler and Dönitz to fight to the end kept Allied sailors and merchant seamen at their battle stations. Because of the Allies' ongoing need to dispatch troops and military hardware to the United Kingdom and liberated French ports after D-Day, the Allied sailors and airmen who had prevailed on the northern convoy runs would endure two more years of arduous service. The merchant seamen would continue to sail in protected convoys until the German capitulation.

Escort Group B-7 continued to escort North Atlantic convoys for four months after Dönitz called off his wolf packs on May 24, 1943. Between June 9 and September 28, the seven warships ferried six convoys totaling 342 merchant ships without a single loss. Then, in October of 1943, Commander Peter Gretton persuaded Admiral Horton and his staff to let B-7 serve as a hunter-killer support group. For three weeks, the destroyers *Duncan* and *Vidette*, frigate *Tay*, and corvettes *Loosestrife, Pink, Snowflake,* and *Sunflower* supported four westbound ON and ONS convoys and one eastbound HX convoy during the U-boat Force's abortive attempt to resume attacks in the North Atlantic in September. None of the U-boat attacks succeeded, however, and Gretton's warships sank two U-boats during the battles, while the *Duncan* itself rescued two survivors from a third U-boat destroyed by an Allied patrol aircraft. Also during that period, Lieutenant Atkinson's crew in the corvette *Pink* conferred further distinction upon B-7 by rescuing the survivors of a VLR Liberator that a U-boat had shot down during an attempted attack on a convoy.

In the spring of 1944, as part of a naval reorganization in preparation for the Normandy invasion set for June 6, Western Approaches Command disbanded Escort Group B-7. Commander Gretton found himself in a shore billet at Admiralty headquarters, while his subordinate captains and their ships proceeded to new assignments. By war's end, Gretton and his six fellow B-7 commanders—Lieutenant Raymond Hart of the *Vidette*, Lieutenant-Commander Robert E. Sherwood of the *Tay*, Lieutenant Robert Atkinson of the *Pink*, Lieutenant Herbert A. Stonehouse of the *Loosestrife*, Lieutenant Harold Chesterman of the *Snowflake*, and Lieutenant-Commander James Plomer of the *Sunflower*—had racked up a total of fifteen U-boat kills, giving B-7 the second-highest score in the Allied services.[23]

After V-E Day on May 8, 1945, three of B-7's warship commanders continued their naval careers, but the majority demobilized to return to civilian life. Commander Peter Gretton chose to remain in the Royal Navy, rising to the rank of vice-admiral before his retirement in May 1963. He had survived and earned recognition from his Royal Navy peers, but he and his family had not escaped the war unscathed. Gretton's younger brother, Richard, had been serving as an officer in the British 18th Cavalry in 1941 when the Afrika Korps overran his unit near Tobruk, Libya. Richard Gretton was killed in a firefight, and his body was never recovered.[24]

Like Peter Gretton, Lieutenant Raymond Hart on the destroyer *Vidette* and Lieutenant James Plomer on the *Sunflower* also continued to serve in the Royal Navy after the end of the war. Hart left the *Vidette* in March 1944 but served as commander of two other warships: the destroyer *Havelock* from Convoy SC122 fame and the frigate *HMS Conn*. While serving in those warships, Hart sank another three U-boats, bringing his personal tally to seven. Hart remained on active duty after the war, retiring as a captain in January 1963. Lieutenant Plomer left the *Sunflower* in March 1944, but remained on active duty in the Royal Canadian Navy after V-E Day. During the early 1950s, he commanded the Canadian aircraft carrier *HMCS Bonaventure*, finally retiring as a captain in September 1962.

The other B-7 commanders opted to pursue careers outside the military. Lieutenant-Commander Robert Sherwood stepped down as commander of the *Tay* on June 25, 1945, relieved by his Escort Group B-7 comrade Robert Atkinson, who by then was an acting lieutenant-commander. After six months as executive officer of a Royal Navy air station, Sherwood left active service and returned to the civilian merchant fleet as a master on the British Railways shipping line. Atkinson left active duty that year as well, but remained in the Royal Navy Reserve, retiring in 1955. After obtaining a postgraduate degree in mathematics, he embarked on a wide-ranging career in marine engineering, steel manufacturing, and later in merchant banking that culminated with an appointment as chairman of the nationalized firm British Shipbuilders during 1980–84. Atkinson presided over twenty-three separate shipyards and 67,500 employees. Like Gretton, Atkinson's family had felt the acute sorrow of wartime loss. All four Atkinson brothers—Robert, Nicholas, Raymond, and Norman—

had gone to sea, two in the merchant fleet and another in the navy. Only Robert survived.[25]

Lieutenant Harold Chesterman left the *Snowflake* in September 1943 to take command of another corvette, *HMS Hurst Castle*. A year later, in 1944, he served a tour ashore, but had one more wartime command, the destroyer *HMS Ambuscade*, from February until July 1945. After the war, Chesterman returned to his native Australia, where he served in the Royal Australian Lifeboat Service before retiring as a captain in 1972. Lieutenant Herbert Stonehouse, who had repaired the *Loosestrife's* reputation upon taking command from the corvette's previous commander in 1943, left the ship to command a newer vessel, the Castle-class corvette *HMS Alnwick Castle*, until December 30, 1945. After a five-month postwar command of a third corvette, *HMS Oakham Castle*, Stonehouse left the Royal Navy and also returned to Australia. He later commanded a civilian lighthouse service ship, the *Cape Leeuwin*.

While the Atlantic Convoy Conference in Washington, D.C. had turned over the northern convoy routes to the British and Canadian navies at the end of March 1943, a number of Americans found themselves still engaged in the Battle of the Atlantic after the reorganization. Ensign John M. Waters and the Coast Guard cutter *Ingham* left the northern convoy routes after the ship's intervention with Convoy SC122 on March 19, 1943. However, the *Ingham* and its proud crew remained active in the next phase of the battle along the Central Atlantic convoy routes connecting Hampton Roads and Gibraltar. For most of the following year, the Coast Guard cutter escorted merchant ships from the U.S. East Coast to North Africa. Waters left the *Ingham* in the fall of 1944 to serve on a navy troopship in the Pacific. Six months later, he assumed command of the destroyer escort *USS Savage*, on which he patrolled the Aleutians and along the East Asia coastline until the spring of 1946. He remained on active duty after the war, becoming an aviator and expert on search-and-rescue operations. Retiring as a captain in 1968, Waters became the first director of public safety for the city of Jacksonville, Florida, and later was a professor at the University of Florida. In his retirement, Waters led a group of the *Ingham* veterans who successfully lobbied Congress to have the cutter, which had remained operational until 1988, designated as a Coast Guard museum ship and the service's World War II memorial.[26]

Most of the merchant seamen and Allied sailors who participated in the climax of the Battle of the Atlantic went on to have varied and diverse wartime experiences. After his return from survivor's leave in Kansas, granted after the U-527 had torpedoed the *Mathew Luckenback* in Convoy HX229, Signalman 3rd Class John Orris Jackson resumed his duties with various Naval Armed Guard detachments. Between May 8, 1943 and September 25, 1945, he made twenty-six Atlantic crossings on more than two dozen different merchant vessels and navy ships. Jackson and his Armed Guard detachment were at sea en route to France to bring home several thousand soldiers from the 6th Armored Division when a message arrived announcing the Japanese surrender on September 2, 1945. Five weeks later, having made thirty-eight separate convoy runs, Jackson left the Brooklyn Naval Armed Guard Center for the last time with a one-way train ticket back to Kansas and civilian life.[27]

Unlike Jackson, Signalman 3rd Class Ted Schorr continued to sail on the same merchant ship for most of his wartime service. He and his Naval Armed Guard detachment remained on the freighter *El Mundo* for the next eighteen months, making twelve Atlantic transits between New York and the British Isles, as well as one round-trip to Venezuela. Between September 1944 and May 1945, he served on two more merchantmen but experienced no U-boat attacks. Discharged in December 1945, Schorr came home to western Pennsylvania with plans to re-enlist in the peacetime navy but ended up returning to the steel mills in Duquesne and never went back to sea.[28]

Like Jackson and Schorr, British merchant seaman Deane Wynne remained at sea for the rest of the war. After the sinking of the *Kingsbury* on March 17, he found work on several British coastal freighters and later transferred to the seagoing salvage tug branch. He made several trans-Atlantic crossings in the tug *Samsonia*, then joined the tug *Assiduous* after the invasion of Normandy. For the next year, he and his fellow crewmen hauled various barges of cargo between the eastern Mediterranean and Indonesia. After a brief illness requiring hospitalization in Ceylon, Wynne joined a third tug, the *Cheerly*, and was serving there when the war in Europe ended. After Japan's surrender four months later, Wynne and several thousand British seamen returned to England on the aircraft carrier *HMS Victorious*. In 1948, after a three-year stint in the merchant navy,

Wynne settled in Australia for another three years, then joined a merchant freighter as fifth engineer to catch a final ride back to England. It was, he later wrote, "the end of my seagoing career."

However, it wasn't the end of Wynne's maritime work. In 1949, Wynne and a friend acquired a forty-foot Dutch herring boat called the *Valkyrien*, and plied the coastal waters of the East Sussex coast, selling their catch from a three-wheeled motorcycle van. Wynne's fishing venture ended as the inadvertent result of a sudden windfall: the British Lion Film Corporation hired Wynne and the *Valkyrien* to appear in a movie based on the 1949 novel, *Green Grow the Rushes*, co-starring a very young Richard Burton as a smuggler's apprentice. During the last day of shooting, the director asked Wynne to go back out in the English Channel for a final round of filming; a sudden storm blew in, waves flooded the engine, and Wynne—alone on the boat—managed to raise its huge lug mainsail. Wynne made it safely back to the bay outside the small Sussex port of Rye, but when the tide receded, the waves pounded the boat's keel on the seabed until it broke, leaving the vessel a total loss. As a result, Deane Wynne proceeded on to several land-based careers.[29]

ON MONDAY, APRIL 30, 1945, with Russian soldiers just several hundred yards away from his underground Führerbunker beneath the Reich Chancellery Building in Berlin, Adolf Hitler sat in his private study gazing at the corpse of his newly wedded wife, Eva Braun. She had committed suicide by taking cyanide. The fifty-six-year-old German dictator then picked up his Walther PPK pistol, placed it against his right temple, and pulled the trigger.

Hitler's suicide triggered the last degraded chapter of the Third Reich and left Grossadmiral Karl Dönitz to complete a final task that he had begun in January 1945. Dönitz had known of mass killings of German civilians by the Red Army in East Prussia as far back as late 1944. With the Red Army steadily advancing west, Dönitz assembled a motley fleet of merchant ships, the few remaining German surface warships, and several dozen U-boats with a mission to evacuate as many German civilians as possible from the approaching Russians. As Germany's war effort ground to a halt and the U-boat war was sputtering out, Dönitz desperately worked to continue the evacuation. Remarkably, 2,020,000 soldiers and refugees were able to flee what would become the Soviet zone of occupation—and later, communist East Germany—in Grossadmiral Dönitz's homemade Dunkirk. With a single gunshot, however, the Führer had now left Dönitz in charge of much more than just the evacuation.[30]

Adolf Hitler had named Grosssadmiral Karl Dönitz his successor as Führer. Dönitz was in a meeting with other German leaders in the town of Plön near the Baltic seacoast when he learned the news. An aide handed him a decrypted message from Hitler's aide Martin Bormann at the Führerbunker in Berlin:

GRAND ADMIRAL DÖNITZ: THE FUHRER HAS APPOINTED YOU, HERR ADMIRAL, AS HIS SUCCESSOR IN PLACE OF REICHSMARSCHALL GÖRING. CONFIRMATION IN WRITING FOLLOWS. YOU ARE HEREBY AUTHORIZED TO TAKE ANY MEASURES WHICH THE SITUATION DEMANDS.

"I assumed," Dönitz later wrote, "that Hitler had nominated me because he wished to clear the way to enable an officer of the Armed Forces to put an end to the war." But Dönitz was mistaken. Hitler had wanted him to continue Germany's *Götterdämmerung* and to lead the nation in a fight to the death, until nothing remained of the Third Reich or its people but ashes. With Hitler's death, however, the dictator's intentions were irrelevant.

Two days after assuming command of the Reich, Dönitz began taking steps to end the war. He relocated Germany's rump government from Berlin to the Naval Academy near Flensburg close to the Danish border. Dönitz dispatched emissaries to the Allied commanders to propose surrendering as many German soldiers as possible to the Americans and British, but not the Russians. But Dönitz's pleas hit a brick wall: Supreme Allied Commander General Dwight D. Eisenhower flatly refused his request, insisting on a simultaneous unconditional surrender to the American, British, and Russian armies.[31]

On May 5, 1945, the grossadmiral transmitted a final message to his U-boat crews at sea, ordering a cease-fire and instructing them to await subsequent instructions for surrendering. He praised them for waging "an heroic fight that knows no equal." Aboard 396 operational U-boats at sea and in port, commanders read out their final orders of the war:

My U-boat men! Six years of U-boat warfare lie behind us. You have fought like lions. A crushing material superiority has compressed us into a very narrow area. A continuation of the struggle is impossible from the bases that remain.

After signing the documents of surrender, Dönitz was arrested and would be put on trial at Nuremberg. He and Grossadmiral Erich Räder, his predecessor as Kriegsmarine commander-in-chief, were charged with: (1) plotting to wage aggressive war, (2) waging aggressive war via the U-boats, and (3) war crimes stemming from several incidents at sea where U-boat commanders were later accused of murdering civilian seamen. Although convicted on all three counts, Dönitz benefited from an aggressive defense. His lawyers obtained a written interrogatory from Pacific Command Admiral Chester W. Nimitz that itemized the harsh tactics American submarines had employed against Japanese merchant ships. At one point during the proceedings, American Judge Francis A. Biddle declared, "Germany waged a much cleaner [submarine] war than we did." Despite sworn denials by Dönitz, Godt, and Hessler that BdU had ever ordered U-boat commanders to kill civilian mariners, seven out of the ten judges voted to convict Dönitz on the third count. In the end, however, the Nuremberg Tribunal gave Dönitz a ten-year sentence, the lightest of all for the twenty-two Nazi leaders who survived the conflict.[32]

Years later, writing his memoirs while serving his ten years at Spandau prison, Dönitz reflected on his career. He noted how for the second time he had fought on the losing side of a war and found himself a prisoner of the enemy. His final observation, delivered with a pedantic deadpan tone, almost comes across as a joke. Referring to the belated introduction of the Type XXI and XXIII U-boats, he wrote, "The new effectiveness of the German U-boat was cut short by the German capitulation, which had become inevitable through the occupation by the enemy of the whole German area." Even in defeat, the admiral had a lingering faith in his fallen U-boat Force.[33]

WHILE THE ALLIES had wrested the initiative from the U-boat Force in the critical turning point in May 1943, the Battle of the Atlantic did not end then; it raged from September 3, 1939 until May 7, 1945, lasting 2,073 days. It was the deadliest naval clash of arms in history. In all theaters of war, the U-boats sank over 3,500 merchant ships totaling 13.5 million tons of shipping, as well as 175 warships or armed auxiliaries. Tens of thousands of merchant seamen, military personnel, and civilian passengers perished. The U-boat men suffered even more.[34]

From the outset of the war, both sides knew that the Atlantic would be the pivotal battlefield that would determine victory or defeat on the Continent. In early 1942, British Admiral Sir Max Horton had written, "Control of the sea is vital to the British Empire. If we lose it, we lose the war." Grossadmiral Karl Dönitz, in launching his *guerre de course*, agreed. As he later wrote, "As long as their island home and their vital [sea] lines of communications were not in mortal danger, the British would see no reason to end the war. . . . We had, I felt, no option but to go on fighting this war against the greatest sea power in the world." Britain's maritime trade, the admiral knew, was responsible for "the very life of the British nation."[35]

Everyone involved in the Battle of the Atlantic, from German U-boat men like Martin Beisheim to Allied escort officers like Peter Gretton, Robert Sherwood, and John Waters, knew what was at stake. They knew that victory and defeat, life and death, would be determined on the open ocean before the grisly end game of the war could play out on land. The men involved in this struggle knew that the repercussions of their actions would be felt for years to come, and they committed themselves accordingly. Their bravery and morale held out until the end—and it was ultimately because of this resolve that their long fight was the bloodiest in naval history. There was, quite simply, no alternative.

ACKNOWLEDGMENTS

I am indebted to many people whose support and help made the research and writing of this book possible.

First and foremost, I would like to thank my wife, Karen Conrad, for her encouragement and assistance in many roles—loving spouse, travel companion, research associate and stern editor. Our daughters, Elaine and Andrea, also provided their love and support.

I also want to express my deepest gratitude to the team at Perseus Books Group and its imprint, Basic Books, for embracing this project, particularly Editorial Director Lara Heimert and Associate Editor Alex Littlefield, two of the finest editors an author could have. They and the rest of the people at Perseus/Basic Books—particularly, Perseus President and CEO David Steinberger, Basic Publisher John Sherer, and Perseus VP Group Managing Editor Robert Kimzey—have created an organization that brings out the best in those writers with whom they work. I also want to thank copy editor Norman MacAfee for his diligent effort to polish and improve my writing.

My talented agent, Deborah Grosvenor, introduced me to Basic Books several years ago, and for that I am forever in her debt.

This book is about the climactic turning point in the Battle of the Atlantic, but in the end it is a series of stories about the people on both sides who fought it. Given that the events recalled here occurred nearly seven decades ago, the challenge was to breathe life into their experiences through detailed research and a comprehensive review of previously written memoirs and histories. Two very pleasant surprises occurred as I set out on this path.

First, I discovered a number of veterans of that great maritime struggle who are still alive and well so many years after the war, and I want to give special thanks to them for recounting experiences that remain vivid in their memories: Former U-758 radioman Martin Beisheim, U.S. Naval Armed Guard signalmen Ted Schorr and John Orris Jackson, and Royal Navy Lieutenant (now Sir) Robert Atkinson, who commanded the corvette HMS Pink.

Many other participants in the convoy fights that this book recounts have long since passed, but I was the beneficiary of both their published memoirs and the official narrative reports they compiled in the course of their wartime service. These included then–Royal Navy Commander Peter W. Gretton, then–U.S. Coast Guard Ensign John M. Waters, and former British merchant sailor Deane Wynne. Thanks to family members of some of these men, I was able to delve deeper into their lives than their printed words would allow. My thanks to Vice-Admiral Michael Gretton, RN (Ret.), who provided me a wealth of information on the Gretton family. Likewise, Dr. Stephen Waters, M.D., allowed me access to his father's personal papers. Richard Wynne was also helpful in providing additional details of his father's experiences.

The second pleasant surprise I experienced in researching this book was to discover a tight community of World War II history buffs who have made the Battle of the Atlantic and the U-boat Force their center of focus. This network of researchers and experts welcomed me with open arms when I asked for help and frequently went the extra mile to help me chase down an elusive fact or when I struggled to reconcile one of the many contradictory accounts of battle that are inevitable in the fog of war. In Germany, journalist Dirk Pohlmann was a stout colleague who helped me locate and obtain vital information from the World War II U-boat Force archives and tracked down U-758 survivor Martin Beisheim. In London, researcher Tony Cooper diligently helped me locate information and photographs that I initially despaired of ever finding. In Victoria, B.C., the second-most-beautiful small city in the world, retired Captain Jerry Mason, USN freely provided knowledge and background about numerous U-boat technical details and shared his own English translations of several U-boat daily war diaries vital to this book that otherwise I would never have seen.

In addition, I need to salute those who have made the fruits of their long research available at several Web sites dedicated to the Battle of the Atlantic, World War II convoys, and the U-boat Force. In particular, I want to thank Icelander Gudmundur Helgason at uboat.net for creating a massive yet user-friendly online archive available to public access. Equally valuable is the Web site uboatarchive.com, whose founder I've already thanked once, Captain Jerry Mason. He has assembled a comprehensive online library that includes the daily war diaries of U-boat Force Head-quarters and a growing list of operational U-boats, as well as formal Allied after-action reports on key U-boat sinkings. Anyone searching for details on particular Allied convoys and the ships that sailed in them will find an easy task thanks to two separate Web sites dedicated to that subject. In an Anglo-American partnership that mirrors the wartime cooperation across the Atlantic, Mike Holdoway, Tony Cooper (thanks again!), and Don Kindell have taken the archive of more than 18,400 Allied convoys com-piled by the late Lieutenant-Commander Arnold Hague, RN (Ret.), and placed it online at convoyweb.org.uk. In Norway, Ms. Siri Lawson Holm has created a comprehensive roster of Allied convoys and related historical data on the Web site warsailors.com. I also wish to thank researchers Can-dace Clifford in Alexandria, Virginia and Owen Cooke in Ottawa, Canada for their help in searching the American and Canadian national archives, respectively.

The Battle of the Atlantic, of course, is a much-told tale, and I was the beneficiary of the hard work that other historians, writers, and veterans have done. I have cited them in the Bibliography for this book. However, if there is one historian whom anyone attempting to write about the U-boats in World War II must acknowledge, it is the late Clay Blair. A U.S. Navy submariner during the war, he later became a prolific writer on mil-itary subjects, and his crowning work was the two-volume encyclopedic history *Hitler's U-boat War*, which remains the most comprehensive ac-count of the U-boat Force from its inception in 1936 until V-E Day. Blair donated his massive personal U-boat archive, assembled over a decade, to the American Heritage Center at the University of Wyoming, where archivists Ginny Kilander, John Waggener, and their colleagues were most helpful to a visiting journalist. Go 'Pokes!

Also, I want to again thank the folks at the Internet-based travel site Indo.com for use of their marvelous latitude-longitude calculator, which transforms the tedious and frustrating effort of computing distances and directions for events at sea into a simple and efficient routine (http://www.indo.com/distance/).

As ever, these people deserve a large share of the credit for this book. Responsibility for its accuracy, however, is mine alone.

Finally, a personal endnote: At the age of two, I moved to Newfoundland with my family when my father, an Air Force officer, received orders to Ernest Harmon Air Force Base. It was a magical place to be a child. I had no knowledge of World War II or the 1943 crisis of the Battle of the Atlantic that was then just seven years past, of course, but for the next three years I soaked up the essence of the North Atlantic: night skies brilliant with the shimmering fire of aurora borealis, leathery fishermen and lobstermen coming in with their catch at Corner Brook, September blizzards that painted the world white, and the rocky headlands above the gleaming, frigid ocean. My hunt through Web site archives, books, and faded microfilm accounts did more than educate me on the titanic struggle that had occurred on the North Atlantic convoy runs. It also awoke a stream of cherished childhood memories that I had long forgotten.

ED OFFLEY
Panama City Beach, Florida

CRITICAL CONVOY SHIPS, MARCH–MAY 1943

KEY:

Ship name in boldface = sunk
Year: when commissioned
Tons: displacement in gross tonnage
Fate: d/ = damaged by U-boat + date
  s/ = sunk by U-boat + date
K/S: killed/survivors

CONVOY SC122

Fifty ships departed New York March 6, 1943; six returned to NYC with storm damage; six detached to Halifax or St. John's; fourteen ships gained from HSC122 from Halifax; fifty-two ships in trans-Atlantic route; attacked by U-boats from wolf packs Gruppe Stürmer and Gruppe Dränger during March 16–19; nine ships sunk totaling 49,023 tons; zero U-boats sunk; guarded by British Escort Group B-5, March 12–23; joined by *USS Babbitt*, *USS (CG) Ingham* March 19–20; forty-three ships arrived Liverpool March 24.

Ship	Flag	Year	Tons	Cargo	Fate	K/S
NYC to Halifax						
Asbjorn	Canada	1935	4,733	Ballast	arrived Halifax 03/08/43	
Permian	Panama	1931	8,890	FFO	arrived Halifax 03/08/43	
NYC to St. John's						
Livingston	British	1928	2,140	General	returned 03/09/43	
Polarland	Norway	1923	1,591	General	returned 03/09/43	
Sevilla	British	1900	7,022	Fuel oil	arrived St. John's 03/12/43	
NYC to Iceland						
Alcedo	Panama	1937	1,392	General	returned Halifax 03/08/43	
Askepot	Norway	1937	1,312	Army supplies		
Cartago	USA	1908	4,732	Frig		
Eastern Guide	USA	1919	3,704	Ammunition	returned Halifax 03/08/43	
Godafoss	Iceland	1921	1,542	General		
Granville	Panama	1930	5,745	General	s/ U-338 03/17/43	13/34
Gudvor	Norway	1928	2,280	General	returned Halifax 03/08/43	
NYC to UK						
Alderamin	Dutch	1920	7,886	General, oil, seed	s/ U-338 03/17/43	15/49
Atland	Sweden	1910	5,203	Iron ore	arrived Loch Ewe	
Aymeric	British	1919	5,196	Iron ore	arrived Loch Ewe	
Baron Elgin	British	1933	3,942	Sugar	arrived Loch Ewe	
Baron Semple	British	1939	4,573	General	arrived Belfast/Loch Ewe	
Baron Stranraer	British	1929	3,668	Iron ore	arrived Loch Ewe	
Beaconoil	Panama	1919	6,893	Diesel oil	arrived Clyde	
Benedick	British	1920	9,503	Admiralty fuel	arrived Clyde	
Bonita	Panama	1918	4,929	Steel, tobacco	arrived U.K.	
Boston City	British	1920	2,870	General, explosives	arrived Belfast	
Bridgepool	British	1924	4,845	Linseed	arrived Loch Ewe	

Ship	Flag	Year	Tons	Cargo	Fate	K/S
Carras	Greece	1918	5,234	Wheat	d/ U-666 s/ U-333 03/19/43	00/31
Carso	British	1937	6,275	Steel, food	arrived Loch Ewe	
Christian Holm	Danish/Br	1927	9,119	Fuel oil	arrived Belfast	
Clarissa Radcliffe	British	1915	5,754	Iron ore	s/ U-663 3/18/43	55/00
Dolius	British	1924	5,507	Bauxite, general	arrived Belfast	
Empire Dunstan	British	1942	2,887	Sugar	arrived Liverpool	
Empire Galahad	British	1942	7,046	General, meat,	arrived Liverpool	
Empire Summer	British	1941	6,949	Explosives, 8 A/C	returned 03/09/43	
English Monarch	British	1924	4,557	Explosives, general	returned 03/09/43	
Filleigh	British	1928	4,856	General, mail	arrived Liverpool	
Fort Cedar Lake	British	1942	7,134	Explosives, general	d/ U-338 s/ U-665 03/17/43	00/50
Georgios P.	Greece	1903	4,052	Sugar	returned NYC 03/03/43	
Glenapp	British	1920	9,503	Africa produce	arrived Liverpool	
Gloxinia	British	1920	3,336	Lube oil	arrived Liverpool	
Historian	British	1924	5,074	General	arrived Liverpool	
Innesmoor	British	1928	4,392	Wheat	arrived Loch Ewe	
Kedoe	Dutch	1921	3,684	Wheat, zinc ore	arrived Belfast	
King Gruffydd	British	1919	5,072	Steel, explosives	s/ U-338 03/17/43	24/25
Kingsbury	British	1937	4,898	Produce, bauxite	s/ U-338 03/17/43	04/44
Losada	British	1921	6,520	General, mail	arrived Liverpool	
LST 305	USA	1943	1,490	Tanks, food	arrived Clyde	
LST 365	USA	1943	1,490	Tanks, food, steel	arrived Liverpool	
McKeesport	USA	1919	6,198	General, grain	returned NYC 03/08/43	
Orminister	British	1914	5,712	Iron ore	arrived Loch Ewe	
Shirvan	British	1925	2,870	Gasoline	arrived Belfast/Mersey	
Vinriver	British	1917	3,881	Sugar	arrived Loch Ewe	
Vistula	USA	1920	8,537	Petroleum	arrived Belfast	

Halifax to Iceland

Fjallfoss	Iceland	1919	1,451	Timber, food	arrived Reykjavik	
Selfoss	Iceland	1914	775	Timber	arrived Reykjavik	

Halifax to UK

Badjestan	British	1928	5,573	Grain	arrived Clyde	
Drakepool	British	1924	4,838	General	arrived Loch Ewe	
Empire Morn	British	1941	7,092	Grain	arrived U.K.	
Franka	Yugoslavia	1918	5,273	General	arrived Loch Ewe	
Helencrest	British	—	—	Grain	arrived Belfast	
Ogmore Castle	British	1919	2,481	Flour	arrived Loch Ewe	
Parkhaven	Dutch	1920	4,803	General	arrived Loch Ewe	
PLM 13	British	1921	3,754	Steel, lumber	returned St. John's	
Polarland	Norway	1923	1,591	General	returned 03/09/43	
Porjus	Sweden	1906	2,965	Steel, pulp	arrived Mersey	
Port Auckland	British	1928	8,789	Frig; general	s/ U-305 03/17/43	08/110
Zamalek	British	1921	1,567	None	Rescue Ship	
Zouave	British	1930	4,256	Iron ore	s/ U-305 03/17/43	13/30

St. John's to UK

Reaveley	British	1940	4,998	None given	arrived Mersey	

CONVOY HX229

Departed New York March 8, 1943; forty ships attacked by U-boats from wolf packs Gruppe Raubgraf, Gruppe Stürmer, and Gruppe Dränger during March 16–19; thirteen ships totaling 93,502 tons sunk; one U-boat sunk (U-384); guarded by British Escort Group B-4 March 11–22, with three individual ships augmenting the escort March 18–19; arrived Liverpool March 23.

Ship	Flag	Year	Tons	Cargo	Fate	K/S
Abraham Lincoln	Norway	1929	5,740	General	arrived Belfast	
Antar	British	1941	7,742	General	arrived Mersey	
Belgian Gulf	Panama	1929	8,401	Lub Oil	arrived Mersey	
Canadian Star	British	1939	8,293	Frig	s/ U-221 03/18/43	34/59
Cape Breton	British	1940	6,044	Linseed	arrived Clyde	
City of Agra	British	1936	6,361	General, explosives	arrived Mersey	
Clan Matheson	British	1919	5,613	General	returned Halifax 03/12/43	
Coracero	British	1923	7,252	Frig	d/ U-384 s/ U-631 03/17/43	06/51
Daniel Webster	USA	1942	7,176	General	arrived Belfast	
El Mundo	Panama	1910	6,008	General	arrived Belfast/Newport	
Elin K.	Norway	1937	5,214	Manganese, wheat	s/ U-603 03/16/43	00/40
Empire Cavalier	British	1942	9,891	Burning oil	arrived Mersey	
Empire Knight	British	1942	7,244	General	arrived Clyde	
Fort Anne	British	1942	7,134	Lead, lumber	arrived Loch Ewe	
Gulf Disc	USA	1938	7,141	FFO	arrived Clyde	
Harry Luckenbach	USA	1919	6,366	General	s/ U-91 03/17/43	80/00
Hugh Williamson	USA	1942	7,176	General	arrived destination	
Irénée Du Pont	USA	1941	6,125	General, oil	d/ U-600 s/ U-91 03/17/43	24/70
James Oglethorpe	USA	1942	7,176	General, A/C	d/ U-758 s/ U-91 03/17/43	44/30
Jean	USA	1918	4,902	General	arrived Mersey	
Kaipara	British	1938	5,882	Frig	arrived Mersey	
Kofreisi	USA	1920	4,934	Stores	arrived Mersey	
Luculus	British	1929	6,546	Petrol	arrived Belfast	
Magdala	Dutch	1931	8,248	Avgas	arrived Belfast	
Margaret Lykes	USA	1919	3,537	Grain, general	arrived Mersey	
Mathew Luckenbach	USA	1918	5,848	General	d/ U-527 s/ U-523 03/19/43	00/68
Nariva	British	1920	8,714	Frig	d/ U-600 s/ U-91 03/17/43	00/94

Ship	Flag	Year	Tons	Cargo	Fate	K/S
Nebraska	British	1920	8,261	Frig	arrived Mersey	
Nicania	British	1942	8,179	Petrol	arrived Mersey	
Pan Rhode Island	USA	1941	7,742	Avgas	arrived Mersey	
Regent Panther	British	1937	9,556	Avgas	arrived Mersey	
Robert Howe	USA	1942	7,176	General	arrived Mersey	
San Veronica	British	1943	8,600	Petrol	arrived Mersey	
Southern Princess	British	1915	12,156	Fuel oil	s/ U-600 03/17/43	06/94
Stephen C. Foster	USA	1943	7,196	Sugar, stores	returned 03/13/43	
Tekoa	British	1922	8,695	Frig, general	arrived Mersey	
Terkoelei	Dutch	1923	5,158	Wheat, zinc	d/ U-384 s/ U-631 03/17/43	36/00
Walter Q. Gresham	USA	1943	7,191	Food	s/ U-221 03/18/43	28/42
William Eustis	USA	1943	7,196	Sugar	d/ U-435 s/ U-91 03/17/43	00/72
Zaanland	Dutch	1921	6,813	Frig, wheat, zinc	s/ U-758 03/17/43	00/53

Note: A third convoy, HX229A, was formed at New York at the same time as HX229 and SC122, consisting of twenty-eight ships that departed on March 9, 1943 under local escort; six were destined for Halifax and two for St. John's; three ships returned to port with storm damage; sixteen more ships joined from Halifax and one from St. John's, making a total of thirty-four vessels making the trans-Atlantic crossing protected by British Escort Group 40 beginning on March 15. HX229A took a far northerly route to Great Britain, eluding the U-boat wolf packs in mid-ocean; one ship, the 14,795-ton British fuel tanker *Svend Foyn*, sank after striking an iceberg on March 19, resulting in the drowning deaths of 43 crewmen and passengers from a total complement aboard of 195; rest of convoy safely arrived Liverpool on March 26.

CONVOY ONS5

Departed Liverpool April 21, 1943; forty-five ships including two escort oilers; joined by Escort Group B-7 off Oversay on April 22; one ship returned with defects; two more ships detached April 26; attacked by wolf packs Gruppe Star (during April 28–30) and Gruppes Fink, Amsel 1 and Amsel 2 (May 4–6); 13 ships sunk totaling 61,958 tons; six U-boats sunk + two more sunk en route homeport + seven damaged; guarded by British Escort Group B-7 April 22–May 7; reinforced by British 3rd and 1st Support Groups May 2–7; arrived Halifax May 12 (less several stragglers).

Ship	Flag	Year	Tons	Cargo	Fate	K/S
Agios Georgios	Greece	1911	4,248	Unk; prob in ballast*	arrived Halifax	
Argon	USA	1920	6,952	Oil	arrived Halifax	
Baron Elgin	British	1933	3,942	Unk; prob in ballast	arrived Halifax	
Baron Graham	British	1925	3,242	Unk; prob in ballast	arrived Halifax	
Baron Semple	British	1939	4,573	Unk; prob in ballast	arrived Halifax	
Bengkalis	Dutch	1918	6,453	Unk; prob in ballast	arrived Halifax	
Berkel	Dutch	1930	2,130	Unk; prob in ballast	arrived Halifax	
Bonde	Norway	1936	1,570	Coal	s/ U-266 05/05/43	14/12
Bornholm	British	1930	3,177	Unk; prob in ballast	arrived Halifax	
Bosworth	British	1919	6,672	Unk; prob in ballast	arrived Halifax	
Bristol City	British	1920	2,864	General cargo	s/ U-358 05/05/43	15/34
British Lady	British	1923	6,098	Oil	arrived Halifax	
Campus	British	1925	3,667	Unk; prob in ballast	arrived Halifax	
Comm. Dorise	British	1917	5,529	Unk; prob in ballast	arrived Halifax	
Cydonia	British	1927	3,517	Unk; prob in ballast	arrived Halifax	
Director	British	1926	5,107	Unk; prob in ballast	arrived Halifax	
Dolius	British	1924	5,507	In ballast	s/ U-638 05/05/43	04/66
Dunsley	British	1929	3,862	Unk; prob in ballast	arrived Halifax	
Empire Advocate	British	1913	5,787	Unk; prob in ballast	Returned Clyde	
Empire Gazelle	British	1920	4,848	Unk; prob in ballast	arrived Halifax	
Empire Planet	British	1923	4,290	Unk; prob in ballast	arrived Halifax	
Fana	Norway	1939	1,375	Unk; prob in ballast	arrived Halifax	
Gharinda	British	1919	5,306	In ballast	s/ U-266 05/05/43	00/92
Gudvor	Norway	1928	2,280	In ballast	arrived Halifax	
Harbury	British	1928	5,081	Coal	s/ U-628 05/05/43	07/42
Harperley	British	1933	4,586	Coal and mail	s/ U-264 05/05/43	10/38
Isobel	Panama	1929	1,515	Unk; prob in ballast	arrived Halifax	
Ivan Topic	Yugoslavia	1920	4,943	Unk; prob in ballast	arrived Halifax	
Lorient	British	1921	4,737	In ballast	s/ U-125 05/04/43	40/00
Lornaston	British	1925	4,934	Unk; prob in ballast	arrived Halifax	
Losada	British	1921	6,520	Unk; prob in ballast	arrived Halifax	

*Unk; prob in ballast = Unknown; probably in ballast

Ship	Flag	Year	Tons	Cargo	Fate	K/S
Mano	British	1925	1,418	Unk; prob in ballast	arrived Halifax	
Mckeesport	USA	1919	6,198	In ballast	s/ U-258 04/29/43	01/67
Merton	British	1941	7,150	Unk; prob in ballast	arrived Halifax	
Modlin	Poland	1906	3,569	Unk; prob in ballast	returned	
Nicolas	Greece	1910	4,540	Unk; prob in ballast	arrived Halifax	
North Britain	British	1940	4,635	Bricks and clay	s/ U-707 05/05/43	35/11
Omega	British	1912	3,788	Unk; prob in ballast	arrived Halifax	
Ottinge	British	1940	2,870	Unk; prob in ballast	arrived Halifax	
Penhale	British	1924	4,071	Unk; prob in ballast	straggled to Reykjavik	
Rena	Norway	1924	5,242	Unk; prob in ballast	arrived Halifax	
Sapelo	USA	1919	16,500	Unk; prob in ballast	arrived Halifax	
Selvistan	British	1924	5,136	In ballast	s/ U-266 05/05/43	06/40
Temple Arch	British	1940	5,138	Unk; prob in ballast	arrived Halifax	
Wentworth	British	1919	5,212	In ballast	s/ U-358 05/05/43	05/42
West Madaket	USA	1918	5,565	In ballast	s/ U-584 05/05/43	00/61
West Maximus	USA	1919	5,561	In ballast	s/ U-264 05/05/43	06/56
Yearby	British	1918	5,666	Unk; prob in ballast	arrived Halifax	

CONVOY SC130

Departed New York May 11, 1943; thirty-seven ships plus rescue ship; guarded by British Escort Group B-7 during May 15–25; attempted attacks by wolf pack Gruppen Donau 1 and Donau 2 during May 18–21; zero ships sunk; four U-boats sunk, one damaged; arrived Liverpool May 26; this was the last North Atlantic convoy to face a concerted U-boat threat prior to Admiral Dönitz's May 24 order canceling the U-boat offensive.

Ship	Flag	Year	Tons	Cargo	Fate
A.C. Bedford	USA	1918	9,485	Fuel oil	arrived United Kingdom
Amstel	Dutch	1925	2,115	Pulp	arrived United Kingdom
Beaconoil	British	1919	6,893	Sun Fuel	arrived United Kingdom
Benedick	British	1928	6,978	FFO	arrived United Kingdom
Bente Maersk	Danish	1928	5,722	Petrol	arrived United Kingdom
Calmar	USA	1920	5,787	Stores, explosives	arrived United Kingdom
Cathlamat	USA	1919	5,869	General	arrived United Kingdom
Cetus	Norway	1920	2,614	Pulp	arrived United Kingdom
Christine Marie	British	1919	3,895	General, ammunition	arrived United Kingdom
Colytto	Dutch	1926	4,408	Grain	arrived United Kingdom
Dalemoor	British	1922	5,835	Grain, general	arrived United Kingdom
Dallington Court	British	1929	6,889	Grain, general	arrived United Kingdom
Daylight	USA	1931	9,180	Fuel oil	arrived United Kingdom
Dynastic	USA	1919	5,773	General, explosives	arrived United Kingdom
E.G. Seubert	USA	1918	9,181	FFO, stores	arrived United Kingdom
Empire Melody	British	1942	2,883	Sugar	arrived United Kingdom
Empire Meteor	British	1940	7,457	Steel, lumber	arrived United Kingdom
Empire Spartan	British	1942	7,009	Steel, lumber	arrived United Kingdom
Empire Tristram	British	1942	7,167	Wheat, general	arrived United Kingdom
Estrella	Norway	1920	3,888	Grain, lumber	arrived United Kingdom
Exchester	USA	1919	4,999	General, stores	arrived United Kingdom
Fjalfoss	Iceland	1919	1,451	General	arrived United Kingdom
Fort Bedford	British	1943	7,127	General	arrived United Kingdom
Gitano	British	1921	3,956	General, explosives	arrived United Kingdom
Graiglas	British	1940	4,312	Steel, lumber	arrived United Kingdom
Henrik Ibsen	Norway	1906	4,671	Grain, general	arrived United Kingdom
Ingman	British	1907	3,169	Grain, general	arrived United Kingdom
Katla	Iceland	1911	1,209	General	arrived United Kingdom
Lagarfoss	Iceland	1904	1,211	General	arrived United Kingdom
Narbo	USA	1920	6,005	General	arrived United Kingdom
Olivebank	British	1926	5,154	General, explosives	arrived United Kingdom
Ravnefjell	Norway	1938	1,339	General	arrived United Kingdom
Sheaf Holme	British	1929	4,814	Steel, general	arrived United Kingdom
Stanlodge	British	1943	5,977	Grain, general	arrived United Kingdom
Tamaha	British	1914	6,946	FFO	arrived United Kingdom
West Honaker	USA	1920	5,428	Grain, general	arrived United Kingdom
Winona	USA	1919	6,197	Phospates	arrived United Kingdom
Zamalek	British	1921	1,565	Rescue Ship	arrived United Kingdom

Sources: Gretton, Peter, Vice Adm., RN (Ret), *Convoy Escort Commander*, Cassell, London, 1964; Middlebrook, Martin, *Convoy*, William Morrow, New York, 1976; Rohwer, Jürgen, *The Critical Convoy Battles of March 1943*, Naval Institute Press, Annapolis, MD, 1977; Syrett, David, *The Defeat of the German U-Boats: The Battle of the Atlantic*, University of South Carolina Press, Columbia, 1994; ConvoyWeb.org: Arnold Hague Convoy Database at http://www.convoyweb.org.uk/hague/index.html; North Atlantic Convoy Rosters at Warsailors.com; Convoy Battles roster and individual merchant ship records at Uboat.net.

NORTH ATLANTIC CONVOYS AT SEA, MARCH 1–MAY 24, 1943

KEY:

HX = NYC/Halifax-Liverpool: Eastbound Fast Convoy
SC = NYC/Halifax-Liverpool: Eastbound Slow Convoy
ON = Outbound North: Liverpool-NYC: Westbound Fast Convoy
ONS = Outbound North Slow: Liverpool/Halifax/Boston: Westbound Slow Convoy
Days: Days at sea
Depart: mm/dd/yy
Arrive: mm/dd/yy
Ship 1: No. of ships at departure
Ship 2: No. of ships arriving (includes ships to Iceland or Canada and stragglers)
SS s/: Ships sunk by U-boats
Tonnage: Tonnage of shipping safely arrived
Tons Lost: gross tonnage losses from U-boats or storm sinkings
UB s/: U-boats sunk
Escort: Convoy Escort Group
Reinforcement: Support Groups

Note: Outbound North (Slow) Convoys (ONS) shared the same numbering tabulation with faster Outbound North convoys until March 13, 1943, when they were split with the slower convoys now starting as ONS1, ONS2, etc. Also, westbound Convoy ON185 scheduled around May 20, 1943 was canceled, leaving a missing number in the roster.

	Convoy	Depart	From	Arrive	To	Days at Sea	Ship 1	Ship 2	SS s/
1	ON166	02/11/43	Liverpool	03/03/43	NYC	20	55	36	14
2	SC120	02/13/43	NYC	03/05/43	Liverpool	20	65	61	0
3	ON167	02/14/43	Liverpool	03/08/43	NYC	22	35	31	2
4	ONS168	02/21/43	Liverpool	03/12/43	Boston	19	60	49	2
5	ONS169	02/22/43	Liverpool	03/21/43	NYC	27	45	41	1
6	SC121	02/23/43	NYC	03/14/43	Liverpool	19	80	74	12
7	HX228	02/28/43	NYC	03/15/43	Liverpool	15	80	62	5
8	ON170	03/03/43	Liverpool	03/20/43	NYC	17	49	47	0
9	ONS171	03/04/43	Liverpool	03/23/43	Halifax	19	43	41	0
10	SC122	03/05/43	NYC	03/24/43	Liverpool	19	50	50	9
11	HX229	03/08/43	NYC	03/23/43	Liverpool	15	40	27	13
12	HX229A	03/09/43	NYC	03/26/43	Liverpool	17	45	39	0
13	ON172	03/09/43	Liverpool	03/27/43	NYC	18	15	13	0
14	ON173	03/13/43	Liverpool	03/29/43	Halifax	16	37	35	0
15	SC123	03/14/43	NYC	04/03/43	Liverpool	21	50	46	0
16	ONS1	03/15/43	Liverpool	04/04/43	Halifax	20	39	39	0
17	HX230	03/18/43	NYC	04/02/43	Liverpool	15	46	43	1
18	ON174	03/20/43	Liverpool	04/08/43	NYC	19	40	40	0
19	SC124	03/20/43	NYC	04/09/43	Liverpool	20	38	36	0
20	ON175	03/24/43	Liverpool	04/16/43	NYC	23	40	39	0
21	HX231	03/25/43	NYC	04/10/43	Liverpool	16	48	38	6
22	ONS2	03/28/43	Liverpool	04/19/43	Halifax	22	41	38	1
23	ON176	03/31/43	Liverpool	04/20/43	NYC	20	46	44	2
24	SC125	03/31/43	Halifax	04/15/43	Liverpool	15	40	35	0
25	HX232	04/01/43	NYC	04/16/43	Liverpool	15	47	44	4
26	ONS3	04/05/43	Liverpool	04/28/43	Halifax	23	23	20	2
27	HX233	04/06/43	NYC	04/21/43	Liverpool	15	58	56	1
28	ON177	04/06/43	Liverpool	04/23/43	NYC	17	27	27	0
29	SC126	04/08/43	Halifax	04/23/43	Liverpool	15	40	38	0
30	HX234	04/12/43	NYC	04/29/43	Liverpool	17	46	40	2
31	ON178	04/12/43	Liverpool	05/02/43	NYC	20	58	56	1
32	ONS4	04/13/43	Liverpool	05/05/43	Halifax	22	42	37	0
33	SC127	04/16/43	Halifax	05/03/43	Liverpool	17	56	56	0
34	HX235	04/18/43	NYC	05/05/43	Liverpool	17	40	35	0
35	ON179	04/18/43	Liverpool	05/06/43	NYC	18	54	52	0
36	ONS5	04/22/43	Liverpool	05/12/43	Halifax	21	46	31	13
37	HX236	04/24/43	NYC	05/09/43	Liverpool	15	45	45	0
38	ON180	04/24/43	Liverpool	05/14/43	NYC	20	64	59	0
39	SC128	04/25/43	Halifax	05/13/43	Liverpool	18	32	31	0
40	ONS6	04/29/43	Liverpool	05/17/43	Halifax	18	32	31	0
41	ON181	04/30/43	Liverpool	05/18/43	NYC	18	48	47	0
42	HX237	05/01/43	NYC	05/17/43	Liverpool	16	47	42	3
43	SC129	05/02/43	Halifax	05/21/43	Liverpool	19	25	23	2
44	ON182	05/06/43	Liverpool	05/22/43	NYC	16	53	52	0
45	HX238	05/07/43	NYC	05/22/43	Liverpool	15	44	42	0
46	ONS7	05/07/43	Liverpool	05/25/43	Halifax	18	50	47	1
47	ON183	05/10/43	Liverpool	05/25/43	NYC	15	32	30	0
48	SC130	05/11/43	Halifax	05/26/43	Liverpool	15	37	35	0
49	HX239	05/13/43	NYC	05/28/43	Liverpool	15	41	39	0
50	ON184	05/15/43	Liverpool	05/31/43	Liverpool	16	36	36	0
51	ONS8	05/17/43	Liverpool	06/01/43	Halifax	15	53	53	0
52	HX240	05/19/43	NYC	06/04/43	Liverpool	16	54	53	0
53	ON186	05/24/43	Liverpool	06/07/43	NYC	14	39	39	0

Sources: ConvoyWeb.org; Warsailors.com.; Uboat.net.

Tonnage	Tons Lost	Wolf Pack	UBs/	Escort	Reinforcement
247,738	88,001	Ritter		A-3	
313,699	0			B-7	
170,766	13,466			B-3	
350,862	13,713	Raubgraf		B-5	
216,836	3,355	Raubgraf		B-4	
256,782	55,661	Westmark, Ostmark		A-3	
566,130	24,175	Neuland, Westmark	2	B-3	6th SG (Bogue), 3/5–10
332,493	0	Raubgraf		B-2	
204,024	0			B-1	
248,923	53,094	Raubgraf, Sturmer, Dranger	0	B-5	
284,613	93,502	Raubgraf	1	B-4	
293,133	0		0	40th EG	
115,384	0			C-3	
256,530	0			B-7	
225,647	0			B-2	3rd SG, 6th SG (Bogue), 3/21–26
225,333	0			B-6	
317,122	7,176	Seeteufel	0	B-1	3rd SG, 3/29–31
287,780	0			B-3	
196,374	0			C-3	
248,438	0			A-3	
427,399	41,494	Löwenherz	2	B-7	4th SG, 4/6–8
164,218	3,835	Adler		C-1	
291,741	3,129	Adler		B-4	
168,291	0	Adler	0	B-6	
312,860	24,300	Adler, Lerche		B-3	4th SG, 4/12–15
106,781	10,403	Meise		40th EG	
384,710	7,131			A-3	3rd SG, 4/17–18
174,819	0			C-4	
200,774	0			B-5	3rd SG, 4/19–21
293,478	17,394	Meise		B-4	3rd SG, 4/25; 4th SG 4/15
351,789	3,025	Meise		B-1	5th SG (Biter), 4/13–15
205,286	0			B-2	5th SG (Biter), 4/23–26; 1st SG, 4/26–28
279,438	0	Specht		C-1	1st SG, 4/24–25; 3rd SG, 4/27–30 4th SG 4/27–30
263,501	0	Specht		C-4	6th SG (Bogue), 4/25–30
372,419	0			C-2	
149,257	61,958	Fink, Amsel 1, Amsel 2, Star	8	B-7	3rd SG, 5/2–6; 1st SG, 5/6–8
345,666	0			B-1	2nd SG, 5/1–5
425,696	0			C-3	
167,632	0			40th EG	
167,348	0			B-6	1st SG, 5/9-10, Archer 5/9–14
330,713	0			B-3	
312,400	21,389	Drossel		C-2	5th SG (Biter), 5/7–13
114,575	7,627	Drossel, Elbe 2		B-2	5th SG (Biter), 5/14–16
378,897	0			C-5	Archer, 5/12–14
319,141	0			C-3	
235,783	5,196		5	B-5	
215,424	0			B-4	
192,993	0	Donau	3	B-7	1st SG, 5–19–22
312,588	0	Mosel		B-3	4th SG (Archer), 5/21–24
248,475	0	Mosel		C-1	6th SG (Bogue), 5/19–25
237,724	0			C-4	2nd SG 5/22–25
410,995	0			C-5	
305,046	0			C-2	

GERMAN U-BOATS
OF WORLD WAR II

PART 1 – THE WORKHORSE U-BOATS

The Type VII and Type IX boats were the primary models used in the Battle of the Atlantic. The Type XIV "Milch Cow" was a specially designed tanker whose primary mission was to refuel other U-boats at sea to extend the length of their war patrols.

Type VII

General Characteristics (Type VIIC):

First Built: 1936
Total Commissioned: 568
Displacement: 781 tons surfaced; 885 tons submerged
Length: 220 feet 2 inches
Beam: 20 feet 4 inches
Draft: 15 feet 6 inches
Complement: 4 officers, 40–48 enlisted crewmen
Propulsion: 2 supercharged Germaniawerft or MAN 6-cylinder diesel motors; 2 AEG
   GU 460/8-276 electric motors
Speed: 17.7 knots surfaced; 7.6 knots submerged
Range: 8,190 nautical miles at 10 knots surfaced; 81 nautical miles at 4 knots
   submerged

Test depth: 750 feet

Armament: Five 21-inch torpedo tubes (4 bow, 1 stern); 14 torpedoes; 26 TMA mines or 39 TMB mines; One C35 88-mm deck gun with 220 rounds; later, 4-barrel 20-mm cannon

Type VII Variants, Number Built, and Notes:

VIIA: 10 built

VIIB: 24 built; additional fuel capacity (39 tons) extended range by 2,500 miles

VIIC: 568 built; slightly longer (1.64 feet) and heavier (16 tons) than the VIIB

VIIC/41: 91 built; a stronger pressure hull gave this model a test depth of 820 feet, 66 greater than the VIIC design

VIID: 6 built; hull extended 32 feet to incorporate 15 vertical tubes for launching mines

VIIF: 4 built; used as torpedo transport with capacity for up to 39 torpedoes; carried no deck guns

Notes: In June 1943, four VIIC U-boats were converted into "U-flak" boats carrying two 20-mm quadruple-barrel anti-aircraft guns and a 37-mm cannon to serve as escorts for other U-boats transiting the Bay of Biscay. The experiment was terminated in November 1943 and the four U-boats were converted back to the VIIC design.

Type IX

General Characteristics (Type IXC/40):

First Built: 1937

Total Built: 193

Displacement: 1,120 tons surfaced; 1,232 tons submerged

Length: 252 feet

Beam: 22 feet 8 inches

Draft: 15 feet 5 inches

Complement: 4 officers, 44–52 enlisted crewmen

Propulsion: 2 MAB supercharged 9-cvlinder diesel engines; 2 SSW electric motors

Speed: 19 knots surfaced; 7.3 knots submerged

Range: 25,620 nautical miles at 10 knots surfaced; 117 nautical miles submerged at 4 knots

Test depth: 656 feet

Armament: Six 21-inch torpedo tubes (4 bow and 2 stern); 22 torpedoes or 44 TMA/66 TMB mines; One 105-mm deck gun with 110 rounds; various secondary flak guns

Type IX Variants, Number Built and Notes:

IXA: 8 built

IXB: 14 built; range 2,775 nautical miles greater than IXA
IXC: 54 built; added fuel capacity provided maximum range of 25,620 nautical miles
IXC/40: 87 built; improved fuel capacity and 19-knot flank speed on surface
IXD: 30 built; hull lengthened to 287 feet to accommodate a second pair of diesel
engines; variants included IXD1, IXD2, and IXD/42

Type XIV

General Characteristics:

Modified Type IXD; no torpedo tunes installed; extra fuel tanks and storage capacity
enabled "Milch Cow" to provide 400 tons of diesel fuel, four torpedoes, and
fresh food to a deployed U-boat to extend its patrol
First Commissioned: 1941
Total Built: 10
Displacement: 1,695 tons surfaced; 1,932 tons submerged
Length: 220 feet 2 inches
Beam: 30 feet 8 inches
Height: 38 feet 5 inches
Draft: 21 feet 4 inches
Complement: 53–60
Propulsion: 2 Germaniawerft F46 supercharged 6-cylinder diesel motors;
2 SSW double-acting electric motors
Speed: 14.9 knots surfaced; 6.2 knots submerged
Range: 12,350 nautical miles at 10 knots surfaced; 55 nautical miles at
4 knots submerged
Test depth: 790 feet
Armament: Two 37-mm anti-aircraft guns; two 20-mm anti-aircraft guns

PART 2 – OTHER U-BOAT MODELS

Type II

General Characteristics (Type IIB):

Originally designed as a coastal patrol U-boat; used primarily in training U-boat crews
First Commissioned: 1935
Total Built: 51
Displacement: 283 tons surfaced; 333 tons submerged
Length: 140 feet 1 inch
Beam: 13 feet 5 inches
Height: 28 feet 3 inches
Draft: 12 feet 10 inches
Complement: 22-24
Propulsion: 2 MWM 8-cylinder diesel engines; 2 SSW double-acting electric motors

Speed: 13 knots surfaced; 7 knots submerged

Range: 2,700 nautical miles at 8 knots surfaced; 38 nautical miles at 4 knots submerged

Test depth: 490 feet

Armament: Three 21-inch torpedo tubes (2 bow, 1 stern), maximum 5 torpedoes

Notes: Four classes were built, the IIA, IIB, IIC, and IID, each successive model slightly longer and heavier than its predecessor.

Type XXI

General Characteristics: Known for its increased underwater operating capability.

First Built: 1943

Total Built: 118, although only 4 were rated as combat-ready before the war ended

Displacement: 1,621 tons standard; 2,100 tons fully loaded

Length: 251 feet 8 inches

Beam: 26 feet 3 inches

Height: 37 feet 2 inches

Draft: 17 feet 5 inches

Complement: 57

Propulsion: 2 MAN supercharged 6-cylinder diesel engines, 4 SSW electric motors (2 double-acting, 2 silent running)

Speed: 15.6 knots surfaced (on diesel), 17.9 knots surfaced on e-motors; 17.2 knots submerged (double-acting e-motors), 6.1 knots submerged (silent-running e-motors)

Range: 15,500 nautical miles at 10 knots surfaced; 340 nautical miles at 6.1 knots submerged

Test depth: 1,140 (design test depth)

Armament: Six 21-inch torpedo tubes (all in bow compartment), total 23 torpedoes or 17 torpedoes and 12 mines; Four 20-mm deck cannon

Notes: Innovations in design included a streamlined, clean hull design for high submerged speed allowing a sprint ability to position for attack without surfacing; three times the electric battery capacity of the Type VIIC; a new hydraulic torpedo-loading system allowed all 6 torpedo tubes to be reloaded in less time than a Type VIIC could reload a single tube; torpedo firing rate was 18 torpedoes in less than 20 minutes; Type XXI also featured a crew's shower and freezer to preserve foods.

Type XXIII

General Characteristics: Smaller "Electro-boat" design for coastal waters and the Mediterranean; hull design, battery capacity and snorkel permitted near-continuous submerged operations; built to replace the Type II U-boat

First Commissioned: June 12, 1944; first war patrol January 18, 1945

Total Built: 61 of 280 ordered

Displacement: 284 tons
Length: 113 feet 10 inches
Beam: 9 feet 10 inches
Draft: 12 feet 0 inches
Complement: 14–18
Propulsion: 1 MWM 6-cylinder diesel motor; 1 AEG double-acting electric motor; 1 BBC "creeping" electric motor
Speed: 9.7 knots surfaced; 12.5 knots submerged
Range: 2,600 nautical miles at 8 knots surfaced; 194 nautical miles at 4 knots submerged
Test depth: 590 feet
Armament: Two 21-inch bow torpedo tubes; maximum load 2 torpedoes
Note: Only 6 Type XXIII U-boats ever carried out a war patrol before the war ended.

Sources: Friedman, Norman, *Submarine Design and Development*, Naval Institute Press, Annapolis, MD, 1984; Worth, Richard, *Fleets of World War II*, Da Capo Press, New York, 2001; U-boat.net.

ESCORT WARSHIPS

KEY:

Displacement in short tons (2,000 lb.) for U.S., long tons (2,240 lb.) for British warships
AA = anti-aircraft gun
D/C = depth-charge racks
CVE = escort carrier
SHP = shaft horsepower

The following escort warship types participated in the critical convoy battles of Battle of the Atlantic in the spring of 1943 and the central Atlantic offensive of June–July 1943.

Selected ships in Class: Ships serving as escorts for Convoys SC122, HX229, ONS5 and SC130, and escort carriers operating in the Atlantic in early- to mid-1943.

BRITISH/CANADIAN ESCORT WARSHIPS

Long Island Class escort aircraft carrier

Constructed: 1941–42
Displacement: 15,120 tons
Length: 492 feet
Complement: 550 crewmen
Aircraft: 15 Martlet or Sea Hurricane fighters/Swordfish or Avenger bombers
Armament: 3 4/50 guns; 19 20mm AA guns
Maximum Speed: 16.5 knots
Engines/Power: Doxford diesel, 1 shaft; 8,500 SHP
Notes on Class: Constructed in the United States for the Royal Navy
Selected ships in Class: HMS Biter

D Class destroyer

Constructed: 1932–33
Displacement: 1,375 tons
Length: 329 feet
Complement: 145 crewmen
Armament: 4 4.7-inch guns; 2 AA, 8 21-inch torpedo tubes, D/C
Maximum Speed: 36 knots
Engines/Power: Geared turbines, 2 shafts; 36,000 SHP
Maximum Range: 5,870 miles at 15 knots
Notes on Class: Variant of B and C Classes; maximum range 5,500 miles at 15 knots;
   HMS Duncan was modified to be a flotilla leader, with a total complement of 175.
Selected ships in Class: HMS Duncan

E Class destroyer

Similar in overall specifications to the D Class; constructed 1934–35
Selected ships in Class: HMS Eclipse

F Class destroyer

Similar in overall specifications to the D Class
Selected ships in Class: HMS Fury

Havant Class destroyer

Constructed: 1939–40
Displacement: 1,340 tons
Length: 323 feet
Complement: 145 crewmen
Armament: 3 4.7-inch guns; 8 5-inch AA (2 x 4); 8 21-inch torpedo tubes; D/C
Maximum Speed: 36 knots
   Engines/Power: Geared turbines, 2 shafts; 38,000 SHP
Maximum Range: 5,530 miles at 15 knots
Notes on Class: Modified H Class, derivative of G Class; originally built for Brazil but
   transferred to Royal Navy in 1939
Selected ships in Class: HMS Harvester, HMS Havelock, HMS Hesperus, HMS Highlander

I Class destroyer

Notes on Class: Same as H Class destroyer with minor alterations; constructed 1937–
   38; HMS Inglefield converted to flotilla leader with 2 additional 4.7-inch guns,
   complement of 175
Selected ships in Class: HMS Inglefield, HMS Icarus, HMS Impulsive

O Class destroyer

Constructed: 1941–42
Displacement: 1,540 tons
Length: 345 feet
 Complement: 175 crewmen
Armament: 4 4.7-inch guns; 6 AA guns; 8 21-inch torpedo tubes; D/C
Maximum Speed: 37 knots
Engines/Power: Geared turbines, 2 shafts; 40,000 SHP
Maximum Range: 5,850 miles at 20 knots
Notes on Class: HMS Oribi had 5th 4.7-inch gun between stacks, 4 torpedo tubes
Selected ships in Class: HMS Offa, HMS Oribi

P Class destroyer

Similar in overall specifications to O Class
Selected ships in Class: HMS Panther, HMS Penn

Town Class destroyer
(ex-Clemson Class, ex-Wickes Class U.S. Navy destroyer)

	Clemson	Wickes
Constructed:	1917–20	1919
Displacement:	1,215 tons	1060 tons
Length:	314.5 feet	314.4 feet
Complement:	101 crewmen	149
Armament:	4 4-inch/.50-cal. guns; 1 3-inch gun; 12 torpedo tubes; D/C (both)	
Maximum Speed:	35 knots	
Engines/Power:	Geared turbines, 2 shafts; 27,000 SHP	
Maximum Range:	4,900 miles at 15 knots	

Notes on Class: 50 of these "flush deck" destroyers transferred to Royal Navy as part of
 the 1940 "destroyers for bases" agreement; Clemson Class a follow-on to the World
 War I–era Wickes Class destroyer with improved fuel capacity; considered inferior
 as a convoy escort because difficult to handle: narrow, V-shaped sterns made for a
 large turning radius at high speed; some armament removed to allow increased
 D/C capacity
Selected ships in Class: HMS Beverley (Wickes), HMS Mansfield (Clemson), HMS Ripley
 (Clemson)

V&W Class destroyer

Constructed: 1916–18
Displacement: 1,188 tons
 Length: 312 feet
Complement: 134 crewmen

Armament: 2 x 4-inch guns; 1 3-inch AA gun; 1 Hedgehog; D/C
Maximum Speed: 34 knots
Engines/Power: Geared turbines, 2 shafts; 30,000 SHP
Maximum Range: 3,500 miles at 15 knots
Notes on Class: To increase range, one boiler and funnel removed to provide increased fuel storage capacity; torpedo tubes removed to increase D/C capacity
Selected ships in Class: HMS Vega, HMS Vidette, HMS Vimy, HMS Volunteer, HMS Walker, HMS Warwick, HMS Winchelsea, HMS Witherington,

River Class frigate

Constructed: 1941–44
Displacement: 1,370 tons
Length: 301 feet
Complement: 140 crewmen
Armament: 2 x 4-inch guns; 10 20-mm guns (2 x 2, 6 x 1); 150 D/C; Hedgehog
Maximum Speed: 20 knots
Engines/Power: 2 shaft reciprocating; 5,500 SHP
Maximum Range: 7,500 miles at 12 knots
Notes on Class: Class constructed to augment Flower-class corvettes as convoy escorts
Selected ships in Class: HMS Jed, HMS Rother, HMS Spey, HMS Swale, HMS Tay, HMS Wear

Banff Class sloop (ex-USCG Lakes Class cutter)

Constructed: 1927–31
Displacement: 1,546 tons
Length: 250 feet
Complement: 200 crewmen
Armament: 1 5-inch/.51-cal. gun; 2 3-inch/.50-cal. guns; 4 20mm AA; D/C
Maximum Speed: 16 knots
Engines/Power: 2 boilers, single shaft
Maximum Range: n/a
Notes on Class: Considered inferior as convoy escorts because their speed was slower than that of a surfaced U-boat; ten Lakes Class cutters loaned to Royal Navy, two expended in a commando raid in Oran
Selected ships in Class: HMS Sennen

Egret Class sloop

Constructed: 1938
Displacement: 1,200 tons
Length: 276 feet
Complement: 188
Armament: 8 x 4-inch AA guns; 4 x .5-inch AA guns (1 x 4); D/C

Maximum Speed: 19.25 knots
Engines/Power: Geared steam turbines, 2 shafts; 3,600 SHP
Maximum Range: n/a
Notes on Class: Only 3 built
Selected ships in Class: HMS Pelican

Flower Class corvette

Constructed: 1939–40
Displacement: 925 tons
Length: 205 feet
Complement: 85 crewmen
Armament: 1 4-inch gun; 1 AA gun; 4 .303 AA; D/C
Maximum Speed: 16 knots
Engines/Power: Reciprocating engine, 1 shaft; 2,750 SHP
Maximum Range: 3,500 miles at 12 knots
Notes on Class: Mass-produced at start of war based on commercial whaler design
with existing ASW equipment installed; speed less than a surfaced U-boat
made ASW work difficult; short length and shallow draft made corvettes ex-
tremely uncomfortable to live in during rough weather; operated by Royal
Navy (including several manned by Free French and Free Belgian crews),
U.S. Coast Guard and U.S. Navy (as patrol gunboats)
Selected ships in Class: HMS Abelia, HMS Alisma, HMS Anemone, HMS Asphodel,
HMS Buttercup, HMS Clover, HMS Godetia, HMS Lavender, HMS Loosestrife,
HMS Pennywort, HMS Pimpernel, HMS Pink, HMS Saxifrage, HMCS Sher-
brooke, HMS Snowflake, HMS Sunflower

Isles Class ASW trawler

Constructed: 1940–44
Displacement: 545 tons
Length: 164 feet
Complement: 40 crewmen
Armament: 1 12-lb. AA gun; 3 x 20mm AA gun; D/C
Maximum Speed: 12 knots
Engines/Power: Reciprocating engine, 1 shaft; 850 SHP
Maximum Range: n/a
Notes on Class: 122 constructed, used by Royal Navy and Royal Canadian Navy
Selected ships in Class: *HMS Campobello*

Misc ASW Trawlers

HMS Northern Gem and *HMS Northern Spray* were small commercial steam trawlers
requisitioned by the Royal Navy and used as convoy rescue ships

AMERICAN ESCORT WARSHIPS

Bogue Class escort aircraft carrier

Constructed: 1942–44
Displacement: 7,800 tons
Length: 495 feet
Complement: 890 crewmen
Aircraft: 24 FM2 Wildcat/TBF Avenger
    Armament: 2 x 5-inch guns
Maximum Speed: 18 knots
Engines/Power: Steam turbines, 1 shaft; 8,500 SHP
Maximum Range: n/a
Notes on Class: Decisive convoy escort defense weapon (*USS Bogue* alone credited
    with 8 U-boat kills, and its escorts another 5); 11 built for U.S. Navy; 34 con-
    structed in the U.S. for the Royal Navy with design modifications and different
    armament (2 x 5-inch guns; 4 x 2 40mm AA; 10 x 1 20mm AA)
Selected ships in Class: USS Bogue, USS Card

Wickes Class destroyer

Constructed: 1918–20
Displacement: 1,220 tons
Length: 314
Complement: 113
Armament: 4 x 1 4-inch guns; 2 3-lb. AA; 12 21-inch torpedo tubes; D/C
Maximum Speed: 35 knots
Engines/Power: Geared turbines, 2 shafts; 27,000 SHP
Maximum Range: 4,900 miles at 15 knots
Notes on Class: 50 Wickes- and Clemson-class destroyers transferred to the Royal
    Navy in the 1940 "destroyers for bases" agreement; considered inferior as a con-
    voy escort because difficult to handle: their narrow, V-shaped sterns made for a
    large turning radius at high speed; some armament removed to allow increased
    D/C capacity
Selected ships in Class: USS Babbitt, USS Upshur

Treasury Class cutter

Constructed: 1936–37
Displacement: 2,482 tons
Length: 327 feet
Complement: 125 crewmen
Armament: 1–4 5-inch guns; various .50-cal. machine guns; D/C
Maximum Speed: 20 knots
Engines/Power: 2 oil-fueled boilers, 2 shafts; 6,200 SHP

Maximum Range: 8,270 miles

Notes on Class: Considered a superior ASW weapon because of its speed and endurance; *USS (CG) Ingham* served in World War II, Korea, Vietnam, and upon decommissioning in 1988 was the oldest commissioned U.S. warship

Selected ships in Class: USS (CG) Campbell, USS (CG) Duane, USS (CG) Ingham, USS (CG) Spencer

Sources: Middlebrook, Martin, *Convoy,* William Morrow, New York, 1976; Polmar, Norman, and Allen, Thomas B., *World War II: America at War,* Random House, New York, 1991; Rohwer, Jurgen, *The Critical Convoy Battles of March 1943,* Naval Institute Press, Annapolis, MD, 1977; Worth, Richard, *Fleets of World War II,* Da Capo Press, New York, 2001; escort ship details from U-boat.net at http://www.uboat.net/ and www.naval-history.net/

EQUIVALENT WORLD WAR II NAVAL OFFICER RANKS

U.S. Navy	Royal Navy	German Navy
Fleet Admiral	Admiral of the Fleet	Grossadmiral +
Admiral	Admiral	Generaladmiral
Vice Admiral	Vice-Admiral	Vizeadmiral
Rear Admiral	Rear-Admiral	Konteradmiral
Captain	Captain	Kapitän zur See
n/a	n/a	Fregattenkapitän *
Commander	Commander	Korvettenkapitän
Lieutenant Commander	Lieutenant-Commander	Kapitänleutnant
Lieutenant	Lieutenant	Oberleutnant zur See #
Lieutenant (junior grade)	Lieutenant (junior grade)	Leutnant zur See
Ensign	Sublieutenant	Oberfähnrich zur See
Midshipman	Midshipman	Fähnrich zur See

+ English translation: Grand Admiral
* English translation: Junior Captain
# English translation: Senior Lieutenant

Sources: U-boat.net; Showall, Jak Mallmann, *Hitler's Navy: A Reference Guide to the Kriegsmarine, 1935–1945*, Seaworth Publishing, London, 2009.

NOTES

INTRODUCTION: A FIGHT IN THE DARK

1. Churchill, Winston S., *The Second World War*, Vol. V, p. 6, Houghton Mifflin, New York, 1948–53.

2. Convoy SC129 details from ConvoyWeb.org.

3. The convoys at sea on May 11, 1943, from ConvoyWeb.org archive. They included the eastbound Convoys SC128, thirty-one ships; SC129, twenty-two ships; SC130, thirty-five ships; HX237, forty-two ships; and HX238, forty-three ships; westbound convoys included ON179, fifty-four ships; ON180, fifty-nine ships; ONS6, thirty-two ships; ON181, forty-seven ships; ON182, fifty-two ships; ONS7, forty-seven ships; and ON183, twenty-nine ships.

4. U-boat deployment figures from Busch, Harald, *U-boats at War*, Ballantine Books, New York, 1953, p. 288; also U-boat Force daily war diaries (Kriegstagebücher, translated into English and posted online at U-boat Archive.net; henceforth KTB) for March 1 force levels each year.

5. Location of U-boats on May 11, 1943 cited in U-boat Force KTB, identified by position on the German Naval Grid; U-boats plotted on a copy of that nautical chart by the author.

6. Description of the attempted U-boat attack against Convoy SC129 by U-223 and other boats from Gruppe Elbe II comes from a variety of official sources and historical accounts. These include the U-boat Headquarters KTB, for May 5–13, 1943; records of Convoy SC129 from ConvoyWeb.org; also MacIntyre, Donald, Captain RN (Ret.), *U-boat Killer*, W. W. Norton, London, 1956, Chapter 11; Blair, Clay, *Hitler's U-Boat War, Vol. 2: The Hunted: 1942–1945*, Random House, New York, 1998, pp. 326–331; Hessler, Günter, *The U-boat War in the Atlantic: 1939–1945*, Her Majesty's Stationery Office, London, 1989, pp. 108–109; additional details on HMS *Hesperus* from Worth, Richard, *Fleets of World War II*, Da Capo Press, New York, 2001, p. 111, and "Allied Warships" at U-boat.net; histories of Gruppe Elbe II U-boats from individual histories at U-boat.net and from Wynn, Kenneth, *U-boat Operations of the Second World War, Vol. 1: Career Histories, U-1-U-510*, Naval Institute Press, Annapolis, MD, 1997, and *Vol. 2: Career Histories U-511-UIT-25*, Naval Institute Press, Annapolis, MD, 1998; biographical details of U-boat commanders Otto Kretschmer, Hans-Joachim Schepke, and Karl-Jurg Wächter from Busch, Rainer and Roll, Hans-Joachim, *German U-boat Commanders of World War II*, Naval Institute Press, Annapolis, MD, 1999, and "U-boat Commanders" at U-boat.net; SC129 base course plotted via the latitude-longitude calculator at Indo.com.

7. Teamwork comments from MacIntyre, *U-boat Killer*, p. xii.

8. Details on escort ship weapons from Campbell, John, *Naval Weapons of World War II*, Naval Institute Press, Annapolis, MD, 1985, pp. 88–91; British scientists learned of the Type VIIC's actual

depth capability after the crew of U-570 surrendered when caught on the surface on August 27, 1941. Scientists went over the U-boat with a fine-toothed comb and learned much about its various combat systems and design. See Blair, Clay, *Hitler's U-Boat War, Vol. 1: The Hunters: 1939–1942*, Random House, New York, 1996, p. 339–348.

9. Details of the sinking of U-99 from MacIntyre, *U-boat Killer*, pp. 50–54; also Kretschmer biography in "Top U-boat Aces" at U-boat.net.

10. MacIntyre's rage over losing two ships from MacIntyre, *U-boat Killer*, p. 164.

11. Escort Group B-2 convoy successes and days at sea compiled from convoy reports filed at ConvoyWeb.org; notes on HF/DF from MacIntyre, *U-boat Killer*, pp. 96–99; U-402 and its victims from U-boat.net.

12. Wächter descriptions of Hesperus attack from U-223 KTB for May 11–12, 1943, translated by U-boat Archive.net from the originals in storage at the German Bundesarchiv, Freiberg; U-223's engineer officer identity from U-223 crew roster at ubootwaffe.net.

13. The "tall columns of gleaming, phosphorescent water" from MacIntyre, *U-boat Killer*, pp. 166–167.

14. The Mark VII "heavy" depth charge with an additional 150-pound cast-iron weight attached had an initial descent rate of 7.7 feet per second that increased to its terminal descent velocity of 16.8 feet per second by a depth of 250 feet; from Campbell, *Naval Weapons*, p. 89.

15. Description of events inside U-223 from U-223's KTB war diary; also MacIntyre, *U-boat Killer*.

16. Hesperus collision with U-357 in MacIntyre, *U-boat Killer*, pp. 116–117.

17. U-223 KTB.

18. The saga of U-223 has a footnote that is almost as amazing as its ordeal and survival after the showdown with the *HMS Hesperus*. Maschinenobergefreiter Zeiger, who had mistakenly jumped overboard, floated for several hours in the dark, rough ocean. He had abandoned hope of rescue when to his astonishment, U-359 suddenly surfaced just fifty yards away. His shouts attracted the crew's attention, and Oberleutnant zur See Heinz Forster quickly dispatched a rescue party to fish him out of the Atlantic, returning him to his amazed comrades on U-223 when the two U-boats rendezvoused at sea several days later.

19. In what must be one of the greatest understatements of the Battle of the Atlantic, this is how U-boat headquarters described U-223's experience against SC129: "U-223 was depth charged, was unable to dive and moved away from the convoy; she reported again later and was able to do without assistance. . . . The operation against the convoy is being continued. . . . U-223 has been too badly damaged to be able to take further part." From BdU KTB, May 11, 1943.

20. U.S. Merchant Marine losses from "American Merchant Marine at War," posted at the Web site of the American Merchant Marine Veterans at usmm.org; British, Commonwealth, Nazi-occupied, and neutral casualties from Admiralty casualty figures cited in Middlebrook, Martin, *Convoy*, William Morrow and Company, New York, 1976, p. 298.

21. Athenia sinking from Syrett, David, "The Battle of the Atlantic: 1943, the Year of Decision," *The American* Neptune, Salem, MA, Winter 1985; Avondale Park sinking from U-boat.net; number of operational U-boats from U-boat.net; total Allied shipping losses from Blair, *U-Boat War, Vol. 1*, p. 771 and Blair, *U-boat War, Vol. 2*, p. 820; U-boat losses from U-boat.net; personnel casualties from Gannon, Michael, *Black May*, Dell Publishing, New York, 1998, p. 421; the crews of 222 U-boats intentionally scuttled their boats after Grossadmiral Dönitz's announcement on May 5 of the impending cease-fire, including two on May 8.

22. Phases of the Battle of the Atlantic drawn from Jacobsen, H. A. and Rowher, Jurgen, Editors, *The Decisive Battles of World War II: The German View*, G.P. Putnam's Sons, New York, 1965; Blair, *U-Boat War, Vol. 1*, passim, and Blair, *U-Boat War, Vol. 2*, passim.

23. Early voyagers from Morison, Samuel Eliot, *The European Discovery of America: The Northern Voyages (Vol. 1)*, Oxford University Press, New York, 1971, pp. 13–29 and 61; Spanish Armada fate from Catholic Encyclopedia, "The Spanish Armada," Robert Appleton Company, New York, 1913; "Westerly Wind" from Conrad, Joseph, *The Mirror of the Sea*, Harper and Brothers, Publishers, New

York, 1906, reproduced in Buchheim, Lother-Gunther, *The Boat*, Dell Publishing/Bantam, 1973, p. 236.

24. British dependence on imports from Hughes, Terry, and Costello, John, *The Battle of the Atlantic*, Dial Press, New York, 1977, p. 215.

CHAPTER 1: A CITY AT WAR

1. New York weather on March 6, 1943 from Weather-Warehouse.com; general scenes of New York from Middlebrook, *Convoy*, pp. 76–79; "nearly 200 ships" from ConvoyWeb.org. These included 118 ships assigned to Convoys SC122, HX229 and HX229A, as well as another seventy-seven assigned to Convoys SC123 and HX230 scheduled to sail on March 14 and 18, respectively.

2. Wartime incidents for the first week of 1943 drawn from editions of *The New York Times* for March 1–7.

3. Worldwide battlefield situation in early March 1943 from Polmar, Norman, and Allen, Thomas B., *World War II: America at War*, Random House, New York, 1991: Guadalcanal, pp. 356–357; North Africa events, pp. 590–594; Stalingrad siege, pp. 763–764.

4. Goebbels "Total war" speech from Calvin College archive at www.calvin.edu.

5. Operational U-boats on September 3, 1939 from Blair, *U-boat War, Vol. 1*, p. 54; growth of U-boat Force between 1939 and 1943 from Busch, *U-boats at War*; shortage of Allied defenses from Syrett, "Year of Decision," *Naval History*.

6. U.S. Navy moves in 1941 from Abbazia, Patrick, *Mr. Roosevelt's Navy: The Private War of the U.S. Atlantic Fleet, 1939–1942*, Naval Institute Press, Annapolis, MD, 1975, pp. 142–143, 197–212; also Blair, *U-boat War, Vol. 1*, pp. 225–228; value of Lend-Lease aid to Britain in 2010 dollars from USInflationCalculator.com.

7. Greer incident from Abbazia, *Roosevelt's Navy*, 223–231; U-652 history from Wynn, *U-boat Operations, Vol. 2*, pp. 108–109; also U-boat.net.

8. *USS Kearny* incident from Blair, *U-Boat War, Vol. 1*, pp. 369–370; *Reuben James* sinking from pp. 374–375.

9. U-123 attacks on inshore shipping from Gannon, Michael, *Operation Drumbeat*, Harper & Row, New York, 1990, pp. 208–223.

10. Plan for Operation Sledgehammer from Perrett, Geoffrey, *There's a War to Be Won: The U.S. Army in World War II*, Random House, New York, 1991, pp. 130–131.

11. Food shortages and Lend-Lease shipments from Hughes and Costello, *Battle of the Atlantic*, pp. 128 and 173; diversion of 1st Infantry Division and supplies in U.K. to North Africa from Perrett, *War to Be* Won, p. 303.

12. For initial convoy procedures, see Barlow, Jeffrey C., "The Navy's Atlantic War Learning Curve," *Naval History* magazine, Annapolis, MD, June 2008.

13. See Appendix 2; British convoy officials had strong second thoughts about eighty ships in Convoy HX228, and ordered fifteen of them to divert to Halifax to join a later convoy; analysis of North Atlantic convoys based on British Admiralty records posted at ConvoyWeb.org and War-Sailors.com; collisions in New York from Blair, *U-Boat War, Vol. 2*, p. 241.

14. Ships from German-occupied nations from Middlebrook, *Convoy*, p. 36.

15. Nationalities of ships in SC122, HX229 and HX229A from analysis of sailing forms at ConvoyWeb.org.

16. Details of individual ships in New York from ConvoyWeb.org., sailing forms for Convoys SC122, HX229 and HX229A; details on ship movements from Middlebrook, *Convoy*, pp. 92–95.

17. SC122 Sailing Conference details from Convoy and Routing procedures from Middlebrook, *Convoy*, pp. 80–82, 92–95; convoy composition from ConvoyWeb.org.

18. Distance from New York to Cape Race, Newfoundland, and from Newfoundland to Rockall, from latitude-longitude calculator at Indo.com.

19. Routes for SC122, HX229, and HX229A from Convoy and Routing procedures from Middlebrook, *Convoy*, p. 88.

20. Deane Wynne's account of his life and wartime experiences in the British Merchant Navy from his autobiography, Wynne, Deane, *Recollections from Below the Mast*, self-published, 2003; *Kingsbury* description from "Allied Ships Sunk" at U-boat.net; description of *Zaanland–Elin K.* collision from Middlebrook, *Convoy*, p. 82.

21. Convoy ONS154 and SC121 details from "Convoy Battles" at U-boat.net.

22. SC122 local escorts from New York to Newfoundland were the corvettes *HMCS Rimouski, HMCS The Pas,* and *HMCS New Westminster* and the minesweeper *HMCS Blairmore.*

23. Convoy SC122 cruising order from ConvoyWeb.org and Rohwer, Jürgen, *The Critical Convoy Battles of March 1943*, Naval Institute Press, Annapolis, MD, 1977, p. 63.

24. White sending message to Dutch freighter *Kedoe* from Middlebrook, *Convoy*, p. 102; few histories of the Battle of the Atlantic cite the Bible Code practice among British mariners. John Waters in his memoir, *Bloody Winter* (D. Van Nostrand Co., New York, 1967), made a brief reference to it, citing the Hebrews 13:8 message. Other examples and Bayley reminiscence from an online discussion group at http://www.navy-net.co.uk/Forums.

25. Wartime experiences and background of Signalman 3rd Class Theodore Schorr from an extensive written interview with the author in January 2010, supplemented by various navy documents provided by Mr. Schorr (hereafter Schorr interview).

26. Growth of U.S. Navy from King, Ernest J., Admiral, *U.S. Navy at War 1941–1945: Official Reports to the Secretary of the Navy*, U.S. Navy Department, Washington, DC, 1946, p. 217.

27. Shipping figures from Behrens, C.B.A., *Merchant Shipping and the Demands of War*, H.M. Stationery Office, London, UK, 1955, p. 23; background of the Naval Armed Guard from "History of the Armed Guard Afloat," United States Naval Administration in World War II, OPNAV-P421–514, prepared by the Director of Naval History, 1946, p. 140.

28. "History of the Armed Guard Afloat," p. 117; loudspeaker announcements cited in Gleichauf, Justin F., *Unsung Sailors: The Naval Armed Guard in World War II*, Naval Institute Press, Annapolis, MD, 1990, p. 171.

29. Mayall background from "Royal Naval Reserve (RNR) Officers 1939–1945" at www.unithistories.com.

30. The local escorts for HX229 were the *USS Kendrick, HMS Chelsea, HMCS Fredericton,* and *HMCS Oakville.*

31. Schorr on *El Mundo* from Schorr interview.

32. *SS Mathew Luckenbach* description from the Web site NavSource.org; Able Seaman Pasquale Civitillo quoted in Middlebrook, *Convoy*, p. 96; armament and Armed Guard Detachment figures from "Supplementary Report of Supplies and/or Personnel Issued by Port Director to *SS Mathew Luckenbach*," Third Naval District, March 11, 1943.

33. Details of Convoy KMS4 from convoy commodore sailing list, posted at Warsailors.com; convoy passage from the Clyde anchorage to Gibraltar from Gretton, Peter, *Convoy Escort Commander*, Cassell & Co., London, 1964, pp. 104–105.

CHAPTER 2: THE ADVERSARIES

1. Composition of mid-ocean escort groups from Rohwer, *Critical Convoy Battles*, pp. 40–42.

2. Background of Admiral Horton and Western Approaches Command drawn from a number of historical accounts, particularly Chalmers, W. S., Rear-Admiral RN (Ret.), *Max Horton and the Western Approaches*, Hodder and Stoughton, London, 1954, passim; Gannon, *Black May*, passim; Gretton, *Escort Commander*, passim, and *Crisis Convoy: The Story of HX231*, Naval Institute Press, Annapolis, MD, 1974, passim.

3. Horton memorandum from Chalmers, *Horton*, pp. 274–279.

4. Horton's demeanor and daily schedule from *Horton*, pp. 150–152.

5. Account of the fight between the *Harvester, Aconit,* U-444, and U-432 from Blair, *U-boat War, Vol. 2*, pp. 256–257, and Uboat.net.

6. Because the maximum flight range from each airbase formed the radius of a circle, the unprotected zone of the Atlantic between North America and the British Isles was narrower in the north-

ern latitudes closer to Iceland and Northern Ireland. The more southerly a convoy's route plotted on a nautical chart, the wider was the area without any land-based air coverage. See map on pp. 134–135.

7. Conversion of the B-24D to the VLR model from Gannon, *Black May*, pp. 79–80.

8. Difficulty of long-range VLR Liberator flights from Middlebrook, *Convoy*, p. 54.

9. B-24 production and operational use in World War II from Eden, Paul, General Editor, *The Encyclopedia of Aircraft of WWII*, Aerospace Publishing, London, 2004, pp. 80–93.

10. U.S. Army–U.S. Navy dispute over land-based aircraft in Buell, Thomas B., *Master of Sea Power: A Biography of Fleet Admiral Ernest J. King*, Little, Brown and Company, Boston, 1980, pp. 286–288; Blair, *U-boat War, Vol. 2*, pp. 462–465; and Waters, *Bloody Winter*, pp. 257–262.

11. "First charge" on resources at Casablanca from Morison, Samuel E., *U.S. Naval Operations in World War II: Vol. X: The Atlantic Battle Won*, Little, Brown, New York, 1951, p. 16; British casualties at Gallipoli from Carylon, Les, *Gallipoli*, Pan Macmillan, Sydney, Australia, 2001, p. 515.

12. Atlantic Convoy Conference decisions from Blair, *U-boat War, Vol. 1*, pp. 239–242.

13. Seventy of 112 Navy VLR Liberators in the Pacific from Waters, *Bloody Winter*, p. 261.

14. The U-boat reports for SC121 and HX228 were surprisingly accurate, given the poor visibility and stormy waters that hampered close observation. The actual losses were twelve ships for 55,661 tons (plus two 143-ton landing craft carried as cargo) and one 3,700-ton ship damaged in SC121, and four ships (plus one landing craft) totaling 24,466 tons and the 1,340-ton *HMS Harvester* lost from HX228; see Blair, *U-boat War, Vol. 2*, pp. 254 and 257; also Convoys SC121 and HX228 in "Convoy Battles" at U-boat.net.

15. Physical description of Dönitz by historian John Toland in the Foreword to Dönitz, Karl, Grand Admiral, *Memoirs: Ten Years and Twenty Days*, Da Capo Press, New York, 1997, p. xvii.

16. German Naval Grid Chart described in Kahn, David, *Seizing the Enigma*, Random House, New York, 1991, pp. 203–205. To further confuse enemy code breakers, the U-boat Force provided separate two-letter bigram codes to disguise both the two-letter quadrant numbers and the four-digit position indicators.

17. U-boat deployment figures from Busch, *U-boats at War*, p. 288; also KTB for March 1 force levels each year; number of U-boats total from Hessler, *U-boat War*, Appendix 2, p. 112; number of boats in the North Atlantic on March 12, 1943, from BdU KTB on that date posted at U-boatarchive.net. The daily disposition of the U-boat force for that date totaled 113 boats at sea. BdU Headquarters at that time was unaware of six U-boat losses that had occurred between March 4 and 12, including the Atlantic boats U-432, U-444, and U-633. In addition to the fifty-eight U-boats actually on patrol in the North Atlantic, there were another fifteen (less U-432) returning to port and another thirty-four (less U-83, U-130, and U-156) operating elsewhere than the North Atlantic.

18. Godt career background from U-boat.net; Dönitz description of Godt from *Memoirs*, p. 64.

19. Backgrounds of Korvettenkapitän Hessler, Kapitänleutnant Schnee, and Kapitänleutnant Cremer from U-boat.net and Busch and Roll, *U-boat Commanders*, pp. 102, 228–229, and 48–49, respectively.

20. Number of U-boats and personnel total from Hessler, *U-boat War*, Appendix 2, p. 112.

21. Dönitz order on daylight submerged attacks from BdU KTB for March 5, 1943, p. 135, posted at U-boatArchive.net.

22. Development of centimetric radar from Polmar and Allen, *World War II*, pp. 673–674; also Gannon, *Black May*, pp. 75–78;.

23. Forty-six U-boats against Convoys SC122 and HX229 from "Wolf Packs" at U-boat.net.

CHAPTER 3: MOVEMENT TO CONTACT

1. Convoy planners intentionally separated the assigned meeting points of successive convoys to avoid congestion and to prevent creating a lucrative target for the U-boats. The WOMP for Convoy HX229 was 152 nautical miles due east of St. John's, about 105 miles away from SC122's; from "Report of Proceedings" of Convoys SC122 and HX229, with distances from the latitude-longitude calculator at Indo.com.

2. Forty-five-mile perimeter calculated by standard convoy escort screen situated five miles distant from the main body; the eleven rows of ships in SC122's main body formed a rectangular box five miles wide and about two miles deep. Rendezvous details from "Record of Proceedings, Convoy SC122 Report of Commodore S.N. White," declassified from Secret, Public Records Office, London, PRO/ADM 199/580; other details from Middlebrook, *Convoy*, pp. 119–120.

3. Wynne comments from Wynne, *Recollections*, passim.

4. Boyle background from Middlebrook, *Convoy*, p. 114; details of Convoy TM1 catastrophe from Blair, *U-boat War, Vol. 2*, pp. 145–148; "Convoy Battles" at Uboat.net; desperation signal from *Havelock* to U-boat in Middlebrook, *Convoy*, p. 114; Convoy TM1 illustrated the frequent exaggeration by U-boat commanders of their attack results despite Dönitz's insistence that they report "honest" results. German propaganda broadcasts claimed from BdU reports that TM1 had lost fifteen ships totaling 142,000 tons, while the actual results were much smaller, albeit still a major loss: seven of nine tankers for 61,457 tons.

5. Convoy ONS168 passage from Blair, *U-boat War, Vol. 2*, pp. 258–259; Escort Group B-5 ships from Rohwer, *Critical Convoy Battles*, p. 40, and ConvoyWeb.org; Wynne description of *Zamalek* from Wynne, *Recollections*, passim.

6. MacKenzie confrontation with crewmen from Schorr interview.

7. Jackson comments from interview with the author; Jackson papers.

8. Description of Day and Day's request to delay Convoy HX229 in Placentia Bay from Middlebrook, *Convoy*, pp. 115–116.

9. Profiles of Escort Groups B-4 and B-5 from Rohwer, *Critical Convoy Battles*, pp. 73 and 77–78; Middlebrook, *Convoy*, pp. 113–117; and Blair, *U-boat, Vol. 2*, pp. 258–260; also various naval messages from COMINCH and area commands reporting status and material condition of escort ships.

10. The role that HF/DF played in convoy defense and the German failure to understand Allied HF/DF gains from Blair, *U-boat War, Vol. 2*, pp. 791–792; Rohwer, *Critical Convoy Battles*, pp. 99–100; and Waters, *Bloody Winter*, pp. 246–247.

11. Scientists at a French subsidiary of ITT had conducted research on HF/DF technology before the war, and after the German invasion of France in June 1940, a dozen of them escaped to the United States via Portugal, where they re-established their operation; see Blair, *U-boat War, Vol. 2*, p. 791.

12. MacIntyre the first British commander to get HF/DF from Blair, *U-boat War, Vol. 2*, p. 791; MacIntyre praise of his HF/DF operator's skills from MacIntyre, *U-boat Killer*, pp. 96–97; Germans wrongfully think HF detection is impossible from Gannon, *Black May*, p. 73.

13. Diversion of Convoy HX229A from Middlebrook, *Convoy*, p. 130.

14. Escort Group B-4 late for rendezvous from Rohwer, *Critical Convoy Battles*, p. 103.

15. Sullivan brothers tragedy from Polmar and Allen, *World War II*, p. 779.

16. Story of the Stilinovich brothers from Gleichauf, *Unsung Sailors*, pp. 239–242; additional details from Mrs. Gladys Stilinovich, widow of Bill Stilinovich, in interview with the author in March 2009.

CHAPTER 4: THE U-BOAT

1. Description of U-boat at sea from Gannon, *Black May*, pp. 37–38.

2. "The wind punished us," from Werner, Herbert A., *Iron Coffins*, Bantam Books, New York, 1978, p. 90. Werner in 1943 was 1st watch officer of U-230, which took part in two wolf pack operations against allied convoys during the critical months of February–March 1943.

3. Information on Martin Beisheim's life and wartime service in the U-boat Force from extended interviews conducted during March and April 2009 (hereafter Beisheim interviews); additional information on the second war patrol of U-758 from the daily war diaries of U-boat Headquarters (BdU KTB); daily war diary of U-758 during February 14–March 30, 1943; also Wynn, *U-boat Operations, Vol. 2*, pp. 153–155; additional biographical information on Kapitänleutnant Helmut

Manseck from Busch and Roll, *U-boat Commanders*, p. 156; details of "beta" message announcing discovery of a convoy from Kahn, *Enigma*, p. 197.

4. U-758 details, including the 448th Type VIIC, from U-boat.net.

5. G7s Falke torpedo on U-758 from Uboat.net; two other U-boats carrying this new weapon were U-603 and U-221.

6. German World War II–era torpedoes and mines from Gannon, *Black May*, pp. 9–10.

7. The Knight's Cross (Ritterkreuz) was a higher-degree version of the German Iron Cross decoration for valor in combat, normally presented to a U-boat commander when he surpassed sinking 50,000 tons of Allied shipping or for a feat of extraordinary bravery in combat (see more details in Appendix 1).

8. Kapitänleutnant Manseck biography from Busch and Roll, *U-boat Commanders*, p. 156; U-758 history from Wynn, *U-boat Operations*, *Vol. 2*, pp. 153–155.

9. U-67 details from Wynn, *U-boat Operations*, *Vol. 1*, pp. 48–49; different times for the Type VIIC and IXC U-boats to submerge from Gannon, *Black May*, p. 7; the U-boat Force operated a total of 709 Type VIICs and only 159 Type IX boats during the war, a three-to-one ratio. April 1943 U-boat losses from BdU KTB on May 1, 1943.

10. Details on Convoy SL87 battle from Beisheim interviews; "Convoy Battles" at U-boat.net; Blair, *U-Boat, Vol. 1*, pp. 381–384, and BdU KTB for September 24–28, 1941; loss of U-67 from Wynn, *U-boat Operations, Vol. 1*, pp. 48–49.

11. Details of wolf packs Bürggraf, Wildfang, Neptun, and Neuland from U-boat.net; other details from Blair, *U-Boat, Vol. 2*, p. 252; also Hessler, *U-boat War, Vol. 2*, pp. 91–93.

12. Beisheim transcription of 2018 encrypted message from U-758 KTB for March 15, 1943, translated by U-boat Archive.net from the originals in storage at the German Bundesarchiv, Freiberg, Germany.

13. Metox incident from Beisheim interviews.

14. Radioman tasks from Beisheim interviews.

CHAPTER 5: THE BATTLE OF THE CODES

1. During the 1960s, the U.S. Navy operated one encryption system still using a mechanical rotor system similar to the Enigma. The KLB-47 used eight of twelve rotors provided to each unit for encrypting and decrypting messages. When Navy Warrant Officer John Walker, a communications officer, began spying for the Soviet KGB in the mid-1960s, the first thing his handlers did was to provide Walker with a hand-held "rotor reader" device that would map the internal wiring in each rotor. This information enabled the Soviets to build their own machine to decrypt KLB47 messages. See Hunter, Robert W., *Spy Hunter*, Naval Institute Press, Annapolis, MD, 1999, pp. 84–85.

2. Naval Enigma machine design and operating procedures from Beisheim interviews; Kahn, *Enigma*, pp. 195–198 and pp. 285–290; and Gannon *Drumbeat*, pp. 425–426.

3. 2018 message cited in U-758 KTB for March 15, 1943; U-91 only three patrol line positions away from U-758 from Middlebrook, *Convoy*, p. 144; distance from U-758 to convoy from measurement of naval grid square quadrants on 1870G Nord-Atlantischer Ozean chart.

4. BdU order to U-758 (Manseck), U-664 (Oberleutnant Adolf Gräf), U-84 (Kapitänleutnant Horst Uphoff), and U-91 (Walkerling) from U-758 KTB, March 15, 1943.

5. The Allied intelligence war against the German Naval Enigma was revealed only with the publication in 1974 of *The Ultra Secret* by retired Royal Air Force Group Captain Frederick Winterbotham (Weidenfield & Nicolson, London). As a result, many postwar naval histories were found to have significant lapses given the vital role the decryption campaigns on both sides had played.

6. Background on B-dienst service from Showall, Jak Mallmann, *German Naval Codebreakers*, Ian Allen Publishing, Surrey, 2003, pp. 147–148, and Middlebrook, *Convoy*, pp. 74–75. In one of the great ironies of history, the German Navy's decision in the 1920s to reorganize its code-breaking and secure communications effort around the B-dienst stemmed from a shocking revelation in a post–World War I British history of how the Royal Navy had broken the German Navy's codes and ciphers in 1914. Three weeks after Britain declared war on imperial Germany on August 4 of that

year, the German light cruiser *Magdeburg* ran aground off the Russian coast while attempting to penetrate the Gulf of Finland from the Baltic Sea. Unable to free the warship, its commander ordered scuttling charges set and for the crew to prepare to abandon ship. When a sailor accidentally lit the fuse to the explosives, the crew panicked and fled the ship in disorder, failing to destroy a number of codebooks. The Russians captured several codebooks and cipher tables and sent a naval delegation to London to hand them over to the First Lord of the Admiralty. Within several months, British naval intelligence officers were reading the encoded messages of the German Navy. The codebreaking success was one of the most closely guarded secrets of World War I, but in 1923, the first volume of Winston Churchill's *The World Crisis* appeared, in which its author in great detail disclosed how the Russians had retrieved the Magdeburg's codebooks and ciphers and given them to him personally. As one historian later noted, the shocked German Navy immediately realized that the service "needed to fundamentally transform its system of secret communications," setting the stage for the development of the naval Enigma system. Winston Churchill's scoop would later return to haunt him when as prime minister during the Battle of the Atlantic he oversaw the struggle by Bletchley Park to unlock the secrets of naval Enigma. For a detailed account of the Magdeburg revelation, see Kahn, *Enigma*, pp. 36–39.

7. German surface raider *Atlantis* seizure of British codebooks from Kahn, David, *The Codebreakers*, Scribner, New York, 1967 and 1996, pp. 465–466; reading Naval Cypher No. 3 from Gannon, *Black May*, p. 56; B-dienst provided "fifty percent" of all intelligence to BdU from Kahn, *Enigma*, pp. 262–263; B-dienst role in battle of Convoy SC107 from Kahn, *Enigma*, p. 212.

8. B-dienst decryption of Convoy SC122 stragggglers and Convoy HX229 course changes from Middlebrook, *Convoy*, pp. 111–113; ironically, the B-dienst also intercepted messages concerning the ad hoc Convoy HX229A, but never realized that it was a separate formation from HX229. This would create much confusion in Berlin when subsequent messages seemed to indicate that the formation was both traveling due north along the Newfoundland-Labrador coast and northeast into the open Atlantic.

9. Bletchley Park attempts to replicate the German naval Enigma from Kahn, *Enigma*, pp. 5 and 94–98.

10. U-67 at Tarrafal Bay from Beisheim interviews; also Blair, *U-boat War, Vol. 1*, pp. 386–387; "one out of ten . . . one out of four convoys," from Kahn, *Enigma*, p. 216; tonnage losses in the last half of 1941 and 1942 from Blair, *U-boat War, Vol. 1*, p. 771, and Blair, *U-boat War, Vol. 2*, p. 820.

11. Seizure of U-559 Enigma documents from Kahn, *Enigma*, pp. 226–227. British and U.S. Navy communications intelligence organizations from Kahn, *Enigma*, pp. 238–244; and Beesly, Patrick, *Very Special Intelligence: The Story of the Admiralty's Operational Intelligence Centre, 1939–1945*, Hamish Hamilton Ltd., London, 1977, pp. 58–60; British "bombe" decryption details from Kahn, *Enigma*, pp. 230–235; breakdown of successful days of decryption from Bray, Jeffrey K., Editor, *Ultra in the Atlantic: Allied Communication Intelligence and the Battle of the Atlantic*, Aegean Park Press, Walnut Creek, CA, 1996, pp. xxi–xxiv and pp. 18–20.

12. Details of Convoys ONS169 and ON170 from ConvoyWeb.org.

13. Rerouting of Convoy SC121 from Blair, *U-boat War, Vol. 2*, p. 252.

CHAPTER 6: THE SIGHTING

1. U-653 operations in its sixth war patrol from Wynn, *U-boat Operations, Vol. 2*, pp. 109–110; also BdU War Diary (BdU KTB) for February 23–25; Middlebrook, *Convoy*, pp. 141–142; additional information from U-653 profile on Uboat.net.

2. U-653 sighting of Convoy HX229 from "Greatest Convoy Battles" at Uboat.net; Theen comments from Middlebrook, *Convoy*, p. 142; the first Gruppe Raubgraf U-boats ordered in to attack HX229 were U-91, U-84, U-664, U-758, U-600, U-615, U-603, U-435, U-616, and U-229. See BdU KTB for March 16, 1943; Manseck orders chase from U-758 KTB for second war patrol, March 16, 1943, translated by U-boat Archive.net from the originals in storage at the German Bundesarchiv, Freiberg.

3. Stürmer-Dränger orientation on March 15 from BdU KTB for March 14, 1943.

4. Allied and German gaps in knowledge from Middlebrook, *Convoy*, p. 144–146; Beesly, *Special Intelligence*, p. 177, and Blair, *U-Boat War, Vol. 2*, pp. 260–261.

5. Change in weather conditions and visibility from U-758 KTB for March 16, 1943.

6. The thirteen Raubgraf U-boats were U-84, U-89, U-91, U-435, U-468, U-600, U-603, U-615, U-621, U-638, U-653, U-664, and U-758; the nineteen Stürmer U-boats were U-134, U-190, U-229, U-305, U-338, U-384, U-439, U-523, U-526, U-527, U-530, U-598, U-616, U-618, U-631, U-641, U-642, U-665, and U-666; see Convoy HX229 at "Greatest Convoy Battles" at U-boat.net.

7. U-758 KTB for March 16, 1943.

8. Beisheim description from Beisheim interviews.

9. Zweigle description of lookout duty from Middlebrook, *Convoy*, p. 156; Bertelsmann background from U-boat.net and Busch and Roll, *U-boat Commanders*, p. 31.

10. U-758 shadowing HX229 from Beisheim interviews; Manseck comments from Middlebrook, *Convoy*, p. 160.

11. *Ingham* at Reykjavik on March 16, 1943, from ship's deck logs for that date.

12. U.S. Atlantic Fleet moves in 1941 from Abbazia, *Roosevelt's Navy*, pp. 142–143 and 197–212; also Blair, *U-Boat War, Vol. 1*, pp. 225–228.

13. Waters as troopship passenger from Waters, *Bloody Winter*, p. 51; "Sight . . . never forget," remarks by Capt. John M. Waters USCG (Ret.) at the decommissioning ceremony of the *USCGC Ingham*, May 27, 1988, videotape of ceremony provided to the author by Dr. Stephen Waters, M.D.

14. Details of ship from "*USCGC Ingham* History" at http://www.uscg.mil/history/webcutters/ Ingham_WPG_35.asp.

15. Convoy SC121 losses from U-boat.net.

16. *Ingham* departure from deck logs for March 16, 1943; Waters description of the critical stakes from Waters, *Bloody Winter*, p. 205.

17. SC122 events from Blair, *U-Boat War, Vol. 2*, p. 260; Middlebrook, *Convoy*, pp. 154–155.

18. Weather and sea conditions late on March 16 from U-758 KTB on that date.

19. HX229 position, course, and speed at 12 midnight GMT from Middlebrook, *Convoy*, p. 155; distances and convoy route waypoints from various U.S. Navy Convoy and Routing messages dispatched to HX229 during March 12–20, 1943 contained in Convoy HX229 Record of Proceedings, Public Records Office, London, ADM 199/576; nautical miles calculated at Indo.com.

20. Escort Group B-4 dispositions the night of March 16 from Rohwer, *Critical Convoy Battles*, p. 119.

21. HX229 at night and U-603 approach from Middlebrook, *Convoy*, pp. 155–157; U-603 war patrol record from Wynn, *U-boat Operations, Vol. 2*, pp. 156–158.

CHAPTER 7: THE BATTLE OF ST. PATRICK'S DAY

1. History and wartime voyages of the *Elin K.* from warsailors.com, ConvoyWeb.org, and Uboat.net; transfer of Norwegian and other foreign-flagged vessels into the British Merchant Fleet from Middlebrook, *Convoy*, pp. 26 and 34–36; German-occupied foreign-flag vessels in Convoys SC122, HX229, and HX229A from ConvoyWeb.org.

2. Details of *Elin K.* crew from "*Elin K.*" profile at WarSailors.com; safe evacuation and *Terkoelei* ignoring lifeboats from Middlebrook, *Convoy*, pp. 158–159.

3. U-603 message in BdU KTB for March 16, 1943. In the confusion of attack and escape, it was not uncommon for U-boat commanders to confuse the sounds of ships breaking up or escort depth-charge explosions for their own torpedoes striking a target.

4. Manseck comments from Middlebrook, *Convoy*, p. 160.

5. Details of U-758 attack from U-758 KTB; Beisheim interviews; Manseck inaccurately claimed three ships sunk and one damaged according to the BdU KTB for March 16, 1943; Rohwer, *Critical Convoy Battles*, pp. 121–123 and 219; and Middlebrook, *Convoy*, pp. 160–164.

6. Schorr confusion over attacks from Schorr interview.

7. Details of U-758 attack on *Zaanland* and *James Oglethorpe* from U-758 KTB for March 16–17, 1943; additional details from Middlebrook, *Convoy*, pp. 160–164; also Rohwer, *Critical Convoy Battles*, pp. 123–124.

8. Manseck claims three ships sunk and a fourth damaged from U-758 KTB and BdU KTB for March 16, 1943.

9. Attacks by U-758, U-435, and U-91 from Beisheim, interviews; U-758 KTB notes; Rohwer, *Critical Convoy Battles*, pp. 124–129; Middlebrook, *Convoy*, pp. 159–170; *Mathew Luckenbach* scene from "Voyage Report of SS *Mathew Luckenbach*," by Ensign James H. Hammond, April 15, 1943, forwarded to the Vice Chief of Naval Operations, including statements by Master Antwood N. Borden, National Archives and Records Service 968/133 (hereafter the Hammond report); John Orris Jackson comments from Jackson papers. Bill Stilinovich witnessing his brother's ship sinking from Gleichauf, *Unsung Sailors*, pp. 239–242; additional details from Mrs. Gladys Stilinovich, widow of Bill Stilinovich, in interview with the author in March 2009.

10. Details of U-338 war patrol from U-boat's KTB for February 23–March 23, translated from the German; U-338 history from Wynn, *U-boat Operations, Vol.1*, p. 227; Kinzel background from Busch and Roll, *U-boat Commanders*, p. 126; Zeissler comments from Middlebrook, *Convoy*, p. 136.

11. Discovery of SC122 from U-338 KTB.

12. Kinzel sighting report of Convoy SC122 from U-338 KTB; Godt clarification of two convoys from BdU KTB for March 17, 1943.

13. Two ships torpedoed from U-338 KTB.

14. Details of U-338 war patrol from U-boat's KTB for February 23–March 23; U-338 history from Wynn, *U-boat Operations, Vol. 1*, p. 227; Kinzel background from Busch and Roll, *U-boat Commanders*, p. 126; description of attack from U-338 KTB for First War Patrol, February 23–March 24, 1943, translated by U-boat Archive.net from the originals in storage at the German Bundesarchiv, Freiberg; also Middlebrook, *Convoy*, p. 180.

15. Wynne's account of the sinking of the *Kingsbury* from Wynne, *Recollections*, passim. Additional details of the *Kingsbury* loss from Blair, *U-Boat War, Vol. 2*, p. 262; Middlebrook, *Convoy*, pp. 180–182, and "Ships Hit by U-boats" at Uboat.net; phase of the moon on March 16, 1943, from "Moon Phase Calculator" at StarDate.org.

16. Wynne rescue from Wynne, *Recollections*.

17. U-600 attack on HX229 including eyewitness accounts from Schorr interview; Middlebrook, *Convoy*, pp. 172–175; Kapitänleutnant Zurmühlen background from Busch and Roll, *U-boat Commanders*, p. 282; details of *Irénée du Pont, Nariva*, and *Southern Princess* from Uboat.net; Stilinovich comments from Gleichauf, *Unsung Sailors*, pp. 240–241.

CHAPTER 8: HEAVY LOSSES

1. Luther comments from "Report of Proceedings for Convoy HX229," ADM 199/575, Public Record Office, London.

2. *Nariva* and *Irénée Du Pont* abandoned, finished off from Rohwer, *Critical Convoy Battles*, pp. 129–130; additional details from Middlebrook, *Convoy*, pp. 200–201; Koitschka biographical information from "U-boat commanders" at Uboat.net; history of U-616 from Wynn, *U-boat Operations, Vol. 2*, pp. 84–85.

3. HX229 reorganization from Middlebrook, *Convoy*, pp. 204–205.

4. HMS *Volunteer's* limited HF/DF capability from Rohwer, *Critical Convoy Battles*, p. 142.

5. Nine Raubgraf boats—U-89, U-91, U-435, U-468, U-600, U-638, U-653, U-664, and U-758—broke off action during March 17. So did two boats from Gruppe Stürmer—U-530 and U-665, and one independent, U-616.

6. U-384 and U-631 operational histories from Wynn, *U-boat Operations, Vol. 1*, pp. 256–257; also Wynn, *U-boat Operations, Vol. 2*, pp. 95–96; U-boat commanders' biographical information from Busch and Roll, *U-boat Commanders*, pp. 136 and 215; *Terkoelei* and *Coracero* details from "Allied Merchants Hit" at Uboat.net.

7. McRae description of attack from Middlebrook, *Convoy*, pp. 205–206. The casualty count from the sinking of the *Irénée Du Pont, Terkoelei,* and *Coracero* illustrates the difficulty of determining the actual numbers of those killed and survivors from such a chaotic situation. The *HMS Mansfield* in a message to Western Approaches Command at 1330 on March 18 reported it had rescued 126 men from the three ships, 55 from the Dutch freighter, 52 from the *Coracero,* and 19 from the *Irénée Du Pont;* the Web site Uboat.net, which also cites British Admiralty archival records, put the *Mansfield's* survivor count at 130: 61 for the *Terkoelei,* 53 for the *Coracero,* and 16 for the *Irénée Du Pont,* of which one man died after being recovered.

8. Luther message from "Report of Proceedings, Convoy HX229," Report of Commodore M. J. D. Mayall RNR, declassified from Secret, Public Records Office, London, PRO/ADM 199/576.

9. HX229 escort reinforcement positions at 1300 March 17 from various position reports; *Ingham* position, course, and speed on March 17 from ship's deck log; course and distance to SC122 derived from latitude-longitude calculator at www.Indo.com.

10. Deane Wynne on *Zamalek* from Wynne, *Recollections.*

11. SC122 daytime events of March 17 from Rohwer, *Critical Convoy Battles,* pp. 145–149; U-439 encounter with Liberator from Middlebrook, *Convoy,* pp. 194–195; background on U-666 and U-439 from Wynn, *U-boat Operations, Vol. 1,* pp. 291–292, and *Vol. 2,* pp. 118–119; Engel and von Tippelskirch biographical details from Busch and Roll, *U-boat Commanders,* pp. 62 and 259.

12. M/86 mission to SC122 from Rohwer, *Critical Convoy Battles,* pp. 145–147; Burcher attack message intercepted from Middlebrook, *Convoy,* p. 195; the BdU KTB for March 17 cited "strong air activity" by the enemy throughout the day that caused many U-boats to lose contact with SC122.

13. VLR Liberator U-boat contact messages in Rohwer, *Critical Convoy Battles,* p. 226.

14. Kinzel in his war diary inaccurately claimed three hits on three ships, but his only actual hit was on the *Granville;* SC122 noon position based on report of *Granville* sinking in "Allied Merchants Hit" at Uboat.net; distance calculation to St. John's and North Channel entrance from latitude-longitude calculator at Indo.com; details of *Granville* sinking from Middlebrook, *Convoy,* pp. 196–197; details of U-338 attack from Rohwer, *Critical Convoy Battles,* p. 221; *Granville* sinking details from "Ships Hit by U-boats" at uboat.net.

15. Afternoon chase of U-boats from Rohwer, *Critical Convoy Battles,* pp. 149–150.

16. Attack on *Port Auckland* and *Zouave* from Rohwer, *Critical Convoy Battles,* pp. 150–152; additional details from "Ships Hit by U-boats" at Uboat.net.

17. U-221 collision with U-254 from Blair, *U-Boat War, Vol. 2,* p. 125.

18. U-221 KTB entry for March 10, 1943, from Dönitz, *Memoirs,* p. 327.

19. "I go" message from Middlebrook, *Convoy,* p. 212; also Rohwer, Critical *Convoy Battles,* p. 144.

20. *City of Agra* message from Middlebrook, *Convoy,* p. 208.

CHAPTER 9: CRISIS IN THE NORTH ATLANTIC

1. Weather on March 17–18 and comments on enemy aircraft from BdU KTB for that date; U-boats in action and VLR missions from Rohwer, *Critical Convoy Battles,* pp. 154–158.

2. King and Roosevelt relationship from Buell, *Sea Power,* various, pp. 240–263; Marshall on FDR preference for the navy from oral interviews with Dr. Forrest C. Pogue cited in Perrett, *War to Be Won,* p. 121; naming of USS *Shangri-La* from Buell, *Sea Power,* p. 243; FDR rejection of King reorganizing naval bureaus from Buell, *Sea Power,* pp. 234–236; Dönitz reliance on Hitler for every decision from "Fuehrer Conferences," in *Brassey's Naval Annual,* 1948, pp. 318 and 333.

3. FDR intervention into VLR Liberator dispute from Middlebrook, *Convoy,* p. 284; number of VLR bombers increased in Waters, *Bloody Winter,* pp. 260–261; this confrontation is curiously absent from many accounts of Admiral King's career, suggestive that the admiral culled his files to redact embarrassing information. Neither King in his official report on the conduct of the war, *U.S. Navy at War, 1941–1945;* nor his postwar memoirs, *Fleet Admiral King: A Naval Record;* nor Thomas B. Buell in his 1980 biography of King based on the admiral's private papers, *Master of Sea Power;* nor Samuel Eliot Morison's fifteen-volume *History of United States Naval Operations in World War II* mentions the protracted struggle over the VLR Liberators.

4. *Mathew Luckenbach* scene from Jackson papers.

5. HX229 events of May 18 from Rohwer, *Critical Convoy Battles*, pp. 141–144, also Middlebrook, *Convoy*, pp. 226–230.

6. Master Antwood Borden comments on HX229 attacks and decision to romp from Hammond report; also group statement by *SS Mathew Luckenbach* officers regarding its torpedoing, National Archives and Records Service RG 968/133; Civitillo comments from Middlebrook, *Convoy*, p. 233; Jackson comments from Jackson papers; Hammond refusal to sign statement from "Hammond Report."

7. Day-Borden exchange in Middlebrook, *Convoy*, p. 234; *Mathew Luckenbach* slower maximum speed from "*Mathew Luckenbach* officers."

8. Events of early March 19 from Rohwer, *Critical Convoy Battles*, pp. 174–175; also Middlebrook, *Convoy*, pp. 241–243; U-666 sinking of *Carras* from "Ships Hit by U-boats" at uboat.net; BdU order to U-boats from BdU KTB for March 19, 1943 posted online at uboatarchive.net.

9. U-527 history from Wynn, *U-boat Operations, Vol. 2*, pp. 15–16; Kapitänleutnant Uhlig background from Busch and Roll, *U-boat Commanders*, p. 261; attack on *Mathew Luckenbach* from U-527 KTB for March 19, 1943, in Waters, *Bloody Winter*, p. 213.

10. Jackson description of torpedo hits from Jackson papers; Civitillo comments from Middlebrook, *Convoy*, p. 243; *Ingham* rescue of crew and Waters as OOD from *USS Ingham* deck logs, for March 19, 1943, and Waters, *Bloody Winter*, pp. 211–215.

11. Sinking of U-384 from Middlebrook, *Convoy*, pp. 246–247; U-663 sinking of *Clarissa Radcliffe* from BdU KTB for March 19, 1943, also in "Ships Hit by U-boats" at uboat.net; *Carras* and *Mathew Luckenbach* finished off from "Ships Hit by U-boats" at uboat.net.

12. Details of end of Convoys HX229 and SC122 from Rohwer, *Critical Convoy Battles*, p. 197, Middlebrook, *Convoy*, pp. 262–269; transfer of Iceland-based escorts to central Atlantic from Waters, *Bloody Winter*, p. 220; *El Mundo* passage to Newport from Schorr interview; HX229 ships returning in Convoy ON177 from ConvoyWeb.org.

13. Wynne experiences at Gourock and London from Wynne, *Recollections*.

14. *Mathew Luckenbach* survivors' experiences from Middlebrook, *Convoy*, pp. 267–268; Jackson papers.

15. Bill Stilinovich forced to keep secret his brother's fate from Gleichauf, *Unsung Sailors*, p. 242; additional details from Gladys Stilinovich interview.

16. The first U-boat that had been scheduled to return to France from the battle was the Gruppe Stürmer U-665 under Oberleutnant zur See Hans-Jurgen Haupt, which had finished off the torpedoed *Fort Cedar Lake* on March 17. However, a Coastal Command Wellington bomber sank U-665 south of Ireland on March 22, killing all forty-six crewmen.

17. There are conflicting accounts of the prisoner. Martin Beisheim, who talked with the Dutchman at length, identified him as Van der Toos. U-boat.net, however, citing German records, said the prisoner's name was G. van der Vuurst.

18. U-758 return to Bordeaux from Beisheim, interview; also U-758 history from Wynn, *U-boat Operations, Vol. 2*, pp. 153–154.

19. German *Sondermeldung* on March 20 from Middlebrook, *Convoy*, p. 271; British bulletin on HX229-SC122 battle from Bracker, Milton, "U-boat Pack Loses Furious 4-day Fight," *The New York Times*, April 20, 1943.

20. The U-boats sank 126 Allied merchant ships totaling 802,160 gross tons in November 1942, and 136 ships for a smaller total loss of 636,926 gross tons in June 1942; see Blair, *Hitler's U-Boat War, Vol. 2*, p. 820 and *Hitler's U-Boat War, Vol. 1*, p. 771 for monthly shipping loss figures; Allied convoy fatalities in March 1943 compiled from individual ship loss reports at Uboat.net.

21. Assessment that the Ultra blackout would last "months" from Blair, *U-boat War, Vol. 2*, p. 240; assessment of U-boat Force growth to 613 U-boats by the end of 1943 based on projected addition of 320 new U-boats in 1943 on top of the existing force of 417 boats, less an estimated 124 boats that the Allies calculated would be sunk during 1943; see Blair, *U-boat War, Vol. 2*, pp. 241–242.

22. "Germans never came so near" from British Admiralty "Monthly A/S [Anti-Submarine] Report," December 1943, p. 3, cited in Morison, Samuel E., *U.S. Naval Operations in World War II*,

Vol. I, The Battle of the Atlantic, Little Brown & Co., New York, 1947, p. 344; Roskill analysis on Battle of the Atlantic crisis from Roskill, Stephen W., Captain RN (Ret.), *The War at Sea, Vol. II,* The Naval & Military Press Ltd., Uckfield, East Sussex, U.K., 1956–1960, pp. 366–367.

23. U.S. and Canadian Army divisions in the United Kingdom between 1942 and 1944 from "Order of Battle of the United States Army in World War II—European Theater of Operations," Office of the Theater Historian, December 1945.

CHAPTER 10: THE ALLIES FIGHT BACK

1. Admirals Noble and Horton attempts to obtain Support Group destroyers from Chalmers, *Horton,* pp. 158–160.

2. Horton comments to Hill in Middlebrook, *Convoy,* p. 267.

3. Captain Lake memorandum recounting Anti-U-boat Committee cited in Middlebrook, *Convoy,* p. 289.

4. Horton observations to Admiral Darke in Chalmers, *Horton,* p. 188.

5. *USS Bogue* escort operations from Blair, *U-boat War, Vol. 2,* pp. 269 and 286–288; HX230 encounter with hurricane-force storm from "Battle of the Atlantic—U-boat Operations, December 1942–May 1945," SRH-008, National Security Agency, declassified, Chapter 3, pp. 39–41.

6. 3rd and 4th Support Group compositions from Chalmers, *Horton,* p. 188, and ConvoyWeb sailing rosters for particular convoys.

7. Gretton remarks on value of support groups from Gretton, *Escort Commander,* p. 118.

8. Support Group ships and operational ready dates from various sources, including individual ships' histories at U-boat.net and the Royal Navy History Homepage at http://www.naval-history.net; also Atlantic Convoy Conference decisions at Blair, *U-boat War, Vol. 2,* p. 245; Support Group convoy escort missions from individual convoy reports at ConvoyWeb.org/uk; Captain Frederick "Johnny" Walker became the Royal Navy's top U-boat killer during World War II. While commanding two separate Support Groups during March 1941 and 1944, his ships were credited with the sinking of twenty U-boats.

9. Allied merchant losses from Blair, *U-boat War, Vol. 1,* Appendix 18, p. 977, and *U-boat War, Vol. 2,* Appendix 20, p. 820; monthly U-boat losses from "Losses by Year" at U-boat.net; Dönitz comments from "Grand Admiral Dönitz on the U-boat War," British Anti-Submarine Warfare archive, 1945, p. 28, Public Record Office, ADM 199/2062; Dönitz fears of losing "tonnage war" from *Memoirs,* p. 343; Dönitz congratulatory message from *U-boat War, Vol. 2,* p. 266.

10. Numbers of U-boats in the North Atlantic on April 20 and May 3, 1943, from BdU KTB entries for those dates; figures do not include U-boats returning to port from North Atlantic operations.

11. Number of U-boats at sea from analysis of BdU KTBs (Daily War Diaries) for March 1, March 29, and May 3, 1943. This excludes outbound U-boats not yet on station and those returning to port; other details from Blair, *U-boat War, Vol. 2,* p. 273; Cremer remarks on convoy crisis from Cremer, *U-boat Commander,* p. 130.

12. The convoys that sailed between March 16 and April 21 included eleven eastbound convoys, HX230 through HX235 from Halifax to Liverpool, and SC123 through SC127 from New York and Halifax. Also twelve westbound convoys sailed from Liverpool, ON172 through ON179 and ONS1 through ONS4; ship totals from analysis of convoy rosters at ConvoyWeb.org; convoy losses and percentage sunk from "All Convoys Hit by U-boats" at U-boat.net.

13. Gruppen Meise, Lerche, and Specht formation from "Wolf packs" at U-boat.net.

14. Dönitz comments on Convoy HX230 from BdU KTB for March 30, 1943.

15. Sighting of *USS Bogue* by U-664 from "Battle of the Atlantic—Allied Communications Intelligence, December 1942–May 1945," SRH-009, National Security Agency, transcribed for online posting at the HyperWar Foundation at http://www.ibiblio.org/hyperwar/ETO/Ultra/SRH-009/index.html, Chapter 3, p. 39; Dönitz comment on Convoy HX233 from *Memoirs,* p. 336.

16. Status of VLR Liberator aircraft in the spring of 1943 from Syrett, David, *The Defeat of the German U-boats*, University of South Carolina Press, Columbia, 1994, p. 14, and Gannon, *Black May*, pp. 80–81.

17. Declassified Enigma intercepts of BdU messages to the Atlantic U-boats prompted authorities to reroute Convoys ON172, ON173, SC125, HX232, SC126, HX234, ON178, ONS4, SC127, HX235, and ON179 during their passages; from Syrett, *Defeat*, p. 33 and 40–43; also Blair, *U-boat War, Vol. 2*, pp. 280 and 287.

18. Details on Convoys HX234, ONS4, and ON178 from sailing lists at ConvoyWeb; other details from Blair, *U-boat War, Vol. 2*, pp. 283–286; also "Communications Intelligence," Chapter 4, pp. 57–58.

19. Dönitz comments on Trotha from Enigma message transmitted at 2230 GMT on April 23; "without attacking . . . worthless" message sent 1531 GMT on April 24, both intercepted and decrypted by the Allies, cited in "Communications Intelligence," pp. 56–57.

20. Oversay and North Channel geographical descriptions from *British Islands Pilot*, Vol. 4, Hydrographic Office No. 147, published under the Authority of the Secretary of the Navy, Washington, D.C., 1917; also Gretton, *Escort Commander*, pp. 134–135; additional scene details from Seth, Ronald, *The Fiercest Battle*, W. W. Norton, New York, 1962, pp. 21–22; ONS5 composition from ConvoyWeb.org.

21. Varying size of convoys and profiles of individual ships from individual sailing lists at ConvoyWeb.org; formation of Convoy ONS5 from "Convoy ONS5: Report of Proceedings, Senior Officer in *HMS Duncan*" and "Report of Proceedings, Commodore Convoy ONS5," Public Records Office, London, U.K., declassified from Most Secret, PRO ADM 223/16; composition of ONS5 from ConvoyWeb.org and WarSailors.com.

22. Details on Norwegian ship *Rena* from Warsailors.com. Commodore J. Kenneth Brook background from Gannon, *Black May*, pp. 124–125, and Seth, *Fiercest Battle*, p. 124.

23. Gretton background from "Notes on the Gretton Family"; additional material as cited from his two postwar memoirs, *Crisis Convoy*, passim, and *Escort Commander*, passim.

24. HMS *Wolverine* involvement in Malta operation and sinking of *Dagabur* from Gretton, *Escort Commander*, pp. 87–94.

25. Escort Group B-7 composition and commanders, group training and preparations for Convoy ONS5 from Gretton, *Escort Commander*, pp. 131–133 and 209.

26. Gretton sending test messages in Latin and questioning Atkinson on helm order from Atkinson, Robert, Oral Interview, undated, Imperial War Museum, London, U.K., Oral History Collection Accession No. 116/93.

27. Gretton evaluation of B-7 performance with Convoy HX231 from Gretton, *Crisis Convoy*, p. 135.

28. Escort Group B-7 new escort commanders, from Gretton, *Escort Commander*, pp. 131–133 and 209.

29. HMS *Duncan* equipment upgrades from Gretton, *Escort Commander*; also Gannon, *Black May*, p. 130.

30. Convoy ONS5 rendezvous from Seth, *Fiercest Battle*, p. 77, and Gannon, *Black May*, p. 124.

31. The seven convoys steaming in the central North Atlantic on April 22, 1943 were eastbound Convoys HX233, HX234, HX235, and SC127, and westbound Convoys ONS3, ON178 and ONS4. Four other convoys were either just departing from or close to arriving at New York, Halifax, or Liverpool but were not threatened by any wolf packs. Sailing data from individual convoy files at ConvoyWeb.org.

32. HMS *Biter* and 5th Support Group details from "Allied Warships" section at U-boat.net, and Blair, *U-boat War, Vol. 2*, p. 285.

33. U-732 report of biplane attack from BdU KTB for April 23; U-404 erroneous claim to have sunk carrier USS *Ranger* from BdU KTB for April 26; Dönitz initial reaction and exchange of messages from "Communications Intelligence," p. 58; Hessler comments on Dönitz's "irritated" reaction from sinking of U-203 from Hessler, *U-boat War*, p. 103; sinking of U-203 and HMS *Pathfinder* from Blair, *U-boat War, Vol. 2*, p. 286; Dönitz and his staff would not realize that U-203 was lost until May 6, when he noted the presumed sinking in the BdU KTB.

34. Dönitz "honest firm" comment from Dönitz, *Memoirs*, p. 338; claimed merchant ship sinkings and tonnages from the BdU KTB during March 20 and May 2, 1943; actual convoy losses from British maritime archives at "All Convoys Hit by U-boats" at U-boat.net.

35. Allied loss of Enigma from Blair, *U-boat War, Vol. 2*, p. 288; Gruppe Star formed and Dönitz comment from BdU KTB for April 27, 1943; the six new VIIC boats were U-231, U-270, U-386, U-648, U-650, U-710, and U-954; the six veteran VIICs were U-209, U-258, U-378, U-381, U-413, and U-552; the five new Type IXC40 boats were U-192, U-528, U-531, U-532, and U-533; see BdU KTB for April 27, 1943; U-710 sinking from U-boat.net.

36. Gruppe Star formation from BdU KTB for April 27, 1943.

CHAPTER 11: THE FIRST SKIRMISHES

1. The convoy's plotted waypoints, labeled XA to XY, charted the planned course from the mouth of the North Channel to the Western Ocean Meeting point east of St. John's, Newfoundland. Convoy ONS5 course track and daily positions from "Convoy ONS5, Report of Proceedings, Senior Escort Officer Escort Group B-7," Public Records Office, London, declassified from Most Secret, PRO ADM 223/16 (hereafter "B-7 Report").

2. HMS *Duncan* refueling difficulties from "B-7 Report"; collision of *Bornholm* and *Berkel* from Seth, *Fiercest*, p. 87, and Gannon, *Black May*, p. 134; Commodore Brook comment from "Narrative of Voyage, ONS5," in ONS5 archive.

3. ONS5 refueling from Gannon, *Black May*, p. 134.

4. Convoy course change from 270 degrees to 247 degrees 30 minutes from "B-7 Report"; Gruppe Star formed and Dönitz comment from BdU KTB for April 27, 1943.

5. U-710 presumed loss entered in BdU KTB on April 28, 1943; Von Witzendorff background from Busch and Roll, *U-boat Commanders*, p. 274 and "U-boat commanders" at U-boat.net; U-650 history from Wynn, *U-boat Operations, Vol. 2*, pp. 106–108.

6. Gretton complaint about atmospheric interference and interception of U-boat contact message for Convoy SC127 from "B-7 Report."

7. U-650 message and BdU reply to U-650 from Gannon, *Black May*, p. 140.

8. U-650 KTB for April 28.

9. Cat-and-mouse game with B-7 and U-650 from U-650 KTB, and Gretton, *Escort Commander*, pp. 136–137.

10. ONS5 evasive maneuver from "B-7 Report," p. 2; also Syrett, *Defeat*, p. 66, and Seth, *Fiercest*, p. 91; von Witzendorff complaint from U-650 KTB.

11. Scene at BdU operations, and next four Gruppe Star boats to report contact from BdU KTB for April 28.

12. Atkinson's description of the CINCWA message from Atkinson, Sir Robert, *Some Experiences of an Ancient Mariner*, Itchen Abbas and Avington Village News, U.K., 2006, p. 12.

13. Atkinson remarks to crew from Atkinson oral history.

14. Escort Group B-7 night stations from "B-7 Report," p. 2.

15. *Duncan* attack on first U-boat from "B-7 Report," Appendix B.

16. *Sunflower* prosecution of U-boat contact from "Report of Proceedings, Convoy ONS5," HMS *Sunflower*, appended to "B-7 Report"; Plomer angry comments from Seth, *Fiercest*, p. 95.

17. *Duncan* pursues four U-boats from "*HMS Duncan's* Report of Attacks on U-boats," in "B-7 Report," Annex B; comments on depth-charge crew from Gretton, *Escort Commander*, pp. 136–139.

18. Chesterman later determined that the helmsman had heard a different order passed to the Asdic operator and mistakenly thought he had been ordered to make a hard turn to starboard; from *Snowflake* initial night attack from "Report of Proceedings, Commanding Officer, HMS *Snowflake*," Appendix A(2) to "B-7 Report."

19. Ottoheinrich Junker career background from Busch and Roll, *U-boat Commanders*, p. 118, and "U-boat commanders" at U-boat.net; U-532 history from Wynn, *U-boat Operations, Vol. 2*, pp. 17–18; German torpedo crisis from Dönitz, *Memoirs*, pp. 85–88.

20. *Snowflake* attack on U-532 from *Snowflake* "Report of Proceedings"; other details from Gannon, *Black May,* pp. 147–148.

21. Gretton comments on Duncan crew from "B-7 Report," and Gretton, *Escort Commander,* p. 138.

22. Junker description of battle damage from U-532 KTB, cited in Gannon, *Black May,* p. 148; credit for two hits in BdU KTB for May 2, 1943.

23. 3rd Support Group ships ordered to ONS5 from "Report of Proceedings, 3rd Support Group, Commanding Officer, *HMS Offa,*" Public Records Office, London, declassified from Most Secret, PRO ADM 223/16 (hereafter "3SG Report"); also "Report of Proceedings, Commanding Officer, *HMS Oribi*" (hereafter "*Oribi* Report"), appendix to "3SG Report."

24. Gretton orders day stations and sends message to Brook in "B-7 Report."

25. *McKeesport* background from "Ships Sunk by U-boats" at U-boat.net; other details from Gannon, *Black May,* pp. 150–151.

26. Duncan reaction to *McKeesport* torpedoing from "B-7 Report"; *West Maximus* straggled from Seth, *Fiercest,* p. 101.

27. U-258 history from Wynn, *U-boat Operations, Vol. 1,* pp. 181–182; Kapitänleutnant Wilhelm von Mässenhausen career from Busch and Roll, *U-boat Commanders,* p. 154, and "U-boat commanders" at U-boat.net.

28. Events of late April 29 from "B-7 Report"; three *Oribi* crewmen injured from Atkinson, *Ancient Mariner,* p. 14.

29. *Oribi* rendezvous from "B-7 Report"; failed fueling attempt from Gannon, *Black May,* p. 154.

30. B-7 events the night of April 30–May 1 from "B-7 Report."

31. 3rd Escort Group night movements from "3SG Report."

32. *HMS Pink* escorting six merchantmen from "Report of Proceedings for ONS5 (Straggler Portion), Commander *HMS Pink,*" in "B-7 Report" (hereafter "*Pink* Straggler Report").

33. Atkinson on watch from Gannon, *Black May,* p. 154; comments on duffel coat from Atkinson oral histories.

34. Description of May 1 storm from Brook, "Narrative of Voyage"; "B-7 Report," and Gretton, *Escort Commander,* pp. 141–142.

35. Dönitz decision to call off Gruppe Star from BdU KTB for May 1, 1943.

36. Number of ships in convoy from Brook, "Narrative of Voyage"; Liberator flight to ONS5 from convoy position at 0800 on May 2 using the latitude-longitude calculator at Indo.com.

37. Duncan fueling woes from "B-7 Report."

38. 3rd Support Group arrival from "3SG Report"; Gretton comments from *Escort Commander,* p. 143.

39. Escort Group B-7 030801Z [GMT] message to CINCWA, from "B-7 Report."

40. Sherwood biographical background and personal profile from Lund, Paul, and Ludlam, Harry, *Night of the U-boats,* W. Foulsham & Co., London, 1973, pp. 75–76; Seth, *Fiercest,* p. 113; Gretton comment about Sherwood from *Escort Commander,* p. 146.

41. Gretton decision to depart from *Escort Commander,* p. 144; detachment of B-7 and 3SG warships from "Convoy ONS5, Continuation of Report by Commanding Officer, *HMS Tay,* S.O.," from "B-7 Report" (hereafter "Tay Report").

CHAPTER 12: THE MÊLÉE AT 55 NORTH 042 WEST

1. The five convoys besides ONS5 in the mid-Atlantic on May 1 included eastbound Convoys HX236 and SC129 and westbound ON180 and ONS6; in its fifteen days of operation during April 19–May 4, Gruppe Specht would constantly change in size as individual U-boats joined or broke off from the group on BdU's orders. Initially comprising eight U-boats, the wolf pack doubled in size to sixteen two days later when Dönitz assigned eight more U-boats from two recently dissolved wolf packs, Meise and Lerche. The total continued to change during the next seven days as eight more U-boats joined the formation while another six broke off to return to port at the end of their individual war patrols. See BdU KTB reports during that period.

2. Three Gruppe Star boats—U-386, U-528, and U-532—had aborted their patrols with serious battle damage during the skirmish with ONS5 on April 29–30, leaving thirteen boats still on patrol; details on the Specht-Amsel patrol line from Bdu KTB, May 3, 1943; latitude-longitude boundaries of Specht-Amsel line and Dönitz exhortation from Gannon, *Black May*, p. 167; calculation of length, orientation, and U-boat spacing from the latitude-longitude calculator at Indo.com.; distances and orientation of patrol lines determined from latitude-longitude calculator at Indo.com; Dönitz exhortation from "Convoy ONS5: Analysis of U-boat Operations," Operational Intelligence Center, British Admiralty (hereafter OIC Analysis).

3. Dönitz organizing Gruppen Amsel 1–4 from BdU KTB for May 3, 1943.

4. SC128 and HX236 evasion of U-boats from Blair, *U-boat War, Vol. 2*, p. 291; Dönitz praise for the SC128 escorts' "feint" from *Memoirs*, p. 338.

5. Gruppe Fink patrol line latitude-longitude from Gannon, *Black May*, p. 168, distance and intervals between U-boats from latitude-longitude calculator at Indo.com; Convoy ONS5 course and speed from "*Tay* Report."

6. Ironically, the Germans had retrieved a similar device from an RAF bomber shot down over Rotterdam on February 2, and by March 5, Admiral Dönitz, citing the radar found on the downed aircraft, openly lamented in the BdU daily war diary, "The enemy is working on carrier frequencies outside the frequency range of the present [Metox radar warning] receivers."

7. Attacks by two RCAF Canso A aircraft on U-209 and U-630 from Blair, *U-boat War, Vol. 2*, pp. 290–291 and Seth, *Fiercest*, pp. 117–119; Heinsohn and Brodda messages to BdU from Gannon, *Black May*, p. 175; details on U-438 and U-209 from U-boat.net.

8. U-438 attack from Gannon, *Black May*, p. 175; Blair, *U-boat War, Vol. 2*, p. 291, and Seth, *Fiercest*, pp. 118–119; U-438 background from U-boat.net.

9. Hasenschar sighting of ONS5 from BdU KTB for May 4, 1943; four U-boats sight ONS5 or its escorts from OIC Analysis.

10. Daytime events for ONS5 from "*Tay* Report," and "3SG Report," p. 2.

11. ONS5 situation at dusk on May 4 from "*Tay* Report," also "Report of Proceedings, Senior Officer, 1st Support Group in *HMS Pelican*" (hereafter "1SG Report"), Public Records Office, London, declassified from Most Secret, PRO ADM 223/16; the U-boats closing in on ONS5 included twenty-seven from Gruppen Specht and Star reorganized as Gruppe Fink; and twelve from Gruppe Amsel reformed into Amsel 1 and Amsel 2 with six boats apiece. Another twelve Amsel boats in Gruppen Amsel 3 and 4 were operating farther south against a different convoy; from BdU KTB for May 3, 1943; three U-boats in contact with ONS5 from OIC Analysis.

12. Dönitz exhortation transmitted at 2213 GMT on May 4 was intercepted by British codebreakers and cited in OIC Analysis.

13. Gretschel description of attack on ONS5 from U-707 KTB cited in Gannon, *Black May*, pp. 180–182; *Oribi* and *Offa* search from "*Oribi* Report"; details on *North Britain* sinking from "Allied Merchants Hit" at U-boat.net.

14. Escort Group B-7 response to U-707 attack from "*Tay* Report"; U-514 and Aufferman details from U-boat.net; *Vidette* hunt for three U-boats from *Vidette* attack summaries in "B-7 Report," Appendix B; U-514 damaged from Gannon, *Black May*, p. 190. U-662 history and Kapitänleutnant Müller background information from U-boat.net; attack on Convoy SL126 from Blair, *U-boat War, Vol. 2*, p. 271; U-732 and Oberleutnant Carlsen background information from U-boat.net; Carlsen aborts patrol from Gannon, *Black May*, p. 190.

15. Seven U-boats in contact with ONS5 from OIC Analysis; details of *Harbury* sinking from "Interview with the Master, Captain W. E. Cook," Shipping Casualties Division, Admiralty Trade Division, June 16, 1943.

16. U-264 attack on *West Maximus* and *Harperley* from "Allied Merchants Hit" at U-boat.net; *Harperley* details from "Interview with the Master, Captain Joseph E. Turgoose," Shipping Casualties Division, Admiralty Trade Division, June 16, 1943 (hereafter "Turgoose interview"); Kapitänleutnant Looks background from Busch and Roll, *U-boat Commanders*, p. 150; Looks commentary on attacks from U-264 KTB, cited in Gannon, *Black May*, pp. 185–186.

17. Details of *Harperley* sinking from Turgoose interview; *West Maximus* sinking details from Gannon, *Black May*, p. 187.

18. Corvette *Snowflake* pursuit of U-boats from "Report of Proceedings, Commanding Officer, HMS *Snowflake*" (hereafter "*Snowflake* Report"), Appendix A-2 to "B-7 Report."

19. U-358 history from U-boat.net and Wynn, *U-boat Operations, Vol. 1*, pp. 236–237; Kapitänleutnant Manke background from Busch and Roll, *U-boat Commanders*, p. 155; Manke claimed in his KTB that the *Bristol City* had stopped to pick up survivors from lifeboats in the area, but no other accounts citing the masters of those ships confirm that.

20. *Wentworth* sinking details from Seth, *Fiercest*, pp. 137–138; Gannon, *Black May*, pp. 197–199.

21. Destroyer *Offa* attack on U-boat from "3SG Report."

22. History of U-270 from U-boat.net and Wynn, *U-boat Operations, Vol. 1*, pp. 191–192; Kapitänleutnant Otto background from Busch and Roll, *U-boat Commanders*, p. 193; Otto description of damage from U-270 KTB for May 5, 1943, cited in Gannon, *Black May*, p. 194.

23. Total convoy losses from "Convoy Battles" at U-boat.net; U-boats sunk, forced to abort, damaged, and driven off from Gannon, *Black May*, pp.199–200; Folkers message on *Lorient* from Gannon, *Black May*, p. 179.

24. BdU exhortation to U-boats from "Communications Intelligence," Chapter 4, p. 60.

25. Convoy ONS5 morning position, course and speed from "B-7 Report"; *Pink* stragglers' group position, course and speed from "*Pink* Straggler Report,"; refueling attempt from "*Tay* Report"; *Oribi* hunts three destroyers from "*Oribi* Report."

26. *Dolius* description and sinking from "Report of an Interview with the Master, M.V. *Dolius*, Captain C. R. Cheetham," Shipping Casualties Section, Admiralty Trade Division, June 15, 1943, in Convoy ONS5 Archive; also "Allied Merchants Hit" at U-boat.net.

27. U-638 history from Wynn, *U-boat Operations, Vol. 2*, p. 100, and U-boat.net; Kapitänleutnant Staudinger background from Busch and Roll, *U-boat Commanders*, p. 247; little is known of U-638's performance in the ONS5 attack because the U-boat and its entire crew were sunk by the corvette *Sunflower* immediately after striking the *Dolius*; evacuation of *Dolius* crew from "Interview with the Master, M.V. *Dolius*."

28. *Sunflower* attack on U-638 and Plomer remarks on *Dolius* survivors from "Report of Proceedings, Commanding Officer, HMS *Sunflower*," Appendix A-3 to "B-7 Report."

29. British convoy escort instructions from Chalmers, *Horton*, p. 167.

30. HMS *Pink* escorting stragglers and attack on U-boat from "*Pink* Straggler Report"; *Pink* forced to shut down one boiler from Gannon, *Black May*, p. 204; *Pink* attack on U-boat from "Narrative of Attack by HMS *Pink* on U-boat," Appendix to "*Pink* Straggler Report."

31. The identity and fate of the corvette *Pink*'s daylight attack on May 5 long eluded postwar researchers and typified the difficulty in reconstructing specific incidents that occurred in a swirling, chaotic battle. The Admiralty initially credited Atkinson with the sinking of the recently commissioned Type IXC40 U-192, commanded by Oberleutnant zur See Werner Happe, which went down with all hands sometime during the ONS5 battle. A later postwar analysis of Admiralty and U-boat records led a 1991 panel to determine that *Pink* had crippled but not sunk the Type VIIC U-358, and that the corvette *Loosestrife* sank the U-192 during the furious battle on the night of May 5–6. Atkinson himself states that the Admiralty had subsequently identified his victim as the Type IXB U-109, which other reports say was sunk on May 4 northeast of the Azores by a Royal Air Force 86 Squadron VLR Liberator; Kapitänleutnant Manke survey of attack and damages from U-358 KTB for May 5, 1943, cited in Gannon, *Black May*, p. 209.

32. The U.S. government's response to the attempted sabotage was swift and brutal. All eight were under arrest within two weeks, and six of them were executed on August 8, 1942 after a military commission trial. The two who betrayed their teammates received lengthy prison sentences but were granted executive clemency by President Truman and deported back to Germany in 1948. See Blair, *U-boat War, Vol. 1*, pp. 603–605.

33. Radio communications between the *Tay* and the VLR Liberator from "R/T [Radio-telephone] Log HMS *Tay*, Convoy ONS5," and from "*Tay* Report"; convoy course, speed, and formation from "*Tay* Report."

34. U-266 history from Wynn, *U-boat Operations, Vol. 1*, p. 188, and U-boat.net; Kapitänleut-nant von Jessen background from Busch and Roll, *U-boat Commanders*, p. 117, and U-boat.net; Amsel 2 patrol line described in Syrett, *Defeat*, p. 73.

35. Description of *Selvistan* loss including weather conditions on May 5 from "Report of an In-terview with the First Officer . . . S.S. *Selvistan*," Shipping Casualties Section, Admiralty Trade Divi-sion, July 27, 1943, in ONS Archive.

36. U-boat periscope seen inside ONS5 from Gannon, *Black May*, p. 213.

37. *Gharinda* and *Bonde* sinkings from "Report of an Interview with the Master . . . S.S. *Gharinda*," Admiralty Trade Division, July 17, 1943, in ONS5 Archive.

38. HMS *Tay* response to U-266 attacks from "*Tay* Report"; *Oribi* and *Offa* hunt U-266 in "3SG Report."

39. *Gharinda* and *Bonde* casualties from "Allied Merchants Hit," at Uboat.net.

40. No records from U-266 survived the battle because an RAF 58 Squadron Halifax bomber at-tacked and sank the U-boat, killing all forty-seven men aboard at a point north of the Azores on May 15 as von Jessen was heading back to St. Nazaire. This marked the first sinking of a U-boat by the Top Secret air-dropped Mark XXIV homing torpedo. U-266 damage report message to BdU in NARA RG457, SRGN 17195; German records show the boat recovered sufficiently to hunt in a subsequent wolf pack, Gruppe Elbe, between May 7 and 10, before heading back to port; from Wynn, *U-boat Operations, Vol. 1*, p. 188.

CHAPTER 13: BATTLE IN THE FOG

1. Nine U-boats in firm contact from OIC Analysis.

2. Weather conditions at dusk on May 5, 1932, from "*Tay* Report."

3. Escort Group B-7 and 3rd Support Group night stations from "*Tay* Report."

4. Dönitz's messages to the Fink and Amsel U-boats were intercepted and decrypted by Allied code breakers; cited in "Communications Intelligence," Chapter 4, p. 60, also OIC Analysis.

5. Gretschel comment on visibility from U-707 KTB for May 5, 1943, cited in Gannon, *Black May*, p. 219.

6. Description of *Sunflower* chase of three U-boats from "*Sunflower* Report"; Plomer-Sherwood radio exchange from "R/T [Radio-telephone] Log–HMS *Tay*"; *Snowflake* chase of U-boats from "*Snowflake* Report."

7. U-531 history from Wynn, *U-boat Operations, Vol. 2*, p. 17; U-30 history and role in sinking the SS *Athenia* from Wynn, *U-boat Operations, Vol. 1*, pp. 20–21; also Blair, *U-Boat, Vol. 1*, pp. 66–69; Neckel background from Busch and Roll, *U-boat Commanders*, p. 186.

8. HMS *Vidette* attack on U-531 from "Report of Attack–Vid Five," in "B-7 Report."

9. U-630 history from Wynn, *U-boat Operations, Vol. 2*, p. 95; Oberleutnant Winkler background from Busch and Roll, *U-boat Commanders*, p. 272; U-630 sinking of the British freighter HX231 merchantman *Shillong* in Gretton, *Escort Commander*, p. 120.

10. HMS *Vidette* attack on U-531 from "Report of Attack–Vid Seven," in "Report of Proceed-ing . . . Escort Group B-7."

11. Sherwood description of tactics from "*Tay* Report."

12. HMS *Loosestrife* sinks U-192 from "Report of Proceedings, Commanding Officer, HMS *Loosestrife*," in "B-7 Report," Appendix A.

13. HMS *Oribi* rams U-125 from "*Oribi* Report," p. 4; Folkers message to BdU and BdU re-sponse from Gannon, *Black May*, p. 228; *Snowflake* attack on U-125 and sinking from "*Snowflake* Report"; Sherwood denial of request to pick up survivors from "R/T [Radio-telephone] Log–HMS *Tay*, Convoy ONS5," from "*Tay* Report."

14. HMS *Sunflower* ramming of U-533 from "*Sunflower* Report."

15. HMS *Pelican* sinking of U-438 and Brewer assessment from "1SG Report."

16. HMS *Spey* attack on U-634 from "Report of Proceedings, Commanding Officer, HMS *Spey*," in "1SG Report."

17. Summary of Convoy ONS5 battle from several sources, including Appendices A and B from "*Tay* Report" and "Convoy ONS5" at U-boat.net.

18. Dönitz calls off ONS5 attack from BdU KTB for May 6, 1943.

CHAPTER 14: DEFEAT OF THE U-BOATS

1. Escort Group B-7 at St. John's and *HMS Duncan* cleanup from Gretton, *Escort Commander*, p. 149; St. John's description from Signalman A. H. Dossett, quoted in Middlebrook, *Convoy*, p. 43; the seven ships in B-7 carried around 50 officers and about 700 enlisted crewmen, tabulated from "Allied Warships" at U-boat.net.

2. As the reader can surmise, these "Records of Proceedings" constitute the main repository of raw data on Convoy ONS5 from the time it formed off Oversay until it reached the Canadian ports.

3. Recommendations and endorsements of Convoy ONS5 escorts from "*Tay* Report"; "B-7 Report"; "Convoy ONS5," Commander-in-Chief, Canadian Northwest Atlantic, July 9, 1943, in Convoy ONS5 Archive; "Remarks by Commodore (D), Western Approaches, Convoy ONS5," June 20, 1943, in Convoy ONS5 Archive; Horton comments to Admiralty in "CINCWA to Lords Commissioners of the Admiralty," July 20, 1943, ADM 237/113.

4. U-732 inaccurately reported sinking a 6,000-ton freighter, while U-264 erroneously reported sinking a third, 5,000-ton merchant ship after torpedoing the *West Maximum* and *Harperley.* See BdU KTB for May 5, 1943.

5. Assessment of ONS5 from BdU KTB for May 6, 1943; U-boat crew casualties compiled from Wynn, *U-boat Operations, Vols. 1* and 2, from individual U-boat histories; Kapitänleutnant Folkers background from "U-boat Commanders" at U-boat.net.

6. Hessler analysis of ONS5 from Hessler, *U-boat War*, p. 106.

7. Addressing the radar threat from BdU KTB for May 6, 1943.

8. Deployment of the Mark XXIV homing torpedo from Gannon, *Black May*, pp. 367–369; Admiral Horton and the aircraft-launched rocket from Chalmers, *Horton*, pp. 193–194.

9. B-dienst interception of messages identifying Allied escort ships with HF/DF from Rohwer, *Critical Convoy Battles*, p. 199: they were the cutter *USS (CG) Spencer* in Escort Group A-3, the destroyer *HMS Churchill* in Escort Group C-4, and the destroyer *HMS Hurricane* in Escort Group B-1; moreover, German agents in Spain photographed the HF/DF antennas on a number of Allied warships, but German analysts mistakenly thought they were part of the ships' radar system.

10. Hessler on exaggerated sinking claims from Hessler, *U-boat War*, p. 100.

11. The convoys were eastbound SC128, HX237, SC129, HX238, SC130, and HX239; and westbound ON180, ONS6, ON181, ON182, ONS7, and ON183; number of convoys, total of merchant ships, and total tonnage at sea or preparing for departure from ConvoyWeb.org; number of U-boats on Atlantic patrol the week of May 3, 1943 from BdU KTB for that date; the other thirty-two operational U-boats were serving in other areas such as the Mediterranean, the South Atlantic, or on Arctic patrols.

12. Formation of Elbe-Rhein patrol line from BdU KTB for May 7, 1943.

13. Composition of Convoys HX237 and SC129 from ConvoyWeb.org; the Escort Group C-2 consisted of the destroyer *HMS Broadway*; the frigate *HMS Lagan*; corvettes *HMCS Chambly, HMCS Drumheller, HMCS Modern,* and *HMS Primrose*; ASW trawler *HMS Vizalma*; and seagoing tug *Dexterous.* Ships in Escort Group B-2 were the destroyers *HMS Hesperus* and *HMS Whitehall*; corvettes *HMS Campanula, HMS Clematis, HMS Gentian, HMS Heather,* and *HMS Sweetbriar,* and the ASW trawlers *HMS Lady Madeleine* and *HMS Sapper.*

14. Of the twelve Rhein U-boats, five joined Elbe 1 and six went into Elbe 2, with U-403 breaking off to return to port; of the sixteen Elbe boats, eight joined Elbe 1 and seven joined Elbe 2, while U-266 left to refuel from a U-tanker and was sunk by an *HMS Biter* aircraft on May 14. See Uboat.net.

15. U-403 attempt against HX237 from BdU KTB for May 10, 1943; also Syrett, *Defeat*, p. 105.

16. U-230 attacked by *Swordfish* in Werner, *Iron Coffins*, p. 122; assessment of air cover over HX237 from BdU war diary for May 12, 1943.

17. Fido homing torpedo attack against U-456 from Gannon, *Black May*, p. 370; HX237 sinkings from "Wolf Packs" at U-boat.net; Admiral Godt was in day-to-day command of the U-boat Force during May 12–15 because Admiral Dönitz was on a formal trip as commander-in-chief of the Kriegsmarine to Italy, where he met with his Italian counterparts and dictator Benito Mussolini; see "Führer Conferences," pp. 320–322.

18. HMS *Hesperus* attacks on U-223 and U-186 from MacIntyre, *U-boat Killer*, Chapter 11; U-boat operations called off against HX237 and SC129 in Syrett, *Defeat*, p. 115.

19. Gruppe Drossel suffered an unusually high number of losses during its seventeen days of operations in the central and North Atlantic. In addition to the three boats lost against HX237, the wolf pack lost another five boats, including two that collided off the coast of Spain on May 4.

20. Distance between the Rhein-Elbe-Drossel operation and the Isar-Iller-Inn-Lech-Naab patrol lines calculated from May 13 position reports using the latitude-longitude calculator at Indo.com; composition of northern wolf packs and identities of eight U-boats in the ONS5 battle from U-boat.net.

21. U-640 sighting of convoy from BdU KTB for May 12, 1943; U-640 and U-657 fates from Blair, *U-boat, Vol. 2*, p. 331; U-646 and U-273 fates from Blair, *U-boat, Vol. 2*, p. 332.

22. Donau 1 and Donau 2 formed, Allied U-boat Situation Report intercepted by B-Dienst, and Convoy SC130 anticipated, from BdU KTB for May 15, 1943.

23. Escort Group B-7 makeup on March 14, 1943 from Syrett, *Defeat*, p. 122; rescue ship *Zamalek* record from "Convoy SC130" at Warsailors.com.

24. First days of SC130 from Gretton, *Escort Commander*, pp. 150–151; additional details from "Gretton Family Notes."

25. Iceberg scare from Gretton, *Escort Commander*, pp. 151–152.

26. Events on May 16 and 17 from Syrett, *Defeat*, pp. 123–125, and Gretton, *Escort Commander*, p. 152.

27. Initial skirmishes with U-boats the night of May 18–19 from Gretton, *Escort Commander*, pp. 154–155, and Syrett, *Defeat*, p. 125; Godt comments from BdU KTB for May 18, 1943.

28. VLR Liberator attack and *Tay* hunt for U-731, and daytime events from Syrett, *Defeat*, pp. 125–127. Citing German and Allied archives, Syrett credited "T/120" with the sinking of the Type VIIC U-954, but a 1991 re-examination of the records led officials to conclude that the aircraft had actually attacked U-731, which escaped. The sinking of U-954 is discussed later in this chapter; other details from Blair, *U-boat War, Vol. 2*, p. 333; and Gretton, *Escort Commander*, pp. 154–155.

29. Since the Hedgehog mortar shells only detonated upon impact with a U-boat, Gretton's eyewitness account led the Admiralty to credit the *Duncan* and *Snowflake* with the sinking of U-381. However, a later analysis indicated that the two escorts had attacked two different U-boats—most likely U-304 and U-636—causing fatal damage to neither. The cause of loss of U-381 remains unknown; see Gannon, *Black May*, p. 384.

30. Gretton comments on *Snowflake* from *Escort Commander*, pp. 156–157.

31. U-256 and U-954 histories from Wynn, *U-boat Operations, Vol. 1*, pp. 179–180, and *U-boat Operations, Vol. 2*, pp. 189–190; Kapitänleutnant Loewe background from Busch and Roll, *U-boat Commanders*, p. 149.

32. Attack on U-954 by 1st Support Group ships *Jed, Wear*, and *Sennen* from Syrett, *Defeat*, pp. 128–129.

33. U-boats frustrated by air coverage of SC130 from Syrett, *Defeat*, p. 130; also Gannon, *Black May*, p. 384.

34. BdU message to U-boats from PRO, DEFE 3/718, intercepted and decrypted communications, cited in Syrett, *Defeat*, p. 130.

35. Events of the night of May 19–20 and sinking of U-258 from Gannon, *Black May*, pp. 384–385.

36. End of the struggle for SC130 from Gretton, *Escort Commander*, pp. 160–161; Escort Group B-7 arrival in the United Kingdom from Gannon, *Black May*, p. 386.

37. Dönitz message of 1910 GMT May 21 from "Communications Intelligence," Chapter 4, p. 65.

38. U-boat losses and Allied merchant ship sinkings during April 29–May 21 from U-boat.net: the convoys were eastbound HX236, SC128, HX237, SC129, HX238, SC130, and HX239, and westbound ON180, ONS6, ON181, ON182, ONS7, ON183, and ON184; the U-boats were able to locate eastbound HX237, SC129, and SC130, as well as westbound ONS5, ONS6, and ONS7.

39. BdU announcement on U-boat withdrawal from the North Atlantic and Dönitz message to his commanders in BdU KTB for May 24, 1943.

40. "Lost the battle" from Dönitz, *Memoirs*, p. 341.

EPILOGUE

1. Biographical details on Field Marshal Keitel from Polmar and Allen, *World War II*, pp. 466–467; substance of Dönitz-Hitler meeting on May 31, 1943, from "Führer Conferences," pp. 330–336.

2. Dönitz estimate of Allied aircraft and warships from Blair, *U-boat War, Vol. 2*, p. 354.

3. Details of "Walter" U-boat from Blair, *U-boat War, Vol. 2*, pp. 312–313, and "The Walter U-boats" at uboat.net; Type XXI and Type XXIII U-boat characteristics from "U-boat Types" at Uboat.net.

4. Decision to send U-boats to the central Atlantic from Hessler, *U-boat War, Vol. 2*, p. 113.

5. Organization of central Atlantic convoys from Blair, *U-boat War Vol. 2*, p. 341; convoy details from ConvoyWeb.org.

6. U.S. Navy warships escorting the central Atlantic convoys included a number of battleships and cruisers in addition to several destroyer squadrons.

7. U-boats assigned to Gruppe Trutz from the North Atlantic included U-92, U-211, U-217, U-221, U-228, U-232, U-336, U-435, U-558, U-569, U-603, U-608, U-641, U-642, U-666, U-951, and U-953; they were joined by two U-boats outbound on patrol from port, the Type XIV U-488, a U-tanker, and the Type IXC40 U-193.

8. U-boats from the North Atlantic that took part in the deception mission were U-91, U-202, U-304, U-378, U-413, U-552, U-575, U-621, U-636, U-645, U-650, U-664, and U-731; newly deployed U-467 was assigned to the operation but was sunk before it arrived; see BdU KTB for May 24, 1943.

9. Deception operation and Gruppe Trutz losses from Uboat.net.

10. Horton message to CINCWA units in Chalmers, *Horton*, pp. 199–200.

11. North Atlantic convoys without combat losses were HX238 to HX256 and SC131 to SC141; numerical analysis from individual convoy records at ConvoyWeb.org.

12. Churchill quote from Morison, *Atlantic Battle Won*, pp. 135–138.

13. ASW reinforcements arrive from Blair, *U-boat War, Vol. 2*, pp. 343–344; also Morison, *Atlantic Battle Won*, pp. 27–28; Tenth Fleet organized in Farago, Ladislas, *The Tenth Fleet*, Ivan Oblensky, Inc., New York, 1962, pp. 163–165; Allies learn of Cypher No. 3 penetration in Polmar and Allen, *World War II*, pp. 146–147.

14. Other wartime events during June–September 1943 from Polmar and Allen, *World War II*, pp. 32–33, 368–369, 481, and 732–733.

15. Escort carrier aircraft tactics against U-boats from Y'Blood, William T., *Hunter-Killer: U.S. Escort Carriers in the Battle of the Atlantic*, Naval Institute Press, Annapolis, MD, 1983, pp. 54–55.

16. *Zaunkönig* attacks against Convoy ON202 escorts from Blair, *U-boat War, Vol. 2*, pp. 422–423; convoy losses from "Convoy ON202" at Uboat.net.

17. Werner experiences from Werner, *Iron Coffins*, pp. 82, 107, 135, 159, 187, and 274.

18. Further U-boat setbacks from Blair, *U-boat War, Vol. 2*, pp. 608–610; limited operation of Type XXI and Type XXIII boats from U-boat.net.

19. Merchant ship losses in 1943 from Blair, *U-boat War, Vol. 2*, p. 820; new American shipping deliveries in 1943 from Lane, Frederick, *Ships for Victory: A History of Shipbuilding under the U.S. Maritime Commission in World War II*, Johns Hopkins University Press, Baltimore, 1951, p. 7.

20. U-boat losses from May 1943 through May 1945 from U-boat.net; personnel casualties from Gannon, *Black May*, p. 421.

21. Analysis of U-boat losses and fatality rates from a compendium of the U-boats that fought against Convoys HX229, SC122, ONS5 and SC130; individual data for each U-boat at U-boat.net, also Wynn, *U-boat Operations*, *Vols. 1* and *2*, for individual U-boat histories.

22. Final patrols of U-758 and Beisheim experiences from Wynn, *U-boat Operations*, *Vol. 2*, pp. 153–154, and Beisheim interviews.

23. The highest-ranking U-boat killer was Royal Navy Captain F. J. "Johnnie" Walker, who received individual credit for three U-boats during 1941–42, and while in command of the 2nd Support Group sank another fifteen U-boats during 1943–44; see "Allied Warship Commanders" at Uboat.net.

24. Gretton postwar service and death of his brother from Gretton Papers.

25. Later war service of Escort Group B-7 from Gretton, *Escort Commander*, pp. 172–175; U-boat kills from "Allied Warship Commanders" at U-boat.net; Atkinson brothers perished: from Robert Atkinson correspondence with the author, August 21, 2009.

26. Waters later wartime service and postwar career from *A Different War* (unpublished manuscript).

27. Jackson later wartime service from Jackson papers.

28. Schoor later wartime service from Schorr interview.

29. Wynne postwar career from Wynne, *Below the Mast*, pp. 207–225, with additional details from Richard Wynne, correspondence, December 2, 2010.

30. The German evacuation from the eastern provinces did not proceed without losses. In separate attacks on January 30 and February 10, 1945, the Soviet submarine S-13 torpedoed two merchant vessels crammed with refugees, killing more than 6,000; see Weir, Gary E., and Boyne, Walter J., *Rising Tide: The Untold Story of the Russian Submarines That Fought the Cold War*, New American Library, New York, 2004, pp. 27–33.

31. Dönitz fear of Russian atrocities from Dönitz, *Memoirs*, p. 431.

32. See Blair, *U-boat War*, *Vol. 2*, pp. 700–704; of nineteen former Nazis convicted by the international court, twelve received death sentences, three were given life sentences (including Grossadmiral Räder, who was released after nine years due to poor health), two more received twenty-year sentences, one received a fifteen-year prison term; two were acquitted.

33. Dönitz appointed chief of state from *Memoirs*, pp. 441–442; last message to U-boats from Blair, *U-boat War*, *Vol. 2*, pp. 699–700; "occupation by the enemy" from "Grand Admiral Dönitz on the U-boat War," in "Monthly Anti-Submarine Warfare Report," Admiralty Intelligence Division, Vol. 6, ADM 199/2062; of the 396 operational U-boats, German commanders scuttled 222 of them in various Norwegian and German ports to prevent the Allies from seizing the boats; the remaining 174 U-boats surrendered to the Allies as directed. The location of those U-boats on May 7, 1945 confirms how constricted the U-boat Force had become due to overwhelming Allied naval supremacy: the vast majority surrendered in place at their bases in Norway (eighty-two) and Germany (thirty-four), while another thirty-eight surrendered at ports in the United Kingdom. Another twenty boats were farther afield, including six in the Far East that the Japanese Navy commandeered after V-E Day, three that surrendered in French ports, five in the United States, two in Canada, two at Gibraltar, and two in Argentina. See Blair, *U-boat War*, *Vol. 2*, Appendix 19, pp. 818–819.

34. Calculation of deadliest naval battle first made by retired Coast Guard Captain John M. Waters Jr., in his postwar memoir, *Bloody Winter*, p. 237.

35. Vice-Admiral Max Horton, report to the Admiralty on "Sea Power and the R.A.F.," February 26, 1942, in Chalmers, *Horton*, p. 276; Dönitz comments in Dönitz, *Memoirs*, pp. 114–115.

GLOSSARY

1WO   Abbreviation for First Watch Officer, the second-in-command of a U-boat

2WO   Abbreviation for Second Watch Officer, a junior officer on a U-boat

AA   Anti-aircraft

ABC-1 Conference   See Conferences.

Action Stations   British naval term for the signal issued to a warship crew that combat with the enemy is imminent

"Adder"   See Convoy Escort Aircraft Maneuvers.

air gap   Area in central North Atlantic Ocean spanning about 600 miles southeast of Greenland and Iceland outside of most allied land-based aircraft range during 1939–43; called the "Black Pit" by U-boat crewmen

Aldis lamp   A fixed or portable plug-in, high-powered Morse Code signaling lamp; named after its inventor, Arthur C. W. Aldis

"Alligator"   See Convoy Escort Aircraft Maneuvers.

Arcadia   See Conferences.

"Artichoke"   See Convoy Escort Ship Maneuvers.

Asdic   British term for early sonar–stands for "Allied Submarine Detection Investigating Committee," a World War I panel that first researched this technology

ASV II   Metric radar

ASV III   Centimetric radar

ASW   Anti-Submarine Warfare (also known by British term "A/S")

Atlantic Charter   See Treaties and Other Agreements.

Atlantic Conference   See Conferences.

Atlantic Convoy Conference   See Conferences.

A.U. Committee   British War Cabinet Anti-U-Boat Warfare Committee

Ballast Tanks   Tanks outside the pressure hull of a submarine that, when flooded with water, enabled the submarine to dive

BAMS   Broadcasts for Allied Merchant Ships—A special Allied message system for transmitting information to convoys at sea that was continuously broken by the German Navy cryptologic service until mid-1943

Baubelehrung   "Boat familiarization"—U-boat Force program that assigned the officers an enlisted crewmen to a U-boat under construction from the time its keel was laid through commissioning for the purpose of training and getting used to all aspects of the boat

B-Dienst   *Funkbeobachtungsdienst*—German Navy cryptologic service

444

BdU   *Befehlshaber der Unterseeboote*—Commander in Chief U-Boats (Admiral Karl Dönitz); the abbreviation also commonly used to identify the admiral's staff or U-boat Headquarters

BdU Zug   Special passenger train for U-boat personnel on leave

"Beta Search"   See Convoy Escort Ship Maneuvers.

Bletchley Park   A mansion and grounds in Buckinghamshire, England (northwest of London), officially termed the Government Code and Cypher School, where cryptanalysts "broke" intercepts of encrypted German wireless radio traffic

Bolero   See Military Operations, Allied. .

Bombe   Nickname for the electromechanical scanning device at Bletchley Park used to decrypt the German Enigma cipher

CAM   Catapult Armed Merchantman—Merchant ship equipped with a short flight deck and aircraft catapult with one or more fighter aircraft used on one-way missions against attacking U-boats; aircraft ditch alongside ship and pilot rescued after flight

Canso   Canadian version of the PBY Catalina flying boat

Captain (D)   Royal Navy title for a captain commanding a flotilla of warships; in the Western Approaches Command responsible for North Atlantic convoy escorts, the officer responsible for that group held the rank of commodore and was known by the title Commodore (D)

CHOP   Change of Operational control—a designated location where command and control of a convoy or naval unit shifts from one headquarters to another

CINCLANTFLT   Commander-in-Chief, U.S. Atlantic Fleet

CINCCNWA   Commander-in-Chief, Canadian Northwest Atlantic Command, established after Atlantic Convoy Conference to replace U.S. Navy Task Force 24

CINCWA   Commander-in-Chief, Western Approaches Command

CNO   Chief of Naval Operations—The senior uniformed officer in the U.S. Navy. Prior to World War II, the CNO was the service's chief planner, but subordinate to the Commander-in-Chief, U.S. Fleet, at the time the No. 1-ranking admiral; both positions were merged early in World War II with Adm. Ernest J. King holding both titles.

"Cobra"   See Convoy Escort Aircraft Maneuvers.

COMINCH   Commander-in-Chief, U.S. Fleet–Senior-most U.S. Navy admiral; position merged in 1942 with Chief of Naval Operations under Adm. Ernest J. King

CONFERENCES

ABC-1 Conference   Code name for American-British military staff conferences held in Washington during Jan.–Mar. 1941 to develop a joint strategy against the Axis.

Arcadia   Code name for U.S.-British leadership conference in Washington during Dec. 1941–Jan. 1942.

Atlantic Conference   Meeting between President Franklin D. Roosevelt and British Prime Minister Winston Churchill and their military staffs on naval warships in Placentia Bay, Newfoundland, Aug. 9–12, 1941; during the meetings the allied leaders assigned top priority toward defeating the U-boat threat in the Atlantic.

Atlantic Convoy Conference   (Also known as Washington Convoy Conference) Organized as a result of the Casablanca Conference two months earlier, representatives from the British, Canadian, and U.S. navies, and the Royal Air Force and U.S. Army Air Forces met from Mar. 1–12, 1943 to identify improvements to North Atlantic Convoy defense. The decisions included the U.S. Navy's pullout from convoy escort groups, but assignment of escort aircraft carriers to several support groups, and agreement to provide 20 VLR land-based bombers to close the Greenland air gap, and to expand HF/DF (high-frequency direction-finding) network on both sides of the Atlantic.

Symbol   Code name for U.S.-British conference in Casablanca, Morocco between Roosevelt and Churchill and their staffs Jan. 14–24, 1943; reached several agreements included Allied call for unconditional surrender of the Axis powers; invasion of Sicily in 1943; postponement of invasion of Europe, and highest priority to defeating U-boat attacks on North Atlantic convoys.

CONVOY ESCORT AIRCRAFT MANEUVERS

"**Adder**"   Daytime aircraft patrol 8–12 miles ahead of convoy; patrol path 15 miles either side of convoy centerline; used when daylight attack expected

"**Alligator**"   Patrol on either port or starboard side of convoy at a distance of 10 miles; patrol path 10 miles ahead and astern of convoy

"**Cobra**"   Daytime aircraft search on both flanks and ahead of a convoy at a directed distance searching for surfaced U-boats; used when U-boats suspected in area but no firm sighting

"**Crocodile**"   Aircraft patrol ahead of a convoy from one bearing to another from the convoy; used to support fast convoys

"**Frog**"   Aircraft sweep across the stern of a convoy formation at a directed distance; patrol path two miles on either side of convoy centerline; used at dusk to detect U-boats trailing the convoy, prior to a convoy course change

"**Lizard**"   Search pre-designated sector to a directed distance out from the convoy; when a special area of ocean suspected to have U-boats; may be used at night

"**Mamba**"   Aircraft search for 30 miles out from the convoy along a particular compass bearing (in response to an HF/DF intercept of a U-boat radio transmission)

"**Python**"   Search on specific compass bearing at designated distance from convoy; conduct square search for 20 minutes; used when HF/DF has a bearing to a U-boat transmission but distance from convoy is unknown

"**Reptile**"   Search on designated bearing to a directed distance for a U-boat detected by D/F bearing. If nothing is sighted, act in accordance with previous instructions; used when U-boat has been detected by D/F bearings

"**Viper**"   Patrol around convoy at range of visibility to convoy; used in daytime if poor visibility or at night

CONVOY ESCORT SHIP MANEUVERS

"**Artichoke**"   Used when a ship in convoy is torpedoed: The escort in the position "Su" astern of the convoy heads for the torpedoed ship at maximum speed in which its sonar/Asdic listening device works; meanwhile, escorts in the forward line of the convoy turn outward until reaching a course opposite the convoy's heading, then conduct a listening search as they pass down the columns of ships, with the lead escort proceeding down the center of the convoy and the outer ships passing close aboard the outermost columns of ships. This maneuver continues until the escorts reach a point 6,000 yards astern of the convoy position at the time of attack

"**Beta Search**"   Anti-submarine tactical measure after sighting U-boat

"**Half-Raspberry**"   Nighttime escort maneuver where upon a U-boat attack, some of the escort warships turn outward from the convoy body and sweep their own patrol sectors with radar and sonar and firing illuminating starshells if ordered

"**Operation Observant**"   an Asdic square search of two-mile sides with the "datum point" (contact point) at the center, usually conducted by two escort ships; one of the escorts could either reinforce the square (sometimes called the box) or operate within it. In event of a ship being torpedoed the site of the attack constituted the "Datum Point."

"Raspberry"   Nighttime escort maneuver where all warships turn outwards from convoy body and sweep their own patrol sectors with radar and sonar while also firing illuminating starshells

"Pineapple"   ASW tactical measure using illumination rounds

"Strawberry"   ASW deployment after U-boat attack

"Crocodile"   See Convoy Escort Aircraft Maneuvers.

Cryptography   The study of code and cipher systems employed for secret communication

CVE   escort aircraft carrier—used in convoy protection beginning in late February 1943

D/C   Depth charge—An anti-submarine weapon dropped or fired by special launcher from a naval warship. During World War II Allied depth charges had 300 or 600 pounds of high explosives with firing mechanisms that would detonate them at a pre-set depth. A special 1,000-pound depth charge fired from a ship's torpedo tubes was used in limited numbers.

Dead reckoning   The calculation of one's position at sea based on course, speed, and elapsed time since the last observed position, factoring in ocean currents, winds, and compass declinations

Enigma   German communications encryption device—used mechanical rotors to scramble clear-text message and to reverse encryption back to clear-text at receiving station (see Ultra). Formal name for the German naval cipher machine was the Schlüssel M, or Marine-Funkschlüssel-Maschine M. Other terms relating to the Allied-German struggle over penetrating the enemy's encrypted communications include:

Bombe   Electromechanical machine used to simulate Enigma settings and decrypt messages

Pinch   a Top Secret military operation to seize Enigma machines, rotors, and other material from German ships without the adversary learning of the compromise

Short signal or *Kurzsignale*   a code that used brief letter-numeral designations to provide routine reports such as weather conditions, fuel state, etc.

Triton   Advanced naval Enigma using four changeable rotors in the machine rather than three; operational in February 1942

ESF   Eastern Sea Frontier—New York–based U.S. Navy headquarters responsible for coastal defense and convoys

Fächer   (fan shot)—simultaneous firing of two or more torpedoes

FAT/G7   *Federapparattorpedo*—See Torpedoes, German.

FFO   fuel furnace oil—a form of fuel oil used in World War II–era naval ships

FIDO   (also Mark XXIV Mine)—See Torpedoes, Allied.

Flak   German acronym from *Fliegerabwehrkanone*–term for anti-aircraft gun or gunfire

Foc's'le   (contraction of forecastle, pronounced "folk-suhl")—A partial deck above the upper deck and at the head of the vessel; traditionally the sailors' living quarters. The name is derived from the castle fitted to medieval ships to bear archers in time of war.

Foxer   Towed noise-generator designed to decoy acoustic torpedoes (See Torpedoes, German)

"Frog"   See Convoy Escort Aircraft Maneuvers.

Funkspruch   Wireless radio signal

General Quarters   U.S. Navy signal that combat with an enemy is imminent

GMT   Greenwich Mean Time

"Half-Raspberry"   See Convoy Escort Ship Maneuvers.

Hawse pipe   The shaft or hole in the side of a vessel's bow through which the anchor chain passes

Hearse   Allied code word for German U-boat

Hedgehog   Anti-submarine projectile with contact fuse fired ahead of escort ship toward suspected U-boat location

HF/DF (prononced "Huff-Duff")—High Frequency Direction-Finding–a system of shore stations and/or ship-mounted direction-finding gear to pinpoint U-boat locations via intercepted bearings to source of high-frequency radio transmissions

Home Fleet Traditional name of that part of the Royal Navy assigned to defend the home waters of the United Kingdom. Resurrected in 1932 as the new name for the British Atlantic Fleet. During World War II its chief function was to prevent the German surface naval forces from breaking out of the Baltic Sea. At its height the fleet had three aircraft carriers, a battleship squadron, two cruiser squadrons, and dozens of destroyers and other escorts.

Husky See Military Operations, Allied.

Hydrophone Underwater sound detection device employed by both U-boats and surface warships. In German, *Gruppenhorchgerat*, or GHG

Hydrophone effect Underwater sound such as propeller cavitation of a surface ship or U-boat, detected and shown on instruments as having a certain bearing and range

JCS U.S. Joint Chiefs of Staff—Panel consisting of the commanders of the U.S. Army, Navy, and Army Air Forces with a fourth four-star officer selected as Chairman (initially Adm. William D. Leahy). The group was initially created in early 1941 as a counterpart to the British Combined Chiefs of Staff for military planning purposes, but was retained after World War II as the uniformed military leadership organization for the U.S. armed forces.

Kaleun (sometimes Kaleu) Contraction of *kapitänleutnant*

K-gun Launcher that fires a depth-charge canister off to the side of an attacking escort ship

Knights Cross *Ritterkreuz*—Variation of the German Iron Cross decoration for valor in combat. There were seven grades of the decoration, and to receive a higher class, one had to have previously earned the next-lower medal. The levels, and number awarded to U-boat sailors, were:

> Iron Cross second class (unknown);
> Iron Cross first class (unknown);
> Knights Cross with Oak Leaves (146 awarded);
> Knights Cross with Oak Leaves and Crossed Swords (only 29 awarded);
> Knights Cross with Oak Leaves, Crossed Swords, and Diamonds (only 5 awarded);
> Knights Cross with Golden Oak Leaves, Crossed Swords, and Diamonds (None).

Knot Unit of speed equivalent to one nautical mile (1.1516 statute miles) per hour

Kriegsmarine Term for the German Navy used between 1935 and 1945

KTB *Kriegstagebüch*—German daily war diary kept by ships and U-boats at sea, and by shore-based headquarters staffs

Leigh Light Powerful aircraft-mounted searchlight used by British aircrews to illuminate surfaced U-boats at night

Lend-Lease Act See Treaties and Other Agreements.

LI *Leitender Ingenieur*—Chief Engineering Officer on a U-boat

"Lizard" See Convoy Escort Aircraft Maneuvers.

Luftwaffe Term for the German Air Force used between 1935 and 1945

LuT *Lagenunabhängiger Torpedo*—see Torpedoes, German.

"Mamba" See Convoy Escort Aircraft Maneuvers.

MERSIG Contraction for Merchant Ship Signals—a system of wireless telegraphy codes used by Allied merchant convoys

Metox French-built radar search receivers installed on U-boats from August 1942. Formally called FuMB, for *Funkmessbeobachtergerät*

"Milch Cow" *Milchkuh*—U-boat designed as refueling tanker for other submarines

MILITARY OPERATIONS, ALLIED

Bolero Buildup of U.S. troops and equipment in Great Britain for the planned invasion of Europe

Husky Invasion of Sicily, 1943

Overlord Invasion of Normandy, June 6, 1944

Pedestal Royal Navy resupply of Malta, August 1942

Roundup Invasion of Europe planned for 1943; canceled

Torch Invasion of French North Africa, November 1942

MILITARY OPERATIONS, GERMAN

Pastorius U-boat operation where U-202 and U-548 landed eight saboteurs ashore at Amagansett, Long Island, and Ponte Vedra, Florida, in June 1942. All were captured and six executed after trial by a U.S. military commission.

Paukenschlag (Drumbeat) U-boat offensive against U.S. East Coast, January 1942

See-Lowe (Sea Lion) Planned 1940 German invasion of England, called off

Naxos U Advanced radar detector used by U-boats against Allied ten-centimeter radar; its performance was poor and rendered useless by a new Allied three-centimeter wavelength radar introduced in 1943

OIC Operational Intelligence Centre—British Admiralty unit responsible for tracking U-boat operations from a wide variety of sources, primarily decrypted communications intercepts

OKM Acronym for *Oberbefehlshaber der Kriegsmarine*—Commander-in-Chief of the German Navy

OMP ("Ocean Meeting Point") Specified location where a convoy rendezvoused with its assigned escort group; also known by specific area—WESTOMP for Western OMP, EASTOMP for Eastern OMP, HOMP for Halifax OMP, and ICOMP for Iceland OMP

OKW *Oberkommando der Wehrmacht*—supreme headquarters of German armed forces

"Operation Observant" See Convoy Escort Ship Maneuvers.

Overlord See Military Operations, Allied.

Pastorius See Military Operations, German.

Paukenschlag (Drumbeat) See Military Operations, German.

Pedestal See Military Operations, Allied.

Periscope Extendable tube-like optical device containing an arrangement of prisms, mirrors, and lenses that enabled a U-boat to view the surface of the sea or the sky from a submerged position

"Pineapple" See Convoy Escort Ship Maneuvers.

"Python" See Convoy Escort Aircraft Maneuvers.

Pressure hull Cylindrical steel hull containing personnel and essential operating systems designed to withstand many atmospheres of water pressure when a U-boat is submerged

Radar ("Radio Direction and Ranging"; also "RDF") a detection system that uses electromagnetic waves to identify the range, altitude, direction, and/or or speed of both moving and fixed objects such as aircraft or ships

"Raspberry" See Convoy Escort Ship Maneuvers.

"Reptile" See Convoy Escort Aircraft Maneuvers.

Romper A merchant ship that leaves a convoy to steam independently toward its destination

Roundup See Military Operations, Allied.

Die Rudeltaktik Wolf Tactics–Tactical doctrine in which U-boat Force headquarters would assign a large group of U-boats into an extended picket line athwart a convoy's anticipated course track. Once a U-boat sighted the formation it would become "contact keeper" and bring up additional boats with radio signals. When a sufficient number of boats were in contact with the convoy, they would then launch a mass attack, usually at night while operating on the surface for maximum speed.

Schlüssel M   German naval version of the Enigma electromechanical cipher machine

Schnorchel   Snorkel—Retractable breathing tube installed on U-boats late in World War II that enabled them to use their diesel engines while running submerged

See-Löwe (Sealion)   See Military Operations, German.

Snowflake   Ship-launched rocket that fires an illumination warhead to provide night-time detection of a surfaced U-boat

Snuggler   A merchant ship that leaves its assigned position within a convoy attempting to protect itself by steaming very close to another ship or ships

Special Intelligence   Code for intercepted and decrypted German military communications; also called Ultra

"Strawberry"   See Convoy Escort Ship Maneuvers.

Submarine Protocol   See Treaties and Other Agreements.

Support Group   Formation of destroyers employed as a mobile reserve force to defend North Atlantic Convoys from U-boat attacks

Swordfish   British carrier-launched biplane used in convoy escort

Symbol   See Conferences.

TBS   (for "Talk Between Ships")—Very High Frequency (VHF) FM radio transmitter-receiver installed on Allied warships to allow direct voice communication without interception by the enemy

Tenth Fleet   Special U.S. Navy command established in Washington, D.C. headquarters in May 1943 to direct the control and routing of convoys, coordinate and direct all anti-submarine operations against U-boats, and supervision of all U.S. Navy ASW training and development

Tonnage War   *Tonnageschlacht*—U-boat strategy devised by Admiral Karl Dönitz whose goal was to destroy Allied shipping at a rate exceeding the American and British shipyards' ability to replace lost merchant vessels

Torch   See Military Operations, Allied.

TORPEDOES, ALLIED

FIDO   (also Mark XXIV Mine)—air-dropped homing torpedo

TORPEDOES, GERMAN

FAT/G7   *Federapparattorpedo*—new steering device attached to the G7a (compressed air) or G7e (electric drive) torpedo that after a pre-set distance changed the weapon's straight-path course into a looping path to increase the chances of hitting a ship in convoy. First deployed on December 28, 1942

LUT   *Lagenunabhängiger Torpedo*—Advanced looping torpedo that could be set to fire in any direction (developed very late in the war)

Zaunkönig (Wren) T5   Homing torpedo designed to seek out the sound of a ship's propeller

Torpex   Military high-explosive combination of Cyclonite, TNT, and aluminum flakes

TREATIES AND OTHER AGREEMENTS

Atlantic Charter   Declaration of U.S. and British war objectives following the Atlantic Conference of August 1941 between President Roosevelt and British Prime Minister Winston Churchill at Placentia Bay, Newfoundland. This laid the foundation for their wartime alliance.

Lend-Lease Act   Approved by Congress in March 1941, this program initially enabled the United States to send military aid to Great Britain while still remaining officially neutral; later expanded to 44 allied nations with the Soviet Union receiving the second-largest share; a total of $50 billion worth of equipment distributed during the war.

Submarine Protocol   1930 international agreement, signed by Germany in 1936, that prohibited sinking civilian ships without warning except in a limited number of cases, including troopships, vessels in convoy, and civilian ships assisting military operations.

Tripartite Pact   Treaty between Germany, Italy, and Japan signed on Sept. 27, 1940 that called on each signatory to provide military assistance in case of attack by a nation not yet in the war (e.g. the United States); Hungary later signed the treaty.

Triton   Variant of Kriegsmarine Enigma system that used four rather than three rotors to encrypt and decrypt messages; operational fleetwide in February 1942 causing a 10-month blackout for Allied code-breakers

Ubootwaffe   German for U-boat Force

Ultra   Code for British decrypts from the German Enigma system

UZO   Contraction of *Uboot-Zieloptik*—Surface target-aiming binoculars with luminous reticules attached to a bridge post that automatically fed target line-of-sight bearing and range to a calculator inside the U-boat conning tower; in turn, this fed attack course headings into the gyroscopes of the torpedoes

V-E Day   "Victory in Europe Day," May 8, 1945—date of German surrender to allies

VLR   Very Long Range—B-24D and LB-30 Mk III Liberators modified with extra fuel tanks for a maximum flight range of 2,300 miles; assigned to long-range patrols against U-boats in the North Atlantic and Mediterranean

"Viper"   See Convoy Escort Aircraft Maneuvers.

Vorhaltrechner   U-boat calculator for determining the course of a torpedo upon firing (see UZO)

WAVES   Women Accepted for Volunteer Emergency Service—A women's reserve corps of the U.S. Navy established in 1942 to fulfill staff assignments in the Navy Department

Western Approaches Command   shortened to CINCWA—Royal Navy headquarters established in November 1941, responsible for defense of trans-Atlantic convoys

Wolf Pack   *Gruppe*—Formation of deployed U-boats directed from BdU headquarters to hunt for a specific allied convoy or to patrol a specific area of the ocean

WRNS   Known as "Wrens"—Women's Royal Naval Service—auxiliary to Royal Navy

Zaunkönig (Wren)—See Torpedoes, German.

BIBLIOGRAPHY

BOOKS

Abbazia, Patrick, *Mr. Roosevelt's Navy: The Private War of the U.S. Atlantic Fleet, 1939–1942*, Naval Institute Press, Annapolis, MD, 1975

Ambrose, Stephen E., *D-Day: The Climactic Battle of World War II*, Simon & Schuster, New York NY, 1994

Anonymous, *British Islands Pilot, Vol. 4, Hydrographic Office No. 147*, published under the Authority of the Secretary of the Navy, Washington, D.C., 1917

Atkinson, Sir Robert, *Some Experiences of an Ancient Mariner*, Itchen Abbas and Avington Village News, U.K., 2006

Bailey, Chris Howard, *The Corvettes and Their Crews: An Oral History*, a Royal Naval Museum Book of the Battle of the Atlantic, Alan Sutton Publishing Ltd., published in the United States by the U.S. Naval Institute Press, Annapolis MD, 1995

Beesly, Patrick, *Very Special Intelligence: The Story of the Admiralty's Operational Intelligence Centre, 1939–1945*, Hamish Hamilton Ltd., London, 1977

Behrens, C. B. A., *Merchant Shipping and the Demands of War*, H.M. Stationery Office, London, 1955

Blair, Clay, *Hitler's U-Boat War, Vol. 1: The Hunters: 1939–1942*, Random House, New York, 1996

Blair, Clay, *Hitler's U-Boat War, Vol. 2: The Hunted: 1942–1945*, Random House, New York, 1998

Bray, Jeffrey K., editor, *Ultra in the Atlantic: Allied Communication Intelligence and the Battle of the Atlantic*, Aegean Park Press, Walnut Creek, CA, 1996

Buell, Thomas B., *Master of Sea Power: A Biography of Fleet Admiral Ernest J. King*, Little, Brown and Company, Boston, 1980

Busch, Harald, *U-boats at War*, Ballantine Books, New York, 1953

Busch, Rainer and Roll, Hans-Joachim, *German U-boat Commanders of World War II*, Naval Institute Press, Annapolis, MD, 1999

Campbell, John, *Naval Weapons of World War II*, Naval Institute Press, Annapolis, MD, 1985

Carylon, Les, *Gallipoli*, Pan Macmillan, Sydney, Australia, 2001

Chalmers, W.S., Rear-Admiral RN (Ret.), *Max Horton and the Western Approaches*, Hodder and Stoughton, London, 1954

Churchill, Winston S., *Memoirs of the Second World War* (Abridgement of the Six Volumes of *The Second World War*), Houghton Mifflin Co., New York, 1987

Colledge, J. J. and Warlow, Ben, *Ships of the Royal Navy: The Complete Record of All Fighting Ships*, Vol. 1, Chatham, London 1969

Conrad, Joseph, *The Mirror of the Sea*, Harper and Brothers, New York, 1906; reprint, The Marlboro Press, Marlboro, VT, 1988

Cremer, Peter, *U-boat Commander*, Naval Institute Press, Annapolis, MD, 1984

Dönitz, Karl, Grand Admiral, *Memoirs: Ten Years and Twenty Days*, Da Capo Press, New York, 1997

Eden, Paul, General Editor, *The Encyclopedia of Aircraft of WWII*, Aerospace Publishing, London, U.K., 2004

Farago, Ladislas, *The Tenth Fleet*, Ivan Oblensky, Inc., New York, 1962

Gannon, Michael, *Operation Drumbeat*, Harper & Row, New York, 1990

Gannon, Michael, *Black May*, Dell Publishing, New York, 1998

Gleichauf, Justin F., *Unsung Sailors: The Naval Armed Guard in World War II*, Naval Institute Press, Annapolis, MD, 1990

Graves, Donald E., *In Peril on the Sea: The Royal Canadian Navy and the Battle of the Atlantic*, Robin Brass Studio, Toronto, 2003

Gretton, Peter, Vice Adm. RN (Ret.), *Convoy Escort Commander*, Cassell & Co. Ltd., London, 1964

Gretton, Peter, Vice Adm. RN (Ret.), *Crisis Convoy: The Story of HX231*, Naval Institute Press, Annapolis, MD, 1974

Hessler, Günter, *The U-boat War in the Atlantic: 1939–1945*, Her Majesty's Stationery Office, London, 1989

Howarth, Stephen and Law, Derek, editors, *The Battle of the Atlantic 1939–1945: The 50th Anniversary International Naval Conference*, Greenhill Books, London 1994.

Hughes, Terry, and Costello, John, *The Battle of the Atlantic*, Dial Press, New York NY, 1977

Hunter, Robert W., *Spy Hunter*, Naval Institute Press, Annapolis, MD, 1999

Kahn, David, *The Codebreakers*, Scribner, New York, 1967, 1996

Kahn, David, *Seizing the Enigma*, Random House, New York, 1991

Keegan, John, *The Price of Admiralty: The Evolution of Naval Warfare*, Viking Penguin, Inc., New York, 1989

King, Fleet Admiral Ernest J., *U.S. Navy at War, 1941–1945: Official Reports to the Secretary of the Navy*, United States Navy Department, Washington, D.C., 1946

King, Ernest J. and Whitehill, Walter Muir, *Fleet Admiral King: A Naval Record*, W. W. Norton, 1952

Kohl, Fritz and Rossler, Eberhard, *The Type XXI U-Boat*, Naval Institute Press, Annapolis, MD, 1991

Lane, Frederick, *Ships for Victory: A History of Shipbuilding under the U.S. Maritime Commission in World War II*, Johns Hopkins University Press, Baltimore, 1951

Lund, Paul, and Ludlam, Harry, *Night of the U-boats*, W. Foulsham & Co. Ltd., London, 1973

MacIntyre, Donald, Captain RN (Ret.), *The Battle of the Atlantic*, B. T. Batsford Ltd., London, 1961

MacIntyre, Donald, Captain RN (Ret.), *U-boat Killer*, W. W. Norton, London, 1956

Middlebrook, Martin, *Convoy*, William Morrow, New York, 1976

Milner, Marc, *The U-Boat Hunters*, Naval Institute Press, Annapolis, MD, 1994

Morison, Samuel Eliot, *The European Discovery of America: The Northern Voyages* (Vol. 1), Oxford University Press, New York, 1971

Morison, Samuel Eliot, *The Two-Ocean War: A Short History of the United States Navy in the Second World War*, Little, Brown, Boston, 1963

Morison, Samuel Eliot, *U.S. Naval Operations in World War II, Vol. I : The Battle of the Atlantic*, Little Brown, New York, 1947

Morison, Samuel Eliot, *U.S. Naval Operations in World War II, Vol. X: The Atlantic Battle Won*, Little Brown, New York, 1951

Mosley, Leonard, *Marshall: Hero for Our Times*, Hearst Books, New York, 1982

Perrett, Geoffrey, *There's a War to Be Won: The U.S. Army in World War II*, Random House, New York, 1991

Perrett, Geoffrey, *Eisenhower*, Random House, New York, 1999

Polmar, Norman, and Allen, Thomas B., *World War II: America at War*, Random House, New York, 1991

Rohwer, Jürgen, *The Critical Convoy Battles of March 1943*, Naval Institute Press, Annapolis, MD, 1977

Roskill, Stephen W., Captain RN (Ret.), *The War at Sea*, Vols. I–III, Naval & Military Press Ltd., Uckfield, East Sussex, U.K., 1956–1960

Seth, Ronald, *The Fiercest Battle*, W. W. Norton, New York, 1962

Showall, Jak Mallmann, *German Naval Codebreakers*, Ian Allan Publishing, Surrey, UK 2003

Showall, Jak Mallmann, *Hitler's Navy: A Reference Guide to the Kriegsmarine, 1935–1945*, Seaworth Publishing, London, 2009

Slessor, Sir John, Marshal of the Royal Air Force, *The Central Blue: Recollections and Reflections*, Cassell, 1956

Staff, Central Office of Information, *The Battle of the Atlantic: The Official Account of the Fight against the U-boats, 1939–1945*, His Majesty's Stationery Office, London, 1946

Strachey, William, "A True Reportory of the Wreck and Redemption of Sir Thomas Gates, Knight," circa 1625, reprinted in *A Voyage to Virginia in 1609*, Louis B. Wright, editor, University Press of Virginia, Charlottesville, 1964

Syrett, David, *The Defeat of the German U-Boats: The Battle of the Atlantic*, University of South Carolina Press, Columbia, 1994

Tarrant, V.E., *The U-boat Offensive: 1914–1945*, Naval Institute Press, Annapolis MD, 1989

Thursfield, H. G., Rear Admiral RN, editor, "Fuehrer Conferences on Naval Affairs—1939–1945," *Brassey's Naval Annual*, The MacMillan Company, New York NY, 1948

Waters, John M. Jr., Capt. USCG (Ret.), *Bloody Winter*, D. Van Nostrand Co., New York, 1967, reprinted by the Naval Institute Press, Annapolis, MD, 1987

Weir, Gary E., and Boyne, Walter J., *Rising Tide: The Untold Story of the Russian Submarines That Fought the Cold War*, New American Library, New York, 2004

Werner, Herbert A., *Iron Coffins*, Bantam Books, New York, 1978

Westwood, David, *The Type VII U-Boat*, Naval Institute Press, Annapolis, MD, 1984

Williamson, Gordon, *U-Boats of the Kaiser's Navy*, Osprey Publishing, Oxford, 2002

Winterbotham, F.W., Group Captain RAF (Ret.), *The Ultra Secret*, Dell, New York, 1975

Woodman, Richard, *The Real Cruel Sea: The Merchant Navy in the Battle of the Atlantic 1939–1943*, John Murray/Hodder Healine, London, 2004

Worth, Richard, *Fleets of World War II*, Da Capo Press, New York, 2001

Wynn, Kenneth, *U-boat Operations of the Second World War, Vol. 1: Career Histories, U-1–U-510*, Naval Institute Press, Annapolis, MD, 1997

Wynn, Kenneth, *U-boat Operations of the Second World War, Vol. 2: Career Histories, U-511–UIT-25*, Naval Institute Press, Annapolis, MD, 1998

Wynne, Deane, *Recollections from Below the Mast*, Rowe The Printers, Imperial Works Guildford Road, Hayle, UK, 2003

Y'Blood, William T., *Hunter-Killer: U.S. Escort Carriers in the Battle of the Atlantic*, Naval Institute Press, Annapolis, MD, 1983

MILITARY AND INTELLIGENCE DOCUMENTS AND REPORTS

"Battle of the Atlantic—U-boat Operations, December 1942–May 1945," SRH-008, National Security Agency, transcribed for online posting at the HyperWar Foundation at http://www.ibiblio.org/hyperwar/ETO/Ultra/SRH-009/index.html

"Battle of the Atlantic—Allied Communications Intelligence, December 1942–May 1945," SRH-009, National Security Agency, transcribed for online posting at the HyperWar Foundation at http://www.ibiblio.org/hyperwar/ETO/Ultra/SRH-009/index.html

"B-dienst" (Radio Intelligence), Spot Item Report, OP-20-G (Office of Naval Intelligence), Nov. 12, 1943, declassified from Secret

"Convoy HX231: Analysis of U-boat Operations," Operational Intelligence Centre, London, U.K., declassified from Most Secret, Public Records Office, London, PRO ADM 223/16

"Convoy ONS5: Analysis of U-boat Operations," Operational Intelligence Centre, London, U.K., declassified from Most Secret, Public Records Office, London, PRO ADM 223/16

Deck Logs, USS (CG) Ingham, February–March 1943, from National Archives and Records Service, Adelphi, MD

"Escort-of-Convoy Instructions," LANTFLT 9A, revised Nov. 17, 1941, declassified from Confidential

"Functions of the 'Secret Room' (F-211) of COMINCH Combat Intelligence," undated

"German Prisoners of War," to Chief of Naval Operations (ONI) from Commanding Officer, USS Osmond Ingram (AVD 9), June 19, 1943, declassified from Secret

"German Radio Intercepts and Cryptanalysts," Commander, Naval Forces Germany, Sept. 18, 1950, declassified from Top Secret

"German U-boats from which Prisoners Were Taken during Hostilities by British and American Forces," by E.G.N. Rushbrooke, British Office of Naval Intelligence, undated, declassified from Restricted

"Grand Admiral Doenitz on the U-boat War," in "Monthly Anti-Submarine Warfare Report," Admiralty Intelligence Division, Vol. 6, 1945, Public Records Office, London, ADM 199/2062

"History of the Armed Guard Afloat," United States Naval Administration in World War II, OP-NAV-P421–514, prepared by the Director of Naval History, 1946

"History of the Eastern Sea Frontier," Department of the Navy, Washington, D.C., undated (mid-1940s)

"History of U-boat Policy—1939–1945," (excerpts of Führer Naval Conferences with Grand Admiral Eric Räder, subsequently Grand Admiral Karl Dönitz), C.B. 4051, British Admiralty, London, February 1946

"Interrogation of German Naval Survivors—1941–1944," British Admiralty, Public Records Office, London, ADM186/808, posted at Ubootwaffe.net

Kriegstagebüch (KTB)—Daily War Patrol Diaries for selected U-boats, translated by U-boat Archive.net from the originals in storage at the German Bundesarchiv, Freiberg, Germany

U-223: KTB for Second War Patrol, April 15–May 24, 1943

U-338: KTB for First War Patrol, February 23–March 24, 1943

U-758: KTB for Second War Patrol, February 14–March 30, 1943

"Memorandum for the Director of Naval History," by Lt. Cmdr. Kenneth A. Knowles USN, Oct. 23, 1945

"Minutes of Meeting, Atlantic Convoy Conference Held at Washington, D.C.," U.S. Navy, March 1943, declassified from Secret.

"Monthly Anti-Submarine Warfare Reports," Vol. 6 (1945), British Admiralty, ADM 199/2062

"Order of Battle of the United States Army in World War II—European Theater of Operations," Office of the Theater Historian, December 1945

Pound, Adm. of the Fleet Sir Dudley, message to Adm. William Stark on allied convoy procedures, Jan. 29, 1942, declassified from Secret, Public Records Office, London, UK

"Prisoner-of-War Mail Code Censorship," Memorandum from Lt. J.S. Marriner RNVR, OP-16, Oct. 12, 1943, declassified from Secret

"Report of Proceedings, Convoy HX229," Report of Commodore M. J. D. Mayall RNR, declassified from Secret, Public Records Office, London, PRO/ADM 199/576

"Report of Proceedings, Convoy ONS5," Commodore (D), Western Approaches, 20 June 1943, Public Records Office, London, PRO/ADM 237/113

"Report of Proceedings [Convoy ONS5], Senior Officer [British Escort Group B-7] in HMS Duncan, declassified from Secret, Public Records Office, London, PRO/ADM 237/113

"Report of Proceedings, [Convoy ONS5], Continuation of report by Commanding Officer, HMS Tay, S.O. [Senior Officer] Close Escort in absence of HMS Duncan," declassified from Secret, Public Records Office, London, PRO/ADM 237/113

"Report of Proceedings, Convoy SC122," Report of Commodore S.N. White, declassified from Secret, Public Records Office, London, PRO/ADM 199/580

"Solving the Enigma: History of the Cryptanalytic Bombe," by Jennifer Wilcox, Center for Cryptologic History, National Security Agency, Revised 2004

"Special Intelligence Summary: Convoys HX229 and SC122," British Operational Intelligence Centre, March 1943, declassified from Most Secret, Public Records Office, London, PRO/ADM 233/16

"Special Intelligence Summary: Convoy ONS5," British Operational Intelligence Centre, Apr. 29–May 5, 1943, declassified from Most Secret, Public Records Office, London, PRO/ADM 223/15

"Special Short Situation Report of Commander-in-Chief German Navy to the U-boat Arm," translated from German, special report from Commander-in-Chief U.S. Fleet, Oct. 22, 1944, declassified from Top Secret Ultra

"Statistical Review: World War II," Army Services Forces, published by the U.S. War Department, Washington, D.C., undated, posted at HyperWar.com

"Ultra and the Battle of the Atlantic—the British View," by Patrick Beesly, paper, Naval Symposium, U.S. Naval Academy, Annapolis MD, Oct. 28, 1977

U.S. Coast Guard, "WWII Reports Concerning Merchant Vessels Sinking, 1938–2002," NARA, Record Group 26, Box 22

"U.S. Naval Activities, World War Two, By State, U.S. Naval Historical Center, Washington, D.C., 1945

U.S. Strategic Bombing Survey, "Interview No. 59—Grand Admiral Karl Dönitz," July 7, 1945, declassified from Confidential

"Use of Special Intelligence in the Battle of the Atlantic," British Naval Intelligence analysis, 1945

"Voyage Report of SS Mathew Luckenbach," by Ensign James H. Hammond, April 15, 1943, forwarded to the Vice Chief of Naval Operations, including statements by Master Antwood N. Borden; also group statement by SS Mathew Luckenbach officers regarding its torpedoing, National Archives and Records Service 968/133.

"The War at Sea," essay by Rear Adm. Eberhard Godt, British Office of Naval Intelligence, Nov. 3, 1945, declassified from Restricted

ARTICLES AND MANUSCRIPTS

Advertisement, The New York Times, "Official O.C.D. Stirrup Pumps," March 7, 1943

Ancell, Robert M. Jr., Lt.j.g. USN, "Grand Admiral Karl Dönitz: Reflections at 80," U.S. Naval Institute Proceedings, Annapolis MD, March 1973

Andrews, Lewis M. Jr., Lt. (USN), "Wild, Cold Ruthless—That's the Atlantic," The New York Times, March 7, 1943

Associated Press, "8 Die in Bomber Crash," The New York Times, March 5, 1943

Associated Press, "13 Ships Are Sunk by U.S. Submarine," The New York Times, March 7, 1943

Associated Press, "678 Lost on Ship Torpedoed in Cold," The New York Times, March 5, 1943

Associated Press, "Gaullist Craft Rams 2 U-boats; Avenges Lost British Destroyer," The New York Times, Apr. 10, 1943

Associated Press, "Knox Assails Acts That Pass 'Piracy,'" The New York Times, Nov. 2, 1941

Associated Press, "Navy Lists 23 Casualties," The New York Times, March 7, 1943

Associated Press, "Navy Spikes DiMaggio Rumor," The New York Times, March 5, 1943

Associated Press, "'Some Recent Visitors Will Never Enjoy Return Trip,' Says Spokesman," The New York Times, Jan. 24, 1942

Associated Press, "U-boat Toll Rises; 'Tough,' Says Knox," The New York Times, April 7, 1943

Barlow, Jeffrey G., "The Navy's Atlantic War Learning Curve," Naval History, Annapolis, MD, June 2008

Belke, T. J., Lt.j.g., "Roll of Drums," U.S. Naval Institute Proceedings, Annapolis, MD, April 1983

Beesly, Patrick, "Convoy PQ17: A Study of Intelligence and Decision-Making," Intelligence and National Security, April 1990

Bracker, Milton, "U-boat Pack Loses Furious 4-day Fight," The New York Times, April 20, 1943

Decker, Hans Joachim, "404 Days! The War Patrol Life of U-505," *U.S. Naval Institute Proceedings*, Annapolis MD, March 1960

Editorial, "The Sea War," *The New York Times*, April 7, 1943

Friedland, Klaus, "Raiding Merchant Shipping: U-boats on the North American Coast, 1942," *The American Neptune*, Salem, MA, Spring 1991

Heinrichs, Waldo, "President Franklin D. Roosevelt's Intervention in the Battle of the Atlantic, 1941," *Diplomatic History*, Fall 1986

Hulen, Bertram, "Our Stand Clear, Officials Insist," *The New York Times*, Nov. 2, 1941

Kurzak, Karl Heniz, "German U-boat Construction," *Naval Institute Proceedings*, Annapolis MD, April 1955

Lundeberg, Philip K., "American Anti-Submarine Operations in the Atlantic, May 1943–May 1945," Ph.D. Dissertation, Harvard University, Cambridge MA, 1963

Milner, Marc, "The Battle That Had to Be Won," *Naval History*, Annapolis, MD, June 2008

Nasuti, Guy, "The Hitler Youth: An Effective Organization for Total War," published at Military-HistoryOnline.com.

O'Connor, Jerome M., "FDR's Undeclared War," *Naval History*, Annapolis, MD, February 2004

Offley, Ed, "Wartime Foes Reunite As Friends," (U-701), *The Ledger-Star*, Norfolk, VA, July 7, 1982

Offley, Ed, "Chesapeake Bay Mined, War Came Close to Home," (U-701), *The Ledger-Star*, Norfolk, VA, July 8, 1982

Offley, Ed, "Confrontation in the Atlantic: The Death of U-701," *The Ledger-Star*, Norfolk, VA, July 9, 1982

Rempel, Gerhard, "The political System of the Third Reich," posted at the Western New England College Web site at http://mars.wnec.edu/~grempel/courses/ger-many/lectures/29nazipolitics.html

Rohwer, Jürgen, "Allied and Axis Radio-Intelligence in the Battle of the Atlantic—a Comparative Analysis," *The Intelligence Revolution—a Historical Perspective*, proceedings of the Thirteenth Military History Symposium, U.S. Air Force Academy, Colorado Springs, CO, Oct. 12–14, 1988

Rohwer, Jürgen, "The Operational Use of Ultra in the Battle of the Atlantic," *Intelligence and International Relations*, Andrew, Christopher and Noales, Jeremy, editors, University of Exeter Press, Exeter 1987

Rohwer, Jürgen, "The U-boat War against the Allied Supply Lines," in *The Decisive Battles of World War II: The German View*, G.P. Putnam's Sons, New York, 1965

Shearer, Lloyd, Sgt. USA, "The Service Man's New York," *The New York Times*, March 7, 1943

Syrett, David, "The Battle of the Atlantic: 1943, the Year of Decision," *The American Neptune*, Salem, MA, Winter 1985

Syrett, David, "The Safe and Timely Arrival of Convoy SC130," *The American Neptune*, Salem, MA, Summer 1990

Taylor, Blaine, "The Onetime U-boat Commander's Career Ladder Led All the Way to the Top—as Hitler's Own Successor," *World War II Magazine*, March 1988

Trussell, C.P. "Navy Called Slow in Submarine War," *The New York Times*, April 21, 1943

Unattributed, "5,500 War Planes Made in February," *The New York Times*, March 5, 1943

Unattributed, "275,000 of 700,000 Buildings in City Fail to Provide Protection Against Raid Fires," *The New York Times*, March 2, 1943

Unattributed, "The Best Selling Books, Here and Elsewhere," *The New York Times*, March 7, 1943

Unattributed, "'Double Red' Drill to Be Held Tonight," *The New York Times*, March 2, 1943

Unattributed, "'Gas' Denied to Navy Hero, He Gets Use of Police Car," *The New York Times*, March 5, 1943

Unattributed, "Gets Stiff 'Gas' Penalty," *The New York Times*, March 5, 1943

Unattributed, "Housewives Cling to Ration Coupons," *The New York Times*, March 1, 1943

Unattributed, "Knox Hits Reports on Ship Sinkings," *The New York Times*, April 24, 1943

Unattributed, "Navy Strikes 'Strong' Blows As U-boats Continue Attack," *The New York Times*, January 21, 1942

Unattributed, "The News of the Week in Review," *The New York Times*, March 7, 1943

Unattributed, "Reprisal Air Raids Here Hinted by German Radio," *The New York Times*, March 2, 1943

Unattributed, "The Spanish Armada," *Catholic Encyclopedia*, Robert Appleton Company, New York, 1913

Unattributed, "War Industry Portrayed: Metropolitan Museum Opens Exhibition of 70 Pictures," *The New York Times*, March 5, 1943

United Press, "313 More Army Men on Casualty Roll," *The New York Times*, March 7, 1943

United Press, "Nazis Now Building 2 U-boats for Every One the Allies Sink," *The New York Times*, January 20, 1943

United Press, "Robert Montgomery Promoted," *The New York Times*, March 8, 1943

United Press, "Single U.S. Air Group Downs 129 Japanese," *The New York Times*, March 5, 1943

Walling, Michael G., "Dangerous Duty in the North Atlantic," *Naval History*, Annapolis, MD, June 2008

Watt, D. C., "The Anglo-German Naval Agreement of 1935: An Interim Judgement," p. 155–175 from "Journal of Modern History," Volume 28, Issue #2, June 1956

UNPUBLISHED OR PRIVATE MANUSCRIPTS

Degen, Horst, "U-701: Glory and Tragedy," unpublished manuscript, 1965

Gretton, Peter, "Notes on the Gretton Family," unpublished manuscript, undated

Low, Francis S., Adm. USN (Ret.), "A Personal Narrative of Association with Fleet Admiral Ernest J. King, U.S. Navy," unpublished essay, 1961

Poyer, David C., "Death of a U-Boat," April 1982 (manuscript provided by the author)

Waters, John M. Jr., Capt. USCG (Ret.), "A Different War," unpublished memoir of his war service years 1943–45, updated 1988

ORAL HISTORY INTERVIEWS

Atkinson, Sir Robert, Oral Interview with Brown, Ray, Imperial War Museum, London, U.K., July 8, 2002; also Royal Naval Museum, Greenwich, UK, Oral History Collection Accession No. 116/93

Chesterman, Harold G., Royal Naval Museum Oral History Collection Accession No. 174/93, Greenwich, UK

"Reminiscences of Vice Admiral George C. Dyer USN (Ret.)," Oral History Collection, U.S. Naval Institute, Annapolis, MD, 1973

"Reminiscences of Vice Admiral John L. McRea USN (Ret.)," Oral History Collection, U.S. Naval Institute, Annapolis, MD, 1990

"Reminiscences of Vice Admiral William R. Smedberg III USN (Ret.)," Oral History Collection, U.S. Naval Institute, Annapolis, MD, undated

ONLINE SOURCES

American Merchant Marine at War, at www.usmm.org

Befehlshaber der Unterseeboote (Commander in Chief, Submarines), Daily War Logs, 1939–1945, translated from the German, posted at http://www.uboatarchive.net/BDUKTB.htm.

ConvoyWeb, Individual Allied Convoy reports, posted at ConvoyWeb at http://www.convoyweb.org.uk/

"Cradle of the Navy," history of the San Diego Naval Training Center, at http://www.quarterdeck.org/

Feldgrau.com (German armed forces 1918–1945) at http://feldgrau.com/

FleetSubmarine.com at http://www.fleetsubmarine.com

"HMS Firedrake History" at http://www.hmsfiredrake.co.uk/

HyperWar: Hypertext History of World War II at http://www.ibiblio.org/hyperwar/

Latitude-longitude calculator at Indo.com: http://www.indo.com/distance/

Naval-History.net at http://www.naval-history.net/index.htm

NavSource.org at http://www.navsource.org

Shipbuilding History.com at http://shipbuildinghistory.com/

U.S. Coast Guard Oral History Program, "Journal of Joseph Matte III on Board the *USS Ingham* While on Convoy Duty in the North Atlantic from 16 February 1942 to 19 April 1943," posted at http://www.uscg.mil/History/weboralhistory/MatteonIngham.asp

U-boat Archive at http://www.uboatarchive.net/

U-boat.net at http://www.uboat.net/

Ubootwaffe.net at http://www.ubootwaffe.net/

Warsailors.com at http://warsailors.com/

Wrecksite.eu at http://www.wrecksite.eu/wrecksite.aspx

INDEX